Writings of Nietzsche:
Volume II

By Friedrich Nietzsche
Edited by Anthony Uyl

Devoted Publishing
Woodstock, Ontario, 2016

Writings of Nietzsche: Volume II

By Friedrich Nietzsche

Edited by Anthony Uyl

The text of Writings of Nietzsche: Volume II is all in the Public Domain. This edition is published by Devoted Publishing a division of 2165467 Ontario Inc.

What kind of philosophies do you have?
Let us know!

Contact us at: devotedpub@hotmail.com
Visit us on Facebook: @DevotedPublishing
Get other print products on our website: www.devotedpublishing.com
Published in Woodstock, Ontario, Canada 2016.

ISBN: 978-1-988297-66-8

Table of Contents

The Birth of Tragedy or Hellenism and Pessimism

Translated by WM. A. Haussmann, PH.D.

Originally Published by:
T.N. FOULIS, 13 & 15 FREDERICK STREET, EDINBURGH: AND LONDON, 1910

TRANSLATOR'S NOTE.

While the translator flatters himself that this version of Nietzsche's early work--having been submitted to unsparingly scrutinising eyes--is not altogether unworthy of the original, he begs to state that he holds twentieth-century English to be a rather unsatisfactory vehicle for philosophical thought. Accordingly, in conjunction with his friend Dr. Ernest Lacy, he has prepared a second, more unconventional translation,--in brief, a translation which will enable one whose knowledge of English extends to, say, the period of Elizabeth, to appreciate Nietzsche in more forcible language, because the language of a stronger age. It is proposed to provide this second translation with an appendix, containing many references to the translated writings of Wagner and Schopenhauer; to the works of Pater, Browning, Burckhardt, Rohde, and others, and a summmary and index.

For help in preparing the present translation, the translator wishes to express his thanks to his friends Dr. Ernest Lacy, Litt.D.; Dr. James Waddell Tupper, Ph.D.; Prof. Harry Max Ferren; Mr. James M'Kirdy, Pittsburg; and Mr. Thomas Common, Edinburgh.

WILLIAM AUGUST HAUSSMANN, A.B., Ph.D.

INTRODUCTION [1]

Frederick Nietzsche was born at Röcken near Lützen, in the Prussian province of Saxony, on the 15th of October 1844, at 10 a.m. The day happened to be the anniversary of the birth of Frederick-William IV., then King of Prussia, and the peal of the local church-bells which was intended to celebrate this event, was, by a happy coincidence, just timed to greet my brother on his entrance into the world. In 1841, at the time when our father was tutor to the Altenburg Princesses, Theresa of Saxe-Altenburg, Elizabeth, Grand Duchess of Olden-burg, and Alexandra, Grand Duchess Constantine of Russia, he had had the honour of being presented to his witty and pious sovereign. The meeting seems to have impressed both parties very favourably; for, very shortly after it had taken place, our father received his living at Röcken "by supreme command." His joy may well be imagined, therefore, when a first son was born to him on his beloved and august patron's birthday, and at the christening ceremony he spoke as follows:--"Thou blessed month of October!--for many years the most decisive events in my life have occurred within thy thirty-one days, and now I celebrate the greatest and most glorious of them all by baptising my little boy! O blissful moment! O exquisite festival! O unspeakably holy duty! In the Lord's name I bless thee!--With all my heart I utter these words: Bring me this, my beloved child, that I may consecrate it unto the Lord. My son, Frederick William, thus shalt thou be named on earth, as a memento of my royal benefactor on whose birthday thou wast born!"

Our father was thirty-one years of age, and our mother not quite nineteen, when my brother was born. Our mother, who was the daughter of a clergyman, was good-looking and healthy, and was one of a very large family of sons and daughters. Our paternal grandparents, the Rev. Oehler and his wife, in Pobles, were typically healthy people. Strength, robustness, lively dispositions, and a cheerful outlook on life, were among the qualities which every one was pleased to observe in them. Our grandfather Oehler was a bright, clever man, and quite the old style of comfortable country parson, who thought it no sin to go hunting. He scarcely had a day's illness in his life, and would certainly not have met with his end as early as he did--that is to say, before his seventieth year--if his careless disregard of all caution, where his health was concerned, had not led to his catching a severe and fatal cold. In regard to our grand-mother Oehler, who died in her eighty-second year, all that can be said is, that if all German women were possessed of the health she enjoyed, the German nation would excel all others from the standpoint of vitality. She bore our grandfather eleven children; gave each of them the breast for nearly the whole of its first year, and reared them all It is said that the sight of these eleven children, at ages varying from nineteen years to one month, with their powerful build, rosy cheeks, beaming eyes, and wealth of curly locks, provoked the admiration of all visitors. Of course, despite their extraordinarily good health, the life of this family was not by any means all sunshine. Each of the children was very spirited, wilful, and obstinate, and it was therefore no simple matter to keep them in order. Moreover, though they always showed the utmost respect and most implicit obedience to their parents--even as middle-aged men and women--misunderstandings between themselves were of constant occurrence. Our Oehler grandparents were fairly well-to-do; for our grandmother hailed from a very old family, who had been extensive land-owners in the neighbourhood of Zeitz for centuries, and her father owned the baronial estate of Wehlitz and a magnificent seat near Zeitz in Pacht. When she married, her father gave her carriages and horses, a coachman, a cook, and a kitchenmaid, which for the wife of a German minister was then, and is still, something quite exceptional. As a result of the wars in the beginning of the nineteenth century, however, our great-grandfather lost the greater part of his property.

Our father's family was also in fairly comfortable circumstances, and likewise very large. Our grandfather Dr. Nietzsche (D.D. and Superintendent) married twice, and had in all twelve children, of whom three died young. Our grandfather on this side, whom I never knew, must certainly have been a distinguished, dignified, very learned and reserved man; his second wife--our beloved grandmother--was an active-minded, intelligent, and exceptionally good-natured woman. The whole of our father's family, which I only got to know when they were very advanced in years, were remarkable for their great power of self-control, their lively interest in intellectual matters, and a strong sense of family unity, which manifested itself both in their splendid readiness to help one another and in their very excellent relations with each other. Our father was the youngest son, and, thanks to his uncommonly lovable disposition, together with other gifts, which only tended to become more marked as he grew older, he was quite the favourite of the family. Blessed with a thoroughly sound constitution, as all averred who knew him at the convent-school in Rossleben, at the University, or later at the ducal court of Altenburg, he was tall and slender, possessed an undoubted gift for poetry and real musical talent, and was moreover a man of delicate sensibilities, full of consideration for his whole family, and distinguished in his manners.

My brother often refers to his Polish descent, and in later years he even instituted research-work with the view of establishing it, which met with partial success. I know nothing definite concerning these investigations, because a large number of valuable documents were unfortunately destroyed after his breakdown in Turin. The family tradition was that a certain Polish nobleman Nicki (pronounced Nietzky) had obtained the special favour of Augustus the Strong, King of Poland, and had received the rank of Earl from him.. When, however, Stanislas Leszcysski the Pole became king, our supposed ancestor became involved in a conspiracy in favour of the Saxons and Protestants. He was sentenced to death; but, taking flight, according to the evidence of the documents, he was ultimately befriended by a certain Earl of Brühl, who gave him a small post in an obscure little provincial town. Occasionally our aged aunts would speak of our great-grandfather Nietzsche, who was said to have died in his ninety-first year, and words always seemed to fail them when they attempted to describe his handsome appearance, good breeding, and vigour. Our ancestors, both on the Nietzsche and the Oehler side, were very long-lived. Of the four pairs of great-grandparents, one great-grandfather reached the age of ninety, five great-grandmothers and-fathers died between eighty-two and eighty-six years of age, and two only failed to reach their seventieth year.

The sorrow which hung as a cloud over our branch of the family was our father's death, as the result of a heavy fall, at the age of thirty-eight. One night, upon leaving some friends whom he had accompanied home, he was met at the door of the vicarage by our little dog. The little animal must have got between his feet, for he stumbled and fell backwards down seven stone steps on to the paving-stones of the vicarage courtyard. As a result of this fall, he was laid up with concussion of the brain, and, after a lingering illness, which lasted eleven months, he died on the 30th of July 1849. The early death of our beloved and highly-gifted father spread gloom over the whole of our childhood. In 1850 our mother withdrew with us to Naumburg on the Saale, where she took up her abode with our widowed grandmother Nietzsche; and there she brought us up with Spartan severity and simplicity, which, besides being typical of the period, was quite de rigeur in her family. Of course, Grand-mamma Nietzsche helped somewhat to temper her daughter-in-law's severity, and in this respect our Oehler grandparents, who were less rigorous with us, their eldest grandchildren, than with their own children, were also very influential. Grandfather Oehler was the first who seems to have recognised the extraordinary talents of his eldest grandchild.

From his earliest childhood upwards, my brother was always strong and healthy; he often declared that he must have been taken for a peasant-boy throughout his childhood and youth, as he was so plump, brown, and rosy. The thick fair hair which fell picturesquely over his shoulders tended somewhat to modify his robust appearance. Had he not possessed those wonderfully beautiful, large, and expressive eyes, however, and had he not been so very ceremonious in his manner, neither his teachers nor his relatives would ever have noticed anything at all remarkable about the boy; for he was both modest and reserved.

He received his early schooling at a preparatory school, and later at a grammar school in Naumburg. In the autumn of 1858, when he was fourteen years of age, he entered the Pforta school, so famous for the scholars it has produced. There, too, very severe discipline prevailed, and much was exacted from the pupils, with the view of inuring them to great mental and physical exertions. Thus, if my brother seems to lay particular stress upon the value of rigorous training, free from all sentimentality, it should be remembered that he speaks from experience in this respect. At Pforta he followed the regular school course, and he did not enter a university until the comparatively late age of twenty. His extraordinary gifts manifested themselves chiefly in his independent and private studies and artistic efforts. As a boy his musical talent had already been so noticeable, that he himself and other competent judges were doubtful as to whether he ought not perhaps to devote himself altogether to music. It is, however, worth noting that everything he did in his later years, whether in Latin, Greek, or German work, bore the stamp of perfection--subject of course to the limitation imposed upon him by his years. His talents came very suddenly to the fore, because he had allowed them to grow for such a long time in concealment. His very first performance in philology, executed while he was a student under Ritschl, the famous philologist, was also typical of him in this respect, seeing that it was ordered to be printed for the Rheinische Museum. Of course this was done amid general and grave expressions of doubt; for, as Dr. Ritschl often declared, it was an unheard-of occurrence for a student in his third term to prepare such an excellent treatise.

Being a great lover of out-door exercise, such as swimming, skating, and walking, he developed into a very sturdy lad. Rohde gives the following description of him as a student: with his healthy complexion, his outward and inner cleanliness, his austere chastity and his solemn aspect, he was the image of that delightful youth described by Adalbert Stifter.

Though as a child he was always rather serious, as a lad and a man he was ever inclined to see the humorous side of things, while his whole being, and everything he said or did, was permeated by an extraordinary harmony. He belonged to the very few who could control even a bad mood and conceal it from others. All his friends are unanimous in their praise of his exceptional evenness of temper and behaviour, and his warm, hearty, and pleasant laugh that seemed to come from the very depths of his benevolent and affectionate nature. In him it might therefore be said, nature had produced a being who in body and spirit was a harmonious whole: his unusual intellect was fully in keeping with his uncommon bodily strength.

The only abnormal thing about him, and something which we both inherited from our father, was short-sightedness, and this was very much aggravated in my brother's case, even in his earliest schooldays, owing to that indescribable anxiety to learn which always characterised him. When one listens to accounts given by his friends and schoolfellows, one is startled by the multiplicity of his studies even in his schooldays.

In the autumn of 1864, he began his university life in Bonn, and studied philology and theology; at the end of six months he gave up theology, and in the autumn of 1865 followed his famous teacher Ritschl to the University of Leipzig. There he became an ardent philologist, and diligently sought to acquire a masterly grasp of this branch of knowledge. But in this respect it would be unfair to forget that the school of Pforta, with its staff of excellent teachers--scholars that would have adorned the chairs of any University--had already afforded the best of preparatory trainings to any one intending to take up philology as a study, more particularly as it gave all pupils ample scope to indulge any individual tastes they might have for any particular branch of ancient history. The last important Latin thesis which my brother wrote for the Landes-Schule, Pforta, dealt with the Megarian poet Theognis, and it was in the rôle of a lecturer on this very subject that, on the 18th January 1866, he made his first appearance in public before the philological society he had helped to found in Leipzig. The paper he read disclosed his investigations on the subject of Theognis the moralist and aristocrat, who, as is well known, described and dismissed the plebeians of his time in terms of the heartiest contempt The aristocratic ideal, which was always so dear to my brother, thus revealed itself for the first time. Moreover, curiously enough, it was precisely this scientific thesis which was the cause of Ritschl's recognition of my brother and fondness for him.

The whole of his Leipzig days proved of the utmost importance to my brother's career. There he was plunged into the very midst of a torrent of intellectual influences which found an impressionable medium in the fiery youth, and to which he eagerly made himself accessible. He did not, however, forget to discriminate among them, but tested and criticised the currents of thought he encountered, and selected accordingly. It is certainly of great importance to ascertain what those influences precisely were to which he yielded, and how long they maintained their sway over him, and it is likewise necessary to discover exactly when the matured mind threw off these fetters in order to work out its own salvation.

The influences that exercised power over him in those days may be described in the three following terms: Hellenism, Schopenhauer, Wagner. His love of Hellenism certainly led him to philology; but, as a matter of fact, what concerned him most was to obtain a wide view of things in general, and this he hoped to derive from that science; philology in itself, with his splendid method and thorough way of going to work, served him only as a means to an end.

If Hellenism was the first strong influence which already in Pforta obtained a sway over my brother, in the winter of 1865-66, a completely new, and therefore somewhat subversive, influence was introduced into his life with Schopenhauer's philosophy. When he reached Leipzig in the autumn of 1865, he was very downcast; for the experiences that had befallen him during his one year of student life in Bonn had deeply depressed him. He had sought at first to adapt himself to his surroundings there, with the hope of ultimately elevating them to his lofty views on things; but both these efforts proved vain, and now he had come to Leipzig with the purpose of framing his own manner of life. It can easily be imagined how the first reading of Schopenhauer's The World as Will and Idea worked upon this man, still stinging from the bitterest experiences and disappointments. He writes: "Here I saw a mirror in which I espied the world, life, and my own nature depicted with frightful grandeur." As my brother, from his very earliest childhood, had always missed both the parent and the educator through our father's untimely death, he began to regard Schopenhauer with almost filial love and respect. He did not venerate him quite as other men did; Schopenhauer's personality was what attracted and enchanted him. From the first he was never blind to the faults in his master's system, and in proof of this we have only to refer to an essay he wrote in the autumn of 1867, which actually contains a criticism of Schopenhauer's philosophy.

Now, in the autumn of 1865, to these two influences, Hellenism and Schopenhauer, a third influence was added--one which was to prove the strongest ever exercised over my brother--and it began with his personal introduction to Richard Wagner. He was introduced to Wagner by the latter's sister, Frau Professor Brockhaus, and his description of their first meeting, contained in a letter to Erwin Rohde, is really most affecting. For years, that is to say, from the time Billow's arrangement of Tristan and Isolde for the pianoforte, had appeared, he had already been a passionate admirer of Wagner's music; but now that the artist himself entered upon the scene of his life, with the whole fascinating strength of his strong will, my brother felt that he was in the presence of a being whom he, of all modern men, resembled most in regard to force of character.

Again, in the case of Richard Wagner, my brother, from the first, laid the utmost stress upon the man's personality, and could only regard his works and views as an expression of the artist's whole being, despite the fact that he by no means understood every one of those works at that time. My brother was the first who ever manifested such enthusiastic affection for Schopenhauer and Wagner, and he was also the first of that numerous band of young followers who ultimately inscribed the two great names upon their banner. Whether Schopenhauer and Wagner ever really corresponded to the glorified pictures my brother painted of them, both in his letters and other writings, is a question which we can no longer answer in the affirmative. Perhaps what he saw in them was only what he himself wished to be some day.

The amount of work my brother succeeded in accomplishing, during his student days, really seems almost incredible. When we examine his record for the years 1865-67, we can scarcely believe it refers to only two years' industry, for at a guess no one would hesitate to suggest four years at least. But in those days, as he himself declares, he still possessed the constitution of a bear. He knew neither what headaches nor indigestion meant, and, despite his short sight, his eyes were able to endure the greatest strain without giving him the smallest trouble. That is why, regardless of seriously interrupting his studies, he was so glad at the thought of becoming a soldier in the forthcoming autumn of 1867; for he was particularly anxious to discover some means of employing his bodily strength.

He discharged his duties as a soldier with the utmost mental and physical freshness, was the crack rider among the recruits of his year, and was sincerely sorry when, owing to an accident, he was compelled to leave the colours before the completion of his service. As a result of this accident he had his first dangerous illness.

While mounting his horse one day, the beast, which was an uncommonly restive one, suddenly reared, and, causing him to strike his chest sharply against the pommel of the saddle, threw him to the ground. My brother then made a second attempt to mount, and succeeded this time, notwithstanding the fact that he had severely sprained and torn two muscles in his chest, and had seriously bruised the adjacent ribs. For a whole day he did his utmost to pay no heed to the injury, and to overcome the pain it caused him; but in the end he only swooned, and a dangerously acute inflammation of the injured tissues was the result. Ultimately he was obliged to consult the famous specialist, Professor Volkmann, in Halle, who quickly put him right.

In October 1868, my brother returned to his studies in Leipzig with double joy. These were his plans: to get his doctor's degree as soon as possible; to proceed to Paris, Italy, and Greece, make a lengthy stay in each place, and then to return to Leipzig in order to settle there as a privat docent. All these plans were, however, suddenly frustrated owing to his premature call to the University of Bale, where he was invited to assume the duties of professor. Some of the philological essays he had written in his student days, and which were published by the Rheinische Museum, had attracted the attention of the Educational Board at Bale. Ratsherr Wilhelm Vischer, as representing this body, appealed to Ritschl for fuller information. Now Ritschl, who had early recognised my brother's extraordinary talents, must have written a letter of such enthusiastic praise ("Nietzsche is a genius: he can do whatever he chooses to put his mind to"), that one of the more cautious members of the council is said to have observed: "If the proposed candidate be really such a genius, then it were better did we not appoint him; for, in any case, he would only stay à short time at the little University of Bale." My brother ultimately accepted the appointment, and, in view of his published philological works, he was immediately granted the doctor's degree by the University of Leipzig. He was twenty-four years and six months old when he took up his position as professor in Bale,--and it was with a heavy heart that he proceeded there, for he knew "the golden period of untrammelled activity" must cease. He was, however, inspired by the deep wish of being able "to transfer to his pupils some of that Schopenhauerian earnestness which is stamped on the brow of the sublime man." "I should like to be something more than a mere trainer of capable philologists: the present generation of teachers, the care of the growing broods,--all this is in my mind. If we must live, let us at least do so in such wise that others may bless our life once we have been peacefully delivered from its toils."

When I look back upon that month of May 1869, and ask both of friends and of myself, what the figure of this youthful University professor of four-and-twenty meant to the world at that time, the reply is naturally, in the first place: that he was one of Ritschl's best pupils; secondly, that he was an exceptionally capable exponent of classical antiquity with a brilliant career before him; and thirdly, that he was a passionate adorer of Wagner and Schopenhauer. But no one has any idea of my brother's independent attitude to the science he had selected, to his teachers and to his ideals, and he deceived both himself and us when he passed as a "disciple" who really shared all the views of his respected master.

On the 28th May 1869, my brother delivered his inaugural address at Bale University, and it is said to have deeply impressed the authorities. The subject of the address was "Homer and Classical Philology."

Musing deeply, the worthy councillors and professors walked homeward. What had they just heard? A young scholar discussing the very justification of his own science in a cool and philosophically critical spirit! A man able to impart so much artistic glamour to his subject, that the once stale and arid study of philology suddenly struck them--and they were certainly not impressionable men--as the messenger of the gods: "and just as the Muses descended upon the dull and tormented Boeotian peasants, so philology comes into a world full of gloomy colours and pictures, full of the deepest, most incurable woes, and speaks to men comfortingly of the beautiful and brilliant godlike figure of a distant, blue, and happy fairyland."

"We have indeed got hold of a rare bird, Herr Ratsherr," said one of these gentlemen to his companion, and the latter heartily agreed, for my brother's appointment had been chiefly his doing.

Even in Leipzig, it was reported that Jacob Burckhardt had said: "Nietzsche is as much an artist as a scholar." Privy-Councillor Ritschl told me of this himself, and then he added, with a smile: "I always said so; he can make his scientific discourses as palpitatingly interesting as a French novelist his novels."

"Homer and Classical Philology"--my brother's inaugural address at the University--was by no means the first literary attempt he had made; for we have already seen that he had had papers published by the Rheinische Museum; still, this particular discourse is important, seeing that it practically contains the programme of many other subsequent essays. I must, however, emphasise this fact here, that neither "Homer and Classical Philology," nor The Birth of Tragedy, represents a beginning in my brother's career. It is really surprising to see how very soon he actually began grappling with the questions which were to prove the problems of his life. If a beginning to his intellectual development be sought at all, then it must be traced to the years 1865-67 in Leipzig. The Birth of Tragedy, his maiden attempt at book-writing, with which he began his twenty-eighth year, is the last link of a long chain of developments, and the first fruit that was a long time coming to maturity. Nietzsche's was a polyphonic nature, in which the most different and apparently most antagonistic talents had come together. Philosophy, art, and science--in the form of philology, then--each certainly possessed a part of him. The most wonderful feature--perhaps it might even be called the real Nietzschean feature--of this versatile creature, was the fact that no eternal strife resulted from the juxtaposition of these inimical traits, that not one of them strove to dislodge, or to get the upper hand of, the others. When Nietzsche renounced the musical career, in order to devote himself to philology, and gave himself up to the most strenuous study, he did not find it essential completely to suppress his other tendencies: as before, he continued both to compose and derive pleasure from music, and even studied counterpoint somewhat seriously. Moreover, during his years at Leipzig, when he consciously gave himself up to philological research, he began to engross himself in Schopenhauer, and was thereby won by philosophy for ever. Everything that could find room took up its abode in him, and these juxtaposed factors, far from interfering with one another's existence, were rather mutually fertilising and stimulating. All those who have read the first volume of the biography with attention must have been struck with the perfect way in which the various impulses in his nature combined in the end to form one general torrent, and how this flowed with ever greater force in the direction of a single goal. Thus science, art, and philosophy developed and became ever more closely related in him, until, in The Birth of Tragedy, they brought forth a "centaur," that is to say, a work which would have been an impossible achievement to a man with only a single, special talent. This polyphony of different talents, all coming to utterance together and producing the richest and boldest of harmonies, is the fundamental feature not only of Nietzsche's early days, but of his whole development. It is once again the artist, philosopher, and man of science, who as one man in later years, after many wanderings, recantations, and revulsions of feeling, produces that other and rarer Centaur of highest rank--Zarathustra.

The Birth of Tragedy requires perhaps a little explaining--more particularly as we have now ceased to use either Schopenhauerian or Wagnerian terms of expression. And it was for this reason that five years after its appearance, my brother wrote an introduction to it, in which he very plainly expresses his doubts concerning the views it contains, and the manner in which they are presented. The kernel of its thought he always recognised as perfectly correct; and all he deplored in later days was that he had spoiled the grand problem of Hellenism, as he understood it, by adulterating it with ingredients taken from the world of most modern ideas. As time went on, he grew ever more and more anxious to define the deep meaning of this book with greater precision and clearness. A very good elucidation of its aims, which unfortunately was never published, appears among his notes of the year 1886, and is as follows:--

"Concerning The Birth of Tragedy.--A book consisting of mere experiences relating to pleasurable and unpleasurable æsthetic states, with a metaphysico-artistic background. At the same time the confession of a romanticist the sufferer feels the deepest longing for beauty--he begets it; finally, a product of youth, full of youthful courage and melancholy.

"Fundamental psychological experiences: the word 'Apollonian' stands for that state of rapt repose in the presence of a visionary world, in the presence of the world of beautiful appearance designed as a deliverance from becoming; the word Dionysos, on the other hand, stands for strenuous becoming, grown self-conscious, in the form of the rampant voluptuousness of the creator, who is also perfectly conscious of the violent anger of the destroyer.

"The antagonism of these two attitudes and the desires that underlie them. The first-named would have the vision it conjures up eternal: in its light man must be quiescent, apathetic, peaceful, healed, and on friendly terms with himself and all existence; the second strives after creation, after the voluptuousness of wilful creation, i.e. constructing and destroying. Creation felt and explained as an instinct would be merely the unremitting inventive action of a dissatisfied being, overflowing with wealth and living at high tension and high pressure,--of a God who would overcome the sorrows of existence by means only of continual changes and transformations,--appearance as a transient and momentary deliverance; the world as an apparent sequence of godlike visions and deliverances.

"This metaphysico-artistic attitude is opposed to Schopenhauer's one-sided view which values art, not from the artist's standpoint but from the spectator's, because it brings salvation and deliverance by means of the joy produced by unreal as opposed to the existing or the real (the experience only of him who is suffering and is in despair owing to himself and everything existing).--Deliverance in the form and its eternity (just as Plato may have pictured it, save that he rejoiced in a complete subordination of all too excitable sensibilities, even in the idea itself). To this is opposed the second point of view--art regarded as a phenomenon of the artist, above all of the musician; the torture of being obliged to create, as a Dionysian instinct.

"Tragic art, rich in both attitudes, represents the reconciliation of Apollo and Dionysos. Appearance is given the greatest importance by Dionysos; and yet it will be denied and cheerfully denied. This is directed against Schopenhauer's teaching of Resignation as the tragic attitude towards the world.

"Against Wagner's theory that music is a means and drama an end.

"A desire for tragic myth (for religion and even pessimistic religion) as for a forcing frame in which certain plants flourish.

"Mistrust of science, although its ephemerally soothing optimism be strongly felt; the 'serenity' of the theoretical man.

"Deep antagonism to Christianity. Why? The degeneration of the Germanic spirit is ascribed to its influence.

"Any justification of the world can only be an æsthetic one. Profound suspicions about morality (--it is part and parcel of the world of appearance).

"The happiness of existence is only possible as the happiness derived from appearance. ('Being' is a fiction invented by those who suffer from becoming.)

"Happiness in becoming is possible only in the annihilation of the real, of the 'existing,' of the beautifully visionary,--in the pessimistic dissipation of illusions:--with the annihilation of the most beautiful phenomena in the world of appearance, Dionysian happiness reaches its zenith."

The Birth of Tragedy is really only a portion of a much greater work on Hellenism, which my brother had always had in view from the time of his student days. But even the portion it represents was originally designed upon a much larger scale than the present one; the reason probably being, that Nietzsche desired only to be of service to Wagner. When a certain portion of the projected work on Hellenism was ready and had received the title Greek Cheerfulness, my brother happened to call upon Wagner at Tribschen in April 1871, and found him very low-spirited in regard to the mission of his life. My brother was very anxious to take some decisive step to help him, and, laying the plans of his great work on Greece aside, he selected a small portion from the already completed manuscript--a portion dealing with one distinct side of Hellenism,--to wit, its tragic art. He then associated Wagner's music with it and the name Dionysos, and thus took the first step towards that world-historical view through which we have since grown accustomed to regard Wagner.

From the dates of the various notes relating to it, The Birth of Tragedy must have been written between the autumn of 1869 and November 1871--a period during which "a mass of æsthetic questions and answers" was fermenting in Nietzsche's mind. It was first published in January 1872 by E. W. Fritsch, in Leipzig, under the title The Birth of Tragedy out of the Spirit of Music. Later on the title was changed to The Birth of Tragedy, or Hellenism and Pessimism.

ELIZABETH FORSTER-NIETZSCHE.
WEIMAR, September 1905.

Footnote:

1. This Introduction by E. Förster-Nietzsche, which appears in the front of the first volume of Naumann's Pocket Edition of Nietzsche, has been translated and arranged by Mr. A. M. Ludovici.

AN ATTEMPT AT SELF-CRITICISM

1

Whatever may lie at the bottom of this doubtful book must be a question of the first rank and attractiveness, moreover a deeply personal question,--in proof thereof observe the time in which it originated, in spite of which it originated, the exciting period of the Franco-German war of 1870-71. While the thunder of the battle of Wörth rolled over Europe, the ruminator and riddle-lover, who had to be the parent of this book, sat somewhere in a nook of the Alps, lost in riddles and ruminations, consequently very much concerned and unconcerned at the same time, and wrote down his meditations on the Greeks,--the kernel of the curious and almost inaccessible book, to which this belated prologue (or epilogue) is to be devoted. A few weeks later: and he found himself under the walls of Metz, still wrestling with the notes of interrogation he had set down concerning the alleged "cheerfulness" of the Greeks and of Greek art; till at last, in that month of deep suspense, when peace was debated at Versailles, he too attained to peace with himself, and, slowly recovering from a disease brought home from the field, made up his mind definitely regarding the "Birth of Tragedy from the Spirit of Music."--From music? Music and Tragedy? Greeks and tragic music? Greeks and the Art-work of pessimism? A race of men, well-fashioned, beautiful, envied, life-inspiring, like no other race hitherto, the Greeks--indeed? The Greeks were in need of tragedy? Yea--of art? Wherefore--Greek art?...

We can thus guess where the great note of interrogation concerning the value of existence had been set. Is pessimism necessarily the sign of decline, of decay, of failure, of exhausted and weakened instincts?--as was the case with the Indians, as is, to all appearance, the case with us "modern" men and Europeans? Is there a pessimism of strength? An intellectual predilection for what is hard, awful, evil, problematical in existence, owing to well-being, to exuberant health, to fullness of existence? Is there perhaps suffering in overfullness itself? A seductive fortitude with the keenest of glances, which yearns for the terrible, as for the enemy, the worthy enemy, with whom it may try its strength? from whom it is willing to learn what "fear" is? What means tragic myth to the Greeks of the best, strongest, bravest era? And the prodigious phenomenon of the Dionysian? And that which was born thereof, tragedy?--And again: that of which tragedy died, the Socratism of morality, the dialectics, contentedness and cheerfulness of the theoretical man--indeed? might not this very Socratism be a sign of decline, of weariness, of disease, of anarchically disintegrating instincts? And the "Hellenic cheerfulness" of the later Hellenism merely a glowing sunset? The Epicurean will counter to pessimism merely a precaution of the sufferer? And science itself, our science--ay, viewed as a symptom of life, what really signifies all science? Whither, worse still, whence--all science? Well? Is scientism perhaps only fear and evasion of pessimism? A subtle defence against--truth! Morally speaking, something like falsehood and cowardice? And, unmorally speaking, an artifice? O Socrates, Socrates, was this perhaps thy secret? Oh mysterious ironist, was this perhaps thine--irony?...

2

What I then laid hands on, something terrible and dangerous, a problem with horns, not necessarily a bull itself, but at all events a new problem: I should say to-day it was the problem of science itself--science conceived for the first time as problematic, as questionable. But the book, in which my youthful ardour and suspicion then discharged themselves--what an impossible book must needs grow out of a task so disagreeable to youth. Constructed of nought but precocious, unripened self-experiences, all of which lay close to the threshold of the communicable, based on the groundwork of art--for the problem of science cannot be discerned on the groundwork of science,--a book perhaps for artists, with collateral analytical and retrospective aptitudes (that is, an exceptional kind of artists, for whom one must seek and does not even care to seek ...), full of psychological innovations and artists' secrets, with an artists' metaphysics in the background, a work of youth, full of youth's mettle and youth's melancholy, independent, defiantly self-sufficient even when it seems to bow to some authority and self-veneration; in short, a firstling-work, even in every bad sense of the term; in spite of its senile problem, affected with every fault of youth, above all with youth's prolixity and youth's "storm and stress": on the other hand, in view of the success it had (especially with the great artist to whom it addressed itself, as it were, in a duologue, Richard Wagner) a demonstrated book, I mean a book which, at any rate, sufficed "for the best of its time." On this account, if for no other reason, it should be treated with some consideration and reserve; yet I shall not altogether conceal how disagreeable it now appears to me, how after sixteen years it stands a total stranger before me,--before an eye which is more mature, and a hundred times more fastidious, but which has by no means grown colder nor lost any of its interest in that self-same task essayed for the first time by this daring book,--to view science through the optics of the artist, and art moreover through the optics of life....

3

I say again, to-day it is an impossible book to me,--I call it badly written, heavy, painful, image-angling and image-entangling, maudlin, sugared at times even to femininism, uneven in tempo, void of the will to logical cleanliness, very convinced and therefore rising above the necessity of demonstration, distrustful even of the propriety of demonstration, as being a book for initiates, as "music" for those who are baptised with the name of Music, who are united from the beginning of things by common ties of rare experiences in art, as a countersign for blood-relations in artibus.--a haughty and fantastic book, which from the very first withdraws even more from the profanum vulgus of the "cultured" than from the "people," but which also, as its effect has shown and still shows, knows very well how to seek fellow-enthusiasts and lure them to new by-ways and dancing-grounds. Here, at any rate--thus much was acknowledged with curiosity as well as with aversion--a strange voice spoke, the disciple of a still "unknown God," who for the time being had hidden himself under the hood of the scholar, under the German's gravity and disinclination for dialectics, even under the bad manners of the Wagnerian; here was a spirit with strange and still nameless needs, a memory bristling with questions, experiences and obscurities, beside which stood the name Dionysos like one more note of interrogation; here spoke--people said to themselves with misgivings--something like a mystic and almost mænadic soul, which, undecided whether it should disclose or conceal itself, stammers with an effort and capriciously as in a strange tongue. It should have sung, this "new soul"--and not spoken! What a pity, that I did not dare to say what I then had to say, as a poet: I could have done so perhaps! Or at least as a philologist:--for even at the present day well-nigh everything in this domain remains to be discovered and disinterred by the philologist! Above all the problem, that here there is a problem before us,--and that, so long as we have no answer to the question "what is Dionysian?" the Greeks are now as ever wholly unknown and inconceivable....

4

Ay, what is Dionysian?--In this book may be found an answer,--a "knowing one" speaks here, the votary and disciple of his god. Perhaps I should now speak more guardedly and less eloquently of a psychological question so difficult as the origin of tragedy among the Greeks. A fundamental question is the relation of the Greek to pain, his degree of sensibility,--did this relation remain constant? or did it veer about?--the question, whether his ever-increasing longing for beauty, for festivals, gaieties, new cults, did really grow out of want, privation, melancholy, pain? For suppose even this to be true--and Pericles (or Thucydides) intimates as much in the great Funeral Speech:--whence then the opposite longing, which appeared first in the order of time, the longing for the ugly, the good, resolute desire of the Old Hellene for pessimism, for tragic myth, for the picture of all that is terrible, evil, enigmatical, destructive, fatal at the basis of existence,--whence then must tragedy have sprung? Perhaps from joy, from strength, from exuberant health, from over-fullness. And what then, physiologically speaking, is the meaning of that madness, out of which comic as well as tragic art has grown, the Dionysian madness? What? perhaps madness is not necessarily the symptom of degeneration, of decline, of belated culture? Perhaps there are--a question for alienists--neuroses of health? of folk-youth and youthfulness? What does that synthesis of god and goat in the Satyr point to? What self-experience what "stress," made the Greek think of the Dionysian reveller and primitive man as a satyr? And as regards the origin of the tragic chorus: perhaps there were endemic ecstasies in the eras when the Greek body bloomed and the Greek soul brimmed over with life? Visions and hallucinations, which took hold of entire communities, entire cult-assemblies? What if the Greeks in the very wealth of their youth had the will to be tragic and were pessimists? What if it was madness itself, to use a word of Plato's, which brought the greatest blessings upon Hellas? And what if, on the other hand and conversely, at the very time of their dissolution and weakness, the Greeks became always more optimistic, more superficial, more histrionic, also more ardent for logic and the logicising of the world,--consequently at the same time more "cheerful" and more "scientific"? Ay, despite all "modern ideas" and prejudices of the democratic taste, may not the triumph of optimism, the common sense that has gained the upper hand, the practical and theoretical utilitarianism, like democracy itself, with which it is synchronous--be symptomatic of declining vigour, of approaching age, of physiological weariness? And not at all--pessimism? Was Epicurus an optimist--because a sufferer?... We see it is a whole bundle of weighty questions which this book has taken upon itself,--let us not fail to add its weightiest question! Viewed through the optics of life, what is the meaning of--morality?...

5

Already in the foreword to Richard Wagner, art---and not morality--is set down as the properly metaphysical activity of man; in the book itself the piquant proposition recurs time and again, that the existence of the world is justified only as an æsthetic phenomenon. Indeed, the entire book recognises only an artist-thought and artist-after-thought behind all occurrences,--a "God," if you will, but certainly only an altogether thoughtless and unmoral artist-God, who, in construction as in destruction, in good as in evil, desires to become conscious of his own equable joy and sovereign glory; who, in creating worlds, frees himself from the anguish of fullness and overfullness, from the suffering of the contradictions concentrated within him. The world, that is, the redemption of God attained at every moment, as the perpetually changing, perpetually new vision of the most suffering, most antithetical, most contradictory being, who contrives to redeem himself only in appearance: this entire artist-metaphysics, call it arbitrary, idle, fantastic, if you will,--the point is, that it already betrays a spirit, which is determined some day, at all hazards, to make a stand against the moral interpretation and significance of life. Here, perhaps for the first time, a pessimism "Beyond Good and Evil" announces itself, here that "perverseness of disposition" obtains expression and formulation, against which Schopenhauer never grew tired of hurling beforehand his angriest imprecations and thunderbolts,--a philosophy which dares to put, derogatorily put, morality itself in the world of phenomena, and not only among "phenomena" (in the sense of the idealistic terminus technicus), but among the "illusions," as appearance, semblance, error, interpretation, accommodation, art. Perhaps the depth of this antimoral tendency may be best estimated from the guarded and hostile silence with which Christianity is treated throughout this book,--Christianity, as being the most extravagant burlesque of the moral theme to which mankind has hitherto been obliged to listen. In fact, to the purely æsthetic world-interpretation and justification taught in this book, there is no greater antithesis than the Christian dogma, which is only and will be only moral, and which, with its absolute standards, for instance, its truthfulness of God, relegates--that is, disowns, convicts, condemns--art, all art, to the realm of falsehood. Behind such a mode of thought and valuation, which, if at all genuine, must be hostile to art, I always experienced what was hostile to life, the wrathful, vindictive counterwill to life itself: for all life rests on appearance, art, illusion, optics, necessity of perspective and error. From the very first Christianity was, essentially and thoroughly, the nausea and surfeit of Life for Life, which only disguised, concealed and decked itself out under the belief in "another" or "better" life. The hatred of the "world," the curse on the affections, the fear of beauty and sensuality, another world, invented for the purpose of slandering this world the more, at bottom a longing for. Nothingness, for the end, for rest, for the "Sabbath of Sabbaths"--all this, as also the unconditional will of Christianity to recognise only moral values, has always appeared to me as the most dangerous and ominous of all possible forms of a "will to perish"; at the least, as the symptom of a most fatal disease, of profoundest weariness, despondency, exhaustion, impoverishment of life,--for before the tribunal of morality (especially Christian, that is, unconditional morality) life must constantly and inevitably be the loser, because life is something essentially unmoral,--indeed, oppressed with the weight of contempt and the everlasting No, life must finally be regarded as unworthy of desire, as in itself unworthy. Morality itself what?--may not morality be a "will to disown life," a secret instinct for annihilation, a principle of decay, of depreciation, of slander, a beginning of the end? And, consequently, the danger of dangers?... It was against morality, therefore, that my instinct, as an intercessory-instinct for life, turned in this questionable book, inventing for itself a fundamental counter--dogma and counter-valuation of life, purely artistic, purely anti-Christian. What should I call it? As a philologist and man of words I baptised it, not without some liberty--for who could be sure of the proper name of the Antichrist?--with the name of a Greek god: I called it Dionysian.

6

You see which problem I ventured to touch upon in this early work?... How I now regret, that I had not then the courage (or immodesty?) to allow myself, in all respects, the use of an individual language for such individual contemplations and ventures in the field of thought--that I laboured to express, in Kantian and Schopenhauerian formulæ, strange and new valuations, which ran fundamentally counter to the spirit of Kant and Schopenhauer, as well as to their taste! What, forsooth, were Schopenhauer's views on tragedy? "What gives"--he says in Welt als Wille und Vorstellung, II. 495--"to all tragedy that singular swing towards elevation, is the awakening of the knowledge that the world, that life, cannot satisfy us thoroughly, and consequently is not worthy of our attachment In this consists the tragic spirit: it therefore leads to resignation." Oh, how differently Dionysos spoke to me! Oh how far from me then was just this entire resignationism!--But there is something far worse in this book, which I now regret even more than having obscured and spoiled Dionysian anticipations with Schopenhauerian formulæ: to wit, that, in general, I spoiled the grand Hellenic problem, as it had opened up before me, by the admixture of the most modern things! That I entertained hopes, where nothing was to be hoped for, where everything pointed all-too-clearly to an approaching end! That, on the basis of our latter-day German music, I began to fable about the "spirit of Teutonism," as if it were on the point of discovering and returning to itself,--ay, at the very time that the German spirit which not so very long before had had the will to the lordship over Europe, the strength to lead and govern Europe, testamentarily and conclusively resigned and, under the pompous pretence of empire-founding, effected its transition to mediocritisation, democracy, and "modern ideas." In very fact, I have since learned to regard this "spirit of Teutonism" as something to be despaired of and unsparingly treated, as also our present German music, which is Romanticism through and through and the most un-Grecian of all possible forms of art: and moreover a first-rate nerve-destroyer, doubly dangerous for a people given to drinking and revering the unclear as a virtue, namely, in its twofold capacity of an intoxicating and stupefying narcotic. Of course, apart from all precipitate hopes and faulty applications to matters specially modern, with which I then spoiled my first book, the great Dionysian note of interrogation, as set down therein, continues standing on and on, even with reference to music: how must we conceive of a music, which is no longer of Romantic origin, like the German; but of Dionysian?...

7

--But, my dear Sir, if your book is not Romanticism, what in the world is? Can the deep hatred of the present, of "reality" and "modern ideas" be pushed farther than has been done in your artist-metaphysics?--which would rather believe in Nothing, or in the devil, than in the "Now"? Does not a radical bass of wrath and annihilative pleasure growl on beneath all your contrapuntal vocal art and aural seduction, a mad determination to oppose all that "now" is, a will which is not so very far removed from practical nihilism and which seems to say: "rather let nothing be true, than that you should be in the right, than that your truth should prevail!" Hear, yourself, my dear Sir Pessimist and art-deifier, with ever so unlocked ears, a single select passage of your own book, that not ineloquent dragon-slayer passage, which may sound insidiously rat-charming to young ears and hearts. What? is not that the true blue romanticist-confession of 1830 under the mask of the pessimism of 1850? After which, of course, the usual romanticist finale at once strikes up,--rupture, collapse, return and prostration before an old belief, before the old God.... What? is not your pessimist book itself a piece of anti-Hellenism and Romanticism, something "equally intoxicating and befogging," a narcotic at all events, ay, a piece of music, of German music? But listen:

> Let us imagine a rising generation with this undauntedness of vision, with this heroic impulse towards the prodigious, let us imagine the bold step of these dragon-slayers, the proud daring with which they turn their backs on all the effeminate doctrines of optimism, in order "to live resolutely" in the Whole and in the Full: would it not be necessary for the tragic man of this culture, with his self-discipline to earnestness and terror, to desire a new art, the art of metaphysical comfort, tragedy as the Helena belonging to him, and that he should exclaim with
>
> Faust:
>
> "Und sollt ich nicht, sehnsüchtigster Gewalt,
> In's Leben ziehn die einzigste Gestalt?"[1]

"Would it not be necessary?" ... No, thrice no! ye young romanticists: it would not be necessary! But it is very probable, that things may end thus, that ye may end thus, namely "comforted," as it is written, in spite of all self-discipline to earnestness and terror; metaphysically comforted, in short, as

Romanticists are wont to end, as Christians.... No! ye should first of all learn the art of earthly comfort, ye should learn to laugh, my young friends, if ye are at all determined to remain pessimists: if so, you will perhaps, as laughing ones, eventually send all metaphysical comfortism to the devil--and metaphysics first of all! Or, to say it in the language of that Dionysian ogre, called Zarathustra:

> "Lift up your hearts, my brethren, high, higher! And do not forget your legs! Lift up also your legs, ye good dancers--and better still if ye stand also on your heads!
>
> "This crown of the laughter, this rose-garland crown--I myself have put on this crown; I myself have consecrated my laughter. No one else have I found to-day strong enough for this.
>
> "Zarathustra the dancer, Zarathustra the light one, who beckoneth with his pinions, one ready for flight, beckoning unto all birds, ready and prepared, a blissfully light-spirited one:--
>
> "Zarathustra the soothsayer, Zarathustra the sooth-laugher, no impatient one, no absolute one, one who loveth leaps and side-leaps: I myself have put on this crown!
>
> "This crown of the laughter, this rose-garland crown--to you my brethren do I cast this crown! Laughing have I consecrated: ye higher men, learn, I pray you--to laugh!"
>
> Thus spake Zarathustra, lxxiii. 17, 18, and 20.
> SILS-MARIA, OBERENGADIN, August 1886.

Footnote:

1.
And shall not I, by mightiest desire,
In living shape that sole fair form acquire?
SWANWICK, trans. of Faust.

THE BIRTH OF TRAGEDY
FROM THE SPIRIT OF MUSIC

FOREWORD TO RICHARD WAGNER

In order to keep at a distance all the possible scruples, excitements, and misunderstandings to which the thoughts gathered in this essay will give occasion, considering the peculiar character of our æsthetic publicity, and to be able also Co write the introductory remarks with the same contemplative delight, the impress of which, as the petrifaction of good and elevating hours, it bears on every page, I form a conception of the moment when you, my highly honoured friend, will receive this essay; how you, say after an evening walk in the winter snow, will behold the unbound Prometheus on the title-page, read my name, and be forthwith convinced that, whatever this essay may contain, the author has something earnest and impressive to say, and, moreover, that in all his meditations he communed with you as with one present and could thus write only what befitted your presence. You will thus remember that it was at the same time as your magnificent dissertation on Beethoven originated, viz., amidst the horrors and sublimities of the war which had just then broken out, that I collected myself for these thoughts. But those persons would err, to whom this collection suggests no more perhaps than the antithesis of patriotic excitement and æsthetic revelry, of gallant earnestness and sportive delight. Upon a real perusal of this essay, such readers will, rather to their surprise, discover how earnest is the German problem we have to deal with, which we properly place, as a vortex and turning-point, in the very midst of German hopes. Perhaps, however, this same class of readers will be shocked at seeing an æsthetic problem taken so seriously, especially if they can recognise in art no more than a merry diversion, a readily dispensable court-jester to the "earnestness of existence": as if no one were aware of the real meaning of this confrontation with the "earnestness of existence." These earnest ones may be informed that I am convinced that art is the highest task and the properly metaphysical activity of this life, as it is understood by the man, to whom, as my sublime protagonist on this path, I would now dedicate this essay.

BASEL, end of the year 1871.

1

We shall have gained much for the science of æsthetics, when once we have perceived not only by logical inference, but by the immediate certainty of intuition, that the continuous development of art is bound up with the duplexity of the Apollonian and the Dionysian: in like manner as procreation is dependent on the duality of the sexes, involving perpetual conflicts with only periodically intervening reconciliations. These names we borrow from the Greeks, who disclose to the intelligent observer the profound mysteries of their view of art, not indeed in concepts, but in the impressively clear figures of their world of deities. It is in connection with Apollo and Dionysus, the two art-deities of the Greeks, that we learn that there existed in the Grecian world a wide antithesis, in origin and aims, between the art of the shaper, the Apollonian, and the non-plastic art of music, that of Dionysus: both these so heterogeneous tendencies run parallel to each other, for the most part openly at variance, and continually inciting each other to new and more powerful births, to perpetuate in them the strife of this antithesis, which is but seemingly bridged over by their mutual term "Art"; till at last, by a metaphysical miracle of the Hellenic will, they appear paired with each other, and through this pairing eventually generate the equally Dionysian and Apollonian art-work of Attic tragedy.

In order to bring these two tendencies within closer range, let us conceive them first of all as the separate art-worlds of dreamland and drunkenness; between which physiological phenomena a contrast may be observed analogous to that existing between the Apollonian and the Dionysian. In dreams, according to the conception of Lucretius, the glorious divine figures first appeared to the souls of men, in dreams the great shaper beheld the charming corporeal structure of superhuman beings, and the Hellenic poet, if consulted on the mysteries of poetic inspiration, would likewise have suggested dreams and would have offered an explanation resembling that of Hans Sachs in the Meistersingers:--

Mein Freund, das grad' ist Dichters Werk,
dass er sein Träumen deut' und merk'.
Glaubt mir, des Menschen wahrster Wahn
wird ihm im Traume aufgethan:
all' Dichtkunst und Poeterei
ist nichts als Wahrtraum-Deuterei.[1]

The beauteous appearance of the dream-worlds, in the production of which every man is a perfect artist, is the presupposition of all plastic art, and in fact, as we shall see, of an important half of poetry also. We take delight in the immediate apprehension of form; all forms speak to us; there is nothing indifferent, nothing superfluous. But, together with the highest life of this dream-reality we also have, glimmering through it, the sensation of its appearance: such at least is my experience, as to the frequency, ay, normality of which I could adduce many proofs, as also the sayings of the poets. Indeed, the man of philosophic turn has a foreboding that underneath this reality in which we live and have our being, another and altogether different reality lies concealed, and that therefore it is also an appearance; and Schopenhauer actually designates the gift of occasionally regarding men and things as mere phantoms and dream-pictures as the criterion of philosophical ability. Accordingly, the man susceptible to art stands in the same relation to the reality of dreams as the philosopher to the reality of existence; he is a close and willing observer, for from these pictures he reads the meaning of life, and by these processes he trains himself for life. And it is perhaps not only the agreeable and friendly pictures that he realises in himself with such perfect understanding: the earnest, the troubled, the dreary, the gloomy, the sudden checks, the tricks of fortune, the uneasy presentiments, in short, the whole "Divine Comedy" of life, and the Inferno, also pass before him, not merely like pictures on the wall--for he too lives and suffers in these scenes,--and yet not without that fleeting sensation of appearance. And perhaps many a one will, like myself, recollect having sometimes called out cheeringly and not without success amid the dangers and terrors of dream-life: "It is a dream! I will dream on!" I have likewise been told of persons capable of continuing the causality of one and the same dream for three and even more successive nights: all of which facts clearly testify that our innermost being, the common substratum of all of us, experiences our dreams with deep joy and cheerful acquiescence.

This cheerful acquiescence in the dream-experience has likewise been embodied by the Greeks in their Apollo: for Apollo, as the god of all shaping energies, is also the soothsaying god. He, who (as the etymology of the name indicates) is the "shining one," the deity of light, also rules over the fair appearance of the inner world of fantasies. The higher truth, the perfection of these states in contrast to the only partially intelligible everyday world, ay, the deep consciousness of nature, healing and helping in sleep and dream, is at the same time the symbolical analogue of the faculty of soothsaying and, in general, of the arts, through which life is made possible and worth living. But also that delicate line, which the dream-picture must not overstep--lest it act pathologically (in which case appearance, being reality pure and simple, would impose upon us)--must not be wanting in the picture of Apollo: that measured limitation, that freedom from the wilder emotions, that philosophical calmness of the sculptor-god. His eye must be "sunlike," according to his origin; even when it is angry and looks displeased, the sacredness of his beauteous appearance is still there. And so we might apply to Apollo, in an eccentric sense, what Schopenhauer says of the man wrapt in the veil of Mâyâ[2]: Welt als Wille und Vorstellung, I. p. 416: "Just as in a stormy sea, unbounded in every direction, rising and falling with howling mountainous waves, a sailor sits in a boat and trusts in his frail barque: so in the midst of a world of sorrows the individual sits quietly supported by and trusting in his principium individuationis." Indeed, we might say of Apollo, that in him the unshaken faith in this principium and the quiet sitting of the man wrapt therein have received their sublimest expression; and we might even designate Apollo as the glorious divine image of the principium individuationis, from out of the gestures and looks of which all the joy and wisdom of "appearance," together with its beauty, speak to us.

In the same work Schopenhauer has described to us the stupendous awe which seizes upon man, when of a sudden he is at a loss to account for the cognitive forms of a phenomenon, in that the principle of reason, in some one of its manifestations, seems to admit of an exception. Add to this awe the blissful ecstasy which rises from the innermost depths of man, ay, of nature, at this same collapse of the principium individuationis, and we shall gain an insight into the being of the Dionysian, which is brought within closest ken perhaps by the analogy of drunkenness. It is either under the influence of the narcotic draught, of which the hymns of all primitive men and peoples tell us, or by the powerful approach of spring penetrating all nature with joy, that those Dionysian emotions awake, in the augmentation of which the subjective vanishes to complete self-forgetfulness. So also in the German Middle Ages singing and dancing crowds, ever increasing in number, were borne from place to place under this same Dionysian power. In these St. John's and St. Vitus's dancers we again perceive the

Bacchic choruses of the Greeks, with their previous history in Asia Minor, as far back as Babylon and the orgiastic Sacæa. There are some, who, from lack of experience or obtuseness, will turn away from such phenomena as "folk-diseases" with a smile of contempt or pity prompted by the consciousness of their own health: of course, the poor wretches do not divine what a cadaverous-looking and ghastly aspect this very "health" of theirs presents when the glowing life of the Dionysian revellers rushes past them.

Under the charm of the Dionysian not only is the covenant between man and man again established, but also estranged, hostile or subjugated nature again celebrates her reconciliation with her lost son, man. Of her own accord earth proffers her gifts, and peacefully the beasts of prey approach from the desert and the rocks. The chariot of Dionysus is bedecked with flowers and garlands: panthers and tigers pass beneath his yoke. Change Beethoven's "jubilee-song" into a painting, and, if your imagination be equal to the occasion when the awestruck millions sink into the dust, you will then be able to approach the Dionysian. Now is the slave a free man, now all the stubborn, hostile barriers, which necessity, caprice, or "shameless fashion" has set up between man and man, are broken down. Now, at the evangel of cosmic harmony, each one feels himself not only united, reconciled, blended with his neighbour, but as one with him, as if the veil of Mâyâ has been torn and were now merely fluttering in tatters before the mysterious Primordial Unity. In song and in dance man exhibits himself as a member of a higher community, has forgotten how to walk and speak, and is on the point of taking a dancing flight into the air. His gestures bespeak enchantment. Even as the animals now talk, and as the earth yields milk and honey, so also something super-natural sounds forth from him: he feels himself a god, he himself now walks about enchanted and elated even as the gods whom he saw walking about in his dreams. Man is no longer an artist, he has become a work of art: the artistic power of all nature here reveals itself in the tremors of drunkenness to the highest gratification of the Primordial Unity. The noblest clay, the costliest marble, namely man, is here kneaded and cut, and the chisel strokes of the Dionysian world-artist are accompanied with the cry of the Eleusinian mysteries: "Ihr stürzt nieder, Millionen? Ahnest du den Schöpfer, Welt?"[3]

Footnotes:

1.

My friend, just this is poet's task:
His dreams to read and to unmask.
Trust me, illusion's truths thrice sealed
In dream to man will be revealed.
All verse-craft and poetisation
Is but soothdream interpretation.

2. Cf. World and Will as Idea, 1. 455 ff., trans, by Haldane and Kemp.

3.

Ye bow in the dust, oh millions?
Thy maker, mortal, dost divine? Cf. Schiller's "Hymn to Joy"; and Beethoven, Ninth Symphony.--TR.

2

Thus far we have considered the Apollonian and his antithesis, the Dionysian, as artistic powers, which burst forth from nature herself, without the mediation of the human artist, and in which her art-impulses are satisfied in the most immediate and direct way: first, as the pictorial world of dreams, the perfection of which has no connection whatever with the intellectual height or artistic culture of the unit man, and again, as drunken reality, which likewise does not heed the unit man, but even seeks to destroy the individual and redeem him by a mystic feeling of Oneness. Anent these immediate art-states of nature every artist is either an "imitator," to wit, either an Apollonian, an artist in dreams, or a Dionysian, an artist in ecstasies, or finally--as for instance in Greek tragedy--an artist in both dreams and ecstasies: so we may perhaps picture him, as in his Dionysian drunkenness and mystical self-abnegation, lonesome and apart from the revelling choruses, he sinks down, and how now, through Apollonian dream-inspiration, his own state, i.e., his oneness with the primal source of the universe, reveals itself to him in a symbolical dream-picture.

After these general premisings and contrastings, let us now approach the Greeks in order to learn in what degree and to what height these art-impulses of nature were developed in them: whereby we shall be enabled to understand and appreciate more deeply the relation of the Greek artist to his archetypes, or, according to the Aristotelian expression, "the imitation of nature." In spite of all the dream-literature and the numerous dream-anecdotes of the Greeks, we can speak only conjecturally, though with a fair degree of certainty, of their dreams. Considering the incredibly precise and unerring plastic power of their eyes, as also their manifest and sincere delight in colours, we can hardly refrain (to the shame of every one born later) from assuming for their very dreams a logical causality of lines and contours, colours and groups, a sequence of scenes resembling their best reliefs, the perfection of which would certainly justify us, if a comparison were possible, in designating the dreaming Greeks as Homers and Homer as a dreaming Greek: in a deeper sense than when modern man, in respect to his dreams, ventures to compare himself with Shakespeare.

On the other hand, we should not have to speak conjecturally, if asked to disclose the immense gap which separated the Dionysian Greek from the Dionysian barbarian. From all quarters of the Ancient World--to say nothing of the modern--from Rome as far as Babylon, we can prove the existence of Dionysian festivals, the type of which bears, at best, the same relation to the Greek festivals as the bearded satyr, who borrowed his name and attributes from the goat, does to Dionysus himself. In nearly every instance the centre of these festivals lay in extravagant sexual licentiousness, the waves of which overwhelmed all family life and its venerable traditions; the very wildest beasts of nature were let loose here, including that detestable mixture of lust and cruelty which has always seemed to me the genuine "witches' draught." For some time, however, it would seem that the Greeks were perfectly secure and guarded against the feverish agitations of these festivals (--the knowledge of which entered Greece by all the channels of land and sea) by the figure of Apollo himself rising here in full pride, who could not have held out the Gorgon's head to a more dangerous power than this grotesquely uncouth Dionysian. It is in Doric art that this majestically-rejecting attitude of Apollo perpetuated itself. This opposition became more precarious and even impossible, when, from out of the deepest root of the Hellenic nature, similar impulses finally broke forth and made way for themselves: the Delphic god, by a seasonably effected reconciliation, was now contented with taking the destructive arms from the hands of his powerful antagonist. This reconciliation marks the most important moment in the history of the Greek cult: wherever we turn our eyes we may observe the revolutions resulting from this event. It was the reconciliation of two antagonists, with the sharp demarcation of the boundary-lines to be thenceforth observed by each, and with periodical transmission of testimonials;--in reality, the chasm was not bridged over. But if we observe how, under the pressure of this conclusion of peace, the Dionysian power manifested itself, we shall now recognise in the Dionysian orgies of the Greeks, as compared with the Babylonian Sacæa and their retrogression of man to the tiger and the ape, the significance of festivals of world-redemption and days of transfiguration. Not till then does nature attain her artistic jubilee; not till then does the rupture of the principium individuationis become an artistic phenomenon. That horrible "witches' draught" of sensuality and cruelty was here powerless: only the curious blending and duality in the emotions of the Dionysian revellers reminds one of it--just as medicines remind one of deadly poisons,--that phenomenon, to wit, that pains beget joy, that jubilation wrings painful sounds out of the breast. From the highest joy sounds the cry of horror or the yearning wail over an irretrievable loss. In these Greek festivals a sentimental trait, as it were, breaks forth from nature, as if she must sigh over her dismemberment into individuals. The song and pantomime of such dually-minded revellers was something new and unheard-of in the Homeric-Grecian world; and the Dionysian music in particular excited awe and horror. If music, as it would seem, was previously known as an Apollonian art, it was, strictly speaking, only as the wave-beat of rhythm, the formative power of which was developed to the representation of Apollonian conditions. The music of Apollo was Doric architectonics in tones, but in merely suggested tones, such as those of the cithara. The very element which forms the essence of Dionysian music (and hence of music in general) is carefully excluded as un-Apollonian; namely, the thrilling powèr of the tone, the uniform stream of the melos, and the thoroughly incomparable world of harmony. In the Dionysian dithyramb man is incited to the highest exaltation of all his symbolic faculties; something never before experienced struggles for utterance--the annihilation of the veil of Mâyâ, Oneness as genius of the race, ay, of nature. The essence of nature is now to be expressed symbolically; a new world of symbols is required; for once the entire symbolism of the body, not only the symbolism of the lips, face, and speech, but the whole pantomime of dancing which sets all the members into rhythmical motion. Thereupon the other symbolic powers, those of music, in rhythmics, dynamics, and harmony, suddenly become impetuous. To comprehend this collective discharge of all the symbolic powers, a man must have already attained that height of self-abnegation, which wills to express itself symbolically through these powers: the Dithyrambic votary of Dionysus is therefore understood only by those like himself! With what astonishment must the Apollonian Greek have beheld him! With an astonishment, which was all the greater the more it was mingled with the shuddering suspicion that all this was in reality not so very foreign to him, yea, that, like unto a veil, his Apollonian consciousness only hid this Dionysian world from his view.

3

In order to comprehend this, we must take down the artistic structure, of the Apollonian culture, as it were, stone by stone, till we behold the foundations on which it rests. Here we observe first of all the glorious Olympian figures of the gods, standing on the gables of this structure, whose deeds, represented in far-shining reliefs, adorn its friezes. Though Apollo stands among them as an individual deity, side by side with others, and without claim to priority of rank, we must not suffer this fact to mislead us. The same impulse which embodied itself in Apollo has, in general, given birth to this whole Olympian world, and in this sense we may regard Apollo as the father thereof. What was the enormous need from which proceeded such an illustrious group of Olympian beings?

Whosoever, with another religion in his heart, approaches these Olympians and seeks among them for moral elevation, even for sanctity, for incorporeal spiritualisation, for sympathetic looks of love, will soon be obliged to turn his back on them, discouraged and disappointed. Here nothing suggests asceticism, spirituality, or duty: here only an exuberant, even triumphant life speaks to us, in which everything existing is deified, whether good or bad. And so the spectator will perhaps stand quite bewildered before this fantastic exuberance of life, and ask himself what magic potion these madly merry men could have used for enjoying life, so that, wherever they turned their eyes, Helena, the ideal image of their own existence "floating in sweet sensuality," smiled upon them. But to this spectator, already turning backwards, we must call out: "depart not hence, but hear rather what Greek folk-wisdom says of this same life, which with such inexplicable cheerfulness spreads out before thee." There is an ancient story that king Midas hunted in the forest a long time for the wise Silenus, the companion of Dionysus, without capturing him. When at last he fell into his hands, the king asked what was best of all and most desirable for man. Fixed and immovable, the demon remained silent; till at last, forced by the king, he broke out with shrill laughter into these words: "Oh, wretched race of a day, children of chance and misery, why do ye compel me to say to you what it were most expedient for you not to hear? What is best of all is for ever beyond your reach: not to be born, not to be, to be nothing. The second best for you, however, is soon to die."

How is the Olympian world of deities related to this folk-wisdom? Even as the rapturous vision of the tortured martyr to his sufferings.

Now the Olympian magic mountain opens, as it were, to our view and shows to us its roots. The Greek knew and felt the terrors and horrors of existence: to be able to live at all, he had to interpose the shining dream-birth of the Olympian world between himself and them. The excessive distrust of the titanic powers of nature, the Moira throning inexorably over all knowledge, the vulture of the great philanthropist Prometheus, the terrible fate of the wise Œdipus, the family curse of the Atridæ which drove Orestes to matricide; in short, that entire philosophy of the sylvan god, with its mythical exemplars, which wrought the ruin of the melancholy Etruscans--was again and again surmounted anew by the Greeks through the artistic middle world of the Olympians, or at least veiled and withdrawn from sight. To be able to live, the Greeks had, from direst necessity, to create these gods: which process we may perhaps picture to ourselves in this manner: that out of the original Titan thearchy of terror the Olympian thearchy of joy was evolved, by slow transitions, through the Apollonian impulse to beauty, even as roses break forth from thorny bushes. How else could this so sensitive people, so vehement in its desires, so singularly qualified for sufferings have endured existence, if it had not been exhibited to them in their gods, surrounded with a higher glory? The same impulse which calls art into being, as the complement and consummation of existence, seducing to a continuation of life, caused also the Olympian world to arise, in which the Hellenic "will" held up before itself a transfiguring mirror. Thus do the gods justify the life of man, in that they themselves live it--the only satisfactory Theodicy! Existence under the bright sunshine of such gods is regarded as that which is desirable in itself, and the real grief of the Homeric men has reference to parting from it, especially to early parting: so that we might now say of them, with a reversion of the Silenian wisdom, that "to die early is worst of all for them, the second worst is--some day to die at all." If once the lamentation is heard, it will ring out again, of the short-lived Achilles, of the leaf-like change and vicissitude of the human race, of the decay of the heroic age. It is not unworthy of the greatest hero to long for a continuation of life, ay, even as a day-labourer. So vehemently does the "will," at the Apollonian stage of development, long for this existence, so completely at one does the Homeric man feel himself with it, that the very lamentation becomes its song of praise.

Here we must observe that this harmony which is so eagerly contemplated by modern man, in fact, this oneness of man with nature, to express which Schiller introduced the technical term "naïve," is by no means such a simple, naturally resulting and, as it were, inevitable condition, which must be found at the gate of every culture leading to a paradise of man: this could be believed only by an age which sought to picture to itself Rousseau's Émile also as an artist, and imagined it had found in Homer such an artist Émile, reared at Nature's bosom. Wherever we meet with the "naïve" in art, it behoves us to recognise the highest effect of the Apollonian culture, which in the first place has always to overthrow some Titanic empire and slay monsters, and which, through powerful dazzling representations and pleasurable illusions, must have triumphed over a terrible depth of world-contemplation and a most keen susceptibility to suffering. But how seldom is the naïve--that complete absorption, in the beauty of appearance--attained! And hence how inexpressibly sublime is Homer, who, as unit being, bears the same relation to this Apollonian folk-culture as the unit dream-artist does to the dream-faculty of the people and of Nature in general. The Homeric "naïveté" can be comprehended only as the complete triumph of the Apollonian illusion: it is the same kind of illusion as Nature so frequently employs to compass her ends. The true goal is veiled by a phantasm: we stretch out our hands for the latter, while Nature attains the former through our illusion. In the Greeks the "will" desired to contemplate itself in the transfiguration of the genius and the world of art; in order to glorify themselves, its creatures had to feel themselves worthy of glory; they had to behold themselves again in a higher sphere, without this consummate world of contemplation acting as an imperative or reproach. Such is the sphere of beauty, in which, as in a mirror, they saw their images, the Olympians. With this mirroring of beauty the Hellenic will combated its talent--correlative to the artistic--for suffering and for the wisdom of suffering: and, as a monument of its victory, Homer, the naïve artist, stands before us.

4

Concerning this naïve artist the analogy of dreams will enlighten us to some extent. When we realise to ourselves the dreamer, as, in the midst of the illusion of the dream-world and without disturbing it, he calls out to himself: "it is a dream, I will dream on"; when we must thence infer a deep inner joy in dream-contemplation; when, on the other hand, to be at all able to dream with this inner joy in contemplation, we must have completely forgotten the day and its terrible obtrusiveness, we may, under the direction of the dream-reading Apollo, interpret all these phenomena to ourselves somewhat as follows. Though it is certain that of the two halves of life, the waking and the dreaming, the former appeals to us as by far the more preferred, important, excellent and worthy of being lived, indeed, as that which alone is lived: yet, with reference to that mysterious ground of our being of which we are the phenomenon, I should, paradoxical as it may seem, be inclined to maintain the very opposite estimate of the value of dream life. For the more clearly I perceive in nature those all-powerful art impulses, and in them a fervent longing for appearance, for redemption through appearance, the more I feel myself driven to the metaphysical assumption that the Verily-Existent and Primordial Unity, as the Eternally Suffering and Self-Contradictory, requires the rapturous vision, the joyful appearance, for its continuous salvation: which appearance we, who are completely wrapt in it and composed of it, must regard as the Verily Non-existent,--i.e., as a perpetual unfolding in time, space and causality,--in other words, as empiric reality. If we therefore waive the consideration of our own "reality" for the present, if we conceive our empiric existence, and that of the world generally, as a representation of the Primordial Unity generated every moment, we shall then have to regard the dream as an appearance of appearance, hence as a still higher gratification of the primordial desire for appearance. It is for this same reason that the innermost heart of Nature experiences that indescribable joy in the naïve artist and in the naïve work of art, which is likewise only "an appearance of appearance." In a symbolic painting, Raphael, himself one of these immortal "naïve" ones, has represented to us this depotentiating of appearance to appearance, the primordial process of the naïve artist and at the same time of Apollonian culture. In his Transfiguration, the lower half, with the possessed boy, the despairing bearers, the helpless, terrified disciples, shows to us the reflection of eternal primordial pain, the sole basis of the world: the "appearance" here is the counter-appearance of eternal Contradiction, the father of things. Out of this appearance then arises, like an ambrosial vapour, a visionlike new world of appearances, of which those wrapt in the first appearance see nothing--a radiant floating in purest bliss and painless Contemplation beaming from wide-open eyes. Here there is presented to our view, in the highest symbolism of art, that Apollonian world of beauty and its substratum, the terrible wisdom of Silenus, and we comprehend, by intuition, their necessary interdependence. Apollo, however, again appears to us as the apotheosis of the principium individuationis, in which alone the perpetually attained end of the Primordial Unity, its redemption through appearance, is consummated: he shows us, with sublime attitudes, how the entire world of torment is necessary, that thereby the individual may be impelled to realise the redeeming vision, and then, sunk in contemplation thereof, quietly sit in his fluctuating barque, in the midst of the sea.

This apotheosis of individuation, if it be at all conceived as imperative and laying down precepts, knows but one law--the individual, i.e., the observance of the boundaries of the individual, measure in the Hellenic sense. Apollo, as ethical deity, demands due proportion of his disciples, and, that this may be observed, he demands self-knowledge. And thus, parallel to the æsthetic necessity for beauty, there run the demands "know thyself" and "not too much," while presumption and undueness are regarded as the truly hostile demons of the non-Apollonian sphere, hence as characteristics of the pre-Apollonian age, that of the Titans, and of the extra-Apollonian world, that of the barbarians. Because of his Titan-like love for man, Prometheus had to be torn to pieces by vultures; because of his excessive wisdom, which solved the riddle of the Sphinx, Œdipus had to plunge into a bewildering vortex of monstrous crimes: thus did the Delphic god interpret the Grecian past.

So also the effects wrought by the Dionysian appeared "titanic" and "barbaric" to the Apollonian Greek: while at the same time he could not conceal from himself that he too was inwardly related to these overthrown Titans and heroes. Indeed, he had to recognise still more than this: his entire existence, with all its beauty and moderation, rested on a hidden substratum of suffering and of knowledge, which was again disclosed to him by the Dionysian. And lo! Apollo could not live without Dionysus! The "titanic" and the "barbaric" were in the end not less necessary than the Apollonian. And now let us imagine to ourselves how the ecstatic tone of the Dionysian festival sounded in ever more luring and bewitching strains into this artificially confined world built on appearance and moderation, how in these strains all the undueness of nature, in joy, sorrow, and knowledge, even to the transpiercing shriek, became audible: let us ask ourselves what meaning could be attached to the psalmodising artist of Apollo, with the phantom harp-sound, as compared with this demonic folk-song! The muses of the arts of "appearance" paled before an art which, in its intoxication, spoke the truth, the wisdom of Silenus cried "woe! woe!" against the cheerful Olympians. The individual, with all his boundaries and due proportions, went under in the self-oblivion of the Dionysian states and forgot the Apollonian precepts. The Undueness revealed itself as truth, contradiction, the bliss born of pain, declared itself but of the heart of nature. And thus, wherever the Dionysian prevailed, the Apollonian was routed and annihilated. But it is quite as certain that, where the first assault was successfully withstood, the authority and majesty of the Delphic god exhibited itself as more rigid and menacing than ever. For I can only explain to myself the Doric state and Doric art as a permanent war-camp of the Apollonian: only by incessant opposition to the titanic-barbaric nature of the Dionysian was it possible for an art so defiantly-prim, so encompassed with bulwarks, a training so warlike and rigorous, a constitution so cruel and relentless, to last for any length of time.

Up to this point we have enlarged upon the observation made at the beginning of this essay: how the Dionysian and the Apollonian, in ever new births succeeding and mutually augmenting one another, controlled the Hellenic genius: how from out the age of "bronze," with its Titan struggles and rigorous folk-philosophy, the Homeric world develops under the fostering sway of the Apollonian impulse to beauty, how this "naïve" splendour is again overwhelmed by the inbursting flood of the Dionysian, and how against this new power the Apollonian rises to the austere majesty of Doric art and the Doric view of things. If, then, in this way, in the strife of these two hostile principles, the older Hellenic history falls into four great periods of art, we are now driven to inquire after the ulterior purpose of these unfoldings and processes, unless perchance we should regard the last-attained period, the period of Doric art, as the end and aim of these artistic impulses: and here the sublime and highly celebrated art-work of Attic tragedy and dramatic dithyramb presents itself to our view as the common goal of both these impulses, whose mysterious union, after many and long precursory struggles, found its glorious consummation in such a child,--which is at once Antigone and Cassandra.

5

We now approach the real purpose of our investigation, which aims at acquiring a knowledge of the Dionyso-Apollonian genius and his art-work, or at least an anticipatory understanding of the mystery of the aforesaid union. Here we shall ask first of all where that new germ which subsequently developed into tragedy and dramatic dithyramb first makes itself perceptible in the Hellenic world. The ancients themselves supply the answer in symbolic form, when they place Homer and Archilochus as the forefathers and torch-bearers of Greek poetry side by side on gems, sculptures, etc., in the sure conviction that only these two thoroughly original compeers, from whom a stream of fire flows over the whole of Greek posterity, should be taken into consideration. Homer, the aged dreamer sunk in himself, the type of the Apollonian naïve artist, beholds now with astonishment the impassioned genius of the warlike votary of the muses, Archilochus, violently tossed to and fro on the billows of existence: and modern æsthetics could only add by way of interpretation, that here the "objective" artist is confronted by the first "subjective" artist. But this interpretation is of little service to us, because we know the subjective artist only as the poor artist, and in every type and elevation of art we demand specially and first of all the conquest of the Subjective, the redemption from the "ego" and the cessation of every individual will and desire; indeed, we find it impossible to believe in any truly artistic production, however insignificant, without objectivity, without pure, interestless contemplation. Hence our æsthetics must first solve the problem as to how the "lyrist" is possible as an artist: he who according to the experience of all ages continually says "I" and sings off to us the entire chromatic scale of his passions and desires. This very Archilochus appals us, alongside of Homer, by his cries of hatred and scorn, by the drunken outbursts of his desire. Is not just he then, who has been called the first subjective artist, the non-artist proper? But whence then the reverence which was shown to him--the poet--in very remarkable utterances by the Delphic oracle itself, the focus of "objective" art?

Schiller has enlightened us concerning his poetic procedure by a psychological observation, inexplicable to himself, yet not apparently open to any objection. He acknowledges that as the preparatory state to the act of poetising he had not perhaps before him or within him a series of pictures with co-ordinate causality of thoughts, but rather a musical mood ("The perception with me is at first without a clear and definite object; this forms itself later. A certain musical mood of mind precedes, and only after this does the poetical idea follow with me.") Add to this the most important phenomenon of all ancient lyric poetry, the union, regarded everywhere as natural, of the lyrist with the musician, their very identity, indeed,--compared with which our modern lyric poetry is like the statue of a god without a head,--and we may now, on the basis of our metaphysics of æsthetics set forth above, interpret the lyrist to ourselves as follows. As Dionysian artist he is in the first place become altogether one with the Primordial Unity, its pain and contradiction, and he produces the copy of this Primordial Unity as music, granting that music has been correctly termed a repetition and a recast of the world; but now, under the Apollonian dream-inspiration, this music again becomes visible to him as in a symbolic dream-picture. The formless and intangible reflection of the primordial pain in music, with its redemption in appearance, then generates a second mirroring as a concrete symbol or example. The artist has already surrendered his subjectivity in the Dionysian process: the picture which now shows to him his oneness with the heart of the world, is a dream-scene, which embodies the primordial contradiction and primordial pain, together with the primordial joy, of appearance. The "I" of the lyrist sounds therefore from the abyss of being: its "subjectivity," in the sense of the modern æsthetes, is a fiction. When Archilochus, the first lyrist of the Greeks, makes known both his mad love and his contempt to the daughters of Lycambes, it is not his passion which dances before us in orgiastic frenzy: we see Dionysus and the Mænads, we see the drunken reveller Archilochus sunk down to sleep--as Euripides depicts it in the Bacchæ, the sleep on the high Alpine pasture, in the noonday sun:--and now Apollo approaches and touches him with the laurel. The Dionyso-musical enchantment of the sleeper now emits, as it were, picture sparks, lyrical poems, which in their highest development are called tragedies and dramatic dithyrambs.

The plastic artist, as also the epic poet, who is related to him, is sunk in the pure contemplation of pictures. The Dionysian musician is, without any picture, himself just primordial pain and the primordial re-echoing thereof. The lyric genius is conscious of a world of pictures and symbols--growing out of the state of mystical self-abnegation and oneness,--which has a colouring causality and velocity quite different from that of the world of the plastic artist and epic poet. While the latter lives in these pictures, and only in them, with joyful satisfaction, and never grows tired of contemplating them with love, even in their minutest characters, while even the picture of the angry Achilles is to him but a picture, the angry expression of which he enjoys with the dream-joy in appearance--so that, by this mirror of appearance, he is guarded against being unified and blending with his figures;--the pictures of the lyrist on the other hand are nothing but his very self and, as it were, only different projections of himself, on account of which he as the moving centre of this world is entitled to say "I": only of course this self is not the same as that of the waking, empirically real man, but the only verily existent and eternal self resting at the basis of things, by means of the images whereof the lyric genius sees through even to this basis of things. Now let us suppose that he beholds himself also among these images as non-genius, i.e., his subject, the whole throng of subjective passions and impulses of the will directed to a definite object which appears real to him; if now it seems as if the lyric genius and the allied non-genius were one, and as if the former spoke that little word "I" of his own accord, this appearance will no longer be able to lead us astray, as it certainly led those astray who designated the lyrist as the subjective poet. In truth, Archilochus, the passionately inflamed, loving and hating man, is but a vision of the genius, who by this time is no longer Archilochus, but a genius of the world, who expresses his primordial pain symbolically in the figure of the man Archilochus: while the subjectively willing and desiring man, Archilochus, can never at any time be a poet. It is by no means necessary, however, that the lyrist should see nothing but the phenomenon of the man Archilochus before him as a reflection of eternal being; and tragedy shows how far the visionary world of the lyrist may depart from this phenomenon, to which, of course, it is most intimately related.

Schopenhauer, who did not shut his eyes to the difficulty presented by the lyrist in the philosophical contemplation of art, thought he had found a way out of it, on which, however, I cannot accompany him; while he alone, in his profound metaphysics of music, held in his hands the means whereby this difficulty could be definitely removed: as I believe I have removed it here in his spirit and to his honour. In contrast to our view, he describes the peculiar nature of song as follows[4] (Welt als Wille und Vorstellung, I. 295):--"It is the subject of the will, i.e., his own volition, which fills the consciousness of the singer; often as an unbound and satisfied desire (joy), but still more often as a restricted desire (grief), always as an emotion, a passion, or an agitated frame of mind. Besides this, however, and along with it, by the sight of surrounding nature, the singer becomes conscious of himself as the subject of pure will-less knowing, the unbroken, blissful peace of which now appears, in contrast to the stress of desire, which is always restricted and always needy. The feeling of this contrast, this alternation, is really what the song as a whole expresses and what principally constitutes the lyrical state of mind. In it pure knowing comes to us as it were to deliver us from desire and the stress thereof: we follow, but only for an instant; for desire, the remembrance of our personal ends, tears us anew from peaceful contemplation; yet ever again the next beautiful surrounding in which the pure will-less knowledge presents itself to us, allures us away from desire. Therefore, in song and in the lyrical mood, desire (the personal interest of the ends) and the pure perception of the surrounding which presents itself, are wonderfully mingled with each other; connections between them are sought for and imagined; the subjective disposition, the affection of the will, imparts its own hue to the contemplated surrounding, and conversely, the surroundings communicate the reflex of their colour to the will. The true song is the expression of the whole of this mingled and divided state of mind."

Who could fail to see in this description that lyric poetry is here characterised as an imperfectly attained art, which seldom and only as it were in leaps arrives at its goal, indeed, as a semi-art, the essence of which is said to consist in this, that desire and pure contemplation, i.e., the unæsthetic and the æsthetic condition, are wonderfully mingled with each other? We maintain rather, that this entire antithesis, according to which, as according to some standard of value, Schopenhauer, too, still classifies the arts, the antithesis between the subjective and the objective, is quite out of place in æsthetics, inasmuch as the subject i.e., the desiring individual who furthers his own egoistic ends, can be conceived only as the adversary, not as the origin of art. In so far as the subject is the artist, however, he has already been released from his individual will, and has become as it were the medium, through which the one verily existent Subject celebrates his redemption in appearance. For this one thing must above all be clear to us, to our humiliation and exaltation, that the entire comedy of art is not at all performed, say, for our betterment and culture, and that we are just as little the true authors of this art-world: rather we may assume with regard to ourselves, that its true author uses us as pictures and artistic projections, and that we have our highest dignity in our significance as works of art--for only as an æsthetic phenomenon is existence and the world eternally justified:--while of course our consciousness of this our specific significance hardly differs from the kind of consciousness which the soldiers painted on canvas have of the battle represented thereon. Hence all our knowledge of art is at bottom quite illusory, because, as knowing persons we are not one and identical with the Being who, as the sole author and spectator of this comedy of art, prepares a perpetual entertainment for himself. Only in so far as the genius in the act of artistic production coalesces with this primordial artist of the world, does he get a glimpse of the eternal essence of art, for in this state he is, in a marvellous manner, like the weird picture of the fairy-tale which can at will turn its eyes and behold itself; he is now at once subject and object, at once poet, actor, and spectator.

Footnote:

4. World as Will and Idea, I. 323, 4th ed. of Haldane and Kemp's translation. Quoted with a few changes.

With reference to Archilochus, it has been established by critical research that he introduced the folk-song into literature, and, on account thereof, deserved, according to the general estimate of the Greeks, his unique position alongside of Homer. But what is this popular folk-song in contrast to the wholly Apollonian epos? What else but the perpetuum vestigium of a union of the Apollonian and the Dionysian? Its enormous diffusion among all peoples, still further enhanced by ever new births, testifies to the power of this artistic double impulse of nature: which leaves its vestiges in the popular song in like manner as the orgiastic movements of a people perpetuate themselves in its music. Indeed, one might also furnish historical proofs, that every period which is highly productive in popular songs has been most violently stirred by Dionysian currents, which we must always regard as the substratum and prerequisite of the popular song.

First of all, however, we regard the popular song as the musical mirror of the world, as the Original melody, which now seeks for itself a parallel dream-phenomenon and expresses it in poetry. Melody is therefore primary and universal, and as such may admit of several objectivations, in several texts. Likewise, in the naïve estimation of the people, it is regarded as by far the more important and necessary. Melody generates the poem out of itself by an ever-recurring process. The strophic form of the popular song points to the same phenomenon, which I always beheld with astonishment, till at last I found this explanation. Any one who in accordance with this theory examines a collection of popular songs, such as "Des Knaben Wunderhorn," will find innumerable instances of the perpetually productive melody scattering picture sparks all around: which in their variegation, their abrupt change, their mad precipitance, manifest a power quite unknown to the epic appearance and its steady flow. From the point of view of the epos, this unequal and irregular pictorial world of lyric poetry must be simply condemned: and the solemn epic rhapsodists of the Apollonian festivals in the age of Terpander have certainly done so.

Accordingly, we observe that in the poetising of the popular song, language is strained to its utmost to imitate music; and hence a new world of poetry begins with Archilochus, which is fundamentally opposed to the Homeric. And in saying this we have pointed out the only possible relation between poetry and music, between word and tone: the word, the picture, the concept here seeks an expression analogous to music and now experiences in itself the power of music. In this sense we may discriminate between two main currents in the history of the language of the Greek people, according as their language imitated either the world of phenomena and of pictures, or the world of music. One has only to reflect seriously on the linguistic difference with regard to colour, syntactical structure, and vocabulary in Homer and Pindar, in order to comprehend the significance of this contrast; indeed, it becomes palpably clear to us that in the period between Homer and Pindar the orgiastic flute tones of Olympus must have sounded forth, which, in an age as late as Aristotle's, when music was infinitely more developed, transported people to drunken enthusiasm, and which, when their influence was first felt, undoubtedly incited all the poetic means of expression of contemporaneous man to imitation. I here call attention to a familiar phenomenon of our own times, against which our æsthetics raises many objections. We again and again have occasion to observe how a symphony of Beethoven compels the individual hearers to use figurative speech, though the appearance presented by a collocation of the different pictorial world generated by a piece of music may be never so fantastically diversified and even contradictory. To practise its small wit on such compositions, and to overlook a phenomenon which is certainly worth explaining, is quite in keeping with this æsthetics. Indeed, even if the tone-poet has spoken in pictures concerning a composition, when for instance he designates a certain symphony as the "pastoral" symphony, or a passage therein as "the scene by the brook," or another as the "merry gathering of rustics," these are likewise only symbolical representations born out of music--and not perhaps the imitated objects of music--representations which can give us no information whatever concerning the Dionysian content of music, and which in fact have no distinctive value of their own alongside of other pictorical expressions. This process of a discharge of music in pictures we have now to transfer to some youthful, linguistically productive people, to get a notion as to how the strophic popular song originates, and how the entire faculty of speech is stimulated by this new principle of imitation of music.

If, therefore, we may regard lyric poetry as the effulguration of music in pictures and concepts, we can now ask: "how does music appear in the mirror of symbolism and conception?" It appears as will, taking the word in the Schopenhauerian sense, i.e., as the antithesis of the æsthetic, purely contemplative, and passive frame of mind. Here, however, we must discriminate as sharply as possible between the concept of essentiality and the concept of phenominality; for music, according to its essence, cannot be will, because as such it would have to be wholly banished from the domain of art--for the will is the unæsthetic-in-itself;--yet it appears as will. For in order to express the phenomenon of music in pictures, the lyrist requires all the stirrings of passion, from the whispering of infant desire to the roaring of madness. Under the impulse to speak of music in Apollonian symbols, he conceives of all nature, and himself therein, only as the eternally willing, desiring, longing existence. But in so far as he interprets music by means of pictures, he himself rests in the quiet calm of Apollonian contemplation, however much all around him which he beholds through the medium of music is in a state of confused and violent motion. Indeed, when he beholds himself through this same medium, his own image appears to him in a state of unsatisfied feeling: his own willing, longing, moaning and rejoicing are to him symbols by which he interprets music. Such is the phenomenon of the lyrist: as Apollonian genius he interprets music through the image of the will, while he himself, completely released from the avidity of the will, is the pure, undimmed eye of day.

Our whole disquisition insists on this, that lyric poetry is dependent on the spirit of music just as music itself in its absolute sovereignty does not require the picture and the concept, but only endures them as accompaniments. The poems of the lyrist can express nothing which has not already been contained in the vast universality and absoluteness of the music which compelled him to use figurative speech. By no means is it possible for language adequately to render the cosmic symbolism of music, for the very reason that music stands in symbolic relation to the primordial contradiction and primordial pain in the heart of the Primordial Unity, and therefore symbolises a sphere which is above all appearance and before all phenomena. Rather should we say that all phenomena, compared with it, are but symbols: hence language, as the organ and symbol of phenomena, cannot at all disclose the innermost essence, of music; language can only be in superficial contact with music when it attempts to imitate music; while the profoundest significance of the latter cannot be brought one step nearer to us by all the eloquence of lyric poetry.

7

We shall now have to avail ourselves of all the principles of art hitherto considered, in order to find our way through the labyrinth, as we must designate the origin of Greek tragedy. I shall not be charged with absurdity in saying that the problem of this origin has as yet not even been seriously stated, not to say solved, however often the fluttering tatters of ancient tradition have been sewed together in sundry combinations and torn asunder again. This tradition tells us in the most unequivocal terms, that tragedy sprang from the tragic chorus, and was originally only chorus and nothing but chorus: and hence we feel it our duty to look into the heart of this tragic chorus as being the real proto-drama, without in the least contenting ourselves with current art-phraseology--according to which the chorus is the ideal spectator, or represents the people in contrast to the regal side of the scene. The latter explanatory notion, which sounds sublime to many a politician--that the immutable moral law was embodied by the democratic Athenians in the popular chorus, which always carries its point over the passionate excesses and extravagances of kings--may be ever so forcibly suggested by an observation of Aristotle: still it has no bearing on the original formation of tragedy, inasmuch as the entire antithesis of king and people, and, in general, the whole politico-social sphere, is excluded from the purely religious beginnings of tragedy; but, considering the well-known classical form of the chorus in Æschylus and Sophocles, we should even deem it blasphemy to speak here of the anticipation of a "constitutional representation of the people," from which blasphemy others have not shrunk, however. The ancient governments knew of no constitutional representation of the people in praxi, and it is to be hoped that they did not even so much as "anticipate" it in tragedy.

Much more celebrated than this political explanation of the chorus is the notion of A. W. Schlegel, who advises us to regard the chorus, in a manner, as the essence and extract of the crowd of spectators,--as the "ideal spectator." This view when compared with the historical tradition that tragedy was originally only chorus, reveals itself in its true character, as a crude, unscientific, yet brilliant assertion, which, however, has acquired its brilliancy only through its concentrated form of expression, through the truly Germanic bias in favour of whatever is called "ideal," and through our momentary astonishment. For we are indeed astonished the moment we compare our well-known theatrical public with this chorus, and ask ourselves if it could ever be possible to idealise something analogous to the Greek chorus out of such a public. We tacitly deny this, and now wonder as much at the boldness of Schlegel's assertion as at the totally different nature of the Greek public. For hitherto we always believed that the true spectator, be he who he may, had always to remain conscious of having before him a work of art, and not an empiric reality: whereas the tragic chorus of the Greeks is compelled to recognise real beings in the figures of the stage. The chorus of the Oceanides really believes that it sees before it the Titan Prometheus, and considers itself as real as the god of the scene. And are we to own that he is the highest and purest type of spectator, who, like the Oceanides, regards Prometheus as real and present in body? And is it characteristic of the ideal spectator that he should run on the stage and free the god from his torments? We had believed in an æsthetic public, and considered the individual spectator the better qualified the more he was capable of viewing a work of art as art, that is, æsthetically; but now the Schlegelian expression has intimated to us, that the perfect ideal spectator does not at all suffer the world of the scenes to act æsthetically on him, but corporeo-empirically. Oh, these Greeks! we have sighed; they will upset our æsthetics! But once accustomed to it, we have reiterated the saying of Schlegel, as often as the subject of the chorus has been broached.

But the tradition which is so explicit here speaks against Schlegel: the chorus as such, without the stage,--the primitive form of tragedy,--and the chorus of ideal spectators do not harmonise. What kind of art would that be which was extracted from the concept of the spectator, and whereof we are to regard the "spectator as such" as the true form? The spectator without the play is something absurd. We fear that the birth of tragedy can be explained neither by the high esteem for the moral intelligence of the multitude nor by the concept of the spectator without the play; and we regard the problem as too deep to be even so much as touched by such superficial modes of contemplation.

An infinitely more valuable insight into the signification of the chorus had already been displayed by Schiller in the celebrated Preface to his Bride of Messina, where he regarded the chorus as a living wall which tragedy draws round herself to guard her from contact with the world of reality, and to preserve her ideal domain and poetical freedom.

It is with this, his chief weapon, that Schiller combats the ordinary conception of the natural, the illusion ordinarily required in dramatic poetry. He contends that while indeed the day on the stage is merely artificial, the architecture only symbolical, and the metrical dialogue purely ideal in character, nevertheless an erroneous view still prevails in the main: that it is not enough to tolerate merely as a poetical license that which is in reality the essence of all poetry. The introduction of the chorus is, he says, the decisive step by which war is declared openly and honestly against all naturalism in art.--It is, methinks, for disparaging this mode of contemplation that our would-be superior age has coined the disdainful catchword "pseudo-idealism." I fear, however, that we on the other hand with our present worship of the natural and the real have landed at the nadir of all idealism, namely in the region of cabinets of wax-figures. An art indeed exists also here, as in certain novels much in vogue at present: but let no one pester us with the claim that by this art the Schiller-Goethian "Pseudo-idealism" has been vanquished.

It is indeed an "ideal" domain, as Schiller rightly perceived, upon--which the Greek satyric chorus, the chorus of primitive tragedy, was wont to walk, a domain raised far above the actual path of mortals. The Greek framed for this chorus the suspended scaffolding of a fictitious natural state and placed thereon fictitious natural beings. It is on this foundation that tragedy grew up, and so it could of course dispense from the very first with a painful portrayal of reality. Yet it is, not an arbitrary world placed by fancy betwixt heaven and earth; rather is it a world possessing the same reality and trustworthiness that Olympus with its dwellers possessed for the believing Hellene. The satyr, as being the Dionysian chorist, lives in a religiously acknowledged reality under the sanction of the myth and cult. That tragedy begins with him, that the Dionysian wisdom of tragedy speaks through him, is just as surprising a phenomenon to us as, in general, the derivation of tragedy from the chorus. Perhaps we shall get a starting-point for our inquiry, if I put forward the proposition that the satyr, the fictitious natural being, is to the man of culture what Dionysian music is to civilisation. Concerning this latter, Richard Wagner says that it is neutralised by music even as lamplight by daylight. In like manner, I believe, the Greek man of culture felt himself neutralised in the presence of the satyric chorus: and this is the most immediate effect of the Dionysian tragedy, that the state and society, and, in general, the gaps between man and man give way to an overwhelming feeling of oneness, which leads back to the heart of nature. The metaphysical comfort,--with which, as I have here intimated, every true tragedy dismisses us--that, in spite of the perpetual change of phenomena, life at bottom is indestructibly powerful and pleasurable, this comfort appears with corporeal lucidity as the satyric chorus, as the chorus of natural beings, who live ineradicable as it were behind all civilisation, and who, in spite of the ceaseless change of generations and the history of nations, remain for ever the same.

With this chorus the deep-minded Hellene, who is so singularly qualified for the most delicate and severe suffering, consoles himself:--he who has glanced with piercing eye into the very heart of the terrible destructive processes of so-called universal history, as also into the cruelty of nature, and is in danger of longing for a Buddhistic negation of the will. Art saves him, and through art life saves him--for herself.

For we must know that in the rapture of the Dionysian state, with its annihilation of the ordinary bounds and limits of existence, there is a lethargic element, wherein all personal experiences of the past are submerged. It is by this gulf of oblivion that the everyday world and the world of Dionysian reality are separated from each other. But as soon as this everyday reality rises again in consciousness, it is felt as such, and nauseates us; an ascetic will-paralysing mood is the fruit of these states. In this sense the Dionysian man may be said to resemble Hamlet: both have for once seen into the true nature of things,--they have perceived, but they are loath to act; for their action cannot change the eternal nature of things; they regard it as shameful or ridiculous that one should require of them to set aright the time which is out of joint. Knowledge kills action, action requires the veil of illusion--it is this lesson which Hamlet teaches, and not the cheap wisdom of John-a-Dreams who from too much reflection, as it were from a surplus of possibilities, does not arrive at action at all. Not reflection, no!--true knowledge, insight into appalling truth, preponderates over all motives inciting to action, in Hamlet as well as in the Dionysian man. No comfort avails any longer; his longing goes beyond a world after death, beyond the gods themselves; existence with its glittering reflection in the gods, or in an immortal other world is abjured. In the consciousness of the truth he has perceived, man now sees everywhere only the awfulness or the absurdity of existence, he now understands the symbolism in the fate of Ophelia, he now discerns the wisdom of the sylvan god Silenus: and loathing seizes him.

Here, in this extremest danger of the will, art approaches, as a saving and healing enchantress; she alone is able to transform these nauseating reflections on the awfulness or absurdity of existence into representations wherewith it is possible to live: these are the representations of the sublime as the artistic subjugation of the awful, and the comic as the artistic delivery from the nausea of the absurd. The satyric chorus of dithyramb is the saving deed of Greek art; the paroxysms described above spent their force in the intermediary world of these Dionysian followers.

8

The satyr, like the idyllic shepherd of our more recent time, is the offspring of a longing after the Primitive and the Natural; but mark with what firmness and fearlessness the Greek embraced the man of the woods, and again, how coyly and mawkishly the modern man dallied with the flattering picture of a tender, flute-playing, soft-natured shepherd! Nature, on which as yet no knowledge has been at work, which maintains unbroken barriers to culture--this is what the Greek saw in his satyr, which still was not on this account supposed to coincide with the ape. On the contrary: it was the archetype of man, the embodiment of his highest and strongest emotions, as the enthusiastic reveller enraptured By the proximity of his god, as the fellow-suffering companion in whom the suffering of the god repeats itself, as the herald of wisdom speaking from the very depths of nature, as the emblem of the sexual omnipotence of nature, which the Greek was wont to contemplate with reverential awe. The satyr was something sublime and godlike: he could not but appear so, especially to the sad and wearied eye of the Dionysian man. He would have been offended by our spurious tricked-up shepherd, while his eye dwelt with sublime satisfaction on the naked and unstuntedly magnificent characters of nature: here the illusion of culture was brushed away from the archetype of man; here the true man, the bearded satyr, revealed himself, who shouts joyfully to his god. Before him the cultured man shrank to a lying caricature. Schiller is right also with reference to these beginnings of tragic art: the chorus is a living bulwark against the onsets of reality, because it--the satyric chorus--portrays existence more truthfully, more realistically, more perfectly than the cultured man who ordinarily considers himself as the only reality. The sphere of poetry does not lie outside the world, like some fantastic impossibility of a poet's imagination: it seeks to be the very opposite, the unvarnished expression of truth, and must for this very reason cast aside the false finery of that supposed reality of the cultured man. The contrast between this intrinsic truth of nature and the falsehood of culture, which poses as the only reality, is similar to that existing between the eternal kernel of things, the thing in itself, and the collective world of phenomena. And even as tragedy, with its metaphysical comfort, points to the eternal life of this kernel of existence, notwithstanding the perpetual dissolution of phenomena, so the symbolism of the satyric chorus already expresses figuratively this primordial relation between the thing in itself and phenomenon. The idyllic shepherd of the modern man is but a copy of the sum of the illusions of culture which he calls nature; the Dionysian Greek desires truth and nature in their most potent form;--he sees himself metamorphosed into the satyr.

The revelling crowd of the votaries of Dionysus rejoices, swayed by such moods and perceptions, the power of which transforms them before their own eyes, so that they imagine they behold themselves as reconstituted genii of nature, as satyrs. The later constitution of the tragic chorus is the artistic imitation of this natural phenomenon, which of course required a separation of the Dionysian spectators from the enchanted Dionysians. However, we must never lose sight of the fact that the public of the Attic tragedy rediscovered itself in the chorus of the orchestra, that there was in reality no antithesis of public and chorus: for all was but one great sublime chorus of dancing and singing satyrs, or of such as allowed themselves to be represented by the satyrs. The Schlegelian observation must here reveal itself to us in a deeper sense. The chorus is the "ideal spectator"[5] in so far as it is the only beholder,[6] the beholder of the visionary world of the scene. A public of spectators, as known to us, was unknown to the Greeks. In their theatres the terraced structure of the spectators' space rising in concentric arcs enabled every one, in the strictest sense, to overlook the entire world of culture around him, and in surfeited contemplation tó imagine himself a chorist. According to this view, then, we may call the chorus in its primitive stage in proto-tragedy, a self-mirroring of the Dionysian man: a phenomenon which may be best exemplified by the process of the actor, who, if he be truly gifted, sees hovering before his eyes with almost tangible perceptibility the character he is to represent. The satyric chorus is first of all a vision of the Dionysian throng, just as the world of the stage is, in turn, a vision of the satyric chorus: the power of this vision is great enough to render the eye dull and insensible to the impression of "reality," to the presence of the cultured men occupying the tiers of seats on every side. The form of the Greek theatre reminds one of a lonesome mountain-valley: the architecture of the scene appears like a luminous cloud-picture which the Bacchants swarming on the mountains behold from the heights, as the splendid encirclement in the midst of which the image of Dionysus is revealed to them.

Owing to our learned conception of the elementary artistic processes, this artistic proto-phenomenon, which is here introduced to explain the tragic chorus, is almost shocking: while nothing can be more certain than that the poet is a poet only in that he beholds himself surrounded by forms which live and act before him, into the innermost being of which his glance penetrates. By reason of a strange defeat in our capacities, we modern men are apt to represent to ourselves the æsthetic proto-phenomenon as too complex and abstract. For the true poet the metaphor is not a rhetorical figure, but a vicarious image which actually hovers before him in place of a concept. The character is not for him an aggregate composed of a studied collection of particular traits, but an irrepressibly live person appearing before his eyes, and differing only from the corresponding vision of the painter by its ever continued life and action. Why is it that Homer sketches much more vividly[7] than all the other poets? Because he contemplates[8] much more. We talk so abstractly about poetry, because we are all wont to be bad poets. At bottom the æsthetic phenomenon is simple: let a man but have the faculty of perpetually seeing a lively play and of constantly living surrounded by hosts of spirits, then he is a poet: let him but feel the impulse to transform himself and to talk from out the bodies and souls of others, then he is a dramatist.

The Dionysian excitement is able to impart to a whole mass of men this artistic faculty of seeing themselves surrounded by such a host of spirits, with whom they know themselves to be inwardly one. This function of the tragic chorus is the dramatic proto-phenomenon: to see one's self transformed before one's self, and then to act as if one had really entered into another body, into another character. This function stands at the beginning of the development of the drama. Here we have something different from the rhapsodist, who does not blend with his pictures, but only sees them, like the painter, with contemplative eye outside of him; here we actually have a surrender of the individual by his entering into another nature. Moreover this phenomenon appears in the form of an epidemic: a whole throng feels itself metamorphosed in this wise. Hence it is that the dithyramb is essentially different from every other variety of the choric song. The virgins, who with laurel twigs in their hands solemnly proceed to the temple of Apollo and sing a processional hymn, remain what they are and retain their civic names: the dithyrambic chorus is a chorus of transformed beings, whose civic past and social rank are totally forgotten: they have become the timeless servants of their god that live aloof from all the spheres of society. Every other variety of the choric lyric of the Hellenes is but an enormous enhancement of the Apollonian unit-singer: while in the dithyramb we have before us a community of unconscious actors, who mutually regard themselves as transformed among one another.

This enchantment is the prerequisite of all dramatic art. In this enchantment the Dionysian reveller sees himself as a satyr, and as satyr he in turn beholds the god, that is, in his transformation he sees a new vision outside him as the Apollonian consummation of his state. With this new vision the drama is complete.

According to this view, we must understand Greek tragedy as the Dionysian chorus, which always disburdens itself anew in an Apollonian world of pictures. The choric parts, therefore, with which tragedy is interlaced, are in a manner the mother-womb of the entire so-called dialogue, that is, of the whole stage-world, of the drama proper. In several successive outbursts does this primordial basis of tragedy beam forth the vision of the drama, which is a dream-phenomenon throughout, and, as such, epic in character: on the other hand, however, as objectivation of a Dionysian state, it does not represent the Apollonian redemption in appearance, but, conversely, the dissolution of the individual and his unification with primordial existence. Accordingly, the drama is the Apollonian embodiment of Dionysian perceptions and influences, and is thereby separated from the epic as by an immense gap.

The chorus of Greek tragedy, the symbol of the mass of the people moved by Dionysian excitement, is thus fully explained by our conception of it as here set forth. Whereas, being accustomed to the position of a chorus on the modern stage, especially an operatic chorus, we could never comprehend why the tragic chorus of the Greeks should be older, more primitive, indeed, more important than the "action" proper,--as has been so plainly declared by the voice of tradition; whereas, furthermore, we could not reconcile with this traditional paramount importance and primitiveness the fact of the chorus' being composed only of humble, ministering beings; indeed, at first only of goatlike satyrs; whereas, finally, the orchestra before the scene was always a riddle to us; we have learned to comprehend at length that the scene, together with the action, was fundamentally and originally conceived only as a vision, that the only reality is just the chorus, which of itself generates the vision and speaks thereof with the entire symbolism of dancing, tone, and word. This chorus beholds in the vision its lord and master Dionysus, and is thus for ever the serving chorus: it sees how he, the god, suffers and glorifies himself, and therefore does not itself act. But though its attitude towards the god is throughout the attitude of ministration, this is nevertheless the highest expression, the Dionysian expression of Nature, and therefore, like Nature herself, the chorus utters oracles and wise sayings when transported with enthusiasm: as fellow-sufferer it is also the sage proclaiming truth from out the heart of Nature. Thus, then, originates the fantastic figure, which seems so shocking, of the wise and enthusiastic satyr, who is at the same time "the dumb man" in contrast to the god: the image of Nature and her strongest impulses, yea, the symbol of Nature, and at the same time the herald of her art and wisdom: musician, poet, dancer, and visionary in one person.

Agreeably to this view, and agreeably to tradition, Dionysus, the proper stage-hero and focus of vision, is not at first actually present in the oldest period of tragedy, but is only imagined as present: i.e., tragedy is originally only "chorus" and not "drama." Later on the attempt is made to exhibit the god as real and to display the visionary figure together with its glorifying encirclement before the eyes of all; it is here that the "drama" in the narrow sense of the term begins. To the dithyrambic chorus is now assigned the task of exciting the minds of the hearers to such a pitch of Dionysian frenzy, that, when the tragic hero appears on the stage, they do not behold in him, say, the unshapely masked man, but a visionary figure, born as it were of their own ecstasy. Let us picture Admetes thinking in profound meditation of his lately departed wife Alcestis, and quite consuming himself in spiritual contemplation thereof--when suddenly the veiled figure of a woman resembling her in form and gait is led towards him: let us picture his sudden trembling anxiety, his agitated comparisons, his instinctive conviction--and we shall have an analogon to the sensation with which the spectator, excited to Dionysian frenzy, saw the god approaching on the stage, a god with whose sufferings he had already become identified. He involuntarily transferred the entire picture of the god, fluttering magically before his soul, to this masked figure and resolved its reality as it were into a phantasmal unreality. This is the Apollonian dream-state, in which the world of day is veiled, and a new world, clearer, more intelligible, more striking than the former, and nevertheless more shadowy, is ever born anew in perpetual change before our eyes. We accordingly recognise in tragedy a thorough-going stylistic contrast: the language, colour, flexibility and dynamics of the dialogue fall apart in the Dionysian lyrics of the chorus on the one hand, and in the Apollonian dream-world of the scene on the other, into entirely separate spheres of expression. The Apollonian appearances, in which Dionysus objectifies himself, are no longer "ein ewiges Meer, ein wechselnd Weben, ein glühend Leben,"[9] as is the music of the chorus, they are no longer the forces merely felt, but not condensed into a picture, by which the inspired votary of Dionysus divines the proximity of his god: the clearness and firmness of epic form now speak to him from the scene, Dionysus now no longer speaks through forces, but as an epic hero, almost in the language of Homer.

Footnotes:

5. Zuschauer.
6. Schauer.
7. Anschaulicher.
8. Anschaut.
9. An eternal sea, A weaving, flowing, Life, all glowing. Faust, trans. of Bayard Taylor.--TR.

9

Whatever rises to the surface in the dialogue of the Apollonian part of Greek tragedy, appears simple, transparent, beautiful. In this sense the dialogue is a copy of the Hellene, whose nature reveals itself in the dance, because in the dance the greatest energy is merely potential, but betrays itself nevertheless in flexible and vivacious movements. The language of the Sophoclean heroes, for instance, surprises us by its Apollonian precision and clearness, so that we at once imagine we see into the innermost recesses of their being, and marvel not a little that the way to these recesses is so short. But if for the moment we disregard the character of the hero which rises to the surface and grows visible--and which at bottom is nothing but the light-picture cast on a dark wall, that is, appearance through and through,--if rather we enter into the myth which projects itself in these bright mirrorings, we shall of a sudden experience a phenomenon which bears a reverse relation to one familiar in optics. When, after a vigorous effort to gaze into the sun, we turn away blinded, we have dark-coloured spots before our eyes as restoratives, so to speak; while, on the contrary, those light-picture phenomena of the Sophoclean hero,--in short, the Apollonian of the mask,--are the necessary productions of a glance into the secret and terrible things of nature, as it were shining spots to heal the eye which dire night has seared. Only in this sense can we hope to be able to grasp the true meaning of the serious and significant notion of "Greek cheerfulness"; while of course we encounter the misunderstood notion of this cheerfulness, as resulting from a state of unendangered comfort, on all the ways and paths of the present time.

The most sorrowful figure of the Greek stage, the hapless Œdipus, was understood by Sophocles as the noble man, who in spite of his wisdom was destined to error and misery, but nevertheless through his extraordinary sufferings ultimately exerted a magical, wholesome influence on all around him, which continues effective even after his death. The noble man does not sin; this is what the thoughtful poet wishes to tell us: all laws, all natural order, yea, the moral world itself, may be destroyed through his action, but through this very action a higher magic circle of influences is brought into play, which establish a new world on the ruins of the old that has been overthrown. This is what the poet, in so far as he is at the same time a religious thinker, wishes to tell us: as poet, he shows us first of all a wonderfully complicated legal mystery, which the judge slowly unravels, link by link, to his own destruction. The truly Hellenic delight at this dialectical loosening is so great, that a touch of surpassing cheerfulness is thereby communicated to the entire play, which everywhere blunts the edge of the horrible presuppositions of the procedure. In the "Œdipus at Colonus" we find the same cheerfulness, elevated, however, to an infinite transfiguration: in contrast to the aged king, subjected to an excess of misery, and exposed solely as a sufferer to all that befalls him, we have here a supermundane cheerfulness, which descends from a divine sphere and intimates to us that in his purely passive attitude the hero attains his highest activity, the influence of which extends far beyond his life, while his earlier conscious musing and striving led him only to passivity. Thus, then, the legal knot of the fable of Œdipus, which to mortal eyes appears indissolubly entangled, is slowly unravelled--and the profoundest human joy comes upon us in the presence of this divine counterpart of dialectics. If this explanation does justice to the poet, it may still be asked whether the substance of the myth is thereby exhausted; and here it turns out that the entire conception of the poet is nothing but the light-picture which healing nature holds up to us after a glance into the abyss. Œdipus, the murderer of his father, the husband of his mother, Œdipus, the interpreter of the riddle of the Sphinx! What does the mysterious triad of these deeds of destiny tell us? There is a primitive popular belief, especially in Persia, that a wise Magian can be born only of incest: which we have forthwith to interpret to ourselves with reference to the riddle-solving and mother-marrying Œdipus, to the effect that when the boundary of the present and future, the rigid law of individuation and, in general, the intrinsic spell of nature, are broken by prophetic and magical powers, an extraordinary counter-naturalness--as, in this case, incest--must have preceded as a cause; for how else could one force nature to surrender her secrets but by victoriously opposing her, i.e., by means of the Unnatural? It is this intuition which I see imprinted in the awful triad of the destiny of Œdipus: the very man who solves the riddle of nature--that double-constituted Sphinx--must also, as the murderer of his father and husband of his mother, break the holiest laws of nature. Indeed, it seems as if the myth sought to whisper into our ears that wisdom, especially Dionysian wisdom, is an unnatural abomination, and that whoever, through his knowledge, plunges nature into an abyss of annihilation, must also experience the dissolution of nature in himself. "The sharpness of wisdom turns round upon the sage: wisdom is a crime against nature": such terrible expressions does the myth call out to us: but the Hellenic poet touches like a sunbeam the sublime and formidable Memnonian statue of the myth, so that it suddenly begins to sound--in Sophoclean melodies.

With the glory of passivity I now contrast the glory of activity which illuminates the Prometheus of Æschylus. That which Æschylus the thinker had to tell us here, but which as a poet he only allows us to surmise by his symbolic picture, the youthful Goethe succeeded in disclosing to us in the daring words of his Prometheus:--

"Hier sitz' ich, forme Menschen
Nach meinem Bilde,
Ein Geschlecht, das mir gleich sei,
Zu leiden, zu weinen,
Zu geniessen und zu freuen sich,
Und dein nicht zu achten,
Wie ich!"[10]

Man, elevating himself to the rank of the Titans, acquires his culture by his own efforts, and compels the gods to unite with him, because in his self-sufficient wisdom he has their existence and their limits in his hand. What is most wonderful, however, in this Promethean form, which according to its fundamental conception is the specific hymn of impiety, is the profound Æschylean yearning for justice: the untold sorrow of the bold "single-handed being" on the one hand, and the divine need, ay, the foreboding of a twilight of the gods, on the other, the power of these two worlds of suffering constraining to reconciliation, to metaphysical oneness--all this suggests most forcibly the central and main position of the Æschylean view of things, which sees Moira as eternal justice enthroned above gods and men. In view of the astonishing boldness with which Æschylus places the Olympian world on his scales of justice, it must be remembered that the deep-minded Greek had an immovably firm substratum of metaphysical thought in his mysteries, and that all his sceptical paroxysms could be discharged upon the Olympians. With reference to these deities, the Greek artist, in particular, had an obscure feeling as to mutual dependency: and it is just in the Prometheus of Æschylus that this feeling is symbolised. The Titanic artist found in himself the daring belief that he could create men and at least destroy Olympian deities: namely, by his superior wisdom, for which, to be sure, he had to atone by eternal suffering. The splendid "can-ing" of the great genius, bought too cheaply even at the price of eternal suffering, the stern pride of the artist: this is the essence and soul of Æschylean poetry, while Sophocles in his Œdipus preludingly strikes up the victory-song of the saint. But even this interpretation which Æschylus has given to the myth does not fathom its astounding depth of terror; the fact is rather that the artist's delight in unfolding, the cheerfulness of artistic creating bidding defiance to all calamity, is but a shining stellar and nebular image reflected in a black sea of sadness. The tale of Prometheus is an original possession of the entire Aryan family of races, and documentary evidence of their capacity for the profoundly tragic; indeed, it is not improbable that this myth has the same characteristic significance for the Aryan race that the myth of the fall of man has for the Semitic, and that there is a relationship between the two myths like that of brother and sister. The presupposition of the Promethean myth is the transcendent value which a naïve humanity attach to fire as the true palladium of every ascending culture: that man, however, should dispose at will of this fire, and should not receive it only as a gift from heaven, as the igniting lightning or the warming solar flame, appeared to the contemplative primordial men as crime and robbery of the divine nature. And thus the first philosophical problem at once causes a painful, irreconcilable antagonism between man and God, and puts as it were a mass of rock at the gate of every culture. The best and highest that men can acquire they obtain by a crime, and must now in their turn take upon themselves its consequences, namely the whole flood of sufferings and sorrows with which the offended celestials must visit the nobly aspiring race of man: a bitter reflection, which, by the dignity it confers on crime, contrasts strangely with the Semitic myth of the fall of man, in which curiosity, beguilement, seducibility, wantonness,--in short, a whole series of pre-eminently feminine passions,--were regarded as the origin of evil. What distinguishes the Aryan representation is the sublime view of active sin as the properly Promethean virtue, which suggests at the same time the ethical basis of pessimistic tragedy as the justification of human evil--of human guilt as well as of the suffering incurred thereby. The misery in the essence of things--which the contemplative Aryan is not disposed to explain away--the antagonism in the heart of the world, manifests itself to him as a medley of different worlds, for instance, a Divine and a human world, each of which is in the right individually, but as a separate existence alongside of another has to suffer for its individuation. With the heroic effort made by the individual for universality, in his attempt to pass beyond the bounds of individuation and become the one universal being, he experiences in himself the primordial contradiction concealed in the essence of things, i.e., he trespasses and suffers. Accordingly crime[11] is understood by the Aryans to be a man, sin[12] by the Semites a woman; as also, the original crime is committed by man, the original sin by woman. Besides, the witches' chorus says:

"Wir nehmen das nicht so genau:
Mit tausend Schritten macht's die Frau;
Doch wie sie auch sich eilen kann
Mit einem Sprunge macht's der Mann."[13]

He who understands this innermost core of the tale of Prometheus--namely the necessity of crime imposed on the titanically striving individual--will at once be conscious of the un-Apollonian nature of this pessimistic representation: for Apollo seeks to pacify individual beings precisely by drawing boundary lines between them, and by again and again calling attention thereto, with his requirements of self-knowledge and due proportion, as the holiest laws of the universe. In order, however, to prevent the form from congealing to Egyptian rigidity and coldness in consequence of this Apollonian tendency, in order to prevent the extinction of the motion of the entire lake in the effort to prescribe to the individual wave its path and compass, the high tide of the Dionysian tendency destroyed from time to time all the little circles in which the one-sided Apollonian "will" sought to confine the Hellenic world. The suddenly swelling tide of the Dionysian then takes the separate little wave-mountains of individuals on its back, just as the brother of Prometheus, the Titan Atlas, does with the earth. This Titanic impulse, to become as it were the Atlas of all individuals, and to carry them on broad shoulders higher and higher, farther and farther, is what the Promethean and the Dionysian have in common. In this respect the Æschylean Prometheus is a Dionysian mask, while, in the afore-mentioned profound yearning for justice, Æschylus betrays to the intelligent observer his paternal descent from Apollo, the god of individuation and of the boundaries of justice. And so the double-being of the Æschylean Prometheus, his conjoint Dionysian and Apollonian nature, might be thus expressed in an abstract formula: "Whatever exists is alike just and unjust, and equally justified in both."

Das ist deine Welt! Das heisst eine Welt![14]

Footnotes:

10.
"Here sit I, forming mankind
In my image,
A race resembling me,--
To sorrow and to weep,
To taste, to hold, to enjoy,
And not have need of thee,
As I!"
(Translation in Hæckel's History of the Evolution of Man.)

11. Der Frevel.]
12. Die Sünde.
13.

We do not measure with such care:
Woman in thousand steps is there,
But howsoe'er she hasten may.
Man in one leap has cleared the way.
Faust, trans. of Bayard Taylor.--TR.

14. This is thy world, and what a world!--Faust.

10

It is an indisputable tradition that Greek tragedy in its earliest form had for its theme only the sufferings of Dionysus, and that for some time the only stage-hero therein was simply Dionysus himself. With the same confidence, however, we can maintain that not until Euripides did Dionysus cease to be the tragic hero, and that in fact all the celebrated figures of the Greek stage--Prometheus, Œdipus, etc.--are but masks of this original hero, Dionysus. The presence of a god behind all these masks is the one essential cause of the typical "ideality," so oft exciting wonder, of these celebrated figures. Some one, I know not whom, has maintained that all individuals are comic as individuals and are consequently un-tragic: from whence it might be inferred that the Greeks in general could not endure individuals on the tragic stage. And they really seem to have had these sentiments: as, in general, it is to be observed that the Platonic discrimination and valuation of the "idea" in contrast to the "eidolon," the image, is deeply rooted in the Hellenic being. Availing ourselves of Plato's terminology, however, we should have to speak of the tragic figures of the Hellenic stage somewhat as follows. The one truly real Dionysus appears in a multiplicity of forms, in the mask of a fighting hero and entangled, as it were, in the net of an individual will. As the visibly appearing god now talks and acts, he resembles an erring, striving, suffering individual: and that, in general, he appears with such epic precision and clearness, is due to the dream-reading Apollo, who reads to the chorus its Dionysian state through this symbolic appearance. In reality, however, this hero is the suffering Dionysus of the mysteries, a god experiencing in himself the sufferings of individuation, of whom wonderful myths tell that as a boy he was dismembered by the Titans and has been worshipped in this state as Zagreus:[15] whereby is intimated that this dismemberment, the properly Dionysian suffering, is like a transformation into air, water, earth, and fire, that we must therefore regard the state of individuation as the source and primal cause of all suffering, as something objectionable in itself. From the smile of this Dionysus sprang the Olympian gods, from his tears sprang man. In his existence as a dismembered god, Dionysus has the dual nature of a cruel barbarised demon, and a mild pacific ruler. But the hope of the epopts looked for a new birth of Dionysus, which we have now to conceive of in anticipation as the end of individuation: it was for this coming third Dionysus that the stormy jubilation-hymns of the epopts resounded. And it is only this hope that sheds a ray of joy upon the features of a world torn asunder and shattered into individuals: as is symbolised in the myth by Demeter sunk in eternal sadness, who rejoices again only when told that she may once more give birth to Dionysus In the views of things here given we already have all the elements of a profound and pessimistic contemplation of the world, and along with these we have the mystery doctrine of tragedy: the fundamental knowledge of the oneness of all existing things, the consideration of individuation as the primal cause of evil, and art as the joyous hope that the spell of individuation may be broken, as the augury of a restored oneness.

It has already been intimated that the Homeric epos is the poem of Olympian culture, wherewith this culture has sung its own song of triumph over the terrors of the war of the Titans. Under the predominating influence of tragic poetry, these Homeric myths are now reproduced anew, and show by this metempsychosis that meantime the Olympian culture also has been vanquished by a still deeper view of things. The haughty Titan Prometheus has announced to his Olympian tormentor that the extremest danger will one day menace his rule, unless he ally with him betimes. In Æschylus we perceive the terrified Zeus, apprehensive of his end, in alliance with the Titan. Thus, the former age of the Titans is subsequently brought from Tartarus once more to the light of day. The philosophy of wild and naked nature beholds with the undissembled mien of truth the myths of the Homeric world as they dance past: they turn pale, they tremble before the lightning glance of this goddess--till the powerful fist[16] of the Dionysian artist forces them into the service of the new deity. Dionysian truth takes over the entire domain of myth as symbolism of its knowledge, which it makes known partly in the public cult of tragedy and partly in the secret celebration of the dramatic mysteries, always, however, in the old mythical garb. What was the power, which freed Prometheus from his vultures and transformed the myth into a vehicle of Dionysian wisdom? It is the Heracleian power of music: which, having reached its highest manifestness in tragedy, can invest myths with a new and most profound significance, which we have already had occasion to characterise as the most powerful faculty of music. For it is the fate of every myth to insinuate itself into the narrow limits of some alleged historical reality, and to be treated by some later generation as a solitary fact with historical claims: and the Greeks were already fairly on the way to restamp the whole of their mythical juvenile dream sagaciously and arbitrarily into a historico-pragmatical juvenile history. For this is the manner in which religions are wont to die out: when of course under the stern, intelligent eyes of an orthodox dogmatism, the mythical presuppositions of a religion are systematised as a completed sum of historical events, and when one begins apprehensively to defend the credibility of the myth, while at the same time opposing all continuation of their natural vitality and luxuriance; when, accordingly, the feeling for myth dies out, and its place is taken by the claim of religion to historical foundations. This dying myth was now seized by the new-born genius of Dionysian music, in whose hands it bloomed once more, with such colours as it had never yet displayed, with a fragrance that awakened a longing anticipation of a metaphysical world. After this final effulgence it collapses, its leaves wither, and soon the scoffing Lucians of antiquity catch at the discoloured and faded flowers which the winds carry off in every direction. Through tragedy the myth attains its profoundest significance, its most expressive form; it rises once more like a wounded hero, and the whole surplus of vitality, together with the philosophical calmness of the Dying, burns in its eyes with a last powerful gleam.

What meantest thou, oh impious Euripides, in seeking once more to enthral this dying one? It died under thy ruthless hands: and then thou madest use of counterfeit, masked myth, which like the ape of Heracles could only trick itself out in the old finery. And as myth died in thy hands, so also died the genius of music; though thou couldst covetously plunder all the gardens of music--thou didst only realise a counterfeit, masked music. And because thou hast forsaken Dionysus. Apollo hath also forsaken thee; rout up all the passions from their haunts and conjure them into thy sphere, sharpen and polish a sophistical dialectics for the speeches of thy heroes--thy very heroes have only counterfeit, masked passions, and speak only counterfeit, masked music.

Footnotes:

15. See article by Mr. Arthur Symons in The Academy, 30th August 1902.
16. Die mächtige Faust.--Cf. Faust, Chorus of Spirits.--TR.

11

Greek tragedy had a fate different from that of all her older sister arts: she died by suicide, in consequence of an irreconcilable conflict; accordingly she died tragically, while they all passed away very calmly and beautifully in ripe old age. For if it be in accordance with a happy state of things to depart this life without a struggle, leaving behind a fair posterity, the closing period of these older arts exhibits such a happy state of things: slowly they sink out of sight, and before their dying eyes already stand their fairer progeny, who impatiently lift up their heads with courageous mien. The death of Greek tragedy, on the other hand, left an immense void, deeply felt everywhere. Even as certain Greek sailors in the time of Tiberius once heard upon a lonesome island the thrilling cry, "great Pan is dead": so now as it were sorrowful wailing sounded through the Hellenic world: "Tragedy is dead! Poetry itself has perished with her! Begone, begone, ye stunted, emaciated epigones! Begone to Hades, that ye may for once eat your fill of the crumbs of your former masters!"

But when after all a new Art blossomed forth which revered tragedy as her ancestress and mistress, it was observed with horror that she did indeed bear the features of her mother, but those very features the latter had exhibited in her long death-struggle. It was Euripides who fought this death-struggle of tragedy; the later art is known as the New Attic Comedy. In it the degenerate form of tragedy lived on as a monument of the most painful and violent death of tragedy proper.

This connection between the two serves to explain the passionate attachment to Euripides evinced by the poets of the New Comedy, and hence we are no longer surprised at the wish of Philemon, who would have got himself hanged at once, with the sole design of being able to visit Euripides in the lower regions: if only he could be assured generally that the deceased still had his wits. But if we desire, as briefly as possible, and without professing to say aught exhaustive on the subject, to characterise what Euripides has in common with Menander and Philemon, and what appealed to them so strongly as worthy of imitation: it will suffice to say that the spectator was brought upon the stage by Euripides. He who has perceived the material of which the Promethean tragic writers prior to Euripides formed their heroes, and how remote from their purpose it was to bring the true mask of reality on the stage, will also know what to make of the wholly divergent tendency of Euripides. Through him the commonplace individual forced his way from the spectators' benches to the stage itself; the mirror in which formerly only great and bold traits found expression now showed the painful exactness that conscientiously reproduces even the abortive lines of nature. Odysseus, the typical Hellene of the Old Art, sank, in the hands of the new poets, to the figure of the Græculus, who, as the good-naturedly cunning domestic slave, stands henceforth in the centre of dramatic interest. What Euripides takes credit for in the

Aristophanean "Frogs," namely, that by his household remedies he freed tragic art from its pompous corpulency, is apparent above all in his tragic heroes. The spectator now virtually saw and heard his double on the Euripidean stage, and rejoiced that he could talk so well. But this joy was not all: one even learned of Euripides how to speak: he prides himself upon this in his contest with Æschylus: how the people have learned from him how to observe, debate, and draw conclusions according to the rules of art and with the cleverest sophistications. In general it may be said that through this revolution of the popular language he made the New Comedy possible. For it was henceforth no longer a secret, how--and with what saws--the commonplace could represent and express itself on the stage. Civic mediocrity, on which Euripides built all his political hopes, was now suffered to speak, while heretofore the demigod in tragedy and the drunken satyr, or demiman, in comedy, had determined the character of the language. And so the Aristophanean Euripides prides himself on having portrayed the common, familiar, everyday life and dealings of the people, concerning which all are qualified to pass judgment. If now the entire populace philosophises, manages land and goods with unheard-of circumspection, and conducts law-suits, he takes all the credit to himself, and glories in the splendid results of the wisdom with which he inoculated the rabble.

It was to a populace prepared and enlightened in this manner that the New Comedy could now address itself, of which Euripides had become as it were the chorus-master; only that in this case the chorus of spectators had to be trained. As soon as this chorus was trained to sing in the Euripidean key, there arose that chesslike variety of the drama, the New Comedy, with its perpetual triumphs of cunning and artfulness. But Euripides--the chorus-master--was praised incessantly: indeed, people would have killed themselves in order to learn yet more from him, had they not known that tragic poets were quite as dead as tragedy. But with it the Hellene had surrendered the belief in his immortality; not only the belief in an ideal past, but also the belief in an ideal future. The saying taken from the well-known epitaph, "as an old man, frivolous and capricious," applies also to aged Hellenism. The passing moment, wit, levity, and caprice, are its highest deities; the fifth class, that of the slaves, now attains to power, at least in sentiment: and if we can still speak at all of "Greek cheerfulness," it is the cheerfulness of the slave who has nothing of consequence to answer for, nothing great to strive for, and cannot value anything of the past or future higher than the present. It was this semblance of "Greek cheerfulness" which so revolted the deep-minded and formidable natures of the first four centuries of Christianity: this womanish flight from earnestness and terror, this cowardly contentedness with easy pleasure, was not only contemptible to them, but seemed to be a specifically anti-Christian sentiment. And we must ascribe it to its influence that the conception of Greek antiquity, which lived on for centuries, preserved with almost enduring persistency that peculiar hectic colour of cheerfulness--as if there had never been a Sixth Century with its birth of tragedy, its Mysteries, its Pythagoras and Heraclitus, indeed as if the art-works of that great period did not at all exist, which in fact--each by itself--can in no wise be explained as having sprung from the soil of such a decrepit and slavish love of existence and cheerfulness, and point to an altogether different conception of things as their source.

The assertion made a moment ago, that Euripides introduced the spectator on the stage to qualify him the better to pass judgment on the drama, will make it appear as if the old tragic art was always in a false relation to the spectator: and one would be tempted to extol the radical tendency of Euripides to bring about an adequate relation between art-work and public as an advance on Sophocles. But, as things are, "public" is merely a word, and not at all a homogeneous and constant quantity. Why should the artist be under obligations to accommodate himself to a power whose strength is merely in numbers? And if by virtue of his endowments and aspirations he feels himself superior to every one of these spectators, how could he feel greater respect for the collective expression of all these subordinate capacities than for the relatively highest-endowed individual spectator? In truth, if ever a Greek artist treated his public throughout a long life with presumptuousness and self-sufficiency, it was Euripides, who, even when the masses threw themselves at his feet, with sublime defiance made an open assault on his own tendency, the very tendency with which he had triumphed over the masses. If this genius had had the slightest reverence for the pandemonium of the public, he would have broken down long before the middle of his career beneath the weighty blows of his own failures. These considerations here make it obvious that our formula--namely, that Euripides brought the spectator upon the stage, in order to make him truly competent to pass judgment--was but a provisional one, and that we must seek for a deeper understanding of his tendency. Conversely, it is undoubtedly well known that Æschylus and Sophocles, during all their lives, indeed, far beyond their lives, enjoyed the full favour of the people, and that therefore in the case of these predecessors of Euripides the idea of a false relation between art-work and public was altogether excluded. What was it that thus forcibly diverted this highly gifted artist, so incessantly impelled to production, from the path over which shone the sun of the greatest names in poetry and the cloudless heaven of popular favour? What strange consideration for the spectator led him to defy, the spectator? How could he, owing to too much respect for the public --dis-respect the public?

Euripides--and this is the solution of the riddle just propounded--felt himself, as a poet, undoubtedly superior to the masses, but not to two of his spectators: he brought the masses upon the stage; these two spectators he revered as the only competent judges and masters of his art: in compliance with their directions and admonitions, he transferred the entire world of sentiments, passions, and experiences, hitherto present at every festival representation as the invisible chorus on the spectators' benches, into the souls of his stage-heroes; he yielded to their demands when he also sought for these new characters the new word and the new tone; in their voices alone he heard the conclusive verdict on his work, as also the cheering promise of triumph when he found himself condemned as usual by the justice of the public.

Of these two, spectators the one is--Euripides himself, Euripides as thinker, not as poet. It might be said of him, that his unusually large fund of critical ability, as in the case of Lessing, if it did not create, at least constantly fructified a productively artistic collateral impulse. With this faculty, with all the clearness and dexterity of his critical thought, Euripides had sat in the theatre and striven to recognise in the masterpieces of his great predecessors, as in faded paintings, feature and feature, line and line. And here had happened to him what one initiated in the deeper arcana of Æschylean tragedy must needs have expected: he observed something incommensurable in every feature and in every line, a certain deceptive distinctness and at the same time an enigmatic profundity, yea an infinitude, of background. Even the clearest figure had always a comet's tail attached to it, which seemed to suggest the uncertain and the inexplicable. The same twilight shrouded the structure of the drama, especially the significance of the chorus. And how doubtful seemed the solution of the ethical problems to his mind! How questionable the treatment of the myths! How unequal the distribution of happiness and misfortune! Even in the language of the Old Tragedy there was much that was objectionable to him, or at least enigmatical; he found especially too much pomp for simple affairs, too many tropes and immense things for the plainness of the characters. Thus he sat restlessly pondering in the theatre, and as a spectator he acknowledged to himself that he did not understand his great predecessors. If, however, he thought the understanding the root proper of all enjoyment and productivity, he had to inquire and look about to see whether any one else thought as he did, and also acknowledged this incommensurability. But most people, and among them the best individuals, had only a distrustful smile for him, while none could explain why the great masters were still in the right in face of his scruples and objections. And in this painful condition he found that other spectator, who did not comprehend, and therefore did not esteem, tragedy. In alliance with him he could venture, from amid his lonesomeness, to begin the prodigious struggle against the art of Æschylus and Sophocles--not with polemic writings, but as a dramatic poet, who opposed his own conception of tragedy to the traditional one.

12

Before we name this other spectator, let us pause here a moment in order to recall our own impression, as previously described, of the discordant and incommensurable elements in the nature of Æschylean tragedy. Let us think of our own astonishment at the chorus and the tragic hero of that type of tragedy, neither of which we could reconcile with our practices any more than with tradition--till we rediscovered this duplexity itself as the origin and essence of Greek tragedy, as the expression of two interwoven artistic impulses, the Apollonian and the Dionysian.

To separate this primitive and all-powerful Dionysian element from tragedy, and to build up a new and purified form of tragedy on the basis of a non-Dionysian art, morality, and conception of things--such is the tendency of Euripides which now reveals itself to us in a clear light.

In a myth composed in the eve of his life, Euripides himself most urgently propounded to his contemporaries the question as to the value and signification of this tendency. Is the Dionysian entitled to exist at all? Should it not be forcibly rooted out of the Hellenic soil? Certainly, the poet tells us, if only it were possible: but the god Dionysus is too powerful; his most intelligent adversary--like Pentheus in the "Bacchæ"--is unwittingly enchanted by him, and in this enchantment meets his fate. The judgment of the two old sages, Cadmus and Tiresias, seems to be also the judgment of the aged poet: that the reflection of the wisest individuals does not overthrow old popular traditions, nor the perpetually propagating worship of Dionysus, that in fact it behoves us to display at least a diplomatically cautious concern in the presence of such strange forces: where however it is always possible that the god may take offence at such lukewarm participation, and finally change the diplomat--in this case Cadmus--into a dragon. This is what a poet tells us, who opposed Dionysus with heroic valour throughout a long life--in order finally to wind up his career with a glorification of his adversary, and with suicide, like one staggering from giddiness, who, in order to escape the horrible vertigo he can no longer endure, casts himself from a tower. This tragedy--the Bacchæ--is a protest against the practicability of his own tendency; alas, and it has already been put into practice! The surprising thing had happened: when the poet recanted, his tendency had already conquered. Dionysus had already been scared from the tragic stage, and in fact by a demonic power which spoke through Euripides. Even

Euripides was, in a certain sense, only a mask: the deity that spoke through him was neither Dionysus nor Apollo, but an altogether new-born demon, called Socrates. This is the new antithesis: the Dionysian and the Socratic, and the art-work of Greek tragedy was wrecked on it. What if even Euripides now seeks to comfort us by his recantation? It is of no avail: the most magnificent temple lies in ruins. What avails the lamentation of the destroyer, and his confession that it was the most beautiful of all temples? And even that Euripides has been changed into a dragon as a punishment by the art-critics of all ages--who could be content with this wretched compensation?

Let us now approach this Socratic tendency with which Euripides combated and vanquished Æschylean tragedy.

We must now ask ourselves, what could be the ulterior aim of the Euripidean design, which, in the highest ideality of its execution, would found drama exclusively on the non-Dionysian? What other form of drama could there be, if it was not to be born of the womb of music, in the mysterious twilight of the Dionysian? Only the dramatised epos: in which Apollonian domain of art the tragic effect is of course unattainable. It does not depend on the subject-matter of the events here represented; indeed, I venture to assert that it would have been impossible for Goethe in his projected "Nausikaa" to have rendered tragically effective the suicide of the idyllic being with which he intended to complete the fifth act; so extraordinary is the power of the epic-Apollonian representation, that it charms, before our eyes, the most terrible things by the joy in appearance and in redemption through appearance. The poet of the dramatised epos cannot completely blend with his pictures any more than the epic rhapsodist. He is still just the calm, unmoved embodiment of Contemplation whose wide eyes see the picture before them. The actor in this dramatised epos still remains intrinsically rhapsodist: the consecration of inner dreaming is on all his actions, so that he is never wholly an actor.

How, then, is the Euripidean play related to this ideal of the Apollonian drama? Just as the younger rhapsodist is related to the solemn rhapsodist of the old time. The former describes his own character in the Platonic "Ion" as follows: "When I am saying anything sad, my eyes fill with tears; when, however, what I am saying is awful and terrible, then my hair stands on end through fear, and my heart leaps." Here we no longer observe anything of the epic absorption in appearance, or of the unemotional coolness of the true actor, who precisely in his highest activity is wholly appearance and joy in appearance. Euripides is the actor with leaping heart, with hair standing on end; as Socratic thinker he designs the plan, as passionate actor he executes it. Neither in the designing nor in the execution is he an artist pure and simple. And so the Euripidean drama is a thing both cool and fiery, equally capable of freezing and burning; it is impossible for it to attain the Apollonian, effect of the epos, while, on the other hand, it has severed itself as much as possible from Dionysian elements, and now, in order to act at all, it requires new stimulants, which can no longer lie within the sphere of the two unique art-impulses, the Apollonian and the Dionysian. The stimulants are cool, paradoxical thoughts, in place of Apollonian intuitions--and fiery passions--in place Dionysean ecstasies; and in fact, thoughts and passions very realistically copied, and not at all steeped in the ether of art.

Accordingly, if we have perceived this much, that Euripides did not succeed in establishing the drama exclusively on the Apollonian, but that rather his non-Dionysian inclinations deviated into a naturalistic and inartistic tendency, we shall now be able to approach nearer to the character æsthetic Socratism. supreme law of which reads about as follows: "to be beautiful everything must be intelligible," as the parallel to the Socratic proposition, "only the knowing is one virtuous." With this canon in his hands Euripides measured all the separate elements of the drama, and rectified them according to his principle: the language, the characters, the dramaturgic structure, and the choric music. The poetic deficiency and retrogression, which we are so often wont to impute to Euripides in comparison with Sophoclean tragedy, is for the most part the product of this penetrating critical process, this daring intelligibility. The Euripidian prologue may serve us as an example of the productivity of this, rationalistic method. Nothing could be more opposed to the technique of our stage than the prologue in the drama of Euripides. For a single person to appear at the outset of the play telling us who he is, what precedes the action, what has happened thus far, yea, what will happen in the course of the play, would be designated by a modern playwright as a wanton and unpardonable abandonment of the effect of suspense. Everything that is about to happen is known beforehand; who then cares to wait for it actually to happen?--considering, moreover, that here there is not by any means the exciting relation of a predicting dream to a reality taking place later on. Euripides speculated quite differently. The effect of tragedy never depended on epic suspense, on the fascinating uncertainty as to what is to happen now and afterwards: but rather on the great rhetoro-lyric scenes in which the passion and dialectics of the chief hero swelled to a broad and mighty stream. Everything was arranged for pathos, not for action: and whatever was not arranged for pathos was regarded as objectionable. But what interferes most with the hearer's pleasurable satisfaction in such scenes is a missing link, a gap in the texture of the previous history. So long as the spectator has to divine the meaning of this or that person, or the presuppositions of this or that conflict of inclinations and intentions, his complete absorption in the doings and sufferings of the chief persons is impossible, as is likewise breathless fellow-feeling and fellow-fearing.

The Æschyleo-Sophoclean tragedy employed the most ingenious devices in the first scenes to place in the hands of the spectator as if by chance all the threads requisite for understanding the whole: a trait in which that noble artistry is approved, which as it were masks the inevitably formal, and causes it to appear as something accidental. But nevertheless Euripides thought he observed that during these first scenes the spectator was in a strange state of anxiety to make out the problem of the previous history, so that the poetic beauties and pathos of the exposition were lost to him. Accordingly he placed the prologue even before the exposition, and put it in the mouth of a person who could be trusted: some deity had often as it were to guarantee the particulars of the tragedy to the public and remove every doubt as to the reality of the myth: as in the case of Descartes, who could only prove the reality of the empiric world by an appeal to the truthfulness of God and His inability to utter falsehood. Euripides makes use of the same divine truthfulness once more at the close of his drama, in order to ensure to the public the future of his heroes; this is the task of the notorious deus ex machina. Between the preliminary and the additional epic spectacle there is the dramatico-lyric present, the "drama" proper.

Thus Euripides as a poet echoes above all his own conscious knowledge; and it is precisely on this account that he occupies such a notable position in the history of Greek art. With reference to his critico-productive activity, he must often have felt that he ought to actualise in the drama the words at the beginning of the essay of Anaxagoras: "In the beginning all things were mixed together; then came the understanding and created order." And if Anaxagoras with his "νοῦς" seemed like the first sober person among nothing but drunken philosophers, Euripides may also have conceived his relation to the other tragic poets under a similar figure. As long as the sole ruler and disposer of the universe, the νοῦς, was still excluded from artistic activity, things were all mixed together in a chaotic, primitive mess;--it is thus Euripides was obliged to think, it is thus he was obliged to condemn the "drunken" poets as the first "sober" one among them. What Sophocles said of Æschylus, that he did what was right, though unconsciously, was surely not in the mind of Euripides: who would have admitted only thus much, that Æschylus, because he wrought unconsciously, did what was wrong. So also the divine Plato speaks for the most part only ironically of the creative faculty of the poet, in so far as it is not conscious insight, and places it on a par with the gift of the soothsayer and dream-interpreter; insinuating that the poet is incapable of composing until he has become unconscious and reason has deserted him. Like Plato, Euripides undertook to show to the world the reverse of the "unintelligent" poet; his æsthetic principle that "to be beautiful everything must be known" is, as I have said, the parallel to the Socratic "to be good everything must be known." Accordingly we may regard Euripides as the poet of æsthetic Socratism. Socrates, however, was that second spectator who did not comprehend and therefore did not esteem the Old Tragedy; in alliance with him Euripides ventured to be the herald of a new artistic activity. If, then, the Old Tragedy was here destroyed, it follows that æsthetic Socratism was the murderous principle; but in so far as the struggle is directed against the Dionysian element in the old art, we recognise in Socrates the opponent of Dionysus, the new Orpheus who rebels against Dionysus; and although destined to be torn to pieces by the Mænads of the Athenian court, yet puts to flight the overpowerful god himself, who, when he fled from Lycurgus, the king of Edoni, sought refuge in the depths of the ocean--namely, in the mystical flood of a secret cult which gradually overspread the earth.

13

That Socrates stood in close relationship to Euripides in the tendency of his teaching, did not escape the notice of contemporaneous antiquity; the most eloquent expression of this felicitous insight being the tale current in Athens, that Socrates was accustomed to help Euripides in poetising. Both names were mentioned in one breath by the adherents of the "good old time," whenever they came to enumerating the popular agitators of the day: to whose influence they attributed the fact that the old Marathonian stalwart capacity of body and soul was more and more being sacrificed to a dubious enlightenment, involving progressive degeneration of the physical and mental powers. It is in this tone, half indignantly and half contemptuously, that Aristophanic comedy is wont to speak of both of them--to the consternation of modern men, who would indeed be willing enough to give up Euripides, but cannot suppress their amazement that Socrates should appear in Aristophanes as the first and head sophist, as the mirror and epitome of all sophistical tendencies; in connection with which it offers the single consolation of putting Aristophanes himself in the pillory, as a rakish, lying Alcibiades of poetry. Without here defending the profound instincts of Aristophanes against such attacks, I shall now indicate, by means of the sentiments of the time, the close connection between Socrates and Euripides. With this purpose in view, it is especially to be remembered that Socrates, as an opponent of tragic art, did not ordinarily patronise tragedy, but only appeared among the spectators when a new play of Euripides was performed. The most noted thing, however, is the close juxtaposition of the two names in the Delphic oracle, which designated Socrates as the wisest of men, but at the same time decided that the second prize in the contest of wisdom was due to Euripides.

Sophocles was designated as the third in this scale of rank; he who could pride himself that, in comparison with Æschylus, he did what was right, and did it, moreover, because he knew what was right. It is evidently just the degree of clearness of this knowledge, which distinguishes these three men in common as the three "knowing ones" of their age.

The most decisive word, however, for this new and unprecedented esteem of knowledge and insight was spoken by Socrates when he found that he was the only one who acknowledged to himself that he knew nothing while in his critical pilgrimage through Athens, and calling on the greatest statesmen, orators, poets, and artists, he discovered everywhere the conceit of knowledge. He perceived, to his astonishment, that all these celebrities were without a proper and accurate insight, even with regard to their own callings, and practised them only by instinct. "Only by instinct": with this phrase we touch upon the heart and core of the Socratic tendency. Socratism condemns therewith existing art as well as existing ethics; wherever Socratism turns its searching eyes it beholds the lack of insight and the power of illusion; and from this lack infers the inner perversity and objectionableness of existing conditions. From this point onwards, Socrates believed that he was called upon to, correct existence; and, with an air of disregard and superiority, as the precursor of an altogether different culture, art, and morality, he enters single-handed into a world, of which, if we reverently touched the hem, we should count it our greatest happiness.

Here is the extraordinary hesitancy which always seizes upon us with regard to Socrates, and again and again invites us to ascertain the sense and purpose of this most questionable phenomenon of antiquity. Who is it that ventures single-handed to disown the Greek character, which, as Homer, Pindar, and Æschylus, as Phidias, as Pericles, as Pythia and Dionysus, as the deepest abyss and the highest height, is sure of our wondering admiration? What demoniac power is it which would presume to spill this magic draught in the dust? What demigod is it to whom the chorus of spirits of the noblest of mankind must call out: "Weh! Weh! Du hast sie zerstört, die schöne Welt, mit mächtiger Faust; sie stürzt, sie zerfällt!"[17]

A key to the character of Socrates is presented to us by the surprising phenomenon designated as the "daimonion" of Socrates. In special circumstances, when his gigantic intellect began to stagger, he got a secure support in the utterances of a divine voice which then spake to him. This voice, whenever it comes, always dissuades. In this totally abnormal nature instinctive wisdom only appears in order to hinder the progress of conscious perception here and there. While in all productive men it is instinct which is the creatively affirmative force, consciousness only comporting itself critically and dissuasively; with Socrates it is instinct which becomes critic; it is consciousness which becomes creator--a perfect monstrosity per defectum! And we do indeed observe here a monstrous defectus of all mystical aptitude, so that Socrates might be designated as the specific non-mystic, in whom the logical nature is developed, through a superfoetation, to the same excess as instinctive wisdom is developed in the mystic. On the other hand, however, the logical instinct which appeared in Socrates was absolutely prohibited from turning against itself; in its unchecked flow it manifests a native power such as we meet with, to our shocking surprise, only among the very greatest instinctive forces. He who has experienced even a breath of the divine naïveté and security of the Socratic course of life in the Platonic writings, will also feel that the enormous driving-wheel of logical Socratism is in motion, as it were, behind Socrates, and that it must be viewed through Socrates as through a shadow. And that he himself had a boding of this relation is apparent from the dignified earnestness with which he everywhere, and even before his judges, insisted on his divine calling. To refute him here was really as impossible as to approve of his instinct-disintegrating influence. In view of this indissoluble conflict, when he had at last been brought before the fòrum of the Greek state, there was only one punishment demanded, namely exile; he might have been sped across the borders as something thoroughly enigmatical, irrubricable and inexplicable, and so posterity would have been quite unjustified in charging the Athenians with a deed of ignominy. But that the sentence of death, and not mere exile, was pronounced upon him, seems to have been brought about by Socrates himself, with perfect knowledge of the circumstances, and without the natural fear of death: he met his death with the calmness with which, according to the description of Plato, he leaves the symposium at break of day, as the last of the revellers, to begin a new day; while the sleepy companions remain behind on the benches and the floor, to dream of Socrates, the true eroticist. The dying Socrates became the new ideal of the noble Greek youths,--an ideal they had never yet beheld,--and above all, the typical Hellenic youth, Plato, prostrated himself before this scene with all the fervent devotion of his visionary soul.

Footnote:

17.

Woe! Woe!
Thou hast it destroyed,
The beautiful world;
With powerful fist;

In ruin 'tis hurled!
Faust, trans. of Bayard Taylor.--TR.

14

Let us now imagine the one great Cyclopean eye of Socrates fixed on tragedy, that eye in which the fine frenzy of artistic enthusiasm had never glowed--let us think how it was denied to this eye to gaze with pleasure into the Dionysian abysses--what could it not but see in the "sublime and greatly lauded" tragic art, as Plato called it? Something very absurd, with causes that seemed to be without effects, and effects apparently without causes; the whole, moreover, so motley and diversified that it could not but be repugnant to a thoughtful mind, a dangerous incentive, however, to sensitive and irritable souls. We know what was the sole kind of poetry which he comprehended: the Æsopian fable: and he did this no doubt with that smiling complaisance with which the good honest Gellert sings the praise of poetry in the fable of the bee and the hen:--

"Du siehst an mir, wozu sie nützt,
Dem, der nicht viel Verstand besitzt,
Die Wahrheit durch ein Bild zu sagen."[18]

But then it seemed to Socrates that tragic art did not even "tell the truth": not to mention the fact that it addresses itself to him who "hath but little wit"; consequently not to the philosopher: a twofold reason why it should be avoided. Like Plato, he reckoned it among the seductive arts which only represent the agreeable, not the useful, and hence he required of his disciples abstinence and strict separation from such unphilosophical allurements; with such success that the youthful tragic poet Plato first of all burned his poems to be able to become a scholar of Socrates. But where unconquerable native capacities bore up against the Socratic maxims, their power, together with the momentum of his mighty character, still sufficed to force poetry itself into new and hitherto unknown channels.

An instance of this is the aforesaid Plato: he, who in the condemnation of tragedy and of art in general certainly did not fall short of the naïve cynicism of his master, was nevertheless constrained by sheer artistic necessity to create a form of art which is inwardly related even to the then existing forms of art which he repudiated. Plato's main objection to the old art--that it is the imitation of a phantom,[19] and hence belongs to a sphere still lower than the empiric world--could not at all apply to the new art: and so we find Plato endeavouring to go beyond reality and attempting to represent the idea which underlies this pseudo-reality. But Plato, the thinker, thereby arrived by a roundabout road just at the point where he had always been at home as poet, and from which Sophocles and all the old artists had solemnly protested against that objection. If tragedy absorbed into itself all the earlier varieties of art, the same could again be said in an unusual sense of Platonic dialogue, which, engendered by a mixture of all the then existing forms and styles, hovers midway between narrative, lyric and drama, between prose and poetry, and has also thereby broken loose from the older strict law of unity of linguistic form; a movement which was carried still farther by the cynic writers, who in the most promiscuous style, oscillating to and fro betwixt prose and metrical forms, realised also the literary picture of the "raving Socrates" whom they were wont to represent in life. Platonic dialogue was as it were the boat in which the shipwrecked ancient poetry saved herself together with all her children: crowded into a narrow space and timidly obsequious to the one steersman, Socrates, they now launched into a new world, which never tired of looking at the fantastic spectacle of this procession. In very truth, Plato has given to all posterity the prototype of a new form of art, the prototype of the novel which must be designated as the infinitely evolved Æsopian fable, in which poetry holds the same rank with reference to dialectic philosophy as this same philosophy held for many centuries with reference to theology: namely, the rank of ancilla. This was the new position of poetry into which Plato forced it under the pressure of the demon-inspired Socrates.

Here philosophic thought overgrows art and compels it to cling close to the trunk of dialectics. The Apollonian tendency has chrysalised in the logical schematism; just as something analogous in the case of Euripides (and moreover a translation of the Dionysian into the naturalistic emotion) was forced upon our attention. Socrates, the dialectical hero in Platonic drama, reminds us of the kindred nature of the Euripidean hero, who has to defend his actions by arguments and counter-arguments, and thereby so often runs the risk of forfeiting our tragic pity; for who could mistake the optimistic element in the essence of dialectics, which celebrates a jubilee in every conclusion, and can breathe only in cool clearness and consciousness: the optimistic element, which, having once forced its way into tragedy, must gradually overgrow its Dionysian regions, and necessarily impel it to self-destruction--even to the death-leap into the bourgeois drama. Let us but realise the consequences of the Socratic maxims: "Virtue is knowledge; man only sins from ignorance; he who is virtuous is happy": these three fundamental forms of optimism involve the death of tragedy. For the virtuous hero must now be a dialectician; there must now be a necessary, visible connection between virtue and knowledge, between belief and morality; the transcendental justice of the plot in Æschylus is now degraded to the superficial and audacious principle of poetic justice with its usual deus ex machina.

How does the chorus, and, in general, the entire Dionyso-musical substratum of tragedy, now appear in the light of this new Socrato-optimistic stage-world? As something accidental, as a readily dispensable reminiscence of the origin of tragedy; while we have in fact seen that the chorus can be understood only as the cause of tragedy, and of the tragic generally. This perplexity with respect to the chorus first manifests itself in Sophocles--an important sign that the Dionysian basis of tragedy already begins to disintegrate with him. He no longer ventures to entrust to the chorus the main share of the effect, but limits its sphere to such an extent that it now appears almost co-ordinate with the actors, just as if it were elevated from the orchestra into the scene: whereby of course its character is completely destroyed, notwithstanding that Aristotle countenances this very theory of the chorus. This alteration of the position of the chorus, which Sophocles at any rate recommended by his practice, and, according to tradition, even by a treatise, is the first step towards the annihilation of the chorus, the phases of which follow one another with alarming rapidity in Euripides, Agathon, and the New Comedy. Optimistic dialectics drives, music out of tragedy with the scourge of its syllogisms: that is, it destroys the essence of tragedy, which can be explained only as a manifestation and illustration of Dionysian states, as the visible symbolisation of music, as the dream-world of Dionysian ecstasy.

If, therefore, we are to assume an anti-Dionysian tendency operating even before Socrates, which received in him only an unprecedentedly grand expression, we must not shrink from the question as to what a phenomenon like that of Socrates indicates: whom in view of the Platonic dialogues we are certainly not entitled to regard as a purely disintegrating, negative power. And though there can be no doubt whatever that the most immediate effect of the Socratic impulse tended to the dissolution of Dionysian tragedy, yet a profound experience of Socrates' own life compels us to ask whether there is necessarily only an antipodal relation between Socratism and art, and whether the birth of an "artistic Socrates" is in general something contradictory in itself.

For that despotic logician had now and then the feeling of a gap, or void, a sentiment of semi-reproach, as of a possibly neglected duty with respect to art. There often came to him, as he tells his friends in prison, one and the same dream-apparition, which kept constantly repeating to him: "Socrates, practise music." Up to his very last days he solaces himself with the opinion that his philosophising is the highest form of poetry, and finds it hard to believe that a deity will remind him of the "common, popular music." Finally, when in prison, he consents to practise also this despised music, in order thoroughly to unburden his conscience. And in this frame of mind he composes a poem on Apollo and turns a few Æsopian fables into verse. It was something similar to the demonian warning voice which urged him to these practices; it was because of his Apollonian insight that, like a barbaric king, he did not understand the noble image of a god and was in danger of sinning against a deity--through ignorance. The prompting voice of the Socratic dream-vision is the only sign of doubtfulness as to the limits of logical nature. "Perhaps "--thus he had to ask himself--"what is not intelligible to me is not therefore unreasonable? Perhaps there is a realm of wisdom from which the logician is banished? Perhaps art is even a necessary correlative of and supplement to science?"

Footnotes:

18.
In me thou seest its benefit,--
To him who hath but little wit,
Through parables to tell the truth.

19. Scheinbild = ειδολον.--TR.

15

In the sense of these last portentous questions it must now be indicated how the influence of Socrates (extending to the present moment, indeed, to all futurity) has spread over posterity like an ever-increasing shadow in the evening sun, and how this influence again and again necessitates a regeneration of art,--yea, of art already with metaphysical, broadest and profoundest sense,--and its own eternity guarantees also the eternity of art.

Before this could be perceived, before the intrinsic dependence of every art on the Greeks, the Greeks from Homer to Socrates, was conclusively demonstrated, it had to happen to us with regard to these Greeks as it happened to the Athenians with regard to Socrates. Nearly every age and stage of culture has at some time or other sought with deep displeasure to free itself from the Greeks, because in their presence everything self-achieved, sincerely admired and apparently quite original, seemed all of a sudden to lose life and colour and shrink to an abortive copy, even to caricature. And so hearty indignation breaks forth time after time against this presumptuous little nation, which dared to designate as "barbaric" for all time everything not native: who are they, one asks one's self, who, though they possessed only an ephemeral historical splendour, ridiculously restricted institutions, a dubious excellence in their customs, and were even branded with ugly vices, yet lay claim to the dignity and singular position among the peoples to which genius is entitled among the masses. What a pity one has not been so fortunate as to find the cup of hemlock with which such an affair could be disposed of without ado: for all the poison which envy, calumny, and rankling resentment engendered within themselves have not sufficed to destroy that self-sufficient grandeur! And so one feels ashamed and afraid in the presence of the Greeks: unless one prize truth above all things, and dare also to acknowledge to one's self this truth, that the Greeks, as charioteers, hold in their hands the reins of our own and of every culture, but that almost always chariot and horses are of too poor material and incommensurate with the glory of their guides, who then will deem it sport to run such a team into an abyss: which they themselves clear with the leap of Achilles.

In order to assign also to Socrates the dignity of such a leading position, it will suffice to recognise in him the type of an unheard-of form of existence, the type of the theoretical man, with regard to whose meaning and purpose it will be our next task to attain an insight. Like the artist, the theorist also finds an infinite satisfaction in what is and, like the former, he is shielded by this satisfaction from the practical ethics of pessimism with its lynx eyes which shine only in the dark. For if the artist in every unveiling of truth always cleaves with raptured eyes only to that which still remains veiled after the unveiling, the theoretical man, on the other hand, enjoys and contents himself with the cast-off veil, and finds the consummation of his pleasure in the process of a continuously successful unveiling through his own unaided efforts. There would have been no science if it had only been concerned about that one naked goddess and nothing else. For then its disciples would have been obliged to feel like those who purposed to dig a hole straight through the earth: each one of whom perceives that with the utmost lifelong exertion he is able to excavate only a very little of the enormous depth, which is again filled up before his eyes by the labours of his successor, so that a third man seems to do well when on his own account he selects a new spot for his attempts at tunnelling. If now some one proves conclusively that the antipodal goal cannot be attained in this direct way, who will still care to toil on in the old depths, unless he has learned to content himself in the meantime with finding precious stones or discovering natural laws? For that reason Lessing, the most honest theoretical man, ventured to say that he cared more for the search after truth than for truth itself: in saying which he revealed the fundamental secret of science, to the astonishment, and indeed, to the vexation of scientific men. Well, to be sure, there stands alongside of this detached perception, as an excess of honesty, if not of presumption, a profound illusion which first came to the world in the person of Socrates, the imperturbable belief that, by means of the clue of causality, thinking reaches to the deepest abysses of being, and that thinking is able not only to perceive being but even to correct it. This sublime metaphysical illusion is added as an instinct to science and again and again leads the latter to its limits, where it must change into art; which is really the end, to be attained by this mechanism.

If we now look at Socrates in the light of this thought, he appears to us as the first who could not only live, but--what is far more--also die under the guidance of this instinct of science: and hence the picture of the dying, Socrates, as the man delivered from the fear of death by knowledge and argument, is the escutcheon, above the entrance to science which reminds every one of its mission, namely, to make existence appear to be comprehensible, and therefore to be justified: for which purpose, if arguments do not suffice, myth also must be used, which I just now designated even as the necessary consequence, yea, as the end of science.

He who once makes intelligible to himself how, after the death of Socrates, the mystagogue of science, one philosophical school succeeds another, like wave upon wave,--how an entirely unfore-shadowed universal development of the thirst for knowledge in the widest compass of the cultured world (and as the specific task for every one highly gifted) led science on to the high sea from which since then it has never again been able to be completely ousted; how through the universality of this movement a common net of thought was first stretched over the entire globe, with prospects, moreover, of conformity to law in an entire solar system;--he who realises all this, together with the amazingly high pyramid of our present-day knowledge, cannot fail to see in Socrates the turning-point and vortex of so-called universal history. For if one were to imagine the whole incalculable sum of energy which has been used up by that universal tendency,--employed, not in the service of knowledge, but for the practical, i.e., egoistical ends of individuals and peoples,--then probably the instinctive love of life would be so much weakened in universal wars of destruction and incessant migrations of peoples, that, owing to the practice of suicide, the individual would perhaps feel the last remnant of a sense of duty, when, like the native of the Fiji Islands, as son he strangles his parents and, as friend, his friend: a practical pessimism which might even give rise to a horrible ethics of general slaughter out of pity--

which, for the rest, exists and has existed wherever art in one form or another, especially as science and religion, has not appeared as a remedy and preventive of that pestilential breath.

In view of this practical pessimism, Socrates is the archetype of the theoretical optimist, who in the above-indicated belief in the fathomableness of the nature of things, attributes to knowledge and perception the power of a universal medicine, and sees in error and evil. To penetrate into the depths of the nature of things, and to separate true perception from error and illusion, appeared to the Socratic man the noblest and even the only truly human calling: just as from the time of Socrates onwards the mechanism of concepts, judgments, and inferences was prized above all other capacities as the highest activity and the most admirable gift of nature. Even the sublimest moral acts, the stirrings of pity, of self-sacrifice, of heroism, and that tranquillity of soul, so difficult of attainment, which the Apollonian Greek called Sophrosyne, were derived by Socrates, and his like-minded successors up to the present day, from the dialectics of knowledge, and were accordingly designated as teachable. He who has experienced in himself the joy of a Socratic perception, and felt how it seeks to embrace, in constantly widening circles, the entire world of phenomena, will thenceforth find no stimulus which could urge him to existence more forcible than the desire to complete that conquest and to knit the net impenetrably close. To a person thus minded the Platonic Socrates then appears as the teacher of an entirely new form of "Greek cheerfulness" and felicity of existence, which seeks to discharge itself in actions, and will find its discharge for the most part in maieutic and pedagogic influences on noble youths, with a view to the ultimate production of genius.

But now science, spurred on by its powerful illusion, hastens irresistibly to its limits, on which its optimism, hidden in the essence of logic, is wrecked. For the periphery of the circle of science has an infinite number of points, and while there is still no telling how this circle can ever be completely measured, yet the noble and gifted man, even before the middle of his career, inevitably comes into contact with those extreme points of the periphery where he stares at the inexplicable. When he here sees to his dismay how logic coils round itself at these limits and finally bites its own tail--then the new form of perception discloses itself, namely tragic perception, which, in order even to be endured, requires art as a safeguard and remedy.

If, with eyes strengthened and refreshed at the sight of the Greeks, we look upon the highest spheres of the world that surrounds us, we behold the avidity of the insatiate optimistic knowledge, of which Socrates is the typical representative, transformed into tragic resignation and the need of art: while, to be sure, this same avidity, in its lower stages, has to exhibit itself as antagonistic to art, and must especially have an inward detestation of Dionyso-tragic art, as was exemplified in the opposition of Socratism to Æschylean tragedy.

Here then with agitated spirit we knock at the gates of the present and the future: will that "transforming" lead to ever new configurations of genius, and especially of the music-practising Socrates? Will the net of art which is spread over existence, whether under the name of religion or of science, be knit always more closely and delicately, or is it destined to be torn to shreds under the restlessly barbaric activity and whirl which is called "the present day"?--Anxious, yet not disconsolate, we stand aloof for a little while, as the spectators who are permitted to be witnesses of these tremendous struggles and transitions. Alas! It is the charm of these struggles that he who beholds them must also fight them!

16

By this elaborate historical example we have endeavoured to make it clear that tragedy perishes as surely by evanescence of the spirit of music as it can be born only out of this spirit. In order to qualify the singularity of this assertion, and, on the other hand, to disclose the source of this insight of ours, we must now confront with clear vision the analogous phenomena of the present time; we must enter into the midst of these struggles, which, as I said just now, are being carried on in the highest spheres of our present world between the insatiate optimistic perception and the tragic need of art. In so doing I shall leave out of consideration all other antagonistic tendencies which at all times oppose art, especially tragedy, and which at present again extend their sway triumphantly, to such an extent that of the theatrical arts only the farce and the ballet, for example, put forth their blossoms, which perhaps not every one cares to smell, in tolerably rich luxuriance. I will speak only of the Most Illustrious Opposition to the tragic conception of things--and by this I mean essentially optimistic science, with its ancestor Socrates at the head of it. Presently also the forces will be designated which seem to me to guarantee a re-birth of tragedy--and who knows what other blessed hopes for the German genius!

Before we plunge into the midst of these struggles, let us array ourselves in the armour of our hitherto acquired knowledge. In contrast to all those who are intent on deriving the arts from one exclusive principle, as the necessary vital source of every work of art, I keep my eyes fixed on the two artistic deities of the Greeks, Apollo and Dionysus, and recognise in them the living and conspicuous representatives of two worlds of art which differ in their intrinsic essence and in their highest aims. Apollo stands before me as the transfiguring genius of the principium individuationis through which alone the redemption in appearance is to be truly attained, while by the mystical cheer of Dionysus the spell of individuation is broken, and the way lies open to the Mothers of Being,[20] to the innermost heart of things. This extraordinary antithesis, which opens up yawningly between plastic art as the Apollonian and music as the Dionysian art, has become manifest to only one of the great thinkers, to such an extent that, even without this key to the symbolism of the Hellenic divinities, he allowed to music a different character and origin in advance of all the other arts, because, unlike them, it is not a copy of the phenomenon, but a direct copy of the will itself, and therefore represents the metaphysical of everything physical in the world, the thing-in-itself of every phenomenon. (Schopenhauer, Welt als Wille und Vorstellung, I. 310.) To this most important perception of æsthetics (with which, taken in a serious sense, æsthetics properly commences), Richard Wagner, by way of confirmation of its eternal truth, affixed his seal, when he asserted in his Beethoven that music must be judged according to æsthetic principles quite different from those which apply to the plastic arts, and not, in general, according to the category of beauty: although an erroneous æsthetics, inspired by a misled and degenerate art, has by virtue of the concept of beauty prevailing in the plastic domain accustomed itself to demand of music an effect analogous to that of the works of plastic art, namely the suscitating delight in beautiful forms. Upon perceiving this extraordinary antithesis, I felt a strong inducement to approach the essence of Greek tragedy, and, by means of it, the profoundest revelation of Hellenic genius: for I at last thought myself to be in possession of a charm to enable me--far beyond the phraseology of our usual æsthetics--to represent vividly to my mind the primitive problem of tragedy: whereby such an astounding insight into the Hellenic character was afforded me that it necessarily seemed as if our proudly comporting classico-Hellenic science had thus far contrived to subsist almost exclusively on phantasmagoria and externalities.

Perhaps we may lead up to this primitive problem with the question: what æsthetic effect results when the intrinsically separate art-powers, the Apollonian and the Dionysian, enter into concurrent actions? Or, in briefer form: how is music related to image and concept?--Schopenhauer, whom Richard Wagner, with especial reference to this point, accredits with an unsurpassable clearness and perspicuity of exposition, expresses himself most copiously on the subject in the following passage which I shall cite here at full length[21] (Welt als Wille und Vorstellung, I. p. 309): "According to all this, we may regard the phenomenal world, or nature, and music as two different expressions of the same thing,[20] which is therefore itself the only medium of the analogy between these two expressions, so that a knowledge of this medium is required in order to understand that analogy. Music, therefore, if regarded as an expression of the world, is in the highest degree a universal language, which is related indeed to the universality of concepts, much as these are related to the particular things. Its universality, however, is by no means the empty universality of abstraction, but of quite a different kind, and is united with thorough and distinct definiteness. In this respect it resembles geometrical figures and numbers, which are the universal forms of all possible objects of experience and applicable to them all a priori, and yet are not abstract but perceptiple and thoroughly determinate. All possible efforts, excitements and manifestations of will, all that goes on in the heart of man and that reason includes in the wide, negative concept of feeling, may be expressed by the infinite number of possible melodies, but always in the universality of mere form, without the material, always according to the thing-in-itself, not the phenomenon,--of which they reproduce the very soul and essence as it were, without the body. This deep relation which music bears to the true nature of all things also explains the fact that suitable music played to any scene, action, event, or surrounding seems to disclose to us its most secret meaning, and appears as the most accurate and distinct commentary upon it; as also the fact that whoever gives himself up entirely to the impression of a symphony seems to see all the possible events of life and the world take place in himself: nevertheless upon reflection he can find no likeness between the music and the things that passed before his mind. For, as we have said, music is distinguished from all the other arts by the fact that it is not a copy of the phenomenon, or, more accurately, the adequate objectivity of the will, but the direct copy of the will itself, and therefore represents the metaphysical of everything physical in the world, and the thing-in-itself of every phenomenon. We might, therefore, just as well call the world embodied music as embodied will: and this is the reason why music makes every picture, and indeed every scene of real life and of the world, at once appear with higher significance; all the more so, to be sure, in proportion as its melody is analogous to the inner spirit of the given phenomenon. It rests upon this that we are able to set a poem to music as a song, or a perceptible representation as a pantomime, or both as an opera. Such particular pictures of human life, set to the universal language of music, are never bound to it or correspond to it with stringent necessity, but stand to it only in the relation of an example chosen at will to a general concept. In the determinateness of the real they represent that which music expresses in the universality of mere form. For melodies are to a certain extent, like general concepts, an abstraction from the actual. This actual world, then, the world of particular things, affords the object of perception, the special and the individual, the particular case, both to the universality of concepts and to the universality of the melodies. But these two universalities are in a certain respect opposed to each other; for the concepts contain only the forms, which are first of all abstracted from perception,--the separated outward shell of things, as it were,--and hence they are, in the strictest sense of the term, abstracta; music, on the other hand, gives the inmost kernel which precedes all forms, or the heart of things. This relation may be very well expressed in the language of the schoolmen, by saying: the concepts are the universalia post rem, but music gives the universalia ante rem, and the real world the universalia in re.--But that in general a relation is possible between a composition and a perceptible representation rests, as we have said, upon the fact that both are simply different expressions of the same inner being of the world. When now, in the particular case, such a relation is actually given, that is to say, when the composer has been able to express in the universal language of music the emotions of will which constitute the heart of an event, then the melody of the song, the music of the opera, is expressive. But the analogy discovered by the composer between the two must have proceeded from the direct knowledge of the nature of the world unknown to his reason, and must not be an imitation produced with conscious intention by means of conceptions; otherwise the music does not express the inner nature of the will itself, but merely gives an inadequate imitation of its phenomenon: all specially imitative music does this."

We have therefore, according to the doctrine of Schopenhauer, an immediate understanding of music as the language of the will, and feel our imagination stimulated to give form to this invisible and yet so actively stirred spirit-world which speaks to us, and prompted to embody it in an analogous example. On the other hand, image and concept, under the influence of a truly conformable music, acquire a higher significance. Dionysian art therefore is wont to exercise--two kinds of influences, on the Apollonian art-faculty: music firstly incites to the symbolic intuition of Dionysian universality, and, secondly, it causes the symbolic image to stand forth in its fullest significance. From these facts, intelligible in themselves and not inaccessible to profounder observation, I infer the capacity of music to give birth to myth, that is to say, the most significant exemplar, and precisely tragic myth: the myth which speaks of Dionysian knowledge in symbols. In the phenomenon of the lyrist, I have set forth that in him music strives to express itself with regard to its nature in Apollonian images. If now we reflect that music in its highest potency must seek to attain also to its highest symbolisation, we must deem it possible that it also knows how to find the symbolic expression of its inherent Dionysian wisdom; and where shall we have to seek for this expression if not in tragedy and, in general, in the conception of the tragic?

From the nature of art, as it is ordinarily conceived according to the single category of appearance and beauty, the tragic cannot be honestly deduced at all; it is only through the spirit of music that we understand the joy in the annihilation of the individual. For in the particular examples of such annihilation only is the eternal phenomenon of Dionysian art made clear to us, which gives expression to the will in its omnipotence, as it were, behind the principium individuationis, the eternal life beyond all phenomena, and in spite of all annihilation. The metaphysical delight in the tragic is a translation of the instinctively unconscious Dionysian wisdom into the language of the scene: the hero, the highest manifestation of the will, is disavowed for our pleasure, because he is only phenomenon, and because the eternal life of the will is not affected by his annihilation. "We believe in eternal life," tragedy exclaims; while music is the proximate idea of this life. Plastic art has an altogether different object: here Apollo vanquishes the suffering of the individual by the radiant glorification of the eternity of the phenomenon; here beauty triumphs over the suffering inherent in life; pain is in a manner surreptitiously obliterated from the features of nature. In Dionysian art and its tragic symbolism the same nature speaks to us with its true undissembled voice: "Be as I am! Amidst the ceaseless change of phenomena the eternally creative primordial mother, eternally impelling to existence, self-satisfying eternally with this change of phenomena!"

Footnotes:

20. Cf. World and Will as Idea, I. p. 339, trans. by Haldane and Kemp.
21. That is "the will" as understood by Schopenhauer.--TR.

17

Dionysian art, too, seeks to convince us of the eternal joy of existence: only we are to seek this joy not in phenomena, but behind phenomena. We are to perceive how all that comes into being must be ready for a sorrowful end; we are compelled to look into the terrors of individual existence--yet we are not to become torpid: a metaphysical comfort tears us momentarily from the bustle of the transforming figures. We are really for brief moments Primordial Being itself, and feel its indomitable desire for being and joy in existence; the struggle, the pain, the destruction of phenomena, now appear to us as something necessary, considering the surplus of innumerable forms of existence which throng and push one another into life, considering the exuberant fertility of the universal will. We are pierced by the maddening sting of these pains at the very moment when we have become, as it were, one with the immeasurable primordial joy in existence, and when we anticipate, in Dionysian ecstasy, the indestructibility and eternity of this joy. In spite of fear and pity, we are the happy living beings, not as individuals, but as the one living being, with whose procreative joy we are blended.

The history of the rise of Greek tragedy now tells us with luminous precision that the tragic art of the Greeks was really born of the spirit of music: with which conception we believe we have done justice for the first time to the original and most astonishing significance of the chorus. At the same time, however, we must admit that the import of tragic myth as set forth above never became transparent with sufficient lucidity to the Greek poets, let alone the Greek philosophers; their heroes speak, as it were, more superficially than they act; the myth does not at all find its adequate objectification in the spoken word. The structure of the scenes and the conspicuous images reveal a deeper wisdom than the poet himself can put into words and concepts: the same being also observed in Shakespeare, whose Hamlet, for instance, in an analogous manner talks more superficially than he acts, so that the previously mentioned lesson of Hamlet is to be gathered not from his words, but from a more profound contemplation and survey of the whole. With respect to Greek tragedy, which of course presents itself to us only as word-drama, I have even intimated that the incongruence between myth and expression might easily tempt us to regard it as shallower and less significant than it really is, and accordingly to postulate for it a more superficial effect than it must have had according to the testimony of the ancients: for how easily one forgets that what the word-poet did not succeed in doing, namely realising the highest spiritualisation and ideality of myth, he might succeed in doing every moment as creative musician! We require, to be sure, almost by philological method to reconstruct for ourselves the ascendency of musical influence in order to receive something of the incomparable comfort which must be characteristic of true tragedy. Even this musical ascendency, however, would only have been felt by us as such had we been Greeks: while in the entire development of Greek music--as compared with the infinitely richer music known and familiar to us--we imagine we hear only the youthful song of the musical genius intoned with a feeling of diffidence. The Greeks are, as the Egyptian priests say, eternal children, and in tragic art also they are only children who do not know what a sublime play-thing has originated under their hands and--is being demolished.

That striving of the spirit of music for symbolic and mythical manifestation, which increases from the beginnings of lyric poetry to Attic tragedy, breaks off all of a sudden immediately after attaining luxuriant development, and disappears, as it were, from the surface of Hellenic art: while the Dionysian view of things born of this striving lives on in Mysteries and, in its strangest metamorphoses and debasements, does not cease to attract earnest natures. Will it not one day rise again as art out of its mystic depth?

Here the question occupies us, whether the power by the counteracting influence of which tragedy perished, has for all time strength enough to prevent the artistic reawaking of tragedy and of the tragic view of things. If ancient tragedy was driven from its course by the dialectical desire for knowledge and the optimism of science, it might be inferred that there is an eternal conflict between the theoretic and the tragic view of things, and only after the spirit of science has been led to its boundaries, and its claim to universal validity has been destroyed by the evidence of these boundaries, can we hope for a re-birth of tragedy: for which form of culture we should have to use the symbol of the music-practising Socrates in the sense spoken of above. In this contrast, I understand by the spirit of science the belief which first came to light in the person of Socrates,--the belief in the fathomableness of nature and in knowledge as a panacea.

He who recalls the immediate consequences of this restlessly onward-pressing spirit of science will realise at once that myth was annihilated by it, and that, in consequence of this annihilation, poetry was driven as a homeless being from her natural ideal soil. If we have rightly assigned to music the capacity to reproduce myth from itself, we may in turn expect to find the spirit of science on the path where it inimically opposes this mythopoeic power of music. This takes place in the development of the New Attic Dithyramb, the music of which no longer expressed the inner essence, the will itself, but only rendered the phenomenon insufficiently, in an imitation by means of concepts; from which intrinsically degenerate music the truly musical natures turned away with the same repugnance that they felt for the art-destroying tendency of Socrates. The unerring instinct of Aristophanes surely did the proper thing when it comprised Socrates himself, the tragedy of Euripides, and the music of the new Dithyrambic poets in the same feeling of hatred, and perceived in all three phenomena the symptoms of a degenerate culture. By this New Dithyramb, music has in an outrageous manner been made the imitative portrait of phenomena, for instance, of a battle or a storm at sea, and has thus, of course, been entirely deprived of its mythopoeic power. For if it endeavours to excite our delight only by compelling us to seek external analogies between a vital or natural process and certain rhythmical figures and characteristic sounds of music; if our understanding is expected to satisfy itself with the perception of these analogies, we are reduced to a frame of mind in which the reception of the mythical is impossible; for the myth as a unique exemplar of generality and truth towering into the infinite, desires to be conspicuously perceived. The truly Dionysean music presents itself to us as such a general mirror of the universal will: the conspicuous event which is refracted in this mirror expands at once for our consciousness to the copy of an eternal truth. Conversely, such a conspicious event is at once divested of every mythical character by the tone-painting of the New Dithyramb; music has here become a wretched copy of the phenomenon, and therefore infinitely poorer than the phenomenon itself: through which poverty it still further reduces even the phenomenon for our consciousness, so that now, for instance, a musically imitated battle of this sort exhausts itself in marches, signal-sounds, etc., and our imagination is arrested precisely by these superficialities. Tone-painting is therefore in every respect the counterpart of true music with its mythopoeic power: through it the phenomenon, poor in itself, is made still poorer, while through an isolated Dionysian music the phenomenon is evolved and expanded into a picture of the world. It was an immense triumph of the non-Dionysian spirit, when, in the development of the New Dithyramb, it had estranged music from itself and reduced it to be the slave of phenomena. Euripides, who, albeit in a higher sense, must be designated as a thoroughly unmusical nature, is for this very reason a passionate adherent of the New Dithyrambic Music, and with the liberality of a freebooter employs all its effective turns and mannerisms.

In another direction also we see at work the power of this un-Dionysian, myth-opposing spirit, when we turn our eyes to the prevalence of character representation and psychological refinement from Sophocles onwards. The character must no longer be expanded into an eternal type, but, on the contrary, must operate individually through artistic by-traits and shadings, through the nicest precision of all lines, in such a manner that the spectator is in general no longer conscious of the myth, but of the mighty nature-myth and the imitative power of the artist. Here also we observe the victory of the phenomenon over the Universal, and the delight in the particular quasi-anatomical preparation; we actually breathe the air of a theoretical world, in which scientific knowledge is valued more highly than the artistic reflection of a universal law. The movement along the line of the representation of character proceeds rapidly: while Sophocles still delineates complete characters and employs myth for their refined development, Euripides already delineates only prominent individual traits of character, which can express themselves in violent bursts of passion; in the New Attic Comedy, however, there are only masks with one expression: frivolous old men, duped panders, and cunning slaves in untiring repetition. Where now is the mythopoeic spirit of music? What is still left now of music is either excitatory music or souvenir music, that is, either a stimulant for dull and used-up nerves, or tone-painting. As regards the former, it hardly matters about the text set to it: the heroes and choruses of Euripides are already dissolute enough when once they begin to sing; to what pass must things have come with his brazen successors?

The new un-Dionysian spirit, however, manifests itself most clearly in the dénouements of the new dramas. In the Old Tragedy one could feel at the close the metaphysical comfort, without which the delight in tragedy cannot be explained at all; the conciliating tones from another world sound purest, perhaps, in the Œdipus at Colonus. Now that the genius of music has fled from tragedy, tragedy is, strictly speaking, dead: for from whence could one now draw the metaphysical comfort? One sought, therefore, for an earthly unravelment of the tragic dissonance; the hero, after he had been sufficiently tortured by fate, reaped a well-deserved reward through a superb marriage or divine tokens of favour. The hero had turned gladiator, on whom, after being liberally battered about and covered with wounds, freedom was occasionally bestowed. The deus ex machina took the place of metaphysical comfort. I will not say that the tragic view of things was everywhere completely destroyed by the intruding spirit of the un-Dionysian: we only know that it was compelled to flee from art into the under-world as it were, in the degenerate form of a secret cult. Over the widest extent of the Hellenic character, however, there raged the consuming blast of this spirit, which manifests itself in the form of "Greek cheerfulness," which we have already spoken of as a senile, unproductive love of existence; this cheerfulness is the counterpart of the splendid "naïveté" of the earlier Greeks, which, according to the characteristic indicated above, must be conceived as the blossom of the Apollonian culture growing out of a dark abyss, as the victory which the Hellenic will, through its mirroring of beauty, obtains over suffering and the wisdom of suffering. The noblest manifestation of that other form of "Greek cheerfulness," the Alexandrine, is the cheerfulness of the theoretical man: it exhibits the same symptomatic characteristics as I have just inferred concerning the spirit of the un-Dionysian:--it combats Dionysian wisdom and art, it seeks to dissolve myth, it substitutes for metaphysical comfort an earthly consonance, in fact, a deus ex machina of its own, namely the god of machines and crucibles, that is, the powers of the genii of nature recognised and employed in the service of higher egoism; it believes in amending the world by knowledge, in guiding life by science, and that it can really confine the individual within a narrow sphere of solvable problems, where he cheerfully says to life: "I desire thee: it is worth while to know thee."

18

It is an eternal phenomenon: the avidious will can always, by means of an illusion spread over things, detain its creatures in life and compel them to live on. One is chained by the Socratic love of knowledge and the vain hope of being able thereby to heal the eternal wound of existence; another is ensnared by art's seductive veil of beauty fluttering before his eyes; still another by the metaphysical comfort that eternal life flows on indestructibly beneath the whirl of phenomena: to say nothing of the more ordinary and almost more powerful illusions which the will has always at hand. These three specimens of illusion are on the whole designed only for the more nobly endowed natures, who in general feel profoundly the weight and burden of existence, and must be deluded into forgetfulness of their displeasure by exquisite stimulants. All that we call culture is made up of these stimulants; and, according to the proportion of the ingredients, we have either a specially Socratic or artistic or tragic culture: or, if historical exemplifications are wanted, there is either an Alexandrine or a Hellenic or a Buddhistic culture.

Our whole modern world is entangled in the meshes of Alexandrine culture, and recognises as its ideal the theorist equipped with the most potent means of knowledge, and labouring in the service of science, of whom the archetype and progenitor is Socrates. All our educational methods have originally this ideal in view: every other form of existence must struggle onwards wearisomely beside it, as something tolerated, but not intended. In an almost alarming manner the cultured man was here found for a long time only in the form of the scholar: even our poetical arts have been forced to evolve from learned imitations, and in the main effect of the rhyme we still recognise the origin of our poetic form from artistic experiments with a non-native and thoroughly learned language. How unintelligible must Faust, the modern cultured man, who is in himself intelligible, have appeared to a true Greek,--Faust, storming discontentedly through all the faculties, devoted to magic and the devil from a desire for knowledge, whom we have only to place alongside of Socrates for the purpose of comparison, in order to see that modern man begins to divine the boundaries of this Socratic love of perception and longs for a coast in the wide waste of the ocean of knowledge. When Goethe on one occasion said to Eckermann with reference to Napoleon: "Yes, my good friend, there is also a productiveness of deeds," he reminded us in a charmingly naïve manner that the non-theorist is something incredible and astounding to modern man; so that the wisdom of Goethe is needed once more in order to discover that such a surprising form of existence is comprehensible, nay even pardonable.

Now, we must not hide from ourselves what is concealed in the heart of this Socratic culture: Optimism, deeming itself absolute! Well, we must not be alarmed if the fruits of this optimism ripen,--if society, leavened to the very lowest strata by this kind of culture, gradually begins to tremble through wanton agitations and desires, if the belief in the earthly happiness of all, if the belief in the possibility of such a general intellectual culture is gradually transformed into the threatening demand for such an Alexandrine earthly happiness, into the conjuring of a Euripidean deus ex machina. Let us mark this well: the Alexandrine culture requires a slave class, to be able to exist permanently: but, in its optimistic view of life, it denies the necessity of such a class, and consequently, when the effect of its beautifully seductive and tranquillising utterances about the "dignity of man" and the "dignity of labour" is spent, it gradually drifts towards a dreadful destination. There is nothing more terrible than a barbaric slave class, who have learned to regard their existence as an injustice, and now prepare to take vengeance, not only for themselves, but for all generations. In the face of such threatening storms, who dares to appeal with confident spirit to our pale and exhausted religions, which even in their foundations have degenerated into scholastic religions?--so that myth, the necessary prerequisite of every religion, is already paralysed everywhere, and even in this domain the optimistic spirit--which we have just designated as the annihilating germ of society--has attained the mastery.

While the evil slumbering in the heart of theoretical culture gradually begins to disquiet modern man, and makes him anxiously ransack the stores of his experience for means to avert the danger, though not believing very much in these means; while he, therefore, begins to divine the consequences his position involves: great, universally gifted natures have contrived, with an incredible amount of thought, to make use of the apparatus of science itself, in order to point out the limits and the relativity of knowledge generally, and thus definitely to deny the claim of science to universal validity and universal ends: with which demonstration the illusory notion was for the first time recognised as such, which pretends, with the aid of causality, to be able to fathom the innermost essence of things. The extraordinary courage and wisdom of Kant and Schopenhauer have succeeded in gaining the most, difficult, victory, the victory over the optimism hidden in the essence of logic, which optimism in turn is the basis of our culture. While this optimism, resting on apparently unobjectionable æterna veritates, believed in the intelligibility and solvability of all the riddles of the world, and treated space, time, and causality as totally unconditioned laws of the most universal validity, Kant, on the other hand, showed that these served in reality only to elevate the mere phenomenon, the work of Mâyâ, to the sole and highest reality, putting it in place of the innermost and true essence of things, thus making the actual knowledge of this essence impossible, that is, according to the expression of Schopenhauer, to lull the dreamer still more soundly asleep (Welt als Wille und Vorstellung, I. 498). With this knowledge a culture is inaugurated which I venture to designate as a tragic culture; the most important characteristic of which is that wisdom takes the place of science as the highest end,--wisdom, which, uninfluenced by the seductive distractions of the sciences, turns with unmoved eye to the comprehensive view of the world, and seeks to apprehend therein the eternal suffering as its own with sympathetic feelings of love. Let us imagine a rising generation with this undauntedness of vision, with this heroic desire for the prodigious, let us imagine the bold step of these dragon-slayers, the proud and daring spirit with which they turn their backs on all the effeminate doctrines of optimism in order "to live resolutely" in the Whole and in the Full: would it not be necessary for the tragic man of this culture, with his self-discipline to earnestness and terror, to desire a new art, the art of metaphysical comfort,--namely, tragedy, as the Hellena belonging to him, and that he should exclaim with Faust:

Und sollt' ich nicht, sehnsüchtigster Gewalt,
In's Leben ziehn die einzigste Gestalt?[21]

But now that the Socratic culture has been shaken from two directions, and is only able to hold the sceptre of its infallibility with trembling hands,--once by the fear of its own conclusions which it at length begins to surmise, and again, because it is no longer convinced with its former naïve trust of the eternal validity of its foundation, --it is a sad spectacle to behold how the dance of its thought always rushes longingly on new forms, to embrace them, and then, shuddering, lets them go of a sudden, as Mephistopheles does the seductive Lamiæ. It is certainly the symptom of the "breach" which all are wont to speak of as the primordial suffering of modern culture that the theoretical man, alarmed and dissatisfied at his own conclusions, no longer dares to entrust himself to the terrible ice-stream of existence: he runs timidly up and down the bank. He no longer wants to have anything entire, with all the natural cruelty of things, so thoroughly has he been spoiled by his optimistic contemplation. Besides, he feels that a culture built up on the principles of science must perish when it begins to grow illogical, that is, to avoid its own conclusions. Our art reveals this universal trouble: in vain does one seek help by imitating all the great productive periods and natures, in vain does one accumulate the entire "world-literature" around modern man for his comfort, in vain does one place one's self in the midst of the art-styles and artists of all ages, so that one may give names to them as Adam did to the beasts: one still continues the eternal hungerer, the "critic" without joy and energy, the Alexandrine man, who is in the main a librarian and corrector of proofs, and who, pitiable wretch goes blind from the dust of books and printers' errors.

Footnotes:

21. Cf. Introduction, p. 14.

19

We cannot designate the intrinsic substance of Socratic culture more distinctly than by calling it the culture of the opera: for it is in this department that culture has expressed itself with special naïveté concerning its aims and pèrceptions, which is sufficiently surprising when we compare the genesis of the opera and the facts of operatic development with the eternal truths of the Apollonian and Dionysian. I call to mind first of all the origin of the stilo rappresentativo and the recitative. Is it credible that this thoroughly externalised operatic music, incapable of devotion, could be received and cherished with enthusiastic favour, as a re-birth, as it were, of all true music, by the very age in which the ineffably sublime and sacred music of Palestrina had originated? And who, on the other hand, would think of making only the diversion-craving luxuriousness of those Florentine circles and the vanity of their dramatic singers responsible for the love of the opera which spread with such rapidity? That in the same age, even among the same people, this passion for a half-musical mode of speech should awaken alongside of the vaulted structure of Palestrine harmonies which the entire Christian Middle Age had been building up, I can explain to myself only by a co-operating extra-artistic tendency in the essence of the recitative.

The listener, who insists on distinctly hearing the words under the music, has his wishes met by the singer in that he speaks rather than sings, and intensifies the pathetic expression of the words in this half-song: by this intensification of the pathos he facilitates the understanding of the words and surmounts the remaining half of the music. The specific danger which now threatens him is that in some unguarded moment he may give undue importance to music, which would forthwith result in the destruction of the pathos of the speech and the distinctness of the words: while, on the other hand, he always feels himself impelled to musical delivery and to virtuose exhibition of vocal talent. Here the "poet" comes to his aid, who knows how to provide him with abundant opportunities for lyrical interjections, repetitions of words and sentences, etc.,--at which places the singer, now in the purely musical element, can rest himself without minding the words. This alternation of emotionally impressive, yet only half-sung speech and wholly sung interjections, which is characteristic of the stilo rappresentativo, this rapidly changing endeavour to operate now on the conceptional and representative faculty of the hearer, now on his musical sense, is something so thoroughly unnatural and withal so intrinsically contradictory both to the Apollonian and Dionysian artistic impulses, that one has to infer an origin of the recitative foreign to all artistic instincts. The recitative must be defined, according to this description, as the combination of epic and lyric delivery, not indeed as an intrinsically stable combination which could not be attained in the case of such totally disparate elements, but an entirely superficial mosaic conglutination, such as is totally unprecedented in the domain of nature and experience. But this was not the opinion of the inventors of the recitative: they themselves, and their age with them, believed rather that the mystery of antique music had been solved by this stilo rappresentativo, in which, as they thought, the only explanation of the enormous influence of an Orpheus, an Amphion, and even of Greek tragedy was to be found. The new style was regarded by them as the re-awakening of the most effective music, the Old Greek music: indeed, with the universal and popular conception of the Homeric world as the primitive world, they could abandon themselves to the dream of having descended once more into the paradisiac beginnings of mankind, wherein music also must needs have had the unsurpassed purity, power, and innocence of which the poets could give such touching accounts in their pastoral plays. Here we see into the internal process of development of this thoroughly modern variety of art, the opera: a powerful need here acquires an art, but it is a need of an unæsthetic kind: the yearning for the idyll, the belief in the prehistoric existence of the artistic, good man. The recitative was regarded as the rediscovered language of this primitive man; the opera as the recovered land of this idyllically or heroically good creature, who in every action follows at the same time a natural artistic impulse, who sings a little along with all he has to say, in order to sing immediately with full voice on the slightest emotional excitement. It is now a matter of indifference to us that the humanists of those days combated the old ecclesiastical representation of man as naturally corrupt and lost, with this new-created picture of the paradisiac artist: so that opera may be understood as the oppositional dogma of the good man, whereby however a solace was at the same time found for the pessimism to which precisely the seriously-disposed men of that time were most strongly incited, owing to the frightful uncertainty of all conditions of life. It is enough to have perceived that the intrinsic charm, and therefore the genesis, of this new form of art lies in the gratification of an altogether unæsthetic need, in the optimistic glorification of man as such, in the conception of the primitive man as the man naturally good and artistic: a principle of the opera which has gradually changed into a threatening and terrible demand, which, in face of the socialistic movements of the present time, we can no longer ignore. The "good primitive man" wants his rights: what paradisiac prospects!

I here place by way of parallel still another equally obvious confirmation of my view that opera is built up on the same principles as our Alexandrine culture. Opera is the birth of the theoretical man, of the critical layman, not of the artist: one of the most surprising facts in the whole history of art. It was the demand of thoroughly unmusical hearers that the words must above all be understood, so that according to them a re-birth of music is only to be expected when some mode of singing has been discovered in which the text-word lords over the counterpoint as the master over the servant. For the words, it is argued, are as much nobler than the accompanying harmonic system as the soul is nobler than the body. It was in accordance with the laically unmusical crudeness of these views that the combination of music, picture and expression was effected in the beginnings of the opera: in the spirit of this æsthetics the first experiments were also made in the leading laic circles of Florence by the poets and singers patronised there. The man incapable of art creates for himself a species of art precisely because he is the inartistic man as such. Because he does not divine the Dionysian depth of music, he changes his musical taste into appreciation of the understandable word-and-tone-rhetoric of the passions in the stilo rappresentativo, and into the voluptuousness of the arts of song; because he is unable to behold a vision, he forces the machinist and the decorative artist into his service; because he cannot apprehend the true nature of the artist, he conjures up the "artistic primitive man" to suit his taste, that is, the man who sings and recites verses under the influence of passion. He dreams himself into a time when passion suffices to generate songs and poems: as if emotion had ever been able to create anything artistic. The postulate of the opera is a false belief concerning the artistic process, in fact, the idyllic belief that every sentient man is an artist. In the sense of this belief, opera is the expression of the taste of the laity in art, who dictate their laws with the cheerful optimism of the theorist.

Should we desire to unite in one the two conceptions just set forth as influential in the origin of opera, it would only remain for us to speak of an idyllic tendency of the opera: in which connection we may avail ourselves exclusively of the phraseology and illustration of Schiller.[22] "Nature and the ideal," he says, "are either objects of grief, when the former is represented as lost, the latter unattained; or both are objects of joy, in that they are represented as real. The first case furnishes the elegy in its narrower signification, the second the idyll in its widest sense." Here we must at once call attention to the common characteristic of these two conceptions in operatic genesis, namely, that in them the ideal is not regarded as unattained or nature as lost Agreeably to this sentiment, there was a primitive age of man when he lay close to the heart of nature, and, owing to this naturalness, had attained the ideal of mankind in a paradisiac goodness and artist-organisation: from which perfect primitive man all of us were supposed to be descended; whose faithful copy we were in fact still said to be: only we had to cast off some few things in order to recognise ourselves once more as this primitive man, on the strength of a voluntary renunciation of superfluous learnedness, of super-abundant culture. It was to such a concord of nature and the ideal, to an idyllic reality, that the cultured man of the Renaissance suffered himself to be led back by his operatic imitation of Greek tragedy; he made use of this tragedy, as Dante made use of Vergil, in order to be led up to the gates of paradise: while from this point he went on without assistance and passed over from an imitation of the highest form of Greek art to a "restoration of all things," to an imitation of man's original art-world. What delightfully naïve hopefulness of these daring endeavours, in the very heart of theoretical culture!--solely to be explained by the comforting belief, that "man-in-himself" is the eternally virtuous hero of the opera, the eternally fluting or singing shepherd, who must always in the end rediscover himself as such, if he has at any time really lost himself; solely the fruit of the optimism, which here rises like a sweetishly seductive column of vapour out of the depth of the Socratic conception of the world.

The features of the opera therefore do not by any means exhibit the elegiac sorrow of an eternal loss, but rather the cheerfulness of eternal rediscovery, the indolent delight in an idyllic reality which one can at least represent to one's self each moment as real: and in so doing one will perhaps surmise some day that this supposed reality is nothing but a fantastically silly dawdling, concerning which every one, who could judge it by the terrible earnestness of true nature and compare it with the actual primitive scenes of the beginnings of mankind, would have to call out with loathing: Away with the phantom! Nevertheless one would err if one thought it possible to frighten away merely by a vigorous shout such a dawdling thing as the opera, as if it were a spectre. He who would destroy the opera must join issue with Alexandrine cheerfulness, which expresses itself so naïvely therein concerning its favourite representation; of which in fact it is the specific form of art. But what is to be expected for art itself from the operation of a form of art, the beginnings of which do not at all lie in the æsthetic province; which has rather stolen over from a half-moral sphere into the artistic domain, and has been able only now and then to delude us concerning this hybrid origin? By what sap is this parasitic opera-concern nourished, if not by that of true art? Must we not suppose that the highest and indeed the truly serious task of art--to free the eye from its glance into the horrors of night and to deliver the "subject" by the healing balm of appearance from the spasms of volitional agitations--will degenerate under the influence of its idyllic seductions and Alexandrine adulation to an empty dissipating tendency, to pastime? What will become of the eternal truths of the Dionysian and Apollonian in such an amalgamation of styles as I have exhibited in the character of the stilo rappresentativo? where music is regarded as the servant, the text as the master, where music is compared with the body, the text with the soul? where at best the highest aim will be the realisation of a paraphrastic tone-painting, just as formerly in the New Attic Dithyramb? where music is completely alienated from its true dignity of being, the Dionysian mirror of the world, so that the only thing left to it is, as a slave of phenomena, to imitate the formal character thereof, and to excite an external pleasure in the play of lines and proportions. On close observation, this fatal influence of the opera on music is seen to coincide absolutely with the universal development of modern music; the optimism lurking in the genesis of the opera and in the essence of culture represented thereby, has, with alarming rapidity, succeeded in divesting music of its Dionyso-cosmic mission and in impressing on it a playfully formal and pleasurable character: a change with which perhaps only the metamorphosis of the Æschylean man into the cheerful Alexandrine man could be compared.

If, however, in the exemplification herewith indicated we have rightly associated the evanescence of the Dionysian spirit with a most striking, but hitherto unexplained transformation and degeneration of the Hellene--what hopes must revive in us when the most trustworthy auspices guarantee the reverse process, the gradual awakening of the Dionysian spirit in our modern world! It is impossible for the divine strength of Herakles to languish for ever in voluptuous bondage to Omphale. Out of the Dionysian root of the German spirit a power has arisen which has nothing in common with the primitive conditions of Socratic culture, and can neither be explained nor excused thereby, but is rather regarded by this culture as something terribly inexplicable and overwhelmingly hostile,--namely, German music as we have to understand it, especially in its vast solar orbit from Bach to Beethoven, from Beethoven to Wagner. What even under the most favourable circumstances can the knowledge-craving Socratism of our days do with this demon rising from unfathomable depths? Neither by means of the zig-zag and arabesque work of operatic melody, nor with the aid of the arithmetical counting board of fugue and contrapuntal dialectics is the formula to be found, in the trebly powerful light[23] of which one could subdue this demon and compel it to speak. What a spectacle, when our æsthetes, with a net of "beauty" peculiar to themselves, now pursue and clutch at the genius of music romping about before them with incomprehensible life, and in so doing display activities which are not to be judged by the standard of eternal beauty any more than by the standard of the sublime. Let us but observe these patrons of music as they are, at close range, when they call out so indefatigably "beauty! beauty!" to discover whether they have the marks of nature's darling children who are fostered and fondled in the lap of the beautiful, or whether they do not rather seek a disguise for their own rudeness, an æsthetical pretext for their own unemotional insipidity: I am thinking here, for instance, of Otto Jahn. But let the liar and the hypocrite beware of our German music: for in the midst of all our culture it is really the only genuine, pure and purifying fire-spirit from which and towards which, as in the teaching of the great Heraclitus of Ephesus, all things move in a double orbit-all that we now call culture, education, civilisation, must appear some day before the unerring judge, Dionysus.

Let us recollect furthermore how Kant and Schopenhauer made it possible for the spirit of German philosophy streaming from the same sources to annihilate the satisfied delight in existence of scientific Socratism by the delimitation of the boundaries thereof; how through this delimitation an infinitely profounder and more serious view of ethical problems and of art was inaugurated, which we may unhesitatingly designate as Dionysian wisdom comprised in concepts. To what then does the mystery of this oneness of German music and philosophy point, if not to a new form of existence, concerning the substance of which we can only inform ourselves presentiently from Hellenic analogies? For to us who stand on the boundary line between two different forms of existence, the Hellenic prototype retains the immeasurable value, that therein all these transitions and struggles are imprinted in a classically instructive form: except that we, as it were, experience analogically in reverse order the chief epochs of the Hellenic genius, and seem now, for instance, to pass backwards from the Alexandrine age to the period of tragedy. At the same time we have the feeling that the birth of a tragic age betokens only a return to itself of the German spirit, a blessed self-rediscovering after excessive and urgent external influences have for a long time compelled it, living as it did in helpless barbaric formlessness, to servitude under their form. It may at last, after returning to the primitive source of its being, venture to stalk along boldly and freely before all nations without hugging the leading-strings of a Romanic civilisation: if only it can learn implicitly of one people--the Greeks, of whom to learn at all is itself a high honour and a rare distinction. And when did we require these highest of all teachers more than at present, when we experience a re-birth of tragedy and are in danger alike of not knowing whence it comes, and of being unable to make clear to ourselves whither it tends.

Footnotes:

22. Essay on Elegiac Poetry.--TR.
23. See Faust, Part 1.1. 965--TR.

20

It may be weighed some day before an impartial judge, in what time and in what men the German spirit has thus far striven most resolutely to learn of the Greeks: and if we confidently assume that this unique praise must be accorded to the noblest intellectual efforts of Goethe, Schiller, and Winkelmann, it will certainly have to be added that since their time, and subsequently to the more immediate influences of these efforts, the endeavour to attain to culture and to the Greeks by this path has in an incomprehensible manner grown feebler and feebler. In order not to despair altogether of the German spirit, must we not infer therefrom that possibly, in some essential matter, even these champions could not penetrate into the core of the Hellenic nature, and were unable to establish a permanent friendly alliance between German and Greek culture? So that perhaps an unconscious perception of this shortcoming might raise also in more serious minds the disheartening doubt as to whether after such predecessors they could advance still farther on this path of culture, or could reach the goal at all. Accordingly, we see the opinions concerning the value of Greek contribution to culture degenerate since that time in the most alarming manner; the expression of compassionate superiority may be heard in the most heterogeneous intellectual and non-intellectual camps, and elsewhere a totally ineffective declamation dallies with "Greek harmony," "Greek beauty," "Greek cheerfulness." And in the very circles whose dignity it might be to draw indefatigably from the Greek channel for the good of German culture, in the circles of the teachers in the higher educational institutions, they have learned best to compromise with the Greeks in good time and on easy terms, to the extent often of a sceptical abandonment of the Hellenic ideal and a total perversion of the true purpose of antiquarian studies. If there be any one at all in these circles who has not completely exhausted himself in the endeavour to be a trustworthy corrector of old texts or a natural-history microscopist of language, he perhaps seeks also to appropriate Grecian antiquity "historically" along with other antiquities, and in any case according to the method and with the supercilious air of our present cultured historiography. When, therefore, the intrinsic efficiency of the higher educational institutions has never perhaps been lower or feebler than at present, when the "journalist," the paper slave of the day, has triumphed over the academic teacher in all matters pertaining to culture, and there only remains to the latter the often previously experienced metamorphosis of now fluttering also, as a cheerful cultured butterfly, in the idiom of the journalist, with the "light elegance" peculiar thereto--with what painful confusion must the cultured persons of a period like the present gaze at the phenomenon (which can perhaps be comprehended analogically only by means of the profoundest principle of the hitherto unintelligible Hellenic genius) of the reawakening of the Dionysian spirit and the re-birth of tragedy? Never has there been another art-period in which so-called culture and true art have been so estranged and opposed, as is so obviously the case at present. We understand why so feeble a culture hates true art; it fears destruction thereby. But must not an entire domain of culture, namely the Socratic-Alexandrine, have exhausted its powers after contriving to culminate in such a daintily-tapering point as our present culture? When it was not permitted to heroes like Goethe and Schiller to break open the enchanted gate which leads into the Hellenic magic mountain, when with their most dauntless striving they did not get beyond the longing gaze which the Goethean Iphigenia cast from barbaric Tauris to her home across the ocean, what could the epigones of such heroes hope for, if the gate should not open to them suddenly of its own accord, in an entirely different position, quite overlooked in all endeavours of culture hitherto--amidst the mystic tones of reawakened tragic music.

Let no one attempt to weaken our faith in an impending re-birth of Hellenic antiquity; for in it alone we find our hope of a renovation and purification of the German spirit through the fire-magic of music. What else do we know of amidst the present desolation and languor of culture, which could awaken any comforting expectation for the future? We look in vain for one single vigorously-branching root, for a speck of fertile and healthy soil: there is dust, sand, torpidness and languishing everywhere! Under such circumstances a cheerless solitary wanderer could choose for himself no better symbol than the Knight with Death and the Devil, as Dürer has sketched him for us, the mail-clad knight, grim and stern of visage, who is able, unperturbed by his gruesome companions, and yet hopelessly, to pursue his terrible path with horse and hound alone. Our Schopenhauer was such a Dürerian knight: he was destitute of all hope, but he sought the truth. There is not his equal.

But how suddenly this gloomily depicted wilderness of our exhausted culture changes when the Dionysian magic touches it! A hurricane seizes everything decrepit, decaying, collapsed, and stunted; wraps it whirlingly into a red cloud of dust; and carries it like a vulture into the air. Confused thereby, our glances seek for what has vanished: for what they see is something risen to the golden light as from a depression, so full and green, so luxuriantly alive, so ardently infinite. Tragedy sits in the midst of this exuberance of life, sorrow and joy, in sublime ecstasy; she listens to a distant doleful song--it tells of the Mothers of Being, whose names are: Wahn, Wille, Wehe[21]--Yes, my friends, believe with me in Dionysian life and in the re-birth of tragedy. The time of the Socratic man is past: crown yourselves with ivy, take in your hands the thyrsus, and do not marvel if tigers and panthers lie down fawning at your feet. Dare now to be tragic men, for ye are to be redeemed! Ye are to accompany the Dionysian festive procession from India to Greece! Equip yourselves for severe conflict, but believe in the wonders of your god!

21

Gliding back from these hortative tones into the mood which befits the contemplative man, I repeat that it can only be learnt from the Greeks what such a sudden and miraculous awakening of tragedy must signify for the essential basis of a people's life. It is the people of the tragic mysteries who fight the battles with the Persians: and again, the people who waged such wars required tragedy as a necessary healing potion. Who would have imagined that there was still such a uniformly powerful effusion of the simplest political sentiments, the most natural domestic instincts and the primitive manly delight in strife in this very people after it had been shaken to its foundations for several generations by the most violent convulsions of the Dionysian demon? If at every considerable spreading of the Dionysian commotion one always perceives that the Dionysian loosing from the shackles of the individual makes itself felt first of all in an increased encroachment on the political instincts, to the extent of indifference, yea even hostility, it is certain, on the other hand, that the state-forming Apollo is also the genius of the principium individuationis, and that the state and domestic sentiment cannot live without an assertion of individual personality. There is only one way from orgasm for a people,--the way to Indian Buddhism, which, in order to be at all endured with its longing for nothingness, requires the rare ecstatic states with their elevation above space, time, and the individual; just as these in turn demand a philosophy which teaches how to overcome the indescribable depression of the intermediate states by means of a fancy. With the same necessity, owing to the unconditional dominance of political impulses, a people drifts into a path of extremest secularisation, the most magnificent, but also the most terrible expression of which is the Roman imperium.

Placed between India and Rome, and constrained to a seductive choice, the Greeks succeeded in devising in classical purity still a third form of life, not indeed for long private use, but just on that account for immortality. For it holds true in all things that those whom the gods love die young, but, on the other hand, it holds equally true that they then live eternally with the gods. One must not demand of what is most noble that it should possess the durable toughness of leather; the staunch durability, which, for instance, was inherent in the national character of the Romans, does not probably belong to the indispensable predicates of perfection. But if we ask by what physic it was possible for the Greeks, in their best period, notwithstanding the extraordinary strength of their Dionysian and political impulses, neither to exhaust themselves by ecstatic brooding, nor by a consuming scramble for empire and worldly honour, but to attain the splendid mixture which we find in a noble, inflaming, and contemplatively disposing wine, we must remember the enormous power of tragedy, exciting, purifying, and disburdening the entire life of a people; the highest value of which we shall divine only when, as in the case of the Greeks, it appears to us as the essence of all the prophylactic healing forces, as the mediator arbitrating between the strongest and most inherently fateful characteristics of a people.

Tragedy absorbs the highest musical orgasm into itself, so that it absolutely brings music to perfection among the Greeks, as among ourselves; but it then places alongside thereof tragic myth and the tragic hero, who, like a mighty Titan, takes the entire Dionysian world on his shoulders and disburdens us thereof; while, on the other hand, it is able by means of this same tragic myth, in the person of the tragic hero, to deliver us from the intense longing for this existence, and reminds us with warning hand of another existence and a higher joy, for which the struggling hero prepares himself presentiently by his destruction, not by his victories. Tragedy sets a sublime symbol, namely the myth between the universal authority of its music and the receptive Dionysian hearer, and produces in him the illusion that music is only the most effective means for the animation of the plastic world of myth. Relying upon this noble illusion, she can now move her limbs for the dithyrambic dance, and abandon herself unhesitatingly to an orgiastic feeling of freedom, in which she could not venture to indulge as music itself, without this illusion. The myth protects us from the music, while, on the other hand, it alone gives the highest freedom thereto. By way of return for this service, music imparts to tragic myth such an impressive and convincing metaphysical significance as could never be attained by word and image, without this unique aid; and the tragic spectator in particular experiences thereby the sure presentiment of supreme joy to which the path through destruction and negation leads; so that he thinks he hears, as it were, the innermost abyss of things speaking audibly to him.

If in these last propositions I have succeeded in giving perhaps only a preliminary expression, intelligible to few at first, to this difficult representation, I must not here desist from stimulating my friends to a further attempt, or cease from beseeching them to prepare themselves, by a detached example of our common experience, for the perception of the universal proposition. In this example I must not appeal to those who make use of the pictures of the scenic processes, the words and the emotions of the performers, in order to approximate thereby to musical perception; for none of these speak music as their mother-tongue, and, in spite of the aids in question, do not get farther than the precincts of musical perception, without ever being allowed to touch its innermost shrines; some of them, like Gervinus, do not even reach the precincts by this path. I have only to address myself to those who, being immediately allied to music, have it as it were for their mother's lap, and are connected with things almost exclusively by unconscious musical relations. I ask the question of these genuine musicians: whether they can imagine a man capable of hearing the third act of Tristan und Isolde without any aid of word or scenery, purely as a vast symphonic period, without expiring by a spasmodic distention of all the wings of the soul? A man who has thus, so to speak, put his ear to the heart-chamber of the cosmic will, who feels the furious desire for existence issuing therefrom as a thundering stream or most gently dispersed brook, into all the veins of the world, would he not collapse all at once? Could he endure, in the wretched fragile tenement of the human individual, to hear the re-echo of countless cries of joy and sorrow from the "vast void of cosmic night," without flying irresistibly towards his primitive home at the sound of this pastoral dance-song of metaphysics? But if, nevertheless, such a work can be heard as a whole, without a renunciation of individual existence, if such a creation could be created without demolishing its creator--where are we to get the solution of this contradiction?

Here there interpose between our highest musical excitement and the music in question the tragic myth and the tragic hero--in reality only as symbols of the most universal facts, of which music alone can speak directly. If, however, we felt as purely Dionysian beings, myth as a symbol would stand by us absolutely ineffective and unnoticed, and would never for a moment prevent us from giving ear to the re-echo of the universalia ante rem. Here, however, the Apollonian power, with a view to the restoration of the well-nigh shattered individual, bursts forth with the healing balm of a blissful illusion: all of a sudden we imagine we see only Tristan, motionless, with hushed voice saying to himself: "the old tune, why does it wake me?" And what formerly interested us like a hollow sigh from the heart of being, seems now only to tell us how "waste and void is the sea." And when, breathless, we thought to expire by a convulsive distention of all our feelings, and only a slender tie bound us to our present existence, we now hear and see only the hero wounded to death and still not dying, with his despairing cry: "Longing! Longing! In dying still longing! for longing not dying!" And if formerly, after such a surplus and superabundance of consuming agonies, the jubilation of the born rent our hearts almost like the very acme of agony, the rejoicing Kurwenal now stands between us and the "jubilation as such," with face turned toward the ship which carries Isolde. However powerfully fellow-suffering encroaches upon us, it nevertheless delivers us in a manner from the primordial suffering of the world, just as the symbol-image of the myth delivers us from the immediate perception of the highest cosmic idea, just as the thought and word deliver us from the unchecked effusion of the unconscious will. The glorious Apollonian illusion makes it appear as if the very realm of tones presented itself to us as a plastic cosmos, as if even the fate of Tristan and Isolde had been merely formed and moulded therein as out of some most delicate and impressible material.

Thus does the Apollonian wrest us from Dionysian universality and fill us with rapture for individuals; to these it rivets our sympathetic emotion, through these it satisfies the sense of beauty which longs for great and sublime forms; it brings before us biographical portraits, and incites us to a thoughtful apprehension of the essence of life contained therein. With the immense potency of the image, the concept, the ethical teaching and the sympathetic emotion--the Apollonian influence uplifts man from his orgiastic self-annihilation, and beguiles him concerning the universality of the Dionysian process into the belief that he is seeing a detached picture of the world, for instance, Tristan and Isolde, and that, through music, he will be enabled to see it still more clearly and intrinsically. What can the healing magic of Apollo not accomplish when it can even excite in us the illusion that the Dionysian is actually in the service of the Apollonian, the effects of which it is capable of enhancing; yea, that music is essentially the representative art for an Apollonian substance?

With the pre-established harmony which obtains between perfect drama and its music, the drama attains the highest degree of conspicuousness, such as is usually unattainable in mere spoken drama. As all the animated figures of the scene in the independently evolved lines of melody simplify themselves before us to the distinctness of the catenary curve, the coexistence of these lines is also audible in the harmonic change which sympathises in a most delicate manner with the evolved process: through which change the relations of things become immediately perceptible to us in a sensible and not at all abstract manner, as we likewise perceive thereby that it is only in these relations that the essence of a character and of a line of melody manifests itself clearly. And while music thus compels us to see more extensively and more intrinsically than usual, and makes us spread out the curtain of the scene before ourselves like some delicate texture, the world of the stage is as infinitely expanded for our spiritualised, introspective eye as it is illumined outwardly from within. How can the word-poet furnish anything analogous, who strives to attain this internal expansion and illumination of the visible stage-world by a much more imperfect mechanism and an indirect path, proceeding as he does from word and concept? Albeit musical tragedy likewise avails itself of the word, it is at the same time able to place alongside thereof its basis and source, and can make the unfolding of the word, from within outwards, obvious to us.

Of the process just set forth, however, it could still be said as decidedly that it is only a glorious appearance, namely the afore-mentioned Apollonian illusion, through the influence of which we are to be delivered from the Dionysian obtrusion and excess. In point of fact, the relation of music to drama is precisely the reverse; music is the adequate idea of the world, drama is but the reflex of this idea, a detached umbrage thereof. The identity between the line of melody and the lining form, between the harmony and the character-relations of this form, is true in a sense antithetical to what one would suppose on the contemplation of musical tragedy. We may agitate and enliven the form in the most conspicuous manner, and enlighten it from within, but it still continues merely phenomenon, from which there is no bridge to lead us into the true reality, into the heart of the world. Music, however, speaks out of this heart; and though countless phenomena of the kind might be passing manifestations of this music, they could never exhaust its essence, but would always be merely its externalised copies. Of course, as regards the intricate relation of music and drama, nothing can be explained, while all may be confused by the popular and thoroughly false antithesis of soul and body; but the unphilosophical crudeness of this antithesis seems to have become--who knows for what reasons--a readily accepted Article of Faith with our æstheticians, while they have learned nothing concerning an antithesis of phenomenon and thing-in-itself, or perhaps, for reasons equally unknown, have not cared to learn anything thereof.

Should it have been established by our analysis that the Apollonian element in tragedy has by means of its illusion gained a complete victory over the Dionysian primordial element of music, and has made music itself subservient to its end, namely, the highest and clearest elucidation of the drama, it would certainly be necessary to add the very important restriction: that at the most essential point this

Apollonian illusion is dissolved and annihilated. The drama, which, by the aid of music, spreads out before us with such inwardly illumined distinctness in all its movements and figures, that we imagine we see the texture unfolding on the loom as the shuttle flies to and fro,--attains as a whole an effect which transcends all Apollonian artistic effects. In the collective effect of tragedy, the Dionysian gets the upper hand once more; tragedy ends with a sound which could never emanate from the realm of Apollonian art. And the Apollonian illusion is thereby found to be what it is,--the assiduous veiling during the performance of tragedy of the intrinsically Dionysian effect: which, however, is so powerful, that it finally forces the Apollonian drama itself into a sphere where it begins to talk with Dionysian wisdom, and even denies itself and its Apollonian conspicuousness. Thus then the intricate relation of the Apollonian and the Dionysian in tragedy must really be symbolised by a fraternal union of the two deities: Dionysus speaks the language of Apollo; Apollo, however, finally speaks the language of Dionysus; and so the highest goal of tragedy and of art in general is attained.

22

Let the attentive friend picture to himself purely and simply, according to his experiences, the effect of a true musical tragedy. I think I have so portrayed the phenomenon of this effect in both its phases that he will now be able to interpret his own experiences. For he will recollect that with regard to the myth which passed before him he felt himself exalted to a kind of omniscience, as if his visual faculty were no longer merely a surface faculty, but capable of penetrating into the interior, and as if he now saw before him, with the aid of music, the ebullitions of the will, the conflict of motives, and the swelling stream of the passions, almost sensibly visible, like a plenitude of actively moving lines and figures, and could thereby dip into the most tender secrets of unconscious emotions. While he thus becomes conscious of the highest exaltation of his instincts for conspicuousness and transfiguration, he nevertheless feels with equal definitiveness that this long series of Apollonian artistic effects still does not generate the blissful continuance in will-less contemplation which the plasticist and the epic poet, that is to say, the strictly Apollonian artists, produce in him by their artistic productions: to wit, the justification of the world of the individuatio attained in this contemplation,--which is the object and essence of Apollonian art. He beholds the transfigured world of the stage and nevertheless denies it. He sees before him the tragic hero in epic clearness and beauty, and nevertheless delights in his annihilation. He comprehends the incidents of the scene in all their details, and yet loves to flee into the incomprehensible. He feels the actions of the hero to be justified, and is nevertheless still more elated when these actions annihilate their originator. He shudders at the sufferings which will befall the hero, and yet anticipates therein a higher and much more overpowering joy. He sees more extensively and profoundly than ever, and yet wishes to be blind. Whence must we derive this curious internal dissension, this collapse of the Apollonian apex, if not from the Dionysian spell, which, though apparently stimulating the Apollonian emotions to their highest pitch, can nevertheless force this superabundance of Apollonian power into its service? Tragic myth is to be understood only as a symbolisation of Dionysian wisdom by means of the expedients of Apollonian art: the mythus conducts the world of phenomena to its boundaries, where it denies itself, and seeks to flee back again into the bosom of the true and only reality; where it then, like Isolde, seems to strike up its metaphysical swan-song:--

In des Wonnemeeres
wogendem Schwall,
in der Duft-Wellen
tönendem Schall,
in des Weltathems
wehendem All--
ertrinken--versinken
unbewusst--höchste Lust![24]

We thus realise to ourselves in the experiences of the truly æsthetic hearer the tragic artist himself when he proceeds like a luxuriously fertile divinity of individuation to create his figures (in which sense his work can hardly be understood as an "imitation of nature")--and when, on the other hand, his vast Dionysian impulse then absorbs the entire world of phenomena, in order to anticipate beyond it, and through its annihilation, the highest artistic primal joy, in the bosom of the Primordial Unity. Of course, our æsthetes have nothing to say about this return in fraternal union of the two art-deities to the original home, nor of either the Apollonian or Dionysian excitement of the hearer, while they are indefatigable in characterising the struggle of the hero with fate, the triumph of the moral order of the world, or the disburdenment of the emotions through tragedy, as the properly Tragic: an indefatigableness which makes me think that they are perhaps not æsthetically excitable men at all, but only to be regarded as moral beings when hearing tragedy. Never since Aristotle has an explanation of the tragic effect been proposed, by which an æsthetic activity of the hearer could be inferred from artistic circumstances. At one time fear and pity are supposed to be forced to an alleviating discharge through the serious procedure, at another time we are expected to feel elevated and inspired at the triumph of good and noble principles, at the sacrifice of the hero in the interest of a moral conception of things; and however certainly I believe that for countless men precisely this, and only this, is the effect of tragedy, it as obviously follows therefrom that all these, together with their interpreting æsthetes, have had no experience of tragedy as the highest art. The pathological discharge, the catharsis of Aristotle, which philologists are at a loss whether to include under medicinal or moral phenomena, recalls a remarkable anticipation of Goethe. "Without a lively pathological interest," he says, "I too have never yet succeeded in elaborating a tragic situation of any kind, and hence I have rather avoided than sought it. Can it perhaps have been still another of the merits of the ancients that the deepest pathos was with them merely æsthetic play, whereas with us the truth of nature must co-operate in order to produce such a work?" We can now answer in the affirmative this latter profound question after our glorious experiences, in which we have found to our astonishment in the case of musical tragedy itself, that the deepest pathos can in reality be merely æsthetic play: and therefore we are justified in believing that now for the first time the proto-phenomenon of the tragic can be portrayed with some degree of success. He who now will still persist in talking only of those vicarious effects proceeding from ultra-æsthetic spheres, and does not feel himself raised above the pathologically-moral process, may be left to despair of his æsthetic nature: for which we recommend to him, by way of innocent equivalent, the interpretation of Shakespeare after the fashion of Gervinus, and the diligent search for poetic justice.

Thus with the re-birth of tragedy the æsthetic hearer is also born anew, in whose place in the theatre a curious quid pro quo was wont to sit with half-moral and half-learned pretensions,--the "critic." In his sphere hitherto everything has been artificial and merely glossed over with a semblance of life. The performing artist was in fact at a loss what to do with such a critically comporting hearer, and hence he, as well as the dramatist or operatic composer who inspired him, searched anxiously for the last remains of life in a being so pretentiously barren and incapable of enjoyment. Such "critics," however, have hitherto constituted the public; the student, the school-boy, yea, even the most harmless womanly creature, were already unwittingly prepared by education and by journals for a similar perception of works of art. The nobler natures among the artists counted upon exciting the moral-religious forces in such a public, and the appeal to a moral order of the world operated vicariously, when in reality some powerful artistic spell should have enraptured the true hearer. Or again, some imposing or at all events exciting tendency of the contemporary political and social world was presented by the dramatist with such vividness that the hearer could forget his critical exhaustion and abandon himself to similar emotions, as, in patriotic or warlike moments, before the tribune of parliament, or at the condemnation of crime and vice:--an estrangement of the true aims of art which could not but lead directly now and then to a cult of tendency. But here there took place what has always taken place in the case of factitious arts, an extraordinary rapid depravation of these tendencies, so that for instance the tendency to employ the theatre as a means for the moral education of the people, which in Schiller's time was taken seriously, is already reckoned among the incredible antiquities of a surmounted culture. While the critic got the upper hand in the theatre and concert-hall, the journalist in the school, and the press in society, art degenerated into a topic of conversation of the most trivial kind, and æsthetic criticism was used as the cement of a vain, distracted, selfish and moreover piteously unoriginal sociality, the significance of which is suggested by the Schopenhauerian parable of the porcupines, so that there has never been so much gossip about art and so little esteem for it. But is it still possible to have intercourse with a man capable of conversing on Beethoven or Shakespeare? Let each answer this question according to his sentiments: he will at any rate show by his answer his conception of "culture," provided he tries at least to answer the question, and has not already grown mute with astonishment.

On the other hand, many a one more nobly and delicately endowed by nature, though he may have gradually become a critical barbarian in the manner described, could tell of the unexpected as well as totally unintelligible effect which a successful performance of Lohengrin, for example, exerted on him: except that perhaps every warning and interpreting hand was lacking to guide him; so that the incomprehensibly heterogeneous and altogether incomparable sensation which then affected him also remained isolated and became extinct, like a mysterious star after a brief brilliancy. He then divined what the æsthetic hearer is.

Footnote:

24.

In the sea of pleasure's
Billowing roll,
In the ether-waves

Knelling and toll,
In the world-breath's
Wavering whole--
To drown in, go down in--
Lost in swoon--greatest boon!

23

He who wishes to test himself rigorously as to how he is related to the true æsthetic hearer, or whether he belongs rather to the community of the Socrato-critical man, has only to enquire sincerely concerning the sentiment with which he accepts the wonder represented on the stage: whether he feels his historical sense, which insists on strict psychological causality, insulted by it, whether with benevolent concession he as it were admits the wonder as a phenomenon intelligible to childhood, but relinquished by him, or whether he experiences anything else thereby. For he will thus be enabled to determine how far he is on the whole capable of understanding myth, that is to say, the concentrated picture of the world, which, as abbreviature of phenomena, cannot dispense with wonder. It is probable, however, that nearly every one, upon close examination, feels so disintegrated by the critico-historical spirit of our culture, that he can only perhaps make the former existence of myth credible to himself by learned means through intermediary abstractions. Without myth, however, every culture loses its healthy, creative natural power: it is only a horizon encompassed with myths which rounds off to unity a social movement. It is only by myth that all the powers of the imagination and of the Apollonian dream are freed from their random rovings. The mythical figures have to be the invisibly omnipresent genii, under the care of which the young soul grows to maturity, by the signs of which the man gives a meaning to his life and struggles: and the state itself knows no more powerful unwritten law than the mythical foundation which vouches for its connection with religion and its growth from mythical ideas.

Let us now place alongside thereof the abstract man proceeding independently of myth, the abstract education, the abstract usage, the abstract right, the abstract state: let us picture to ourselves the lawless roving of the artistic imagination, not bridled by any native myth: let us imagine a culture which has no fixed and sacred primitive seat, but is doomed to exhaust all its possibilities, and has to nourish itself wretchedly from the other cultures--such is the Present, as the result of Socratism, which is bent on the destruction of myth. And now the myth-less man remains eternally hungering among all the bygones, and digs and grubs for roots, though he have to dig for them even among the remotest antiquities. The stupendous historical exigency of the unsatisfied modern culture, the gathering around one of countless other cultures, the consuming desire for knowledge--what does all this point to, if not to the loss of myth, the loss of the mythical home, the mythical source? Let us ask ourselves whether the feverish and so uncanny stirring of this culture is aught but the eager seizing and snatching at food of the hungerer--and who would care to contribute anything more to a culture which cannot be appeased by all it devours, and in contact with which the most vigorous and wholesome nourishment is wont to change into "history and criticism"?

We should also have to regard our German character with despair and sorrow, if it had already become inextricably entangled in, or even identical with this culture, in a similar manner as we can observe it to our horror to be the case in civilised France; and that which for a long time was the great advantage of France and the cause of her vast preponderance, to wit, this very identity of people and culture, might compel us at the sight thereof to congratulate ourselves that this culture of ours, which is so questionable, has hitherto had nothing in common with the noble kernel of the character of our people. All our hopes, on the contrary, stretch out longingly towards the perception that beneath this restlessly palpitating civilised life and educational convulsion there is concealed a glorious, intrinsically healthy, primeval power, which, to be sure, stirs vigorously only at intervals in stupendous moments, and then dreams on again in view of a future awakening. It is from this abyss that the German Reformation came forth: in the choral-hymn of which the future melody of German music first resounded. So deep, courageous, and soul-breathing, so exuberantly good and tender did this chorale of Luther sound,--as the first Dionysian-luring call which breaks forth from dense thickets at the approach of spring. To it responded with emulative echo the solemnly wanton procession of Dionysian revellers, to whom we are indebted for German music--and to whom we shall be indebted for the re-birth of German myth.

I know that I must now lead the sympathising and attentive friend to an elevated position of lonesome contemplation, where he will have but few companions, and I call out encouragingly to him that we must hold fast to our shining guides, the Greeks. For the rectification of our æsthetic knowledge we previously borrowed from them the two divine figures, each of which sways a separate realm of art, and concerning whose mutual contact and exaltation we have acquired a notion through Greek tragedy. Through a remarkable disruption of both these primitive artistic impulses, the ruin of Greek tragedy seemed to be necessarily brought about: with which process a degeneration and a transmutation of the Greek national character was strictly in keeping, summoning us to earnest reflection as to how closely and necessarily art and the people, myth and custom, tragedy and the state, have coalesced in their bases. The ruin of tragedy was at the same time the ruin of myth. Until then the Greeks had been involuntarily compelled immediately to associate all experiences with their myths, indeed they had to comprehend them only through this association: whereby even the most immediate present necessarily appeared to them sub specie æterni and in a certain sense as timeless. Into this current of the timeless, however, the state as well as art plunged in order to find repose from the burden and eagerness of the moment. And a people--for the rest, also a man--is worth just as much only as its ability to impress on its experiences the seal of eternity: for it is thus, as it were, desecularised, and reveals its unconscious inner conviction of the relativity of time and of the true, that is, the metaphysical significance of life. The contrary happens when a people begins to comprehend itself historically and to demolish the mythical bulwarks around it: with which there is usually connected a marked secularisation, a breach with the unconscious metaphysics of its earlier existence, in all ethical consequences. Greek art and especially Greek tragedy delayed above all the annihilation of myth: it was necessary to annihilate these also to be able to live detached from the native soil, unbridled in the wilderness of thought, custom, and action. Even in such circumstances this metaphysical impulse still endeavours to create for itself a form of apotheosis (weakened, no doubt) in the Socratism of science urging to life: but on its lower stage this same impulse led only to a feverish search, which gradually merged into a pandemonium of myths and superstitions accumulated from all quarters: in the midst of which, nevertheless, the Hellene sat with a yearning heart till he contrived, as Græculus, to mask his fever with Greek cheerfulness and Greek levity, or to narcotise himself completely with some gloomy Oriental superstition.

We have approached this condition in the most striking manner since the reawakening of the Alexandro--Roman antiquity in the fifteenth century, after a long, not easily describable, interlude. On the heights there is the same exuberant love of knowledge, the same insatiate happiness of the discoverer, the same stupendous secularisation, and, together with these, a homeless roving about, an eager intrusion at foreign tables, a frivolous deification of the present or a dull senseless estrangement, all sub speci sæculi, of the present time: which same symptoms lead one to infer the same defect at the heart of this culture, the annihilation of myth. It seems hardly possible to transplant a foreign myth with permanent success, without dreadfully injuring the tree through this transplantation: which is perhaps occasionally strong enough and sound enough to eliminate the foreign element after a terrible struggle; but must ordinarily consume itself in a languishing and stunted condition or in sickly luxuriance. Our opinion of the pure and vigorous kernel of the German being is such that we venture to expect of it, and only of it, this elimination of forcibly ingrafted foreign elements, and we deem it possible that the German spirit will reflect anew on itself. Perhaps many a one will be of opinion that this spirit must begin its struggle with the elimination of the Romanic element: for which it might recognise an external preparation and encouragement in the victorious bravery and bloody glory of the late war, but must seek the inner constraint in the emulative zeal to be for ever worthy of the sublime protagonists on this path, of Luther as well as our great artists and poets. But let him never think he can fight such battles without his household gods, without his mythical home, without a "restoration" of all German things I And if the German should look timidly around for a guide to lead him back to his long-lost home, the ways and paths of which he knows no longer--let him but listen to the delightfully luring call of the Dionysian bird, which hovers above him, and would fain point out to him the way thither.

24

Among the peculiar artistic effects of musical tragedy we had to emphasise an Apollonian illusion, through which we are to be saved from immediate oneness with the Dionysian music, while our musical excitement is able to discharge itself on an Apollonian domain and in an interposed visible middle world. It thereby seemed to us that precisely through this discharge the middle world of theatrical procedure, the drama generally, became visible and intelligible from within in a degree unattainable in the other forms of Apollonian art: so that here, where this art was as it were winged and borne aloft by the spirit of music, we had to recognise the highest exaltation of its powers, and consequently in the fraternal union of Apollo and Dionysus the climax of the Apollonian as well as of the Dionysian artistic aims.

Of course, the Apollonian light-picture did not, precisely with this inner illumination through music, attain the peculiar effect of the weaker grades of Apollonian art. What the epos and the animated stone can do--constrain the contemplating eye to calm delight in the world of the individuatio--could not be realised here, notwithstanding the greater animation and distinctness. We contemplated the drama and penetrated with piercing glance into its inner agitated world of motives--and yet it seemed as if only a symbolic picture passed before us, the profoundest significance of which we almost believed we had divined, and which we desired to put aside like a curtain in order to behold the original behind it. The greatest distinctness of the picture did not suffice us: for it seemed to reveal as well as veil something; and while it seemed, with its symbolic revelation, to invite the rending of the veil for the disclosure of the mysterious background, this illumined all-conspicuousness itself enthralled the eye and prevented it from penetrating more deeply He who has not experienced this,--to have to view, and at the same time to have a longing beyond the viewing,--will hardly be able to conceive how clearly and definitely these two processes coexist in the contemplation of tragic myth and are felt to be conjoined; while the truly æsthetic spectators will confirm my assertion that among the peculiar effects of tragedy this conjunction is the most noteworthy. Now let this phenomenon of the æsthetic spectator be transferred to an analogous process in the tragic artist, and the genesis of tragic myth will have been understood. It shares with the Apollonian sphere of art the full delight in appearance and contemplation, and at the same time it denies this delight and finds a still higher satisfaction in the annihilation of the visible world of appearance. The substance of tragic myth is first of all an epic event involving the glorification of the fighting hero: but whence originates the essentially enigmatical trait, that the suffering in the fate of the hero, the most painful victories, the most agonising contrasts of motives, in short, the exemplification of the wisdom of Silenus, or, æsthetically expressed, the Ugly and Discordant, is always represented anew in such countless forms with such predilection, and precisely in the most youthful and exuberant age of a people, unless there is really a higher delight experienced in all this?

For the fact that things actually take such a tragic course would least of all explain the origin of a form of art; provided that art is not merely an imitation of the reality of nature, but in truth a metaphysical supplement to the reality of nature, placed alongside thereof for its conquest. Tragic myth, in so far as it really belongs to art, also fully participates in this transfiguring metaphysical purpose of art in general: What does it transfigure, however, when it presents the phenomenal world in the guise of the suffering hero? Least of all the "reality" of this phenomenal world, for it says to us: "Look at this! Look carefully! It is your life! It is the hour-hand of your clock of existence!"

And myth has displayed this life, in order thereby to transfigure it to us? If not, how shall we account for the æsthetic pleasure with which we make even these representations pass before us? I am inquiring concerning the æsthetic pleasure, and am well aware that many of these representations may moreover occasionally create even a moral delectation, say under the form of pity or of a moral triumph. But he who would derive the effect of the tragic exclusively from these moral sources, as was usually the case far too long in æsthetics, let him not think that he has done anything for Art thereby; for Art must above all insist on purity in her domain. For the explanation of tragic myth the very first requirement is that the pleasure which characterises it must be sought in the purely æsthetic sphere, without encroaching on the domain of pity, fear, or the morally-sublime. How can the ugly and the discordant, the substance of tragic myth, excite an æsthetic pleasure?

Here it is necessary to raise ourselves with a daring bound into a metaphysics of Art. I repeat, therefore, my former proposition, that it is only as an æsthetic phenomenon that existence and the world, appear justified: and in this sense it is precisely the function of tragic myth to convince us that even the Ugly and Discordant is an artistic game which the will, in the eternal fulness of its joy, plays with itself. But this not easily comprehensible proto-phenomenon of Dionysian Art becomes, in a direct way, singularly intelligible, and is immediately apprehended in the wonderful significance of musical dissonance: just as in general it is music alone, placed in contrast to the world, which can give us an idea as to what is meant by the justification of the world as an æsthetic phenomenon. The joy that the tragic myth excites has the same origin as the joyful sensation of dissonance in music. The Dionysian, with its primitive joy expèrienced in pain itself, is the common source of music and tragic myth.

Is it not possible that by calling to our aid the musical relation of dissonance, the difficult problem of tragic effect may have meanwhile been materially facilitated? For we now understand what it means to wish to view tragedy and at the same time to have a longing beyond the viewing: a frame of mind, which, as regards the artistically employed dissonance, we should simply have to characterise by saying that we desire to hear and at the same time have a longing beyond the hearing. That striving for the infinite, the pinion-flapping of longing, accompanying the highest delight in the clearly-perceived reality, remind one that in both states we have to recognise a Dionysian phenomenon, which again and again reveals to us anew the playful up-building and demolishing of the world of individuals as the efflux of a primitive delight, in like manner as when Heraclitus the Obscure compares the world-building power to a playing child which places stones here and there and builds sandhills only to overthrow them again.

Hence, in order to form a true estimate of the Dionysian capacity of a people, it would seem that we must think not only of their music, but just as much of their tragic myth, the second witness of this capacity. Considering this most intimate relationship between music and myth, we may now in like manner suppose that a degeneration and depravation of the one involves a deterioration of the other: if it be true at all that the weakening of the myth is generally expressive of a debilitation of the Dionysian capacity. Concerning both, however, a glance at the development of the German genius should not leave us in any doubt; in the opera just as in the abstract character of our myth-less existence, in an art sunk to pastime just as in a life guided by concepts, the inartistic as well as life-consuming nature of Socratic optimism had revealed itself to us. Yet there have been indications to console us that nevertheless in some inaccessible abyss the German spirit still rests and dreams, undestroyed, in glorious health, profundity, and Dionysian strength, like a knight sunk in slumber: from which abyss the Dionysian song rises to us to let us know that this German knight even still dreams his primitive Dionysian myth in blissfully earnest visions. Let no one believe that the German spirit has for ever lost its mythical home when it still understands so obviously the voices of the birds which tell of that home. Some day it will find itself awake in all the morning freshness of a deep sleep: then it will slay the dragons, destroy the malignant dwarfs, and waken Brünnhilde--and Wotan's spear itself will be unable to obstruct its course!

My friends, ye who believe in Dionysian music, ye know also what tragedy means to us. There we have tragic myth, born anew from music,--and in this latest birth ye can hope for everything and forget what is most afflicting. What is most afflicting to all of us, however, is--the prolonged degradation in which the German genius has lived estranged from house and home in the service of malignant dwarfs. Ye understand my allusion--as ye will also, in conclusion, understand my hopes.

25

Music and tragic myth are equally the expression of the Dionysian capacity of a people, and are inseparable from each other. Both originate in an ultra Apollonian sphere of art; both transfigure a region in the delightful accords of which all dissonance, just like the terrible picture of the world, dies charmingly away; both play with the sting of displeasure, trusting to their most potent magic; both justify thereby the existence even of the "worst world." Here the Dionysian, as compared with the Apollonian, exhibits itself as the eternal and original artistic force, which in general calls into existence the entire world of phenomena: in the midst of which a new transfiguring appearance becomes necessary, in order to keep alive the animated world of individuation. If we could conceive an incarnation of dissonance--and what is man but that?--then, to be able to live this dissonance would require a glorious illusion which would spread a veil of beauty over its peculiar nature. This is the true function of Apollo as deity of art: in whose name we comprise all the countless manifestations of the fair realm of illusion, which each moment render life in general worth living and make one impatient for the experience of the next moment.

At the same time, just as much of this basis of all existence--the Dionysian substratum of the world--is allowed to enter into the consciousness of human beings, as can be surmounted again by the Apollonian transfiguring power, so that these two art-impulses are constrained to develop their powers in strictly mutual proportion, according to the law of eternal justice. When the Dionysian powers rise with such vehemence as we experience at present, there can be no doubt that, veiled in a cloud, Apollo has already descended to us; whose grandest beautifying influences a coming generation will perhaps behold.

That this effect is necessary, however, each one would most surely perceive by intuition, if once he found himself carried back--even in a dream--into an Old-Hellenic existence. In walking under high Ionic colonnades, looking upwards to a horizon defined by clear and noble lines, with reflections of his transfigured form by his side in shining marble, and around him solemnly marching or quietly moving men, with harmoniously sounding voices and rhythmical pantomime, would he not in the presence of this perpetual influx of beauty have to raise his hand to Apollo and exclaim: "Blessed race of Hellenes! How great Dionysus must be among you, when the Delian god deems such charms necessary to cure you of your dithyrambic madness!"--To one in this frame of mind, however, an aged Athenian, looking up to him with the sublime eye of Æschylus, might answer: "Say also this, thou curious stranger: what sufferings this people must have undergone, in order to be able to become thus beautiful! But now follow me to a tragic play, and sacrifice with me in the temple of both the deities!"

APPENDIX

[Late in the year 1888, not long before he was overcome by his sudden attack of insanity, Nietzsche wrote down a few notes concerning his early work, the Birth of Tragedy. These were printed in his sister's biography (Das Leben Friedrich Nietzsches, vol. ii. pt. i. pp. 102 ff.), and are here translated as likely to be of interest to readers of this remarkable work. They also appear in the Ecce Homo.--TRANSLATOR'S NOTE.]

"To be just to the Birth of Tragedy(1872), one will have to forget some few things. It has wrought effects, it even fascinated through that wherein it was amiss--through its application to Wagnerism, just as if this Wagnerism were symptomatic of a rise and going up. And just on that account was the book an event in Wagner's life: from thence and only from thence were great hopes linked to the name of Wagner. Even to-day people remind me, sometimes right in the midst of a talk on Parsifal, that I and none other have it on my conscience that such a high opinion of the cultural value of this movement came to the top. More than once have I found the book referred to as 'the Re-birth of Tragedy out of the Spirit of Music': one only had an ear for a new formula of Wagner's art, aim, task,--and failed to hear withal what was at bottom valuable therein. 'Hellenism and Pessimism' had been a more unequivocal title: namely, as a first lesson on the way in which the Greeks got the better of pessimism,--on the means whereby they overcame it. Tragedy simply proves that the Greeks were no pessimists: Schopenhauer was mistaken here as he was mistaken in all other things. Considered with some neutrality, the Birth of Tragedy appears very unseasonable: one would not even dream that it was begun amid the thunders of the battle of Wörth. I thought these problems through and through before the walls of Metz in cold September nights, in the midst of the work of nursing the sick; one might even believe the book to be fifty years older. It is politically indifferent--un-German one will say to-day,--it smells shockingly Hegelian, in but a few formulæ does it scent of Schopenhauer's funereal perfume. An 'idea'--the antithesis of 'Dionysian versus Apollonian'--translated into metaphysics; history itself as the evolution of this 'idea'; the antithesis dissolved into oneness in Tragedy; through this optics things that had never yet looked into one another's face, confronted of a sudden, and illumined and comprehended through one another: for instance, Opera and Revolution. The two decisive innovations of the book are, on the one hand, the comprehension of the Dionysian phenomenon among the Greeks (it gives the first psychology thereof, it sees therein the One root of all Grecian art); on the other, the comprehension of Socratism: Socrates diagnosed for the first time as the tool of Grecian dissolution, as a typical decadent. 'Rationality' against instinct! 'Rationality' at any price as a dangerous, as a life-undermining force! Throughout the whole book a deep hostile silence on Christianity: it is neither Apollonian nor Dionysian; it negatives all æsthetic values (the only values recognised by the Birth of Tragedy), it is in the widest sense nihilistic, whereas in the Dionysian symbol the utmost limit of affirmation is reached. Once or twice the Christian priests are alluded to as a 'malignant kind of dwarfs,' as 'subterraneans.'"

2

"This beginning is singular beyond measure. I had for my own inmost experience discovered the only symbol and counterpart of history,--I had just thereby been the first to grasp the wonderful phenomenon of the Dionysian. And again, through my diagnosing Socrates as a decadent, I had given a wholly unequivocal proof of how little risk the trustworthiness of my psychological grasp would run of being weakened by some moralistic idiosyncrasy--to view morality itself as a symptom of decadence is an innovation, a novelty of the first rank in the history of knowledge. How far I had leaped in either case beyond the smug shallow-pate-gossip of optimism contra pessimism! I was the first to see the intrinsic antithesis: here, the degenerating instinct which, with subterranean vindictiveness, turns against life (Christianity, the philosophy of Schopenhauer, in a certain sense already the philosophy of Plato, all idealistic systems as typical forms), and there, a formula of highest affirmation, born of fullness and overfullness, a yea-saying without reserve to suffering's self, to guilt's self, to all that is questionable and strange in existence itself. This final, cheerfullest, exuberantly mad-and-merriest Yea to life is not only the highest insight, it is also the deepest, it is that which is most rigorously confirmed and upheld by truth and science. Naught that is, is to be deducted, naught is dispensable; the phases of existence rejected by the Christians and other nihilists are even of an infinitely higher order in the hierarchy of values than that which the instinct of decadence sanctions, yea durst sanction. To comprehend this courage is needed, and, as a condition thereof, a surplus of strength: for precisely in degree as courage dares to thrust forward, precisely according to the measure of strength, does one approach truth. Perception, the yea-saying to reality, is as much a necessity to the strong as to the weak, under the inspiration of weakness, cowardly shrinking, and flight from reality--the 'ideal.' ... They are not free to perceive: the decadents have need of the lie,--it is one of their conditions of self-preservation. Whoso not only comprehends the word Dionysian, but also grasps his self in this word, requires no refutation of Plato or of Christianity or of Schopenhauer--he smells the putrefaction."

3

"To what extent I had just thereby found the concept 'tragic,' the definitive perception of the psychology of tragedy, I have but lately stated in the Twilight of the Idols, page 139 (1st edit.): 'The affirmation of life, even in its most unfamiliar and severe problems, the will to life, enjoying its own inexhaustibility in the sacrifice of its highest types,--that is what I called Dionysian, that is what I divined as the bridge to a psychology of the tragic poet. Not in order to get rid of terror and pity, not to purify from a dangerous passion by its vehement discharge (it was thus that Aristotle misunderstood it); but, beyond terror and pity, to realise in fact the eternal delight of becoming, that delight which even involves in itself the joy of annihilating![1] In this sense I have the right to understand myself to be the first tragic philosopher--that is, the utmost antithesis and antipode to a pessimistic philosopher. Prior to myself there is no such translation of the Dionysian into the philosophic pathos: there lacks the tragic wisdom,--I have sought in vain for an indication thereof even among the great Greeks of philosophy, the thinkers of the two centuries before Socrates. A doubt still possessed me as touching Heraclitus, in whose proximity I in general begin to feel warmer and better than anywhere else. The affirmation of transiency and annihilation, to wit the decisive factor in a Dionysian philosophy, the yea-saying to antithesis and war, to becoming, with radical rejection even of the concept 'being,'--that I must directly acknowledge as, of all thinking hitherto, the nearest to my own. The doctrine of 'eternal recurrence,' that is, of the unconditioned and infinitely repeated cycle of all things--this doctrine of Zarathustra's might after all have been already taught by Heraclitus. At any rate the portico[2] which inherited well-nigh all its fundamental conceptions from Heraclitus, shows traces thereof."

4

"In this book speaks a prodigious hope. In fine, I see no reason whatever for taking back my hope of a Dionysian future for music. Let us cast a glance a century ahead, let us suppose my assault upon two millenniums of anti-nature and man-vilification succeeds! That new party of life which will take in hand the greatest of all tasks, the upbreeding of mankind to something higher,--add thereto the relentless annihilation of all things degenerating and parasitic, will again make possible on earth that too-much of life, from which there also must needs grow again the Dionysian state. I promise a tragic age: the highest art in the yea-saying to life, tragedy, will be born anew, when mankind have behind them the consciousness of the hardest but most necessary wars, without suffering therefrom. A psychologist might still add that what I heard in my younger years in Wagnerian music had in general naught to do with Wagner; that when I described Wagnerian music I described what I had heard, that I had instinctively to translate and transfigure all into the new spirit which I bore within myself...."

Footnotes:

1. Mr. Common's translation, pp. 227-28.
2. Greek: στοά.

Early Greek Philosophy & Other Essays

Translated by Maximilian A. Mügge

Originally Published by:
T.N. Foulis 13 & 15 Frederick Street, Edinburgh: and London 1911

TRANSLATOR'S PREFACE

The essays contained in this volume treat of various subjects. With the exception of perhaps one we must consider all these papers as fragments. Written during the early Seventies, and intended mostly as prefaces, they are extremely interesting, since traces of Nietzsche's later tenets--like Slave and Master morality, the Superman--can be found everywhere. But they are also very valuable on account of the young philosopher's daring and able handling of difficult and abstruse subjects. "Truth and Falsity," and "The Greek Woman" are probably the two essays which will prove most attractive to the average reader.

In the essay on THE GREEK STATE the two tenets mentioned above are clearly discernible, though the Superman still goes by the Schopenhauerian label "genius." Our philosopher attacks the modern ideas of the "dignity of man" and of the "dignity of labour," because Existence seems to be without worth and dignity. The preponderance of such illusory ideas is due to the political power nowadays vested in the "slaves." The Greeks saw no dignity in labour. They saw the necessity of it, and the necessity of slavery, but felt ashamed of both. Not even the labour of the artist did they admire, although they praised his completed work.

If the Greeks perished through their slavery, one thing is still more certain: we shall perish through the lack of slavery. To the essence of Culture slavery is innate. It is part of it. A vast multitude must labour and "slave" in order that a few may lead an existence devoted to beauty and art.

Strife and war are necessary for the welfare of the State. War consecrates and purines the State. The purpose of the military State is the creating of the military genius, the ruthless conqueror, the War-lord. There also exists a mysterious connection between the State in general and the creating of the genius.

In THE GREEK WOMAN, Nietzsche, the man who said, "One cannot think highly enough of women," delineates his ideal of woman. Penelope, Antigone, Electra are his ideal types.

Plato's dictum that in the perfect State the family would cease to exist, belongs to the most intimate things uttered about the relation between women and the State. The Greek woman as mother had to vegetate in obscurity, to lead a kind of Cranfordian existence for the greater welfare of the body politic. Only in Greek antiquity did woman occupy her proper position, and for this reason she was more honoured than she has ever been since. Pythia was the mouthpiece, the symbol of Greek unity.

ON MUSIC AND WORDS. Music is older, more fundamental than language. Music is an expression of cosmic consciousness. Language is only a gesture-symbolism.

It is true the music of every people was at first allied to lyric poetry; "absolute music" always appeared much later. But that is due to the double nature in the essence of language. The tone of the speaker expresses the basic pleasure- and displeasure-sensations of the individual. These form the tonal subsoil common to all languages; they are comprehensible everywhere. Language itself is a super-structure on that subsoil; it is a gesture-symbolism for all the other conceptions which man adds to that subsoil.

The endeavour to illustrate a poem by music is futile. The text of an opera is therefore quite negligible. Modern opera in its music is therefore often only a stimulant or a remembrancer for set, stereotyped feelings. Great music, i.e., Dionysean music, makes us forget to listen to the words.

HOMER'S CONTEST. The Greek genius acknowledged strife, struggle, contest to be necessary in this life. Only through competition and emulation will the Common-Wealth thrive. Yet there was no unbridled ambition. Everyone's individual endeavours were subordinated to the welfare of the community. The curse of present-day contest is that it does not do the same.

In THE RELATION OF SCHOPENHAUER'S PHILOSOPHY TO A GERMAN CULTURE an amusing and yet serious attack is made on the hollow would-be culture of the German Philistines who after the Franco-Prussian war were swollen with self-conceit, self-sufficiency, and were a great danger to real Culture. Nietzsche points out Schopenhauer's great philosophy as the only possible means of escaping the humdrum of Philistia with its hypocrisy and intellectual ostrichisation.

The essay on GREEK PHILOSOPHY DURING THE TRAGIC AGE is a performance of great interest to the scholar. It brims with ideas. The Hegelian School, especially Zeller, has shown what an important place is held by the earlier thinkers in the history of Greek thought and how necessary a knowledge of their work is for all who wish to understand Plato and Aristotle. Diels' great book: "Die Fragmente der Vorsokratiker", Benn's, Burnet's and Fairbanks' books we may regard as the peristyle through which we enter the temple of Early Greek Philosophy. Nietzsche's essay then is like a beautiful festoon swinging between the columns erected by Diels and the others out of the marble of facts.

Beauty and the personal equation are the two "leitmotive" of Nietzsche's history of the pre-Socratian philosophers. Especially does he lay stress upon the personal equation, since that is the only permanent item of interest, considering that every "System" crumbles into nothing with the appearance of a new thinker. In this way Nietzsche treats of Thales, Anaximander, Heraclitus, Parmenides, Xenophanes, Anaxagoras. There are also some sketches of a draft for an intended but never accomplished continuation, in which Empedocles, Democritus and Plato were to be dealt with.

Probably the most popular of the Essays in this book will prove to be the one on TRUTH AND FALSITY. It is an epistemological rhapsody on the relativity of truth, on "Appearance and Reality," on "perceptual flux" versus--"conceptual conceit."

Man's intellect is only a means in the struggle for existence, a means taking the place of the animal's horns and teeth. It adapts itself especially to deception and dissimulation.

There are no absolute truths. Truth is relative and always imperfect. Yet fictitious values fixed by convention and utility are set down as truth. The liar does not use these standard coins of the realm. He is hated; not out of love for truth, no, but because he is dangerous.

Our words never hit the essence, the "X" of a thing, but indicate only external characteristics. Language is the columbarium of the ideas, the cemetery of perceptions.

Truths are metaphors, illusions, anthropomorph isms about which one has forgotten that they are such. There are different truths to different beings. Like a spider man sits in the web of his truths and ideas. He wants to be deceived. By means of error he mostly lives; truth is often fatal. When the liar, the story-teller, the poet, the rhapsodist lie to him without hurting him he--loves them!--

The text underlying this translation is that of Vol. I. of the "Taschenausgabe." One or two obscure passages I hope my conjectures may have elucidated. The dates following the titles indicate the year when these essays were written.

In no other work have I felt so deeply the great need of the science of Signifies with its ultimate international standardisation of terms, as attempted by Eisler and Baldwin. I hope, however, I have succeeded in conveying accurately the meaning of the author in spite of a certain looseness in his philosophical terminology.

The English language is somewhat at a disadvantage through its lack of a Noun-Infinitive. I can best illustrate this by a passage from Parmenides:

χρὴ τὸ λέγειν τε νοεῖν τ' ἐὸν ἔμμεναι· ἔστι γὰρ εἶναι, μηδὲν δ' οὐκ ἔστιν· τά σ' ἐγὼ ψράζεσθαι ἄνωγα.

In his usual masterly manner Diels translates these lines with: "Das Sagen und Denken musz ein Seiendes sein. Denn das Sein existiert, das Nichts existiert nicht; das heisz ich dich wohl zu beherzigen." On the other hand in Fairbanks' "version" we read: "It is necessary both to say and to think that being is; for it is possible that being is, and it is impossible that not being is; this is what I bid thee ponder." In order to avoid a similar obscurity, throughout the paper on "EARLY GREEK PHILOSOPHY" I have rendered "das Seiende" (τὸ ἐὸν) with "Existent", "das Nicht-Seiende" with "Non-Existent"; "das Sein" (εἶναι) with "Being" and "das Nicht-Sein" with "Not-Being."

I am directly or indirectly indebted for many suggestions to several friends of mine, especially to two of my colleagues, J. Charlton Hipkins, M.A., and R. Miller, B.A., for their patient revision of the whole of the proofs.

M. A. MÜGGE.

LONDON, July 1911.

THE GREEK STATE

Preface to an Unwritten Book (1871)

We moderns have an advantage over the Greeks in two ideas, which are given as it were as a compensation to a world behaving thoroughly slavishly and yet at the same time anxiously eschewing the word "slave": we talk of the "dignity of man" and of the "dignity of labour." Everybody worries in order miserably to perpetuate a miserable existence; this awful need compels him to consuming labour; man (or, more exactly, the human intellect) seduced by the "Will" now occasionally marvels at labour as something dignified. However in order that labour might have a claim on titles of honour, it would be necessary above all, that Existence itself, to which labour after all is only a painful means, should have more dignity and value than it appears to have had, up to the present, to serious philosophies and religions. What else may we find in the labour-need of all the millions but the impulse to exist at any price, the same all-powerful impulse by which stunted plants stretch their roots through earthless rocks!

Out of this awful struggle for existence only individuals can emerge, and they are at once occupied with the noble phantoms of artistic culture, lest they should arrive at practical pessimism, which Nature abhors as her exact opposite. In the modern world, which, compared with the Greek, usually produces only abnormalities and centaurs, in which the individual, like that fabulous creature in the beginning of the Horatian Art of Poetry, is jumbled together out of pieces, here in the modern world in one and the same man the greed of the struggle for existence and the need for art show themselves at the same time: out of this unnatural amalgamation has originated the dilemma, to excuse and to consecrate that first greed before this need for art. Therefore; we believe in the "Dignity of man" and the "Dignity of labour."

The Greeks did not require such conceptual hallucinations, for among them the idea that labour is a disgrace is expressed with startling frankness; and another piece of wisdom, more hidden and less articulate, but everywhere alive, added that the human thing also was an ignominious and piteous nothing and the "dream of a shadow." Labour is a disgrace, because existence has no value in itself; but even though this very existence in the alluring embellishment of artistic illusions shines forth and really seems to have a value in itself, then that proposition is still valid that labour is a disgrace--a disgrace indeed by the fact that it is impossible for man, fighting for the continuance of bare existence, to become an artist. In modern times it is not the art-needing man but the slave who determines the general conceptions, the slave who according to his nature must give deceptive names to all conditions in order to be able to live. Such phantoms as the dignity of man, the dignity of labour, are the needy products of slavedom hiding itself from itself. Woful time, in which the slave requires such conceptions, in which he is incited to think about and beyond himself! Cursed seducers, who have destroyed the slave's state of innocence by the fruit of the tree of knowledge! Now the slave must vainly scrape through from one day to another with transparent lies recognisable to every one of deeper insight, such as the alleged "equal rights of all" or the so-called "fundamental rights of man," of man as such, or the "dignity of labour." Indeed he is not to understand at what stage and at what height dignity can first be mentioned--namely, at the point, where the individual goes wholly beyond himself and no longer has to work and to produce in order to preserve his individual existence.

And even on this height of "labour" the Greek at times is overcome by a feeling, that looks like shame. In one place Plutarch with earlier Greek instinct says that no nobly born youth on beholding the Zeus in Pisa would have the desire to become himself a Phidias, or on seeing the Hera in Argos, to become himself a Polyklet; and just as little would he wish to be Anacreon, Philetas or Archilochus, however much he might revel in their poetry. To the Greek the work of the artist falls just as much under the undignified conception of labour as any ignoble craft. But if the compelling force of the artistic impulse operates in him, then he must produce and submit himself to that need of labour. And as a father admires the beauty and the gift of his child but thinks of the act of procreation with shamefaced dislike, so it was with the Greek. The joyful astonishment at the beautiful has not blinded him as to its origin which appeared to him, like all "Becoming" in nature, to be a powerful necessity, a forcing of itself into existence. That feeling by which the process of procreation is considered as something shamefacedly to be hidden, although by it man serves a higher purpose than his individual preservation, the same feeling veiled also the origin of the great works of art, in spite of the fact that through them a higher form of existence is inaugurated, just as through that other act comes a new generation. The feeling of shame seems therefore to occur where man is merely a tool of manifestations of will infinitely greater than he is permitted to consider himself in the isolated shape of the individual.

Now we have the general idea to which are to be subordinated the feelings which the Greek had with regard to labour and slavery. Both were considered by them as a necessary disgrace, of which one feels ashamed, as a disgrace and as a necessity at the same time. In this feeling of shame is hidden the unconscious discernment that the real aim needs those conditional factors, but that in that need lies the fearful and beast-of-prey-like quality of the Sphinx Nature, who in the glorification of the artistically free culture-life so beautifully stretches forth her virgin-body. Culture, which is chiefly a real need for art, rests upon a terrible basis: the latter however makes itself known in the twilight sensation of shame. In order that there may be a broad, deep, and fruitful soil for the development of art, the enormous majority must, in the service of a minority, be slavishly subjected to life's struggle, to a greater degree than their own wants necessitate. At their cost, through the surplus of their labour, that privileged class is to be relieved from the struggle for existence, in order to create and to satisfy a new world of want.

Accordingly we must accept this cruel sounding truth, that slavery is of the essence of Culture; a truth of course, which leaves no doubt as to the absolute value of Existence. This truth is the vulture, that gnaws at the liver of the Promethean promoter of Culture. The misery of toiling men must still increase in order to make the production of the world of art possible to a small number of Olympian men. Here is to be found the source of that secret wrath nourished by Communists and Socialists of all times, and also by their feebler descendants, the white race of the "Liberals," not only against the arts, but also against classical antiquity. If Culture really rested upon the will of a people, if here inexorable powers did not rule, powers which are law and barrier to the individual, then the contempt for Culture, the glorification of a "poorness in spirit," the iconoclastic annihilation of artistic claims would be more than an insurrection of the suppressed masses against drone-like individuals; it would be the cry of compassion tearing down the walls of Culture; the desire for justice, for the equalization of suffering, would swamp all other ideas. In fact here and there sometimes an exuberant degree of compassion has for a short time opened all the flood gates of Culture-life; a rainbow of compassionate love and of peace appeared with the first radiant rise of Christianity and under it was born Christianity's most beautiful fruit, the gospel according to St John. But there are also instances to show that powerful religions for long periods petrify a given degree of Culture, and cut off with inexorable sickle everything that still grows on strongly and luxuriantly. For it is not to be forgotten that the same cruelty, which we found in the essence of every Culture, lies also in the essence of every powerful religion and in general in the essence of power, which is always evil; so that we shall understand it just as well, when a Culture is shattering, with a cry for liberty or at least justice, a too highly piled bulwark of religious claims. That which in this "sorry scheme" of things will live (i.e., must live), is at the bottom of its nature a reflex of the primal-pain and primal-contradiction, and must therefore strike our eyes--"an organ fashioned for this world and earth"--as an insatiable greed for existence and an eternal self-contradiction, within the form of time, therefore as Becoming. Every moment devours the preceding one, every birth is the death of innumerable beings; begetting, living, murdering, all is one. Therefore we may compare this grand Culture with a blood-stained victor, who in his triumphal procession carries the defeated along as slaves chained to his chariot, slaves whom a beneficent power has so blinded that, almost crushed by the wheels of the chariot, they nevertheless still exclaim: "Dignity of labour!" "Dignity of Man!" The voluptuous Cleopatra-Culture throws ever again the most priceless pearls, the tears of compassion for the misery of slaves, into her golden goblet. Out of the emasculation of modern man has been born the enormous social distress of the present time, not out of the true and deep commiseration for that misery; and if it should be true that the Greeks perished through their slavedom then another fact is much more certain, that we shall perish through the lack of slavery. Slavedom did not appear in any way objectionable, much less abominable, either to early Christianity or to the Germanic race. What an uplifting effect on us has the contemplation of the mediæval bondman, with his legal and moral relations,--relations that were inwardly strong and tender,--towards the man of higher rank, with the profound fencing-in of his narrow existence--how uplifting!--and how reproachful!

He who cannot reflect upon the position of affairs in Society without melancholy, who has learnt to conceive of it as the continual painful birth of those privileged Culture-men, in whose service everything else must be devoured--he will no longer be deceived by that false glamour, which the moderns have spread over the origin and meaning of the State. For what can the State mean to us, if not the means by which that social-process described just now is to be fused and to be guaranteed in its unimpeded continuance? Be the sociable instinct in individual man as strong as it may, it is only the iron clamp of the State that constrains the large masses upon one another in such a fashion that a chemical decomposition of Society, with its pyramid-like super-structure, is bound to take place. Whence however originates this sudden power of the State, whose aim lies much beyond the insight and beyond the egoism of the individual? How did the slave, the blind mole of Culture, originate? The Greeks in their instinct relating to the law of nations have betrayed it to us, in an instinct, which even in the ripest fulness of their civilisation and humanity never ceased to utter as out of a brazen mouth such words as: "to the victor belongs the vanquished, with wife and child, life and property. Power gives the first right and there is no right, which at bottom is not presumption, usurpation, violence."

Here again we see with what pitiless inflexibility Nature, in order to arrive at Society, forges for herself the cruel tool of the State--namely, that conqueror with the iron hand, who is nothing else than the objectivation of the instinct indicated. By the indefinable greatness and power of such conquerors the spectator feels, that they are only the means of an intention manifesting itself through them and yet hiding itself from them. The weaker forces attach themselves to them with such mysterious speed, and transform themselves so wonderfully, in the sudden swelling of that violent avalanche, under the charm of that creative kernel, into an affinity hitherto not existing, that it seems as if a magic will were emanating from them.

Now when we see how little the vanquished trouble themselves after a short time about the horrible origin of the State, so that history informs us of no class of events worse than the origins of those sudden, violent, bloody and, at least in one point, inexplicable usurpations: when hearts involuntarily go out towards the magic of the growing State with the presentiment of an invisible deep purpose, where the calculating intellect is enabled to see an addition of forces only; when now the State is even contemplated with fervour as the goal and ultimate aim of the sacrifices and duties of the individual: then out of all that speaks the enormous necessity of the State, without which Nature might not succeed in coming, through Society, to her deliverance in semblance, in the mirror of the genius. What discernments does the instinctive pleasure in the State not overcome! One would indeed feel inclined to think that a man who looks into the origin of the State will henceforth seek his salvation at an awful distance from it; and where can one not see the monuments of its origin--devastated lands, destroyed cities, brutalised men, devouring hatred of nations! The State, of ignominiously low birth, for the majority of men a continually flowing source of hardship, at frequently recurring periods the consuming torch of mankind--and yet a word, at which we forget ourselves, a battle cry, which has filled men with enthusiasm for innumerable really heroic deeds, perhaps the highest and most venerable object for the blind and egoistic multitude which only in the tremendous moments of State-life has the strange expression of greatness on its face!

We have, however, to consider the Greeks, with regard to the unique sun-height of their art, as the "political men in themselves," and certainly history knows of no second instance of such an awful unchaining of the political passion, such an unconditional immolation of all other interests in the service of this State-instinct; at the best one might distinguish the men of the Renascence in Italy with a similar title for like reasons and by way of comparison. So overloaded is that passion among the Greeks that it begins ever anew to rage against itself and to strike its teeth into its own flesh. This bloody jealousy of city against city, of party against party, this murderous greed of those little wars, the tiger-like triumph over the corpse of the slain enemy, in short, the incessant renewal of those Trojan scenes of struggle and horror, in the spectacle of which, as a genuine Hellene, Homer stands before us absorbed with delight--whither does this naïve barbarism of the Greek State point? What is its excuse before the tribunal of eternal justice? Proud and calm, the State steps before this tribunal and by the hand it leads the flower of blossoming womanhood: Greek society. For this Helena the State waged those wars--and what grey-bearded judge could here condemn?--

Under this mysterious connection, which we here divine between State and art, political greed and artistic creation, battlefield and work of art, we understand by the State, as already remarked, only the cramp-iron, which compels the Social process; whereas without the State, in the natural bellum omnium contra omnes Society cannot strike root at all on a larger scale and beyond the reach of the family. Now, after States have been established almost everywhere, that bent of the bellum omnium contra omnes concentrates itself from time to time into a terrible gathering of war-clouds and discharges itself as it were in rare but so much the more violent shocks and lightning flashes. But in consequence of the effect of that bellum,--an effect which is turned inwards and compressed,--Society is given time during the intervals to germinate and burst into leaf, in order, as soon as warmer days come, to let the shining blossoms of genius sprout forth.

In face of the political world of the Hellenes, I will not hide those phenomena of the present in which I believe I discern dangerous atrophies of the political sphere equally critical for art and society. If there should exist men, who as it were through birth are placed outside the national-and State-instincts, who consequently have to esteem the State only in so far as they conceive that it coincides with their own interest, then such men will necessarily imagine as the ultimate political aim the most undisturbed collateral existence of great political communities possible, which they might be permitted to pursue their own purposes without restriction. With this idea in their heads they will promote that policy which will offer the greatest security to these purposes; whereas it is unthinkable, that they, against their intentions, guided perhaps by an unconscious instinct, should sacrifice themselves for the State-tendency, unthinkable because they lack that very instinct. All other citizens of the State are in the dark about what Nature intends with her State-instinct within them, and they follow blindly; only those who stand outside this instinct know what they want from the State and what the State is to grant them. Therefore it is almost unavoidable that such men should gain great influence in the State because they are allowed to consider it as a means, whereas all the others under the sway of those unconscious purposes of the State are themselves only means for the fulfilment of the State-purpose. In order now to attain, through the medium of the State, the highest furtherance of their selfish aims, it is above all necessary, that the State be wholly freed from those awfully incalculable war-convulsions so that it may be used rationally; and thereby they strive with all their might for a condition of things in which war is an impossibility. For that purpose the thing to do is first to curtail and to enfeeble the political separatisms and factions and through the establishment of large equipoised State-bodies and the mutual safeguarding of them to make the successful result of an aggressive war and consequently war itself the greatest improbability; as on the other hand they will endeavour to wrest the question of war and peace from the decision of individual lords, in order to be able rather to appeal to the egoism of the masses or their representatives; for which purpose they again need slowly to dissolve the monarchic instincts of the nations. This purpose they attain best through the most general promulgation of the liberal optimistic view of the world, which has its roots in the doctrines of French Rationalism and the French Revolution, i.e., in a wholly un-Germanic, genuinely neo-Latin shallow and unmetaphysical philosophy. I cannot help seeing in the prevailing international movements of the present day, and the simultaneous promulgation of universal suffrage, the effects of the fear of war above everything else, yea I behold behind these movements, those truly international homeless money-hermits, as the really alarmed, who, with their natural lack of the State-instinct, have learnt to abuse politics as a means of the Exchange, and State and Society as an apparatus for their own enrichment. Against the deviation of the State-tendency into a money-tendency, to be feared from this side, the only remedy is war and once again war, in the emotions of which this at least becomes obvious, that the State is not founded upon the fear of the war-demon, as a protective institution for egoistic individuals, but in love to fatherland and prince, it produces an ethical impulse, indicative of a much higher destiny. If I therefore designate as a dangerous and characteristic sign of the present political situation the application of revolutionary thought in the service of a selfish State-less money-aristocracy, if at the same time I conceive of the enormous dissemination of liberal optimism as the result of modern financial affairs fallen into strange hands, and if I imagine all evils of social conditions together with the necessary decay of the arts to have either germinated from that root or grown together with it, one will have to pardon my occasionally chanting a Pæan on war. Horribly clangs its silvery bow; and although it comes along like the night, war is nevertheless Apollo, the true divinity for consecrating and purifying the State. First of all, however, as is said in the beginning of the "Iliad," he lets fly his arrow on the mules and dogs. Then he strikes the men themselves, and everywhere pyres break into flames. Be it then pronounced that war is just as much a necessity for the State as the slave is for society, and who can avoid this verdict if he honestly asks himself about the causes of the never-equalled Greek art-perfection?

He who contemplates war and its uniformed possibility, the soldier's profession, with respect to the hitherto described nature of the State, must arrive at the conviction, that through war and in the profession of arms is placed before our eyes an image, or even perhaps the prototype of the State. Here we see as the most general effect of the war-tendency an immediate decomposition and division of the chaotic mass into military castes, out of which rises, pyramid-shaped, on an exceedingly broad base of slaves the edifice of the "martial society." The unconscious purpose of the whole movement constrains every individual under its yoke, and produces also in heterogeneous natures as it were a chemical transformation of their qualities until they are brought into affinity with that purpose. In the highest castes one perceives already a little more of what in this internal process is involved at the bottom, namely the creation of the military genius--with whom we have become acquainted as the original founder of states. In the case of many States, as, for example, in the Lycurgian constitution of Sparta, one can distinctly perceive the impress of that fundamental idea of the State, that of the creation of the military genius. If we now imagine the military primal State in its greatest activity, at its proper "labour," and if we fix our glance upon the whole technique of war, we cannot avoid correcting our notions picked up from everywhere, as to the "dignity of man" and the "dignity of labour" by the question, whether the idea of dignity is applicable also to that labour, which has as its purpose the destruction of the "dignified" man, as well as to the man who is entrusted with that "dignified labour," or whether in this warlike task of the State those mutually contradictory ideas do not neutralise one another. I should like to think the warlike man to be a means of the military genius and his labour again only a tool in the hands of that same genius; and not to him, as absolute man and non-genius, but to him as a means of the genius--whose pleasure also can be to choose his tool's destruction as a mere pawn sacrificed on the strategist's chessboard--is due a degree of dignity, of that dignity namely, to have been deemed worthy of being a means of the genius. But what is shown here in a single instance is valid in the most general sense; every human being, with his total activity, only has dignity in so far as he is a tool of the genius, consciously or unconsciously; from this we may immediately deduce the ethical conclusion, that "man in himself," the absolute man possesses neither dignity, nor rights, nor duties;

only as a wholly determined being serving unconscious purposes can man excuse his existence.

Plato's perfect State is according to these considerations certainly something still greater than even the warm-blooded among his admirers believe, not to mention the smiling mien of superiority with which our "historically" educated refuse such a fruit of antiquity. The proper aim of the State, the Olympian existence and ever-renewed procreation and preparation of the genius,--compared with which all other things are only tools, expedients and factors towards realisation--is here discovered with a poetic intuition and painted with firmness. Plato saw through the awfully devastated Herma of the then-existing State-life and perceived even then something divine in its interior. He believed that one might be able to take out this divine image and that the grim and barbarically distorted outside and shell did not belong to the essence of the State: the whole fervour and sublimity of his political passion threw itself upon this belief, upon that desire--and in the flames of this fire he perished. That in his perfect State he did not place at the head the genius in its general meaning, but only the genius of wisdom and of knowledge, that he altogether excluded the inspired artist from his State, that was a rigid consequence of the Socratian judgment on art, which Plato, struggling against himself, had made his own. This more external, almost incidental gap must not prevent our recognising in the total conception of the Platonic State the wonderfully great hieroglyph of a profound and eternally to be interpreted esoteric doctrine of the connection between State and Genius. What we believed we could divine of this cryptograph we have said in this preface.

THE GREEK WOMAN

(Fragment, 1871)

Just as Plato from disguises and obscurities brought to light the innermost purpose of the State, so also he conceived the chief cause of the position of the Hellenic Woman with regard to the State; in both cases he saw in what existed around him the image of the ideas manifested to him, and of these ideas of course the actual was only a hazy picture and phantasmagoria. He who according to the usual custom considers the position of the Hellenic Woman to be altogether unworthy and repugnant to humanity, must also turn with this reproach against the Platonic conception of this position; for, as it were, the existing forms were only precisely set forth in this latter conception. Here therefore our question repeats itself: should not the nature and the position of the Hellenic Woman have a necessary relation to the goals of the Hellenic Will?

Of course there is one side of the Platonic conception of woman, which stands in abrupt contrast with Hellenic custom: Plato gives to woman a full share in the rights, knowledge and duties of man, and considers woman only as the weaker sex, in that she will not achieve remarkable success in all things, without however disputing this sex's title to all those things. We must not attach more value to; this strange notion than to the expulsion of the artist out of the ideal State; these are side-lines daringly mis-drawn, aberrations as it were of the hand otherwise so sure and of the so calmly contemplating eye which at times under the influence of the deceased master becomes dim and dejected; in this mood he exaggerates the master's paradoxes and in the abundance of his love gives himself satisfaction by very eccentrically intensifying the latter's doctrines even to foolhardiness.

The most significant word however that Plato as a Greek could say on the relation of woman to the State, was that so objectionable demand, that in the perfect State, the Family was to cease. At present let us take no account of his abolishing even marriage, in order to carry out this demand fully, and of his substituting solemn nuptials arranged by order of the State, between the bravest men and the noblest women, for the attainment of beautiful offspring. In that principal proposition however he has indicated most distinctly--indeed too distinctly, offensively distinctly--an important preparatory step of the Hellenic Will towards the procreation of the genius. But in the customs of the Hellenic people the claim of the family on man and child was extremely limited: the man lived in the State, the child grew up for the State and was guided by the hand of the State. The Greek Will took care that the need of culture could not be satisfied in the seclusion of a small circle. From the State the individual has to receive everything in order to return everything to the State. Woman accordingly means to the State, what sleep does to man. In her nature lies the healing power, which replaces that which has been used up, the beneficial rest in which everything immoderate confines itself, the eternal Same, by which the excessive and the surplus regulate themselves. In her the future generation dreams. Woman is more closely related to Nature than man and in all her essentials she remains ever herself. Culture is with her always something external, a something which does not touch the kernel that is eternally faithful to Nature, therefore the culture of woman might well appear to the Athenian as something indifferent, yea--if one only wanted to conjure it up in one's mind, as something ridiculous. He who at once feels himself compelled from that to infer the position of women among the Greeks as unworthy and all too cruel, should not indeed take as his criterion the "culture" of modern woman and her claims, against which it is sufficient just to point out the Olympian women together with Penelope, Antigone, Elektra. Of course it is true that these are ideal figures, but who would be able to create such ideals out of the present world?--Further indeed is to be considered what sons these women have borne, and what women they must have been to have given birth to such sons! The Hellenic woman as mother had to live in obscurity, because the political instinct together with its highest aim demanded it. She had to vegetate like a plant, in the narrow circle, as a symbol of the Epicurean wisdom λάθε βυώσας. Again, in more recent times, with the complete disintegration of the principle of the State, she had to step in as helper; the family as a makeshift for the State is her work; and in this sense the artistic aim of the State had to abase itself to the level of a domestic art. Thereby it has been brought about, that the passion of love, as the one realm wholly accessible to women, regulates our art to the very core. Similarly, home-education considers itself so to speak as the only natural one and suffers State-education only as a questionable infringement upon the right of home-education: all this is right as far as the modern State only is concerned.--With that the nature of woman withal remains unaltered, but her power is, according to the position which the State takes up with regard to women, a different one. Women have indeed really the power to make good to a certain extent the deficiencies of the State--ever faithful to their nature, which I have compared to sleep. In Greek antiquity they held that position, which the most supreme will of the State assigned to them: for that reason they have been glorified as never since. The goddesses of Greek mythology are their images: the Pythia and the Sibyl, as well as the Socratic Diotima are the priestesses out of whom divine wisdom speaks. Now one understands why the proud resignation of the Spartan woman at the news of her son's death in battle can be no fable. Woman in relation to the State felt herself in her proper position, therefore she had more dignity than woman has ever had since. Plato who through abolishing family and marriage still intensifies the position of woman, feels now so much reverence towards them, that oddly enough he is misled by a subsequent statement of their equality with man, to abolish again the order of rank which is their due: the highest triumph of the woman of antiquity, to have seduced even the wisest!

As long as the State is still in an embryonic condition woman as mother preponderates and determines the grade and the manifestations of Culture: in the same way as woman is destined to complement the disorganised State. What Tacitus says of German women: inesse quin etiam sanctum aliquid et providum putant, nec aut consilia earum aspernantur aut responsa neglegunt, applies on the whole to all nations not yet arrived at the real State. In such stages one feels only the more strongly that which at all times becomes again manifest, that the instincts of woman as the bulwark of the future generation are invincible and that in her care for the preservation of the species Nature speaks out of these instincts very distinctly. How far this divining power reaches is determined, it seems, by the greater or lesser consolidation of the State: in disorderly and more arbitrary conditions, where the whim or the passion of the individual man carries along with itself whole tribes, then woman suddenly comes forward as the warning prophetess. But in Greece too there was a never slumbering care that the terribly overcharged political instinct might splinter into dust and atoms the little political organisms before they attained their goals in any way. Here the Hellenic Will created for itself ever new implements by means of which it spoke, adjusting, moderating, warning: above all it is in the Pythia, that the power of woman to compensate the State manifested itself so clearly, as it has never done since. That a people split up thus into small tribes and municipalities, was yet at bottom whole and was performing the task of its nature within its faction, was assured by that wonderful phenomenon the Pythia and the Delphian oracle: for always, as long as Hellenism created its great works of art, it spoke out of one mouth and as one Pythia. We cannot hold back the portentous discernment that to the Will individuation means much suffering, and that in order to reach those individuals It needs an enormous step-ladder of individuals. It is true our brains reel with the consideration whether the Will in order to arrive at Art, has perhaps effused Itself out into these worlds, stars, bodies, and atoms: at least it ought to become clear to us then, that Art is not necessary for the individuals, but for the Will itself: a sublime outlook at which we shall be permitted to glance once more from another position.

ON MUSIC AND WORDS

(Fragment, 1871)

What we here have asserted of the relationship between language and music must be valid too, for equal reasons concerning the relationship of Mime to Music. The Mime too, as the intensified symbolism of man's gestures, is, measured by the eternal significance of music, only a simile, which brings into expression the innermost secret of music but very superficially, namely on the substratum of the passionately moved human body. But if we include language also in the category of bodily symbolism, and compare the drama, according to the canon advanced, with music, then I venture to think, a proposition of Schopenhauer will come into the clearest light, to which reference must be made again later on. "It might be admissible, although a purely musical mind does not demand it, to join and adapt words or even a clearly represented action to the pure language of tones, although the latter, being self-sufficient, needs no help; so that our perceiving and reflecting intellect, which does not like to be quite idle, may meanwhile have light and analogous occupation also. By this concession to the intellect man's attention adheres even more closely to music, by this at the same time, too, is placed underneath that which the tones indicate in their general metaphorless language of the heart, a visible picture, as it were a schema, as an example illustrating a general idea ... indeed such things will even heighten the effect of music." (Schopenhauer, Parerga, II., "On the Metaphysics of the Beautiful and Æsthetics," § 224.) If we disregard the naturalistic external motivation according to which our perceiving and reflecting intellect does not like to be quite idle when listening to music, and attention led by the hand of an obvious action follows better--then the drama in relation to music has been characterised by Schopenhauer for the best reasons as a schema, as an example illustrating a general idea: and when he adds "indeed such things will even heighten the effect of music" then the enormous universality and originality of vocal music, of the connection of tone with metaphor and idea guarantee the correctness of this utterance. The music of every people begins in closest connection with lyricism and long before absolute music can be thought of, the music of a people in that connection passes through the most important stages of development. If we understand this primal lyricism of a people, as indeed we must, to be an imitation of the artistic typifying Nature, then as the original prototype of that union of music and lyricism must be regarded: the duality in the essence of language, already typified by Nature. Now, after discussing the relation of music to metaphor we will fathom deeper this essence of language.

In the multiplicity of languages the fact at once manifests itself, that word and thing do not necessarily coincide with one another completely, but that the word is a symbol. But what does the word symbolise? Most certainly only conceptions, be these now conscious ones or as in the greater number of cases, unconscious; for how should a word-symbol correspond to that innermost nature of which we and the world are images? Only as conceptions we know that kernel, only in its metaphorical expressions are we familiar with it; beyond that point there is nowhere a direct bridge which could lead us to it. The whole life of impulses, too, the play of feelings, sensations, emotions, volitions, is known to us--as I am forced to insert here in opposition to Schopenhauer--after a most rigid self-examination, not according to its essence but merely as conception; and we may well be permitted to say, that even Schopenhauer's "Will" is nothing else but the most general phenomenal form of a Something otherwise absolutely indecipherable. If therefore we must acquiesce in the rigid necessity of getting nowhere beyond the conceptions we can nevertheless again distinguish two main species within their realm. The one species manifest themselves to us as pleasure-and-displeasure-sensations and accompany all other conceptions as a never-lacking fundamental basis. This most general manifestation, out of which and by which alone we understand all Becoming and all Willing and for which we will retain the name "Will" has now too in language its own symbolic sphere: and in truth this sphere is equally fundamental to the language, as that manifestation is fundamental to all other conceptions. All degrees of pleasure and displeasure--expressions of one primal cause unfathomable to us--symbolise themselves in the tone of the speaker: whereas all the other conceptions are indicated by the gesture-symbolism of the speaker. In so far as that primal cause is the same in all men, the tonal subsoil is also the common one, comprehensible beyond the difference of language. Out of it now develops the more arbitrary gesture-symbolism which is not wholly adequate for its basis: and with which begins the diversity of languages, whose multiplicity we are permitted to consider--to use a simile--as a strophic text to that primal melody of the pleasure-and-displeasure-language. The whole realm of the consonantal and vocal we believe we may reckon only under gesture-symbolism: consonants and vowels without that fundamental tone which is necessary above all else, are nothing but positions of the organs of speech, in short, gestures--; as soon as we imagine the word proceeding out of the mouth of man, then first of all the root of the word, and the basis of that gesture-symbolism, the tonal subsoil, the echo of the pleasure-and-displeasure-sensations originate. As our whole corporeality stands in relation to that original phenomenon, the "Will," so the word built out of its consonants and vowels stands in relation to its tonal basis.

This original phenomenon, the "Will," with its scale of pleasure-and-displeasure-sensations attains in the development of music an ever more adequate symbolic expression: and to this historical process the continuous effort of lyric poetry runs parallel, the effort to transcribe music into metaphors: exactly as this double-phenomenon, according to the just completed disquisition, lies typified in language.

He who has followed us into these difficult contemplations readily, attentively, and with some imagination--and with kind indulgence where the expression has been too scanty or too unconditional--will now have the advantage with us, of laying before himself more seriously and answering more deeply than is usually the case some stirring points of controversy of present-day æsthetics and still more of contemporary artists. Let us think now, after all our assumptions, what an undertaking it must be, to set music to a poem; i.e., to illustrate a poem by music, in order to help music thereby to obtain a language of ideas. What a perverted world! A task that appears to my mind like that of a son wanting to create his father! Music can create metaphors out of itself, which will always however be but schemata, instances as it were of her intrinsic general contents. But how should the metaphor, the conception, create music out of itself! Much less could the idea, or, as one has said, the "poetical idea" do this. As certainly as a bridge leads out of the mysterious castle of the musician into the free land of the metaphors--and the lyric poet steps across it--as certainly is it impossible to go the contrary way, although some are said to exist who fancy they have done so. One might people the air with the phantasy of a Raphael, one might see St. Cecilia, as he does, listening enraptured to the harmonies of the choirs of angels--no tone issues from this world apparently lost in music: even if we imagined that that harmony in reality, as by a miracle, began to sound for us, whither would Cecilia, Paul and Magdalena disappear from us, whither even the singing choir of angels! We should at once cease to be Raphael: and as in that picture the earthly instruments lie shattered on the ground, so our painter's vision, defeated by the higher, would fade and die away.--How nevertheless could the miracle happen? How should the Apollonian world of the eye quite engrossed in contemplation be able to create out of itself the tone, which on the contrary symbolises a sphere which is excluded and conquered just by that very Apollonian absorption in Appearance? The delight at Appearance cannot raise out of itself the pleasure at Non-appearance; the delight of perceiving is delight only by the fact that nothing reminds us of a sphere in which individuation is broken and abolished. If we have characterised at all correctly the Apollonian in opposition to the Dionysean, then the thought which attributes to the metaphor, the idea, the appearance, in some way the power of producing out of itself the tone, must appear to us strangely wrong. We will not be referred, in order to be refuted, to the musician who writes music to existing lyric poems; for after all that has been said we shall be compelled to assert that the relationship between the lyric poem and its setting must in any case be a different one from that between a father and his child. Then what exactly?

Here now we may be met on the ground of a favourite æsthetic notion with the proposition, "It is not the poem which gives birth to the setting but the sentiment created by the poem." I do not agree with that; the more subtle or powerful stirring-up of that pleasure-and-displeasure-subsoil is in the realm of productive art the element which is inartistic in itself; indeed only its total exclusion makes the complete self-absorption and disinterested perception of the artist possible. Here perhaps one might retaliate that I myself just now predicated about the "Will," that in music "Will" came to an ever more adequate symbolic expression. My answer, condensed into an æsthetic axiom, is this: the Will is the object of music but not the origin of it, that is the Will in its very greatest universality, as the most original manifestation, under which is to be understood all Becoming. That, which we call feeling, is with regard to this Will already permeated and saturated with conscious and unconscious conceptions and is therefore no longer directly the object of music; it is unthinkable then that these feelings should be able to create music out of themselves. Take for instance the feelings of love, fear and hope: music can no longer do anything with them in a direct way, every one of them is already so filled with conceptions. On the contrary these feelings can serve to symbolise music, as the lyric poet does who translates for himself into the simile-world of feelings that conceptually and metaphorically unapproachable realm of the Will, the proper content and object of music. The lyric poet resembles all those hearers of music who are conscious of an effect of music on their emotions; the distant and removed power of music appeals, with them, to an intermediate realm which gives to them as it were a foretaste, a symbolic preliminary conception of music proper, it appeals to the intermediate realm of the emotions. One might be permitted to say about them, with respect to the Will, the only object of music, that they bear the same relation to this Will, as the analogous morning-dream, according to Schopenhauer's theory, bears to the dream proper. To all those, however, who are unable to get at music except with their emotions, is to be said, that they will ever remain in the entrance-hall, and will never have access to the sanctuary of music: which, as I said, emotion cannot show but only symbolise.

With regard however to the origin of music, I have already explained that that can never lie in the Will, but must rather rest in the lap of that force, which under the form of the "Will" creates out of itself a visionary world: the origin of music lies beyond all individuation, a proposition, which after our discussion on the Dionysean self-evident. At this point I take the liberty of setting forth again comprehensively side by side those decisive propositions which the antithesis of the Dionysean and Apollonian dealt with has compelled us to enunciate:

The "Will," as the most original manifestation, is the object of music: in this sense music can be called imitation of Nature, but of Nature in its most general form.--

The "Will" itself and the feelings--manifestations of the Will already permeated with conceptions--are wholly incapable of creating music out of themselves, just as on the other hand it is utterly denied to music to represent feelings, or to have feelings as its object, while Will is its only object.--

He who carries away feelings as effects of music has within them as it were a symbolic intermediate realm, which can give him a foretaste of music, but excludes him at the same time from her innermost sanctuaries.--

The lyric poet interprets music to himself through the symbolic world of emotions, whereas he himself, in the calm of the Apollonian contemplation, is exempted from those emotions.--

When, therefore, the musician writes a setting to a lyric poem he is moved as musician neither through the images nor through the emotional language in the text; but a musical inspiration coming from quite a different sphere chooses for itself that song-text as allegorical expression. There cannot therefore be any question as to a necessary relation between poem and music; for the two worlds brought here into connection are too strange to one another to enter into more than a superficial alliance; the song-text is just a symbol and stands to music in the same relation as the Egyptian hieroglyph of bravery did to the brave warrior himself. During the highest revelations of music we even feel involuntarily the crudeness of every figurative effort and of every emotion dragged in for purposes of analogy; for example, the last quartets of Beethoven quite put to shame all illustration and the entire realm of empiric reality. The symbol, in face of the god really revealing himself, has no longer any meaning; moreover it appears as an offensive superficiality.

One must not think any the worse of us for considering from this point of view one item so that we may speak about it without reserve, namely the last movement of Beethoven's Ninth Symphony, a movement which is unprecedented and unanalysable in its charms. To the dithyrambic world-redeeming exultation of this music Schiller's poem "To Joy," is wholly incongruous, yea, like cold moon-light, pales beside that sea of flame. Who would rob me of this sure feeling? Yea, who would be able to dispute that that feeling during the hearing of this music does not find expression in a scream only because we, wholly impotent through music for metaphor and word, already hear nothing at all from Schiller's poem. All that noble sublimity, yea the grandeur of Schiller's verses has, beside the truly naïve-innocent folk-melody of joy, a disturbing, troubling, even crude and offensive effect; only the ever fuller development of the choir's song and the masses of the orchestra preventing us from hearing them, keep from us that sensation of incongruity. What therefore shall we think of that awful æsthetic superstition that Beethoven himself made a solemn statement as to his belief in the limits of absolute music, in that fourth movement of the Ninth Symphony, yea that he as it were with it unlocked the portals of a new art, within which music had been enabled to represent even metaphor and idea and whereby music had been opened to the "conscious mind." And what does Beethoven himself tell us when he has choir-song introduced by a recitative? "Alas friends, let us intonate not these tones but more pleasing and joyous ones!" More pleasing and joyous ones! For that he needed the convincing tone of the human voice, for that he needed the music of innocence in the folk-song. Not the word, but the "more pleasing" sound, not the idea but the most heartfelt joyful tone was chosen by the sublime master in his longing for the most soul-thrilling ensemble of his orchestra. And how could one misunderstand him! Rather may the same be said of this movement as Richard Wagner says of the great "Missa Solemnis" which he calls "a pure symphonic work of the most genuine Beethoven-spirit" (Beethoven, p. 42). "The voices are treated here quite in the sense of human instruments, in which sense Schopenhauer quite rightly wanted these human voices to be considered; the text underlying them is understood by us in these great Church compositions, not in its conceptual meaning, but it serves in the sense of the musical work of art, merely as material for vocal music and does not stand to our musically determined sensation in a disturbing position simply because it does not incite in us any rational conceptions but, as its ecclesiastical character conditions too, only touches us with the impression of well-known symbolic creeds." Besides I do not doubt that Beethoven, had he written the Tenth Symphony--of which drafts are still extant--would have composed just the Tenth Symphony.

Let us now approach, after these preparations, the discussion of the opera, so as to be able to proceed afterwards from the opera to its counterpart in the Greek tragedy. What we had to observe in the last movement of the Ninth, i.e., on the highest level of modern music-development, viz., that the word-content goes down unheard in the general sea of sound, is nothing isolated and peculiar, but the general and eternally valid norm in the vocal music of all times, the norm which alone is adequate to the origin of lyric song. The man in a state of Dionysean excitement has a listener just as little as the orgiastic crowd, a listener to whom he might have something to communicate, a listener as the epic narrator and generally speaking the Apollonian artist, to be sure, presupposes. It is rather in the nature of the Dionysean art, that it has no consideration for the listener: the inspired servant of Dionysos is, as I said in a former place, understood only by his compeers. But if we now imagine a listener at those endemic outbursts of Dionysean excitement then we shall have to prophesy for him a fate similar to that which Pentheus the discovered eavesdropper suffered, namely, to be torn to pieces by the Mænads. The lyric musician sings "as the bird sings,"[1] alone, out of innermost compulsion; when the listener comes to him with a demand he must become dumb. Therefore it would be altogether unnatural to ask from the lyric musician that one should also understand the text-words of his song, unnatural because here a demand is made by the listener, who has no right at all during the lyric outburst to claim anything. Now with the poetry of the great ancient lyric poets in your hand, put the question honestly to yourself whether they can have even thought of making themselves clear to the mass of the people standing around and listening, clear with their world of metaphors and thoughts; answer this serious question with a look at Pindar and the Æschylian choir songs. These most daring and obscure intricacies of thought, this whirl of metaphors, ever impetuously reproducing itself, this oracular tone of the whole, which we, without the diversion of music and orchestration, so often cannot penetrate even with the closest attention--was this whole world of miracles transparent as glass to the Greek crowd, yea, a metaphorical-conceptual interpretation of music? And with such mysteries of thought as are to be found in Pindar do you think the wonderful poet could have wished to elucidate the music already strikingly distinct? Should we here not be forced to an insight into the very nature of the lyricist--the artistic man, who to himself must interpret music through the symbolism of metaphors and emotions, but who has nothing to communicate to the listener; an artist who, in complete aloofness, even forgets those who stand eagerly listening near him. And as the lyricist his hymns, so the people sing the folk-song, for themselves, out of in-most impulse, unconcerned whether the word is comprehensible to him who does not join in the song. Let us think of our own experiences in the realm of higher art-music: what did we understand of the text of a Mass of Palestrina, of a Cantata of Bach, of an Oratorio of Händel, if we ourselves perhaps did not join in singing? Only for him who joins in singing do lyric poetry and vocal music exist; the listener stands before it as before absolute music.

But now the opera begins, according to the clearest testimonies, with the demand of the listener to understand the word.

What? The listener demands? The word is to be understood?

But to bring music into the service of a series of metaphors and conceptions, to use it as a means to an end, to the strengthening and elucidation of such conceptions and metaphors--such a peculiar presumption as is found in the concept of an "opera," reminds me of that ridiculous person who endeavours to lift himself up into the air with his own arms; that which this fool and which the opera according to that idea attempt are absolute impossibilities. That idea of the opera does not demand perhaps an abuse from music but--as I said--an impossibility. Music never can become a means; one may push, screw, torture it; as tone, as roll of the drum, in its crudest and simplest stages, it still defeats poetry and abases the latter to its reflection. The opera as a species of art according to that concept is therefore not only an aberration of music, but an erroneous conception of æsthetics. If I herewith, after all, justify the nature of the opera for æsthetics, I am of course far from justifying at the same time bad opera music or bad opera-verses. The worst music can still mean, as compared with the best poetry, the Dionysean world-subsoil, and the worst poetry can be mirror, image and reflection of this subsoil, if together with the best music: as certainly, namely, as the single tone against the metaphor is already Dionysean, and the single metaphor together with idea and word against music is already Apollonian. Yea, even bad music together with bad poetry can still inform as to the nature of music and poesy.

When therefore Schopenhauer felt Bellini's "Norma," for example, as the fulfilment of tragedy, with regard to that opera's music and poetry, then he, in Dionysean-Apollonian emotion and self-forgetfulness, was quite entitled to do so, because he perceived music and poetry in their most general, as it were, philosophical value, as music and poetry: but with that judgment he showed a poorly educated taste,--for good taste always has historical perspective. To us, who intentionally in this investigation avoid any question of the historic value of an art-phenomenon and endeavour to focus only the phenomenon itself, in its unaltered eternal meaning, and consequently in its highest type, too,--to us the art-species of the "opera" seems to be justified as much as the folk-song, in so far as we find in both that union of the Dionysean and Apollonian and are permitted to assume for the opera--namely for the highest type of the opera--an origin analogous to that of the folk-song. Only in so far as the opera historically known to us has a completely different origin from that of the folk-song do we reject this "opera," which stands in the same relation to that generic notion just defended by us, as the marionette does to a living human being. It is certain, music never can become a means in the service of the text, but must always defeat the text, yet music must become bad when the composer interrupts every Dionysean force rising within himself by an anxious regard for the words and gestures of his marionettes. If the poet of the opera-text has offered him nothing more than the usual schematised figures with their Egyptian regularity, then the freer, more unconditional, more Dionysean is the development of the music; and the more she despises all dramatic requirements, so much the higher will be the value of the opera. In this sense it is true the opera is, at its best, good music, and nothing but music: whereas the jugglery performed at the same time is, as it were, only a fantastic disguise of the orchestra, above all, of the most important instruments the orchestra has: the singers; and from this jugglery the judicious listener turns away laughing. If the mass is diverted by this very jugglery and only permits the music with it, then the mob fares as all those do who value the frame of a good picture higher than the picture itself. Who treats such naïve aberrations with a serious or even pathetic reproach?

But what will the opera mean as "dramatic" music, in its possibly farthest distance from pure music, efficient in itself, and purely Dionysean? Let us imagine a passionate drama full of incidents which carries away the spectator, and which is already sure of success by its plot: what will "dramatic" music be able to add, if it does not take away something? Firstly, it will take away much: for in every moment where for once the Dionysean power of music strikes the listener, the eye is dimmed that sees the action, the eye that became absorbed in the individuals appearing before it: the listener now forgets the drama and becomes alive again to it only when the Dionysean spell over him has been broken. In so far, however, as music makes the listener forget the drama, it is not yet "dramatic" music: but what kind of music is that which is not allowed to exercise any Dionysean power over the listener? And how is it possible? It is possible as purely conventional symbolism, out of which convention has sucked all natural strength: as music which has diminished to symbols of remembrance: and its effect aims at reminding the spectator of something, which at the sight of the drama must not escape him lest he should misunderstand it: as a trumpet signal is an invitation for the horse to trot. Lastly, before the drama commenced and in interludes or during tedious passages, doubtful as to dramatic effect, yea, even in its highest moments, there would still be permitted another species of remembrance-music, no longer purely conventional, namely emotional-music, music, as a stimulant to dull or wearied nerves. I am able to distinguish in the so-called dramatic music these two elements only: a conventional rhetoric and remembrance-music, and a sensational music with an effect essentially physical: and thus it vacillates between the noise of the drum and the signal-horn, like the mood of the warrior who goes into the battle. But now the mind, regaling itself on pure music and educated through comparison, demands a masquerade for those two wrong tendencies of music; "Remembrance" and "Emotion" are to be played, but in good music, which must be in itself enjoyable, yea, valuable; what despair for the dramatic musician, who must mask the big drum by good music, which, however, must nevertheless have no purely musical, but only a stimulating effect! And now comes the great Philistine public nodding its thousand heads and enjoys this "dramatic music" which is ever ashamed of itself, enjoys it to the very last morsel, without perceiving anything of its shame and embarrassment. Rather the public feels its skin agreeably tickled, for indeed homage is being rendered in all forms and ways to the public! To the pleasure-hunting, dull-eyed sensualist, who needs excitement, to the conceited "educated person" who has accustomed himself to good drama and good music as to good food, without after all making much out of it, to the forgetful and absent-minded egoist, who must be led back to the work of art with force and with signal-horns because selfish plans continually pass through his mind aiming at gain or pleasure. Woe-begone dramatic musicians! "Draw near and view your Patrons' faces! The half are coarse, the half are cold."[1] "Why should you rack, poor foolish Bards, for ends like these the gracious Muses?"[2] And that the muses are tormented, even tortured and flayed, these veracious miserable ones do not themselves deny!

We had assumed a passionate drama, carrying away the spectator, which even without music would be sure of its effect. I fear that that in it which is "poetry" and not action proper will stand in relation to true poetry as dramatic music to music in general: it will be remembrance-and emotional-poetry. Poetry will serve as a means, in order to recall in a conventional fashion feelings and passions, the expression of which has been found by real poets and has become celebrated, yea, normal with them. Further, this poetry will be expected in dangerous moments to assist the proper "action,"--whether a criminalistic horror-story or an exhibition of witchery mad with shifting the scenes,--and to spread a covering veil over the crudeness of the action itself. Shamefully conscious, that the poetry is only masquerade which cannot bear the light of day, such a "dramatic" rime-jingle clamours now for "dramatic" music, as on the other hand again the poetaster of such dramas is met after one-fourth of the way by the dramatic musician with his talent for the drum and the signal-horn and his shyness of genuine music, trusting in itself and self-sufficient. And now they see one another; and these Apollonian and Dionysean caricatures, this par nobile fratrum, embrace one another!

Footnotes:

1. A reference to Goethe's ballad, The Minstrel, st. 5:

"I sing as sings the bird, whose note The leafy bough is heard on. The song that falters from my throat For me is ample guerdon." TR.

2. A quotation from Goethe's "Faust": Part I., lines 91, 92, and 95, 96.--TR.

HOMER'S CONTEST

Preface to an Unwritten Book (1872)

When one speaks of "humanity" the notion lies at the bottom, that humanity is that which separates and distinguishes man from Nature. But such a distinction does not in reality exist: the "natural" qualities and the properly called "human" ones have grown up inseparably together. Man in his highest and noblest capacities is Nature and bears in himself her awful twofold character. His abilities generally considered dreadful and inhuman are perhaps indeed the fertile soil, out of which alone can grow forth all humanity in emotions, actions and works.

Thus the Greeks, the most humane men of ancient times, have in themselves a trait of cruelty, of tiger-like pleasure in destruction: a trait, which in the grotesquely magnified image of the Hellene, in Alexander the Great, is very plainly visible, which, however, in their whole history, as well as in their mythology, must terrify us who meet them with the emasculate idea of modern humanity. When Alexander has the feet of Batis, the brave defender of Gaza, bored through, and binds the living body to his chariot in order to drag him about exposed to the scorn of his soldiers, that is a sickening caricature of Achilles, who at night ill-uses Hector's corpse by a similar trailing; but even this trait has for us something offensive, something which inspires horror. It gives us a peep into the abysses of hatred. With the same sensation perhaps we stand before the bloody and insatiable self-laceration of two Greek parties, as for example in the Corcyrean revolution. When the victor, in a fight of the cities, according to the law of warfare, executes the whole male population and sells all the women and children into slavery, we see, in the sanction of such a law, that the Greek deemed it a positive necessity to allow his hatred to break forth unimpeded; in such moments the compressed and swollen feeling relieved itself; the tiger bounded forth, a voluptuous cruelty shone out of his fearful eye. Why had the Greek sculptor to represent again and again war and fights in innumerable repetitions, extended human bodies whose sinews are tightened through hatred or through the recklessness of triumph, fighters wounded and writhing with pain, or the dying with the last rattle in their throat? Why did the whole Greek world exult in the fighting scenes of the "Iliad"? I am afraid, we do not understand them enough in "Greek fashion," and that we should even shudder, if for once we did understand them thus.

But what lies, as the mother-womb of the Hellenic, behind the Homeric world? In the latter, by the extremely artistic definiteness, and the calm and purity of the lines we are already lifted far above the purely material amalgamation: its colours, by an artistic deception, appear lighter, milder, warmer; its men, in this coloured, warm illumination, appear better and more sympathetic--but where do we look, if, no longer guided and protected by Homer's hand, we step backwards into the pre-Homeric world? Only into night and horror, into the products of a fancy accustomed to the horrible. What earthly existence is reflected in the loathsome-awful theogonian lore: a life swayed only by the children of the night, strife, amorous desires, deception, age and death. Let us imagine the suffocating atmosphere of Hesiod's poem, still thickened and darkened and without all the mitigations and purifications, which poured over Hellas from Delphi and the numerous seats of the gods! If we mix this thickened Boeotian air with the grim voluptuousness of the Etruscans, then such a reality would extort from us a world of myths within which Uranos, Kronos and Zeus and the struggles of the Titans would appear as a relief. Combat in this brooding atmosphere is salvation and safety; the cruelty of victory is the summit of life's glories. And just as in truth the idea of Greek law has developed from murder and expiation of murder, so also nobler Civilisation takes her first wreath of victory from the altar of the expiation of murder. Behind that bloody age stretches a wave-furrow deep into Hellenic history. The names of Orpheus, of Musæus, and their cults indicate to what consequences the uninterrupted sight of a world of warfare and cruelty led--to the loathing of existence, to the conception of this existence as a punishment to be borne to the end, to the belief in the identity of existence and indebtedness. But these particular conclusions are not specifically Hellenic; through them Greece comes into contact with India and the Orient generally. The Hellenic genius had ready yet another answer to the question: what does a life of fighting and of victory mean? and gives this answer in the whole breadth of Greek history.

In order to understand the latter we must start from the fact that the Greek genius admitted the existing fearful impulse, and deemed it justified; whereas in the Orphic phase of thought was contained the belief that life with such an impulse as its root would not be worth living. Strife and the pleasure of victory were acknowledged; and nothing separates the Greek world more from ours than the colouring, derived hence, of some ethical ideas, e.g., of Eris and of Envy.

When the traveller Pausanius during his wanderings through Greece visited the Helicon, a very old copy of the first didactic poem of the Greeks, "The Works and Days" of Hesiod, was shown to him, inscribed upon plates of lead and severely damaged by time and weather. However he recognised this much, that, unlike the usual copies, it had not at its head that little hymnus on Zeus, but began at once with the declaration: "Two Eris-goddesses are on earth." This is one of the most noteworthy Hellenic thoughts and worthy to be impressed on the new-comer immediately at the entrance-gate of Greek ethics. "One would like to praise the one Eris, just as much as to blame the other, if one uses one's reason. For these two goddesses have quite different dispositions. For the one, the cruel one, furthers the evil war and feud! No mortal likes her, but under the yoke of need one pays honour to the burdensome Eris, according to the decree of the immortals. She, as the elder, gave birth to black night. Zeus the high-ruling one, however, placed the other Eris upon the roots of the earth and among men as a much better one. She urges even the unskilled man to work, and if one who lacks property beholds another who is rich, then he hastens to sow in similar fashion and to plant and to put his house in order; the neighbour vies with the neighbour who strives after fortune. Good is this Eris to men. The potter also has a grudge against the potter, and the carpenter against the carpenter; the beggar envies the beggar, and the singer the singer."

The two last verses which treat of the odium figulinum appear to our scholars to be incomprehensible in this place. According to their judgment the predicates: "grudge" and "envy" fit only the nature of the evil Eris, and for this reason they do not hesitate to designate these verses as spurious or thrown by chance into this place. For that judgment however a system of Ethics other than the Hellenic must have inspired these scholars unawares; for in these verses to the good Eris Aristotle finds no offence. And not only Aristotle but the whole Greek antiquity thinks of spite and envy otherwise than we do and agrees with Hesiod, who first designates as an evil one that Eris who leads men against one another to a hostile war of extermination, and secondly praises another Eris as the good one, who as jealousy, spite, envy, incites men to activity but not to the action of war to the knife but to the action of contest. The Greek is envious and conceives of this quality not as a blemish, but as the effect of a beneficent deity. What a gulf of ethical judgment between us and him? Because he is envious he also feels, with every superfluity of honour, riches, splendour and fortune, the envious eye of a god resting on himself, and he fears this envy; in this case the latter reminds him of the transitoriness of every human lot; he dreads his very happiness and, sacrificing the best of it, he bows before the divine envy. This conception does not perhaps estrange him from his gods; their significance on the contrary is expressed by the thought that with them man in whose soul jealousy is enkindled against every other living being, is never allowed to venture into contest. In the fight of Thamyris with the Muses, of Marsyas with Apollo, in the heart-moving fate of Niobe appears the horrible opposition of the two powers, who must never fight with one another, man and god.

The greater and more sublime however a Greek is, the brighter in him appears the ambitious flame, devouring everybody who runs with him on the same track. Aristotle once made a list of such contests on a large scale; among them is the most striking instance how even a dead person can still incite a living one to consuming jealousy; thus for example Aristotle designates the relation between the Kolophonian Xenophanes and Homer. We do not understand this attack on the national hero of poetry in all its strength, if we do not imagine, as later on also with Plato, the root of this attack to be the ardent desire to step into the place of the overthrown poet and to inherit his fame. Every great Hellene hands on the torch of the contest; at every great virtue a new light is kindled. If the young Themistocles could not sleep at the thought of the laurels of Miltiades so his early awakened bent released itself only in the long emulation with Aristides in that uniquely noteworthy, purely instinctive genius of his political activity, which Thucydides describes. How characteristic are both question and answer, when a notable opponent of Pericles is asked, whether he or Pericles was the better wrestler in the city, and he gives the answer: "Even if I throw him down he denies that he has fallen, attains his purpose and convinces those who saw him fall."

If one wants to see that sentiment unashamed in its naïve expressions, the sentiment as to the necessity of contest lest the State's welfare be threatened, one should think of the original meaning of Ostracism, as for example the Ephesians pronounced it at the banishment of Hermodor. "Among us nobody shall be the best; if however someone is the best, then let him be so elsewhere and among others." Why should not someone be the best? Because with that the contest would fail, and the eternal life-basis of the Hellenic State would be endangered. Later on Ostracism receives quite another position with regard to the contest; it is applied, when the danger becomes obvious that one of the great contesting politicians and party-leaders feels himself urged on in the heat of the conflict towards harmful and destructive measures and dubious coups d'état. The original sense of this peculiar institution however is not that of a safety-valve but that of a stimulant. The all-excelling individual was to be removed in order that the contest of forces might re-awaken, a thought which is hostile to the "exclusiveness" of genius in the modern sense but which assumes that in the natural order of things there are always several geniuses which incite one another to action, as much also as they hold one another within the bounds of moderation. That is the kernel of the Hellenic contest-conception: it abominates autocracy, and fears its dangers; it desires as a preventive against the genius--a second genius.

Every natural gift must develop itself by contest. Thus the Hellenic national pedagogy demands, whereas modern educators fear nothing as much as, the unchaining of the so-called ambition. Here one fears selfishness as the "evil in itself"--with the exception of the Jesuits, who agree with the Ancients and who, possibly, for that reason, are the most efficient educators of our time. They seem to believe that Selfishness, i.e., the individual element is only the most powerful agens but that it obtains its character as "good" and "evil" essentially from the aims towards which it strives. To the Ancients however the aim of the agonistic education was the welfare of the whole, of the civic society. Every Athenian for instance was to cultivate his Ego in contest, so far that it should be of the highest service to Athens and should do the least harm. It was not unmeasured and immeasurable as modern ambition generally is; the youth thought of the welfare of his native town when he vied with others in running, throwing or singing; it was her glory that he wanted to increase with his own; it was to his town's gods that he dedicated the wreaths which the umpires as a mark of honour set upon his head. Every Greek from childhood felt within himself the burning wish to be in the contest of the towns an instrument for the welfare of his own town; in this his selfishness was kindled into flame, by this his selfishness was bridled and restricted. Therefore the individuals in antiquity were freer, because their aims were nearer and more tangible. Modern man, on the contrary, is everywhere hampered by infinity, like the fleet-footed Achilles in the allegory of the Eleate Zeno: infinity impedes him, he does not even overtake the tortoise.

But as the youths to be educated were brought up struggling against one another, so their educators were in turn in emulation amongst themselves. Distrustfully jealous, the great musical masters, Pindar and Simonides, stepped side by side; in rivalry the sophist, the higher teacher of antiquity meets his fellow-sophist; even the most universal kind of instruction, through the drama, was imparted to the people only under the form of an enormous wrestling of the great musical and dramatic artists. How wonderful! "And even the artist has a grudge against the artist!" And the modern man dislikes in an artist nothing so much as the personal battle-feeling, whereas the Greek recognises the artist only in such a personal struggle. There where the modern suspects weakness of the work of art, the Hellene seeks the source of his highest strength! That, which by way of example in Plato is of special artistic importance in his dialogues, is usually the result of an emulation with the art of the orators, of the sophists, of the dramatists of his time, invented deliberately in order that at the end he could say: "Behold, I can also do what my great rivals can; yea I can do it even better than they. No Protagoras has composed such beautiful myths as I, no dramatist such a spirited and fascinating whole as the Symposion, no orator penned such an oration as I put up in the Georgias--and now I reject all that together and condemn all imitative art! Only the contest made me a poet, a sophist, an orator!" What a problem unfolds itself there before us, if we ask about the relationship between the contest and the conception of the work of art!--If on the other hand we remove the contest from Greek life, then we look at once into the pre-Homeric abyss of horrible savagery, hatred, and pleasure in destruction. This phenomenon alas! shows itself frequently when a great personality was, owing to an enormously brilliant deed, suddenly withdrawn from the contest and became hors de concours according to his, and his fellow-citizens' judgment. Almost without exception the effect is awful; and if one usually draws from these consequences the conclusion that the Greek was unable to bear glory and fortune, one should say more exactly that he was unable to bear fame without further struggle, and fortune at the end of the contest. There is no more distinct instance than the fate of Miltiades. Placed upon a solitary height and lifted far above every fellow-combatant through his incomparable success at Marathon, he feels a low thirsting for revenge awakened within himself against a citizen of Para, with whom he had been at enmity long ago. To satisfy his desire he misuses reputation, the public exchequer and civic honour and disgraces himself. Conscious of his ill-success he falls into unworthy machinations. He forms a clandestine and godless connection with Timo a priestess of Demeter, and enters at night the sacred temple, from which every man was excluded. After he has leapt over the wall and comes ever nearer the shrine of the goddess, the dreadful horror of a panic-like terror suddenly seizes him; almost prostrate and unconscious he feels himself driven back and leaping the wall once more, he falls down paralysed and severely injured. The siege must be raised and a disgraceful death impresses its seal upon a brilliant heroic career, in order to darken it for all posterity. After the battle at Marathon the envy of the celestials has caught him. And this divine envy breaks into flames when it beholds man without rival, without opponent, on the solitary height of glory. He now has beside him only the gods--and therefore he has them against him. These however betray him into a deed of the Hybris, and under it he collapses.

Let us well observe that just as Miltiades perishes so the noblest Greek States perish when they, by merit and fortune, have arrived from the racecourse at the temple of Nike. Athens, which had destroyed the independence of her allies and avenged with severity the rebellions of her subjected foes, Sparta, which after the battle of Ægospotamoi used her preponderance over Hellas in a still harsher and more cruel fashion, both these, as in the case of Miltiades, brought about their ruin through deeds of the Hybris, as a proof that without envy, jealousy, and contesting ambition the Hellenic State like the Hellenic man degenerates. He becomes bad and cruel, thirsting for revenge, and godless; in short, he becomes "pre-Homeric"--and then it needs only a panic in order to bring about his fall and to crush him. Sparta and Athens surrender to Persia, as Themistocles and Alcibiades have done; they betray Hellenism after they have given up the noblest Hellenic fundamental thought, the contest, and Alexander, the coarsened copy and abbreviation of Greek history, now invents the cosmopolitan Hellene, and the so-called "Hellenism."

THE RELATION OF SCHOPENHAUER'S PHILOSOPHY TO A GERMAN CULTURE

Preface to an Unwritten Book (1872)

In dear vile Germany culture now lies so decayed in the streets, jealousy of all that is great rules so shamelessly, and the general tumult of those who race for "Fortune" resounds so deafeningly, that one must have a strong faith, almost in the sense of credo quia absurdum est, in order to hope still for a growing Culture, and above all--in opposition to the press with her "public opinion"--to be able to work by public teaching. With violence must those, in whose hearts lies the immortal care for the people, free themselves from all the inrushing impressions of that which is just now actual and valid, and evoke the appearance of reckoning them indifferent things. They must appear so, because they want to think, and because a loathsome sight and a confused noise, perhaps even mixed with the trumpet-flourishes of war-glory, disturb their thinking, and above all, because they want to believe in the German character and because with this faith they would lose their strength. Do not find fault with these believers if they look from their distant aloofness and from the heights towards their Promised Land! They fear those experiences, to which the kindly disposed foreigner surrenders himself, when he lives among the Germans, and must be surprised how little German life corresponds to those great individuals, works and actions, which, in his kind disposition he has learned to revere as the true German character. Where the German cannot lift himself into the sublime he makes an impression less than the mediocre. Even the celebrated German scholarship, in which a number of the most useful domestic and homely virtues such as faithfulness, self-restriction, industry, moderation, cleanliness appear transposed into a purer atmosphere and, as it were, transfigured, is by no means the result of these virtues; looked at closely, the motive urging to unlimited knowledge appears in Germany much more like a defect, a gap, than an abundance of forces, it looks almost like the consequence of a needy formless atrophied life and even like a flight from the moral narrow-mindedness and malice to which the German without such diversions is subjected, and which also in spite of that scholarship, yea still within scholarship itself, often break forth. As the true virtuosi of philistinism the Germans are at home in narrowness of life, discerning and judging; if any one will carry them above themselves into the sublime, then they make themselves heavy as lead, and as such lead-weights they hang to their truly great men, in order to pull them down out of the ether to the level of their own necessitous indigence. Perhaps this Philistine homeliness may be only the degeneration of a genuine German virtue--a profound submersion into the detail, the minute, the nearest and into the mysteries of the individual--but this virtue grown mouldy is now worse than the most open vice, especially since one has now become conscious, with gladness of the heart, of this quality, even to literary self-glorification. Now the "Educated" among the proverbially so cultured Germans and the "Philistines" among the, as everybody knows, so uncultured Germans shake hands in public and agree with one another concerning the way in which henceforth one will have to write, compose poetry, paint, make music and even philosophise, yea--rule, so as neither to stand too much aloof from the culture of the one, nor to give offence to the "homeliness" of the other. This they call now "The German Culture of our times." Well, it is only necessary to inquire after the characteristic by which that "educated" person is to be recognised; now that we know that his foster-brother, the German Philistine, makes himself known as such to all the world, without bashfulness, as it were, after innocence is lost.

The educated person nowadays is educated above all "historically," by his historic consciousness he saves himself from the sublime in which the Philistine succeeds by his "homeliness." No longer that enthusiasm which history inspires--as Goethe was allowed to suppose--but just the blunting of all enthusiasm is now the goal of these admirers of the nil admirari, when they try to conceive everything historically; to them however we should exclaim: Ye are the fools of all centuries! History will make to you only those confessions, which you are worthy to receive. The world has been at all times full of trivialities and nonentities; to your historic hankering just these and only these unveil themselves. By your thousands you may pounce upon an epoch--you will afterwards hunger as before and be allowed to boast of your sort of starved soundness. Illam ipsam quam iactant sanitatem non firmitate sed iciunio consequuntur. (Dialogus de oratoribus, cap. 25.) History has not thought fit to tell you anything that is essential, but scorning and invisible she stood by your side, slipping into this one's hand some state proceedings, into that one's an ambassadorial report, into another's a date or an etymology or a pragmatic cobweb. Do you really believe yourself able to reckon up history like an addition sum, and do you consider your common intellect and your mathematical education good enough for that? How it must vex you to hear, that others narrate things, out of the best known periods, which you will never conceive, never!

If now to this "education," calling itself historic but destitute of enthusiasm, and to the hostile Philistine activity, foaming with rage against all that is great, is added that third brutal and excited company of those who race after "Fortune"--then that in summa results in such a confused shrieking and such a limb-dislocating turmoil that the thinker with stopped-up ears and blindfolded eyes flees into the most solitary wilderness,--where he may see, what those never will see, where he must hear sounds which rise to him out of all the depths of nature and come down to him from the stars. Here he confers with the great problems floating towards him, whose voices of course sound just as comfortless-awful, as unhistoric-eternal. The feeble person flees back from their cold breath, and the calculating one runs right through them without perceiving them. They deal worst, however, with the "educated man" who at times bestows great pains upon them. To him these phantoms transform themselves into conceptual cobwebs and hollow sound-figures. Grasping after them he imagines he has philosophy; in order to search for them he climbs about in the so-called history of philosophy--and when at last he has collected and piled up quite a cloud of such abstractions and stereotyped patterns, then it may happen to him that a real thinker crosses his path and--puffs them away. What a desperate annoyance indeed to meddle with philosophy as an "educated person"! From time to time it is true it appears to him as if the impossible connection of philosophy with that which nowadays gives itself airs as "German Culture" has become possible; some mongrel dallies and ogles between the two spheres and confuses fantasy on this side and on the other. Meanwhile however one piece of advice is to be given to the Germans, if they do not wish to let themselves be confused. They may put to themselves the question about everything that they now call Culture: is this the hoped-for German Culture, so serious and creative, so redeeming for the German mind, so purifying for the German virtues that their only philosopher in this century, Arthur Schopenhauer, should have to espouse its cause?

Here you have the philosopher--now search for the Culture proper to him! And if you are able to divine what kind of culture that would have to be, which would correspond to such a philosopher, then you have, in this divination, already passed sentence on all your culture and on yourselves!

PHILOSOPHY DURING THE TRAGIC AGE OF THE GREEKS

(1873)

PREFACE

(Probably 1874)

If we know the aims of men who are strangers to us, it is sufficient for us to approve of or condemn them as wholes. Those who stand nearer to us we judge according to the means by which they further their aims; we often disapprove of their aims, but love them for the sake of their means and the style of their volition. Now philosophical systems are absolutely true only to their founders, to all later philosophers they are usually one big mistake, and to feebler minds a sum of mistakes and truths; at any rate if regarded as highest aim they are an error, and in so far reprehensible. Therefore many disapprove of every philosopher, because his aim is not theirs; they are those whom I called "strangers to us." Whoever on the contrary finds any pleasure at all in great men finds pleasure also in such systems, be they ever so erroneous, for they all have in them one point which is irrefutable, a personal touch, and colour; one can use them in order to form a picture of the philosopher, just as from a plant growing in a certain place one can form conclusions as to the soil. That mode of life, of viewing human affairs at any rate, has existed once and is therefore possible; the "system" is the growth in this soil or at least a part of this system....

I narrate the history of those philosophers simplified: I shall bring into relief only that point in every system which is a little bit of personality, and belongs to that which is irrefutable, and indiscussable, which history has to preserve: it is a first attempt to regain and recreate those natures by comparison, and to let the polyphony of Greek nature at least resound once again: the task is, to bring to light that which we must always love and revere and of which no later knowledge can rob us: the great man.

LATER PREFACE

(Towards the end of 1879)

This attempt to relate the history of the earlier Greek philosophers distinguishes itself from similar attempts by its brevity. This has been accomplished by mentioning but a small number of the doctrines of every philosopher, i.e., by incompleteness. Those doctrines, however, have been selected in which the personal element of the philosopher re-echoes most strongly; whereas a complete enumeration of all possible propositions handed down to us--as is the custom in text-books--merely brings about one thing, the absolute silencing of the personal element. It is through this that those records become so tedious; for in systems which have been refuted it is only this personal element that can still interest us, for this alone is eternally irrefutable. It is possible to shape the picture of a man out of three anecdotes. I endeavour to bring into relief three anecdotes out of every system and abandon the remainder.

1

There are opponents of philosophy, and one does well to listen to them; especially if they dissuade the distempered heads of Germans from metaphysics and on the other hand preach to them purification through the Physis, as Goethe did, or healing through Music, as Wagner. The physicians of the people condemn philosophy; he, therefore, who wants to justify it, must show to what purpose healthy nations use and have used philosophy. If he can show that, perhaps even the sick people will benefit by learning why philosophy is harmful just to them. There are indeed good instances of a health which can exist without any philosophy or with quite a moderate, almost a toying use of it; thus the

Romans at their best period lived without philosophy. But where is to be found the instance of a nation becoming diseased whom philosophy had restored to health? Whenever philosophy showed itself helping, saving, prophylactic, it was with healthy people; it made sick people still more ill. If ever a nation was disintegrated and but loosely connected with the individuals, never has philosophy bound these individuals closer to the whole. If ever an individual was willing to stand aside and plant around himself the hedge of self-sufficiency, philosophy was always ready to isolate him still more and to destroy him through isolation. She is dangerous where she is not in her full right, and it is only the health of a nation but not that of every nation which gives her this right.

Let us now look around for the highest authority as to what constitutes the health of a nation. I he Greeks, as the truly healthy nation, have justified philosophy once for all by having philosophised; and that indeed more than all other nations. They could not even stop at the right time, for still in their withered age they comported themselves as heated notaries of philosophy, although they understood by it only the pious sophistries and the sacrosanct hair-splittings of Christian dogmatics. They themselves have much lessened their merit for barbarian posterity by not being able to stop at the right time, because that posterity in its uninstructed and impetuous youth necessarily became entangled in those artfully woven nets and ropes.

On the contrary, the Greek knew how to begin at the right time, and this lesson, when one ought to begin philosophising, they teach more distinctly than any other nation. For it should not be begun when trouble comes as perhaps some presume who derive philosophy from moroseness; no, but in good fortune, in mature manhood, out of the midst of the fervent serenity of a brave and victorious man's estate. The fact that the Greeks philosophised at that time throws light on the nature of philosophy and her task as well as on the nature of the Greeks themselves. Had they at that time been such commonsense and precocious experts and gayards as the learned Philistine of our days perhaps imagines, or had their life been only a state of voluptuous soaring, chiming, breathing and feeling, as the unlearned visionary is pleased to assume, then the spring of philosophy would not have come to light among them. At the best there would have come forth a brook soon trickling away in the sand or evaporating into fogs, but never that broad river flowing forth with the proud beat of its waves, the river which we know as Greek Philosophy.

True, it has been eagerly pointed out how much the Greeks could find and learn abroad, in the Orient, and how many different things they may easily have brought from there. Of course an odd spectacle resulted, when certain scholars brought together the alleged masters from the Orient and the possible disciples from Greece, and exhibited Zarathustra near Heraclitus, the Hindoos near the Eleates, the Egyptians near Empedocles, or even Anaxagoras among the Jews and Pythagoras among the Chinese. In detail little has been determined; but we should in no way object to the general idea, if people did not burden us with the conclusion that therefore Philosophy had only been imported into Greece and was not indigenous to the soil, yea, that she, as something foreign, had possibly ruined rather than improved the Greek. Nothing is more foolish than to swear by the fact that the Greeks had an aboriginal culture; no, they rather absorbed all the culture flourishing among other nations, and they advanced so far, just because they understood how to hurl the spear further from the very spot where another nation had let it rest. They were admirable in the art of learning productively, and so, like them, we ought to learn from our neighbours, with a view to Life not to pedantic knowledge, using everything learnt as a foothold whence to leap high and still higher than our neighbour. The questions as to the beginning of philosophy are quite negligible, for everywhere in the beginning there is the crude, the unformed, the empty and the ugly; and in all things only the higher stages come into consideration. He who in the place of Greek philosophy prefers to concern himself with that of Egypt and Persia, because the latter are perhaps more "original" and certainly older, proceeds just as ill-advisedly as those who cannot be at ease before they have traced back the Greek mythology, so grand and profound, to such physical trivialities as sun, lightning, weather and fog, as its prime origins, and who fondly imagine they have rediscovered for instance in the restricted worship of the one celestial vault among the other Indo-Germans a purer form of religion than the poly-theistic worship of the Greek had been. The road towards the beginning always leads into barbarism, and he who is concerned with the Greeks ought always to keep in mind the fact that the unsubdued thirst for knowledge in itself always barbarises just as much as the hatred of knowledge, and that the Greeks have subdued their inherently insatiable thirst for knowledge by their regard for Life, by an ideal need of Life,--since they wished to live immediately that which they learnt. The Greeks also philosophised as men of culture and with the aims of culture, and therefore saved themselves the trouble of inventing once again the elements of philosophy and knowledge out of some autochthonous conceit, and with a will they at once set themselves to fill out, enhance, raise and purify these elements they had taken over in such a way, that only now in a higher sense and in a purer sphere they became inventors. For they discovered the typical philosopher's genius, and the inventions of all posterity have added nothing essential.

Every nation is put to shame if one points out such a wonderfully idealised company of philosophers as that of the early Greek masters, Thales, Anaximander, Heraclitus, Parmenides,

Anaxagoras, Empedocles, Democritus and Socrates. All those men are integral, entire and self-contained,[1] and hewn out of one stone. Severe necessity exists between their thinking and their character. They are not bound by any convention, because at that time no professional class of philosophers and scholars existed. They all stand before us in magnificent solitude as the only ones who then devoted their life exclusively to knowledge. They all possess the virtuous energy of the Ancients, whereby they excel all the later philosophers in finding their own form and in perfecting it by metamorphosis in its most minute details and general aspect. For they were met by no helpful and facilitating fashion. Thus together they form what Schopenhauer, in opposition to the Republic of Scholars, has called a Republic of Geniuses; one giant calls to another across the arid intervals of ages, and, undisturbed by a wanton, noisy race of dwarfs, creeping about beneath them, the sublime intercourse of spirits continues.

Of this sublime intercourse of spirits I have resolved to relate those items which our modern hardness of hearing might perhaps hear and understand; that means certainly the least of all. It seems to me that those old sages from Thales to Socrates have discussed in that intercourse, although in its most general aspect, everything that constitutes for our contemplation the peculiarly Hellenic. In their intercourse, as already in their personalities, they express distinctly the great features of Greek genius of which the whole of Greek history is a shadowy impression, a hazy copy, which consequently speaks less clearly. If we could rightly interpret the total life of the Greek nation, we should ever find reflected only that picture which in her highest geniuses shines with more resplendent colours. Even the first experience of philosophy on Greek soil, the sanction of the Seven Sages is a distinct and unforgettable line in the picture of the Hellenic. Other nations have their Saints, the Greeks have Sages. Rightly it has been said that a nation is characterised not only by her great men but rather by the manner in which she recognises and honours them. In other ages the philosopher is an accidental solitary wanderer in the most hostile environment, either slinking through or pushing himself through with clenched fists. With the Greek however the philosopher is not accidental; when in the Sixth and Fifth centuries amidst the most frightful dangers and seductions of secularisation he appears and as it were steps forth from the cave of Trophonios into the very midst of luxuriance, the discoverers' happiness, the wealth and the sensuousness of the Greek colonies, then we divine that he comes as a noble warner for the same purpose for which in those centuries Tragedy was born and which the Orphic mysteries in their grotesque hieroglyphics give us to understand. The opinion of those philosophers on Life and Existence altogether means so much more than a modern opinion because they had before themselves Life in a luxuriant perfection, and because with them, unlike us, the sense of the thinker was not muddled by the disunion engendered by the wish for freedom, beauty, fulness of life and the love for truth that only asks: What is the good of Life at all? The mission which the philosopher has to discharge within a real Culture, fashioned in a homogeneous style, cannot be clearly conjectured out of our circumstances and experiences for the simple reason that we have no such culture. No, it is only a Culture like the Greek which can answer the question as to that task of the philosopher, only such a Culture can, as I said before, justify philosophy at all; because such a Culture alone knows and can demonstrate why and how the philosopher is not an accidental, chance wanderer driven now hither, now thither. There is a steely necessity which fetters the philosopher to a true Culture: but what if this Culture does not exist? Then the philosopher is an incalculable and therefore terror-inspiring comet, whereas in the favourable case, he shines as the central star in the solar-system of culture. It is for this reason that the Greeks justify the philosopher, because with them he is no comet.

Footnotes:

1. Cf. Napoleon's word about Goethe: "Voilà un homme!"--TR.

2

After such contemplations it will be accepted without offence if I speak of the pre-Platonic philosophers as of a homogeneous company, and devote this paper to them exclusively. Something quite new begins with Plato; or it might be said with equal justice that in comparison with that Republic of Geniuses from Thales to Socrates, the philosophers since Plato lack something essential.

Whoever wants to express himself unfavourably about those older masters may call them one-sided, and their Epigones, with Plato as head, many-sided. Yet it would be more just and unbiassed to conceive of the latter as philosophic hybrid-characters, of the former as the pure types. Plato himself is the first magnificent hybrid-character, and as such finds expression as well in his philosophy as in his personality. In his ideology are united Socratian, Pythagorean, and Heraclitean elements, and for this reason it is no typically pure phenomenon. As man, too, Plato mingles the features of the royally secluded, all-sufficing Heraclitus, of the melancholy-compassionate and legislatory Pythagoras and of the psycho-expert dialectician Socrates. All later philosophers are such hybrid-characters; wherever something one-sided does come into prominence with them as in the case of the Cynics, it is not type but caricature. Much more important however is the fact that they are founders of sects and that the sects founded by them are all institutions in direct opposition to the Hellenic culture and the unity of its style prevailing up to that time. In their way they seek a redemption, but only for the individuals or at the best for groups of friends and disciples closely connected with them. The activity of the older philosophers tends, although they were unconscious of it, towards a cure and purification on a large scale; the mighty course of Greek culture is not to be stopped; awful dangers are to be removed out of the way of its current; the philosopher protects and defends his native country. Now, since Plato, he is in exile and conspires against his fatherland.

It is a real misfortune that so very little of those older philosophic masters has come down to us and that all complete works of theirs are withheld from us. Involuntarily, on account of that loss, we measure them according to wrong standards and allow ourselves to be influenced unfavourably towards them by the mere accidental fact that Plato and Aristotle never lacked appreciators and copyists. Some people presuppose a special providence for books, a fatum libellorum; such a providence however would at any rate be a very malicious one if it deemed it wise to withhold from us the works of Heraclitus, Empedocles' wonderful poem, and the writings of Democritus, whom the ancients put on a par with Plato, whom he even excels as far as ingenuity goes, and as a substitute put into our hand Stoics, Epicureans and Cicero. Probably the most sublime part of Greek thought and its expression in words is lost to us; a fate which will not surprise the man who remembers the misfortunes of Scotus Erigena or of Pascal, and who considers that even in this enlightened century the first edition of Schopenhauer's "The World As Will And Idea" became waste-paper. If somebody will presuppose a special fatalistic power with respect to such things he may do so and say with Goethe: "Let no one complain about and grumble at things vile and mean, they are the real rulers,--however much this be gainsaid!" In particular they are more powerful than the power of truth. Mankind very rarely produces a good book in which with daring freedom is intonated the battle-song of truth, the song of philosophic heroism; and yet whether it is to live a century longer or to crumble and moulder into dust and ashes, depends on the most miserable accidents, on the sudden mental eclipse of men's heads, on superstitious convulsions and antipathies, finally on fingers not too fond of writing or even on eroding bookworms and rainy weather. But we will not lament but rather take the advice of the reproving and consolatory words which Hamann addresses to scholars who lament over lost works. "Would not the artist who succeeded in throwing a lentil through the eye of a needle have sufficient, with a bushel of lentils, to practise his acquired skill? One would like to put this question to all scholars who do not know how to use the works of the Ancients any better than that man used his lentils." It might be added in our case that not one more word, anecdote, or date needed to be transmitted to us than has been transmitted, indeed that even much less might have been preserved for us and yet we should have been able to establish the general doctrine that the Greeks justify philosophy.

A time which suffers from the so-called "general education" but has no culture and no unity of style in her life hardly knows what to do with philosophy, even if the latter were proclaimed by the very Genius of Truth in the streets and market-places. She rather remains at such a time the learned monologue of the solitary rambler, the accidental booty of the individual, the hidden closet-secret or the innocuous chatter between academic senility and childhood. Nobody dare venture to fulfil in himself the law of philosophy, nobody lives philosophically, with that simple manly faith which compelled an Ancient, wherever he was, whatever he did, to deport himself as a Stoic, when he had once pledged his faith to the Stoa. All modern philosophising is limited politically and regulated by the police to learned semblance. Thanks to governments, churches, academies, customs, fashions, and the cowardice of man, it never gets beyond the sigh: "If only!..." or beyond the knowledge: "Once upon a time there was..." Philosophy is without rights; therefore modern man, if he were at all courageous and conscientious, ought to condemn her and perhaps banish her with words similar to those by which Plato banished the tragic poets from his State. Of course there would be left a reply for her, as there remained to those poets against Plato. If one once compelled her to speak out she might say perhaps: "Miserable Nation! Is it my fault if among you I am on the tramp, like a fortune teller through the land, and must hide and disguise myself, as if I were a great sinner and ye my judges? Just look at my sister, Art! It is with her as with me; we have been cast adrift among the Barbarians and no longer know how to save ourselves. Here we are lacking, it is true, every good right; but the judges before whom we find justice judge you also and will tell you: First acquire a culture; then you shall experience what Philosophy can and will do."--

3

Greek philosophy seems to begin with a preposterous fancy, with the proposition that water is the origin and mother-womb of all things. Is it really necessary to stop there and become serious? Yes, and for three reasons: Firstly, because the proposition does enunciate something about the origin of things; secondly, because it does so without figure and fable; thirdly and lastly, because in it is contained, although only in the chrysalis state, the idea: Everything is one. The first mentioned reason leaves Thales still in the company of religious and superstitious people, the second however takes him out of this company and shows him to us as a natural philosopher, but by virtue of the third, Thales becomes the first Greek philosopher. If he had said: "Out of water earth is evolved," we should only have a scientific hypothesis; a false one, though nevertheless difficult to refute. But he went beyond the scientific. In his presentation of this concept of unity through the hypothesis of water, Thales has not surmounted the low level of the physical discernments of his time, but at the best overleapt them. The deficient and unorganised observations of an empiric nature which Thales had made as to the occurrence and transformations of water, or to be more exact, of the Moist, would not in the least have made possible or even suggested such an immense generalisation. That which drove him to this generalisation was a metaphysical dogma, which had its origin in a mystic intuition and which together with the ever renewed endeavours to express it better, we find in all philosophies,--the proposition: Everything is one!

How despotically such a faith deals with all empiricism is worthy of note; with Thales especially one can learn how Philosophy has behaved at all times, when she wanted to get beyond the hedges of experience to her magically attracting goal. On light supports she leaps in advance; hope and divination wing her feet. Calculating reason too, clumsily pants after her and seeks better supports in its attempt to reach that alluring goal, at which its divine companion has already arrived. One sees in imagination two wanderers by a wild forest-stream which carries with it rolling stones; the one, light-footed, leaps over it using the stones and swinging himself upon them ever further and further, though they precipitously sink into the depths behind him. The other stands helpless there most of the time; he has first to build a pathway which will bear his heavy, weary step; sometimes that cannot be done and then no god will help him across the stream. What therefore carries philosophical thinking so quickly to its goal? Does it distinguish itself from calculating and measuring thought only by its more rapid flight through large spaces? No, for a strange illogical power wings the foot of philosophical thinking; and this power is Fancy. Lifted by the latter, philosophical thinking leaps from possibility to possibility, and these for the time being are taken as certainties; and now and then even whilst on the wing it gets hold of certainties. An ingenious presentiment shows them to the flier; demonstrable certainties are divined at a distance to be at this point. Especially powerful is the strength of Fancy in the lightning-like seizing and illuminating of similarities; afterwards reflection applies its standards and models and seeks to substitute the similarities by equalities, that which was seen side by side by causalities. But though this should never be possible, even in the case of Thales the indemonstrable philosophising has yet its value; although all supports are broken when Logic and the rigidity of Empiricism want to get across to the proposition: Everything is water; yet still there is always, after the demolition of the scientific edifice, a remainder, and in this very remainder lies a moving force and as it were the hope of future fertility.

Of course I do not mean that the thought in any restriction or attenuation, or as allegory, still retains some kind of "truth"; as if, for instance, one might imagine the creating artist standing near a waterfall, and seeing in the forms which leap towards him, an artistically prefiguring game of the water with human and animal bodies, masks, plants, rocks, nymphs, griffins, and with all existing types in general, so that to him the proposition: Everything is water, is confirmed. The thought of Thales has rather its value--even after the perception of its indemonstrableness--in the very fact, that it was meant unmythically and unallegorically. The Greeks among whom Thales became so suddenly conspicuous were the anti-type of all realists by only believing essentially in the reality of men and gods, and by contemplating the whole of nature as if it were only a disguise, masquerade and metamorphosis of these god-men. Man was to them the truth, and essence of things; everything else mere phenomenon and deceiving play. For that very reason they experienced incredible difficulty in conceiving of ideas as ideas. Whilst with the moderns the most personal item sublimates itself into abstractions, with them the most abstract notions became personified. Thales, however, said, "Not man but water is the reality of things "; he began to believe in nature, in so far that he at least believed in water. As a mathematician and astronomer he had grown cold towards everything mythical and allegorical, and even if he did not succeed in becoming disillusioned as to the pure abstraction, Everything is one, and although he left off at a physical expression he was nevertheless among the Greeks of his time a surprising rarity. Perhaps the exceedingly conspicuous Orpheans possessed in a still higher degree than he the faculty of conceiving abstractions and of thinking unplastically; only they did not succeed in expressing these abstractions except in the form of the allegory. Also Pherecydes of Syrus who is a contemporary of

Thales and akin to him in many physical conceptions hovers with the expression of the latter in that middle region where Allegory is wedded to Mythos, so that he dares, for example, to compare the earth with a winged oak, which hangs in the air with spread pinions and which Zeus bedecks, after the defeat of Kronos, with a magnificent robe of honour, into which with his own hands Zeus embroiders lands, water and rivers. In contrast with such gloomy allegorical philosophising scarcely to be translated into the realm of the comprehensible, Thales' are the works of a creative master who began to look into Nature's depths without fantastic fabling. If as it is true he used Science and the demonstrable but soon out-leapt them, then this likewise is a typical characteristic of the philosophical genius. The Greek word which designates the Sage belongs etymologically to sapio, I taste, sapiens, the tasting one, sisyphos, the man of the most delicate taste; the peculiar art of the philosopher therefore consists, according to the opinion of the people, in a delicate selective judgment by taste, by discernment, by significant differentiation. He is not prudent, if one calls him prudent, who in his own affairs finds out the good; Aristotle rightly says: "That which Thales and Anaxagoras know, people will call unusual, astounding, difficult, divine but--useless, since human possessions were of no concern to those two." Through thus selecting and precipitating the unusual, astounding, difficult, and divine, Philosophy marks the boundary-lines dividing her from Science in the same way as she does it from Prudence by the emphasising of the useless. Science without thus selecting, without such delicate taste, pounces upon everything knowable, in the blind covetousness to know all at any price; philosophical thinking however is always on the track of the things worth knowing, on the track of the great and most important discernments. Now the idea of greatness is changeable, as well in the moral as in the æsthetic realm, thus Philosophy begins with a legislation with respect to greatness, she becomes a Nomenclator. "That is great," she says, and therewith she raises man above the blind, untamed covetousness of his thirst for knowledge. By the idea of greatness she assuages this thirst: and it is chiefly by this, that she contemplates the greatest discernment, that of the essence and kernel of things, as attainable and attained. When Thales says, "Everything is water," man is startled up out of his worm-like mauling of and crawling about among the individual sciences; he divines the last solution of things and masters through this divination the common perplexity of the lower grades of knowledge. The philosopher tries to make the total-chord of the universe re-echo within himself and then to project it into ideas outside himself: whilst he is contemplative like the creating artist, sympathetic like the religionist, looking out for ends and causalities like the scientific man, whilst he feels himself swell up to the macrocosm, he still retains the circumspection to contemplate himself coldly as the reflex of the world; he retains that cool-headedness, which the dramatic artist possesses, when he transforms himself into other bodies, speaks out of them, and yet knows how to project this transformation outside himself into written verses. What the verse is to the poet, dialectic thinking is to the philosopher; he snatches at it in order to hold fast his enchantment, in order to petrify it. And just as words and verse to the dramatist are only stammerings in a foreign language, to tell in it what he lived, what he saw, and what he can directly promulgate by gesture and music only, thus the expression of every deep philosophical intuition by means of dialectics and scientific reflection is, it is true, on the one hand the only means to communicate what has been seen, but on the other hand it is a paltry means, and at the bottom a metaphorical, absolutely inexact translation into a different sphere and language. Thus Thales saw the Unity of the "Existent," and when he wanted to communicate this idea he talked of water.

4

Whilst the general type of the philosopher in the picture of Thales is set off rather hazily, the picture of his great successor already speaks much more distinctly to us. Anaximander of Milet, the first philosophical author of the Ancients, writes in the very way that the typical philosopher will always write as long as he is not alienated from ingenuousness and naïveté by odd claims: in a grand lapidarian style of writing, sentence for sentence ... a witness of a new inspiration, and an expression of the sojourning in sublime contemplations. The thought and its form are milestones on the path towards the highest wisdom. With such a lapidarian emphasis Anaximander once said: "Whence things originated, thither, according to necessity, they must return and perish; for they must pay penalty and be judged for their injustices according to the order of time." Enigmatical utterance of a true pessimist, oracular inscription on the boundary-stone of Greek philosophy, how shall we explain thee?

The only serious moralist of our century in the Parergis (Vol. ii., chap. 12, "Additional Remarks on The Doctrine about the Suffering in the World, Appendix of Corresponding Passages") urges on us a similar contemplation: "The right standard by which to judge every human being is that he really is a being who ought not to exist at all, but who is expiating his existence by manifold forms of suffering and death:--What can one expect from such a being? Are we not all sinners condemned to death? We expiate our birth firstly by our life and secondly by our death." He who in the physiognomy of our universal human lot reads this doctrine and already recognises the fundamental bad quality of every human life, in the fact that none can stand a very close and careful contemplation--although our time, accustomed to the biographical epidemic, seems to think otherwise and more loftily about the dignity of man; he who, like Schopenhauer, on "the heights of the Indian breezes" has heard the sacred word about the moral value of existence, will be kept with difficulty from making an extremely anthropomorphic metaphor and from generalizing that melancholy doctrine--at first only limited to human life--and applying it by transmission to the general character of all existence. It may not be very logical, it is however at any rate very human and moreover quite in harmony with the philosophical leaping described above, now with Anaximander to consider all Becoming as a punishable emancipation from eternal "Being," as a wrong that is to be atoned for by destruction. Everything that has once come into existence also perishes, whether we think of human life or of water or of heat and cold; everywhere where definite qualities are to be noticed, we are allowed to prophesy the extinction of these qualities--according to the all-embracing proof of experience. Thus a being that possesses definite qualities and consists of them, can never be the origin and principle of things; the veritable ens, the "Existent," Anaximander concluded, cannot possess any definite qualities, otherwise, like all other things, it would necessarily have originated and perished. In order that Becoming may not cease, the Primordial-being must be indefinite. The immortality and eternity of the Primordial-being lies not in an infiniteness and inexhaustibility--as usually the expounders of Anaximander presuppose--but in this, that it lacks the definite qualities which lead to destruction, for which reason it bears also its name: The Indefinite. The thus labelled Primordial-being is superior to all Becoming and for this very reason it guarantees the eternity and unimpeded course of Becoming. This last unity in that Indefinite, the mother-womb of all things, can, it is true, be designated only negatively by man, as something to which no predicate out of the existing world of Becoming can be allotted, and might be considered a peer to the Kantian "Thing-in-itself."

Of course he who is able to wrangle persistently with others as to what kind of thing that primordial substance really was, whether perhaps an intermediate thing between air and water, or perhaps between air and fire, has not understood our philosopher at all; this is likewise to be said about those, who seriously ask themselves, whether Anaximander had thought of his primordial substance as a mixture of all existing substances. Rather we must direct our gaze to the place where we can learn that Anaximander no longer treated the question of the origin of the world as purely physical; we must direct our gaze towards that first stated lapidarian proposition. When on the contrary he saw a sum of wrongs to be expiated in the plurality of things that have become, then he, as the first Greek, with daring grasp caught up the tangle of the most profound ethical problem. How can anything perish that has a right to exist? Whence that restless Becoming and giving-birth, whence that expression of painful distortion on the face of Nature, whence the never-ending dirge in all realms of existence? Out of this world of injustice, of audacious apostasy from the primordial-unity of things Anaximander flees into a metaphysical castle, leaning out of which he turns his gaze far and wide in order at last, after a pensive silence, to address to all beings this question: "What is your existence worth? And if it is worth nothing why are you there? By your guilt, I observe, you sojourn in this world. You will have to expiate it by death. Look how your earth fades; the seas decrease and dry up, the marine-shell on the mountain shows you how much already they have dried up; fire destroys your world even now, finally it will end in smoke and ashes. But again and again such a world of transitoriness will ever build itself up; who shall redeem you from the curse of Becoming?"

Not every kind of life may have been welcome to a man who put such questions, whose upward-soaring thinking continually broke the empiric ropes, in order to take at once to the highest, superlunary flight. Willingly we believe tradition, that he walked along in especially dignified attire and showed a truly tragic hauteur in his gestures and habits of life. He lived as he wrote; he spoke as solemnly as he dressed himself, he raised his hand and placed his foot as if this existence was a tragedy, and he had been born in order to co-operate in that tragedy by playing the rôle of hero. In all that he was the great model of Empedocles. His fellow-citizens elected him the leader of an emigrating colony--perhaps they were pleased at being able to honour him and at the same time to get rid of him. His thought also emigrated and founded colonies; in Ephesus and in Elea they could not get rid of him; and if they could not resolve upon staying at the spot where he stood, they nevertheless knew that they had been led there by him, whence they now prepared to proceed without him.

Thales shows the need of simplifying the empire of plurality, and of reducing it to a mere expansion or disguise of the one single existing quality, water. Anaximander goes beyond him with two steps. Firstly he puts the question to himself: How, if there exists an eternal Unity at all, is that Plurality possible? and he takes the answer out of the contradictory, self-devouring and denying character of this Plurality. The existence of this Plurality becomes a moral phenomenon to him; it is not justified, it expiates itself continually through destruction. But then the questions occur to him: Yet why has not everything that has become perished long ago, since, indeed, quite an eternity of time has already gone by? Whence the ceaseless current of the River of Becoming? He can save himself from these questions only by mystic possibilities: the eternal Becoming can have its origin only in the eternal "Being," the conditions for that apostasy from that eternal "Being" to a Becoming in injustice are ever the same, the constellation of things cannot help itself being thus fashioned, that no end is to be seen of that stepping forth of the individual being out of the lap of the "Indefinite." At this Anaximander stayed; that is, he remained within the deep shadows which like gigantic spectres were lying on the mountain range of such a world-perception. The more one wanted to approach the problem of solving how out of the Indefinite the Definite, out of the Eternal the Temporal, out of the Just the Unjust could by secession ever originate, the darker the night became.----

5

Towards the midst of this mystic night, in which Anaximander's problem of the Becoming was wrapped up, Heraclitus of Ephesus approached and illuminated it by a divine flash of lightning. "I contemplate the Becoming," he exclaimed,--"and nobody has so attentively watched this eternal wave-surging and rhythm of things. And what do I behold? Lawfulness, infallible certainty, ever equal paths of Justice, condemning Erinyes behind all transgressions of the laws, the whole world the spectacle of a governing justice and of demoniacally omnipresent natural forces subject to justice's sway. I do not behold the punishment of that which has become, but the justification of Becoming. When has sacrilege, when has apostasy manifested itself in inviolable forms, in laws esteemed sacred? Where injustice sways, there is caprice, disorder, irregularity, contradiction; where however Law and Zeus' daughter, Dike, rule alone, as in this world, how could the sphere of guilt, of expiation, of judgment, and as it were the place of execution of all condemned ones be there?"

From this intuition Heraclitus took two coherent negations, which are put into the right light only by a comparison with the propositions of his predecessor. Firstly, he denied the duality of two quite diverse worlds, into the assumption of which Anaximander had been pushed; he no longer distinguished a physical world from a metaphysical, a realm of definite qualities from a realm of indefinable indefiniteness. Now after this first step he could neither be kept back any longer from a still greater audacity of denying: he denied "Being" altogether. For this one world which was left to him,--shielded all round by eternal, unwritten laws, flowing up and down in the brazen beat of rhythm,--shows nowhere persistence, indestructibility, a bulwark in the stream. Louder than Anaximander, Heraclitus exclaimed: "I see nothing but Becoming. Be not deceived! It is the fault of your limited outlook and not the fault of the essence of things if you believe that you see firm land anywhere in the ocean of Becoming and Passing. You need names for things, just as if they had a rigid permanence, but the very river in which you bathe a second time is no longer the same one which you entered before."

Heraclitus has as his royal property the highest power of intuitive conception, whereas towards the other mode of conception which is consummated by ideas and logical combinations, that is towards reason, he shows himself cool, apathetic, even hostile, and he seems to derive a pleasure when he is able to contradict reason by means of a truth gained intuitively, and this he does in such propositions as: "Everything has always its opposite within itself," so fearlessly that Aristotle before the tribunal of Reason accuses him of the highest crime, of having sinned against the law of opposition. Intuitive representation however embraces two things: firstly, the present, motley, changing world, pressing on us in all experiences, secondly, the conditions by means of which alone any experience of this world becomes possible: time and space. For these are able to be intuitively apprehended, purely in themselves and independent of any experience; i.e., they can be perceived, although they are without definite contents. If now Heraclitus considered time in this fashion, dissociated from all experiences, he had in it the most instructive monogram of all that which falls within the realm of intuitive conception. Just as he conceived of time, so also for instance did Schopenhauer, who repeatedly says of it: that in it every instant exists only in so far as it has annihilated the preceding one, its father, in order to be itself effaced equally quickly; that past and future are as unreal as any dream; that the present is only the dimensionless and unstable boundary between the two; that however, like time, so space, and again like the latter, so also everything that is simultaneously in space and time, has only a relative existence, only through and for the sake of a something else, of the same kind as itself, i.e., existing only under the same limitations. This truth is in the highest degree self-evident, accessible to everyone, and just for that very reason, abstractly and rationally, it is only attained with great difficulty. Whoever has this truth before his eyes must however also proceed at once to the next Heraclitean consequence and say that the whole essence of actuality is in fact activity, and that for actuality there is no other kind of existence and reality, as Schopenhauer has likewise expounded ("The World As Will And Idea," Vol. I., Bk. I, sec. 4): "Only as active does it fill space and time: its action upon the immediate object determines the perception in which alone it exists: the effect of the action of any material object upon any other, is known only in so far as the latter acts upon the immediate object in a different way from that in which it acted before; it consists in this alone. Cause and effect thus constitute the whole nature of matter; its true being is its action. The totality of everything material is therefore very appropriately called in German

Wirklichkeit (actuality)--a word which is far more expressive than Realität (reality).[2] That upon which actuality acts is always matter; actuality's whole 'Being' and essence therefore consist only in the orderly change, which one part of it causes in another, and is therefore wholly relative, according to a relation which is valid only within the boundary of actuality, as in the case of time and space."

The eternal and exclusive Becoming, the total instability of all reality and actuality, which continually works and becomes and never is, as Heraclitus teaches--is an awful and appalling conception, and in its effects most nearly related to that sensation, by which during an earthquake one loses confidence in the firmly-grounded earth. It required an astonishing strength to translate this effect into its opposite, into the sublime, into happy astonishment. Heraclitus accomplished this through an observation of the proper course of all Becoming and Passing, which he conceived of under the form of polarity, as the divergence of a force into two qualitatively different, opposite actions, striving after reunion. A quality is set continually at variance with itself and separates itself into its opposites: these opposites continually strive again one towards another. The common people of course think to recognise something rigid, completed, consistent; but the fact of the matter is that at any instant, bright and dark, sour and sweet are side by side and attached to one another like two wrestlers of whom sometimes the one succeeds, sometimes the other. According to Heraclitus honey is at the same time sweet and bitter, and the world itself an amphora whose contents constantly need stirring up. Out of the war of the opposites all Becoming originates; the definite and to us seemingly persistent qualities express only the momentary predominance of the one fighter, but with that the war is not at an end; the wrestling continues to all eternity. Everything happens according to this struggle, and this very struggle manifests eternal justice. It is a wonderful conception, drawn from the purest source of Hellenism, which considers the struggle as the continual sway of a homogeneous, severe justice bound by eternal laws. Only a Greek was able to consider this conception as the fundament of a Cosmodicy; it is Hesiod's good Eris transfigured into the cosmic principle, it is the idea of a contest, an idea held by individual Greeks and by their State, and translated out of the gymnasia and palæstra, out of the artistic agonistics, out of the struggle of the political parties and of the towns into the most general principle, so that the machinery of the universe is regulated by it. Just as every Greek fought as though he alone were in the right, and as though an absolutely sure standard of judicial opinion could at any instant decide whither victory is inclining, thus the qualities wrestle one with another, according to inviolable laws and standards which are inherent in the struggle. The Things themselves in the permanency of which the limited intellect of man and animal believes, do not "exist" at all; they are as the fierce flashing and fiery sparkling of drawn swords, as the stars of Victory rising with a radiant resplendence in the battle of the opposite qualities.

That struggle which is peculiar to all Becoming, that eternal interchange of victory is again described by Schopenhauer: ("The World As Will And Idea," Vol. I., Bk. 2, sec. 27) "The permanent matter must constantly change its form; for under the guidance of causality, mechanical, physical, chemical, and organic phenomena, eagerly striving to appear, wrest the matter from each other, for each desires to reveal its own Idea. This strife may be followed up through the whole of nature; indeed nature exists only through it." The following pages give the most noteworthy illustrations of this struggle, only that the prevailing tone of this description ever remains other than that of Heraclitus in so far as to Schopenhauer the struggle is a proof of the Will to Life falling out with itself; it is to him a feasting on itself on the part of this dismal, dull impulse, as a phenomenon on the whole horrible and not at all making for happiness. The arena and the object of this struggle is Matter,--which some natural forces alternately endeavour to disintegrate and build up again at the expense of other natural forces,--as also Space and Time, the union of which through causality is this very matter.

Footnote:

2. Mira in quibusdam rebus verborum proprietas est, et consuetudo sermonis antiqui quædam efficacissimis notis signat (Seneca, Epist. 81).--TR.

6

Whilst the imagination of Heraclitus measured the restlessly moving universe, the "actuality" (Wirklichkeit), with the eye of the happy spectator, who sees innumerable pairs wrestling in joyous combat entrusted to the superintendence of severe umpires, a still higher presentiment seized him, he no longer could contemplate the wrestling pairs and the umpires, separated one from another; the very umpires seemed to fight, and the fighters seemed to be their own judges--yea, since at the bottom he conceived only of the one Justice eternally swaying, he dared to exclaim: "The contest of The Many is itself pure justice. And after all: The One is The Many. For what are all those qualities according to their nature? Are they immortal gods? Are they separate beings working for themselves from the beginning and without end? And if the world which we see knows only Becoming and Passing but no Permanence, should perhaps those qualities constitute a differently fashioned metaphysical world, true, not a world of unity as Anaximander sought behind the fluttering veil of plurality, but a world of eternal and essential pluralities?" Is it possible that however violently he had denied such duality, Heraclitus has after all by a round-about way accidentally got into the dual cosmic order, an order with an Olympus of numerous immortal gods and demons,--viz., many realities,--and with a human world, which sees only the dust-cloud of the Olympic struggle and the flashing of divine spears,--i.e., only a Becoming? Anaximander had fled just from these definite qualities into the lap of the metaphysical "Indefinite"; because the former became and passed, he had denied them a true and essential existence; however should it not seem now as if the Becoming is only the looming-into-view of a struggle of eternal qualities? When we speak of the Becoming, should not the original cause of this be sought in the peculiar feebleness of human cognition--whereas in the nature of things there is perhaps no Becoming, but only a co-existing of many true increate indestructible realities?

These are Heraclitean loop-holes and labyrinths; he exclaims once again: "The 'One' is the 'Many'." The many perceptible qualities are neither eternal entities, nor phantasmata of our senses (Anaxagoras conceives them later on as the former, Parmenides as the latter), they are neither rigid, sovereign "Being" nor fleeting Appearance hovering in human minds. The third possibility which alone was left to Heraclitus nobody will be able to divine with dialectic sagacity and as it were by calculation, for what he invented here is a rarity even in the realm of mystic incredibilities and unexpected cosmic metaphors.--The world is the Game of Zeus, or expressed more physically, the game of fire with itself, the "One" is only in this sense at the same time the "Many."--

In order to elucidate in the first place the introduction of fire as a world-shaping force, I recall how Anaximander had further developed the theory of water as the origin of things. Placing confidence in the essential part of Thales' theory, and strengthening and adding to the latter's observations, Anaximander however was not to be convinced that before the water and, as it were, after the water there was no further stage of quality: no, to him out of the Warm and the Cold the Moist seemed to form itself, and the Warm and the Cold therefore were supposed to be the preliminary stages, the still more original qualities. With their issuing forth from the primordial existence of the "Indefinite," Becoming begins. Heraclitus who as physicist subordinated himself to the importance of Anaximander, explains to himself this Anaximandrian "Warm" as the respiration, the warm breath, the dry vapours, in short as the fiery element: about this fire he now enunciates the same as Thales and Anaximander had enunciated about the water: that in innumerable metamorphoses it was passing along the path of Becoming, especially in the three chief aggregate stages as something Warm, Moist, and Firm. For water in descending is transformed into earth, in ascending into fire: or as Heraclitus appears to have expressed himself more exactly: from the sea ascend only the pure vapours which serve as food to the divine fire of the stars, from the earth only the dark, foggy ones, from which the Moist derives its nourishment. The pure vapours are the transitional stage in the passing of sea into fire, the impure the transitional stage in the passing of earth into water. Thus the two paths of metamorphosis of the fire run continuously side by side, upwards and downwards, to and fro, from fire to water, from water to earth, from earth back again to water, from water to fire. Whereas Heraclitus is a follower of Anaximander in the most important of these conceptions, e.g., that the fire is kept up by the evaporations, or herein, that out of the water is dissolved partly earth, partly fire; he is on the other hand quite independent and in opposition to Anaximander in excluding the "Cold" from the physical process, whilst Anaximander had put it side by side with the "Warm" as having the same rights, so as to let the "Moist" originate out of both. To do so, was of course a necessity to Heraclitus, for if everything is to be fire, then, however many possibilities of its transformation might be assumed, nothing can exist that would be the absolute antithesis to fire; he has, therefore, probably interpreted only as a degree of the "Warm" that which is called the "Cold," and he could justify this interpretation without difficulty. Much more important than this deviation from the doctrine of Anaximander is a further agreement; he, like the latter, believes in an end of the world periodically repeating itself and in an ever-renewed emerging of another world out of the all-destroying world-fire. The period during which the world hastens towards that world-fire and the dissolution into pure fire is characterised by him most strikingly as a demand and a need; the state of being completely swallowed up by the fire as satiety; and now to us remains the question as to how he understood and named the newly awakening impulse for world-creation, the pouring-out-of-itself into the forms of plurality. The Greek proverb seems to come to our assistance with the thought that "satiety gives birth to crime" (the Hybris) and one may indeed ask oneself for a minute whether perhaps Heraclitus has derived that return to plurality out of the Hybris. Let us just take this thought seriously: in its light the face of Heraclitus changes before our eyes, the proud gleam of his eyes dies out, a wrinkled expression of painful resignation, of impotence becomes distinct, it seems that we know why later antiquity called him the "weeping philosopher." Is not the whole world-process now an act of punishment of the Hybris? The plurality the result of a crime? The transformation of the pure into the impure, the consequence of injustice? Is not the guilt now shifted into the essence of the things and indeed, the world of Becoming and of individuals accordingly exonerated from guilt; yet at the same time are they not condemned for ever and ever to bear the consequences of guilt?

7

That dangerous word, Hybris, is indeed the touchstone for every Heraclitean; here he may show whether he has understood or mistaken his master. Is there in this world: Guilt, injustice, contradiction, suffering?

Yes, exclaims Heraclitus, but only for the limited human being, who sees divergently and not convergently, not for the contuitive god; to him everything opposing converges into one harmony, invisible it is true to the common human eye, yet comprehensible to him who like Heraclitus resembles the contemplative god. Before his fiery eye no drop of injustice is left in the world poured out around him, and even that cardinal obstacle--how pure fire can take up its quarters in forms so impure--he masters by means of a sublime simile. A Becoming and Passing, a building and destroying, without any moral bias, in perpetual innocence is in this world only the play of the artist and of the child. And similarly, just as the child and the artist play, the eternally living fire plays, builds up and destroys, in innocence--and this game the Æon plays with himself. Transforming himself into water and earth, like a child he piles heaps of sand by the sea, piles up and demolishes; from time to time he recommences the game. A moment of satiety, then again desire seizes him, as desire compels the artist to create. Not wantonness, but the ever newly awakening impulse to play, calls into life other worlds. The child throws away his toys; but soon he starts again in an innocent frame of mind. As soon however as the child builds he connects, joins and forms lawfully and according to an innate sense of order.

Thus only is the world contemplated by the æsthetic man, who has learned from the artist and the genesis of the latter's work, how the struggle of plurality can yet bear within itself law and justice, how the artist stands contemplative above, and working within the work of art, how necessity and play, antagonism and harmony must pair themselves for the procreation of the work of art.

Who now will still demand from such a philosophy a system of Ethics with the necessary imperatives--Thou Shalt,--or even reproach Heraclitus with such a deficiency. Man down to his last fibre is Necessity and absolutely "unfree "--if by freedom one understands the foolish claim to be able to change at will one's essentia like a garment, a claim, which up to the present every serious philosophy has rejected with due scorn. That so few human beings live with consciousness in the Logos and in accordance with the all-overlooking artist's eye originates from their souls being wet and from the fact that men's eyes and ears, their intellect in general is a bad witness when "moist ooze fills their souls." Why that is so, is not questioned any more than why fire becomes water and earth. Heraclitus is not compelled to prove (as Leibnitz was) that this world was even the best of all; it was sufficient for him that the world is the beautiful, innocent play of the Æon. Man on the whole is to him even an irrational being, with which the fact that in all his essence the law of all-ruling reason is fulfilled does lot clash. He does not occupy a specially favoured position in nature, whose highest phenomenon is not simple-minded man, but fire, for instance, as stars. In so far as man has through necessity received a share of fire, he is a little more rational; as far as he consists of earth and water it stands badly with his reason. He is not compelled to take cognisance of the Logos simply because he is a human being. Why is there water, why earth? This to Heraclitus is a much more serious problem than to ask, why men are so stupid and bad. In the highest and the most perverted men the same inherent lawfulness and justice manifest themselves. If however one would ask Heraclitus the question "Why is fire not always fire, why is it now water, now earth?" then he would only just answer: "It is a game, don't take it too pathetically and still less, morally." Heraclitus describes only the existing world and has the same contemplative pleasure in it which the artist experiences when looking at his growing work. Only those who have cause to be discontented with his natural history of man find him gloomy, melancholy, tearful, sombre, atrabilarious, pessimistic and altogether hateful. He however would take these discontented people, together with their antipathies and sympathies, their hatred und their love, as negligible and perhaps answer them with some such comment as: "Dogs bark at anything they do not know," or, "To the ass chaff is preferable to gold."

With such discontented persons also originate the numerous complaints as to the obscurity of the Heraclitean style; probably no man has ever written clearer and more illuminatingly; of course, very abruptly, and therefore naturally obscure to the racing readers. But why a philosopher should intentionally write obscurely--a thing habitually said about Heraclitus--is absolutely inexplicable; unless he has some cause to hide his thoughts or is sufficiently a rogue to conceal his thoughtlessness underneath words. One is, as Schopenhauer says, indeed compelled by lucid expression to prevent misunderstandings even in affairs of practical every-day life, how then should one be allowed to express oneself indistinctly, indeed puzzlingly in the most difficult, most abstruse, scarcely attainable object of thinking, the tasks of philosophy? With respect to brevity however Jean Paul gives a good precept: "On the whole it is right that everything great--of deep meaning to a rare mind--should be uttered with brevity and (therefore) obscurely so that the paltry mind would rather proclaim it to be nonsense than translate it into the realm of his empty-headedness. For common minds have an ugly ability to perceive in the deepest and richest saying nothing but their own every-day opinion." Moreover and in spite of it Heraclitus has not escaped the "paltry minds"; already the Stoics have "re-expounded" him into the shallow and dragged down his æsthetic fundamental-perception as to the play of the world to the miserable level of the common regard for the practical ends of the world and more explicitly for the advantages of man, so that out of his Physics has arisen in those heads a crude optimism, with the continual invitation to Dick, Tom, and Harry, "Plaudite amici!"

8

Heraclitus was proud; and if it comes to pride with a philosopher then it is a great pride. His work never refers him to a "public," the applause of the masses and the hailing chorus of contemporaries. To wander lonely along his path belongs to the nature of the philosopher. His talents are the most rare, in a certain sense the most unnatural and at the same time exclusive and hostile even toward kindred talents. The wall of his self-sufficiency must be of diamond, if it is not to be demolished and broken, for everything is in motion against him. His journey to immortality is more cumbersome and impeded than any other and yet nobody can believe more firmly than the philosopher that he will attain the goal by that journey--because he does not know where he is to stand if not on the widely spread wings of all time; for the disregard of everything present and momentary lies in the essence of the great philosophic nature. He has truth; the wheel of time may roll whither it pleases, never can it escape from truth. It is important to hear that such men have lived. Never for example would one be able to imagine the pride of Heraclitus as an idle possibility. In itself every endeavour after knowledge seems by its nature to be eternally unsatisfied and unsatisfactory. Therefore nobody unless instructed by history will like to believe in such a royal self-esteem and conviction of being the only wooer of truth. Such men live in their own solar-system--one has to look for them there. A Pythagoras, an Empedocles treated themselves too with a super-human esteem, yea, with almost religious awe; but the tie of sympathy united with the great conviction of the metempsychosis and the unity of everything living, led them back to other men, for their welfare and salvation. Of that feeling of solitude, however, which permeated the Ephesian recluse of the Artemis Temple, one can only divine something, when growing benumbed in the wildest mountain desert. No paramount feeling of compassionate agitation, no desire to help, heal and save emanates from him. He is a star without an atmosphere. His eye, directed blazingly inwards, looks outward, for appearance's sake only, extinct and icy. All around him, immediately upon the citadel of his pride beat the waves of folly and perversity: with loathing he turns away from them. But men with a feeling heart would also shun such a Gorgon monster as cast out of brass; within an out-of-the-way sanctuary, among the statues of gods, by the side of cold composedly-sublime architecture such a being may appear more comprehensible. As man among men Heraclitus was incredible; and though he was seen paying attention to the play of noisy children, even then he was reflecting upon what never man thought of on such an occasion: the play of the great world-child, Zeus. He had no need of men, not even for his discernments. He was not interested in all that which one might perhaps ascertain from them, and in what the other sages before him had been endeavouring to ascertain. He spoke with disdain of such questioning, collecting, in short "historic" men. "I sought and investigated myself," he said, with a word by which one designates the investigation of an oracle; as if he and no one else were the true fulfiller and achiever of the Delphic precept: "Know thyself."

What he learned from this oracle, he deemed immortal wisdom, and eternally worthy of explanation, of unlimited effect even in the distance, after the model of the prophetic speeches of the Sibyl. It is sufficient for the latest mankind: let the latter have that expounded to her, as oracular sayings, which he like the Delphic god "neither enunciates nor conceals." Although it is proclaimed by him, "without smiles, finery and the scent of ointments," but rather as with "foaming mouth," it must force its way through the millenniums of the future. For the world needs truth eternally, therefore she needs also Heraclitus eternally; although he has no need of her. What does his fame matter to him?--fame with "mortals ever flowing on!" as he exclaims scornfully. His fame is of concern to man, not to himself; the immortality of mankind needs him, not he the immortality of the man Heraclitus. That which he beheld, the doctrine of the Law in the Becoming, and of the Play in the Necessity, must henceforth be beheld eternally; he has raised the curtain of this greatest stage-play.

9

Whereas in every word of Heraclitus are expressed the pride and the majesty of truth, but of truth caught by intuitions, not scaled by the rope-ladder of Logic, whereas in sublime ecstasy he beholds but does not espy, discerns but does not reckon, he is contrasted with his contemporary Parmenides, a man likewise with the type of a prophet of truth, but formed as it were out of ice and not out of fire, and shedding around himself cold, piercing light.

Parmenides once had, probably in his later years, a moment of the very purest abstraction, undimmed by any reality, perfectly lifeless; this moment--un-Greek, like no other in the two centuries of the Tragic Age--the product of which is the doctrine of "Being," became a boundary-stone for his own life, which divided it into two periods; at the same time however the same moment divides the pre-Socratic thinking into two halves, of which the first might be called the Anaximandrian, the second the Parmenidean. The first period in Parmenides' own philosophising bears still the signature of Anaximander; this period produced a detailed philosophic-physical system as answer to Anaximander's questions. When later that icy abstraction-horror caught him, and the simplest proposition treating of "Being" and "Not-Being" was advanced by him, then among the many older doctrines thrown by him upon the scrap heap was also his own system. However he does not appear to have lost all paternal piety towards the strong and well-shapen child of his youth, and he saved himself therefore by saying: "It is true there is only one right way; if one however wants at any time to betake oneself to another, then my earlier opinion according to its purity and consequence alone is right." Sheltering himself with this phrase he has allowed his former physical system a worthy and extensive space in his great poem on Nature, which really was to proclaim the new discernment as the only signpost to truth. This fatherly regard, even though an error should have crept in through it, is a remainder of human feeling, in a nature quite petrified by logical rigidity and almost changed into a thinking-machine.

Parmenides, whose personal intercourse with Anaximander does not seem incredible to me, and whose starting from Anaximander's doctrine is not only credible but evident, had the same distrust for the complete separation of a world which only is, and a world which only becomes, as had also caught Heraclitus and led to a denying of "Being" altogether. Both sought a way out from that contrast and divergence of a dual order of the world. That leap into the Indefinite, Indefinable, by which once for all Anaximander had escaped from the realm of Becoming and from the empirically given qualities of such realm, that leap did not become an easy matter to minds so independently fashioned as those of Heraclitus and Parmenides; first they endeavoured to walk as far as they could and reserved to themselves the leap for that place, where the foot finds no more hold and one has to leap, in order not to fall. Both looked repeatedly at that very world, which Anaximander had condemned in so melancholy a way and declared to be the place of wanton crime and at the same time the penitentiary cell for the injustice of Becoming. Contemplating this world Heraclitus, as we know already, had discovered what a wonderful order, regularity and security manifest themselves in every Becoming; from that he concluded that the Becoming could not be anything evil and unjust. Quite a different outlook had Parmenides; he compared the qualities one with another, and believed that they were not all of the same kind, but ought to be classified under two headings. If for example he compared bright and dark, then the second quality was obviously only the negation of the first; and thus he distinguished positive and negative qualities, seriously endeavouring to rediscover and register that fundamental antithesis in the whole realm of Nature. His method was the following: He took a few antitheses, e.g., light and heavy, rare and dense, active and passive, and compared them with that typical antithesis of bright and dark: that which corresponded with the bright was the positive, that which corresponded with the dark the negative quality. If he took perhaps the heavy and light, the light fell to the side of the bright, the heavy to the side of the dark; and thus "heavy" was to him only the negation of "light," but the "light" a positive quality. This method alone shows that he had a defiant aptitude for abstract logical procedure, closed against the suggestions of the senses. The "heavy" seems indeed to offer itself very forcibly to the senses as a positive quality; that did not keep Parmenides from stamping it as a negation. Similarly he placed the earth in opposition to the fire, the "cold" in opposition to the "warm," the "dense" in opposition to the "rare," the "female" in opposition to the "male," the "passive" in opposition to the "active," merely as negations: so that before his gaze our empiric world divided itself into two separate spheres, into that of the positive qualities--with a bright, fiery, warm, light, rare, active-masculine character--and into that of the negative qualities. The latter express really only the lack, the absence of the others, the positive ones. He therefore described the sphere in which the positive qualities are absent as dark, earthy, cold, heavy, dense and altogether as of feminine-passive character. Instead of the expressions "positive" and "negative" he used the standing term "existent" and "non-existent" and had arrived with this at the proposition, that, in contradiction to Anaximander, this our world itself contains something "existent," and of course something "non-existent." One is not to seek that "existent" outside the world and as it were above our horizon; but before us, and everywhere in every Becoming, something "existent" and active is contained.

With that however still remained to him the task of giving the more exact answer to the question: What is the Becoming? and here was the moment where he had to leap, in order not to fall, although perhaps to such natures as that of Parmenides, even any leaping means a falling. Enough! we get into fog, into the mysticism of qualitates occultæ, and even a little into mythology. Parmenides, like Heraclitus, looks at the general Becoming and Not-remaining and explains to himself a Passing only thus, that the "Non-Existent" bore the guilt. For how should the "Existent" bear the guilt of Passing? Likewise, however, the Originating, i.e., the Becoming, must come about through the assistance of the "Non-Existent"; for the "Existent" is always there and could not of itself first originate and it could not explain any Originating, any Becoming. Therefore the Originating, the Becoming as well as the Passing and Perishing have been brought about by the negative qualities. But that the originating "thing" has a content, and the passing "thing" loses a content, presupposes that the positive qualities--and that just means that very content--participate likewise in both processes. In short the proposition results: "For the Becoming the 'Existent' as well as the 'Non-Existent' is necessary; when they co-operate then a Becoming results." But how come the "positive" and the "negative" to one another? Should they not on the contrary eternally flee one another as antitheses and thereby make every Becoming impossible? Here Parmenides appeals to a qualitas occulta, to a mystic tendency of the antithetical pairs to approach and attract one another, and he allegorises that peculiar contrariety by the name of Aphrodite, and by the empirically known relation of the male and female principle. It is the power of Aphrodite which plays the matchmaker between the antithetical pair, the "Existent" and the "Non-Existent." Passion brings together the antagonistic and antipathetic elements: the result is a Becoming. When Desire has become satiated, Hatred and the innate antagonism again drive asunder the "Existent" and the "Non-Existent"--then man says: the thing perishes, passes.

10

But no one with impunity lays his profane hands on such awful abstractions as the "Existent" and the "Non-Existent"; the blood freezes slowly as one touches them. There was a day upon which an odd idea suddenly occurred to Parmenides, an idea which seemed to take all value away from his former combinations, so that he felt inclined to throw them aside, like a money bag with old worn-out coins. It is commonly believed that an external impression, in addition to the centrifugal consequence of such ideas as "existent" and "non-existent," has also been co-active in the invention of that day; this impression was an acquaintance with the theology of the old roamer and rhapsodist, the singer of a mystic deification of Nature, the Kolophonian Xenophanes. Throughout an extraordinary life Xenophanes lived as a wandering poet and became through his travels a well-informed and most instructive man who knew how to question and how to narrate, for which reason Heraclitus reckoned him amongst the polyhistorians and above all amongst the "historic" natures, in the sense mentioned. Whence and when came to him the mystic bent into the One and the eternally Resting, nobody will be able to compute; perhaps it is only the conception of the finally settled old man, to whom, after the agitation of his erratic wanderings, and after the restless learning and searching for truth, the vision of a divine rest, the permanence of all things within a pantheistic primal peace appears as the highest and greatest ideal. After all it seems to me quite accidental that in the same place in Elea two men lived together for a time, each of whom carried in his head a conception of unity; they formed no school and had nothing in common which perhaps the one might have learned from the other and then might have handed on. For, in the case of these two men, the origin of that conception of unity is quite different, yea opposite; and if either of them has become at all acquainted with the doctrine of the other then, in order to understand it at all, he had to translate it first into his own language. With this translation however the very specific element of the other doctrine was lost. Whereas Parmenides arrived at the unity of the "Existent" purely through an alleged logical consequence and whereas he span that unity out of the ideas "Being" and "Not-Being," Xenophanes was a religious mystic and belonged, with that mystic unity, very properly to the Sixth Century. Although he was no such revolutionising personality as Pythagoras he had nevertheless in his wanderings the same bent and impulse to improve, purify, and cure men. He was the ethical teacher, but still in the stage of the rhapsodist; in a later time he would have been a sophist. In the daring disapproval of the existing customs and valuations he had not his equal in Greece; moreover he did not, like Heraclitus and Plato, retire into solitude but placed himself before the very public, whose exulting admiration of Homer, whose passionate propensity for the honours of the gymnastic festivals, whose adoration of stones in human shape, he criticised severely with wrath and scorn, yet not as a brawling Thersites. The freedom of the individual was with him on its zenith; and by this almost limitless stepping free from all conventions he was more closely related to Parmenides than by that last divine unity, which once he had beheld, in a visionary state worthy of that century. His unity scarcely had expression and word in common with the one "Being" of Parmenides, and certainly had not the same origin.

It was rather an opposite state of mind in which Parmenides found his doctrine of "Being," On that day and in that state he examined his two co-operating antitheses, the "Existent" and the "Non-Existent," the positive and the negative qualities, of which Desire and Hatred constitute the world and the Becoming. He was suddenly caught up, mistrusting, by the idea of negative quality, of the "Non-Existent." For can something which does not exist be a quality? or to put the question in a broader sense: can anything indeed which does not exist, exist? The only form of knowledge in which we at once put unconditional trust and the disapproval of which amounts to madness, is the tautology A = A. But this very tautological knowledge called inexorably to him: what does not exist, exists not! What is, is! Suddenly he feels upon his life the load of an enormous logical sin; for had he not always without hesitation assumed that there were existing negative qualities, in short a "Non-Existent," that therefore, to express it by a formula, A = Not-A, which indeed could only be advanced by the most out and out perversity of thinking. It is true, as he recollected, the whole great mass of men judge with the same perversity; he himself has only participated in the general crime against logic. But the same moment which charges him with this crime surrounds him with the light of the glory of an invention, he has found, apart from all human illusion, a principle, the key to the world-secret, he now descends into the abyss of things, guided by the firm and fearful hand of the tautological truth as to "Being."

On the way thither he meets Heraclitus--an unfortunate encounter! Just now Heraclitus' play with antinomies was bound to be very hateful to him, who placed the utmost importance upon the severest separation of "Being" and "Not-Being"; propositions like this: "We are and at the same time we are not" --"'Being' and 'Not-Being' is at the same time the same thing and again not the same thing," propositions through which all that he had just elucidated and disentangled became again dim and inextricable, incited him to wrath. "Away with the men," he exclaimed, "who seem to have two heads and yet know nothing! With them truly everything is in flux, even their thinking! They stare at things stupidly, but they must be deaf as well as blind so to mix up the opposites"! The want of judgment on the part of the masses, glorified by playful antinomies and praised as the acme of all knowledge was to him a painful and incomprehensible experience.

Now he dived into the cold bath of his awful abstractions. That which is true must exist in eternal presence, about it cannot be said "it was," "it will be." The "Existent" cannot have become; for out of what should it have become? Out of the "Non-Existent"? But that does not exist and can produce nothing. Out of the "Existent"? This would not produce anything but itself. The same applies to the Passing, it is just as impossible as the Becoming, as any change, any increase, any decrease. On the whole the proposition is valid: Everything about which it can be said: "it has been" or "it will be" does not exist; about the "Existent" however it can never be said "it does not exist." The "Existent" is indivisible, for where is the second power, which should divide it? It is immovable, for whither should it move itself? It cannot be infinitely great nor infinitely small, for it is perfect and a perfectly given infinitude is a contradiction. Thus the "Existent" is suspended, delimited, perfect, immovable, everywhere equally balanced and such equilibrium equally perfect at any point, like a globe, but not in a space, for otherwise this space would be a second "Existent." But there cannot exist several "Existents," for in order to separate them, something would have to exist which was not existing, an assumption which neutralises itself. Thus there exists only the eternal Unity.

If now, however, Parmenides turned back his gaze to the world of Becoming, the existence of which he had formerly tried to understand by such ingenious conjectures, he was wroth at his eye seeing the Becoming at all, his ear hearing it. "Do not follow the dim-sighted eyes," now his command runs, "not the resounding ear nòr the tongue, but examine only by the power of the thought." Therewith he accomplished the extremely important first critique of the apparatus of knowledge, although this critique was still inadequate and proved disastrous in its consequences. By tearing entirely asunder the senses and the ability to think in abstractions, i.e. reason, just as if they were two thoroughly separate capacities, he demolished the intellect itself, and incited people to that wholly erroneous separation of "mind" and "body" which, especially since Plato, lies like a curse on philosophy. All sense perceptions, Parmenides judges, cause only illusions and their chief illusion is their deluding us to believe that even the "Non-Existent" exists, that even the Becoming has a "Being." All that plurality, diversity and variety of the empirically known world, the change of its qualities, the order in its ups and downs, is thrown aside mercilessly as mere appearance and delusion; from there nothing is to be learnt, therefore all labour is wasted which one bestows upon this false, through-and-through futile world, the conception of which has been obtained by being hum-bugged by the senses. He who judges in such generalisations as Parmenides did, ceases therewith to be an investigator of natural philosophy in detail; his interest in phenomena withers away; there develops even a hatred of being unable to get rid of this eternal fraud of the senses. Truth is now to dwell only in the most faded, most abstract generalities, in the empty husks of the most indefinite words, as in a maze of cobwebs; and by such a "truth" now the philosopher sits, bloodless as an abstraction and surrounded by a web of formulæ. The spider undoubtedly wants the blood of its victims; but the Parmenidean philosopher hates the very blood of his victims, the blood of

Empiricism sacrificed by him.

11

And that was a Greek who "flourished" about the time of the outbreak of the Ionic Revolution. At that time it was possible for a Greek to flee out of the superabundant reality, as out of a mere delusive schematism of the imaginative faculties--not perhaps like Plato into the land of the eternal ideas, into the workshop of the world-creator, in order to feast the eyes on unblemished, unbreakable primal-forms of things--but into the rigid death-like rest of the coldest and emptiest conception, that of the "Being." We will indeed beware of interpreting such a remarkable fact by false analogies. That flight was not a world-flight in the sense of Indian philosophers; no deep religious conviction as to the depravity, transitoriness and accursedness of Existence demanded that flight--that ultimate goal, the rest in the "Being," was not striven after as the mystic absorption in one all-sufficing enrapturing conception which is a puzzle and a scandal to common men. The thought of Parmenides bears in itself not the slightest trace of the intoxicating mystical Indian fragrance, which is perhaps not wholly imperceptible in Pythagoras and Empedocles; the strange thing in that fact, at this period, is rather the very absence of fragrance, colour, soul, form, the total lack of blood, religiosity and ethical warmth, the abstract-schematic--in a Greek!--above all however our philosopher's awful energy of striving after Certainty, in a mythically thinking and highly emotional--fantastic age is quite remarkable. "Grant me but a certainty, ye gods!"is the prayer of Parmenides, "and be it, in the ocean of Uncertainty, only a board, broad enough to lie on! Everything becoming, everything luxuriant, varied, blossoming, deceiving, stimulating, living, take all that for yourselves, and give to me but the single poor empty Certainty!"

In the philosophy of Parmenides the theme of ontology forms the prelude. Experience offered him nowhere a "Being" as he imagined it to himself, but from the fact that he could conceive of it he concluded that it must exist; a conclusion which rests upon the supposition that we have an organ of knowledge which reaches into the nature of things and is independent of experience. The material of our thinking according to Parmenides does not exist in perception at all but is brought in from somewhere else, from an extra-material world to which by thinking we have a direct access. Against all similar chains of reasoning Aristotle has already asserted that existence never belongs to the essence, never belongs to the nature of a thing. For that very reason from the idea of "Being"--of which the essentia precisely is only the "Being"--cannot be inferred an existentia of the "Being" at all. The logical content of that antithesis "Being" and "Not-Being" is perfectly nil, if the object lying at the bottom of it, if the precept cannot be given from which this antithesis has been deduced by abstraction; without this going back to the precept the antithesis is only a play with conceptions, through which indeed nothing is discerned. For the merely logical criterion of truth, as Kant teaches, namely the agreement of a discernment with the general and the formal laws of intellect and reason is, it is true, the conditio sine qua non, consequently the negative condition of all truth; further however logic cannot go, and logic cannot discover by any touchstone the error which pertains not to the form but to the contents. As soon, however, as one seeks the content for the logical truth of the antithesis: "That which is, is; that which is not, is not," one will find indeed not a simple reality, which is fashioned rigidly according to that antithesis: about a tree I can say as well "it is" in comparison with all the other things, as well "it becomes" in comparison with itself at another moment of time as finally also "it is not," e.g.," it is not yet tree," as long as I perhaps look at the shrub. Words are only symbols for the relations of things among themselves and to`us, and nowhere touch absolute truth; and now to crown all, the word "Being" designates only the most general relation, which connects all things, and so does the word "Not-Being." If however the Existence of the things themselves be unprovable, then the relation of the things among themselves, the so-called "Being" and "Not-Being," will not bring us any nearer to the land of truth. By means of words and ideas we shall never get behind the wall of the relations, let us say into some fabulous primal cause of things, and even in the pure forms of the sensitive faculty and of the intellect, in space, time and causality we gain nothing, which might resemble a "Veritas æterna?" It is absolutely impossible for the subject to see and discern something beyond himself, so impossible that Cognition and "Being" are the most contradictory of all spheres. And if in the uninstructed naïveté of the then critique of the intellect Parmenides was permitted to fancy that out of the eternally subjective idea he had come to a "Being-In-itself," then it is to-day, after Kant, a daring ignorance, if here and there, especially among badly informed theologians who want to play the philosopher, is proposed as the task of philosophy: "to conceive the Absolute by means of consciousness," perhaps even in the form: "the Absolute is already extant, else how could it be sought?" as Hegel has expressed himself, or with the saying of Beneke: "that the 'Being' must be given somehow, must be attainable for us somehow, since otherwise we could not even have the idea of 'Being.'" The idea of "Being"! As though that idea did not indicate the most miserable empiric origin already in the etymology of the word. For esse means at the bottom: "to breathe," if man uses it of all other things, then he transmits the conviction that he himself breathes and lives by means of a metaphor, i.e., by means of something illogical to the other things and conceives of their Existence as a Breathing according to human analogy. Now the original meaning of the word soon becomes effaced; so much however still remains that man conceives of the existence of other things according to the analogy of his own existence, therefore anthropomorphically, and at any rate by means of an illogical transmission. Even to man, therefore apart from that transmission, the proposition: "I breathe, therefore a 'Being' exists" is quite insufficient since against it the same objection must be made, as against the ambulo, ergo sum, or ergo est.

12

The other idea, of greater import than that of the "Existent," and likewise invented already by Parmenides, although not yet so clearly applied as by his disciple Zeno is the idea of the Infinite. Nothing Infinite can exist; for from such an assumption the contradictory idea of a perfect Infinitude would result. Since now our actuality, our existing world everywhere shows the character of that perfect Infinitude, our world signifies in its nature a contradiction against logic and therewith also against reality and is deception, lie, fantasma. Zeno especially applied the method of indirect proof; he said for example, "There can be no motion from one place to another; for if there were such a motion, then an Infinitude would be given as perfect, this however is an impossibility." Achilles cannot catch up the tortoise which has a small start in a race, for in order to reach only the point from which the tortoise began, he would have had to run through innumerable, infinitely many spaces, viz., first half of that space, then the fourth, then the sixteenth, and so on ad infinitum. If he does in fact overtake the tortoise then this is an illogical phenomenon, and therefore at any rate not a truth, not a reality, not real "Being," but only a delusion. For it is never possible to finish the infinite. Another popular expression of this doctrine is the flying and yet resting arrow. At any instant of its flight it has a position; in this position it rests. Now would the sum of the infinite positions of rest be identical with motion? Would now the Resting, infinitely often repeated, be Motion, therefore its own opposite? The Infinite is here used as the aqua fortis of reality, through it the latter is dissolved. If however the Ideas are fixed, eternal and entitative--and for Parmenides "Being" and Thinking coincide--if therefore the Infinite can never be perfect, if Rest can never become Motion, then in fact the arrow has not flown at all; it never left its place and resting position; no moment of time has passed. Or expressed in another way: in this so-called yet only alleged Actuality there exists neither time, nor space, nor motion. Finally the arrow itself is only an illusion; for it originates out of the Plurality, out of the phantasmagoria of the "Non-One" produced by the senses. Suppose the arrow had a "Being," then it would be immovable, timeless, increate, rigid and eternal--an impossible conception! Supposing that Motion was truly real, then there would be no rest, therefore no position for the arrow, therefore no space--an impossible conception! Supposing that time were real, then it could not be of an infinite divisibility; the time which the arrow needed, would have to consist of a limited number of time-moments, each of these moments would have to be an Atomon--an impossible conception! All our conceptions, as soon as their empirically-given content, drawn out of this concrete world, is taken as a Veritas æterna, lead to contradictions. If there is absolute motion, then there is no space; if there is absolute space then there is no motion; if there is absolute "Being," then there is no Plurality; if there is an absolute Plurality, then there is no Unity. It should at least become clear to us how little we touch the heart of things or untie the knot of reality with such ideas, whereas Parmenides and Zeno inversely hold fast to the truth and omnivalidity of ideas and condemn the perceptible world as the opposite of the true and omnivalid ideas, as an objectivation of the illogical and contradictory. With all their proofs they start from the wholly undemonstrable, yea improbable assumption that in that apprehensive faculty we possess the decisive, highest criterion of "Being" and "Not-Being," i.e., of objective reality and its opposite; those ideas are not to prove themselves true, to correct themselves by Actuality, as they are after all really derived from it, but on the contrary they are to measure and to judge Actuality, and in case of a contradiction with logic, even to condemn. In order to concede to them this judicial competence Parmenides had to ascribe to them the same "Being," which alone he allowed in general as the "Being"; Thinking and that one increate perfect ball of the "Existent" were now no longer to be conceived as two different kinds of "Being," since there was not permitted a duality of "Being." Thus the over-risky flash of fancy had become necessary to declare Thinking and "Being" identical. No form of perceptibility, no symbol, no simile could possibly be of any help here; the fancy was wholly inconceivable, but it was necessary, yea in the lack of every possibility of illustration it celebrated the highest triumph over the world and the claims of the senses. Thinking and that clod-like, ball-shaped, through-and-through dead-massive, and rigid-immovable "Being," must, according to the Parmenidean imperative, dissolve into one another and be the same in every respect, to the horror of fantasy. What does it matter that this identity contradicts the senses! This contradiction is just the guarantee that such an identity is not borrowed from the senses.

13

Moreover against Parmenides could be produced a strong couple of argumenta ad hominem or ex concessis, by which, it is true, truth itself could not be brought to light, but at any rate the untruth of that absolute separation of the world of the senses and the world of the ideas, and the untruth of the identity of "Being" and Thinking could be demonstrated. Firstly, if the Thinking of Reason in ideas is real, then also Plurality and Motion must have reality, for rational Thinking is mobile; and more precisely, it is a motion from idea to idea, therefore within a plurality of realities. There is no subterfuge against that; it is quite impossible to designate Thinking as a rigid Permanence, as an eternally immobile, intellectual Introspection of Unity. Secondly, if only fraud and illusion come from the senses, and if in reality there exists only the real identity of "Being" and Thinking, what then are the senses themselves? They too are certainly Appearance only since they do not coincide with the Thinking, and their product, the world of senses, does not coincide with "Being." If however the senses themselves are Appearance to whom then are they Appearance? How can they, being unreal, still deceive? The "Non-Existent" cannot even deceive. Therefore the Whence? of deception and Appearance remains an enigma, yea, a contradiction. We call these argumenta ad hominem: The Objection Of The Mobile Reason and that of The Origin Of Appearance. From the first would result the reality of Motion and of Plurality, from the second the impossibility of the Parmenidean Appearance, assuming that the chief-doctrine of Parmenides on the "Being" were accepted as true. This chief-doctrine however only says: The "Existent" only has a "Being," the "Non-Existent" does not exist. If Motion however has such a "Being," then to Motion applies what applies to the "Existent" in general: it is increate, eternal, indestructible, without increase or decrease. But if the "Appearance" is denied and a belief in it made untenable, by means of that question as to the Whence? of the "Appearance," if the stage of the so-called Becoming, of change, our many-shaped, restless, coloured and rich Existence is protected from the Parmenidean rejection, then it is necessary to characterise this world of change and alteration as a sum of such really existing Essentials, existing simultaneously into all eternity. Of a change in the strict sense, of a Becoming there cannot naturally be any question even with this assumption. But now Plurality has a real "Being," all qualities have a real "Being" and motion not less; and of any moment of this world--although these moments chosen at random lie at a distance of millenniums from one another--it would have to be possible to say: all real Essentials extant in this world are without exception co-existent, unaltered, undiminished, without increase, without decrease. A millennium later the world is exactly the same. Nothing has altered. If in spite of that the appearance of the world at the one time is quite different from that at the other time, then that is no deception, nothing merely apparent, but the effect of eternal motion. The real "Existent" is moved sometimes thus, sometimes thus: together, asunder, upwards, downwards, into one another, pell-mell.

14

With this conception we have already taken a step into the realm of the doctrine of Anaxagoras. By him both objections against Parmenides are raised in full strength; that of the mobile Thinking and that of the Whence? of "Appearance"; but in the chief proposition Parmenides has subjugated him as well as all the younger philosophers and nature-explorers. They all deny the possibility of Becoming and Passing, as the mind of the people conceives them and as Anaximander and Heraclitus had assumed with greater circumspection and yet still heedlessly. Such a mythological Originating out of the Nothing, such a Disappearing into the Nothing, such an arbitrary Changing of the Nothing into the Something, such a random exchanging, putting on and putting off of the qualities was henceforth considered senseless; but so was, and for the same reasons, an originating of the Many out of the One, of the manifold qualities out of the one primal-quality, in short the derivation of the world out of a primary substance, as argued by Thales and Heraclitus. Rather was now the real problem advanced of applying the doctrine of increate imperishable "Being" to this existing world, without taking one's refuge in the theory of appearance and deception. But if the empiric world is not to be Appearance, if the things are not to be derived out of Nothing and just as little out of the one Something, then these things must contain in themselves a real "Being," their matter and content must be unconditionally real, and all change can refer only to the form, i.e., to the position, order, grouping, mixing, separation of these eternally co-existing Essentials. It is just as in a game of dice; they are ever the same dice; but falling sometimes thus, sometimes thus, they mean to us something different. All older theories had gone back to a primal element, as womb and cause of Becoming, be this water, air, fire or the Indefinite of Anaximander. Against that Anaxagoras now asserts that out of the Equal the Unequal could never come forth, and that out of the one "Existent" the change could never be explained. Whether now one were to imagine that assumed matter to be rarefied or condensed, one would never succeed by such a condensation or rarefaction in explaining the problem one would like to explain: the plurality of qualities. But if the world in fact is full of the most different qualities then these must, in case they are not appearance, have a "Being," i.e., must be eternal, increate, imperishable and ever co-existing. Appearance, however, they cannot be, since the question as to the Whence? of Appearance remains unanswered, yea answers itself in the negative! The earlier seekers after Truth had intended to simplify the problem of Becoming by advancing only one substance, which bore in its bosom the possibilities of all Becoming; now on the contrary it is asserted: there are innumerable substances, but never more, never less, and never new ones. Only Motion, playing dice with them throws them into ever new combinations. That Motion however is a truth and not Appearance, Anaxagoras proved in opposition to Parmenides by the indisputable succession of our conceptions in thinking. We have therefore in the most direct fashion the insight into the truth of motion and succession in the fact that we think and have conceptions. Therefore at any rate the one rigid, resting, dead "Being" of Parmenides has been removed out of the way, there are many "Existents" just as surely as all these many "Existents" (existing things, substances) are in motion. Change is motion--but whence originates motion? Does this motion leave perhaps wholly untouched the proper essence of those many independent, isolated substances, and, according to the most severe idea of the "Existent," must not motion in itself be foreign to them? Or does it after all belong to the things themselves? We stand here at an important decision; according to which way we turn, we shall step into the realm either of Anaxagoras or of Empedocles or of Democritus. The delicate question must be raised: if there are many substances, and if these many move, what moves them? Do they move one another? Or is it perhaps only gravitation? Or are there magic forces of attraction and repulsion within the things themselves? Or does the cause of motion lie outside these many real substances? Or putting the question more pointedly: if two things show a succession, a mutual change of position, does that originate from themselves? And is this to be explained mechanically or magically? Or if this should not be the case is it a third something which moves them? It is a sorry problem, for Parmenides would still have been able to prove against Anaxagoras the impossibility of motion, even granted that there are many substances. For he could say: Take two Substances existing of themselves, each with quite differently fashioned, autonomous, unconditioned "Being"--and of such kind are the Anaxagorean substances--they can never clash together, never move, never attract one another, there exists between them no causality, no bridge, they do not come into contact with one another, do not disturb one another, they do not interest one another, they are utterly indifferent. The impact then is just as inexplicable as the magic attraction: that which is utterly foreign cannot exercise any effect upon another, therefore cannot move itself nor allow itself to be moved. Parmenides would even have added: the only way of escape which is left to you is this, to ascribe motion to the things themselves; then however all that you know and see as motion is indeed only a deception and not true motion, for the only kind of motion which could belong to those absolutely original substances, would be merely an autogenous motion limited to themselves without any effect. But you assume motion in order to explain those effects of change, of the disarrangement in space, of alteration, in short the causalities and relations of the things among themselves. But these very effects would not be explained and would remain as problematic as ever; for this reason one cannot conceive why it should be necessary to assume a motion since it does not perform that which you demand from it. Motion does not belong to the nature of things and is eternally foreign to them.

Those opponents of the Eleatean unmoved Unity were induced to make light of such an argument by prejudices of a perceptual character. It seems so irrefutable that each veritable "Existent" is a space-filling body, a lump of matter, large or small but in any case spacially dimensioned; so that two or more such lumps cannot be in one space. Under this hypothesis Anaxagoras, as later on Democritus, assumed that they must knock against each other; if in their motions they came by chance upon one another, that they would dispute the same space with each other, and that this struggle was the very cause of all Change. In other words: those wholly isolated, thoroughly heterogeneous and eternally unalterable substances were after all not conceived as being absolutely heterogeneous but all had in addition to a specific, wholly peculiar quality, also one absolutely homogeneous substratum: a piece of space-filling matter. In their participation in matter they all stood equal and therefore could act upon one another, i.e., knock one another. Moreover all Change did not in the least depend on the heterogeneity of those substances but on their homogeneity, as matter. At the bottom of the assumption of Anaxagoras is a logical oversight; for that which is the "Existent-In-Itself" must be wholly unconditional and coherent, is therefore not allowed to assume as its cause anything,--whereas all those Anaxagorean substances have still a conditioning Something: matter, and already assume its existence; the substance "Red" for example was to Anaxagoras not just merely red in itself but also in a reserved or suppressed way a piece of matter without any qualities. Only with this matter the "Red-In-Itself" acted upon other substances, not with the "Red," but with that which is not red, not coloured, nor in any way qualitatively definite. If the "Red" had been taken strictly as "Red," as the real substance itself, therefore without that substratum, then Anaxagoras would certainly not have dared to speak of an effect of the "Red" upon other substances, perhaps even with the phrase that the "Red-In-Itself" was transmitting the impact received from the "Fleshy-In-Itself." Then it would be clear that such an "Existent" par excellence could never be moved.

15

One has to glance at the opponents of the Eleates, in order to appreciate the extraordinary advantages in the assumption of Parmenides. What embarrassments,--from which Parmenides had escaped,--awaited Anaxagoras and all who believed in a plurality of substances, with the question, How many substances? Anaxagoras made the leap, closed his eyes and said, "Infinitely many"; thus he had flown at least beyond the incredibly laborious proof of a definite number of elementary substances. Since these "Infinitely Many" had to exist without increase and unaltered for eternities, in that assumption was given the contradiction of an infinity to be conceived as completed and perfect. In short, Plurality, Motion, Infinity driven into flight by Parmenides with the amazing proposition of the one "Being," returned from their exile and hurled their projectiles at the opponents of Parmenides, causing them wounds for which there is no cure. Obviously those opponents have no real consciousness and knowledge as to the awful force of those Eleatean thoughts, "There can be no time, no motion, no space; for all these we can only think of as infinite, and to be more explicit, firstly infinitely large, then infinitely divisible; but everything infinite has no 'Being,' does not exist," and this nobody doubts, who takes the meaning of the word "Being" severely and considers the existence of something contradictory impossible, e.g., the existence of a completed infinity. If however the very Actuality shows us everything under the form of the completed infinity then it becomes evident that it contradicts itself and therefore has no true reality. If those opponents however should object: "but in your thinking itself there does exist succession, therefore neither could your thinking be real and consequently could not prove anything," then Parmenides perhaps like Kant in a similar case of an equal objection would have answered: "I can, it is true, say my conceptions follow upon one another, but that means only that we are not conscious of them unless within a chronological order, i.e., according to the form of the inner sense. For that reason time is not a something in itself nor any order or quality objectively adherent to things." We should therefore have to distinguish between the Pure Thinking, that would be timeless like the one Parmenidean "Being," and the consciousness of this thinking, and the latter would already translate the thinking into the form of appearance, i.e., of succession, plurality and motion. It is probable that Parmenides would have availed himself of this loophole; however, the same objection would then have to be raised against him which is raised against Kant by A. Spir ("Thinking And Reality," 2nd ed., vol. i., pp. 209, &c). "Now, in the first place however it is clear, that I cannot know anything of a succession as such, unless I have the successive members of the same simultaneously in my consciousness. Thus the conception of a succession itself is not at all successive, hence also quite different from the succession of our conceptions. Secondly Kant's assumption implies such obvious absurdities that one is surprised that he could leave them unnoticed. Cæsar and Socrates according to this assumption are not really dead, they still live exactly as they did two thousand years ago and only seem to be dead, as a consequence of an organisation of my inner sense." Future men already live and if they do not now step forward as living that organisation of the "inner sense" is likewise the cause of it. Here above all other things the question is to be put: How can the beginning and the end of conscious life itself, together with all its internal and external senses, exist merely in the conception of the inner sense? The fact is indeed this, that one certainly cannot deny the reality of Change. If it is thrown out through the window it slips in again through the keyhole. If one says: "It merely seems to me, that conditions and conceptions change,"--then this very semblance and appearance itself is something objectively existing and within it without doubt the succession has objective reality, some things in it really do succeed one another.--Besides one must observe that indeed the whole critique of reason only has cause and right of existence under the assumption that to us our conceptions themselves appear exactly as they are. For if the conceptions also appeared to us otherwise than they really are, then one would not be able to advance any solid proposition about them, and therefore would not be able to accomplish any gnosiology or any "transcendental" investigation of objective validity. Now it remains however beyond all doubt that our conceptions themselves appear to us as successive."

The contemplation of this undoubted succession and agitation has now urged Anaxagoras to a memorable hypothesis. Obviously the conceptions themselves moved themselves, were not pushed and had no cause of motion outside themselves. Therefore he said to himself, there exists a something which bears in itself the origin and the commencement of motion; secondly, however, he notices that this conception was moving not only itself but also something quite different, the body. He discovers therefore, in the most immediate experience an effect of conceptions upon expansive matter, which makes itself known as motion in the latter. That was to him a fact; and only incidentally it stimulated him to explain this fact. Let it suffice that he had a regulative schema for the motion in the world,--this motion he now understood either as a motion of the true isolated essences through the Conceptual

Principle, the Nous, or as a motion through a something already moved. That with his fundamental assumption the latter kind, the mechanical transmission of motions and impacts likewise contained in itself a problem, probably escaped him; the commonness and every-day occurrence of the effect through impact most probably dulled his eye to the mysteriousness of impact. On the other hand he certainly felt the problematic, even contradictory nature of an effect of conceptions upon substances existing in themselves and he also tried therefore to trace this effect back to a mechanical push and impact which were considered by him as quite comprehensible. For the Nous too was without doubt such a substance existing in itself and was characterised by him as a very delicate and subtle matter, with the specific quality of thinking. With a character assumed in this way, the effect of this matter upon other matter had of course to be of exactly the same kind as that which another substance exercises upon a third, i.e., a mechanical effect, moving by pressure and impact. Still the philosopher had now a substance which moves itself and other things, a substance of which the motion did not come from outside and depended on no one else: whereas it seemed almost a matter of indifference how this automobilism was to be conceived of, perhaps similar to that pushing themselves hither and thither of very fragile and small globules of quicksilver. Among all questions which concern motion there is none more troublesome than the question as to the beginning of motion. For if one may be allowed to conceive of all remaining motions as effect and consequences, then nevertheless the first primal motion is still to be explained; for the mechanical motions, the first link of the chain certainly cannot lie in a mechanical motion, since that would be as good as recurring to the nonsensical idea of the causa sui. But likewise it is not feasible to attribute to the eternal, unconditional things a motion of their own, as it were from the beginning, as dowry of their existence. For motion cannot be conceived without a direction whither and whereupon, therefore only as relation and condition; but a thing is no longer "entitative-in-itself" and "unconditional," if according to its nature it refers necessarily to something existing outside of it. In this embarrassment Anaxagoras thought he had found an extraordinary help and salvation in that Nous, automobile and otherwise independent; the nature of that Nous being just obscure and veiled enough to produce the deception about it, that its assumption also involves that forbidden causa sui. To empiric observation it is even an established fact that Conception is not a causa sui but the effect of the brain, yea, it must appear to that observation as an odd eccentricity to separate the "mind," the product of the brain, from its causa and still to deem it existing after this severing. This Anaxagoras did; he forgot the brain, its marvellous design, the delicacy and intricacy of its convolutions and passages and he decreed the "Mind-In-Itself." This "Mind-In-Itself" alone among all substances had Free-will,--a grand discernment! This Mind was able at any odd time to begin with the motion of the things outside it; on the other hand for ages and ages it could occupy itself with itself--in short Anaxagoras was allowed to assume a first moment of motion in some primeval age, as the Chalaza of all so-called Becoming; i.e., of all Change, namely of all shifting and rearranging of the eternal substances and their particles, Although the Mind itself is eternal, it is in no way compelled to torment itself for eternities with the shifting about of grains of matter; and certainly there was a time and a state of those matters--it is quite indifferent whether that time was of long or short duration--during which the Nous had not acted upon them, during which they were still unmoved. That is the period of the Anaxagorean chaos.

16

The Anaxagorean chaos is not an immediately evident conception; in order to grasp it one must have understood the conception which our philosopher had with respect to the so-called "Becoming." For in itself the state of all heterogeneous "Elementary-existences" before all motion would by no means necessarily result in an absolute mixture of all "seeds of things," as the expression of Anaxagoras runs, an intermixture, which he imagined as a complete pell-mell, disordered in its smallest parts, after all these "Elementary-existences" had been, as in a mortar, pounded and resolved into atoms of dust, so that now in that chaos, as in an amphora, they could be whirled into a medley. One might say that this conception of the chaos did not contain anything inevitable, that one merely needed rather to assume any chance position of all those "existences," but not an infinite decomposition of them; an irregular side-by-side arrangement was already sufficient; there was no need of a pell-mell, let alone such a total pell-mell. What therefore put into Anaxagoras' head that difficult and complex conception? As already said: his conception of the empirically given Becoming. From his experience he drew first a most extraordinary proposition on the Becoming, and this proposition necessarily resulted in that doctrine of the chaos, as its consequence.

The observation of the processes of evolution in nature, not a consideration of an earlier philosophical system, suggested to Anaxagoras the doctrine, that All originated from All; this was the conviction of the natural philosopher based upon a manifold, and at the bottom, of course, excessively inadequate induction. He proved it thus: if even the contrary could originate out of the contrary, e.g., the Black out of the White, everything is possible; that however did happen with the dissolution of white snow into black water. The nourishment of the body he explained to himself in this way: that in the articles of food there must be invisibly small constituents of flesh or blood or bone which during alimentation became disengaged and united with the homogeneous in the body. But if All can become out of All, the Firm out of the Liquid, the Hard out of the Soft, the Black out of the White, the Fleshy out of Bread, then also All must be contained in All. The names of things in that case express only the preponderance of the one substance over the other substances to be met with in smaller, often imperceptible quantities. In gold, that is to say, in that which one designates a potiore by the name "gold," there must be also contained silver, snow, bread, and flesh, but in very small quantities; the whole is called after the preponderating item, the gold-substance.

But how is it possible, that one substance preponderates and fills a thing in greater mass than the others present? Experience shows, that this preponderance is gradually produced only through Motion, that the preponderance is the result of a process, which we commonly call Becoming. On the other hand, that "All is in All" is not the result of a process, but, on the contrary, the preliminary condition of all Becoming and all Motion, and is consequently previous to all Becoming. In other words: experience teaches, that continually the like is added to the like, e.g., through nourishment, therefore originally those homogeneous substances were not together and agglomerated, but they were separate. Rather, in all empiric processes coming before our eyes, the homogeneous is always segregated from the heterogeneous and transmitted (e.g., during nourishment, the particles of flesh out of the bread, &c), consequently the pell-mell of the different substances is the older form of the constitution of things and in point of time previous to all Becoming and Moving. If all so-called Becoming is a segregating and presupposes a mixture, the question arises, what degree of intermixture this pell-mell must have had originally. Although the process of a moving on the part of the homogeneous to the homogeneous--i.e., Becoming--has already lasted an immense time, one recognises in spite of that, that even yet in all things remainders and seed-grains of all other things are enclosed, waiting for their segregation, and one recognises further that only here and there a preponderance has been brought about; the primal mixture must have been a complete one, i.e., going down to the infinitely small, since the separation and unmixing takes up an infinite length of time. Thereby strict adherence is paid to the thought: that everything which possesses an essential "Being" is infinitely divisible, without forfeiting its specificum.

According to these hypotheses Anaxagoras conceives of the world's primal existence: perhaps as similar to a dust-like mass of infinitely small, concrete particles of which every one is specifically simple and possesses one quality only, yet so arranged that every specific quality is represented in an infinite number of individual particles. Such particles Aristotle has called Homoiomere in consideration of the fact that they are the Parts, all equal one to another, of a Whole which is homogeneous with its Parts. One would however commit a serious mistake to equate this primal pell-mell of all such particles, such "seed-grains of things" to the one primal matter of Anaximander; for the latter's primal matter called the "Indefinite" is a thoroughly coherent and peculiar mass, the former's primal pell-mell is an aggregate of substances. It is true one can assert about this Aggregate of Substances exactly the same as about the Indefinite of Anaximander, as Aristotle does: it could be neither white nor grey, nor black, nor of any other colour; it was tasteless, scentless, and altogether as a Whole defined neither quantitatively nor qualitatively: so far goes the similarity of the Anaximandrian Indefinite and the Anaxagorean Primal Mixture. But disregarding this negative equality they distinguish themselves one from another positively by the latter being a compound, the former a unity. Anaxagoras had by the assumption of his Chaos at least so much to his advantage, that he was not compelled to deduce the Many from the One, the Becoming out of the "Existent."

Of course with his complete intermixture of the "seeds" he had to admit one exception: the Nous was not then, nor is It now admixed with any thing. For if It were admixed with only one "Existent," It would have, in infinite divisions, to dwell in all things. This exception is logically very dubious, especially considering the previously described material nature of the Nous, it has something mythological in itself and seems arbitrary, but was however, according to Anaxagorean prœmissa, a strict necessity. The Mind, which is moreover infinitely divisible like any other matter, only not through other matters but through Itself, has, if It divides Itself, in dividing and conglobating sometimes in large, sometimes in small masses, Its equal mass and quality from all eternity; and that which at this minute exists as Mind in animals, plants, men, was also Mind without a more or less, although distributed in another way a thousand years ago. But wherever It had a relation to another substance, there It never was admixed with it, but voluntarily seized it, moved and pushed it arbitrarily--in short, ruled it. Mind, which alone has motion in Itself, alone possesses ruling power in this world and shows it through moving the grains of matter. But whither does It move them? Or is a motion conceivable, without direction, without path? Is Mind in Its impacts just as arbitrary as it is, with regard to the time when It pushes, and when It does not push? In short, does Chance, i.e., the blindest option, rule within Motion? At this boundary we step into the Most Holy within the conceptual realm of Anaxagoras.

17

What had to be done with that chaotic pell-mell of the primal state previous to all motion, so that out of it, without any increase of new substances and forces, the existing world might originate, with its regular stellar orbits, with its regulated forms of seasons and days, with its manifold beauty and order,--in short, so that out of the Chaos might come a Cosmos? This can be only the effect of Motion, and of a definite and well-organised motion. This Motion itself is the means of the Nous, Its goal would be the perfect segregation of the homogeneous, a goal up to the present not yet attained, because the disorder and the mixture in the beginning was infinite. This goal is to be striven after only by an enormous process, not to be realized suddenly by a mythological stroke of the wand. If ever, at an infinitely distant point of time, it is achieved that everything homogeneous is brought together and the "primal-existences" undivided are encamped side by side in beautiful order, and every particle has found its comrades and its home, and the great peace comes about after the great division and splitting up of the substances, and there will be no longer anything that is divided ind split up, then the Nous will again return into Its automobilism and, no longer Itself divided, roam through the world, sometimes in larger, sometimes in smaller masses, as plant-mind or animal-mind, and no longer will It take up Its new dwelling-place in other matter. Meanwhile the task has not been completed; but the kind of motion which the Nous has thought out, in order to solve the task, shows a marvellous suitableness, for by this motion the task is further solved in each new moment. For this motion has the character of concentrically progressive circular motion; it began at some one point of the chaotic mixture, in the form of a little gyration, and in ever larger paths this circular movement traverses all existing "Being," jerking forth everywhere the homogeneous to the homogeneous. At first this revolution brings everything Dense to the Dense, everything Rare to the Rare, and likewise all that is Dark, Bright, Moist, Dry to their kind; above these general groups or classifications there are again two still more comprehensive, namely Ether, that is to say everything that is Warm, Bright, Rare, and Aër, that is to say everything that is Dark, Cold, Heavy, Firm. Through the segregation of the ethereal masses from the aërial, there is formed, as the most immediate effect of that epicycle whose centre moves along in the circumference of ever greater circles, a something as in an eddy made in standing water; heavy compounds are led towards the middle and compressed. Just in the same way that travelling waterspout in chaos forms itself on the outer side out of the Ethereal, Rare, Bright Constituents, on the inner side out of the Cloudy, Heavy, Moist Constituents. Then in the course of this process out of that Aërial mass, conglomerating in its interior, water is separated, and again out of the water the earthy element, and then out of the earthy element, under the effect of the awful cold are separated the stones. Again at some juncture masses of stone, through the momentum of the rotation, are torn away sideways from the earth and thrown into the realm of the hot light Ether; there in the latter's fiery element they are made to glow and, carried along in the ethereal rotation, they irradiate light, and as sun and stars illuminate and warm the earth, in herself dark and cold. The whole conception is of a wonderful daring and simplicity and has nothing of that clumsy and anthropomorphical teleology, which has been frequently connected with the name of Anaxagoras. That conception has its greatness just in this, that it derives the whole Cosmos of Becoming out of the moved circle, whereas Parmenides contemplated the true "Existent" as a resting, dead ball. Once that circle is put into motion and caused to roll by the Nous, then all the order, law and beauty of the world is the natural consequence of that first impetus. How very much one wrongs Anaxagoras if one reproaches him for the wise abstention from teleology which shows itself in this conception and talks scornfully of his Nous as of a deus ex machina. Rather, on account of the elimination of mythological and theistic miracle-working and anthropomorphic ends and utilities, Anaxagoras might have made use of proud words similar to those which Kant used in his Natural History of the Heavens. For it is indeed a sublime thought, to retrace that grandeur of the cosmos and the marvellous arrangement of the orbits of the stars, to retrace all that, in all forms to a simple, purely mechanical motion and, as it were, to a moved mathematical figure, and therefore not to reduce all that to purposes and intervening hands of a machine-god, but only to a kind of oscillation, which, having once begun, is in its progress necessary and definite, and effects result which resemble the wisest computation of sagacity and extremely well thought-out fitness without being anything of the sort. "I enjoy the pleasure," says Kant, of seeing how a well-ordered whole produces itself without the assistance of arbitrary fabrications, under the impulse of fixed laws of motion--a well-ordered whole which looks so similar to that world-system which is ours, that I cannot abstain from considering it to be the same. It seems to me that one might say here, in a certain sense without presumption: 'Give me matter and I will build a world out of it.'"

18

Suppose now, that for once we allow that primal mixture as rightly concluded, some considerations especially from Mechanics seem to oppose the grand plan of the world edifice. For even though the Mind at a point causes a circular movement its continuation is only conceivable with great difficulty, especially since it is to be infinite and gradually to make all existing masses rotate. As a matter of course one would assume that the pressure of all the remaining matter would have crushed out this small circular movement when it had scarcely begun; that this does not happen presupposes on the part of the stimulating Nous, that the latter began to work suddenly with awful force, or at any rate so quickly, that we must call the motion a whirl: such a whirl as Democritus himself imagined. And since this whirl must be infinitely strong in order not to be checked through the whole world of the Infinite weighing heavily upon it, it will be infinitely quick, for strength can manifest itself originally only in speed. On the contrary the broader the concentric rings are, the slower will be this motion; if once the motion could reach the end of the infinitely extended world, then this motion would have already infinitely little speed of rotation. Vice versa, if we conceive of the motion as infinitely great, i.e., infinitely quick, at the moment of the very first beginning of motion, then the original circle must have been infinitely small; we get therefore as the beginning a particle rotated round itself, a particle with an infinitely small material content. This however would not at all explain the further motion; one might imagine even all particles of the primal mass to rotate round themselves and yet the whole mass would remain unmoved and unseparated. If, however, that material particle of infinite smallness, caught and swung by the Nous, was not turned round itself but described a circle somewhat larger than a point, this would cause it to knock against other material particles, to move them on, to hurl them, to make them rebound and thus gradually to stir up a great and spreading tumult within which, as the next result, that separation of the aërial masses from the ethereal had to take place. Just as the commencement of the motion itself is an arbitrary act of the Nous, arbitrary also is the manner of this commencement in so far as the first motion circumscribes a circle of which the radius is chosen somewhat larger than a point.

19

Here of course one might ask, what fancy had at that time so suddenly occurred to the Nous, to knock against some chance material particle out of that number of particles and to turn it around in whirling dance and why that did not occur to It earlier. Whereupon Anaxagoras would answer: "The Nous has the privilege of arbitrary action; It may begin at any chance time, It depends on Itself, whereas everything else is determined from outside. It has no duty, and no end which It might be compelled to pursue; if It did once begin with that motion and set Itself an end, this after all was only--the answer is difficult, Heraclitus would say--play!"

That seems always to have been the last solution or answer hovering on the lips of the Greek. The Anaxagorean Mind is an artist and in truth the most powerful genius of mechanics and architecture, creating with the simplest means the most magnificent forms and tracks and as it were a mobile architecture, but always out of that irrational arbitrariness which lies in the soul of the artist. It is as though Anaxagoras was pointing at Phidias and in face of the immense work of art, the Cosmos, was calling out to us as he would do in front of the Parthenon: "The Becoming is no moral, but only an artistic phenomenon." Aristotle relates that, to the question what made life worth living, Anaxagoras had answered: "Contemplating the heavens and the total order of the Cosmos." He treated physical things so devotionally, and with that same mysterious awe, which we feel when standing in front of an antique temple; his doctrine became a species of free-thinking religious exercise, protecting itself through the odi profanum vulgus et arceo and choosing its adherents with precaution out of the highest and noblest society of Athens. In the exclusive community of the Athenian Anaxagoreans the mythology of the people was allowed only as a symbolic language; all myths, all gods, all heroes were considered here only as hieroglyphics of the interpretation of nature, and even the Homeric epic was said to be the canonic song of the sway of the Nous and the struggles and laws of Nature. Here and there a note from this society of sublime free-thinkers penetrated to the people; and especially Euripides, the great and at all times daring Euripides, ever thinking of something new, dared to let many things become known by means of the tragic mask, many things which pierced like an arrow through the senses of the masses and from which the latter freed themselves only by means of ludicrous caricatures and ridiculous re-interpretations.

The greatest of all Anaxagoreans however is Pericles, the mightiest and worthiest man of the world; and Plato bears witness that the philosophy of Anaxagoras alone had given that sublime flight to the genius of Pericles. When as a public orator he stood before his people, in the beautiful rigidity and immobility of a marble Olympian and now, calm, wrapped in his mantle, with unruffled drapery, without any change of facial expression, without smile, with a voice the strong tone of which remained ever the same, and when he now spoke in an absolutely un-Demosthenic but merely Periclean fashion, when he thundered, struck with lightnings, annihilated and redeemed--then he was the epitome of the Anaxagorean Cosmos, the image of the Nous, who has built for Itself the most beautiful and dignified receptacle, then Pericles was as it were the visible human incarnation of the building, moving, eliminating, ordering, reviewing, artistically-undetermined force of the Mind. Anaxagoras himself said man was the most rational being or he must necessarily shelter the Nous within himself in greater fulness than all other beings, because he had such admirable organs as his hands; Anaxagoras concluded therefore, that that Nous, according to the extent to which It made Itself master of a material body, was always forming for Itself out of this material the tools corresponding to Its degree of power, consequently the Nous made the most beautiful and appropriate tools, when It was appearing in his greatest fulness. And as the most wondrous and appropriate action of the Nous was that circular primal-motion, since at that time the Mind was still together, undivided, in Itself, thus to the listening Anaxagoras the effect of the Periclean speech often appeared perhaps as a simile of that circular primal-motion; for here too he perceived a whirl of thoughts moving itself at first with awful force but in an orderly manner, which in concentric circles gradually caught and carried away the nearest and farthest and which, when it reached its end, had reshaped--organising and segregating--the whole nation.

To the later philosophers of antiquity the way in which Anaxagoras made use of his Nous for the interpretation of the world was strange, indeed scarcely pardonable; to them it seemed as though he had found a grand tool but had not well understood it and they tried to retrieve what the finder had neglected. They therefore did not recognise what meaning the abstention of Anaxagoras, inspired by the purest spirit of the method of natural science, had, and that this abstention first of all in every case puts to itself the question: "What is the cause of Something"? (causa efficiens)--and not "What is the purpose of Something"? (causa finalis). The Nous has not been dragged in by Anaxagoras for the purpose of answering the special question: "What is the cause of motion and what causes regular motions?"; Plato however reproaches him, that he ought to have, but had not shown that everything was in its own fashion and its own place the most beautiful, the best and the most appropriate. But this Anaxagoras would not have dared to assert in any individual case, to him the existing world was not even the most conceivably perfect world, for he saw everything originate out of everything, and he found the segregation of the substances through the Nous complete and done with, neither at the end of the filled space of the world nor in the individual beings. For his understanding it was sufficient that he had found a motion, which, by simple continued action could create the visible order out of a chaos mixed through and through; and he took good care not to put the question as to the Why? of the motion, as to the rational purpose of motion. For if the Nous had to fulfil by means of motion a purpose innate in the noumenal essence, then it was no longer in Its free will to commence the motion at any chance time; in so far as the Nous is eternal, It had also to be determined eternally by this purpose, and then no point of time could have been allowed to exist in which motion was still lacking, indeed it would have been logically forbidden to assume a starting point for motion: whereby again the conception of original chaos, the basis of the whole Anaxagorean interpretation of the world would likewise have become logically impossible. In order to escape such difficulties, which teleology creates, Anaxagoras had always to emphasise and asseverate that the Mind has free will; all Its actions, including that of the primal motion, were actions of the "free will," whereas on the contrary after that primeval moment the whole remaining world was shaping itself in a strictly determined, and more precisely, mechanically determined form. That absolutely free will however can be conceived only as purposeless, somewhat after the fashion of children's play or the artist's bent for play. It is an error to ascribe to Anaxagoras the common confusion of the teleologist, who, marvelling at the extraordinary appropriateness, at the agreement of the parts with the whole, especially in the realm of the organic, assumes that that which exists for the intellect had also come into existence through intellect, and that that which man brings about only under the guidance of the idea of purpose, must have been brought about by Nature through reflection and ideas of purpose. (Schopenhauer, "The World As Will And Idea," vol. ii., Second Book, chap. 26: On Teleology). Conceived in the manner of Anaxagoras, however, the order and appropriateness of things on the contrary is nothing but the immediate result of a blind mechanical motion; and only in order to cause this motion, in order to get for once out of the dead-rest of the Chaos, Anaxagoras assumed the free-willed Nous who depends only on Itself. He appreciated in the Nous just the very quality of being a thing of chance, a chance agent, therefore of being able to act unconditioned, undetermined, guided neither by causes nor by purposes.

Notes for a Continuation

(Early Part of 1873)

1

That this total conception of the Anaxagorean doctrine must be right, is proved most clearly by the way in which the successors of Anaxagoras, the Agrigentine Empedocles and the atomic teacher Democritus in their counter-systems actually criticised and improved that doctrine. The method of this critique is more than anything a continued renunciation in that spirit of natural science mentioned above, the law of economy applied to the interpretation of nature. That hypothesis, which explains the existing world with the smallest expenditure of assumptions and means is to have preference: for in such a hypothesis is to be found the least amount of arbitrariness, and in it free play with possibilities is prohibited. Should there be two hypotheses which both explain the world, then a strict test must be applied as to which of the two better satisfies that demand of economy. He who can manage this explanation with the simpler and more known forces, especially the mechanical ones, he who deduces the existing edifice of the world out of the smallest possible number of forces, will always be preferred to him who allows the more complicated and less-known forces, and these moreover in greater number, to carry on a world-creating play. So then we see Empedocles endeavouring to remove the superfluity of hypotheses from the doctrine of Anaxagoras.

The first hypothesis which falls as unnecessary is that of the Anaxagorean Nous, for its assumption is much too complex to explain anything so simple as motion. After all it is only necessary to explain the two kinds of motion: the motion of a body towards another, and the motion away from another.

2

If our present Becoming is a segregating, although not a complete one, then Empedocles asks: what prevents complete segregation? Evidently a force works against it, i.e., a latent motion of attraction.

Further: in order to explain that Chaos, a force must already have been at work; a movement is necessary to bring about this complicated entanglement.

Therefore periodical preponderance of the one and the other force is certain. They are opposites.

The force of attraction is still at work; for otherwise there would be no Things at all, everything would be segregated.

This is the actual fact: two kinds of motion. The Nous does not explain them. On the contrary, Love and Hatred; indeed we certainly see that these move as well as that the Nous moves.

Now the conception of the primal state undergoes a change: it is the most blessed. With Anaxagoras it was the chaos before the architectural work, the heap of stones as it were upon the building site.

3

Empedocles had conceived the thought of a tangential force originated by revolution and working against gravity ("de coelo," i., p. 284), Schopenhauer, "W. A. W.," ii. 390.

He considered the continuation of the circular movement according to Anaxagoras impossible. It would result in a whirl, i.e., the contrary of ordered motion.

If the particles were infinitely mixed, pell-mell, then one would be able to break asunder the bodies without any exertion of power, they would not cohere or hold together, they would be as dust.

The forces, which press the atoms against one another, and which give stability to the mass, Empedocles calls "Love." It is a molecular force, a constitutive force of the bodies.

4

Against Anaxagoras.

1. The Chaos already presupposes motion.
2. Nothing prevented the complete segregation.
3. Our bodies would be dust-forms. How can motion exist, if there are not counter-motions in all bodies?
4. An ordered permanent circular motion impossible; only a whirl. He assumes the whirl itself to be an effect of the νεῖκος.--ἀπορροιαί. How do distant things operate on one another, sun upon earth? If everything were still in a whirl, that would be impossible. Therefore at least two moving powers: which must be inherent in Things.
5. Why infinite ὄντα? Transgression of experience. Anaxagoras meant the chemical atoms. Empedocles tried the assumption of four kinds of chemical atoms. He took the aggregate states to be essential, and heat to be co-ordinated. Therefore the aggregate states through repulsion and attraction; matter in four forms.
6. The periodical principle is necessary.
7. With the living beings Empedocles will also deal still on the same principle. Here also he denies purposiveness. His greatest deed. With Anaxagoras a dualism.

5

The symbolism of sexual love. Here as in the Platonic fable the longing after Oneness shows itself, and here, likewise, is shown that once a greater unity already existed; were this greater unity established, then this would again strive after a still greater one. The conviction of the unity of everything living guarantees that once there was an immense Living Something, of which we are pieces; that is probably the Sphairos itself. He is the most blessed deity. Everything was connected only through love, therefore in the highest degree appropriate. Love has been torn to pieces and splintered by hatred, love has been divided into her elements and killed--bereft of life. In the whirl no living individuals originate. Eventually everything is segregated and now our period begins. (He opposes the Anaxagorean Primal Mixture by a Primal Discord.) Love, blind as she is, with furious haste again throws the elements one against another endeavouring to see whether she can bring them back to life again or not. Here and there she is successful. It continues. A presentiment originates in the living beings, that they are to strive after still higher unions than home and the primal state. Eros. It is a terrible crime to kill life, for thereby one works back to the Primal Discord. Some day everything will be again one single life, the most blissful state.

The Pythagorean-orphean doctrine re-interpreted in the manner of natural science. Empedocles consciously masters both means of expression, therefore he is the first rhetor. Political aims.

The double-nature--the agonal and the loving, the compassionate.

Attempt of the Hellenic total reform.

All inorganic matter has originated out of organic, it is dead organic matter. Corpse and man.

6

DEMOCRITUS

The greatest possible simplification of the hypotheses.

1. There is motion, therefore vacuum, therefore a "Non-Existent." Thinking is motion.
2. If there is a "Non-Existent" it must be indivisible, i.e., absolutely filled. Division is only explicable in case of empty spaces and pores. The "Non-Existent" alone is an absolutely porous thing.
3. The secondary qualities of matter, νόμῳ, not of Matter-In-Itself.
4. Establishment of the primary qualities of the ἄτομα. Wherein homogeneous, wherein heterogeneous?
5. The aggregate-states of Empedocles (four elements) presuppose only the homogeneous atoms, they themselves cannot therefore be ὄντα.
6. Motion is connected indissolubly with the atoms, effect of gravity. Epicur. Critique: what does gravity signify in an infinite vacuum?
7. Thinking is the motion of the fire-atoms. Soul, life, perceptions of the senses.

Value of materialism and its embarrassment.

Plato and Democritus.

The hermit-like homeless noble searcher for truth. Democritus and the Pythagoreans together find the basis of natural sciences.

What are the causes which have interrupted a flourishing science of experimental physics in antiquity after Democritus?

7

Anaxagoras has taken from Heraclitus the idea that in every Becoming and in every Being the opposites are together.

He felt strongly the contradiction that a body has many qualities and he pulverised it in the belief that he had now dissolved it into its true qualities.

. Plato: first Heraclitean, later Sceptic: Everything, even Thinking, is in a state of flux.

Brought through Socrates to the permanence of the good, the beautiful.

These assumed as entitative.

All generic ideals partake of the idea of the good, the beautiful, and they too are therefore entitative, being (as the soul partakes of the idea of Life). The idea is formless.

Through Pythagoras' metempsychosis has been answered the question: how we can know anything about the ideas.

Plato's end: scepticism in Parmenides. Refutation of ideology.

8

CONCLUSION

Greek thought during the tragic age is pessimistic or artistically optimistic.

Their judgment about life implies more.

The One, flight from the Becoming. Aut unity, aut artistic play.

Deep distrust of reality: nobody assumes a good god, who has made everything optime.

{Pythagoreans, religious sect.
{Anaximander.
{Empedocles.

Eleates.
{Anaxagoras.
{Heraclitus.

Democritus: the world without moral and æsthetic meaning, pessimism of chance.

If one placed a tragedy before all these, the three former would see in it the mirror of the fatality of existence, Parmenides a transitory appearance, Heraclitus and Anaxagoras an artistic edifice and image of the world-laws, Democritus the result of machines.

With Socrates Optimism begins, an optimism no longer artistic, with teleology and faith in the good god; faith in the enlightened good man. Dissolution of the instincts, Socrates breaks with the hitherto prevailing knowledge and culture; he intends returning to the old citizen-virtue and to the State.

Plato dissociates himself from the State, when he observes that the State has become identical with the new Culture.

The Socratic scepticism is a weapon against the hitherto prevailing culture and knowledge.

ON TRUTH AND FALSITY IN THEIR ULTRAMORAL SENSE

(1873)

In some remote corner of the universe, effused into innumerable solar-systems, there was once a star upon which clever animals invented cognition. It was the haughtiest, most mendacious moment in the history of this world, but yet only a moment. After Nature had taken breath awhile the star congealed and the clever animals had to die.--Someone might write a fable after this style, and yet he would not have illustrated sufficiently, how wretched,; shadow-like, transitory, purposeless and fanciful the human intellect appears in Nature. There were eternities during which this intellect did not exist, and when it has once more passed away there will be nothing to show that it has existed. For this intellect is not concerned with any further mission transcending the sphere of human life. No, it is purely human and none but its owner and procreator regards it so pathetically as to suppose that the world revolves around it. If, however, we and the gnat could understand each other we should learn that even the gnat swims through the air with the same pathos, and feels within itself the flying centre of the world. Nothing in Nature is so bad or so insignificant that it will not, at the smallest puff of that force cognition, immediately swell up like a balloon, and just as a mere porter wants to have his admirer, so the very proudest man, the philosopher, imagines he sees from all sides the eyes of the universe telescopically directed upon his actions and thoughts.

It is remarkable that this is accomplished by the intellect, which after all has been given to the most unfortunate, the most delicate, the most transient beings only as an expedient, in order to detain them for a moment in existence, from which without that extra-gift they would have every cause to flee as swiftly as Lessing's son.[1] That haughtiness connected with cognition and sensation, spreading blinding fogs before the eyes and over the senses of men, deceives itself therefore as to the value of existence owing to the fact that it bears within itself the most flattering evaluation of cognition. Its most general effect is deception; but even its most particular effects have something of deception in their nature.

The intellect, as a means for the preservation of the individual, develops its chief power in dissimulation; for it is by dissimulation that the feebler, and less robust individuals preserve themselves, since it has been denied them to fight the battle of existence with horns or the sharp teeth of beasts of prey. In man this art of dissimulation reaches its acme of perfection: in him deception, flattery, falsehood and fraud, slander, display, pretentiousness, disguise, cloaking convention, and acting to others and to himself in short, the continual fluttering to and fro around the one flame--Vanity: all these things are so much the rule, and the law, that few things are more incomprehensible than the way in which an honest and pure impulse to truth could have arisen among men. They are deeply immersed in illusions and dream-fancies; their eyes glance only over the surface of things and see "forms"; their sensation nowhere leads to truth, but contents itself with receiving stimuli and, so to say, with playing hide-and-seek on the back of things. In addition to that, at night man allows his dreams to lie to him a whole life-time long, without his moral sense ever trying to prevent them; whereas men are said to exist who by the exercise of a strong will have overcome the habit of snoring. What indeed does man know about himself? Oh! that he could but once see himself complete, placed as it were in an illuminated glass-case! Does not nature keep secret from him most things, even about his body, e.g., the convolutions of the intestines, the quick flow of the blood-currents, the intricate vibrations of the fibres, so as to banish and lock him up in proud, delusive knowledge? Nature threw away the key; and woe co the fateful curiosity which might be able for a moment to look out and down through a crevice in the chamber of consciousness, and discover that man, indifferent to his own ignorance, is resting on the pitiless, the greedy, the insatiable, the murderous, and, as it were, hanging in dreams on the back of a tiger. Whence, in the wide world, with this state of affairs, arises the impulse to truth?

As far as the individual tries to preserve himself against other individuals, in the natural state of things he uses the intellect in most cases only for dissimulation; since, however, man both from necessity and boredom wants to exist socially and gregariously, he must needs make peace and at least endeavour to cause the greatest bellum omnium contra omnes to disappear from his world. This first conclusion of peace brings with it a something which looks like the first step towards the attainment of that enigmatical bent for truth. For that which henceforth is to be "truth" is now fixed; that is to say, a uniformly valid and binding designation of things is invented and the legislature of language also gives the first laws of truth: since here, for the first time, originates the contrast between truth and falsity. The liar uses the valid designations, the words, in order to make the unreal appear as real; e.g., he says, "I am rich," whereas the right designation for his state would be "poor." He abuses the fixed conventions by convenient substitution or even inversion of terms. If he does this in a selfish and moreover harmful fashion, society will no longer trust him but will even exclude him. In this way men avoid not so much being defrauded, but being injured by fraud. At bottom, at this juncture too, they hate not deception, but the evil, hostile consequences of certain species of deception. And it is in a similarly limited sense only that man desires truth: he covets the agreeable, life-preserving consequences of truth; he is indifferent towards pure, ineffective knowledge; he is even inimical towards truths which possibly might prove harmful or destroying. And, moreover, what after all are those conventions op language? Are they possibly products of knowledge, of the love of truth; do the designations and the things coincide? Is language the adequate expression of all realities?

Only by means of forgetfulness can man ever arrive at imagining that he possesses "truth" in that degree just indicated. If he does not mean to content himself with truth in the shape of tautology, that is, with empty husks, he will always obtain illusions instead of truth. What is a word? The expression of a nerve-stimulus in sounds. But to infer a cause outside us from the nerve-stimulus is already the result of a wrong and unjustifiable application of the proposition of causality. How should we dare, if truth with the genesis of language, if the point of view of certainty with the designations had alone been decisive; how indeed should we dare to say: the stone is hard; as if "hard" was known to us otherwise; and not merely as an entirely subjective stimulus! We divide things according to genders; we designate the tree as masculine,[2] the plant as feminine:[3] what arbitrary metaphors! How far flown beyond the canon of certainty! We speak of a "serpent";[4] the designation fits nothing but the sinuosity, and could therefore also appertain to the worm. What arbitrary demarcations! what one-sided preferences given sometimes to this, sometimes to that quality of a thing! The different languages placed side by side show that with words truth or adequate expression matters little: for otherwise there would not be so many languages. The "Thing-in-itself" (it is just this which would be the pure ineffective truth) is also quite incomprehensible to the creator of language and not worth making any great endeavour to obtain. He designates only the relations of things to men and for their expression he calls to his help the most daring metaphors. A nerve-stimulus, first transformed into a percept! First metaphor! The percept again copied into a sound! Second metaphor! And each time he leaps completely out of one sphere right into the midst of an entirely different one. One can imagine a man who is quite deaf and has never had a sensation of tone and of music; just as this man will possibly marvel at Chladni's sound figures in the sand, will discover their cause in the vibrations of the string, and will then proclaim that now he knows what man calls "tone"; even so does it happen to us all with language. When we talk about trees, colours, snow and flowers, we believe we know something about the things themselves, and yet we only possess metaphors of the things, and these metaphors do not in the least correspond to the original essentials. Just as the sound shows itself as a sand-figure, in the same way the enigmatical x of the Thing-in-itself is seen first as nerve-stimulus, then as percept, and finally as sound. At any rate the genesis of language did not therefore proceed on logical lines, and the whole material in which and with which the man of truth, the investigator, the philosopher works and builds, originates, if not from Nephelococcygia, cloud-land, at any rate not from the essence of things.

Let us especially think about the formation of ideas. Every word becomes at once an idea not by having, as one might presume, to serve as a reminder for the original experience happening but once and absolutely individualised, to which experience such word owes its origin, no, but by having simultaneously to fit innumerable, more or less similar (which really means never equal, therefore altogether unequal) cases. Every idea originates through equating the unequal. As certainly as no one leaf is exactly similar to any other, so certain is it that the idea "leaf" has been formed through an arbitrary omission of these individual differences, through a forgetting of the differentiating qualities, and this idea now awakens the notion that in nature there is, besides the leaves, a something called the "leaf," perhaps a primal form according to which all leaves were woven, drawn, accurately measured, coloured, crinkled, painted, but by unskilled hands, so that no copy had turned out correct and trustworthy as a true copy of the primal form. We call a man "honest"; we ask, why has he acted so honestly to-day? Our customary answer runs, "On account of his honesty." The Honesty! That means again: the "leaf" is the cause of the leaves. We really and truly do not know anything at all about an essential quality which might be called the honesty, but we do know about numerous individualised, and therefore unequal actions, which we equate by omission of the unequal, and now designate as honest actions; finally out of them we formulate a qualitas occulta with the name "Honesty." The disregarding of the individual and real furnishes us with the idea, as it likewise also gives us the form; whereas nature knows of no forms and ideas, and therefore knows no species but only an x, to us inaccessible and indefinable. For our antithesis of individual and species is anthropomorphic too and does not come from the essence of things, although on the other hand we do not dare to say that it does not correspond to it; for that would be a dogmatic assertion and as such just as undemonstrable as its contrary.

What therefore is truth? A mobile army of metaphors, metonymies, anthropomorphisms: in short a sum of human relations which became poetically and rhetorically intensified, metamorphosed, adorned, and after long usage seem to a nation fixed, canonic and binding; truths are illusions of which one has forgotten that they are illusions; worn-out metaphors which have become powerless to affect the senses; coins which have their obverse effaced and now are no longer of account as coins but merely as metal.

Still we do not yet know whence the impulse to truth comes, for up to now we have heard only about the obligation which society imposes in order to exist: to be truthful, that is, to use the usual metaphors, therefore expressed morally: we have heard only about the obligation to lie according to a fixed convention, to lie gregariously in a style binding for all. Now man of course forgets that matters are going thus with him; he therefore lies in that fashion pointed out unconsciously and according to habits of centuries' standing--and by this very unconsciousness, by this very forgetting, he arrives at a sense for truth. Through this feeling of being obliged to designate one thing as "red," another as "cold," a third one as "dumb," awakes a moral emotion relating to truth. Out of the antithesis "liar" whom nobody trusts, whom all exclude, man demonstrates to himself the venerableness, reliability, usefulness of truth. Now as a "rational" being he submits his actions to the sway of abstractions; he no longer suffers himself to be carried away by sudden impressions, by sensations, he first generalises all these impressions into paler, cooler ideas, in order to attach to them the ship of his life and actions. Everything which makes man stand out in bold relief against the animal depends on this faculty of volatilising the concrete metaphors into a schema, and therefore resolving a perception into an idea. For within the range of those schemata a something becomes possible that never could succeed under the first perceptual impressions: to build up a pyramidal order with castes and grades, to create a new world of laws, privileges, sub-orders, delimitations, which now stands opposite the other perceptual world of first impressions and assumes the appearance of being the more fixed, general, known, human of the two and therefore the regulating and imperative one. Whereas every metaphor of perception is individual and without its equal and therefore knows how to escape all attempts to classify it, the great "edifice of ideas shows the rigid regularity of a Roman Columbarium and in logic breathes forth the sternness and coolness which we find in mathematics. He who has been breathed upon by this coolness will scarcely believe, that the idea too, bony and hexa-hedral, and permutable as a die, remains however only as the residuum of a metaphor, and that the illusion of the artistic metamorphosis of a nerve-stimulus into percepts is, if not the mother, then the grand-mother of every idea. Now in this game of dice, "Truth" means to use every die as it is designated, to count its points carefully, to form exact classifications, and never lo violate the order of castes and the sequences of rank. Just as the Romans and Etruscans for their benefit cut up the sky by means of strong mathematical lines and banned a god as it were into a templum, into a space limited in this fashion, so every nation has above its head such a sky of ideas divided up mathematically, and it understands the demand for truth to mean that every conceptual god is to be looked for only in his own sphere. One may here well admire man, who succeeded in piling up an infinitely complex dome of ideas on a movable foundation and as it were on running water, as a powerful genius of architecture. Of course in order to obtain hold on such a foundation it must be as an edifice piled up out of cobwebs, so fragile, as to be carried away by the waves: so firm, as not to be blown asunder by every wind. In this way man as an architectural genius rises high above the bee; she builds with wax, which she brings together out of nature; he with the much more delicate material of ideas, which he must first manufacture within himself. He is very much to be admired here--but not on account of his impulse for truth, his bent for pure cognition of things. If somebody hides a thing behind a bush, seeks it again and finds it in the self-same place, then there is not much to boast of, respecting this seeking and finding; thus, however, matters stand with the seeking and finding of "truth" within the realm of reason. If I make the definition of the mammal and then declare after inspecting a camel, "Behold a mammal," then no doubt a truth is brought to light thereby, but it is of very limited value, I mean it is anthropomorphic through and through, and does not contain one single point which is "true-in-itself," real and universally valid, apart from man. The seeker after such truths seeks at the bottom only the metamorphosis of the world in man, he strives for an understanding of the world as a human-like thing and by his battling gains at best the feeling of an assimilation. Similarly, as the astrologer contemplated the stars in the service of man and in connection with their happiness and unhappiness, such a seeker contemplates the whole world as related to man, as the infinitely protracted echo of an original sound: man; as the multiplied copy of the one arch-type: man. His procedure is to apply man as the measure of all things, whereby he starts from the error of believing that he has these things immediately before him as pure objects. He therefore forgets that the original metaphors of perception are metaphors, and takes them for the things themselves.

Only by forgetting that primitive world of metaphors, only by the congelation and coagulation of an original mass of similes and percepts pouring forth as a fiery liquid out of the primal faculty of human fancy, only by the invincible faith, that this sun, this window, this table is a truth in itself: in short only by the fact that man forgets himself as subject, and what is more as an artistically creating subject: only by all this does he live with some repose, safety and consequence. If he were able to get out of the prison walls of this faith, even for an instant only, his "self-consciousness would be destroyed at once. Already it costs him some trouble to admit to himself that the insect and the bird perceive a world different from his own, and that the question, which of the two world-perceptions is more accurate, is quite a senseless one, since to decide this question it would be necessary to apply the standard of right perception, i.e., to apply a standard which does not exist. On the whole it seems to me that the "right perception"--which would mean the adequate expression of an object in the subject--is a nonentity full of contradictions: for between two utterly different spheres, as between subject and object, there is no causality, no accuracy, no expression, but at the utmost an æsthetical relation, I mean a suggestive metamorphosis, a stammering translation into quite a distinct foreign language, for which purpose however there is needed at any rate an intermediate sphere, an intermediate force, freely composing and freely inventing. The word "phenomenon" contains many seductions, and on that account I avoid it as much as possible, for it is not true that the essence of things appears in the empiric world. A painter who had no hands and wanted to express the picture distinctly present to his mind by the agency of song, would still reveal much more with this permutation of spheres, than the empiric world reveals about the essence of things. The very relation of a nerve-stimulus to the produced percept is in itself no necessary one; but if the same percept has been reproduced millions of times and has been the inheritance of many successive generations of man, and in the end appears each time to all mankind as the result of the same cause, then it attains finally for man the same importance as if it were the unique, necessary percept and as if that relation between the original nerve-stimulus and the percept produced were a close relation of causality: just as a dream eternally repeated, would be perceived and judged as though real. But the congelation and coagulation of a metaphor does not at all guarantee the necessity and exclusive justification of that metaphor.

Surely every human being who is at home with such contemplations has felt a deep distrust against any idealism of that kind, as often as he has distinctly convinced himself of the eternal rigidity, omni-presence, and infallibility of nature's laws: he has arrived at the conclusion that as far as we can penetrate the heights of the telescopic and the depths of the microscopic world, everything is quite secure, complete, infinite, determined, and continuous. Science will have to dig in these shafts eternally and successfully and all things found are sure to have to harmonise and not to contradict one another. How little does this resemble a product of fancy, for if it were one it would necessarily betray somewhere its nature of appearance and unreality. Against this it may be objected in the first place that if each of us had for himself a different sensibility, if we ourselves were only able to perceive sometimes as a bird, sometimes as a worm, sometimes as a plant, or if one of us saw the same stimulus as red, another as blue, if a third person even perceived it as a tone, then nobody would talk of such an orderliness of nature, but would conceive of her only as an extremely subjective structure. Secondly, what is, for us in general, a law of nature? It is not known in itself but only in its effects, that is to say in its relations to other laws of nature, which again are known to us only as sums of relations. Therefore all these relations refer only one to another and are absolutely incomprehensible to us in their essence; only that which we add: time, space, i.e., relations of sequence and numbers, are really known to us in them. Everything wonderful, however, that we marvel at in the laws of nature, everything that demands an explanation and might seduce us into distrusting idealism, lies really and solely in the mathematical rigour and inviolability of the conceptions of time and space. These however we produce within ourselves and throw them forth with that necessity with which the spider spins; since we are compelled to conceive all things under these forms only, then it is no longer wonderful that in all things we actually conceive none but these forms: for they all must bear within themselves the laws of number, and this very idea of number is the most marvellous in all things. All obedience to law which impresses us so forcibly in the orbits of stars and in chemical processes coincides at the bottom with those qualities which we ourselves attach to those things, so that it is we who thereby make the impression upon ourselves. Whence it clearly follows that that artistic formation of metaphors, with which every sensation in us begins, already presupposes those forms, and is therefore only consummated within them; only out of the persistency of these primal forms the possibility explains itself, how afterwards--out of the metaphors themselves a structure of ideas, could again be compiled. For the latter is an imitation of the relations of time, space and number in the realm of metaphors.

Footnote:

1. The German poet, Lessing, had been married for just a little over one year to Eva König. A son was born and died the same day, and the mother's life was despaired of. In a letter to his friend Eschenburg the poet wrote: "... and I lost him so unwillingly, this son! For he had so much understanding! so much understanding! Do not suppose that the few hours of fatherhood have made me an ape of a father! I know what I say. Was it not understanding, that they had to drag him into the world with a pair of forceps? that he so soon suspected the evil of this world? Was it not understanding, that

he seized the first opportunity to get away from it?..."

Eva König died a week later.--TR.

2. In German the tree--der Baum--is masculine.--TR.

3. In German the plant--die Pflanze---is feminine--TR.

4. Cf. the German die Schlange and schlingen, the English serpent from the Latin serpere.--TR.

2

As we saw, it is language which has worked originally at the construction of ideas; in later times it is science. Just as the bee works at the same time at the cells and fills them with honey, thus science works irresistibly at that great columbarium of ideas, the cemetery of perceptions, builds ever newer and higher storeys; supports, purifies, renews the old cells, and endeavours above all to fill that gigantic framework and to arrange within it the whole of the empiric world, i.e., the anthropomorphic world. And as the man of action binds his life to reason and its ideas, in order to avoid being swept away and losing himself, so the seeker after truth builds his hut close to the towering edifice of science in order to collaborate with it and to find protection. And he needs protection. For there are awful powers which continually press upon him, and which hold out against the "truth" of science "truths" fashioned in quite another way, bearing devices of the most heterogeneous character.

That impulse towards the formation of metaphors, mat fundamental impulse of man, which we cannot reason away for one moment--for thereby we should reason away man himself--is in truth not defeated nor even subdued by the fact that out of its evaporated products, the ideas, a regular and rigid new world has been built as a stronghold for it. This impulse seeks for itself a new realm of action and another river-bed, and finds it in Mythos and more generally in Art. This impulse constantly confuses the rubrics and cells of the ideas, by putting up new figures of speech, metaphors, metonymies; it constantly shows its passionate longing for shaping the existing world of waking man as motley, irregular, inconsequentially incoherent, attractive, and eternally new as the world of dreams is. For indeed, waking man per se is only clear about his being awake through the rigid and orderly woof of ideas, and it is for this very reason that he sometimes comes to believe that he was dreaming when that woof of ideas has for a moment been torn by Art. Pascal is quite right, when he asserts, that if the same dream came to us every night we should be just as much occupied by it as by the things which we see every day; to quote his words, "If an artisan were certain that he would dream every night for fully twelve hours that he was a king, I believe that he would be just as happy as a king who dreams every night for twelve hours that he is an artisan." The wide-awake day of a people mystically excitable, let us say of the earlier Greeks, is in fact through the continually-working wonder, which the mythos presupposes, more akin to the dream than to the day of the thinker sobered by science. If every tree may at some time talk as a nymph, or a god under the disguise of a bull, carry away virgins, if the goddess Athene herself be suddenly seen as, with a beautiful team, she drives, accompanied by Pisistratus, through the markets of Athens--and every honest Athenian did believe this--at any moment, as in a dream, everything is possible; and all nature swarms around man as if she were nothing but the masquerade of the gods, who found it a huge joke to deceive man by assuming all possible forms.

Man himself, however, has an invincible tendency to let himself be deceived, and he is like one enchanted with happiness when the rhapsodist narrates to him epic romances in such a way that they appear real or when the actor on the stage makes the king appear more kingly than reality shows him. Intellect, that master of dissimulation, is free and dismissed from his service as slave, so long as It is able to deceive without injuring, and then It celebrates Its Saturnalia. Never is It richer, prouder, more luxuriant, more skilful and daring; with a creator's delight It throws metaphors into confusion, shifts the boundary-stones of the abstractions, so that for instance It designates the stream as the mobile way which carries man to that place whither he would otherwise go. Now It has thrown off Its shoulders the emblem of servitude. Usually with gloomy officiousness It endeavours to point out the way to a poor individual coveting existence, and It fares forth for plunder and booty like a servant for his master, but now It Itself has become a master and may wipe from Its countenance the expression of indigence. Whatever It now does, compared with Its former doings, bears within itself dissimulation, just as Its former doings bore the character of distortion. It copies human life, but takes it for a good thing and seems to rest quite satisfied with it. That enormous framework and hoarding of ideas, by clinging to which needy man saves himself through life, is to the freed intellect only a scaffolding and a toy for Its most daring feats, and when It smashes it to pieces, throws it into confusion, and then puts it together ironically, pairing the strangest, separating the nearest items, then It manifests that It has no use for those makeshifts of misery, and that It is now no longer led by ideas but by intuitions. From these intuitions no regular road leads into the land of the spectral schemata, the abstractions; for them the word is not made, when man sees them he is dumb, or speaks in forbidden metaphors and in unheard-of combinations of ideas, in order to correspond creatively with the impression of the powerful present intuition at least by destroying and jeering at the old barriers of ideas.

There are ages, when the rational and the intuitive man stand side by side, the one full of fear of the intuition, the other full of scorn for the abstraction; the latter just as irrational as the former is inartistic. Both desire to rule over life; the one by knowing how to meet the most important needs with foresight, prudence, regularity; the other as an "over-joyous" hero by ignoring those needs and taking that life only as real which simulates appearance and beauty. Wherever intuitive man, as for instance in the earlier history of Greece, brandishes his weapons more powerfully and victoriously than his opponent, there under favourable conditions, a culture can develop and art can establish her rule over life. That dissembling, that denying of neediness, that splendour of metaphorical notions and especially that directness of dissimulation accompany all utterances of such a life. Neither the house of man, nor his way of walking, nor his clothing, nor his earthen jug suggest that necessity invented them; it seems as if they all were intended as the expressions of a sublime happiness, an Olympic cloudlessness, and as it were a playing at seriousness. Whereas the man guided by ideas and abstractions only wards off misfortune by means of them, without even enforcing for himself happiness out of the abstractions; whereas he strives after the greatest possible freedom from pains, the intuitive man dwelling in the midst of culture has from his intuitions a harvest: besides the warding off of evil, he attains a continuous in-pouring of enlightenment, enlivenment and redemption. Of course when he does suffer, he suffers more: and he even suffers more frequently since he cannot learn from experience, but again and again falls into the same ditch into which he has fallen before. In suffering he is just as irrational as in happiness; he cries aloud and finds no consolation. How different matters are in the same misfortune with the Stoic, taught by experience and ruling himself by ideas! He who otherwise only looks for uprightness, truth, freedom from deceptions and shelter from ensnaring and sudden attack, in his misfortune performs the masterpiece of dissimulation, just as the other did in his happiness; he shows no twitching mobile human face but as it were a mask with dignified, harmonious features; he does not cry out and does not even alter his voice; when a heavy thundercloud bursts upon him, he wraps himself up in his cloak and with slow and measured step walks away from beneath it.

THE END.

On the Future of Our Educational Institutions: Homer and Classical Philology

Translated, With Introduction, by J.M. Kennedy

Originally Published by:
T.N. Foulis, 13 & 15 Frederick Street, Edinburgh: and London, 1909

TRANSLATOR'S INTRODUCTION

"On the Future of our Educational Institutions" comprehends a series of five lectures delivered by Nietzsche when Professor of Classical Philology at Băle University. As they were prepared when he was only twenty-seven years of age, we can scarcely expect to find in them that broad, "good European" point of view which we meet with in his later works. These lectures, however, are not only highly interesting in themselves; but indispensable for those who wish to trace the gradual development of Nietzsche's thought.

Nietzsche's aim, as is now pretty well known, was the elevation of the type man. At this period of his life he believed that this end could be best attained by the protection and careful development of men of genius, Hence his antagonism in the following lectures towards the purely time-serving German schools and colleges of his age, in which culture was not only neglected but not even known--the one aim of the teachers being to instruct the pupils in the art of "getting on," of playing a successful part in the struggle for existence, of becoming useful citizens. Of course, Nietzsche was too little of a wild reformer to be adverse to a schooling of this nature. He freely admits that a bread-winning education is necessary for the majority, and that officials are necessary to the State; but he adds that everything learnt as a preparation for taking part in the commercial or political battle of life has nothing to do with culture. True culture is only for a few select minds, which it is necessary to bring together under the protecting roof of an institution that shall prepare them for culture, and for culture only. Such an institution, he goes on to say, does not yet exist; but we must have it if the delicate flower of the German mind is no longer to be choked by the noxious weeds which have gathered round it. As instances of minds thus "choked," Nietzsche mentions Lessing, Winckelmann, and Schiller.

The standard of culture to be aimed at by the man of genius Nietzsche had in mind was to be found in the model literary and artistic works which have come down to us from ancient Greece. To understand these works, of course, the classical authors had to be studied in the original, and the methods of teaching then in vogue paid too much attention to inconsequential points (<i>e.g.</i> variant readings) instead of dealing with the subject in a broad-minded philosophical spirit. Nietzsche endeavoured to counteract this tendency in the "Homer and Classical Philology," his inaugural address at Băle University, by outlining a much vaster conception of philology than his fellow-teachers had ever dreamt of, laying stress upon the <i>artistic</i> results which would accrue if the science were applied on a wider scale--results which would be of a much higher order than those obtained by the narrow pedantry then prevailing.

It is a very superficial comment on these lectures to say that Nietzsche was merely referring to the German schools and colleges of his time. It would be even shallower to suggest that his remarks do not apply to the schools and teachers of present-day England and America; for we likewise do not possess the cultural institution, the <i>real</i> educational establishment, that Nietzsche longed for. Broadly speaking, the English public schools, the older English universities, and the American high schools, train their scholars to be useful to the State: the modern universities and the remaining schools give that instructionin bread-winning which Nietzsche admits to be necessary for the majority; but in no case is an attempt made to pick out a few higher minds and train them for culture. Our crude methods of teaching the classical languages are too well known to be commented upon; and an insight into classical antiquity, with the good taste, the firm principles, and the lofty aims obtained therefrom, is exactly what our various educational institutions do not aim at giving. Yet, as Nietzsche truly says, no progress in any other direction, no matter how brilliant, can deliver our students from the curse of an education which adapts itself more and more to the needs of the age, and thus loses all its power of guiding the age. Let the student who, as the victim of this system, suffers more from it than his teachers care to admit, read the paragraph on pp. 132 and 133 containing the sentences--

> He feels that he can neither lead nor help himself.... His condition is undignified, even dreadful: he keeps between the two extremes of work at high pressure and a state of melancholy enervation.... He seeks consolation in hasty and incessant action so as to hide himself from himself, etc.,

and then let him confess that Nietzsche's insight into his psychology is profound and decisive. The whole paragraph might have been written by Nietzsche after a visit to present-day England.

As bearing upon the same subject, the reader will find it interesting to compare the lectures here translated with Matthew Arnold's prose writings passim, particularly the <i>Essays in Criticism, Mixed Essays,</i> and <i>Culture and Anarchy</i>.

J. M. KENNEDY.
LONDON, May 1909.

On the Future of Our Educational Institutions

PREFACE

The reader from whom I expect something must possess three qualities: he must be calm and must read without haste; he must not be ever interposing his own personality and his own special "culture"; and he must not expect as the ultimate results of his study of these pages that he will be presented with a set of new formulæ. I do not propose to furnish formulæ or new plans of study for Gymnasia or other schools; and I am much more inclined to admire the extraordinary power of those who are able to cover the whole distance between the depths of empiricism and the heights of special culture-problems, and who again descend to the level of the driest rules and the most neatly expressed formulæ. I shall be content if only I can ascend a tolerably lofty mountain, from the summit of which, after having recovered my breath, I may obtain a general survey of the ground; for I shall never be able, in this book, to satisfy the votaries of tabulated rules. Indeed, I see a time coming when serious men, working together in the service of a completely rejuvenated and purified culture, may again become the directors of a system of everyday instruction, calculated to promote that culture; and they will probably be compelled once more to draw up sets of rules: but how remote this time now seems! And what may not happen meanwhile! It is just possible that between now and then all Gymnasia--yea, and perhaps all universities, may be destroyed, or have become so utterly transformed that their very regulations may, in the eyes of future generations, seem to be but the relics of the cave-dwellers' age.

This book is intended for calm readers,--for men who have not yet been drawn into the mad headlong rush of our hurry-skurrying age, and who do not experience any idolatrous delight in throwing themselves beneath its chariot-wheels. It is for men, therefore, who are not accustomed to estimate the value of everything according to the amount of time it either saves or wastes. In short, it is for the few. These, we believe, "still have time." Without any qualms of conscience they may improve the most fruitful and vigorous hours of their day in meditating on the future of our education; they may even believe when the evening has come that they have used their day in the most dignified and useful way, namely, in the meditatio generis futuri. No one among them has yet forgotten to think while reading a book; he still understands the secret of reading between the lines, and is indeed so generous in what he himself brings to his study, that he continues to reflect upon what he has read, perhaps long after he has laid the book aside. And he does this, not because he wishes to write a criticism about it or even another book; but simply because reflection is a pleasant pastime to him. Frivolous spendthrift! Thou art a reader after my own heart; for thou wilt be patient enough to accompany an author any distance, even though he himself cannot yet see the goal at which he is aiming,--even though he himself feels only that he must at all events honestly believe in a goal, in order that a future and possibly very remote generation may come face to face with that towards which we are now blindly and instinctively groping. Should any reader demur and suggest that all that is required is prompt and bold reform; should he imagine that a new "organisation" introduced by the State, were all that is necessary, then we fear he would have misunderstood not only the author but the very nature of the problem under consideration.

The third and most important stipulation is, that he should in no case be constantly bringing himself and his own "culture" forward, after the style of most modern men, as the correct standard and measure of all things. We would have him so highly educated that he could even think meanly of his education or despise it altogether. Only thus would he be able to trust entirely to the author's guidance; for it is only by virtue of ignorance and his consciousness of ignorance, that the latter can dare to make himself heard. Finally, the author would wish his reader to be fully alive to the specific character of our present barbarism and of that which distinguishes us, as the barbarians of the nineteenth century, from other barbarians.

Now, with this book in his hand, the writer seeks all those who may happen to be wandering, hither and thither, impelled by feelings similar to his own. Allow yourselves to be discovered--ye lonely ones in whose existence I believe! Ye unselfish ones, suffering in yourselves from the corruption of the German spirit! Ye contemplative ones who cannot, with hasty glances, turn your eyes swiftly from one surface to another! Ye lofty thinkers, of whom Aristotle said that ye wander through life vacillating and inactive so long as no great honour or glorious Cause calleth you to deeds! It is you I summon! Refrain this once from seeking refuge in your lairs of solitude and dark misgivings. Bethink you that this book was framed to be your herald. When ye shall go forth to battle in your full panoply, who among you will not rejoice in looking back upon the herald who rallied you?

INTRODUCTION

The title I gave to these lectures ought, like all titles, to have been as definite, as plain, and as significant as possible; now, however, I observe that owing to a certain excess of precision, in its present form it is too short and consequently misleading. My first duty therefore will be to explain the title, together with the object of these lectures, to you, and to apologise for being obliged to do this. When I promised to speak to you concerning the future of our educational institutions, I was not thinking especially of the evolution of our particular institutions in Bâle. However frequently my general observations may seem to bear particular application to our own conditions here, I personally have no desire to draw these inferences, and do not wish to be held responsible if they should be drawn, for the simple reason that I consider myself still far too much an inexperienced stranger among you, and much too superficially acquainted with your methods, to pretend to pass judgment upon any such special order of scholastic establishments, or to predict the probable course their development will follow. On the other hand, I know full well under what distinguished auspices I have to deliver these lectures--namely, in a city which is striving to educate and enlighten its inhabitants on a scale so magnificently out of proportion to its size, that it must put all larger cities to shame. This being so, I presume I am justified in assuming that in a quarter where so much is done for the things of which I wish to speak, people must also think a good deal about them. My desire--yea, my very first condition, therefore, would be to become united in spirit with those who have not only thought very deeply upon educational problems, but have also the will to promote what they think to be right by all the means in their power. And, in view of the difficulties of my task and the limited time at my disposal, to such listeners, alone, in my audience, shall I be able to make myself understood--and even then, it will be on condition that they shall guess what I can do no more than suggest, that they shall supply what I am compelled to omit; in brief, that they shall need but to be reminded and not to be taught. Thus, while I disclaim all desire of being taken for an uninvited adviser on questions relating to the schools and the University of Bâle, I repudiate even more emphatically still the rôle of a prophet standing on the horizon of civilisation and pretending to predict the future of education and of scholastic organisation. I can no more project my vision through such vast periods of time than I can rely upon its accuracy when it is brought too close to an object under examination. With my title: Our Educational Institutions, I wish to refer neither to the establishments in Bâle nor to the incalculably vast number of other scholastic institutions which exist throughout the nations of the world to-day; but I wish to refer to German institutions of the kind which we rejoice in here. It is their future that will now engage our attention, i.e. the future of German elementary, secondary, and public schools (Gymnasien) and universities. While pursuing our discussion, however, we shall for once avoid all comparisons and valuations, and guard more especially against that flattering illusion that our conditions should be regarded as the standard for all others and as surpassing them. Let it suffice that they are our institutions, that they have not become a part of ourselves by mere accident, and were not laid upon us like a garment; but that they are living monuments of important steps in the progress of civilisation, in some respects even the furniture of a bygone age, and as such link us with the past of our people, and are such a sacred and venerable legacy that I can only undertake to speak of the future of our educational institutions in the sense of their being a most probable approximation to the ideal spirit which gave them birth. I am, moreover, convinced that the numerous alterations which have been introduced into these institutions within recent years, with the view of bringing them up-to-date, are for the most part but distortions and aberrations of the originally sublime tendencies given to them at their foundation. And what we dare to hope from the future, in this behalf, partakes so much of the nature of a rejuvenation, a reviviscence, and a refining of the spirit of Germany that, as a result of this very process, our educational institutions may also be indirectly remoulded and born again, so as to appear at once old and new, whereas now they only profess to be "modern" or "up-to-date."

Now it is only in the spirit of the hope above mentioned that I wish to speak of the future of our educational institutions: and this is the second point in regard to which I must tender an apology from the outset. The "prophet" pose is such a presumptuous one that it seems almost ridiculous to deny that I have the intention of adopting it. No one should attempt to describe the future of our education, and the means and methods of instruction relating thereto, in a prophetic spirit, unless he can prove that the picture he draws already exists in germ to-day, and that all that is required is the extension and development of this embryo if the necessary modifications are to be produced in schools and other educational institutions. All I ask, is, like a Roman haruspex, to be allowed to steal glimpses of the future out of the very entrails of existing conditions, which, in this case, means no more than to hand the laurels of victory to any one of the many forces tending to make itself felt in our present educational system, despite the fact that the force in question may be neither a favourite, an esteemed, nor a very extensive one. I confidently assert that it will be victorious, however, because it has the strongest and mightiest of all allies in nature herself; and in this respect it were well did we not forget that scores of the very first principles of our modern educational methods are thoroughly artificial, and that the most fatal weaknesses of the present day are to be ascribed to this artificiality. He who feels in complete harmony with the present state of affairs and who acquiesces in it as something "selbstverständliches,"[1] excites our envy neither in regard to his faith nor in regard to that egregious word "selbstverständlich," so frequently heard in fashionable circles.

He, however, who holds the opposite view and is therefore in despair, does not need to fight any longer: all he requires is to give himself up to solitude in order soon to be alone. Albeit, between those who take everything for granted and these anchorites, there stand the fighters--that is to say, those who still have hope, and as the noblest and sublimest example of this class, we recognise Schiller as he is described by Goethe in his "Epilogue to the Bell."

"Brighter now glow'd his cheek, and still more bright
With that unchanging, ever youthful glow:--
That courage which o'ercomes, in hard-fought fight,
Sooner or later ev'ry earthly foe,--
That faith which soaring to the realms of light,
Now boldly presseth on, now bendeth low,
So that the good may work, wax, thrive amain,
So that the day the noble may attain."[2]

I should like you to regard all I have just said as a kind of preface, the object of which is to illustrate the title of my lectures and to guard me against any possible misunderstanding and unjustified criticisms. And now, in order to give you a rough outline of the range of ideas from which I shall attempt to form a judgment concerning our educational institutions, before proceeding to disclose my views and turning from the title to the main theme, I shall lay a scheme before you which, like a coat of arms, will serve to warn all strangers who come to my door, as to the nature of the house they are about to enter, in case they may feel inclined, after having examined the device, to turn their backs on the premises that bear it. My scheme is as follows:--

Two seemingly antagonistic forces, equally deleterious in their actions and ultimately combining to produce their results, are at present ruling over our educational institutions, although these were based originally upon very different principles. These forces are: a striving to achieve the greatest possible extension of education on the one hand, and a tendency to minimise and to weaken it on the other. The first-named would fain spread learning among the greatest possible number of people, the second would compel education to renounce its highest and most independent claims in order to subordinate itself to the service of the State. In the face of these two antagonistic tendencies, we could but give ourselves up to despair, did we not see the possibility of promoting the cause of two other contending factors which are fortunately as completely German as they are rich in promises for the future; I refer to the present movement towards limiting and concentrating education as the antithesis of the first of the forces above mentioned, and that other movement towards the strengthening and the independence of education as the antithesis of the second force. If we should seek a warrant for our belief in the ultimate victory of the two last-named movements, we could find it in the fact that both of the forces which we hold to be deleterious are so opposed to the eternal purpose of nature as the concentration of education for the few is in harmony with it, and is true, whereas the first two forces could succeed only in founding a culture false to the root.

Footnotes:

1. Selbstverständlich = "granted or self-understood."
2. The Poems of Goethe. Edgar Alfred Bowring's Translation. (Ed. 1853.)

FIRST LECTURE

(Delivered on the 16th of January 1872.)

Ladies and Gentlemen,--The subject I now propose to consider with you is such a serious and important one, and is in a sense so disquieting, that, like you, I would gladly turn to any one who could proffer some information concerning it,--were he ever so young, were his ideas ever so improbable--provided that he were able, by the exercise of his own faculties, to furnish some satisfactory and sufficient explanation. It is just possible that he may have had the opportunity of hearing sound views expressed in reference to the vexed question of the future of our educational institutions, and that he may wish to repeat them to you; he may even have had distinguished teachers, fully qualified to foretell what is to come, and, like the haruspices of Rome, able to do so after an inspection of the entrails of the Present.

Indeed, you yourselves may expect something of this kind from me. I happened once, in strange but perfectly harmless circumstances, to overhear a conversation on this subject between two remarkable men, and the more striking points of the discussion, together with their manner of handling the theme, are so indelibly imprinted on my memory that, whenever I reflect on these matters, I invariably find myself falling into their grooves of thought. I cannot, however, profess to have the same courageous confidence which they displayed, both in their daring utterance of forbidden truths, and in the still more daring conception of the hopes with which they astonished me. It therefore seemed to me to be in the highest degree important that a record of this conversation should be made, so that others might be incited to form a judgment concerning the striking views and conclusions it contains: and, to this end, I had special grounds for believing that I should do well to avail myself of the opportunity afforded by this course of lectures.

I am well aware of the nature of the community to whose serious consideration I now wish to commend that conversation--I know it to be a community which is striving to educate and enlighten its members on a scale so magnificently out of proportion to its size that it must put all larger cities to shame. This being so, I presume I may take it for granted that in a quarter where so much is done for the things of which I wish to speak, people must also think a good deal about them. In my account of the conversation already mentioned, I shall be able to make myself completely understood only to those among my audience who will be able to guess what I can do no more than suggest, who will supply what I am compelled to omit, and who, above all, need but to be reminded and not taught.

Listen, therefore, ladies and gentlemen, while I recount my harmless experience and the less harmless conversation between the two gentlemen whom, so far, I have not named.

Let us now imagine ourselves in the position of a young student--that is to say, in a position which, in our present age of bewildering movement and feverish excitability, has become an almost impossible one. It is necessary to have lived through it in order to believe that such careless self-lulling and comfortable indifference to the moment, or to time in general, are possible. In this condition I, and a friend about my own age, spent a year at the University of Bonn on the Rhine,--it was a year which, in its complete lack of plans and projects for the future, seems almost like a dream to me now--a dream framed, as it were, by two periods of growth. We two remained quiet and peaceful, although we were surrounded by fellows who in the main were very differently disposed, and from time to time we experienced considerable difficulty in meeting and resisting the somewhat too pressing advances of the young men of our own age. Now, however, that I can look upon the stand we had to take against these opposing forces, I cannot help associating them in my mind with those checks we are wont to receive in our dreams, as, for instance, when we imagine we are able to fly and yet feel ourselves held back by some incomprehensible power.

I and my friend had many reminiscences in common, and these dated from the period of our boyhood upwards. One of these I must relate to you, since it forms a sort of prelude to the harmless experience already mentioned. On the occasion of a certain journey up the Rhine, which we had made together one summer, it happened that he and I independently conceived the very same plan at the same hour and on the same spot, and we were so struck by this unwonted coincidence that we determined to carry the plan out forthwith. We resolved to found a kind of small club which would consist of ourselves and a few friends, and the object of which would be to provide us with a stable and binding organisation directing and adding interest to our creative impulses in art and literature; or, to put it more plainly: each of us would be pledged to present an original piece of work to the club once a month,--

either a poem, a treatise, an architectural design, or a musical composition, upon which each of the others, in a friendly spirit, would have to pass free and unrestrained criticism.

We thus hoped, by means of mutual correction, to be able both to stimulate and to chasten our creative impulses and, as a matter of fact, the success of the scheme was such that we have both always felt a sort of respectful attachment for the hour and the place at which it first took shape in our minds.

This attachment was very soon transformed into a rite; for we all agreed to go, whenever it was possible to do so, once a year to that lonely spot near Rolandseck, where on that summer's day, while sitting together, lost in meditation, we were suddenly inspired by the same thought. Frankly speaking, the rules which were drawn up on the formation of the club were never very strictly observed; but owing to the very fact that we had many sins of omission on our conscience during our student-year in Bonn, when we were once more on the banks of the Rhine, we firmly resolved not only to observe our rule, but also to gratify our feelings and our sense of gratitude by reverently visiting that spot near Rolandseck on the day appointed.

It was, however, with some difficulty that we were able to carry our plans into execution; for, on the very day we had selected for our excursion, the large and lively students' association, which always hindered us in our flights, did their utmost to put obstacles in our way and to hold us back. Our association had organised a general holiday excursion to Rolandseck on the very day my friend and I had fixed upon, the object of the outing being to assemble all its members for the last time at the close of the half-year and to send them home with pleasant recollections of their last hours together.

The day was a glorious one; the weather was of the kind which, in our climate at least, only falls to our lot in late summer: heaven and earth merged harmoniously with one another, and, glowing wondrously in the sunshine, autumn freshness blended with the blue expanse above. Arrayed in the bright fantastic garb in which, amid the gloomy fashions now reigning, students alone may indulge, we boarded a steamer which was gaily decorated in our honour, and hoisted our flag on its mast. From both banks of the river there came at intervals the sound of signal-guns, fired according to our orders, with the view of acquainting both our host in Rolandseck and the inhabitants in the neighbourhood with our approach. I shall not speak of the noisy journey from the landing-stage, through the excited and expectant little place, nor shall I refer to the esoteric jokes exchanged between ourselves; I also make no mention of a feast which became both wild and noisy, or of an extraordinary musical production in the execution of which, whether as soloists or as chorus, we all ultimately had to share, and which I, as musical adviser of our club, had not only had to rehearse, but was then forced to conduct. Towards the end of this piece, which grew ever wilder and which was sung to ever quicker time, I made a sign to my friend, and just as the last chord rang like a yell through the building, he and I vanished, leaving behind us a raging pandemonium.

In a moment we were in the refreshing and breathless stillness of nature. The shadows were already lengthening, the sun still shone steadily, though it had sunk a good deal in the heavens, and from the green and glittering waves of the Rhine a cool breeze was wafted over our hot faces. Our solemn rite bound us only in so far as the latest hours of the day were concerned, and we therefore determined to employ the last moments of clear daylight by giving ourselves up to one of our many hobbies.

At that time we were passionately fond of pistol-shooting, and both of us in later years found the skill we had acquired as amateurs of great use in our military career. Our club servant happened to know the somewhat distant and elevated spot which we used as a range, and had carried our pistols there in advance. The spot lay near the upper border of the wood which covered the lesser heights behind Rolandseck: it was a small uneven plateau, close to the place we had consecrated in memory of its associations. On a wooded slope alongside of our shooting-range there was a small piece of ground which had been cleared of wood, and which made an ideal halting-place; from it one could get a view of the Rhine over the tops of the trees and the brushwood, so that the beautiful, undulating lines of the Seven Mountains and above all of the Drachenfels bounded the horizon against the group of trees, while in the centre of the bow formed by the glistening Rhine itself the island of Nonnenwörth stood out as if suspended in the river's arms. This was the place which had become sacred to us through the dreams and plans we had had in common, and to which we intended to withdraw, later in the evening,--nay, to which we should be obliged to withdraw, if we wished to close the day in accordance with the law we had imposed on ourselves.

At one end of the little uneven plateau, and not very far away, there stood the mighty trunk of an oak-tree, prominently visible against a background quite bare of trees and consisting merely of low undulating hills in the distance. Working together, we had once carved a pentagram in the side of this tree-trunk. Years of exposure to rain and storm had slightly deepened the channels we had cut, and the figure seemed a welcome target for our pistol-practice. It was already late in the afternoon when we reached our improvised range, and our oak-stump cast a long and attenuated shadow across the barren heath. All was still: thanks to the lofty trees at our feet, we were unable to catch a glimpse of the valley of the Rhine below. The peacefulness of the spot seemed only to intensify the loudness of our pistol-shots--and I had scarcely fired my second barrel at the pentagram when I felt some one lay hold of my arm and noticed that my friend had also some one beside him who had interrupted his loading.

Turning sharply on my heels I found myself face to face with an astonished old gentleman, and felt what must have been a very powerful dog make a lunge at my back. My friend had been approached by a somewhat younger man than I had; but before we could give expression to our surprise the older of the two interlopers burst forth in the following threatening and heated strain: "No! no!" he called to us, "no duels must be fought here, but least of all must you young students fight one. Away with these pistols and compose yourselves. Be reconciled, shake hands! What?--and are you the salt of the earth, the intelligence of the future, the seed of our hopes--and are you not even able to emancipate yourselves from the insane code of honour and its violent regulations? I will not cast any aspersions on your hearts, but your heads certainly do you no credit. You, whose youth is watched over by the wisdom of Greece and Rome, and whose youthful spirits, at the cost of enormous pains, have been flooded with the light of the sages and heroes of antiquity,--can you not refrain from making the code of knightly honour--that is to say, the code of folly and brutality--the guiding principle of your conduct?--Examine it rationally once and for all, and reduce it to plain terms; lay its pitiable narrowness bare, and let it be the touchstone, not of your hearts but of your minds. If you do not regret it then, it will merely show that your head is not fitted for work in a sphere where great gifts of discrimination are needful in order to burst the bonds of prejudice, and where a well-balanced understanding is necessary for the purpose of distinguishing right from wrong, even when the difference between them lies deeply hidden and is not, as in this case, so ridiculously obvious. In that case, therefore, my lads, try to go through life in some other honourable manner; join the army or learn a handicraft that pays its way."

To this rough, though admittedly just, flood of eloquence, we replied with some irritation, interrupting each other continually in so doing: "In the first place, you are mistaken concerning the main point; for we are not here to fight a duel at all; but rather to practise pistol-shooting. Secondly, you do not appear to know how a real duel is conducted;--do you suppose that we should have faced each other in this lonely spot, like two highwaymen, without seconds or doctors, etc. etc.? Thirdly, with regard to the question of duelling, we each have our own opinions, and do not require to be waylaid and surprised by the sort of instruction you may feel disposed to give us."

This reply, which was certainly not polite, made a bad impression upon the old man. At first, when he heard that we were not about to fight a duel, he surveyed us more kindly: but when we reached the last passage of our speech, he seemed so vexed that he growled. When, however, we began to speak of our point of view, he quickly caught hold of his companion, turned sharply round, and cried to us in bitter tones: "People should not have points of view, but thoughts!" And then his companion added: "Be respectful when a man such as this even makes mistakes!"

Meanwhile, my friend, who had reloaded, fired a shot at the pentagram, after having cried: "Look out!" This sudden report behind his back made the old man savage; once more he turned round and looked sourly at my friend, after which he said to his companion in a feeble voice: "What shall we do? These young men will be the death of me with their firing."--"You should know," said the younger man, turning to us, "that your noisy pastimes amount, as it happens on this occasion, to an attempt upon the life of philosophy. You observe this venerable man,--he is in a position to beg you to desist from firing here. And when such a man begs----" "Well, his request is generally granted," the old man interjected, surveying us sternly.

As a matter of fact, we did not know what to make of the whole matter; we could not understand what our noisy pastimes could have in common with philosophy; nor could we see why, out of regard for polite scruples, we should abandon our shooting-range, and at this moment we may have appeared somewhat undecided and perturbed. The companion noticing our momentary discomfiture, proceeded to explain the matter to us.

"We are compelled," he said, "to linger in this immediate neighbourhood for an hour or so; we have a rendezvous here. An eminent friend of this eminent man is to meet us here this evening; and we had actually selected this peaceful spot, with its few benches in the midst of the wood, for the meeting. It would really be most unpleasant if, owing to your continual pistol-practice, we were to be subjected to an unending series of shocks; surely your own feelings will tell you that it is impossible for you to continue your firing when you hear that he who has selected this quiet and isolated place for a meeting with a friend is one of our most eminent philosophers."

This explanation only succeeded in perturbing us the more; for we saw a danger threatening us which was even greater than the loss of our shooting-range, and we asked eagerly, "Where is this quiet spot? Surely not to the left here, in the wood?"

"That is the very place."

"But this evening that place belongs to us," my friend interposed. "We must have it," we cried together.

Our long-projected celebration seemed at that moment more important than all the philosophies of the world, and we gave such vehement and animated utterance to our sentiments that in view of the incomprehensible nature of our claims we must have cut a somewhat ridiculous figure. At any rate, our philosophical interlopers regarded us with expressions of amused inquiry, as if they expected us to proffer some sort of apology. But we were silent, for we wished above all to keep our secret.

Thus we stood facing one another in silence, while the sunset dyed the tree-tops a ruddy gold. The philosopher contemplated the sun, his companion contemplated him, and we turned our eyes towards our nook in the woods which to-day we seemed in such great danger of losing. A feeling of sullen anger took possession of us. What is philosophy, we asked ourselves, if it prevents a man from being by himself or from enjoying the select company of a friend,--in sooth, if it prevents him from becoming a philosopher? For we regarded the celebration of our rite as a thoroughly philosophical performance. In celebrating it we wished to form plans and resolutions for the future, by means of quiet reflections we hoped to light upon an idea which would once again help us to form and gratify our spirit in the future, just as that former idea had done during our boyhood. The solemn act derived its very significance from this resolution, that nothing definite was to be done, we were only to be alone, and to sit still and meditate, as we had done five years before when we had each been inspired with the same thought. It was to be a silent solemnisation, all reminiscence and all future; the present was to be as a hyphen between the two. And fate, now unfriendly, had just stepped into our magic circle--and we knew not how to dismiss her;--the very unusual character of the circumstances filled us with mysterious excitement.

Whilst we stood thus in silence for some time, divided into two hostile groups, the clouds above waxed ever redder and the evening seemed to grow more peaceful and mild; we could almost fancy we heard the regular breathing of nature as she put the final touches to her work of art--the glorious day we had just enjoyed; when, suddenly, the calm evening air was rent by a confused and boisterous cry of joy which seemed to come from the Rhine. A number of voices could be heard in the distance--they were those of our fellow-students who by that time must have taken to the Rhine in small boats. It occurred to us that we should be missed and that we should also miss something: almost simultaneously my friend and I raised our pistols: our shots were echoed back to us, and with their echo there came from the valley the sound of a well-known cry intended as a signal of identification. For our passion for shooting had brought us both repute and ill-repute in our club. At the same time we were conscious that our behaviour towards the silent philosophical couple had been exceptionally ungentlemanly; they had been quietly contemplating us for some time, and when we fired the shock made them draw close up to each other. We hurried up to them, and each in our turn cried out: "Forgive us. That was our last shot, and it was intended for our friends on the Rhine. They have understood us, do you hear? If you insist upon having that place among the trees, grant us at least the permission to recline there also. You will find a number of benches on the spot: we shall not disturb you; we shall sit quite still and shall not utter a word: but it is now past seven o'clock and we must go there at once.

"That sounds more mysterious than it is," I added after a pause; "we have made a solemn vow to spend this coming hour on that ground, and there were reasons for the vow. The spot is sacred to us, owing to some pleasant associations, it must also inaugurate a good future for us. We shall therefore endeavour to leave you with no disagreeable recollections of our meeting--even though we have done much to perturb and frighten you."

The philosopher was silent; his companion, however, said: "Our promises and plans unfortunately compel us not only to remain, but also to spend the same hour on the spot you have selected. It is left for us to decide whether fate or perhaps a spirit has been responsible for this extraordinary coincidence."

"Besides, my friend," said the philosopher, "I am not half so displeased with these warlike youngsters as I was. Did you observe how quiet they were a moment ago, when we were contemplating the sun? They neither spoke nor smoked, they stood stone still, I even believe they meditated."

Turning suddenly in our direction, he said: "Were you meditating? Just tell me about it as we proceed in the direction of our common trysting-place." We took a few steps together and went down the slope into the warm balmy air of the woods where it was already much darker. On the way my friend openly revealed his thoughts to the philosopher, he confessed how much he had feared that perhaps to-day for the first time a philosopher was about to stand in the way of his philosophising.

The sage laughed. "What? You were afraid a philosopher would prevent your philosophising? This might easily happen: and you have not yet experienced such a thing? Has your university life been free from experience? You surely attend lectures on philosophy?"

This question discomfited us; for, as a matter of fact, there had been no element of philosophy in our education up to that time. In those days, moreover, we fondly imagined that everybody who held the post and possessed the dignity of a philosopher must perforce be one: we were inexperienced and badly informed. We frankly admitted that we had not yet belonged to any philosophical college, but that we would certainly make up for lost time.

"Then what," he asked, "did you mean when you spoke of philosophising?" Said I, "We are at a loss for a definition. But to all intents and purposes we meant this, that we wished to make earnest endeavours to consider the best possible means of becoming men of culture." "That is a good deal and at the same time very little," growled the philosopher; "just you think the matter over. Here are our benches, let us discuss the question exhaustively: I shall not disturb your meditations with regard to how you are to become men of culture. I wish you success and--points of view, as in your duelling questions; brand-new, original, and enlightened points of view. The philosopher does not wish to prevent your philosophising: but refrain at least from disconcerting him with your pistol-shots. Try to imitate the Pythagoreans to-day: they, as servants of a true philosophy, had to remain silent for five years--possibly you may also be able to remain silent for five times fifteen minutes, as servants of your own future culture, about which you seem so concerned."

We had reached our destination: the solemnisation of our rite began. As on the previous occasion, five years ago, the Rhine was once more flowing beneath a light mist, the sky seemed bright and the woods exhaled the same fragrance. We took our places on the farthest corner of the most distant bench; sitting there we were almost concealed, and neither the philosopher nor his companion could see our faces. We were alone: when the sound of the philosopher's voice reached us, it had become so blended with the rustling leaves and with the buzzing murmur of the myriads of living things inhabiting the wooded height, that it almost seemed like the music of nature; as a sound it resembled nothing more than a distant monotonous plaint. We were indeed undisturbed.

Some time elapsed in this way, and while the glow of sunset grew steadily paler the recollection of our youthful undertaking in the cause of culture waxed ever more vivid. It seemed to us as if we owed the greatest debt of gratitude to that little society we had founded; for it had done more than merely supplement our public school training; it had actually been the only fruitful society we had had, and within its frame we even placed our public school life, as a purely isolated factor helping us in our general efforts to attain to culture.

We knew this, that, thanks to our little society, no thought of embracing any particular career had ever entered our minds in those days. The all too frequent exploitation of youth by the State, for its own purposes--that is to say, so that it may rear useful officials as quickly as possible and guarantee their unconditional obedience to it by means of excessively severe examinations--had remained quite foreign to our education. And to show how little we had been actuated by thoughts of utility or by the prospect of speedy advancement and rapid success, on that day we were struck by the comforting consideration that, even then, we had not yet decided what we should be--we had not even troubled ourselves at all on this head. Our little society had sown the seeds of this happy indifference in our souls and for it alone we were prepared to celebrate the anniversary of its foundation with hearty gratitude. I have already pointed out, I think, that in the eyes of the present age, which is so intolerant of anything that is not useful, such purposeless enjoyment of the moment, such a lulling of one's self in the cradle of the present, must seem almost incredible and at all events blameworthy. How useless we were! And how proud we were of being useless! We used even to quarrel with each other as to which of us should have the glory of being the more useless. We wished to attach no importance to anything, to have strong views about nothing, to aim at nothing; we wanted to take no thought for the morrow, and desired no more than to recline comfortably like good-for-nothings on the threshold of the present; and we did--bless us!

--That, ladies and gentlemen, was our standpoint then!--

Absorbed in these reflections, I was just about to give an answer to the question of the future of our Educational Institutions in the same self-sufficient way, when it gradually dawned upon me that the "natural music," coming from the philosopher's bench had lost its original character and travelled to us in much more piercing and distinct tones than before. Suddenly I became aware that I was listening, that I was eavesdropping, and was passionately interested, with both ears keenly alive to every sound. I nudged my friend who was evidently somewhat tired, and I whispered: "Don't fall asleep! There is something for us to learn over there. It applies to us, even though it be not meant for us."

For instance, I heard the younger of the two men defending himself with great animation while the philosopher rebuked him with ever increasing vehemence. "You are unchanged," he cried to him, "unfortunately unchanged. It is quite incomprehensible to me how you can still be the same as you were seven years ago, when I saw you for the last time and left you with so much misgiving. I fear I must once again divest you, however reluctantly, of the skin of modern culture which you have donned meanwhile;--and what do I find beneath it? The same immutable 'intelligible' character forsooth, according to Kant; but unfortunately the same unchanged 'intellectual' character, too--which may also be a necessity, though not a comforting one. I ask myself to what purpose have I lived as a philosopher, if, possessed as you are of no mean intelligence and a genuine thirst for knowledge, all the years you have spent in my company have left no deeper impression upon you. At present you are behaving as if you had not even heard the cardinal principle of all culture, which I went to such pains to inculcate upon you during our former intimacy. Tell me,--what was that principle?"

"I remember," replied the scolded pupil, "you used to say no one would strive to attain to culture if he knew how incredibly small the number of really cultured people actually is, and can ever be. And even this number of really cultured people would not be possible if a prodigious multitude, from reasons opposed to their nature and only led on by an alluring delusion, did not devote themselves to education. It were therefore a mistake publicly to reveal the ridiculous disproportion between the number of really cultured people and the enormous magnitude of the educational apparatus. Here lies the whole secret of culture--namely, that an innumerable host of men struggle to achieve it and work hard to that end, ostensibly in their own interests, whereas at bottom it is only in order that it may be possible for the few to attain to it."

"That is the principle," said the philosopher,--"and yet you could so far forget yourself as to believe that you are one of the few? This thought has occurred to you--I can see. That, however, is the result of the worthless character of modern education. The rights of genius are being democratised in order that people may be relieved of the labour of acquiring culture, and their need of it. Every one wants if possible to recline in the shade of the tree planted by genius, and to escape the dreadful necessity of working for him, so that his procreation may be made possible. What? Are you too proud to be a teacher? Do you despise the thronging multitude of learners? Do you speak contemptuously of the teacher's calling? And, aping my mode of life, would you fain live in solitary seclusion, hostilely isolated from that multitude? Do you suppose that you can reach at one bound what I ultimately had to win for myself only after long and determined struggles, in order even to be able to live like a philosopher? And do you not fear that solitude will wreak its vengeance upon you? Just try living the life of a hermit of culture. One must be blessed with overflowing wealth in order to live for the good of all on one's own resources! Extraordinary youngsters! They felt it incumbent upon them to imitate what is precisely most difficult and most high,--what is possible only to the master, when they, above all, should know how difficult and dangerous this is, and how many excellent gifts may be ruined by attempting it!"

"I will conceal nothing from you, sir," the companion replied. "I have heard too much from your lips at odd times and have been too long in your company to be able to surrender myself entirely to our present system of education and instruction. I am too painfully conscious of the disastrous errors and abuses to which you used to call my attention--though I very well know that I am not strong enough to hope for any success were I to struggle ever so valiantly against them. I was overcome by a feeling of general discouragement; my recourse to solitude was the result neither of pride nor arrogance. I would fain describe to you what I take to be the nature of the educational questions now attracting such enormous and pressing attention. It seemed to me that I must recognise two main directions in the forces at work--two seemingly antagonistic tendencies, equally deleterious in their action, and ultimately combining to produce their results: a striving to achieve the greatest possible expansion of education on the one hand, and a tendency to minimise and weaken it on the other. The first-named would, for various reasons, spread learning among the greatest number of people; the second would compel education to renounce its highest, noblest and sublimest claims in order to subordinate itself to some other department of life--such as the service of the State.

"I believe I have already hinted at the quarter in which the cry for the greatest possible expansion of education is most loudly raised. This expansion belongs to the most beloved of the dogmas of modern political economy. As much knowledge and education as possible; therefore the greatest possible supply and demand--hence as much happiness as possible:--that is the formula. In this case utility is made the object and goal of education,--utility in the sense of gain--the greatest possible pecuniary gain. In the quarter now under consideration culture would be defined as that point of vantage which enables one to 'keep in the van of one's age,' from which one can see all the easiest and best roads to wealth, and with which one controls all the means of communication between men and nations. The purpose of education, according to this scheme, would be to rear the most 'current' men possible,--'current' being used here in the sense in which it is applied to the coins of the realm. The greater the number of such men, the happier a nation will be; and this precisely is the purpose of our modern educational institutions: to help every one, as far as his nature will allow, to become 'current'; to develop him so that his particular degree of knowledge and science may yield him the greatest possible amount of happiness and pecuniary gain. Every one must be able to form some sort of estimate of himself; he must know how much he may reasonably expect from life. The 'bond between intelligence and property' which this point of view postulates has almost the force of a moral principle. In this quarter all culture is loathed which isolates, which sets goals beyond gold and gain, and which requires time: it is customary to dispose of such eccentric tendencies in education as systems of 'Higher Egotism,' or of 'Immoral Culture--Epicureanism.' According to the morality reigning here, the demands are quite different; what is required above all is 'rapid education,' so that a money-earning creature may be produced with all speed; there is even a desire to make this education so thorough that a creature may be reared that will be able to earn a great deal of money. Men are allowed only the precise amount of culture which is compatible with the interests of gain; but that amount, at least, is expected from them. In short: mankind has a necessary right to happiness on earth--that is why culture is necessary--but on that account alone!"

"I must just say something here," said the philosopher. "In the case of the view you have described so clearly, there arises the great and awful danger that at some time or other the great masses may overleap the middle classes and spring headlong into this earthly bliss. That is what is now called 'the social question.' It might seem to these masses that education for the greatest number of men was only a means to the earthly bliss of the few: the 'greatest possible expansion of education' so enfeebles education that it can no longer confer privileges or inspire respect. The most general form of culture is simply barbarism. But I do not wish to interrupt your discussion."

The companion continued: "There are yet other reasons, besides this beloved economical dogma, for the expansion of education that is being striven after so valiantly everywhere. In some countries the fear of religious oppression is so general, and the dread of its results so marked, that people in all classes of society long for culture and eagerly absorb those elements of it which are supposed to scatter the religious instincts. Elsewhere the State, in its turn, strives here and there for its own preservation, after the greatest possible expansion of education, because it always feels strong enough to bring the most determined emancipation, resulting from culture, under its yoke, and readily approves of everything which tends to extend culture, provided that it be of service to its officials or soldiers, but in the main to itself, in its competition with other nations. In this case, the foundations of a State must be sufficiently broad and firm to constitute a fitting counterpart to the complicated arches of culture which it supports, just as in the first case the traces of some former religious tyranny must still be felt for a people to be driven to such desperate remedies. Thus, wherever I hear the masses raise the cry for an expansion of education, I am wont to ask myself whether it is stimulated by a greedy lust of gain and property, by the memory of a former religious persecution, or by the prudent egotism of the State itself.

"On the other hand, it seemed to me that there was yet another tendency, not so clamorous, perhaps, but quite as forcible, which, hailing from various quarters, was animated by a different desire,--the desire to minimise and weaken education.

"In all cultivated circles people are in the habit of whispering to one another words something after this style: that it is a general fact that, owing to the present frantic exploitation of the scholar in the service of his science, his education becomes every day more accidental and more uncertain. For the study of science has been extended to such interminable lengths that he who, though not exceptionally gifted, yet possesses fair abilities, will need to devote himself exclusively to one branch and ignore all others if he ever wish to achieve anything in his work. Should he then elevate himself above the herd by means of his speciality, he still remains one of them in regard to all else,--that is to say, in regard to all the most important things in life. Thus, a specialist in science gets to resemble nothing so much as a factory workman who spends his whole life in turning one particular screw or handle on a certain instrument or machine, at which occupation he acquires the most consummate skill. In Germany, where we know how to drape such painful facts with the glorious garments of fancy, this narrow specialisation on the part of our learned men is even admired, and their ever greater deviation from the path of true culture is regarded as a moral phenomenon. 'Fidelity in small things,' 'dogged faithfulness,' become expressions of highest eulogy, and the lack of culture outside the speciality is flaunted abroad as a sign of noble sufficiency.

"For centuries it has been an understood thing that one alluded to scholars alone when one spoke of cultured men; but experience tells us that it would be difficult to find any necessary relation between the two classes to-day. For at present the exploitation of a man for the purpose of science is accepted everywhere without the slightest scruple. Who still ventures to ask, What may be the value of a science which consumes its minions in this vampire fashion? The division of labour in science is practically struggling towards the same goal which religions in certain parts of the world are consciously striving after,--that is to say, towards the decrease and even the destruction of learning. That, however, which, in the case of certain religions, is a perfectly justifiable aim, both in regard to their origin and their history, can only amount to self-immolation when transferred to the realm of science. In all matters of a general and serious nature, and above all, in regard to the highest philosophical problems, we have now already reached a point at which the scientific man, as such, is no longer allowed to speak. On the other hand, that adhesive and tenacious stratum which has now filled up the interstices between the sciences--Journalism--believes it has a mission to fulfil here, and this it does, according to its own particular lights--that is to say, as its name implies, after the fashion of a day-labourer.

"It is precisely in journalism that the two tendencies combine and become one. The expansion and the diminution of education here join hands. The newspaper actually steps into the place of culture, and he who, even as a scholar, wishes to voice any claim for education, must avail himself of this viscous stratum of communication which cements the seams between all forms of life, all classes, all arts, and all sciences, and which is as firm and reliable as news paper is, as a rule. In the newspaper the peculiar educational aims of the present culminate, just as the journalist, the servant of the moment, has stepped into the place of the genius, of the leader for all time, of the deliverer from the tyranny of the moment. Now, tell me, distinguished master, what hopes could I still have in a struggle against the general topsy-turvification of all genuine aims for education; with what courage can I, a single teacher, step forward, when I know that the moment any seeds of real culture are sown, they will be mercilessly crushed by the roller of this pseudo-culture? Imagine how useless the most energetic work on the part of the individual teacher must be, who would fain lead a pupil back into the distant and evasive Hellenic world and to the real home of culture, when in less than an hour, that same pupil will have recourse to a newspaper, the latest novel, or one of those learned books, the very style of which already bears the revolting impress of modern barbaric culture----"

"Now, silence a minute!" interjected the philosopher in a strong and sympathetic voice. "I understand you now, and ought never to have spoken so crossly to you. You are altogether right, save in your despair. I shall now proceed to say a few words of consolation."

SECOND LECTURE

(Delivered on the 6th of February 1872.)

LADIES AND GENTLEMEN,--Those among you whom I now have the pleasure of addressing for the first time and whose only knowledge of my first lecture has been derived from reports will, I hope, not mind being introduced here into the middle of a dialogue which I had begun to recount on the last occasion, and the last points of which I must now recall. The philosopher's young companion was just pleading openly and confidentially with his distinguished tutor, and apologising for having so far renounced his calling as a teacher in order to spend his days in comfortless solitude. No suspicion of superciliousness or arrogance had induced him to form this resolve.

"I have heard too much from your lips at various times," the straightforward pupil said, "and have been too long in your company, to surrender myself blindly to our present systems of education and instruction. I am too painfully conscious of the disastrous errors and abuses to which you were wont to call my attention; and yet I know that I am far from possessing the requisite strength to meet with success, however valiantly I might struggle to shatter the bulwarks of this would-be culture. I was overcome by a general feeling of depression: my recourse to solitude was not arrogance or superciliousness." Whereupon, to account for his behaviour, he described the general character of modern educational methods so vividly that the philosopher could not help interrupting him in a voice full of sympathy, and crying words of comfort to him.

"Now, silence for a minute, my poor friend," he cried; "I can more easily understand you now, and should not have lost my patience with you. You are altogether right, save in your despair. I shall now proceed to say a few words of comfort to you. How long do you suppose the state of education in the schools of our time, which seems to weigh so heavily upon you, will last? I shall not conceal my views on this point from you: its time is over; its days are counted. The first who will dare to be quite straightforward in this respect will hear his honesty re-echoed back to him by thousands of courageous souls. For, at bottom, there is a tacit understanding between the more nobly gifted and more warmly disposed men of the present day. Every one of them knows what he has had to suffer from the condition of culture in schools; every one of them would fain protect his offspring from the need of enduring similar drawbacks, even though he himself was compelled to submit to them. If these feelings are never quite honestly expressed, however, it is owing to a sad want of spirit among modern pedagogues. These lack real initiative; there are too few practical men among them--that is to say, too few who happen to have good and new ideas, and who know that real genius and the real practical mind must necessarily come together in the same individuals, whilst the sober practical men have no ideas and therefore fall short in practice.

"Let any one examine the pedagogic literature of the present; he who is not shocked at its utter poverty of spirit and its ridiculously awkward antics is beyond being spoiled. Here our philosophy must not begin with wonder but with dread; he who feels no dread at this point must be asked not to meddle with pedagogic questions. The reverse, of course, has been the rule up to the present; those who were terrified ran away filled with embarrassment as you did, my poor friend, while the sober and fearless ones spread their heavy hands over the most delicate technique that has ever existed in art--over the technique of education. This, however, will not be possible much longer; at some time or other the upright man will appear, who will not only have the good ideas I speak of, but who in order to work at their realisation, will dare to break with all that exists at present: he may by means of a wonderful example achieve what the broad hands, hitherto active, could not even imitate--then people will everywhere begin to draw comparisons; then men will at least be able to perceive a contrast and will be in a position to reflect upon its causes, whereas, at present, so many still believe, in perfect good faith, that heavy hands are a necessary factor in pedagogic work."

"My dear master," said the younger man, "I wish you could point to one single example which would assist me in seeing the soundness of the hopes which you so heartily raise in me. We are both acquainted with public schools; do you think, for instance, that in respect of these institutions anything may be done by means of honesty and good and new ideas to abolish the tenacious and antiquated customs now extant? In this quarter, it seems to me, the battering-rams of an attacking party will have to meet with no solid wall, but with the most fatal of stolid and slippery principles. The leader of the assault has no visible and tangible opponent to crush, but rather a creature in disguise that can transform itself into a hundred different shapes and, in each of these, slip out of his grasp, only in order to reappear and to confound its enemy by cowardly surrenders and feigned retreats. It was precisely the public schools which drove me into despair and solitude, simply because I feel that if the struggle here leads to victory all other educational institutions must give in; but that, if the reformer be forced to abandon his cause here, he may as well give up all hope in regard to every other scholastic question. Therefore, dear master, enlighten me concerning the public schools; what can we hope for in the way of their abolition or reform?"

"I also hold the question of public schools to be as important as you do," the philosopher replied. "All other educational institutions must fix their aims in accordance with those of the public school system; whatever errors of judgment it may suffer from, they suffer from also, and if it were ever purified and rejuvenated, they would be purified and rejuvenated too. The universities can no longer lay claim to this importance as centres of influence, seeing that, as they now stand, they are at least, in one important aspect, only a kind of annex to the public school system, as I shall shortly point out to you. For the moment, let us consider, together, what to my mind constitutes the very hopeful struggle of the two possibilities: either that the motley and evasive spirit of public schools which has hitherto been fostered, will completely vanish, or that it will have to be completely purified and rejuvenated. And in order that I may not shock you with general propositions, let us first try to recall one of those public school experiences which we have all had, and from which we have all suffered. Under severe examination what, as a matter of fact, is the present system of teaching German in public schools?

"I shall first of all tell you what it should be. Everybody speaks and writes German as thoroughly badly as it is just possible to do so in an age of newspaper German: that is why the growing youth who happens to be both noble and gifted has to be taken by force and put under the glass shade of good taste and of severe linguistic discipline. If this is not possible, I would prefer in future that Latin be spoken; for I am ashamed of a language so bungled and vitiated.

"What would be the duty of a higher educational institution, in this respect, if not this--namely, with authority and dignified severity to put youths, neglected, as far as their own language is concerned, on the right path, and to cry to them: 'Take your own language seriously! He who does not regard this matter as a sacred duty does not possess even the germ of a higher culture. From your attitude in this matter, from your treatment of your mother-tongue, we can judge how highly or how lowly you esteem art, and to what extent you are related to it. If you notice no physical loathing in yourselves when you meet with certain words and tricks of speech in our journalistic jargon, cease from striving after culture; for here in your immediate vicinity, at every moment of your life, while you are either speaking or writing, you have a touchstone for testing how difficult, how stupendous, the task of the cultured man is, and how very improbable it must be that many of you will ever attain to culture.'

"In accordance with the spirit of this address, the teacher of German at a public school would be forced to call his pupil's attention to thousands of details, and with the absolute certainty of good taste, to forbid their using such words and expressions, for instance, as: 'beanspruchen,' 'vereinnahmen,' 'einer Sache Rechnung tragen,' 'die Initiative ergreifen,' 'selbstverständlich,'[3] etc., cum tædio in infinitum. The same teacher would also have to take our classical authors and show, line for line, how carefully and with what precision every expression has to be chosen when a writer has the correct feeling in his heart and has before his eyes a perfect conception of all he is writing. He would necessarily urge his pupils, time and again, to express the same thought ever more happily; nor would he have to abate in rigour until the less gifted in his class had contracted an unholy fear of their language, and the others had developed great enthusiasm for it.

"Here then is a task for so-called 'formal' education[4] [the education tending to develop the mental faculties, as opposed to 'material' education,[5] which is intended to deal only with the acquisition of facts, e.g. history, mathematics, etc.], and one of the utmost value: but what do we find in the public school--that is to say, in the head-quarters of formal education? He who understands how to apply what he has heard here will also know what to think of the modern public school as a so-called educational institution. He will discover, for instance, that the public school, according to its fundamental principles, does not educate for the purposes of culture, but for the purposes of scholarship; and, further, that of late it seems to have adopted a course which indicates rather that it has even discarded scholarship in favour of journalism as the object of its exertions. This can be clearly seen from the way in which German is taught.

"Instead of that purely practical method of instruction by which the teacher accustoms his pupils to severe self-discipline in their own language, we find everywhere the rudiments of a historico-scholastic method of teaching the mother-tongue: that is to say, people deal with it as if it were a dead language and as if the present and future were under no obligations to it whatsoever. The historical method has become so universal in our time, that even the living body of the language is sacrificed for the sake of anatomical study. But this is precisely where culture begins--namely, in understanding how to treat the quick as something vital, and it is here too that the mission of the cultured teacher begins: in suppressing the urgent claims of 'historical interests' wherever it is above all necessary to do properly and not merely to know properly. Our mother-tongue, however, is a domain in which the pupil must learn how to do properly, and to this practical end, alone, the teaching of German is essential in our scholastic establishments. The historical method may certainly be a considerably easier and more comfortable one for the teacher; it also seems to be compatible with a much lower grade of ability and, in general, with a smaller display of energy and will on his part. But we shall find that this observation holds good in every department of pedagogic life: the simpler and more comfortable method always masquerades in the disguise of grand pretensions and stately titles; the really practical side, the doing, which should belong to culture and which, at bottom, is the more difficult side, meets only with disfavour and contempt. That is why the honest man must make himself and others quite clear concerning this quid pro quo.

"Now, apart from these learned incentives to a study of the language, what is there besides which the German teacher is wont to offer? How does he reconcile the spirit of his school with the spirit of the few that Germany can claim who are really cultured,--i.e. with the spirit of its classical poets and artists? This is a dark and thorny sphere, into which one cannot even bear a light without dread; but even here we shall conceal nothing from ourselves; for sooner or later the whole of it will have to be reformed. In the public school, the repulsive impress of our æsthetic journalism is stamped upon the still unformed minds of youths. Here, too, the teacher sows the seeds of that crude and wilful misinterpretation of the classics, which later on disports itself as art-criticism, and which is nothing but bumptious barbarity. Here the pupils learn to speak of our unique Schiller with the superciliousness of prigs; here they are taught to smile at the noblest and most German of his works--at the Marquis of Posa, at Max and Thekla--at these smiles German genius becomes incensed and a worthier posterity will blush.

"The last department in which the German teacher in a public school is at all active, which is often regarded as his sphere of highest activity, and is here and there even considered the pinnacle of public school education, is the so-called German composition. Owing to the very fact that in this department it is almost always the most gifted pupils who display the greatest eagerness, it ought to have been made clear how dangerously stimulating, precisely here, the task of the teacher must be. German composition makes an appeal to the individual, and the more strongly a pupil is conscious of his various qualities, the more personally will he do his German composition. This 'personal doing' is urged on with yet an additional fillip in some public schools by the choice of the subject, the strongest proof of which is, in my opinion, that even in the lower classes the non-pedagogic subject is set, by means of which the pupil is led to give a description of his life and of his development. Now, one has only to read the titles of the compositions set in a large number of public schools to be convinced that probably the large majority of pupils have to suffer their whole lives, through no fault of their own, owing to this premature demand for personal work--for the unripe procreation of thoughts. And how often are not all a man's subsequent literary performances but a sad result of this pedagogic original sin against the intellect!

"Let us only think of what takes place at such an age in the production of such work. It is the first individual creation; the still undeveloped powers tend for the first time to crystallise; the staggering sensation produced by the demand for self-reliance imparts a seductive charm to these early performances, which is not only quite new, but which never returns. All the daring of nature is hauled out of its depths; all vanities--no longer constrained by mighty barriers--are allowed for the first time to assume a literary form: the young man, from that time forward, feels as if he had reached his consummation as a being not only able, but actually invited, to speak and to converse. The subject he selects obliges him either to express his judgment upon certain poetical works, to class historical persons together in a description of character, to discuss serious ethical problems quite independently, or even to turn the searchlight inwards, to throw its rays upon his own development and to make a critical report of himself: in short, a whole world of reflection is spread out before the astonished young man who, until then, had been almost unconscious, and is delivered up to him to be judged.

"Now let us try to picture the teacher's usual attitude towards these first highly influential examples of original composition. What does he hold to be most reprehensible in this class of work? What does he call his pupil's attention to?--To all excess in form or thought--that is to say, to all that which, at their age, is essentially characteristic and individual. Their really independent traits which, in response to this very premature excitation, can manifest themselves only in awkwardness, crudeness, and grotesque features,--in short, their individuality is reproved and rejected by the teacher in favour of an unoriginal decent average. On the other hand, uniform mediocrity gets peevish praise; for, as a rule, it is just the class of work likely to bore the teacher thoroughly.

"There may still be men who recognise a most absurd and most dangerous element of the public school curriculum in the whole farce of this German composition. Originality is demanded here: but the only shape in which it can manifest itself is rejected, and the 'formal' education that the system takes for granted is attained to only by a very limited number of men who complete it at a ripe age. Here everybody without exception is regarded as gifted for literature and considered as capable of holding opinions concerning the most important questions and people, whereas the one aim which proper education should most zealously strive to achieve would be the suppression of all ridiculous claims to independent judgment, and the inculcation upon young men of obedience to the sceptre of genius. Here a pompous form of diction is taught in an age when every spoken or written word is a piece of barbarism. Now let us consider, besides, the danger of arousing the self-complacency which is so easily awakened in youths; let us think how their vanity must be flattered when they see their literary reflection for the first time in the mirror. Who, having seen all these effects at one glance, could any longer doubt whether all the faults of our public, literary, and artistic life were not stamped upon every fresh generation by the system we are examining: hasty and vain production, the disgraceful manufacture of books; complete want of style; the crude, characterless, or sadly swaggering method of expression; the loss of every æsthetic canon; the voluptuousness of anarchy and chaos--in short, the literary peculiarities of both our journalism and our scholarship.

"None but the very fewest are aware that, among many thousands, perhaps only one is justified in describing himself as literary, and that all others who at their own risk try to be so deserve to be met with Homeric laughter by all competent men as a reward for every sentence they have ever had printed;--for it is truly a spectacle meet for the gods to see a literary Hephaistos limping forward who would pretend to help us to something. To educate men to earnest and inexorable habits and views, in this respect, should be the highest aim of all mental training, whereas the general laisser aller of the 'fine personality' can be nothing else than the hall-mark of barbarism. From what I have said, however, it must be clear that, at least in the teaching of German, no thought is given to culture; something quite different is in view,--namely, the production of the afore-mentioned 'free personality.' And so long as German public schools prepare the road for outrageous and irresponsible scribbling, so long as they do not regard the immediate and practical discipline of speaking and writing as their most holy duty, so long as they treat the mother-tongue as if it were only a necessary evil or a dead body, I shall not regard these institutions as belonging to real culture.

"In regard to the language, what is surely least noticeable is any trace of the influence of classical examples: that is why, on the strength of this consideration alone, the so-called 'classical education' which is supposed to be provided by our public school, strikes me as something exceedingly doubtful and confused. For how could anybody, after having cast one glance at those examples, fail to see the great earnestness with which the Greek and the Roman regarded and treated his language, from his youth onwards--how is it possible to mistake one's example on a point like this one?--provided, of course, that the classical Hellenic and Roman world really did hover before the educational plan of our public schools as the highest and most instructive of all morals--a fact I feel very much inclined to doubt. The claim put forward by public schools concerning the 'classical education' they provide seems to be more an awkward evasion than anything else; it is used whenever there is any question raised as to the competency of the public schools to impart culture and to educate. Classical education, indeed! It sounds so dignified! It confounds the aggressor and staves off the assault--for who could see to the bottom of this bewildering formula all at once? And this has long been the customary strategy of the public school: from whichever side the war-cry may come, it writes upon its shield--not overloaded with honours--one of those confusing catchwords, such as: 'classical education,' 'formal education,' 'scientific education':--three glorious things which are, however, unhappily at loggerheads, not only with themselves but among themselves, and are such that, if they were compulsorily brought together, would perforce bring forth a culture-monster. For a 'classical education' is something so unheard of, difficult and rare, and exacts such complicated talent, that only ingenuousness or impudence could put it forward as an attainable goal in our public schools. The words: 'formal education' belong to that crude kind of unphilosophical phraseology which one should do one's utmost to get rid of; for there is no such thing as 'the opposite of formal education.' And he who regards 'scientific education' as the object of a public school thereby sacrifices 'classical education' and the so-called 'formal education,' at one stroke, as the scientific man and the cultured man belong to two different spheres which, though coming together at times in the same individual, are never reconciled.

"If we compare all three of these would-be aims of the public school with the actual facts to be observed in the present method of teaching German, we see immediately what they really amount to in practice,--that is to say, only to subterfuges for use in the fight and struggle for existence and, often enough, mere means wherewith to bewilder an opponent. For we are unable to detect any single feature in this teaching of German which in any way recalls the example of classical antiquity and its glorious methods of training in languages. 'Formal education,' however, which is supposed to be achieved by this method of teaching German, has been shown to be wholly at the pleasure of the 'free personality,' which is as good as saying that it is barbarism and anarchy. And as for the preparation in science, which is one of the consequences of this teaching, our Germanists will have to determine, in all justice, how little these learned beginnings in public schools have contributed to the splendour of their sciences, and how much the personality of individual university professors has done so.--Put briefly: the public school has hitherto neglected its most important and most urgent duty towards the very beginning of all real culture, which is the mother-tongue; but in so doing it has lacked the natural, fertile soil for all further efforts at culture. For only by means of stern, artistic, and careful discipline and habit, in a language, can the correct feeling for the greatness of our classical writers be strengthened. Up to the present their recognition by the public schools has been owing almost solely to the doubtful æsthetic hobbies of a few teachers or to the massive effects of certain of their tragedies and novels. But everybody should, himself, be aware of the difficulties of the language: he should have learnt them from experience: after long seeking and struggling he must reach the path our great poets trod in order to be able to realise how lightly and beautifully they trod it, and how stiffly and swaggeringly the others follow at their heels.

"Only by means of such discipline can the young man acquire that physical loathing for the beloved and much-admired 'elegance' of style of our newspaper manufacturers and novelists, and for the 'ornate style' of our literary men; by it alone is he irrevocably elevated at a stroke above a whole host of absurd questions and scruples, such, for instance, as whether Auerbach and Gutzkow are really poets, for his disgust at both will be so great that he will be unable to read them any longer, and thus the problem will be solved for him. Let no one imagine that it is an easy matter to develop this feeling to the extent necessary in order to have this physical loathing; but let no one hope to reach sound æsthetic judgments along any other road than the thorny one of language, and by this I do not mean philological research, but self-discipline in one's mother-tongue.

"Everybody who is in earnest in this matter will have the same sort of experience as the recruit in the army who is compelled to learn walking after having walked almost all his life as a dilettante or empiricist. It is a hard time: one almost fears that the tendons are going to snap and one ceases to hope that the artificial and consciously acquired movements and positions of the feet will ever be carried out with ease and comfort. It is painful to see how awkwardly and heavily one foot is set before the other, and one dreads that one may not only be unable to learn the new way of walking, but that one will forget how to walk at all. Then it suddenly become noticeable that a new habit and a second nature have been born of the practised movements, and that the assurance and strength of the old manner of walking returns with a little more grace: at this point one begins to realise how difficult walking is, and one feels in a position to laugh at the untrained empiricist or the elegant dilettante. Our 'elegant' writers, as their style shows, have never learnt 'walking' in this sense, and in our public schools, as our other writers show, no one learns walking either. Culture begins, however, with the correct movement of the language: and once it has properly begun, it begets that physical sensation in the presence of 'elegant' writers which is known by the name of 'loathing.'

"We recognise the fatal consequences of our present public schools, in that they are unable to inculcate severe and genuine culture, which should consist above all in obedience and habituation; and that, at their best, they much more often achieve a result by stimulating and kindling scientific tendencies, is shown by the hand which is so frequently seen uniting scholarship and barbarous taste, science and journalism. In a very large majority of cases to-day we can observe how sadly our scholars fall short of the standard of culture which the efforts of Goethe, Schiller, Lessing, and Winckelmann established; and this falling short shows itself precisely in the egregious errors which the men we speak of are exposed to, equally among literary historians--whether Gervinus or Julian Schmidt--as in any other company; everywhere, indeed, where men and women converse. It shows itself most frequently and painfully, however, in pedagogic spheres, in the literature of public schools. It can be proved that the only value that these men have in a real educational establishment has not been mentioned, much less generally recognised for half a century: their value as preparatory leaders and mystogogues of classical culture, guided by whose hands alone can the correct road leading to antiquity be found.

"Every so-called classical education can have but one natural starting-point--an artistic, earnest, and exact familiarity with the use of the mother-tongue: this, together with the secret of form, however, one can seldom attain to of one's own accord, almost everybody requires those great leaders and tutors and must place himself in their hands. There is, however, no such thing as a classical education that could grow without this inferred love of form. Here, where the power of discerning form and barbarity gradually awakens, there appear the pinions which bear one to the only real home of culture--ancient Greece. If with the solitary help of those pinions we sought to reach those far-distant and diamond-studded walls encircling the stronghold of Hellenism, we should certainly not get very far; once more, therefore, we need the same leaders and tutors, our German classical writers, that we may be borne up, too, by the wing-strokes of their past endeavours--to the land of yearning, to Greece.

"Not a suspicion of this possible relationship between our classics and classical education seems to have pierced the antique walls of public schools. Philologists seem much more eagerly engaged in introducing Homer and Sophocles to the young souls of their pupils, in their own style, calling the result simply by the unchallenged euphemism: 'classical education.' Let every one's own experience tell him what he had of Homer and Sophocles at the hands of such eager teachers. It is in this department that the greatest number of deepest deceptions occur, and whence misunderstandings are inadvertently spread. In German public schools I have never yet found a trace of what might really be called 'classical education,' and there is nothing surprising in this when one thinks of the way in which these institutions have emancipated themselves from German classical writers and the discipline of the German language. Nobody reaches antiquity by means of a leap into the dark, and yet the whole method of treating ancient writers in schools, the plain commentating and paraphrasing of our philological teachers, amounts to nothing more than a leap into the dark.

"The feeling for classical Hellenism is, as a matter of fact, such an exceptional outcome of the most energetic fight for culture and artistic talent that the public school could only have professed to awaken this feeling owing to a very crude misunderstanding. In what age? In an age which is led about blindly by the most sensational desires of the day, and which is not aware of the fact that, once that feeling for Hellenism is roused, it immediately becomes aggressive and must express itself by indulging in an incessant war with the so-called culture of the present. For the public school boy of to-day, the Hellenes as Hellenes are dead: yes, he gets some enjoyment out of Homer, but a novel by Spielhagen interests him much more: yes, he swallows Greek tragedy and comedy with a certain relish, but a thoroughly modern drama, like Freitag's 'Journalists,' moves him in quite another fashion. In regard to all ancient authors he is rather inclined to speak after the manner of the æsthete, Hermann Grimm, who, on one occasion, at the end of a tortuous essay on the Venus of Milo, asks himself: 'What does this goddess's form mean to me? Of what use are the thoughts she suggests to me? Orestes and OEdipus, Iphigenia and Antigone, what have they in common with my heart?'--No, my dear public school boy, the Venus of Milo does not concern you in any way, and concerns your teacher just as little--and that is the misfortune, that is the secret of the modern public school. Who will conduct you to the land of culture, if your leaders are blind and assume the position of seers notwithstanding? Which of you will ever attain to a true feeling for the sacred seriousness of art, if you are systematically spoiled, and taught to stutter independently instead of being taught to speak; to æstheticise on your own account, when you ought to be taught to approach works of art almost piously; to philosophise without assistance, while you ought to be compelled to listen to great thinkers. All this with the result that you remain eternally at a distance from antiquity and become the servants of the day.

"At all events, the most wholesome feature of our modern institutions is to be found in the earnestness with which the Latin and Greek languages are studied over a long course of years. In this way boys learn to respect a grammar, lexicons, and a language that conforms to fixed rules; in this department of public school work there is an exact knowledge of what constitutes a fault, and no one is troubled with any thought of justifying himself every minute by appealing (as in the case of modern German) to various grammatical and orthographical vagaries and vicious forms. If only this respect for language did not hang in the air so, like a theoretical burden which one is pleased to throw off the moment one turns to one's mother-tongue! More often than not, the classical master makes pretty short work of the mother-tongue; from the outset he treats it as a department of knowledge in which one is allowed that indolent ease with which the German treats everything that belongs to his native soil. The splendid practice afforded by translating from one language into another, which so improves and fertilises one's artistic feeling for one's own tongue, is, in the case of German, never conducted with that fitting categorical strictness and dignity which would be above all necessary in dealing with an undisciplined language. Of late, exercises of this kind have tended to decrease ever more and more: people are satisfied to know the foreign classical tongues, they would scorn being able to apply them.

"Here one gets another glimpse of the scholarly tendency of public schools: a phenomenon which throws much light upon the object which once animated them,--that is to say, the serious desire to cultivate the pupil. This belonged to the time of our great poets, those few really cultured Germans,--the time when the magnificent Friedrich August Wolf directed the new stream of classical thought, introduced from Greece and Rome by those men, into the heart of the public schools. Thanks to his bold start, a new order of public schools was established, which thenceforward was not to be merely a nursery for science, but, above all, the actual consecrated home of all higher and nobler culture.

"Of the many necessary measures which this change called into being, some of the most important have been transferred with lasting success to the modern regulations of public schools: the most important of all, however, did not succeed--the one demanding that the teacher, also, should be consecrated to the new spirit, so that the aim of the public school has meanwhile considerably departed from the original plan laid down by Wolf, which was the cultivation of the pupil. The old estimate of scholarship and scholarly culture, as an absolute, which Wolf overcame, seems after a slow and spiritless struggle rather to have taken the place of the culture-principle of more recent introduction, and now claims its former exclusive rights, though not with the same frankness, but disguised and with features veiled. And the reason why it was impossible to make public schools fall in with the magnificent plan of classical culture lay in the un-German, almost foreign or cosmopolitan nature of these efforts in the cause of education: in the belief that it was possible to remove the native soil from under a man's feet and that he should still remain standing; in the illusion that people can spring direct, without bridges, into the strange Hellenic world, by abjuring German and the German mind in general.

"Of course one must know how to trace this Germanic spirit to its lair beneath its many modern dressings, or even beneath heaps of ruins; one must love it so that one is not ashamed of it in its stunted form, and one must above all be on one's guard against confounding it with what now disports itself proudly as 'Up-to-date German culture.' The German spirit is very far from being on friendly times with this up-to-date culture: and precisely in those spheres where the latter complains of a lack of culture the real German spirit has survived, though perhaps not always with a graceful, but more often an ungraceful, exterior. On the other hand, that which now grandiloquently assumes the title of 'German culture' is a sort of cosmopolitan aggregate, which bears the same relation to the German spirit as Journalism does to Schiller or Meyerbeer to Beethoven: here the strongest influence at work is the fundamentally and thoroughly un-German civilisation of France, which is aped neither with talent nor with taste, and the imitation of which gives the society, the press, the art, and the literary style of Germany their pharisaical character. Naturally the copy nowhere produces the really artistic effect which the original, grown out of the heart of Roman civilisation, is able to produce almost to this day in France. Let any one who wishes to see the full force of this contrast compare our most noted novelists with the less noted ones of France or Italy: he will recognise in both the same doubtful tendencies and aims, as also the same still more doubtful means, but in France he will find them coupled with artistic earnestness, at least with grammatical purity, and often with beauty, while in their every feature he will recognise the echo of a corresponding social culture. In Germany, on the other hand, they will strike him as unoriginal, flabby, filled with dressing-gown thoughts and expressions, unpleasantly spread out, and therewithal possessing no background of social form. At the most, owing to their scholarly mannerisms and display of knowledge, he will be reminded of the fact that in Latin countries it is the artistically-trained man, and that in Germany it is the abortive scholar, who becomes a journalist. With this would-be German and thoroughly unoriginal culture, the German can nowhere reckon upon victory: the Frenchman and the Italian will always get the better of him in this respect, while, in regard to the clever imitation of a foreign culture, the Russian, above all, will always be his superior.

"We are therefore all the more anxious to hold fast to that German spirit which revealed itself in the German Reformation, and in German music, and which has shown its enduring and genuine strength in the enormous courage and severity of German philosophy and in the loyalty of the German soldier, which has been tested quite recently. From it we expect a victory over that 'up-to-date' pseudo-culture which is now the fashion. What we should hope for the future is that schools may draw the real school of culture into this struggle, and kindle the flame of enthusiasm in the younger generation, more particularly in public schools, for that which is truly German; and in this way so-called classical education will resume its natural place and recover its one possible starting-point.

"A thorough reformation and purification of the public school can only be the outcome of a profound and powerful reformation and purification of the German spirit. It is a very complex and difficult task to find the border-line which joins the heart of the Germanic spirit with the genius of Greece. Not, however, before the noblest needs of genuine German genius snatch at the hand of this genius of Greece as at a firm post in the torrent of barbarity, not before a devouring yearning for this genius of Greece takes possession of German genius, and not before that view of the Greek home, on which Schiller and Goethe, after enormous exertions, were able to feast their eyes, has become the Mecca of the best and most gifted men, will the aim of classical education in public schools acquire any definition; and they at least will not be to blame who teach ever so little science and learning in public schools, in order to keep a definite and at the same time ideal aim in their eyes, and to rescue their pupils from that glistening phantom which now allows itself to be called 'culture' and 'education.' This is the sad plight of the public school of to-day: the narrowest views remain in a certain measure right, because no one seems able to reach or, at least, to indicate the spot where all these views culminate in error."

"No one?" the philosopher's pupil inquired with a slight quaver in his voice; and both men were silent.

Footnotes:

3. It is not practicable to translate these German solecisms by similar instances of English solecisms. The reader who is interested in the subject will find plenty of material in a book like the Oxford King's English.

4. German: Formelle Bildung.

5. German: Materielle Bildung.

THIRD LECTURE

(Delivered on the 27th of February 1872.)

Ladies and Gentlemen,--At the close of my last lecture, the conversation to which I was a listener, and the outlines of which, as I clearly recollect them, I am now trying to lay before you, was interrupted by a long and solemn pause. Both the philosopher and his companion sat silent, sunk in deep dejection: the peculiarly critical state of that important educational institution, the German public school, lay upon their souls like a heavy burden, which one single, well-meaning individual is not strong enough to remove, and the multitude, though strong, not well meaning enough.

Our solitary thinkers were perturbed by two facts: by clearly perceiving on the one hand that what might rightly be called "classical education" was now only a far-off ideal, a castle in the air, which could not possibly be built as a reality on the foundations of our present educational system, and that, on the other hand, what was now, with customary and unopposed euphemism, pointed to as "classical education" could only claim the value of a pretentious illusion, the best effect of which was that the expression "classical education" still lived on and had not yet lost its pathetic sound. These two worthy men saw clearly, by the system of instruction in vogue, that the time was not yet ripe for a higher culture, a culture founded upon that of the ancients: the neglected state of linguistic instruction; the forcing of students into learned historical paths, instead of giving them a practical training; the connection of certain practices, encouraged in the public schools, with the objectionable spirit of our journalistic publicity--all these easily perceptible phenomena of the teaching of German led to the painful certainty that the most beneficial of those forces which have come down to us from classical antiquity are not yet known in our public schools: forces which would train students for the struggle against the barbarism of the present age, and which will perhaps once more transform the public schools into the arsenals and workshops of this struggle.

On the other hand, it would seem in the meantime as if the spirit of antiquity, in its fundamental principles, had already been driven away from the portals of the public schools, and as if here also the gates were thrown open as widely as possible to the be-flattered and pampered type of our present self-styled "German culture." And if the solitary talkers caught a glimpse of a single ray of hope, it was that things would have to become still worse, that what was as yet divined only by the few would soon be clearly perceived by the many, and that then the time for honest and resolute men for the earnest consideration of the scope of the education of the masses would not be far distant.

After a few minutes' silent reflection, the philosopher's companion turned to him and said: "You used to hold out hopes to me, but now you have done more: you have widened my intelligence, and with it my strength and courage: now indeed can I look on the field of battle with more hardihood, now indeed do I repent of my too hasty flight. We want nothing for ourselves, and it should be nothing to us how many individuals may fall in this battle, or whether we ourselves may be among the first. Just because we take this matter so seriously, we should not take our own poor selves so seriously: at the very moment we are falling some one else will grasp the banner of our faith. I will not even consider whether I am strong enough for such a fight, whether I can offer sufficient resistance; it may even be an honourable death to fall to the accompaniment of the mocking laughter of such enemies, whose seriousness has frequently seemed to us to be something ridiculous. When I think how my contemporaries prepared themselves for the highest posts in the scholastic profession, as I myself have done, then I know how we often laughed at the exact contrary, and grew serious over something quite different----"

"Now, my friend," interrupted the philosopher, laughingly, "you speak as one who would fain dive into the water without being able to swim, and who fears something even more than the mere drowning; not being drowned, but laughed at. But being laughed at should be the very last thing for us to dread; for we are in a sphere where there are too many truths to tell, too many formidable, painful, unpardonable truths, for us to escape hatred, and only fury here and there will give rise to some sort of embarrassed laughter. Just think of the innumerable crowd of teachers, who, in all good faith, have assimilated the system of education which has prevailed up to the present, that they may cheerfully and without over-much deliberation carry it further on. What do you think it will seem like to these men when they hear of projects from which they are excluded beneficio naturæ; of commands which their mediocre abilities are totally unable to carry out; of hopes which find no echo in them; of battles the war-cries of which they do not understand, and in the fighting of which they can take part only as dull and obtuse rank and file? But, without exaggeration, that must necessarily be the position of practically all the teachers in our higher educational establishments: and indeed we cannot wonder at this when we consider how such a teacher originates, how he becomes a teacher of such high status. Such a large number of higher educational establishments are now to be found everywhere that far more teachers will continue to be required for them than the nature of even a highly-gifted people can produce; and thus an inordinate stream of undesirables flows into these institutions, who, however, by their preponderating numbers and their instinct of 'similis simile gaudet' gradually come to determine the nature of these institutions. There may be a few people, hopelessly unfamiliar with pedagogical matters, who believe that our present profusion of public schools and teachers, which is manifestly out of all proportion, can be changed into a real profusion, an ubertas ingenii, merely by a few rules and regulations, and without any reduction in the number of these institutions. But we may surely be unanimous in recognising that by the very nature of things only an exceedingly small number of people are destined for a true course of education, and that a much smaller number of higher educational establishments would suffice for their further development, but that, in view of the present large numbers of educational institutions, those for whom in general such institutions ought only to be established must feel themselves to be the least facilitated in their progress.

"The same holds good in regard to teachers. It is precisely the best teachers--those who, generally speaking, judged by a high standard, are worthy of this honourable name--who are now perhaps the least fitted, in view of the present standing of our public schools, for the education of these unselected youths, huddled together in a confused heap; but who must rather, to a certain extent, keep hidden from them the best they could give: and, on the other hand, by far the larger number of these teachers feel themselves quite at home in these institutions, as their moderate abilities stand in a kind of harmonious relationship to the dullness of their pupils. It is from this majority that we hear the ever-resounding call for the establishment of new public schools and higher educational institutions: we are living in an age which, by ringing the changes on its deafening and continual cry, would certainly give one the impression that there was an unprecedented thirst for culture which eagerly sought to be quenched. But it is just at this point that one should learn to hear aright: it is here, without being disconcerted by the thundering noise of the education-mongers, that we must confront those who talk so tirelessly about the educational necessities of their time. Then we should meet with a strange disillusionment, one which we, my good friend, have often met with: those blatant heralds of educational needs, when examined at close quarters, are suddenly seen to be transformed into zealous, yea, fanatical opponents of true culture, i.e. all those who hold fast to the aristocratic nature of the mind; for, at bottom, they regard as their goal the emancipation of the masses from the mastery of the great few; they seek to overthrow the most sacred hierarchy in the kingdom of the intellect--the servitude of the masses, their submissive obedience, their instinct of loyalty to the rule of genius.

"I have long accustomed myself to look with caution upon those who are ardent in the cause of the so-called 'education of the people' in the common meaning of the phrase; since for the most part they desire for themselves, consciously or unconsciously, absolutely unlimited freedom, which must inevitably degenerate into something resembling the saturnalia of barbaric times, and which the sacred hierarchy of nature will never grant them. They were born to serve and to obey; and every moment in which their limping or crawling or broken-winded thoughts are at work shows us clearly out of which clay nature moulded them, and what trade mark she branded thereon. The education of the masses cannot, therefore, be our aim; but rather the education of a few picked men for great and lasting works. We well know that a just posterity judges the collective intellectual state of a time only by those few great and lonely figures of the period, and gives its decision in accordance with the manner in which they are recognised, encouraged, and honoured, or, on the other hand, in which they are snubbed, elbowed aside, and kept down. What is called the 'education of the masses' cannot be accomplished except with difficulty; and even if a system of universal compulsory education be applied, they can only be reached outwardly: those individual lower levels where, generally speaking, the masses come into contact with culture, where the people nourishes its religious instinct, where it poetises its mythological images, where it keeps up its faith in its customs, privileges, native soil, and language--all these levels can scarcely be reached by direct means, and in any case only by violent demolition. And, in serious matters of this kind, to hasten forward the progress of the education of the people means simply the postponement of this violent demolition, and the maintenance of that wholesome unconsciousness, that sound sleep, of the people, without which counter-action and remedy no culture, with the exhausting strain and excitement of its own actions, can make any headway.

"We know, however, what the aspiration is of those who would disturb the healthy slumber of the people, and continually call out to them: 'Keep your eyes open! Be sensible! Be wise!' we know the aim of those who profess to satisfy excessive educational requirements by means of an extraordinary increase in the number of educational institutions and the conceited tribe of teachers originated thereby. These very people, using these very means, are fighting against the natural hierarchy in the realm of the intellect, and destroying the roots of all those noble and sublime plastic forces which have their material origin in the unconsciousness of the people, and which fittingly terminate in the procreation of genius and its due guidance and proper training. It is only in the simile of the mother that we can grasp the meaning and the responsibility of the true education of the people in respect to genius: its real origin is not to be found in such education; it has, so to speak, only a metaphysical source, a metaphysical home. But for the genius to make his appearance; for him to emerge from among the people; to portray the reflected picture, as it were, the dazzling brilliancy of the peculiar colours of this people; to depict the noble destiny of a people in the similitude of an individual in a work which will last for all time, thereby making his nation itself eternal, and redeeming it from the ever-shifting element of transient things: all this is possible for the genius only when he has been brought up and come to maturity in the tender care of the culture of a people; whilst, on the other hand, without this sheltering home, the genius will not, generally speaking, be able to rise to the height of his eternal flight, but will at an early moment, like a stranger weather-driven upon a bleak, snow-covered desert, slink away from the inhospitable land."

"You astonish me with such a metaphysics of genius," said the teacher's companion, "and I have only a hazy conception of the accuracy of your similitude. On the other hand, I fully understand what you have said about the surplus of public schools and the corresponding surplus of higher grade teachers; and in this regard I myself have collected some information which assures me that the educational tendency of the public school must right itself by this very surplus of teachers who have really nothing at all to do with education, and who are called into existence and pursue this path solely because there is a demand for them. Every man who, in an unexpected moment of enlightenment, has convinced himself of the singularity and inaccessibility of Hellenic antiquity, and has warded off this conviction after an exhausting struggle--every such man knows that the door leading to this enlightenment will never remain open to all comers; and he deems it absurd, yea disgraceful, to use the Greeks as he would any other tool he employs when following his profession or earning his living, shamelessly fumbling with coarse hands amidst the relics of these holy men. This brazen and vulgar feeling is, however, most common in the profession from which the largest numbers of teachers for the public schools are drawn, the philological profession, wherefore the reproduction and continuation of such a feeling in the public school will not surprise us.

"Just look at the younger generation of philologists: how seldom we see in them that humble feeling that we, when compared with such a world as it was, have no right to exist at all: how coolly and fearlessly, as compared with us, did that young brood build its miserable nests in the midst of the magnificent temples! A powerful voice from every nook and cranny should ring in the ears of those who, from the day they begin their connection with the university, roam at will with such self-complacency and shamelessness among the awe-inspiring relics of that noble civilisation: 'Hence, ye uninitiated, who will never be initiated; fly away in silence and shame from these sacred chambers!' But this voice speaks in vain; for one must to some extent be a Greek to understand a Greek curse of excommunication. But these people I am speaking of are so barbaric that they dispose of these relics to suit themselves: all their modern conveniences and fancies are brought with them and concealed among those ancient pillars and tombstones, and it gives rise to great rejoicing when somebody finds, among the dust and cobwebs of antiquity, something that he himself had slyly hidden there not so very long before. One of them makes verses and takes care to consult Hesychius' Lexicon. Something there immediately assures him that he is destined to be an imitator of Æschylus, and leads him to believe, indeed, that he 'has something in common with' Æschylus: the miserable poetaster! Yet another peers with the suspicious eye of a policeman into every contradiction, even into the shadow of every contradiction, of which Homer was guilty: he fritters away his life in tearing Homeric rags to tatters and sewing them together again, rags that he himself was the first to filch from the poet's kingly robe. A third feels ill at ease when examining all the mysterious and orgiastic sides of antiquity: he makes up his mind once and for all to let the enlightened Apollo alone pass without dispute, and to see in the Athenian a gay and intelligent but nevertheless somewhat immoral Apollonian. What a deep breath he draws when he succeeds in raising yet another dark corner of antiquity to the level of his own intelligence!--when, for example, he discovers in Pythagoras a colleague who is as enthusiastic as himself in arguing about politics. Another racks his brains as to why OEdipus was condemned by fate to perform such abominable deeds--killing his father, marrying his mother. Where lies the blame! Where the poetic justice! Suddenly it occurs to him: OEdipus was a passionate fellow, lacking all Christian gentleness--he even fell into an unbecoming rage when Tiresias called him a monster and the curse of the whole country. Be humble and meek! was what Sophocles tried to teach, otherwise you will have to marry your mothers and kill your fathers! Others, again, pass their lives in counting the number of verses written by Greek and Roman poets, and are delighted with the proportions 7:13 = 14:26. Finally, one of them brings forward his solution of a question, such as the Homeric poems considered from the standpoint of prepositions, and thinks he has drawn the truth from the bottom of the well with +ana+ and +kata+. All of them, however, with the most widely separated aims in view, dig and burrow in Greek soil with a restlessness and a blundering awkwardness that must surely be painful to a true friend of antiquity: and thus it comes to pass that I should like to take by the hand every talented or talentless man who feels a certain professional inclination urging him on to the study of antiquity, and harangue him as follows: 'Young sir, do you know what perils threaten you, with your little stock of school learning, before you become a man in the full sense of the word? Have you heard that, according to Aristotle, it is by no means a tragic death to be slain by a statue? Does that surprise you? Know, then, that for centuries philologists have been trying, with ever-failing strength, to re-erect the fallen statue of Greek antiquity, but without success; for it is a colossus around which single individual men crawl like pygmies. The leverage of the united representatives of modern culture is utilised for the purpose; but it invariably happens that the huge column is scarcely more than lifted from the ground when it falls down again, crushing beneath its weight the luckless wights under it. That, however, may be tolerated, for every being must perish by some means or other; but who is there to guarantee that during all these attempts the statue itself will not break in pieces! The philologists are being crushed by the Greeks--perhaps we can put up with this--but antiquity itself threatens to be crushed by these philologists! Think that over, you easy-going young man; and turn back, lest you too should not be an iconoclast!'"

"Indeed," said the philosopher, laughing, "there are many philologists who have turned back as you so much desire, and I notice a great contrast with my own youthful experience. Consciously or unconsciously, large numbers of them have concluded that it is hopeless and useless for them to come into direct contact with classical antiquity, hence they are inclined to look upon this study as barren, superseded, out-of-date. This herd has turned with much greater zest to the science of language: here in this wide expanse of virgin soil, where even the most mediocre gifts can be turned to account, and where a kind of insipidity and dullness is even looked upon as decided talent, with the novelty and uncertainty of methods and the constant danger of making fantastic mistakes--here, where dull regimental routine and discipline are desiderata--here the newcomer is no longer frightened by the majestic and warning voice that rises from the ruins of antiquity: here every one is welcomed with open arms, including even him who never arrived at any uncommon impression or noteworthy thought after a perusal of Sophocles and Aristophanes, with the result that they end in an etymological tangle, or are seduced into collecting the fragments of out-of-the-way dialects--and their time is spent in associating and dissociating, collecting and scattering, and running hither and thither consulting books. And such a usefully employed philologist would now fain be a teacher! He now undertakes to teach the youth of the public schools something about the ancient writers, although he himself has read them without any particular impression, much less with insight! What a dilemma! Antiquity has said nothing to him, consequently he has nothing to say about antiquity. A sudden thought strikes him: why is he a skilled philologist at all! Why did these authors write Latin and Greek! And with a light heart he immediately begins to etymologise with Homer, calling Lithuanian or Ecclesiastical Slavonic, or, above all, the sacred Sanskrit, to his assistance: as if Greek lessons were merely the excuse for a general introduction to the study of languages, and as if Homer were lacking in only one respect, namely, not being written in pre-Indogermanic. Whoever is acquainted with our present public schools well knows what a wide gulf separates their teachers from classicism, and how, from a feeling of this want, comparative philology and allied professions have increased their numbers to such an unheard-of degree."

"What I mean is," said the other, "it would depend upon whether a teacher of classical culture did not confuse his Greeks and Romans with the other peoples, the barbarians, whether he could never put Greek and Latin on a level with other languages: so far as his classicalism is concerned, it is a matter of indifference whether the framework of these languages concurs with or is in any way related to the other languages: such a concurrence does not interest him at all; his real concern is with what is not common to both, with what shows him that those two peoples were not barbarians as compared with the others--in so far, of course, as he is a true teacher of culture and models himself after the majestic patterns of the classics."

"I may be wrong," said the philosopher, "but I suspect that, owing to the way in which Latin and Greek are now taught in schools, the accurate grasp of these languages, the ability to speak and write them with ease, is lost, and that is something in which my own generation distinguished itself--a generation, indeed, whose few survivers have by this time grown old; whilst, on the other hand, the present teachers seem to impress their pupils with the genetic and historical importance of the subject to such an extent that, at best, their scholars ultimately turn into little Sanskritists, etymological spitfires, or reckless conjecturers; but not one of them can read his Plato or Tacitus with pleasure, as we old folk can. The public schools may still be seats of learning: not, however of the learning which, as it were, is only the natural and involuntary auxiliary of a culture that is directed towards the noblest ends; but rather of that culture which might be compared to the hypertrophical swelling of an unhealthy body. The public schools are certainly the seats of this obesity, if, indeed, they have not degenerated into the abodes of that elegant barbarism which is boasted of as being 'German culture of the present!'"

"But," asked the other, "what is to become of that large body of teachers who have not been endowed with a true gift for culture, and who set up as teachers merely to gain a livelihood from the profession, because there is a demand for them, because a superfluity of schools brings with it a superfluity of teachers? Where shall they go when antiquity peremptorily orders them to withdraw?

Must they not be sacrificed to those powers of the present who, day after day, call out to them from the never-ending columns of the press 'We are culture! We are education! We are at the zenith! We are the apexes of the pyramids! We are the aims of universal history!'--when they hear the seductive promises, when the shameful signs of non-culture, the plebeian publicity of the so-called 'interests of culture' are extolled for their benefit in magazines and newspapers as an entirely new and the best possible, full-grown form of culture! Whither shall the poor fellows fly when they feel the presentiment that these promises are not true--where but to the most obtuse, sterile scientificality, that here the shriek of culture may no longer be audible to them? Pursued in this way, must they not end, like the ostrich, by burying their heads in the sand? Is it not a real happiness for them, buried as they are among dialects, etymologies, and conjectures, to lead a life like that of the ants, even though they are miles removed from true culture, if only they can close their ears tightly and be deaf to the voice of the 'elegant' culture of the time."

"You are right, my friend," said the philosopher, "but whence comes the urgent necessity for a surplus of schools for culture, which further gives rise to the necessity for a surplus of teachers?--when we so clearly see that the demand for a surplus springs from a sphere which is hostile to culture, and that the consequences of this surplus only lead to non-culture. Indeed, we can discuss this dire necessity only in so far as the modern State is willing to discuss these things with us, and is prepared to follow up its demands by force: which phenomenon certainly makes the same impression upon most people as if they were addressed by the eternal law of things. For the rest, a 'Culture-State,' to use the current expression, which makes such demands, is rather a novelty, and has only come to a 'self-understanding' within the last half century, i.e. in a period when (to use the favourite popular word) so many 'self-understood' things came into being, but which are in themselves not 'self-understood' at all. This right to higher education has been taken so seriously by the most powerful of modern States--Prussia--that the objectionable principle it has adopted, taken in connection with the well-known daring and hardihood of this State, is seen to have a menacing and dangerous consequence for the true German spirit; for we see endeavours being made in this quarter to raise the public school, formally systematised, up to the so-called 'level of the time.' Here is to be found all that mechanism by means of which as many scholars as possible are urged on to take up courses of public school training: here, indeed, the State has its most powerful inducement--the concession of certain privileges respecting military service, with the natural consequence that, according to the unprejudiced evidence of statistical officials, by this, and by this only, can we explain the universal congestion of all Prussian public schools, and the urgent and continual need for new ones. What more can the State do for a surplus of educational institutions than bring all the higher and the majority of the lower civil service appointments, the right of entry to the universities, and even the most influential military posts into close connection with the public school: and all this in a country where both universal military service and the highest offices of the State unconsciously attract all gifted natures to them. The public school is here looked upon as an honourable aim, and every one who feels himself urged on to the sphere of government will be found on his way to it. This is a new and quite original occurrence: the State assumes the attitude of a mystogogue of culture, and, whilst it promotes its own ends, it obliges every one of its servants not to appear in its presence without the torch of universal State education in their hands, by the flickering light of which they may again recognise the State as the highest goal, as the reward of all their strivings after education.

"Now this last phenomenon should indeed surprise them; it should remind them of that allied, slowly understood tendency of a philosophy which was formerly promoted for reasons of State, namely, the tendency of the Hegelian philosophy: yea, it would perhaps be no exaggeration to say that, in the subordination of all strivings after education to reasons of State, Prussia has appropriated, with success, the principle and the useful heirloom of the Hegelian philosophy, whose apotheosis of the State in this subordination certainly reaches its height."

"But," said the philosopher's companion, "what purposes can the State have in view with such a strange aim? For that it has some State objects in view is seen in the manner in which the conditions of Prussian schools are admired by, meditated upon, and occasionally imitated by other States. These other States obviously presuppose something here that, if adopted, would tend towards the maintenance and power of the State, like our well-known and popular conscription. Where everyone proudly wears his soldier's uniform at regular intervals, where almost every one has absorbed a uniform type of national culture through the public schools, enthusiastic hyperboles may well be uttered concerning the systems employed in former times, and a form of State omnipotence which was attained only in antiquity, and which almost every young man, by both instinct and training, thinks it is the crowning glory and highest aim of human beings to reach."

"Such a comparison," said the philosopher, "would be quite hyperbolical, and would not hobble along on one leg only. For, indeed, the ancient State emphatically did not share the utilitarian point of view of recognising as culture only what was directly useful to the State itself, and was far from wishing to destroy those impulses which did not seem to be immediately applicable. For this very reason the profound Greek had for the State that strong feeling of admiration and thankfulness which is so distasteful to modern men; because he clearly recognised not only that without such State protection the germs of his culture could not develop, but also that all his inimitable and perennial culture had flourished so luxuriantly under the wise and careful guardianship of the protection afforded by the State. The State was for his culture not a supervisor, regulator, and watchman, but a vigorous and muscular companion and friend, ready for war, who accompanied his noble, admired, and, as it were, ethereal friend through disagreeable reality, earning his thanks therefor. This, however, does not happen when a modern State lays claim to such hearty gratitude because it renders such chivalrous service to German culture and art: for in this regard its past is as ignominious as its present, as a proof of which we have but to think of the manner in which the memory of our great poets and artists is celebrated in German cities, and how the highest objects of these German masters are supported on the part of the State.

"There must therefore be peculiar circumstances surrounding both this purpose towards which the State is tending, and which always promotes what is here called 'education'; and surrounding likewise the culture thus promoted, which subordinates itself to this purpose of the State. With the real German spirit and the education derived therefrom, such as I have slowly outlined for you, this purpose of the State is at war, hiddenly or openly: the spirit of education, which is welcomed and encouraged with such interest by the State, and owing to which the schools of this country are so much admired abroad, must accordingly originate in a sphere that never comes into contact with this true German spirit: with that spirit which speaks to us so wondrously from the inner heart of the German Reformation, German music, and German philosophy, and which, like a noble exile, is regarded with such indifference and scorn by the luxurious education afforded by the State. This spirit is a stranger: it passes by in solitary sadness, and far away from it the censer of pseudo-culture is swung backwards and forwards, which, amidst the acclamations of 'educated' teachers and journalists, arrogates to itself its name and privileges, and metes out insulting treatment to the word 'German.' Why does the State require that surplus of educational institutions, of teachers? Why this education of the masses on such an extended scale? Because the true German spirit is hated, because the aristocratic nature of true culture is feared, because the people endeavour in this way to drive single great individuals into self-exile, so that the claims of the masses to education may be, so to speak, planted down and carefully tended, in order that the many may in this way endeavour to escape the rigid and strict discipline of the few great leaders, so that the masses may be persuaded that they can easily find the path for themselves--following the guiding star of the State!

"A new phenomenon! The State as the guiding star of culture! In the meantime one thing consoles me: this German spirit, which people are combating so much, and for which they have substituted a gaudily attired locum tenens, this spirit is brave: it will fight and redeem itself into a purer age; noble, as it is now, and victorious, as it one day will be, it will always preserve in its mind a certain pitiful toleration of the State, if the latter, hard-pressed in the hour of extremity, secures such a pseudo-culture as its associate. For what, after all, do we know about the difficult task of governing men, i.e. to keep law, order, quietness, and peace among millions of boundlessly egoistical, unjust, unreasonable, dishonourable, envious, malignant, and hence very narrow-minded and perverse human beings; and thus to protect the few things that the State has conquered for itself against covetous neighbours and jealous robbers? Such a hard-pressed State holds out its arms to any associate, grasps at any straw; and when such an associate does introduce himself with flowery eloquence, when he adjudges the State, as Hegel did, to be an 'absolutely complete ethical organism,' the be-all and end-all of every one's education, and goes on to indicate how he himself can best promote the interests of the State--who will be surprised if, without further parley, the State falls upon his neck and cries aloud in a barbaric voice of full conviction: 'Yes! Thou art education! Thou art indeed culture!'"

FOURTH LECTURE

(Delivered on the 5th of March 1872.)

LADIES AND GENTLEMEN,--Now that you have followed my tale up to this point, and that we have made ourselves joint masters of the solitary, remote, and at times abusive duologue of the philosopher and his companion, I sincerely hope that you, like strong swimmers, are ready to proceed on the second half of our journey, especially as I can promise you that a few other marionettes will appear in the puppet-play of my adventure, and that if up to the present you have only been able to do little more than endure what I have been telling you, the waves of my story will now bear you more quickly and easily towards the end. In other words we have now come to a turning, and it would be advisable for us to take a short glance backwards to see what we think we have gained from such a varied conversation.

"Remain in your present position," the philosopher seemed to say to his companion, "for you may cherish hopes. It is more and more clearly evident that we have no educational institutions at all; but that we ought to have them. Our public schools--established, it would seem, for this high object--have either become the nurseries of a reprehensible culture which repels the true culture with profound hatred--i.e. a true, aristocratic culture, founded upon a few carefully chosen minds; or they foster a micrological and sterile learning which, while it is far removed from culture, has at least this merit, that it avoids that reprehensible culture as well as the true culture." The philosopher had particularly drawn his companion's attention to the strange corruption which must have entered into the heart of culture when the State thought itself capable of tyrannising over it and of attaining its ends through it; and further when the State, in conjunction with this culture, struggled against other hostile forces as well as against the spirit which the philosopher ventured to call the "true German spirit." This spirit, linked to the Greeks by the noblest ties, and shown by its past history to have been steadfast and courageous, pure and lofty in its aims, its faculties qualifying it for the high task of freeing modern man from the curse of modernity--this spirit is condemned to live apart, banished from its inheritance. But when its slow, painful tones of woe resound through the desert of the present, then the overladen and gaily-decked caravan of culture is pulled up short, horror-stricken. We must not only astonish, but terrify--such was the philosopher's opinion: not to fly shamefully away, but to take the offensive, was his advice; but he especially counselled his companion not to ponder too anxiously over the individual from whom, through a higher instinct, this aversion for the present barbarism proceeded, "Let it perish: the Pythian god had no difficulty in finding a new tripod, a second Pythia, so long, at least, as the mystic cold vapours rose from the earth."

The philosopher once more began to speak: "Be careful to remember, my friend," said he, "there are two things you must not confuse. A man must learn a great deal that he may live and take part in the struggle for existence; but everything that he as an individual learns and does with this end in view has nothing whatever to do with culture. This latter only takes its beginning in a sphere that lies far above the world of necessity, indigence, and struggle for existence. The question now is to what extent a man values his ego in comparison with other egos, how much of his strength he uses up in the endeavour to earn his living. Many a one, by stoically confining his needs within a narrow compass, will shortly and easily reach the sphere in which he may forget, and, as it were, shake off his ego, so that he can enjoy perpetual youth in a solar system of timeless and impersonal things. Another widens the scope and needs of his ego as much as possible, and builds the mausoleum of this ego in vast proportions, as if he were prepared to fight and conquer that terrible adversary, Time. In this instinct also we may see a longing for immortality: wealth and power, wisdom, presence of mind, eloquence, a flourishing outward aspect, a renowned name--all these are merely turned into the means by which an insatiable, personal will to live craves for new life, with which, again, it hankers after an eternity that is at last seen to be illusory.

"But even in this highest form of the ego, in the enhanced needs of such a distended and, as it were, collective individual, true culture is never touched upon; and if, for example, art is sought after, only its disseminating and stimulating actions come into prominence, i.e. those which least give rise to pure and noble art, and most of all to low and degraded forms of it. For in all his efforts, however great and exceptional they seem to the onlooker, he never succeeds in freeing himself from his own hankering and restless personality: that illuminated, ethereal sphere where one may contemplate without the obstruction of one's own personality continually recedes from him--and thus, let him learn, travel, and collect as he may, he must always live an exiled life at a remote distance from a higher life and from true culture. For true culture would scorn to contaminate itself with the needy and covetous individual; it well knows how to give the slip to the man who would fain employ it as a means of attaining to egoistic ends; and if any one cherishes the belief that he has firmly secured it as a means of livelihood, and that he can procure the necessities of life by its sedulous cultivation, then it suddenly steals away with noiseless steps and an air of derisive mockery.[6]

"I will thus ask you, my friend, not to confound this culture, this sensitive, fastidious, ethereal goddess, with that useful maid-of-all-work which is also called 'culture,' but which is only the intellectual servant and counsellor of one's practical necessities, wants, and means of livelihood Every kind of training, however, which holds out the prospect of bread-winning as its end and aim, is not a training for culture as we understand the word; but merely a collection of precepts and directions to show how, in the struggle for existence, a man may preserve and protect his own person. It may be freely admitted that for the great majority of men such a course of instruction is of the highest importance; and the more arduous the struggle is the more intensely must the young man strain every nerve to utilise his strength to the best advantage.

"But--let no one think for a moment that the schools which urge him on to this struggle and prepare him for it are in any way seriously to be considered as establishments of culture. They are institutions which teach one how to take part in the battle of life; whether they promise to turn out civil servants, or merchants, or officers, or wholesale dealers, or farmers, or physicians, or men with a technical training. The regulations and standards prevailing at such institutions differ from those in a true educational institution; and what in the latter is permitted, and even freely held out as often as possible, ought to be considered as a criminal offence in the former.

"Let me give you an example. If you wish to guide a young man on the path of true culture, beware of interrupting his naive, confident, and, as it were, immediate and personal relationship with nature. The woods, the rocks, the winds, the vulture, the flowers, the butterfly, the meads, the mountain slopes, must all speak to him in their own language; in them he must, as it were, come to know himself again in countless reflections and images, in a variegated round of changing visions; and in this way he will unconsciously and gradually feel the metaphysical unity of all things in the great image of nature, and at the same time tranquillise his soul in the contemplation of her eternal endurance and necessity. But how many young men should be permitted to grow up in such close and almost personal proximity to nature! The others must learn another truth betimes: how to subdue nature to themselves. Here is an end of this naive metaphysics; and the physiology of plants and animals, geology, inorganic chemistry, force their devotees to view nature from an altogether different standpoint. What is lost by this new point of view is not only a poetical phantasmagoria, but the instinctive, true, and unique point of view, instead of which we have shrewd and clever calculations, and, so to speak, overreachings of nature. Thus to the truly cultured man is vouchsafed the inestimable benefit of being able to remain faithful, without a break, to the contemplative instincts of his childhood, and so to attain to a calmness, unity, consistency, and harmony which can never be even thought of by a man who is compelled to fight in the struggle for existence.

"You must not think, however, that I wish to withhold all praise from our primary and secondary schools: I honour the seminaries where boys learn arithmetic and master modern languages, and study geography and the marvellous discoveries made in natural science. I am quite prepared to say further that those youths who pass through the better class of secondary schools are well entitled to make the claims put forward by the fully-fledged public school boy; and the time is certainly not far distant when such pupils will be everywhere freely admitted to the universities and positions under the government, which has hitherto been the case only with scholars from the public schools--of our present public schools, be it noted![7] I cannot, however, refrain from adding the melancholy reflection: if it be true that secondary and public schools are, on the whole, working so heartily in common towards the same ends, and differ from each other only in such a slight degree, that they may take equal rank before the tribunal of the State, then we completely lack another kind of educational institutions: those for the development of culture! To say the least, the secondary schools cannot be reproached with this; for they have up to the present propitiously and honourably followed up tendencies of a lower order, but one nevertheless highly necessary. In the public schools, however, there is very much less honesty and very much less ability too; for in them we find an instinctive feeling of shame, the unconscious perception of the fact that the whole institution has been ignominiously degraded, and that the sonorous words of wise and apathetic teachers are contradictory to the dreary, barbaric, and sterile reality. So there are no true cultural institutions! And in those very places where a pretence to culture is still kept up, we find the people more hopeless, atrophied, and discontented than in the secondary schools, where the so-called 'realistic' subjects are taught! Besides this, only think how immature and uninformed one must be in the company of such teachers when one actually misunderstands the rigorously defined philosophical expressions 'real' and 'realism' to such a degree as to think them the contraries of mind and matter, and to interpret 'realism' as 'the road to knowledge, formation, and mastery of reality.'

"I for my own part know of only two exact contraries: institutions for teaching culture and institutions for teaching how to succeed in life. All our present institutions belong to the second class; but I am speaking only of the first."

About two hours went by while the philosophically-minded couple chatted about such startling questions. Night slowly fell in the meantime; and when in the twilight the philosopher's voice had sounded like natural music through the woods, it now rang out in the profound darkness of the night when he was speaking with excitement or even passionately; his tones hissing and thundering far down the valley, and reverberating among the trees and rocks. Suddenly he was silent: he had just repeated, almost pathetically, the words, "we have no true educational institutions; we have no true educational institutions!" when something fell down just in front of him--it might have been a fir-cone--and his dog barked and ran towards it. Thus interrupted, the philosopher raised his head, and suddenly became aware of the darkness, the cool air, and the lonely situation of himself and his companion. "Well! What are we about!" he ejaculated, "it's dark. You know whom we were expecting here; but he hasn't come. We have waited in vain; let us go."

***

I must now, ladies and gentlemen, convey to you the impressions experienced by my friend and myself as we eagerly listened to this conversation, which we heard distinctly in our hiding-place. I have already told you that at that place and at that hour we had intended to hold a festival in commemoration of something: and this something had to do with nothing else than matters concerning educational training, of which we, in our own youthful opinions, had garnered a plentiful harvest during our past life. We were thus disposed to remember with gratitude the institution which we had at one time thought out for ourselves at that very spot in order, as I have already mentioned, that we might reciprocally encourage and watch over one another's educational impulses. But a sudden and unexpected light was thrown on all that past life as we silently gave ourselves up to the vehement words of the philosopher. As when a traveller, walking heedlessly across unknown ground, suddenly puts his foot over the edge of a cliff, so it now seemed to us that we had hastened to meet the great danger rather than run away from it. Here at this spot, so memorable to us, we heard the warning: "Back! Not another step! Know you not whither your footsteps tend, whither this deceitful path is luring you?"

It seemed to us that we now knew, and our feeling of overflowing thankfulness impelled us so irresistibly towards our earnest counsellor and trusty Eckart, that both of us sprang up at the same moment and rushed towards the philosopher to embrace him. He was just about to move off, and had already turned sideways when we rushed up to him. The dog turned sharply round and barked, thinking doubtless, like the philosopher's companion, of an attempt at robbery rather than an enraptured embrace. It was plain that he had forgotten us. In a word, he ran away. Our embrace was a miserable failure when we did overtake him; for my friend gave a loud yell as the dog bit him, and the philosopher himself sprang away from me with such force that we both fell. What with the dog and the men there was a scramble that lasted a few minutes, until my friend began to call out loudly, parodying the philosopher's own words: "In the name of all culture and pseudo-culture, what does the silly dog want with us? Hence, you confounded dog; you uninitiated, never to be initiated; hasten away from us, silent and ashamed!" After this outburst matters were cleared up to some extent, at any rate so far as they could be cleared up in the darkness of the wood. "Oh, it's you!" ejaculated the philosopher, "our duellists! How you startled us! What on earth drives you to jump out upon us like this at such a time of the night?"

"Joy, thankfulness, and reverence," said we, shaking the old man by the hand, whilst the dog barked as if he understood, "we can't let you go without telling you this. And if you are to understand everything you must not go away just yet; we want to ask you about so many things that lie heavily on our hearts. Stay yet awhile; we know every foot of the way and can accompany you afterwards. The gentleman you expect may yet turn up. Look over yonder on the Rhine: what is that we see so clearly floating on the surface of the water as if surrounded by the light of many torches? It is there that we may look for your friend, I would even venture to say that it is he who is coming towards you with all those lights."

And so much did we assail the surprised old man with our entreaties, promises, and fantastic delusions, that we persuaded the philosopher to walk to and fro with us on the little plateau, "by learned lumber undisturbed," as my friend added.

"Shame on you!" said the philosopher, "if you really want to quote something, why choose Faust? However, I will give in to you, quotation or no quotation, if only our young companions will keep still and not run away as suddenly as they made their appearance, for they are like will-o'-the-wisps; we are amazed when they are there and again when they are not there."

My friend immediately recited--

Respect, I hope, will teach us how we may
Our lighter disposition keep at bay.
Our course is only zig-zag as a rule.

The philosopher was surprised, and stood still. "You astonish me, you will-o'-the-wisps," he said; "this is no quagmire we are on now. Of what use is this ground to you? What does the proximity of a philosopher mean to you? For around him the air is sharp and clear, the ground dry and hard. You must find out a more fantastic region for your zig-zagging inclinations."

"I think," interrupted the philosopher's companion at this point, "the gentlemen have already told us that they promised to meet some one here at this hour; but it seems to me that they listened to our comedy of education like a chorus, and truly 'idealistic spectators'--for they did not disturb us; we thought we were alone with each other."

"Yes, that is true," said the philosopher, "that praise must not be withheld from them, but it seems to me that they deserve still higher praise----"

Here I seized the philosopher's hand and said: "That man must be as obtuse as a reptile, with his stomach on the ground and his head buried in mud, who can listen to such a discourse as yours without becoming earnest and thoughtful, or even excited and indignant. Self-accusation and annoyance might perhaps cause a few to get angry; but our impression was quite different: the only thing I do not know is how exactly to describe it. This hour was so well-timed for us, and our minds were so well prepared, that we sat there like empty vessels, and now it seems as if we were filled to overflowing with this new wisdom: for I no longer know how to help myself, and if some one asked me what I am thinking of doing to-morrow, or what I have made up my mind to do with myself from now on, I should not know what to answer. For it is easy to see that we have up to the present been living and educating ourselves in the wrong way--but what can we do to cross over the chasm between to-day and to-morrow?"

"Yes," acknowledged my friend, "I have a similar feeling, and I ask the same question: but besides that I feel as if I were frightened away from German culture by entertaining such high and ideal views of its task; yea, as if I were unworthy to co-operate with it in carrying out its aims. I only see a resplendent file of the highest natures moving towards this goal; I can imagine over what abysses and through what temptations this procession travels. Who would dare to be so bold as to join in it?"

At this point the philosopher's companion again turned to him and said: "Don't be angry with me when I tell you that I too have a somewhat similar feeling, which I have not mentioned to you before. When talking to you I often felt drawn out of myself, as it were, and inspired with your ardour and hopes till I almost forgot myself. Then a calmer moment arrives; a piercing wind of reality brings me back to earth--and then I see the wide gulf between us, over which you yourself, as in a dream, draw me back again. Then what you call 'culture' merely totters meaninglessly around me or lies heavily on my breast: it is like a shirt of mail that weighs me down, or a sword that I cannot wield."

Our minds, as we thus argued with the philosopher, were unanimous, and, mutually encouraging and stimulating one another, we slowly walked with him backwards and forwards along the unencumbered space which had earlier in the day served us as a shooting range. And then, in the still night, under the peaceful light of hundreds of stars, we all broke out into a tirade which ran somewhat as follows:--

"You have told us so much about the genius," we began, "about his lonely and wearisome journey through the world, as if nature never exhibited anything but the most diametrical contraries: in one place the stupid, dull masses, acting by instinct, and then, on a far higher and more remote plane, the great contemplating few, destined for the production of immortal works. But now you call these the apexes of the intellectual pyramid: it would, however, seem that between the broad, heavily burdened foundation up to the highest of the free and unencumbered peaks there must be countless intermediate degrees, and that here we must apply the saying natura non facit saltus. Where then are we to look for the beginning of what you call culture; where is the line of demarcation to be drawn between the spheres which are ruled from below upwards and those which are ruled from above downwards? And if it be only in connection with these exalted beings that true culture may be spoken of, how are institutions to be founded for the uncertain existence of such natures, how can we devise educational establishments which shall be of benefit only to these select few? It rather seems to us that such persons know how to find their own way, and that their full strength is shown in their being able to walk without the educational crutches necessary for other people, and thus undisturbed to make their way through the storm and stress of this rough world just like a phantom."

We kept on arguing in this fashion, speaking without any great ability and not putting our thoughts in any special form: but the philosopher's companion went even further, and said to him: "Just think of all these great geniuses of whom we are wont to be so proud, looking upon them as tried and true leaders and guides of this real German spirit, whose names we commemorate by statues and festivals, and whose works we hold up with feelings of pride for the admiration of foreign lands--how did they obtain the education you demand for them, to what degree do they show that they have been nourished and matured by basking in the sun of national education? And yet they are seen to be possible, they have nevertheless become men whom we must honour: yea, their works themselves justify the form of the development of these noble spirits; they justify even a certain want of education for which we must make allowance owing to their country and the age in which they lived. How could Lessing and Winckelmann benefit by the German culture of their time? Even less than, or at all events just as little as Beethoven, Schiller, Goethe, or every one of our great poets and artists. It may perhaps be a law of nature that only the later generations are destined to know by what divine gifts an earlier generation was favoured."

At this point the old philosopher could not control his anger, and shouted to his companion: "Oh, you innocent lamb of knowledge! You gentle sucking doves, all of you! And would you give the name of arguments to those distorted, clumsy, narrow-minded, ungainly, crippled things? Yes, I have just now been listening to the fruits of some of this present-day culture, and my ears are still ringing with the sound of historical 'self-understood' things, of over-wise and pitiless historical reasonings! Mark this, thou unprofaned Nature: thou hast grown old, and for thousands of years this starry sky has spanned the space above thee--but thou hast never yet heard such conceited and, at bottom, mischievous chatter as the talk of the present day! So you are proud of your poets and artists, my good Teutons? You point to them and brag about them to foreign countries, do you? And because it has given you no trouble to have them amongst you, you have formed the pleasant theory that you need not concern yourselves further with them? Isn't that so, my inexperienced children: they come of their own free will, the stork brings them to you! Who would dare to mention a midwife! You deserve an earnest teaching, eh? You should be proud of the fact that all the noble and brilliant men we have mentioned were prematurely suffocated, worn out, and crushed through you, through your barbarism? You think without shame of Lessing, who, on account of your stupidity, perished in battle against your ludicrous gods and idols, the evils of your theatres, your learned men, and your theologians, without once daring to lift himself to the height of that immortal flight for which he was brought into the world. And what are your impressions when you think of Winckelmann, who, that he might rid his eyes of your grotesque fatuousness, went to beg help from the Jesuits, and whose disgraceful religious conversion recoils upon you and will always remain an ineffaceable blemish upon you? You can even name Schiller without blushing! Just look at his picture! The fiery, sparkling eyes, looking at you with disdain, those flushed, death-like cheeks: can you learn nothing from all that? In him you had a beautiful and divine plaything, and through it was destroyed. And if it had been possible for you to take Goethe's friendship away from this melancholy, hasty life, hunted to premature death, then you would have crushed him even sooner than you did. You have not rendered assistance to a single one of our great geniuses--and now upon that fact you wish to build up the theory that none of them shall ever be helped in future? For each of them, however, up to this very moment, you have always been the 'resistance of the stupid world' that Goethe speaks of in his "Epilogue to the Bell"; towards each of them you acted the part of apathetic dullards or jealous narrow-hearts or malignant egotists. In spite of you they created their immortal works, against you they directed their attacks, and thanks to you they died so prematurely, their tasks only half accomplished, blunted and dulled and shattered in the battle. Who can tell to what these heroic men were destined to attain if only that true German spirit had gathered them together within the protecting walls of a powerful institution?--that spirit which, without the help of some such institution, drags out an isolated, debased, and degraded existence. All those great men were utterly ruined; and it is only an insane belief in the Hegelian 'reasonableness of all happenings' which would absolve you of any responsibility in the matter. And not those men alone! Indictments are pouring forth against you from every intellectual province: whether I look àt the talents of our poets, philosophers, painters, or sculptors--and not only in the case of gifts of the highest order--I everywhere see immaturity, overstrained nerves, or prematurely exhausted energies, abilities wasted and nipped in the bud; I everywhere feel that 'resistance of the stupid world,' in other words, your guiltiness. That is what I am talking about when I speak of lacking educational establishments, and why I think those which at present claim the name in such a pitiful condition. Whoever is pleased to call this an 'ideal desire,' and refers to it as 'ideal' as if he were trying to get rid of it by praising me, deserves the answer that the present system is a scandal and a disgrace, and that the man who asks for warmth in the midst of ice and snow must indeed get angry if he hears this referred to as an 'ideal desire.' The matter we are now discussing is concerned with clear, urgent, and palpably evident realities: a man who knows anything of the question feels that there is a need which must be seen to, just like cold and hunger. But the man who is not affected at all by this matter most certainly has a standard by which to measure the extent of his own culture, and thus to know what I call 'culture,' and where the line should be drawn between that which is ruled from below upwards and that which is ruled from above downwards."

The philosopher seemed to be speaking very heatedly. We begged him to walk round with us again, since he had uttered the latter part of his discourse standing near the tree-stump which had served us as a target. For a few minutes not a word more was spoken. Slowly and thoughtfully we walked to and fro. We did not so much feel ashamed of having brought forward such foolish arguments as we felt a kind of restitution of our personality. After the heated and, so far as we were concerned, very unflattering utterance of the philosopher, we seemed to feel ourselves nearer to him--that we even stood in a personal relationship to him. For so wretched is man that he never feels himself brought into such close contact with a stranger as when the latter shows some sign of weakness, some defect. That our philosopher had lost his temper and made use of abusive language helped to bridge over the gulf created between us by our timid respect for him: and for the sake of the reader who feels his indignation rising at this suggestion let it be added that this bridge often leads from distant hero-worship to personal love and pity. And, after the feeling that our personality had been restored to us, this pity gradually became stronger and stronger. Why were we making this old man walk up and down with us between the rocks and trees at that time of the night? And, since he had yielded to our entreaties, why could we not have thought of a more modest and unassuming manner of having ourselves instructed, why should the three of us have contradicted him in such clumsy terms?

For now we saw how thoughtless, unprepared, and baseless were all the objections we had made, and how greatly the echo of the present was heard in them, the voice of which, in the province of culture, the old man would fain not have heard. Our objections, however, were not purely intellectual ones: our reasons for protesting against the philosopher's statements seemed to lie elsewhere. They arose perhaps from the instinctive anxiety to know whether, if the philosopher's views were carried into effect, our own personalities would find a place in the higher or lower division; and this made it necessary for us to find some arguments against the mode of thinking which robbed us of our self-styled claims to culture. People, however, should not argue with companions who feel the weight of an argument so personally; or, as the moral in our case would have been: such companions should not argue, should not contradict at all.

So we walked on beside the philosopher, ashamed, compassionate, dissatisfied with ourselves, and more than ever convinced that the old man was right and that we had done him wrong. How remote now seemed the youthful dream of our educational institution; how clearly we saw the danger which we had hitherto escaped merely by good luck, namely, giving ourselves up body and soul to the educational system which forced itself upon our notice so enticingly, from the time when we entered the public schools up to that moment. How then had it come about that we had not taken our places in the chorus of its admirers? Perhaps merely because we were real students, and could still draw back from the rough-and-tumble, the pushing and struggling, the restless, ever-breaking waves of publicity, to seek refuge in our own little educational establishment; which, however, time would have soon swallowed up also.

Overcome by such reflections, we were about to address the philosopher again, when he suddenly turned towards us, and said in a softer tone--

"I cannot be surprised if you young men behave rashly and thoughtlessly; for it is hardly likely that you have ever seriously considered what I have just said to you. Don't be in a hurry; carry this question about with you, but do at any rate consider it day and night. For you are now at the parting of the ways, and now you know where each path leads. If you take the one, your age will receive you with open arms, you will not find it wanting in honours and decorations: you will form units of an enormous rank and file; and there will be as many people like-minded standing behind you as in front of you. And when the leader gives the word it will be re-echoed from rank to rank. For here your first duty is this: to fight in rank and file; and your second: to annihilate all those who refuse to form part of the rank and file. On the other path you will have but few fellow-travellers: it is more arduous, winding and precipitous; and those who take the first path will mock you, for your progress is more wearisome, and they will try to lure you over into their own ranks. When the two paths happen to cross, however, you will be roughly handled and thrust aside, or else shunned and isolated.

"Now, take these two parties, so different from each other in every respect, and tell me what meaning an educational establishment would have for them. That enormous horde, crowding onwards on the first path towards its goal, would take the term to mean an institution by which each of its members would become duly qualified to take his place in the rank and file, and would be purged of everything which might tend to make him strive after higher and more remote aims. I don't deny, of course, that they can find pompous words with which to describe their aims: for example, they speak of the 'universal development of free personality upon a firm social, national, and human basis,' or they announce as their goal: 'The founding of the peaceful sovereignty of the people upon reason, education, and justice.'

"An educational establishment for the other and smaller company, however, would be something vastly different. They would employ it to prevent themselves from being separated from one another and overwhelmed by the first huge crowd, to prevent their few select spirits from losing sight of their splendid and noble task through premature weariness, or from being turned aside from the true path, corrupted, or subverted. These select spirits must complete their work: that is the raison d'être of their common institution--a work, indeed, which, as it were, must be free from subjective traces, and must further rise above the transient events of future times as the pure reflection of the eternal and immutable essence of things. And all those who occupy places in that institution must co-operate in the endeavour to engender men of genius by this purification from subjectiveness and the creation of the works of genius. Not a few, even of those whose talents may be of the second or third order, are suited to such co-operation, and only when serving in such an educational establishment as this do they feel that they are truly carrying out their life's task. But now it is just these talents I speak of which are drawn away from the true path, and their instincts estranged, by the continual seductions of that modern 'culture.'

"The egotistic emotions, weaknesses, and vanities of these few select minds are continually assailed by the temptations unceasingly murmured into their ears by the spirit of the age: 'Come with me! There you are servants, retainers, tools, eclipsed by higher natures; your own peculiar characteristics never have free play; you are tied down, chained down, like slaves; yea, like automata: here, with me, you will enjoy the freedom of your own personalities, as masters should, your talents will cast their lustre on yourselves alone, with their aid you may come to the very front rank; an innumerable train of followers will accompany you, and the applause of public opinion will yield you more pleasure than a nobly-bestowed commendation from the height of genius.' Even the very best of men now yield to these temptations: and it cannot be said that the deciding factor here is the degree of talent, or whether a man is accessible to these voices or not; but rather the degree and the height of a certain moral sublimity, the instinct towards heroism, towards sacrifice--and finally a positive, habitual need of culture, prepared by a proper kind of education, which education, as I have previously said, is first and foremost obedience and submission to the discipline of genius. Of this discipline and submission, however, the present institutions called by courtesy 'educational establishments' know nothing whatever, although I have no doubt that the public school was originally intended to be an institution for sowing the seeds of true culture, or at least as a preparation for it. I have no doubt, either, that they took the first bold steps in the wonderful and stirring times of the Reformation, and that afterwards, in the era which gave birth to Schiller and Goethe, there was again a growing demand for culture, like the first protuberance of that wing spoken of by Plato in the Phaedrus, which, at every contact with the beautiful, bears the soul aloft into the upper regions, the habitations of the gods."

"Ah," began the philosopher's companion, "when you quote the divine Plato and the world of ideas, I do not think you are angry with me, however much my previous utterance may have merited your disapproval and wrath. As soon as you speak of it, I feel that Platonic wing rising within me; and it is only at intervals, when I act as the charioteer of my soul, that I have any difficulty with the resisting and unwilling horse that Plato has also described to us, the 'crooked, lumbering animal, put together anyhow, with a short, thick neck; flat-faced, and of a dark colour, with grey eyes and blood-red complexion; the mate of insolence and pride, shag-eared and deaf, hardly yielding to whip or spur.'[8] Just think how long I have lived at a distance from you, and how all those temptations you speak of have endeavoured to lure me away, not perhaps without some success, even though I myself may not have observed it. I now see more clearly than ever the necessity for an institution which will enable us to live and mix freely with the few men of true culture, so that we may have them as our leaders and guiding stars. How greatly I feel the danger of travelling alone! And when it occurred to me that I could save myself by flight from all contact with the spirit of the time, I found that this flight itself was a mere delusion. Continuously, with every breath we take, some amount of that atmosphere circulates through every vein and artery, and no solitude is lonesome or distant enough for us to be out of reach of its fogs and clouds. Whether in the guise of hope, doubt, profit, or virtue, the shades of that culture hover about us; and we have been deceived by that jugglery even here in the presence of a true hermit of culture. How steadfastly and faithfully must the few followers of that culture--which might almost be called sectarian--be ever on the àlert! How they must strengthen and uphold one another! How adversely would any errors be criticised here, and how sympathetically excused! And thus, teacher, I ask you to pardon me, after you have laboured so earnestly to set me in the right path!"

"You use a language which I do not care for, my friend," said the philosopher, "and one which reminds me of a diocesan conference. With that I have nothing to do. But your Platonic horse pleases me, and on its account you shall be forgiven. I am willing to exchange my own animal for yours. But it is getting chilly, and I don't feel inclined to walk about any more just now. The friend I was waiting for is indeed foolish enough to come up here even at midnight if he promised to do so. But I have waited in vain for the signal agreed upon; and I cannot guess what has delayed him. For as a rule he is punctual, as we old men are wont, to be, something that you young men nowadays look upon as old-fashioned. But he has left me in the lurch for once: how annoying it is! Come away with me! It's time to go!"

At this moment something happened.

Footnotes:

6. It will be apparent from these words that Nietzsche is still under the influence of Schopenhauer.--TR.

7. This prophecy has come true.--TR.

8. Phaedrus; Jowett's translation.

FIFTH LECTURE

(Delivered on the 23rd of March 1872.)

LADIES AND GENTLEMEN,--If you have lent a sympathetic ear to what I have told you about the heated argument of our philosopher in the stillness of that memorable night, you must have felt as disappointed as we did when he announced his peevish intention. You will remember that he had suddenly told us he wished to go; for, having been left in the lurch by his friend in the first place, and, in the second, having been bored rather than animated by the remarks addressed to him by his companion and ourselves when walking backwards and forwards on the hillside, he now apparently wanted to put an end to what appeared to him to be a useless discussion. It must have seemed to him that his day had been lost, and he would have liked to blot it out of his memory, together with the recollection of ever having made our acquaintance. And we were thus rather unwillingly preparing to depart when something else suddenly brought him to a standstill, and the foot he had just raised sank hesitatingly to the ground again.

A coloured flame, making a crackling noise for a few seconds, attracted our attention from the direction of the Rhine; and immediately following upon this we heard a slow, harmonious call, quite in tune, although plainly the cry of numerous youthful voices. "That's his signal," exclaimed the philosopher, "so my friend is really coming, and I haven't waited for nothing, after all. It will be a midnight meeting indeed--but how am I to let him know that I am still here? Come! Your pistols; let us see your talent once again! Did you hear the severe rhythm of that melody saluting us? Mark it well, and answer it in the same rhythm by a series of shots."

This was a task well suited to our tastes and abilities; so we loaded up as quickly as we could and pointed our weapons at the brilliant stars in the heavens, whilst the echo of that piercing cry died away in the distance. The reports of the first, second, and third shots sounded sharply in the stillness; and then the philosopher cried "False time!" as our rhythm was suddenly interrupted: for, like a lightning flash, a shooting star tore its way across the clouds after the third report, and almost involuntarily our fourth and fifth shots were sent after it in the direction it had taken.

"False time!" said the philosopher again, "who told you to shoot stars! They can fall well enough without you! People should know what they want before they begin to handle weapons."

And then we once more heard that loud melody from the waters of the Rhine, intoned by numerous and strong voices. "They understand us," said the philosopher, laughing, "and who indeed could resist when such a dazzling phantom comes within range?" "Hush!" interrupted his friend, "what sort of a company can it be that returns the signal to us in such a way? I should say they were between twenty and forty strong, manly voices in that crowd--and where would such a number come from to greet us? They don't appear to have left the opposite bank of the Rhine yet; but at any rate we must have a look at them from our own side of the river. Come along, quickly!"

We were then standing near the top of the hill, you may remember, and our view of the river was interrupted by a dark, thick wood. On the other hand, as I have told you, from the quiet little spot which we had left we could have a better view than from the little plateau on the hillside; and the Rhine, with the island of Nonnenwörth in the middle, was just visible to the beholder who peered over the tree-tops. We therefore set off hastily towards this little spot, taking care, however, not to go too quickly for the philosopher's comfort. The night was pitch dark, and we seemed to find our way by instinct rather than by clearly distinguishing the path, as we walked down with the philosopher in the middle.

We had scarcely reached our side of the river when a broad and fiery, yet dull and uncertain light shot up, which plainly came from the opposite side of the Rhine. "Those are torches," I cried, "there is nothing surer than that my comrades from Bonn are over yonder, and that your friend must be with them. It is they who sang that peculiar song, and they have doubtless accompanied your friend here. See! Listen! They are putting off in little boats. The whole torchlight procession will have arrived here in less than half an hour."

The philosopher jumped back. "What do you say?" he ejaculated, "your comrades from Bonn--students--can my friend have come here with students?"

This question, uttered almost wrathfully, provoked us. "What's your objection to students?" we demanded; but there was no answer. It was only after a pause that the philosopher slowly began to speak, not addressing us directly, as it were, but rather some one in the distance: "So, my friend, even at midnight, even on the top of a lonely mountain, we shall not be alone; and you yourself are bringing a pack of mischief-making students along with you, although you well know that I am only too glad to get out of the way of hoc genus omne. I don't quite understand you, my friend: it must mean something when we arrange to meet after a long separation at such an out-of-the-way place and at such an unusual hour. Why should we want a crowd of witnesses--and such witnesses! What calls us together to-day is least of all a sentimental, soft-hearted necessity; for both of us learnt early in life to live alone in dignified isolation. It was not for our own sakes, not to show our tender feelings towards each other, or to perform an unrehearsed act of friendship, that we decided to meet here; but that here, where I once came suddenly upon you as you sat in majestic solitude, we might earnestly deliberate with each other like knights of a new order. Let them listen to us who can understand us; but why should you bring with you a throng of people who don't understand us! I don't know what you mean by such a thing, my friend!"

We did not think it proper to interrupt the dissatisfied old grumbler; and as he came to a melancholy close we did not dare to tell him how greatly this distrustful repudiation of students vexed us.

At last the philosopher's companion turned to him and said: "I am reminded of the fact that even you at one time, before I made your acquaintance, occupied posts in several universities, and that reports concerning your intercourse with the students and your methods of instruction at the time are still in circulation. From the tone of resignation in which you have just referred to students many would be inclined to think that you had some peculiar experiences which were not at all to your liking; but personally I rather believe that you saw and experienced in such places just what every one else saw and experienced in them, but that you judged what you saw and felt more justly and severely than any one else. For, during the time I have known you, I have learnt that the most noteworthy, instructive, and decisive experiences and events in one's life are those which are of daily occurrence; that the greatest riddle, displayed in full view of all, is seen by the fewest to be the greatest riddle, and that these problems are spread about in every direction, under the very feet of the passers-by, for the few real philosophers to lift up carefully, thenceforth to shine as diamonds of wisdom. Perhaps, in the short time now left us before the arrival of your friend, you will be good enough to tell us something of your experiences of university life, so as to close the circle of observations, to which we were involuntarily urged, respecting our educational institutions. We may also be allowed to remind you that you, at an earlier stage of your remarks, gave me the promise that you would do so. Starting with the public school, you claimed for it an extraordinary importance: all other institutions must be judged by its standard, according as its aim has been proposed; and, if its aim happens to be wrong, all the others have to suffer. Such an importance cannot now be adopted by the universities as a standard; for, by their present system of grouping, they would be nothing more than institutions where public school students might go through finishing courses. You promised me that you would explain this in greater detail later on: perhaps our student friends can bear witness to that, if they chanced to overhear that part of our conversation."

"We can testify to that," I put in. The philosopher then turned to us and said: "Well, if you really did listen attentively, perhaps you can now tell me what you understand by the expression 'the present aim of our public schools.' Besides, you are still near enough to this sphere to judge my opinions by the standard of your own impressions and experiences."

My friend instantly answered, quickly and smartly, as was his habit, in the following words: "Until now we had always thought that the sole object of the public school was to prepare students for the universities. This preparation, however, should tend to make us independent enough for the extraordinarily free position of a university student;[9] for it seems to me that a student, to a greater extent than any other individual, has more to decide and settle for himself. He must guide himself on a wide, utterly unknown path for many years, so the public school must do its best to render him independent."

I continued the argument where my friend left off. "It even seems to me," I said, "that everything for which you have justly blamed the public school is only a necessary means employed to imbue the youthful student with some kind of independence, or at all events with the belief that there is such a thing. The teaching of German composition must be at the service of this independence: the individual must enjoy his opinions and carry out his designs early, so that he may be able to travel alone and without crutches. In this way he will soon be encouraged to produce original work, and still sooner to take up criticism and analysis. If Latin and Greek studies prove insufficient to make a student an enthusiastic admirer of antiquity, the methods with which such studies are pursued are at all events sufficient to awaken the scientific sense, the desire for a more strict causality of knowledge, the passion for finding out and inventing. Only think how many young men may be lured away for ever to the attractions of science by a new reading of some sort which they have snatched up with youthful hands at the public school! The public school boy must learn and collect a great deal of varied information: hence an impulse will gradually be created, accompanied with which he will continue to learn and collect independently at the university. We believe, in short, that the aim of the public school is to prepare and accustom the student always to live and learn independently afterwards, just as beforehand he must live and learn dependently at the public school."

The philosopher laughed, not altogether good-naturedly, and said: "You have just given me a fine example of that independence. And it is this very independence that shocks me so much, and makes any place in the neighbourhood of present-day students so disagreeable to me. Yes, my good friends, you are perfect, you are mature; nature has cast you and broken up the moulds, and your teachers must surely gloat over you. What liberty, certitude, and independence of judgment; what novelty and freshness of insight! You sit in judgment--and the cultures of all ages run away. The scientific sense is kindled, and rises out of you like a flame--let people be careful, lest you set them alight! If I go further into the question and look at your professors, I again find the same independence in a greater and even more charming degree: never was there a time so full of the most sublime independent folk, never was slavery more detested, the slavery of education and culture included.

"Permit me, however, to measure this independence of yours by the standard of this culture, and to consider your university as an educational institution and nothing else. If a foreigner desires to know something of the methods of our universities, he asks first of all with emphasis: 'How is the student connected with the university?' We answer: 'By the ear, as a hearer.' The foreigner is astonished. 'Only by the ear?' he repeats. 'Only by the ear,' we again reply. The student hears. When he speaks, when he sees, when he is in the company of his companions when he takes up some branch of art: in short, when he lives he is independent, i.e. not dependent upon the educational institution. The student very often writes down something while he hears; and it is only at these rare moments that he hangs to the umbilical cord of his alma mater. He himself may choose what he is to listen to; he is not bound to believe what is said; he may close his ears if he does not care to hear. This is the 'acroamatic' method of teaching.

"The teacher, however, speaks to these listening students. Whatever else he may think and do is cut off from the student's perception by an immense gap. The professor often reads when he is speaking. As a rule he wishes to have as many hearers as possible; he is not content to have a few, and he is never satisfied with one only. One speaking mouth, with many ears, and half as many writing hands--there you have to all appearances, the external academical apparatus; the university engine of culture set in motion. Moreover, the proprietor of this one mouth is severed from and independent of the owners of the many ears; and this double independence is enthusiastically designated as 'academical freedom.' And again, that this freedom may be broadened still more, the one may speak what he likes and the other may hear what he likes; except that, behind both of them, at a modest distance, stands the State, with all the intentness of a supervisor, to remind the professors and students from time to time that it is the aim, the goal, the be-all and end-all, of this curious speaking and hearing procedure.

"We, who must be permitted to regard this phenomenon merely as an educational institution, will then inform the inquiring foreigner that what is called 'culture' in our universities merely proceeds from the mouth to the ear, and that every kind of training for culture is, as I said before, merely 'acroamatic.' Since, however, not only the hearing, but also the choice of what to hear is left to the independent decision of the liberal-minded and unprejudiced student, and since, again, he can withhold all belief and authority from what he hears, all training for culture, in the true sense of the term, reverts to himself; and the independence it was thought desirable to aim at in the public school now presents itself with the highest possible pride as 'academical self-training for culture,' and struts about in its brilliant plumage.

"Happy times, when youths are clever and cultured enough to teach themselves how to walk! Unsurpassable public schools, which succeed in implanting independence in the place of the dependence, discipline, sûbordination, and obedience implanted by former generations that thought it their duty to drive away all the bumptiousness of independence! Do you clearly see, my good friends, why I, from the standpoint of culture, regard the present type of university as a mere appendage to the public school? The culture instilled by the public school passes through the gates of the university as something ready and entire, and with its own particular claims: it demands, it gives laws, it sits in judgment. Do not, then, let yourselves be deceived in regard to the cultured student; for he, in so far as he thinks he has absorbed the blessings of education, is merely the public school boy as moulded by the hands of his teacher: one who, since his academical isolation, and after he has left the public school, has therefore been deprived of all further guidance to culture, that from now on he may begin to live by himself and be free.

"Free! Examine this freedom, ye observers of human nature! Erected upon the sandy, crumbling foundation of our present public school culture, its building slants to one side, trembling before the whirlwind's blast. Look at the free student, the herald of self-culture: guess what his instincts are; explain him from his needs! How does his culture appear to you when you measure it by three graduated scales: first, by his need for philosophy; second, by his instinct for art; and third, by Greek and Roman antiquity as the incarnate categorical imperative of all culture?

"Man is so much encompassed about by the most serious and difficult problems that, when they are brought to his attention in the right way, he is impelled betimes towards a lasting kind of philosophical wonder, from which alone, as a fruitful soil, a deep and noble culture can grow forth. His own experiences lead him most frequently to the consideration of these problems; and it is especially in the tempestuous period of youth that every personal event shines with a double gleam, both as the exemplification of a triviality and, at the same time, of an eternally surprising problem, deserving of explanation. At this age, which, as it were, sees his experiences encircled with metaphysical rainbows, man is, in the highest degree, in need of a guiding hand, because he has suddenly and almost instinctively convinced himself of the ambiguity of existence, and has lost the firm support of the beliefs he has hitherto held.

"This natural state of great need must of course be looked upon as the worst enemy of that beloved independence for which the cultured youth of the present day should be trained. All these sons of the present, who have raised the banner of the 'self-understood,' are therefore straining every nerve to crush down these feelings of youth, to cripple them, to mislead them, or to stop their growth altogether; and the favourite means employed is to paralyse that natural philosophic impulse by the so-called "historical culture." A still recent system,[10] which has won for itself a world-wide scandalous reputation, has discovered the formula for this self-destruction of philosophy; and now, wherever the historical view of things is found, we can see such a naive recklessness in bringing the irrational to 'rationality' and 'reason' and making black look like white, that one is even inclined to parody Hegel's phrase and ask: 'Is all this irrationality real?' Ah, it is only the irrational that now seems to be 'real,' i.e. really doing something; and to bring this kind of reality forward for the elucidation of history is reckoned as true 'historical culture.' It is into this that the philosophical impulse of our time has pupated itself; and the peculiar philosophers of our universities seem to have conspired to fortify and confirm the young academicians in it.

"It has thus come to pass that, in place of a profound interpretation of the eternally recurring problems, a historical--yea, even philological--balancing and questioning has entered into the educational arena: what this or that philosopher has or has not thought; whether this or that essay or dialogue is to be ascribed to him or not; or even whether this particular reading of a classical text is to be preferred to that. It is to neutral preoccupations with philosophy like these that our students in philosophical seminaries are stimulated; whence I have long accustomed myself to regard such science as a mere ramification of philology, and to value its representatives in proportion as they are good or bad philologists. So it has come about that philosophy itself is banished from the universities: wherewith our first question as to the value of our universities from the standpoint of culture is answered.

"In what relationship these universities stand to art cannot be acknowledged without shame: in none at all. Of artistic thinking, learning, striving, and comparison, we do not find in them a single trace; and no one would seriously think that the voice of the universities would ever be raised to help the advancement of the higher national schemes of art. Whether an individual teacher feels himself to be personally qualified for art, or whether a professorial chair has been established for the training of æstheticising literary historians, does not enter into the question at all: the fact remains that the university is not in a position to control the young academician by severe artistic discipline, and that it must let happen what happens, willy-nilly--and this is the cutting answer to the immodest pretensions of the universities to represent themselves as the highest educational institutions.

"We find our academical 'independents' growing up without philosophy and without art; and how can they then have any need to 'go in for' the Greeks and Romans?--for we need now no longer pretend, like our forefathers, to have any great regard for Greece and Rome, which, besides, sit enthroned in almost inaccessible loneliness and majestic alienation. The universities of the present time consequently give no heed to almost extinct educational predilections like these, and found their philological chairs for the training of new and exclusive generations of philologists, who on their part give similar philological preparation in the public schools--a vicious circle which is useful neither to philologists nor to public schools, but which above all accuses the university for the third time of not being what it so pompously proclaims itself to be--a training ground for culture. Take away the Greeks, together with philosophy and art, and what ladder have you still remaining by which to ascend to culture? For, if you attempt to clamber up the ladder without these helps, you must permit me to inform you that all your learning will lie like a heavy burden on your shoulders rather than furnishing you with wings and bearing you aloft.

"If you honest thinkers have honourably remained in these three stages of intelligence, and have perceived that, in comparison with the Greeks, the modern student is unsuited to and unprepared for philosophy, that he has no truly artistic instincts, and is merely a barbarian believing himself to be free, you will not on this account turn away from him in disgust, although you will, of course, avoid coming into too close proximity with him. For, as he now is, he is not to blame: as you have perceived him he is the dumb but terrible accuser of those who are to blame.

"You should understand the secret language spoken by this guilty innocent, and then you, too, would learn to understand the inward state of that independence which is paraded outwardly with so much ostentation. Not one of these noble, well-qualified youths has remained a stranger to that restless, tiring, perplexing, and debilitating need of culture: during his university term, when he is apparently the only free man in a crowd of servants and officials, he atones for this huge illusion of freedom by ever-growing inner doubts and convictions. He feels that he can neither lead nor help himself; and then he plunges hopelessly into the workaday world and endeavours to ward off such feelings by study. The most trivial bustle fastens itself upon him; he sinks under his heavy burden. Then he suddenly pulls himself together; he still feels some of that power within him which would have enabled him to keep his head above water. Pride and noble resolutions assert themselves and grow in him. He is afraid of sinking at this early stage into the limits of a narrow profession; and now he grasps at pillars and railings alongside the stream that he may not be swept away by the current. In vain! for these supports give way, and he finds he has clutched at broken reeds. In low and despondent spirits he sees his plans vanish away in smoke. His condition is undignified, even dreadful: he keeps between the two extremes of work at high pressure and a state of melancholy enervation. Then he becomes tired, lazy, afraid of work, fearful of everything great; and hating himself. He looks into his own breast, analyses his faculties, and finds he is only peering into hollow and chaotic vacuity. And then he once more falls from the heights of his eagerly-desired self-knowledge into an ironical scepticism. He divests his struggles of their real importance, and feels himself ready to undertake any class of useful work, however degrading. He now seeks consolation in hasty and incessant action so as to hide himself from himself. And thus his helplessness and the want of a leader towards culture drive him from one form of life into another: but doubt, elevation, worry, hope, despair--everything flings him hither and thither as a proof that all the stars above him by which he could have guided his ship have set.

"There you have the picture of this glorious independence of yours, of that academical freedom, reflected in the highest minds--those which are truly in need of culture, compared with whom that other crowd of indifferent natures does not count at all, natures that delight in their freedom in a purely barbaric sense. For these latter show by their base smugness and their narrow professional limitations that this is the right element for them: against which there is nothing to be said. Their comfort, however, does not counter-balance the suffering of one single young man who has an inclination for culture and feels the need of a guiding hand, and who at last, in a moment of discontent, throws down the reins and begins to despise himself. This is the guiltless innocent; for who has saddled him with the unbearable burden of standing alone? Who has urged him on to independence at an age when one of the most natural and peremptory needs of youth is, so to speak, a self-surrendering to great leaders and an enthusiastic following in the footsteps of the masters?

"It is repulsive to consider the effects to which the violent suppression of such noble natures may lead. He who surveys the greatest supporters and friends of that pseudo-culture of the present time, which I so greatly detest, will only too frequently find among them such degenerate and shipwrecked men of culture, driven by inward despair to violent enmity against culture, when, in a moment of desperation, there was no one at hand to show them how to attain it. It is not the worst and most insignificant people whom we afterwards find acting as journalists and writers for the press in the metamorphosis of despair: the spirit of some well-known men of letters might even be described, and justly, as degenerate studentdom. How else, for example, can we reconcile that once well-known 'young Germany' with its present degenerate successors? Here we discover a need of culture which, so to speak, has grown mutinous, and which finally breaks out into the passionate cry: I am culture! There, before the gates of the public schools and universities, we can see the culture which has been driven like a fugitive away from these institutions. True, this culture is without the erudition of those establishments, but assumes nevertheless the mien of a sovereign; so that, for example, Gutzkow the novelist might be pointed to as the best example of a modern public school boy turned æsthete. Such a degenerate man of culture is a serious matter, and it is a horrifying spectacle for us to see that all our scholarly and journalistic publicity bears the stigma of this degeneracy upon it. How else can we do justice to our learned men, who pay untiring attention to, and even co-operate in the journalistic corruption of the people, how else than by the acknowledgment that their learning must fill a want of their own similar to that filled by novel-writing in the case of others: i.e. a flight from one's self, an ascetic extirpation of their cultural impulses, a desperate attempt to annihilate their own individuality. From our degenerate literary art, as also from that itch for scribbling of our learned men which has now reached such alarming proportions, wells forth the same sigh: Oh that we could forget ourselves! The attempt fails: memory, not yet suffocated by the mountains of printed paper under which it is buried, keeps on repeating from time to time: 'A degenerate man of culture! Born for culture and brought up to non-culture! Helpless barbarian, slave of the day, chained to the present moment, and thirsting for something--ever thirsting!'

"Oh, the miserable guilty innocents! For they lack something, a need that every one of them must have felt: a real educational institution, which could give them goals, masters, methods, companions; and from the midst of which the invigorating and uplifting breath of the true German spirit would inspire them. Thus they perish in the wilderness; thus they degenerate into enemies of that spirit which is at bottom closely allied to their own; thus they pile fault upon fault higher than any former generation ever did, soiling the clean, desecrating the holy, canonising the false and spurious. It is by them that you can judge the educational strength of our universities, asking yourselves, in all seriousness, the question: What cause did you promote through them? The German power of invention, the noble German desire for knowledge, the qualifying of the German for diligence and self-sacrifice--splendid and beautiful things, which other nations envy you; yea, the finest and most magnificent things in the world, if only that true German spirit overspread them like a dark thundercloud, pregnant with the blessing of forthcoming rain. But you are afraid of this spirit, and it has therefore come to pass that a cloud of another sort has thrown a heavy and oppressive atmosphere around your universities, in which your noble-minded scholars breathe wearily and with difficulty.

"A tragic, earnest, and instructive attempt was made in the present century to destroy the cloud I have last referred to, and also to turn the people's looks in the direction of the high welkin of the German spirit. In all the annals of our universities we cannot find any trace of a second attempt, and he who would impressively demonstrate what is now necessary for us will never find a better example. I refer to the old, primitive Burschenschaft.[11]

"When the war of liberation was over, the young student brought back home the unlooked-for and worthiest trophy of battle--the freedom of his fatherland. Crowned with this laurel he thought of something still nobler. On returning to the university, and finding that he was breathing heavily, he became conscious of that oppressive and contaminated air which overhung the culture of the university. He suddenly saw, with horror-struck, wide-open eyes, the non-German barbarism, hiding itself in the guise of all kinds of scholasticism; he suddenly discovered that his own leaderless comrades were abandoned to a repulsive kind of youthful intoxication. And he was exasperated. He rose with the same aspect of proud indignation as Schiller may have had when reciting the Robbers to his companions: and if he had prefaced his drama with the picture of a lion, and the motto, 'in tyrannos,' his follower himself was that very lion preparing to spring; and every 'tyrant' began to tremble. Yes, if these indignant youths were looked at superficially and timorously, they would seem to be little else than Schiller's robbers: their talk sounded so wild to the anxious listener that Rome and Sparta seemed mere nunneries compared with these new spirits. The consternation raised by these young men was indeed far more general than had ever been caused by those other 'robbers' in court circles, of which a German prince, according to Goethe, is said to have expressed the opinion: 'If he had been God, and had foreseen the appearance of the Robbers, he would not have created the world.'

"Whence came the incomprehensible intensity of this alarm? For those young men were the bravest, purest, and most talented of the band both in dress and habits: they were distinguished by a magnanimous recklessness and a noble simplicity. A divine command bound them together to seek harder and more pious superiority: what could be feared from them? To what extent this fear was merely deceptive or simulated or really true is something that will probably never be exactly known; but a strong instinct spoke out of this fear and out of its disgraceful and senseless persecution. This instinct hated the Burschenschaft with an intense hatred for two reasons: first of all on account of its organisation, as being the first attempt to construct a true educational institution, and, secondly, on account of the spirit of this institution, that earnest, manly, stern, and daring German spirit; that spirit of the miner's son, Luther, which has come down to us unbroken from the time of the Reformation.

"Think of the fate of the Burschenschaft when I ask you, Did the German university then understand that spirit, as even the German princes in their hatred appear to have understood it? Did the alma mater boldly and resolutely throw her protecting arms round her noble sons and say: 'You must kill me first, before you tóuch my children?' I hear your answer--by it you may judge whether the German university is an educational institution or not.

"The student knew at that time at what depth a true educational institution must take root, namely, in an inward renovation and inspiration of the purest moral faculties. And this must always be repeated to the student's credit. He may have learnt on the field of battle what he could learn least of all in the sphere of 'academical freedom': that great leaders are necessary, and that all culture begins with obedience. And in the midst of victory, with his thoughts turned to his liberated fatherland, he made the vow that he would remain German. German! Now he learnt to understand his Tacitus; now he grasped the signification of Kant's categorical imperative; now he was enraptured by Weber's "Lyre and Sword" songs.[12] The gates of philosophy, of art, yea, even of antiquity, opened unto him; and in one of the most memorable of bloody acts, the murder of Kotzebue, he revenged--with penetrating insight and enthusiastic short-sightedness--his one and only Schiller, prematurely consumed by the opposition of the stupid world: Schiller, who could have been his leader, master, and organiser, and whose loss he now bewailed with such heartfelt resentment.

"For that was the doom of those promising students: they did not find the leaders they wanted. They gradually became uncertain, discontented, and at variance among themselves; unlucky indiscretions showed only too soon that the one indispensability of powerful minds was lacking in the midst of them: and, while that mysterious murder gave evidence of astonishing strength, it gave no less evidence of the grave danger arising from the want of a leader. They were leaderless--therefore they perished.

"For I repeat it, my friends! All culture begins with the very opposite of that which is now so highly esteemed as 'academical freedom': with obedience, with subordination, with discipline, with subjection. And as leaders must have followers so also must the followers have a leader--here a certain reciprocal predisposition prevails in the hierarchy of spirits: yea, a kind of pre-established harmony. This eternal hierarchy, towards which all things naturally tend, is always threatened by that pseudo-culture which now sits on the throne of the present. It endeavours either to bring the leaders down to the level of its own servitude or else to cast them out altogether. It seduces the followers when they are seeking their predestined leader, and overcomes them by the fumes of its narcotics. When, however, in spite of all this, leader and followers have at last met, wounded and sore, there is an impassioned feeling of rapture, like the echo of an ever-sounding lyre, a feeling which I can let you divine only by means of a simile.

"Have you ever, at a musical rehearsal, looked at the strange, shrivelled-up, good-natured species of men who usually form the German orchestra? What changes and fluctuations we see in that capricious goddess 'form'! What noses and ears, what clumsy, danse macabre movements! Just imagine for a moment that you were deaf, and had never dreamed of the existence of sound or music, and that you were looking upon the orchestra as a company of actors, and trying to enjoy their performance as a drama and nothing more. Undisturbed by the idealising effect of the sound, you could never see enough of the stern, medieval, wood-cutting movement of this comical spectacle, this harmonious parody on the homo sapiens.

"Now, on the other hand, assume that your musical sense has returned, and that your ears are opened. Look at the honest conductor at the head of the orchestra performing his duties in a dull, spiritless fashion: you no longer think of the comical aspect of the whole scene, you listen--but it seems to you that the spirit of tediousness spreads out from the honest conductor over all his companions. Now you see only torpidity and flabbiness, you hear only the trivial, the rhythmically inaccurate, and the melodiously trite. You see the orchestra only as an indifferent, ill-humoured, and even wearisome crowd of players.

"But set a genius--a real genius--in the midst of this crowd; and you instantly perceive something almost incredible. It is as if this genius, in his lightning transmigration, had entered into these mechanical, lifeless bodies, and as if only one demoniacal eye gleamed forth out of them all. Now look and listen--you can never listen enough! When you again observe the orchestra, now loftily storming, now fervently wailing, when you notice the quick tightening of every muscle and the rhythmical necessity of every gesture, then you too will feel what a pre-established harmony there is between leader and followers, and how in the hierarchy of spirits everything impels us towards the establishment of a like organisation. You can divine from my simile what I would understand by a true educational institution, and why I am very far from recognising one in the present type of university."

[From a few MS. notes written down by Nietzsche in the spring and autumn of 1872, and still preserved in the Nietzsche Archives at Weimar, it is evident that he at one time intended to add a sixth and seventh lecture to the five just given. These notes, although included in the latest edition of Nietzsche's works, are utterly lacking in interest and continuity, being mèrely headings and sub-headings of sections in the proposed lectures. They do not, indeed, occupy more than two printed pages, and were deemed too fragmentary for translation in this edition.]

Footnotes:

9. The reader may be reminded that a German university student is subject to very few restrictions, and that much greater liberty is allowed him than is permitted to English students. Nietzsche did not approve of this extraordinary freedom, which, in his opinion, led to intellectual lawlessness.--TR.

10. Hegel's.--TR.

11. A German students' association, of liberal principles, founded for patriotic purposes at Jena in 1813.

12. Weber set one or two of Körner's "Lyre and Sword" songs to music. The reader will remember that these lectures were delivered when Nietzsche was only in his twenty-eighth year. Like Goethe, he afterwards freed himself from all patriotic trammels and prejudices, and aimed at a general European culture. Luther, Schiller, Kant, Körner, and Weber did not continue to be the objects of his veneration for long, indeed, they were afterwards violently attacked by him, and the superficial student who speaks of inconsistency may be reminded of Nietzsche's phrase in stanza 12 of the epilogue to Beyond Good and Evil: "Nur wer sich wandelt, bleibt mit mir verwandt"; i.e. only the changing ones have anything in common with me.--TR.

HOMER AND CLASSICAL PHILOLOGY

(Inaugural Address delivered at Bâle University, 28th of May 1869.)

At the present day no clear and consistent opinion seems to be held regarding Classical Philology. We are conscious of this in the circles of the learned just as much as among the followers of that science itself. The cause of this lies in its many-sided character, in the lack of an abstract unity, and in the inorganic aggregation of heterogeneous scientific activities which are connected with one another only by the name "Philology." It must be freely admitted that philology is to some extent borrowed from several other sciences, and is mixed together like a magic potion from the most outlandish liquors, ores, and bones. It may even be added that it likewise conceals within itself an artistic element, one which, on æsthetic and ethical grounds, may be called imperatival--an element that acts in opposition to its purely scientific behaviour. Philology is composed of history just as much as of natural science or æsthetics: history, in so far as it endeavours to comprehend the manifestations of the individualities of peoples in ever new images, and the prevailing law in the disappearance of phenomena; natural science, in so far as it strives to fathom the deepest instinct of man, that of speech; æsthetics, finally, because from various antiquities at our disposal it endeavours to pick out the so-called "classical" antiquity, with the view and pretension of excavating the ideal world buried under it, and to hold up to the present the mirror of the classical and everlasting standards. That these wholly different scientific and æsthetico-ethical impulses have been associated under a common name, a kind of sham monarchy, is shown especially by the fact that philology at every period from its origin onwards was at the same time pedagogical. From the standpoint of the pedagogue, a choice was offered of those elements which were of the greatest educational value; and thus that science, or at least that scientific aim, which we call philology, gradually developed out of the practical calling originated by the exigencies of that science itself.

These philological aims were pursued sometimes with greater ardour and sometimes with less, in accordance with the degree of culture and the development of the taste of a particular period; but, on the other hand, the followers of this science are in the habit of regarding the aims which correspond to their several abilities as the aims of philology; whence it comes about that the estimation of philology in public opinion depends upon the weight of the personalities of the philologists!

At the present time--that is to say, in a period which has seen men distinguished in almost every department of philology--a general uncertainty of judgment has increased more and more, and likewise a general relaxation of interest and participation in philological problems. Such an undecided and imperfect state of public opinion is damaging to a science in that its hidden and open enemies can work with much better prospects of success. And philology has a great many such enemies. Where do we not meet with them, these mockers, always ready to aim a blow at the philological "moles," the animals that practise dust-eating ex professo, and that grub up and eat for the eleventh time what they have already eaten ten times before. For opponents of this sort, however, philology is merely a useless, harmless, and inoffensive pastime, an object of laughter and not of hate. But, on the other hand, there is a boundless and infuriated hatred of philology wherever an ideal, as such, is feared, where the modern man falls down to worship himself, and where Hellenism is looked upon as a superseded and hence very insignificant point of view. Against these enemies, we philologists must always count upon the assistance of artists and men of artistic minds; for they alone can judge how the sword of barbarism sweeps over the head of every one who loses sight of the unutterable simplicity and noble dignity of the Hellene; and how no progress in commerce or technical industries, however brilliant, no school regulations, no political education of the masses, however widespread and complete, can protect us from the curse of ridiculous and barbaric offences against good taste, or from annihilation by the Gorgon head of the classicist.

Whilst philology as a whole is looked on with jealous eyes by these two classes of opponents, there are numerous and varied hostilities in other directions of philology; philologists themselves are quarrelling with one another; internal dissensions are caused by useless disputes about precedence and mutual jealousies, but especially by the differences--even enmities--comprised in the name of philology, which are not, however, by any means naturally harmonised instincts.

Science has this in common with art, that the most ordinary, everyday thing appears to it as something entirely new and attractive, as if metamorphosed by witchcraft and now seen for the first time. Life is worth living, says art, the beautiful temptress; life is worth knowing, says science. With this contrast the so heartrending and dogmatic tradition follows in a theory, and consequently in the practice of classical philology derived from this theory. We may consider antiquity from a scientific point of view; we may try to look at what has happened with the eye of a historian, or to arrange and compare the linguistic forms of ancient masterpieces, to bring them at all events under a morphological law; but we always lose the wonderful creative force, the real fragrance, of the atmosphere of antiquity; we forget that passionate emotion which instinctively drove our meditation and enjoyment back to the Greeks. From this point onwards we must take notice of a clearly determined and very surprising antagonism which philology has great cause to regret. From the circles upon whose help we must place the most implicit reliance--the artistic friends of antiquity, the warm supporters of Hellenic beauty and noble simplicity--we hear harsh voices crying out that it is precisely the philologists themselves who are the real opponents and destroyers of the ideals of antiquity. Schiller upbraided the philologists with having scattered Homer's laurel crown to the winds. It was none other than Goethe who, in early life a supporter of Wolf's theories regarding Homer, recanted in the verses--

With subtle wit you took away
Our former adoration:
The Iliad, you may us say,
Was mere conglomeration.
Think it not crime in any way:
Youth's fervent adoration
Leads us to know the verity,
And feel the poet's unity.

The reason of this want of piety and reverence must lie deeper; and many are in doubt as to whether philologists are lacking in artistic capacity and impressions, so that they are unable to do justice to the ideal, or whether the spirit of negation has become a destructive and iconoclastic principle of theirs. When, however, even the friends of antiquity, possessed of such doubts and hesitations, point to our present classical philology as something questionable, what influence may we not ascribe to the outbursts of the "realists" and the claptrap of the heroes of the passing hour? To answer the latter on this occasion, especially when we consider the nature of the present assembly, would be highly injudicious; at any rate, if I do not wish to meet with the fate of that sophist who, when in Sparta, publicly undertook to praise and defend Herakles, when he was interrupted with the query: "But who then has found fault with him?" I cannot help thinking, however, that some of these scruples are still sounding in the ears of not a few in this gathering; for they may still be frequently heard from the lips of noble and artistically gifted men--as even an upright philologist must feel them, and feel them most painfully, at moments when his spirits are downcast. For the single individual there is no deliverance from the dissensions referred to; but what we contend and inscribe on our banner is the fact that classical philology, as a whole, has nothing whatsoever to do with the quarrels and bickerings of its individual disciples. The entire scientific and artistic movement of this peculiar centaur is bent, though with cyclopic slowness, upon bridging over the gulf between the ideal antiquity--which is perhaps only the magnificent blossoming of the Teutonic longing for the south--and the real antiquity; and thus classical philology pursues only the final end of its own being, which is the fusing together of primarily hostile impulses that have only forcibly been brought together. Let us talk as we will about the unattainability of this goal, and even designate the goal itself as an illogical pretension--the aspiration for it is very real; and I should like to try to make it clear by an example that the most significant steps of classical philology never lead away from the ideal antiquity, but to it; and that, just when people are speaking unwarrantably of the overthrow of sacred shrines, new and more worthy altars are being erected. Let us then examine the so-called Homeric question from this standpoint, a question the most important problem of which Schiller called a scholastic barbarism.

The important problem referred to is the question of the personality of Homer.

We now meet everywhere with the firm opinion that the question of Homer's personality is no longer timely, and that it is quite a different thing from the real "Homeric question." It may be added that, for a given period--such as our present philological period, for example--the centre of discussion may be removed from the problem of the poet's personality; for even now a painstaking experiment is being made to reconstruct the Homeric poems without the aid of personality, treating them as the work of several different persons. But if the centre of a scientific question is rightly seen to be where the swelling tide of new views has risen up, i.e. where individual scientific investigation comes into contact with the whole life of science and culture--if any one, in other words, indicates a historico-cultural valuation as the central point of the question, he must also, in the province of Homeric criticism, take his stand upon the question of personality as being the really fruitful oasis in the desert of the whole argument. For in Homer the modern world, I will not say has learnt, but has examined, a great historical point of view; and, even without now putting forward my own opinion as to whether this examination has been or can be happily carried out, it was at all events the first example of the application of that productive point of view. By it scholars learnt to recognise condensed beliefs in the apparently firm, immobile figures of the life of ancient peoples; by it they for the first time perceived the wonderful capability of the soul of a people to represent the conditions of its morals and beliefs in the form of a personality. When historical criticism has confidently seized upon this method of evaporating apparently concrete personalities, it is permissible to point to the first experiment as an important event in the history of sciences, without considering whether it was successful in this instance or not.

It is a common occurrence for a series of striking signs and wonderful emotions to precede an epoch-making discovery. Even the experiment I have just referred to has its own attractive history; but it goes back to a surprisingly ancient era. Friedrich August Wolf has exactly indicated the spot where Greek antiquity dropped the question. The zenith of the historico-literary studies of the Greeks, and hence also of their point of greatest importance--the Homeric question--was reached in the age of the Alexandrian grammarians. Up to this time the Homeric question had run through the long chain of a uniform process of development, of which the standpoint of those grammarians seemed to be the last link, the last, indeed, which was attainable by antiquity. They conceived the Iliad and the Odyssey as the creations of one single Homer; they declared it to be psychologically possible for two such different works to have sprung from the brain of one genius, in contradiction to the Chorizontes, who represented the extreme limit of the scepticism of a few detached individuals of antiquity rather than antiquity itself considered as a whole. To explain the different general impression of the two books on the assumption that one poet composed them both, scholars sought assistance by referring to the seasons of the poet's life, and compared the poet of the Odyssey to the setting sun. The eyes of those critics were tirelessly on the lookout for discrepancies in the language and thoughts of the two poems; but at this time also a history of the Homeric poem and its tradition was prepared, according to which these discrepancies were not due to Homer, but to those who committed his words to writing and those who sang them. It was believed that Homer's poem was passed from one generation to another viva voce, and faults were attributed to the improvising and at times forgetful bards. At a certain given date, about the time of Pisistratus, the poems which had been repeated orally were said to have been collected in manuscript form; but the scribes, it is added, allowed themselves to take some liberties with the text by transposing some lines and adding extraneous matter here and there. This entire hypothesis is the most important in the domain of literary studies that antiquity has exhibited; and the acknowledgment of the dissemination of the Homeric poems by word of mouth, as opposed to the habits of a book-learned age, shows in particular a depth of ancient sagacity worthy of our admiration. From those times until the generation that produced Friedrich August Wolf we must take a jump over a long historical vacuum; but in our own age we find the argument left just as it was at the time when the power of controversy departed from antiquity, and it is a matter of indifference to us that Wolf accepted as certain tradition what antiquity itself had set up only as a hypothesis. It may be remarked as most characteristic of this hypothesis that, in the strictest sense, the personality of Homer is treated seriously; that a certain standard of inner harmony is everywhere presupposed in the manifestations of the personality; and that, with these two excellent auxiliary hypotheses, whatever is seen to be below this standard and opposed to this inner harmony is at once swept aside as un-Homeric. But even this distinguishing characteristic, in place of wishing to recognise the supernatural existence of a tangible personality, ascends likewise through all the stages that lead to that zenith, with ever-increasing energy and clearness. Individuality is ever more strongly felt and accentuated; the psychological possibility of a single Homer is ever more forcibly demanded. If we descend backwards from this zenith, step by step, we find a guide to the understanding of the Homeric problem in the person of Aristotle. Homer was for him the flawless and untiring artist who knew his end and the means to attain it; but there is still a trace of infantile criticism to be found in Aristotle--i.e., in the naive concession he made to the public opinion that considered Homer as the author of the original of all comic epics, the Margites. If we go still further backwards from Aristotle, the inability to create a personality is seen to increase; more and more poems are attributed to Homer; and every period lets us see its degree of criticism by how much and what it considers as Homeric. In this backward examination, we instinctively feel that away beyond Herodotus there lies a period in which an immense flood of great epics has been identified with the name of Homer.

Let us imagine ourselves as living in the time of Pisistratus: the word "Homer" then comprehended an abundance of dissimilarities. What was meant by "Homer" at that time? It is evident that that generation found itself unable to grasp a personality and the limits of its manifestations. Homer had now become of small consequence. And then we meet with the weighty question: What lies before this period? Has Homer's personality, because it cannot be grasped, gradually faded away into an empty name? Or had all the Homeric poems been gathered together in a body, the nation naively representing itself by the figure of Homer? Was the person created out of a conception, or the conception out of a person? This is the real "Homeric question," the central problem of the personality.

The difficulty of answering this question, however, is increased when we seek a reply in another direction, from the standpoint of the poems themselves which have come down to us. As it is difficult for us at the present day, and necessitates a serious effort on our part, to understand the law of gravitation clearly--that the earth alters its form of motion when another heavenly body changes its position in space, although no material connection unites one to the other--it likewise costs us some trouble to obtain a clear impression of that wonderful problem which, like a coin long passed from hand to hand, has lost its original and highly conspicuous stamp. Poetical works, which cause the hearts of even the greatest geniuses to fail when they endeavour to vie with them, and in which unsurpassable images are held up for the admiration of posterity--and yet the poet who wrote them with only a hollow, shaky name, whenever we do lay hold on him; nowhere the solid kernel of a powerful personality. "For who would wage war with the gods: who, even with the one god?" asks Goethe even, who, though a genius, strove in vain to solve that mysterious problem of the Homeric inaccessibility.

The conception of popular poetry seemed to lead like a bridge over this problem--a deeper and more original power than that of every single creative individual was said to have become active; the happiest people, in the happiest period of its existence, in the highest activity of fantasy and formative power, was said to have created those immeasurable poems. In this universality there is something almost intoxicating in the thought of a popular poem: we feel, with artistic pleasure, the broad, overpowering liberation of a popular gift, and we delight in this natural phenomenon as we do in an uncontrollable cataract. But as soon as we examine this thought at close quarters, we involuntarily put a poetic mass of people in the place of the poetising soul of the people: a long row of popular poets in whom individuality has no meaning, and in whom the tumultuous movement of a people's soul, the intuitive strength of a people's eye, and the unabated profusion of a people's fantasy, were once powerful: a row of original geniuses, attached to a time, to a poetic genus, to a subject-matter.

Such a conception justly made people suspicious. Could it be possible that that same Nature who so sparingly distributed her rarest and most precious production--genius--should suddenly take the notion of lavishing her gifts in one sole direction? And here the thorny question again made its appearance: Could we not get along with one genius only, and explain the present existence of that unattainable excellence? And now eyes were keenly on the lookout for whatever that excellence and singularity might consist of. Impossible for it to be in the construction of the complete works, said one party, for this is far from faultless; but doubtless to be found in single songs: in the single pieces above all; not in the whole. A second party, on the other hand, sheltered themselves beneath the authority of Aristotle, who especially admired Homer's "divine" nature in the choice of his entire subject, and the manner in which he planned and carried it out. If, however, this construction was not clearly seen, this fault was due to the way the poems were handed down to posterity and not to the poet himself--it was the result of retouchings and interpolations, owing to which the original setting of the work gradually became obscured. The more the first school looked for inequalities, contradictions, perplexities, the more energetically did the other school brush aside what in their opinion obscured the original plan, in order, if possible, that nothing might be left remaining but the actual words of the original epic itself. The second school of thought of course held fast by the conception of an epoch-making genius as the composer of the great works. The first school, on the other hand, wavered between the supposition of one genius plus a number of minor poets, and another hypothesis which assumed only a number of superior and even mediocre individual bards, but also postulated a mysterious discharging, a deep, national, artistic impulse, which shows itself in individual minstrels as an almost indifferent medium. It is to this latter school that we must attribute the representation of the Homeric poems as the expression of that mysterious impulse.

All these schools of thought start from the assumption that the problem of the present form of these epics can be solved from the standpoint of an æsthetic judgment--but we must await the decision as to the authorised line of demarcation between the man of genius and the poetical soul of the people. Are there characteristic differences between the utterances of the man of genius and the poetical soul of the people?

This whole contrast, however, is unjust and misleading. There is no more dangerous assumption in modern æsthetics than that of popular poetry and individual poetry, or, as it is usually called, artistic poetry. This is the reaction, or, if you will, the superstition, which followed upon the most momentous discovery of historico-philological science, the discovery and appreciation of the soul of the people. For this discovery prepared the way for a coming scientific view of history, which was until then, and in many respects is even now, a mere collection of materials, with the prospect that new materials would continue to be added, and that the huge, overflowing pile would never be systematically arranged. The people now understood for the first time that the long-felt power of greater individualities and wills was larger than the pitifully small will of an individual man;[1] they now saw that everything truly great in the kingdom of the will could not have its deepest root in the inefficacious and ephemeral individual will; and, finally, they now discovered the powerful instincts of the masses, and diagnosed those unconscious impulses to be the foundations and supports of the so-called universal history. But the newly-lighted flame also cast its shadow: and this shadow was none other than that superstition already referred to, which popular poetry set up in opposition to individual poetry, and thus enlarged the comprehension of the people's soul to that of the people's mind. By the misapplication of a tempting analogical inference, people had reached the point of applying in the domain of the intellect and artistic ideas that principle of greater individuality which is truly applicable only in the domain of the will. The masses have never experienced more flattering treatment than in thus having the laurel of genius set upon their empty heads. It was imagined that new shells were forming round a small kernel, so to speak, and that those pieces of popular poetry originated like avalanches, in the drift and flow of tradition. They were, however, ready to consider that kernel as being of the smallest possible dimensions, so that they might occasionally get rid of it altogether without losing anything of the mass of the avalanche. According to this view, the text itself and the stories built round it are one and the same thing.

[1] Of course Nietzsche saw afterwards that this was not so.--TR.

Now, however, such a contrast between popular poetry and individual poetry does not exist at all; on the contrary, all poetry, and of course popular poetry also, requires an intermediary individuality. This much-abused contrast, therefore, is necessary only when the term individual poem is understood to mean a poem which has not grown out of the soil of popular feeling, but which has been composed by a non-popular poet in a non-popular atmosphere--something which has come to maturity in the study of a learned man, for example.

With the superstition which presupposes poetising masses is connected another: that popular poetry is limited to one particular period of a people's history and afterwards dies out--which indeed follows as a consequence of the first superstition I have mentioned. According to this school, in the place of the gradually decaying popular poetry we have artistic poetry, the work of individual minds, not of masses of people. But the same powers which were once active are still so; and the form in which they act has remained exactly the same. The great poet of a literary period is still a popular poet in no narrower sense than the popular poet of an illiterate age. The difference between them is not in the way they originate, but it is their diffusion and propagation, in short, tradition. This tradition is exposed to eternal danger without the help of handwriting, and runs the risk of including in the poems the remains of those individualities through whose oral tradition they were handed down.

If we apply all these principles to the Homeric poems, it follows that we gain nothing with our theory of the poetising soul of the people, and that we are always referred back to the poetical individual. We are thus confronted with the task of distinguishing that which can have originated only in a single poetical mind from that which is, so to speak, swept up by the tide of oral tradition, and which is a highly important constituent part of the Homeric poems.

Since literary history first ceased to be a mere collection of names, people have attempted to grasp and formulate the individualities of the poets. A certain mechanism forms part of the method: it must be explained--i.e., it must be deduced from principles--why this or that individuality appears in this way and not in that. People now study biographical details, environment, acquaintances, contemporary events, and believe that by mixing all these ingredients together they will be able to manufacture the wished-for individuality. But they forget that the punctum saliens, the indefinable individual characteristics, can never be obtained from a compound of this nature. The less there is known about the life and times of the poet, the less applicable is this mechanism. When, however, we have merely the works and the name of the writer, it is almost impossible to detect the individuality, at all events, for those who put their faith in the mechanism in question; and particularly when the works are perfect, when they are pieces of popular poetry. For the best way for these mechanicians to grasp individual characteristics is by perceiving deviations from the genius of the people; the aberrations and hidden allusions: and the fewer discrepancies to be found in a poem the fainter will be the traces of the individual poet who composed it.

All those deviations, everything dull and below the ordinary standard which scholars think they perceive in the Homeric poems, were attributed to tradition, which thus became the scapegoat. What was left of Homer's own individual work? Nothing but a series of beautiful and prominent passages chosen in accordance with subjective taste. The sum total of æsthetic singularity which every individual scholar perceived with his own artistic gifts, he now called Homer.

This is the central point of the Homeric errors. The name of Homer, from the very beginning, has no connection either with the conception of æsthetic perfection or yet with the Iliad and the Odyssey. Homer as the composer of the Iliad and the Odyssey is not a historical tradition, but an æsthetic judgment.

The only path which leads back beyond the time of Pisistratus and helps us to elucidate the meaning of the name Homer, takes its way on the one hand through the reports which have reached us concerning Homer's birthplace: from which we see that, although his name is always associated with heroic epic poems, he is on the other hand no more referred to as the composer of the Iliad and the Odyssey than as the author of the Thebais or any other cyclical epic. On the other hand, again, an old tradition tells of the contest between Homer and Hesiod, which proves that when these two names were mentioned people instinctively thought of two epic tendencies, the heroic and the didactic; and that the signification of the name "Homer" was included in the material category and not in the formal. This imaginary contest with Hesiod did not even yet show the faintest presentiment of individuality. From the time of Pisistratus onwards, however, with the surprisingly rapid development of the Greek feeling for beauty, the differences in the æsthetic value of those epics continued to be felt more and more: the Iliad and the Odyssey arose from the depths of the flood and have remained on the surface ever since. With this process of æsthetic separation, the conception of Homer gradually became narrower: the old material meaning of the name "Homer" as the father of the heroic epic poem, was changed into the æsthetic meaning of Homer, the father of poetry in general, and likewise its original prototype. This transformation was contemporary with the rationalistic criticism which made Homer the magician out to be a possible poet, which vindicated the material and formal traditions of those numerous epics as against the unity of the poet, and gradually removed that heavy load of cyclical epics from Homer's shoulders.

So Homer, the poet of the Iliad and the Odyssey, is an æsthetic judgment. It is, however, by no means affirmed against the poet of these epics that he was merely the imaginary being of an æsthetic impossibility, which can be the opinion of only very few philologists indeed. The majority contend that a single individual was responsible for the general design of a poem such as the Iliad, and further that this individual was Homer. The first part of this contention may be admitted; but, in accordance with what I have said, the latter part must be denied. And I very much doubt whether the majority of those who adopt the first part of the contention have taken the following considerations into account.

The design of an epic such as the Iliad is not an entire whole, not an organism; but a number of pieces strung together, a collection of reflections arranged in accordance with æsthetic rules. It is certainly the standard of an artist's greatness to note what he can take in with a single glance and set out in rhythmical form. The infinite profusion of images and incidents in the Homeric epic must force us to admit that such a wide range of vision is next to impossible. Where, however, a poet is unable to observe artistically with a single glance, he usually piles conception on conception, and endeavours to adjust his characters according to a comprehensive scheme.

He will succeed in this all the better the more he is familiar with the fundamental principles of æsthetics: he will even make some believe that he made himself master of the entire subject by a single powerful glance.

The Iliad is not a garland, but a bunch of flowers. As many pictures as possible are crowded on one canvas; but the man who placed them there was indifferent as to whether the grouping of the collected pictures was invariably suitable and rhythmically beautiful. He well knew that no one would ever consider the collection as a whole; but would merely look at the individual parts. But that stringing together of some pieces as the manifestations of a grasp of art which was not yet highly developed, still less thoroughly comprehended and generally esteemed, cannot have been the real Homeric deed, the real Homeric epoch-making event. On the contrary, this design is a later product, far later than Homer's celebrity. Those, therefore, who look for the "original and perfect design" are looking for a mere phantom; for the dangerous path of oral tradition had reached its end just as the systematic arrangement appeared on the scene; the disfigurements which were caused on the way could not have affected the design, for this did not form part of the material handed down from generation to generation.

The relative imperfection of the design must not, however, prevent us from seeing in the designer a different personality from the real poet. It is not only probable that everything which was created in those times with conscious æsthetic insight, was infinitely inferior to the songs that sprang up naturally in the poet's mind and were written down with instinctive power: we can even take a step further. If we include the so-called cyclic poems in this comparison, there remains for the designer of the Iliad and the Odyssey the indisputable merit of having done something relatively great in this conscious technical composing: a merit which we might have been prepared to recognise from the beginning, and which is in my opinion of the very first order in the domain of instinctive creation. We may even be ready to pronounce this synthetisation of great importance. All those dull passages and discrepancies--deemed of such importance, but really only subjective, which we usually look upon as the petrified remains of the period of tradition--are not these perhaps merely the almost necessary evils which must fall to the lot of the poet of genius who undertakes a composition virtually without a parallel, and, further, one which proves to be of incalculable difficulty?

Let it be noted that the insight into the most diverse operations of the instinctive and the conscious changes the position of the Homeric problem; and in my opinion throws light upon it.

We believe in a great poet as the author of the Iliad and the Odyssey--but not that Homer was this poet.

The decision on this point has already been given. The generation that invented those numerous Homeric fables, that poetised the myth of the contest between Homer and Hesiod, and looked upon all the poems of the epic cycle as Homeric, did not feel an æsthetic but a material singularity when it pronounced the name "Homer." This period regards Homer as belonging to the ranks of artists like Orpheus, Eumolpus, Dædalus, and Olympus, the mythical discoverers of a new branch of art, to whom, therefore, all the later fruits which grew from the new branch were thankfully dedicated.

And that wonderful genius to whom we owe the Iliad and the Odyssey belongs to this thankful posterity: he, too, sacrificed his name on the altar of the primeval father of the Homeric epic, Homeros.

Up to this point, gentlemen, I think I have been able to put before you the fundamental philosophical and æsthetic characteristics of the problem of the personality of Homer, keeping all minor details rigorously at a distance, on the supposition that the primary form of this widespread and honeycombed mountain known as the Homeric question can be most clearly observed by looking down at it from a far-off height. But I have also, I imagine, recalled two facts to those friends of antiquity who take such delight in accusing us philologists of lack of piety for great conceptions and an unproductive zeal for destruction. In the first place, those "great" conceptions--such, for example, as that of the indivisible and inviolable poetic genius, Homer--were during the pre-Wolfian period only too great, and hence inwardly altogether empty and elusive when we now try to grasp them. If classical philology goes back again to the same conceptions, and once more tries to pour new wine into old bottles, it is only on the surface that the conceptions are the same: everything has really become new; bottle and mind, wine and word. We everywhere find traces of the fact that philology has lived in company with poets, thinkers, and artists for the last hundred years: whence it has now come about that the heap of ashes formerly pointed to as classical philology is now turned into fruitful and even rich soil.[2]

[2] Nietzsche perceived later on that this statement was, unfortunately, not justified.--TR.

And there is a second fact which I should like to recall to the memory of those friends of antiquity who turn their dissatisfied backs on classical philology. You honour the immortal masterpieces of the Hellenic mind in poetry and sculpture, and think yourselves so much more fortunate than preceding generations, which had to do without them; but you must not forget that this whole fairyland once lay buried under mountains of prejudice, and that the blood and sweat and arduous labour of innumerable followers of our science were all necessary to lift up that world from the chasm into which it had sunk. We grant that philology is not the creator of this world, not the composer of that immortal music; but is it not a merit, and a great merit, to be a mere virtuoso, and let the world for the first time hear that music which lay so long in obscurity, despised and undecipherable? Who was Homer previously to Wolf's brilliant investigations? A good old man, known at best as a "natural genius," at all events the child of a barbaric age, replete with faults against good taste and good morals. Let us hear how a learned man of the first rank writes about Homer even so late as 1783: "Where does the good man live? Why did he remain so long incognito? Apropos, can't you get me a silhouette of him?"

We demand thanks--not in our own name, for we are but atoms--but in the name of philology itself, which is indeed neither a Muse nor a Grace, but a messenger of the gods: and just as the Muses descended upon the dull and tormented Boeotian peasants, so Philology comes into a world full of gloomy colours and pictures, full of the deepest, most incurable woes; and speaks to men comfortingly of the beautiful and godlike figure of a distant, rosy, and happy fairyland.

It is time to close; yet before I do so a few words of a personal character must be added, justified, I hope, by the occasion of this lecture.

It is but right that a philologist should describe his end and the means to it in the short formula of a confession of faith; and let this be done in the saying of Seneca which I thus reverse--

"Philosophia facta est quæ philologia fuit."

By this I wish to signify that all philological activities should be enclosed and surrounded by a philosophical view of things, in which everything individual and isolated is evaporated as something detestable, and in which great homogeneous views alone remain. Now, therefore, that I have enunciated my philological creed, I trust you will give me cause to hope that I shall no longer be a stranger among you: give me the assurance that in working with you towards this end I am worthily fulfilling the confidence with which the highest authorities of this community have honoured me.

The Case Of Wagner, Nietzsche Contra Wagner, Selected Aphorisms

Translated By Anthony M. Ludovici

Originally Published by:
T. N. Foulis 13 & 15 Frederick Street Edinburgh and London 1911

TRANSLATOR' S PREFACE.

Nietzsche wrote the rough draft of "The Case of Wagner" in Turin, during the month of May 1888; he completed it in Sils Maria towards the end of June of the same year, and it was published in the following autumn. "Nietzsche contra Wagner" was written about the middle of December 1888; but, although it was printed and corrected before the New Year, it was not published until long afterwards owing to Nietzsche's complete breakdown in the first days of 1889.

In reading these two essays we are apt to be deceived, by their virulent and forcible tone, into believing that the whole matter is a mere cover for hidden fire,—a mere blind of æsthetic discussion concealing a deep and implacable personal feud which demands and will have vengeance. In spite of all that has been said to the contrary, many people still hold this view of the two little works before us; and, as the actual facts are not accessible to every one, and rumours are more easily believed than verified, the error of supposing that these pamphlets were dictated by personal animosity, and even by Nietzsche's envy of Wagner in his glory, seems to be a pretty common one. Another very general error is to suppose that the point at issue here is not one concerning music at all, but concerning religion. It is taken for granted that the aspirations, the particular quality, the influence, and the method of an art like music, are matters quite distinct from the values and the conditions prevailing in the culture with which it is in harmony, and that however many Christian elements may be discovered in Wagnerian texts, Nietzsche had no right to raise æsthetic objections because he happened to entertain the extraordinary view that these Christian elements had also found their way into Wagnerian music.

To both of these views there is but one reply:—they are absolutely false.

In the "Ecce Homo," Nietzsche's autobiography,—a book which from cover to cover and line for line is sincerity itself—we learn what Wagner actually meant to Nietzsche. On pages 41, 44, 84, 122, 129, &c, we cannot doubt that Nietzsche is speaking from his heart,—and what does he say?—In impassioned tones he admits his profound indebtedness to the great musician, his love for him, his gratitude to him,—how Wagner was the only German who had ever been anything to him—how his friendship with Wagner constituted the happiest and most valuable experience of his life,—how his breach with Wagner almost killed him. And, when we remember, too, that Wagner on his part also declared that he was "alone" after he had lost "that man" (Nietzsche), we begin to perceive that personal bitterness and animosity are out of the question here. We feel we are on a higher plane, and that we must not judge these two men as if they were a couple of little business people who had had a suburban squabble.

Nietzsche declares ("Ecce Homo," p. 24) that he never attacked persons as persons. If he used a name at all, it was merely as a means to an end, just as one might use a magnifying glass in order to make a general, but elusive and intricate fact more clear and more apparent, and if he used the name of David Strauss, without bitterness or spite (for he did not even know the man), when he wished to personify Culture-Philistinism, so, in the same spirit, did he use the name of Wagner, when he wished to personify the general decadence of modern ideas, values, aspirations and Art.

Nietzsche's ambition, throughout his life, was to regenerate European culture. In the first period of his relationship with Wagner, he thought that he had found the man who was prepared to lead in this direction. For a long while he regarded his master as the Saviour of Germany, as the innovator and renovator who was going to arrest the decadent current of his time and lead men to a greatness which had died with antiquity. And so thoroughly did he understand his duties as a disciple, so wholly was he devoted to this cause, that, in spite of all his unquestioned gifts and the excellence of his original achievements, he was for a long while regarded as a mere "literary lackey" in Wagner's service, in all those circles where the rising musician was most disliked.

Gradually, however, as the young Nietzsche developed and began to gain an independent view of life and humanity, it seemed to him extremely doubtful whether Wagner actually was pulling the same way with him. Whereas, theretofore, he had identified Wagner's ideals with his own, it now dawned upon him slowly that the regeneration of German culture, of European culture, and the transvaluation of values which would be necessary for this regeneration, really lay off the track of Wagnerism. He saw that he had endowed Wagner with a good deal that was more his own than Wagner's. In his love he had transfigured the friend, and the composer of "Parsifal" and the man of his imagination were not one. The fact was realised step by step; disappointment upon disappointment, revelation after revelation, ultimately brought it home to him, and though his best instincts at first opposed it, the revulsion of feeling at last became too strong to be scouted, and Nietzsche was plunged into the blackest despair. Had he followed his own human inclinations, he would probably have remained Wagner's friend until the end. As it was, however, he remained loyal to his cause, and this meant denouncing his former idol.

"Joyful Wisdom," "Thus Spake Zarathustra," "Beyond Good and Evil," "The Genealogy of Morals," "The Twilight of the Idols," "The Antichrist"—all these books were but so many exhortations to mankind to step aside from the general track now trodden by Europeans. And what happened? Wagner began to write some hard things about Nietzsche; the world assumed that Nietzsche and Wagner had engaged in a paltry personal quarrel in the press, and the whole importance of the real issue was buried beneath the human, all-too-human interpretations which were heaped upon it.

Nietzsche was a musician of no mean attainments. For a long while, in his youth, his superiors had been doubtful whether he should not be educated for a musical career, so great were his gifts in this art; and if his mother had not been offered a six-years' scholarship for her son at the famous school of Pforta, Nietzsche, the scholar and philologist, would probably have been an able composer. When he speaks about music, therefore, he knows what he is talking about, and when he refers to Wagner's music in particular, the simple fact of his long intimacy with Wagner during the years at Tribschen, is a sufficient guarantee of his deep knowledge of the subject. Now Nietzsche was one of the first to recognise that the principles of art are inextricably bound up with the laws of life, that an æsthetic dogma may therefore promote or depress all vital force, and that a picture, a symphony, a poem or a statue, is just as capable of being pessimistic, anarchic, Christian or revolutionary, as a philosophy or a science is. To speak of a certain class of music as being compatible with the decline of culture, therefore, was to Nietzsche a perfectly warrantable association of ideas, and that is why, throughout his philosophy, so much stress is laid upon æsthetic considerations.

But if in England and America Nietzsche's attack on Wagner's art may still seem a little incomprehensible, let it be remembered that the Continent has long known that Nietzsche was actually in the right. Every year thousands are now added to the large party abroad who have ceased from believing in the great musical revolutionary of the seventies; that he was one with the French Romanticists and rebels has long since been acknowledged a fact in select circles, both in France and Germany, and if we still have Wagner with us in England, if we still consider Nietzsche as a heretic, when he declares that "Wagner was a musician for unmusical people," it is only because we are more removed than we imagine, from all the great movements, intellectual and otherwise, which take place on the Continent.

In Wagner's music, in his doctrine, in his whole concept of art, Nietzsche saw the confirmation, the promotion—aye, even the encouragement, of that decadence and degeneration which is now rampant in Europe; and it is for this reason, although to the end of his life he still loved Wagner, the man and the friend, that we find him, on the very eve of his spiritual death, exhorting us to abjure Wagner the musician and the artist.

Anthony M. Ludovici.

PREFACE TO THE THIRD EDITION[1]

In spite of the adverse criticism with which the above preface has met at the hands of many reviewers since the summer of last year, I cannot say that I should feel justified, even after mature consideration, in altering a single word or sentence it contains. If I felt inclined to make any changes at all, these would take the form of extensive additions, tending to confirm rather than to modify the general argument it advances; but, any omissions of which I may have been guilty in the first place, have been so fully rectified since, thanks to the publication of the English translations of Daniel Halévy's and Henri Lichtenberger's works, "The Life of Friedrich Nietzsche,"[2] and "The Gospel of Superman,"[3] respectively, that, were it not for the fact that the truth about this matter cannot be repeated too often, I should have refrained altogether from including any fresh remarks of my own in this Third Edition.

In the works just referred to (pp. 129 et seq. in Halévy's book, and pp. 78 et seq. in Lichtenberger's book), the statement I made in my preface to "Thoughts out of Season," vol. i., and which I did not think it necessary to repeat in my first preface to these pamphlets, will be found to receive the fullest confirmation.

The statement in question was to the effect that many long years before these pamphlets were even projected, Nietzsche's apparent volte-face in regard to his hero Wagner had been not only foreshadowed but actually stated in plain words, in two works written during his friendship with Wagner,—the works referred to being "The Birth of Tragedy" (1872), and "Wagner in Bayreuth" (1875) of which Houston Stuart Chamberlain declares not only that it possesses "undying classical worth" but that "a perusal of it is indispensable to all who wish to follow the question [of Wagner] to its roots."[4]

The idea that runs through the present work like a leitmotif—the idea that Wagner was at bottom more of a mime than a musician—was so far an ever present thought with Nietzsche that it is ever impossible to ascertain the period when it was first formulated.

In Nietzsche's wonderful autobiography (Ecce Homo, p. 88), in the section dealing with the early works just mentioned, we find the following passage—"In the second of the two essays [Wagner in Bayreuth] with a profound certainty of instinct, I already characterised the elementary factor in Wagner's nature as a theatrical talent which, in all his means and aspirations, draws its final conclusions." And as early as 1874, Nietzsche wrote in his diary—"Wagner is a born actor. Just as Goethe was an abortive painter, and Schiller an abortive orator, so Wagner was an abortive theatrical genius. His attitude to music is that of the actor; for he knows how to sing and speak, as it were out of different souls and from absolutely different worlds (Tristan and the Meistersinger)."

There is, however, no need to multiply examples, seeing, as I have said, that in the translations of Halévy's and Lichtenberger's books the reader will find all the independent evidence he could possibly desire, disproving the popular, and even the learned belief that, in the two pamphlets before us we have a complete, apparently unaccountable, and therefore "demented" volte-face on Nietzsche's part. Nevertheless, for fear lest some doubt should still linger in certain minds concerning this point, and with the view of adding interest to these essays, the Editor considered it advisable, in the Second Edition, to add a number of extracts from Nietzsche's diary of the year 1878 (ten years before "The Case of Wagner," and "Nietzsche contra Wagner" were written) in order to show to what extent those learned critics who complain of Nietzsche's "morbid and uncontrollable recantations and revulsions of feeling," have overlooked even the plain facts of the case when forming their all-too-hasty conclusions. These extracts will be found at the end of "Nietzsche contra Wagner." While reading them, however, it should not be forgotten that they were never intended for publication by Nietzsche himself—a fact which accounts for their unpolished and sketchy form—and that they were first published in vol. xi. of the first German Library Edition (pp. 99-129) only when he was a helpless invalid, in 1897. Since then, in 1901 and 1906 respectively, they have been reprinted, once in the large German Library Edition (vol. xi. pp. 181-202), and once in the German Pocket Edition, as an appendix to "Human-All-too-Human," Part II.

An altogether special interest now attaches to these pamphlets; for, in the first place we are at last in possession of Wagner's own account of his development, his art, his aspirations and his struggles, in the amazing self-revelation entitled My Life;[5] and secondly, we now have Ecce Homo, Nietzsche's autobiography, in which we learn for the first time from Nietzsche's own pen to what extent his history was that of a double devotion—to Wagner on the one hand, and to his own life task, the Transvaluation of all Values, on the other.

Readers interested in the Nietzsche-Wagner controversy will naturally look to these books for a final solution of all the difficulties which the problem presents. But let them not be too sanguine. From first to last this problem is not to be settled by "facts." A good deal of instinctive choice, instinctive aversion, and instinctive suspicion are necessary here. A little more suspicion, for instance, ought to be applied to Wagner's My Life, especially in England, where critics are not half suspicious enough about a continental artist's self-revelations, and are too prone, if they have suspicions at all, to apply them in the wrong place.

An example of this want of finesse in judging foreign writers is to be found in Lord Morley's work on Rousseau,—a book which ingenuously takes for granted everything that a writer like Rousseau cares to say about himself, without considering for an instant the possibility that Rousseau might have practised some hypocrisy. In regard to Wagner's life we might easily fall into the same error—that is to say, we might take seriously all he says concerning himself and his family affairs.

We should beware of this, and should not even believe Wagner when he speaks badly about himself. No one speaks badly about himself without a reason, and the question in this case is to find out the reason. Did Wagner—in the belief that genius was always immoral—wish to pose as an immoral Egotist, in order to make us believe in his genius, of which he himself was none too sure in his innermost heart? Did Wagner wish to appear "sincere" in his biography, in order to awaken in us a belief in the sincerity of his music, which he likewise doubted, but wished to impress upon the world as "true"? Or did he wish to be thought badly of in connection with things that were not true, and that consequently did not affect him, in order to lead us off the scent of true things, things he was ashamed of and which he wished the world to ignore—just like Rousseau (the similarity between the two is more than a superficial one) who barbarously pretended to have sent his children to the foundling hospital, in order not to be thought incapable of having had any children at all? In short, where is the bluff in Wagner's biography? Let us therefore be careful about it, and all the more so because Wagner himself guarantees the truth of it in the prefatory note. If we were to be credulous here, we should moreover be acting in direct opposition to Nietzsche's own counsel as given in the following aphorisms (Nos. 19 and 20, p. 89):—

"It is very difficult to trace the course of Wagner's development,—no trust must be placed in his own description of his soul's experiences. He writes party-pamphlets for his followers.

"It is extremely doubtful whether Wagner is able to bear witness about himself."

While on p. 37 (the note), we read:—"He [Wagner] was not proud enough to be able to suffer the truth about himself. Nobody had less pride than he. Like Victor Hugo he remained true to himself even in his biography,—he remained an actor."

However, as a famous English judge has said—"Truth will come out, even in the witness box," and, as we may add in this case, even in an autobiography. There is one statement in Wagner's My Life which sounds true to my ears at least—a statement which, in my opinion, has some importance, and to which Wagner himself seems to grant a mysterious significance. I refer to the passage on p. 93 of vol i., in which Wagner says:—"Owing to the exceptional vivacity and innate susceptibility of my nature … I gradually became conscious of a certain power of transporting or bewildering my more indolent companions."

This seems innocent enough. When, however, it is read in conjunction with Nietzsche's trenchant criticism, particularly on pp. 14, 15, 16, 17 and 18 of this work, and also with a knowledge of Wagner's music, it becomes one of the most striking passages in Wagner's autobiography, for it records how soon he became conscious of his dominant instinct and faculty.

I know perfectly well that the Wagnerites will not be influenced by these remarks. Their gratitude to Wagner is too great for this. He has supplied the precious varnish wherewith to hide the dull ugliness of our civilisation. He has given to souls despairing over the materialism of this world, to souls despairing of themselves, and longing to be rid of themselves, the indispensable hashish and morphia wherewith to deaden their inner discords. These discords are everywhere apparent nowadays. Wagner is therefore a common need, a common benefactor. As such he is bound to be worshipped and adored in spite of all egotistical and theatrical autobiographies.

Albeit, signs are not wanting—at least among his Anglo-Saxon worshippers who stand even more in need of romanticism than their continental brethren,—which show that, in order to uphold Wagner, people are now beginning to draw distinctions between the man and the artist. They dismiss the man as "human-all-too-human," but they still maintain that there are divine qualities in his music. However distasteful the task of disillusioning these psychological tyros may be, they should be informed that no such division of a man into two parts is permissible, save in Christianity (the body and the soul), but that outside purely religious spheres it is utterly unwarrantable. There can be no such strange divorce between a bloom and the plant on which it blows, and has a black woman ever been known to give birth to a white child?

Wagner, as Nietzsche tells us on p. 19, "was something complete, he was a typical decadent in whom every sign of 'free will' was lacking, in whom every feature was necessary." Wagner, allow me to add, was a typical representative of the nineteenth century, which was the century of contradictory values, of opposed instincts, and of every kind of inner disharmony. The genuine, the classical artists of that period, such men as Heine, Goethe, Stendhal, and Gobineau, overcame their inner strife, and each succeeded in making a harmonious whole out of himself—not indeed without a severe struggle; for everyone of them suffered from being the child of his age, i.e., a decadent. The only difference between them and the romanticists lies in the fact that they (the former) were conscious of what was wrong with them, and possessed the will and the strength to overcome their illness; whereas the romanticists chose the easier alternative—namely, that of shutting their eyes on themselves.

"I am just as much a child of my age as Wagner—i.e., I am a decadent," says Nietzsche. "The only difference is that I recognised the fact, that I struggled against it"[6]

What Wagner did was characteristic of all romanticists and contemporary artists: he drowned and overshouted his inner discord by means of exuberant pathos and wild exaltation. Far be it from me to value Wagner's music in extenso here—this is scarcely a fitting opportunity to do so;—but I think it might well be possible to show, on purely psychological grounds, how impossible it was for a man like Wagner to produce real art. For how can harmony, order, symmetry, mastery, proceed from uncontrolled discord, disorder, disintegration, and chaos? The fact that an art which springs from such a marshy soil may, like certain paludal plants, be "wonderful," "gorgeous," and "overwhelming," cannot be denied; but true art it is not. It is so just as little as Gothic architecture is,—that style which, in its efforts to escape beyond the tragic contradiction in its mediæval heart, yelled its hysterical cry heavenwards and even melted the stones of its structures into a quivering and fluid jet, in order to give adequate expression to the painful and wretched conflict then raging between the body and the soul.

That Wagner, too, was a great sufferer, there can be no doubt; not, however, a sufferer from strength, like a true artist, but from weakness—the weakness of his age, which he never overcame. It is for this reason that he should be rather pitied than judged as he is now being judged by his German and English critics, who, with thoroughly neurotic suddenness, have acknowledged their revulsion of feeling a little too harshly.

"I have carefully endeavoured not to deride, or deplore, or detest…" says Spinoza, "but to understand"; and these words ought to be our guide, not only in the case of Wagner, but in all things.

Inner discord is a terrible affliction, and nothing is so certain to produce that nervous irritability which is so trying to the patient as well as to the outer world, as this so-called spiritual disease. Nietzsche was probably quite right when he said the only real and true music that Wagner ever composed did not consist of his elaborate arias and overtures, but of ten or fifteen bars which, dispersed here and there, gave expression to the composer's profound and genuine melancholy. But this melancholy had to be overcome, and Wagner with the blood of a cabotin in his veins, resorted to the remedy that was nearest to hand—that is to say, the art of bewildering others and himself. Thus he remained ignorant about himself all his life; for there was, as Nietzsche rightly points out (p. 37, note), not sufficient pride in the man for him to desire to know or to suffer gladly the truth concerning his real nature. As an actor his ruling passion was vanity, but in his case it was correlated with a semi-conscious knowledge of the fact that all was not right with him and his art. It was this that caused him to suffer. His egomaniacal behaviour and his almost Rousseauesque fear and suspicion of others were only the external manifestations of his inner discrepancies. But, to repeat what I have already said, these abnormal symptoms are not in the least incompatible with Wagner's music, they are rather its very cause, the root from which it springs.

In reality, therefore, Wagner the man and Wagner the artist were undoubtedly one, and constituted a splendid romanticist. His music as well as his autobiography are proofs of his wonderful gifts in this direction. His success in his time, as in ours, is due to the craving of the modern world for actors, sorcerers, bewilderers and idealists who are able to conceal the ill-health and the weakness that prevail, and who please by intoxicating and exalting. But this being so, the world must not be disappointed to find the hero of a preceding age explode in the next. It must not be astonished to find a disparity between the hero's private life and his "elevating" art or romantic and idealistic gospel. As long as people will admire heroic attitudes more than heroism, such disillusionment is bound to be the price of their error. In a truly great man, life-theory and life-practice, if seen from a sufficiently lofty point of view, must and do always agree, in an actor, in a romanticist, in an idealist, and in a Christian, there is always a yawning chasm between the two, which, whatever well-meaning critics may do, cannot be bridged posthumously by acrobatic feats in psychologicis.

Let anyone apply this point of view to Nietzsche's life and theory. Let anyone turn his life inside out, not only as he gives it to us in his Ecce Homo, but as we find it related by all his biographers, friends and foes alike, and what will be the result? Even if we ignore his works—the blooms which blowed from time to time from his life—we absolutely cannot deny the greatness of the man's private practice, and if we fully understand and appreciate the latter, we must be singularly deficient in instinct and in flair if we do not suspect that some of this greatness is reflected in his life-task.

ANTHONY M. LUDOVICI
London, July 1911.

THE CASE OF WAGNER: A MUSICIAN'S PROBLEM

A LETTER FROM TURIN, MAY 1888
"RIDENDO DICERE SEVERUM...."

Preface

I am writing this to relieve my mind. It is not malice alone which makes me praise Bizet at the expense of Wagner in this essay. Amid a good deal of jesting I wish to make one point clear which does not admit of levity. To turn my back on Wagner was for me a piece of fate, to get to like anything else whatever afterwards was for me a triumph. Nobody, perhaps, had ever been more dangerously involved in Wagnerism, nobody had defended himself more obstinately against it, nobody had ever been so overjoyed at ridding himself of it. A long history!—Shall I give it a name?—If I were a moralist, who knows what I might not call it! Perhaps a piece of self-mastery.—But the philosopher does not like the moralist, neither does he like high-falutin' words....

What is the first and last thing that a philosopher demands of himself? To overcome his age in himself, to become "timeless." With what then does the philosopher have the greatest fight? With all that in him which makes him the child of his time. Very well then! I am just as much a child of my age as Wagner—i.e., I am a decadent. The only difference is that I recognised the fact, that I struggled against it. The philosopher in me struggled against it.

My greatest preoccupation hitherto has been the problem of decadence, and I had reasons for this. "Good and evil" form only a playful subdivision of this problem. If one has trained one's eye to detect the symptoms of decline, one also understands morality,—one understands what lies concealed beneath its holiest names and tables of values: e.g., impoverished life, the will to nonentity, great exhaustion. Morality denies life.... In order to undertake such a mission I was obliged to exercise self-discipline:—I had to side against all that was morbid in myself including Wagner, including Schopenhauer, including the whole of modern humanity.—A profound estrangement, coldness and soberness towards all that belongs to my age, all that was contemporary: and as the highest wish, Zarathustra's eye, an eye which surveys the whole phenomenon—mankind—from an enormous distance,—which looks down upon it.—For such a goal—what sacrifice would not have been worth while? What "self-mastery"! What "self-denial"!

The greatest event of my life took the form of a recovery. Wagner belongs only to my diseases.

Not that I wish to appear ungrateful to this disease. If in this essay I support the proposition that Wagner is harmful, I none the less wish to point out unto whom, in spite of all, he is indispensable—to the philosopher. Anyone else may perhaps be able to get on without Wagner: but the philosopher is not free to pass him by. The philosopher must be the evil conscience of his age,—but to this end he must be possessed of its best knowledge. And what better guide, or more thoroughly efficient revealer of the soul, could be found for the labyrinth of the modern spirit than Wagner? Through Wagner modernity speaks her most intimate language: it conceals neither its good nor its evil: it has thrown off all shame. And, conversely, one has almost calculated the whole of the value of modernity once one is clear concerning what is good and evil in Wagner. I can perfectly well understand a musician of to-day who says: "I hate Wagner but I can endure no other music." But I should also understand a philosopher who said, "Wagner is modernity in concentrated form." There is no help for it, we must first be Wagnerites....

1

Yesterday—would you believe it?—I heard Bizet's masterpiece for the twentieth time. Once more I attended with the same gentle reverence; once again I did not run away. This triumph over my impatience surprises me. How such a work completes one! Through it one almost becomes a "masterpiece" oneself—And, as a matter of fact, each time I heard Carmen it seemed to me that I was more of a philosopher, a better philosopher than at other times: I became so forbearing, so happy, so Indian, so settled.... To sit for five hours: the first step to holiness!—May I be allowed to say that Bizet's orchestration is the only one that I can endure now? That other orchestration which is all the rage at present—the Wagnerian—is brutal, artificial and "unsophisticated" withal, hence its appeal to all the three senses of the modern soul at once. How terribly Wagnerian orchestration affects me! I call it the Sirocco. A disagreeable sweat breaks out all over me. All my fine weather vanishes.

Bizet's music seems to me perfect. It comes forward lightly, gracefully, stylishly. It is lovable, it does not sweat. "All that is good is easy, everything divine runs with light feet": this is the first principle of my æsthetics. This music is wicked, refined, fatalistic, and withal remains popular,—it possesses the refinement of a race, not of an individual. It is rich. It is definite. It builds, organises, completes, and in this sense it stands as a contrast to the polypus in music, to "endless melody". Have more painful, more tragic accents ever been heard on the stage before? And how are they obtained? Without grimaces! Without counterfeiting of any kind! Free from the lie of the grand style!—In short: this music assumes that the listener is intelligent even as a musician,—thereby it is the opposite of Wagner, who, apart from everything else, was in any case the most ill-mannered genius on earth (Wagner takes us as if ... , he repeats a thing so often that we become desperate,—that we ultimately believe it).

And once more: I become a better man when Bizet speaks to me. Also a better musician, a better listener. Is it in any way possible to listen better?—I even burrow behind this music with my ears. I hear its very cause. I seem to assist at its birth. I tremble before the dangers which this daring music runs, I am enraptured over those happy accidents for which even Bizet himself may not be responsible.—And, strange to say, at bottom I do not give it a thought, or am not aware how much thought I really do give it. For quite other ideas are running through my head the while.... Has any one ever observed that music emancipates the spirit? gives wings to thought? and that the more one becomes a musician the more one is also a philosopher? The grey sky of abstraction seems thrilled by flashes of lightning; the light is strong enough to reveal all the details of things; to enable one to grapple with problems; and the world is surveyed as if from a mountain top—With this I have defined philosophical pathos—And unexpectedly answers drop into my lap, a small hailstorm of ice and wisdom, of problems solved. Where am I? Bizet makes me productive. Everything that is good makes me productive. I have gratitude for nothing else, nor have I any other touchstone for testing what is good.

2

Bizet's work also saves; Wagner is not the only "Saviour." With it one bids farewell to the damp north and to all the fog of the Wagnerian ideal. Even the action in itself delivers us from these things. From Merimée it has this logic even in passion, from him it has the direct line, inexorable necessity, but what it has above all else is that which belongs to sub-tropical zones—that dryness of atmosphere, that limpidezza of the air. Here in every respect the climate is altered. Here another kind of sensuality, another kind of sensitiveness and another kind of cheerfulness make their appeal. This music is gay, but not in a French or German way. Its gaiety is African; fate hangs over it, its happiness is short, sudden, without reprieve. I envy Bizet for having had the courage of this sensitiveness, which hitherto in the cultured music of Europe has found no means of expression,—of this southern, tawny, sunburnt sensitiveness.... What a joy the golden afternoon of its happiness is to us! When we look out, with this music in our minds, we wonder whether we have ever seen the sea so calm. And how soothing is this Moorish dancing! How, for once, even our insatiability gets sated by its lascivious melancholy!—And finally love, love translated back into Nature! Not the love of a "cultured girl!"—no Senta-sentimentality.[7] But love as fate, as a fatality, cynical, innocent, cruel,—and precisely in this way Nature! The love whose means is war, whose very essence is the mortal hatred between the sexes!—I know no case in which the tragic irony, which constitutes the kernel of love, is expressed with such severity, or in so terrible a formula, as in the last cry of Don José with which the work ends:

"Yes, it is I who have killed her, I—my adored Carmen!"

—Such a conception of love (the only one worthy of a philosopher) is rare: it distinguishes one work of art from among a thousand others. For, as a rule, artists are no better than the rest of the world, they are even worse—they misunderstand love. Even Wagner misunderstood it. They imagine that they are selfless in it because they appear to be seeking the advantage of another creature often to their own disadvantage. But in return they want to possess the other creature.... Even God is no exception to this rule, he is very far from thinking "What does it matter to thee whether I love thee or not?"—He becomes terrible if he is not loved in return "L'amour—and with this principle one carries one's point against Gods and men—est de tous les sentiments le plus égoiste, et par conséquent, lorsqu'il est blessé, le moins généreux" (B. Constant).

3

Perhaps you are beginning to perceive how very much this music improves me?—Il faut méditerraniser la musique. and I have my reasons for this principle ("Beyond Good and Evil," pp. 216 et seq.) The return to Nature, health, good spirits, youth, virtue!—And yet I was one of the most corrupted Wagnerites.... I was able to take Wagner seriously. Oh, this old magician! what tricks has he not played upon us! The first thing his art places in our hands is a magnifying glass: we look through it, and we no longer trust our own eyes—Everything grows bigger, even Wagner grows bigger.... What a clever rattlesnake. Throughout his life he rattled "resignation," "loyalty," and "purity" about our ears, and he retired from the corrupt world with a song of praise to chastity!—And we believed it all....

—But you will not listen to me? You prefer even the problem of Wagner to that of Bizet? But neither do I underrate it; it has its charm. The problem of salvation is even a venerable problem. Wagner pondered over nothing so deeply as over salvation: his opera is the opera of salvation. Someone always wants to be saved in his operas,—now it is a youth; anon it is a maid,—this is his problem—And how lavishly he varies his leitmotif! What rare and melancholy modulations! If it were not for Wagner, who would teach us that innocence has a preference for saving interesting sinners? (the case in "Tannhauser"). Or that even the eternal Jew gets saved and settled down when he marries? (the case in the "Flying Dutchman"). Or that corrupted old females prefer to be saved by chaste young men? (the case of Kundry). Or that young hysterics like to be saved by their doctor? (the case in "Lohengrin"). Or that beautiful girls most love to be saved by a knight who also happens to be a Wagnerite? (the case in the "Mastersingers"). Or that even married women also like to be saved by a knight? (the case of Isolde). Or that the venerable Almighty, after having compromised himself morally in all manner of ways, is at last delivered by a free spirit and an immoralist? (the case in the "Ring"). Admire, more especially this last piece of wisdom! Do you understand it? I—take good care not to understand it.... That it is possible to draw yet other lessons from the works above mentioned,—I am much more ready to prove than to dispute. That one may be driven by a Wagnerian ballet to desperation—and to virtue! (once again the case in "Tannhauser"). That not going to bed at the right time may be followed by the worst consequences (once again the case of "Lohengrin").—That one can never be too sure of the spouse one actually marries (for the third time, the case of "Lohengrin"). "Tristan and Isolde" glorifies the perfect husband who, in a certain case, can ask only one question: "But why have ye not told me this before? Nothing could be simpler than that!" Reply:

"That I cannot tell thee. And what thou askest, That wilt thou never learn."

"Lohengrin" contains a solemn ban upon all investigation and questioning. In this way Wagner stood for the Christian concept, "Thou must and shalt believe". It is a crime against the highest and the holiest to be scientific.... The "Flying Dutchman" preaches the sublime doctrine that woman can moor the most erratic soul, or to put it into Wagnerian terms "save" him. Here we venture to ask a question. Supposing that this were actually true, would it therefore be desirable?—What becomes of the "eternal Jew" whom a woman adores and enchains? He simply ceases from being eternal, he marries,—that is to say, he concerns us no longer.—Transferred into the realm of reality, the danger for the artist and for the genius—and these are of course the "eternal Jews"—resides in woman: adoring women are their ruin. Scarcely any one has sufficient character not to be corrupted—"saved" when he finds himself treated as a God—he then immediately condescends to woman.—Man is a coward in the face of all that is eternally feminine, and this the girls know.—In many cases of woman's love, and perhaps precisely in the most famous ones, the love is no more than a refined form of parasitism, a making one's nest in another's soul and sometimes even in another's flesh—Ah! and how constantly at the cost of the host!

We know the fate of Goethe in old-maidish moralin-corroded Germany. He was always offensive to Germans, he found honest admirers only among Jewesses. Schiller, "noble" Schiller, who cried flowery words into their ears,—he was a man after their own heart. What did they reproach Goethe with?—with the Mount of Venus, and with having composed certain Venetian epigrams. Even Klopstock preached him a moral sermon; there was a time when Herder was fond of using the word "Priapus" when he spoke of Goethe. Even "Wilhelm Meister" seemed to be only a symptom of decline, of a moral "going to the dogs". The "Menagerie of tame cattle," the worthlessness of the hero in this book, revolted Niebuhr, who finally bursts out in a plaint which Biterolf[8] might well have sung: "nothing so easily makes a painful impression as when a great mind despoils itself of its wings and strives for virtuosity in something greatly inferior, while it renounces more lofty aims." But the most indignant of all was the cultured woman—all smaller courts in Germany, every kind of "Puritanism" made the sign of the cross at the sight of Goethe, at the thought of the "unclean spirit" in Goethe.—This history was what Wagner set to music. He saves Goethe, that goes without saying; but he does so in such a clever way that he also takes the side of the cultured woman. Goethe gets saved: a prayer saves him, a cultured woman draws him out of the mire.

—As to what Goethe would have thought of Wagner?—Goethe once set himself the question, "what danger hangs over all romanticists—the fate of romanticists?"—His answer was: "To choke over the rumination of moral and religious absurdities." In short: Parsifal.... The philosopher writes thereto an epilogue: Holiness—the only remaining higher value still seen by the mob or by woman, the horizon of the ideal for all those who are naturally short-sighted. To philosophers, however, this horizon, like every other, is a mere misunderstanding, a sort of slamming of the door in the face of the real beginning of their world,—their danger, their ideal, their desideratum.... In more polite language: La philosophie ne suffit pas au grand nombre. Il lui faut la sainteté....

4

I shall once more relate the history of the "Ring". This is its proper place. It is also the history of a salvation except that in this case it is Wagner himself who is saved—Half his lifetime Wagner believed in the Revolution as only a Frenchman could have believed in it. He sought it in the runic inscriptions of myths, he thought he had found a typical revolutionary in Siegfried.—"Whence arises all the evil in this world?" Wagner asked himself. From "old contracts": he replied, as all revolutionary ideologists have done. In plain English: from customs, laws, morals, institutions, from all those things upon which the ancient world and ancient society rests. "How can one get rid of the evil in this world? How can one get rid of ancient society?" Only by declaring war against "contracts" (traditions, morality). This Siegfried does. He starts early at the game, very early—his origin itself is already a declaration of war against morality—he is the result of adultery, of incest.... Not the saga, but Wagner himself is the inventor of this radical feature, in this matter he corrected the saga.... Siegfried continues as he began: he follows only his first impulse, he flings all tradition, all respect, all fear to the winds. Whatever displeases him he strikes down. He tilts irreverently at old god-heads. His principal undertaking, however, is to emancipate woman,—"to deliver Brunnhilda."... Siegfried and Brunnhilda, the sacrament of free love, the dawn of the golden age, the twilight of the Gods of old morality—evil is got rid of.... For a long while Wagner's ship sailed happily along this course. There can be no doubt that along it Wagner sought his highest goal.—What happened? A misfortune. The ship dashed on to a reef; Wagner had run aground. The reef was Schopenhauer's philosophy; Wagner had stuck fast on a contrary view of the world. What had he set to music? Optimism? Wagner was ashamed. It was moreover an optimism for which Schopenhauer had devised an evil expression,—unscrupulous optimism. He was more than ever ashamed. He reflected for some time; his position seemed desperate.... At last a path of escape seemed gradually to open before him—what if the reef on which he had been wrecked could be interpreted as a goal, as the ulterior motive, as the actual purpose of his journey? To be wrecked here, this was also a goal:—Bene navigavi cum naufragium feci ... and he translated the "Ring" into Schopenhauerian language. Everything goes wrong, everything goes to wrack and ruin, the new world is just as bad as the old one:—Nonentity, the Indian Circe beckons ... Brunnhilda, who according to the old plan had to retire with a song in honour of free love, consoling the world with the hope of a socialistic Utopia in which "all will be well"; now gets something else to do. She must first study Schopenhauer. She must first versify the fourth book of "The World as Will and Idea." Wagner was saved.... Joking apart, this was a salvation. The service which Wagner owes to Schopenhauer is incalculable. It was the philosopher of decadence who allowed the artist of decadence to find himself.—

5

The artist of decadence. That is the word. And here I begin to be serious. I could not think of looking on approvingly while this décadent spoils our health—and music into the bargain. Is Wagner a man at all? Is he not rather a disease? Everything he touches he contaminates. He has made music sick.

A typical décadent who thinks himself necessary with his corrupted taste, who arrogates to himself a higher taste, who tries to establish his depravity as a law, as progress, as a fulfilment.

And no one guards against it. His powers of seduction attain monstrous proportions, holy incense hangs around him, the misunderstanding concerning him is called the Gospel,—and he has certainly not converted only the poor in spirit to his cause!

I should like to open the window a little:—Air! More air!—

The fact that people in Germany deceive themselves concerning Wagner does not surprise me.

The reverse would surprise me. The Germans have modelled a Wagner for themselves, whom they can honour: never yet have they been psychologists; they are thankful that they misunderstand. But that people should also deceive themselves concerning Wagner in Paris! Where people are scarcely anything else than psychologists. And in Saint Petersburg! Where things are divined, which even Paris has no idea of. How intimately related must Wagner be to the entire decadence of Europe for her not to have felt that he was decadent! He belongs to it, he is its protagonist, its greatest name.... We bring honour on ourselves by elevating him to the clouds—For the mere fact that no one guards against him is in itself already a sign of decadence. Instinct is weakened, what ought to be eschewed now attracts. People actually kiss that which plunges them more quickly into the abyss.—Is there any need for an example? One has only to think of the régime which anæmic, or gouty, or diabetic people prescribe for themselves. The definition of a vegetarian: a creature who has need of a corroborating diet. To recognise what is harmful as harmful, to be able to deny oneself what is harmful, is a sign of youth, of vitality. That which is harmful lures the exhausted: cabbage lures the vegetarian. Illness itself can be a stimulus to life but one must be healthy enough for such a stimulus!—Wagner increases exhaustion—therefore he attracts the weak and exhausted to him. Oh, the rattlesnake joy of the old Master precisely because he always saw "the little children" coming unto him!

I place this point of view first and foremost: Wagner's art is diseased. The problems he sets on the stage are all concerned with hysteria; the convulsiveness of his emotions, his over-excited sensitiveness, his taste which demands ever sharper condimentation, his erraticness which he togged out to look like principles, and, last but not least, his choice of heroes and heroines, considered as physiological types (—a hospital ward!—): the whole represents a morbid picture; of this there can be no doubt. Wagner est une névrose. Maybe, that nothing is better known to-day, or in any case the subject of greater study, than the Protean character of degeneration which has disguised itself here, both as an art and as an artist. In Wagner our medical men and physiologists have a most interesting case, or at least a very complete one. Owing to the very fact that nothing is more modern than this thorough morbidness, this dilatoriness and excessive irritability of the nervous machinery, Wagner is the modern artist par excellence, the Cagliostro of modernity. All that the world most needs to-day, is combined in the most seductive manner in his art,—the three great stimulants of exhausted people: brutality, artificiality and innocence (idiocy).

Wagner is a great corrupter of music. With it, he found the means of stimulating tired nerves,—and in this way he made music ill. In the art of spurring exhausted creatures back into activity, and of recalling half-corpses to life, the inventiveness he shows is of no mean order. He is the master of hypnotic trickery, and he fells the strongest like bullocks. Wagner's success—his success with nerves, and therefore with women—converted the whole world of ambitious musicians into disciples of his secret art. And not only the ambitious, but also the shrewd.... Only with morbid music can money be made to-day; our big theatres live on Wagner.

6

—Once more I will venture to indulge in a little levity. Let us suppose that Wagner's success could become flesh and blood and assume a human form; that, dressed up as a good-natured musical savant, it could move among budding artists. How do you think it would then be likely to express itself?—

My friends, it would say, let us exchange a word or two in private. It is easier to compose bad music than good music. But what, if apart from this it were also more profitable, more effective, more convincing, more exalting, more secure, more Wagnerian?... Pulchrum est paucorum hominum. Bad enough in all conscience! We understand Latin, and perhaps we also understand which side our bread is buttered. Beauty has its drawbacks: we know that. Wherefore beauty then? Why not rather aim at size, at the sublime, the gigantic, that which moves the masses?—And to repeat, it is easier to be titanic than to be beautiful; we know that....

We know the masses, we know the theatre. The best of those who assemble there,—German youths, horned Siegfrieds and other Wagnerites, require the sublime, the profound, and the overwhelming. This much still lies within our power. And as for the others who assemble there,—the cultured crétins, the blasé pigmies, the eternally feminine, the gastrically happy, in short the people—they also require the sublime, the profound, the overwhelming. All these people argue in the same way. "He who overthrows us is strong; he who elevates us is godly; he who makes us wonder vaguely is profound."—Let us make up our mind then, my friends in music: we do want to overthrow them, we do want to elevate them, we do want to make them wonder vaguely. This much still lies within our powers.

In regard to the process of making them wonder: it is here that our notion of "style" finds its starting-point. Above all, no thoughts! Nothing is more compromising than a thought! But the state of mind which precedes thought, the labour of the thought still unborn, the promise of future thought, the world as it was before God created it—a recrudescence of chaos.... Chaos makes people wonder....

In the words of the master: infinity but without melody.

In the second place, with regard to the overthrowing,—this belongs at least in part, to physiology. Let us, in the first place, examine the instruments. A few of them would convince even our intestines (—they throw open doors, as Handel would say), others becharm our very marrow. The colour of the melody is all-important here, the melody itself is of no importance. Let us be precise about this point. To what other purpose should we spend our strength? Let us be characteristic in tone even to the point of foolishness! If by means of tones we allow plenty of scope for guessing, this will be put to the credit of our intellects. Let us irritate nerves, let us strike them dead: let us handle thunder and lightning,—that is what overthrows.....

But what overthrows best, is passion.—We must try and be clear concerning this question of passion. Nothing is cheaper than passion! All the virtues of counterpoint may be dispensed with, there is no need to have learnt anything,—but passion is always within our reach! Beauty is difficult: let us beware of beauty!... And also of melody! However much in earnest we may otherwise be about the ideal, let us slander, my friends, let us slander,—let us slander melody! Nothing is more dangerous than a beautiful melody! Nothing is more certain to ruin taste! My friends, if people again set about loving beautiful melodies, we are lost!...

First principle: melody is immoral. Proof: "Palestrina". Application: "Parsifal." The absence of melody is in itself sanctifying....

And this is the definition of passion. Passion—or the acrobatic feats of ugliness on the tight-rope of enharmonic—My friends, let us dare to be ugly! Wagner dared it! Let us heave the mud of the most repulsive harmonies undauntedly before us. We must not even spare our hands! Only thus, shall we become natural....

And now a last word of advice. Perhaps it covers everything—Let us be idealists!—If not the cleverest, it is at least the wisest thing we can do. In order to elevate men we ourselves must be exalted. Let us wander in the clouds, let us harangue eternity, let us be careful to group great symbols all around us! Sursum! Bumbum!—there is no better advice. The "heaving breast" shall be our argument, "beautiful feelings" our advocates. Virtue still carries its point against counterpoint. "How could he who improves us, help being better than we?" man has ever thought thus. Let us therefore improve mankind!—in this way we shall become good (in this way we shall even become "classics"—Schiller became a "classic"). The straining after the base excitement of the senses, after so-called beauty, shattered the nerves of the Italians: let us remain German! Even Mozart's relation to music—Wagner spoke this word of comfort to us—was at bottom frivolous....

Never let us acknowledge that music "may be a recreation," that it may "enliven," that it may "give pleasure." Never let us give pleasure!—we shall be lost if people once again think of music hedonistically.... That belongs to the bad eighteenth century.... On the other hand, nothing would be more advisable (between ourselves) than a dose of—cant, sit venia verbo. This imparts dignity.—And let us take care to select the precise moment when it would be fitting to have black looks, to sigh openly, to sigh devoutly, to flaunt grand Christian sympathy before their eyes. "Man is corrupt who will save him? what will save him?" Do not let us reply. We must be on our guard. We must control our ambition, which would bid us found new religions. But no one must doubt that it is we who save him, that in our music alone salvation is to be found.... (See Wagner's essay, "Religion and Art.")

7

Enough! Enough! I fear that, beneath all my merry jests, you are beginning to recognise the sinister truth only too clearly—the picture of the decline of art, of the decline of the artist. The latter, which is a decline of character, might perhaps be defined provisionally in the following manner: the musician is now becoming an actor, his art is developing ever more and more into a talent for telling lies. In a certain chapter of my principal work which bears the title "Concerning the Physiology of Art,"[9] I shall have an opportunity of showing more thoroughly how this transformation of art as a whole into histrionics is just as much a sign of physiological degeneration (or more precisely a form of hysteria), as any other individual corruption, and infirmity peculiar to the art which Wagner inaugurated: for instance the restlessness of its optics, which makes it necessary to change one's attitude to it every second. They understand nothing of Wagner who see in him but a sport of nature, an arbitrary mood, a chapter of accidents. He was not the "defective," "ill-fated," "contradictory" genius that people have declared him to be. Wagner was something complete, he was a typical décadent, in whom every sign of "free will" was lacking, in whom every feature was necessary. If there is anything at all of interest in Wagner, it is the consistency with which a critical physiological condition may convert itself, step by step, conclusion after conclusion, into a method, a form of procedure, a reform of all principles, a crisis in taste.

At this point I shall only stop to consider the question of style. How is decadence in literature characterised? By the fact that in it life no longer animates the whole. Words become predominant and leap right out of the sentence to which they belong, the sentences themselves trespass beyond their bounds, and obscure the sense of the whole page, and the page in its turn gains in vigour at the cost of the whole,—the whole is no longer a whole. But this is the formula for every decadent style: there is always anarchy among the atoms, disaggregation of the will,—in moral terms: "freedom of the individual,"—extended into a political theory "equal rights for all." Life, equal vitality, all the vibration and exuberance of life, driven back into the smallest structure, and the remainder left almost lifeless. Everywhere paralysis, distress, and numbness, or hostility and chaos both striking one with ever increasing force the higher the forms of organisation are into which one ascends. The whole no longer lives at all: it is composed, reckoned up, artificial, a fictitious thing.

In Wagner's case the first thing we notice is an hallucination, not of tones, but of attitudes. Only after he has the latter does he begin to seek the semiotics of tone for them. If we wish to admire him, we should observe him at work here: how he separates and distinguishes, how he arrives at small unities, and how he galvanises them, accentuates them, and brings them into pre-eminence. But in this way he exhausts his strength the rest is worthless. How paltry, awkward, and amateurish is his manner of "developing," his attempt at combining incompatible parts. His manner in this respect reminds one of two people who even in other ways are not unlike him in style—the brothers Goncourt; one almost feels compassion for so much impotence. That Wagner disguised his inability to create organic forms, under the cloak of a principle, that he should have constructed a "dramatic style" out of what we should call the total inability to create any style whatsoever, is quite in keeping with that daring habit, which stuck to him throughout his life, of setting up a principle wherever capacity failed him. (In this respect he was very different from old Kant, who rejoiced in another form of daring, i.e.: whenever a principle failed him, he endowed man with a "capacity" which took its place…) Once more let it be said that Wagner is really only worthy of admiration and love by virtue of his inventiveness in small things, in his elaboration of details,—here one is quite justified in proclaiming him a master of the first rank, as our greatest musical miniaturist who compresses an infinity of meaning and sweetness into the smallest space. His wealth of colour, of chiaroscuro, of the mystery of a dying light, so pampers our senses that afterwards almost every other musician strikes us as being too robust. If people would believe me, they would not form the highest idea of Wagner from that which pleases them in him to-day. All that was only devised for convincing the masses, and people like ourselves recoil from it just as one would recoil from too garish a fresco. What concern have we with the irritating brutality of the overture to the "Tannhauser"? Or with the Walkyrie Circus? Whatever has become popular in Wagner's art, including that which has become so outside the theatre, is in bad taste and spoils taste. The "Tannhauser" March seems to me to savour of the Philistine; the overture to the "Flying Dutchman" is much ado about nothing; the prelude to "Lohengrin" was the first, only too insidious, only too successful example of how one can hypnotise with music (—I dislike all music which aspires to nothing higher than to convince the nerves). But apart from the Wagner who paints frescoes and practises magnetism, there is yet another Wagner who hoards small treasures: our greatest melancholic in music, full of side glances, loving speeches, and words of comfort, in which no one ever forestalled him,—the tone-master of melancholy and drowsy happiness…. A lexicon of Wagner's most intimate phrases—a host of short fragments of from five to fifteen bars each, of music which nobody knows…. Wagner had the virtue of décadents,—pity….

8

—"Very good! But how can this décadent spoil one's taste if perchance one is not a musician, if perchance one is not oneself a décadent?"—Conversely! How can one help it! Just you try it!—You know not what Wagner is: quite a great actor! Does a more profound, a more ponderous influence exist on the stage? Just look at these youthlets,—all benumbed, pale, breathless! They are Wagnerites: they know nothing about music,—and yet Wagner gets the mastery of them. Wagner's art presses with the weight of a hundred atmospheres: do but submit, there is nothing else to do…. Wagner the actor is a tyrant, his pathos flings all taste, all resistance, to the winds.

—Who else has this persuasive power in his attitudes, who else sees attitudes so clearly before anything else! This holding-of-its-breath in Wagnerian pathos, this disinclination to have done with an intense feeling, this terrifying habit of dwelling on a situation in which every instant almost chokes one.——

Was Wagner a musician at all? In any case he was something else to a much greater degree—that is to say, an incomparable histrio, the greatest mime, the most astounding theatrical genius that the Germans have ever had, our scenic artist par excellence. He belongs to some other sphere than the history of music, with whose really great and genuine figure he must not be confounded. Wagner and

Beethoven—this is blasphemy—and above all it does not do justice even to Wagner.... As a musician he was no more than what he was as a man, he became a musician, he became a poet, because the tyrant in him, his actor's genius, drove him to be both. Nothing is known concerning Wagner, so long as his dominating instinct has not been divined.

Wagner was not instinctively a musician. And this he proved by the way in which he abandoned all laws and rules, or, in more precise terms, all style in music, in order to make what he wanted with it, i.e., a rhetorical medium for the stage, a medium of expression, a means of accentuating an attitude, a vehicle of suggestion and of the psychologically picturesque. In this department Wagner may well stand as an inventor and an innovator of the first order—he increased the powers of speech of music to an incalculable degree—he is the Victor Hugo of music as language, provided always we allow that under certain circumstances music may be something which is not music, but speech—instrument—ancilla dramaturgica. Wagner's music, not in the tender care of theatrical taste, which is very tolerant, is simply bad music, perhaps the worst that has ever been composed. When a musician can no longer count up to three, he becomes "dramatic," he becomes "Wagnerian"....

Wagner almost discovered the magic which can be wrought even now by means of music which is both incoherent and elementary. His consciousness of this attains to huge proportions, as does also his instinct to dispense entirely with higher law and style. The elementary factors—sound, movement, colour, in short, the whole sensuousness of music—suffice. Wagner never calculates as a musician with a musician's conscience, all he strains after is effect, nothing more than effect. And he knows what he has to make an effect upon!—In this he is as unhesitating as Schiller was, as any theatrical man must be; he has also the latter's contempt for the world which he brings to its knees before him. A man is an actor when he is ahead of mankind in his possession of this one view, that everything which has to strike people as true, must not be true. This rule was formulated by Talma: it contains the whole psychology of the actor, it also contains—and this we need not doubt—all his morality. Wagner's music is never true.

—But it is supposed to be so: and thus everything is as it should be. As long as we are young, and Wagnerites into the bargain, we regard Wagner as rich, even as the model of a prodigal giver, even as a great landlord in the realm of sound. We admire him in very much the same way as young Frenchmen admire Victor Hugo—that is to say, for his "royal liberality." Later on we admire the one as well as the other for the opposite reason: as masters and paragons in economy, as prudent amphitryons. Nobody can equal them in the art of providing a princely board with such a modest outlay.—The Wagnerite, with his credulous stomach, is even sated with the fare which his master conjures up before him. But we others who, in books as in music, desire above all to find substance, and who are scarcely satisfied with the mere representation of a banquet, are much worse off. In plain English, Wagner does not give us enough to masticate. His recitative—very little meat, more bones, and plenty of broth—I christened "alla genovese": I had no intention of flattering the Genoese with this remark, but rather the older recitativo, the recitativo secco. And as to Wagnerian leitmotif, I fear I lack the necessary culinary understanding for it. If hard pressed, I might say that I regard it perhaps as an ideal toothpick, as an opportunity of ridding one's self of what remains of one's meal. Wagner's "arias" are still left over. But now I shall hold my tongue.

Even in his general sketch of the action, Wagner is above all an actor. The first thing that occurs to him is a scene which is certain to produce a strong effect, a real actio,[10] with a basso-relievo of attitudes; an overwhelming scene, this he now proceeds to elaborate more deeply, and out of it he draws his characters. The whole of what remains to be done follows of itself, fully in keeping with a technical economy which has no reason to be subtle. It is not Corneille's public that Wagner has to consider, it is merely the nineteenth century. Concerning the "actual requirements of the stage" Wagner would have about the same opinion as any other actor of to-day, a series of powerful scenes, each stronger than the one that preceded it,—and, in between, all kinds of clever nonsense. His first concern is to guarantee the effect of his work; he begins with the third act, he approves his work according to the quality of its final effect. Guided by this sort of understanding of the stage, there is not much danger of one's creating a drama unawares. Drama demands inexorable logic: but what did Wagner care about logic? Again I say, it was not Corneille's public that he had to consider; but merely Germans! Everybody knows the technical difficulties before which the dramatist often has to summon all his strength and frequently to sweat his blood: the difficulty of making the plot seem necessary and the unravelment as well, so that both are conceivable only in a certain way, and so that each may give the impression of freedom (the principle of the smallest expenditure of energy). Now the very last thing that Wagner does is to sweat blood over the plot; and on this and the unravelment he certainly spends the smallest possible amount of energy. Let anybody put one of Wagner's "plots" under the microscope, and I wager that he will be forced to laugh. Nothing is more enlivening than the dilemma in "Tristan," unless it be that in the "Mastersingers." Wagner is no dramatist; let nobody be deceived on this point. All he did was to love the word "drama"—he always loved fine words. Nevertheless, in his writings the word "drama" is merely a misunderstanding (—and a piece of shrewdness: Wagner always affected superiority in regard to the word "opera"—), just as the word "spirit" is a misunderstanding in the New Testament.—He was not enough of a psychologist for drama; he instinctively avoided a psychological plot—but how?—by always putting idiosyncrasy in its place.... Very modern—eh? Very Parisian! very decadent!... Incidentally, the plots that Wagner knows how to unravel with the help of dramatic inventions, are of quite another kind. For example, let us suppose that Wagner requires a female voice. A whole act without a woman's voice would be impossible! But in this particular instance not one of the heroines happens to be free. What does Wagner do? He emancipates the oldest woman on earth, Erda. "Step up, aged grandmamma! You have got to sing!" And Erda sings. Wagner's end has been achieved. Thereupon he immediately dismisses the old lady. "Why on earth did you come? Off with you! Kindly go to sleep again!" In short, a scene full of mythological awe, before which the Wagnerite wonders all kinds of things....

—"But the substance of Wagner's texts! their mythical substance, their eternal substance"—Question: how is this substance, this eternal substance tested? The chemical analyst replies: Translate Wagner into the real, into the modern,—let us be even more cruel, and say into the bourgeois! And what will then become of him?—Between ourselves, I have tried the experiment. Nothing is more entertaining, nothing more worthy of being recommended to a picnic-party, than to discuss Wagner dressed in a more modern garb: for instance Parsifal, as a candidate in divinity, with a public-school education (—the latter, quite indispensable for pure foolishness). What surprises await one! Would you believe it, that Wagner's heroines one and all, once they have been divested of the heroic husks, are almost indistinguishable from Mdme. Bovary!—just as one can conceive conversely, of Flaubert's being well able to transform all his heroines into Scandinavian or Carthaginian women, and then to offer them to Wagner in this mythologised form as a libretto. Indeed, generally speaking, Wagner does not seem to have become interested in any other problems than those which engross the little Parisian decadents of to-day. Always five paces away from the hospital! All very modern problems, all problems which are at home in big cities! do not doubt it!... Have you noticed (it is in keeping with this association of ideas) that Wagner's heroines never have any children?—They cannot have them.... The despair with which Wagner tackled the problem of arranging in some way for Siegfried's birth, betrays how modern his feelings on this point actually were.—Siegfried "emancipated woman"—but not with any hope of offspring.—And now here is a fact which leaves us speechless: Parsifal is Lohengrin's father! How ever did he do it?—Ought one at this juncture to remember that "chastity works miracles"?...

Wagnerus dixit princeps in castitate auctoritas.

10

And now just a word en passant concerning Wagner's writings: they are among other things a school of shrewdness. The system of procedures of which Wagner disposes, might be applied to a hundred other cases,—he that hath ears to hear let him hear. Perhaps I may lay claim to some public acknowledgment, if I put three of the most valuable of these procedures into a precise form.

Everything that Wagner cannot do is bad.

Wagner could do much more than he does; but his strong principles prevent him.

Everything that Wagner can do, no one will ever be able to do after him, no one has ever done before him, and no one must ever do after him. Wagner is godly.

These three propositions are the quintessence of Wagner's writings;—the rest is merely—"literature".

—Not every kind of music hitherto has been in need of literature; and it were well, to try and discover the actual reason of this. Is it perhaps that Wagner's music is too difficult to understand? Or did he fear precisely the reverse—that it was too easy,—that people might not understand it with sufficient difficulty?—As a matter of fact, his whole life long, he did nothing but repeat one proposition: that his music did not mean music alone! But something more! Something immeasurably more!... "Not music alone"—no musician would speak in this way. I repeat, Wagner could not create things as a whole; he had no choice, he was obliged to create things in bits, with "motives," attitudes, formulæ, duplications, and hundreds of repetitions, he remained a rhetorician in music,—and that is why he was at bottom forced to press "this means" into the foreground. "Music can never be anything else than a means": this was his theory, but above all it was the only practice that lay open to him. No musician however thinks in this way.—Wagner was in need of literature, in order to persuade the whole world to take his music seriously, profoundly, "because it meant an infinity of things", all his life he was the commentator of the "Idea."—What does Elsa stand for? But without a doubt, Elsa is "the unconscious mind of the people" (—"when I realised this, I naturally became a thorough revolutionist"—).

Do not let us forget that, when Hegel and Schelling were misleading the minds of Germany, Wagner was still young: that he guessed, or rather fully grasped, that the only thing which Germans take seriously is—"the idea,"—that is to say, something obscure, uncertain, wonderful; that among Germans lucidity is an objection, logic a refutation. Schopenhauer rigorously pointed out the dishonesty of Hegel's and Schelling's age,—rigorously, but also unjustly, for he himself, the pessimistic old counterfeiter, was in no way more "honest" than his more famous contemporaries. But let us leave morality out of the question, Hegel is a matter of taste.... And not only of German but of European taste!... A taste which Wagner understood!—which he felt equal to! which he has immortalised!—All he did was to apply it to music—he invented a style for himself, which might mean an "infinity of things,"—he was Hegel's heir.... Music as "Idea."—

And how well Wagner was understood!—The same kind of man who used to gush over Hegel, now gushes over Wagner, in his school they even write Hegelian.[11] But he who understood Wagner best, was the German youthlet. The two words "infinity" and "meaning" were sufficient for this: at their sound the youthlet immediately began to feel exceptionally happy. Wagner did not conquer these boys with music, but with the "idea":—it is the enigmatical vagueness of his art, its game of hide-and-seek amid a hundred symbols, its polychromy in ideals, which leads and lures the lads. It is Wagner's genius for forming clouds, his sweeps and swoops through the air, his ubiquity and nullibiety—precisely the same qualities with which Hegel led and lured in his time!—Moreover in the presence of Wagner's multifariousness, plenitude and arbitrariness, they seem to themselves justified—"saved". Tremulously they listen while the great symbols in his art seem to make themselves heard from out the misty distance, with a gentle roll of thunder, and they are not at all displeased if at times it gets a little grey, gruesome and cold. Are they not one and all, like Wagner himself, on quite intimate terms with bad weather, with German weather! Wotan is their God, but Wotan is the God of bad weather.... They are right, how could these German youths—in their present condition,—miss what we others, we halcyonians, miss in Wagner? i.e.: la gaya scienza; light feet, wit, fire, grave, grand logic, stellar dancing, wanton intellectuality, the vibrating light of the South, the calm sea—perfection....

11

—I have mentioned the sphere to which Wagner belongs—certainly not to the history of music. What, however, does he mean historically?—The rise of the actor in music: a momentous event which not only leads me to think but also to fear.

In a word: "Wagner and Liszt." Never yet have the "uprightness" and "genuineness" of musicians been put to such a dangerous test. It is glaringly obvious: great success, mob success is no longer the achievement of the genuine,—in order to get it a man must be an actor!—Victor Hugo and Richard Wagner—they both prove one and the same thing: that in declining civilisations, wherever the mob is allowed to decide, genuineness becomes superfluous, prejudicial, unfavourable. The actor, alone, can still kindle great enthusiasm.—And thus it is his golden age which is now dawning,—his and that of all those who are in any way related to him. With drums and fifes, Wagner marches at the head of all artists in declamation, in display and virtuosity. He began by convincing the conductors of orchestras, the scene-shifters and stage-singers, not to forget the orchestra:—he "delivered" them from monotony.... The movement that Wagner created has spread even to the land of knowledge: whole sciences pertaining to music are rising slowly, out of centuries of scholasticism. As an example of what I mean, let me point more particularly to Riemann's services to rhythmics; he was the first who called attention to the leading idea in punctuation—even for music (unfortunately he did so with a bad word; he called it "phrasing").—All these people, and I say it with gratitude, are the best, the most respectable among Wagner's admirers—they have a perfect right to honour Wagner. The same instinct unites them with one another; in him they recognise their highest type, and since he has inflamed them with his own ardour they feel themselves transformed into power, even into great power. In this quarter, if anywhere, Wagner's influence has really been beneficent. Never before has there been so much thinking, willing, and industry in this sphere. Wagner endowed all these artists with a new conscience: what they now exact and obtain from themselves, they had never exacted before Wagner's time—before then they had been too modest. Another spirit prevails on the stage since Wagner rules there the most difficult things are expected, blame is severe, praise very scarce,—the good and the excellent have become the rule. Taste is no longer necessary, nor even is a good voice. Wagner is sung only with ruined voices: this has a more "dramatic" effect. Even talent is out of the question. Expressiveness at all costs, which is what the Wagnerian ideal—the ideal of decadence—demands, is hardly compatible with talent. All that is required for this is virtue—that is to say, training, automatism, "self-denial". Neither taste, voices, nor gifts, Wagner's stage requires but one thing: Germans!… The definition of a German: an obedient man with long legs…. There is a deep significance in the fact that the rise of Wagner should have coincided with the rise of the "Empire": both phenomena are a proof of one and the same thing—obedience and long legs.—Never have people been more obedient, never have they been so well ordered about. The conductors of Wagnerian orchestras, more particularly, are worthy of an age, which posterity will one day call, with timid awe, the classical age of war.

Wagner understood how to command; in this respect, too, he was a great teacher. He commanded as a man who had exercised an inexorable will over himself—as one who had practised lifelong discipline: Wagner was, perhaps, the greatest example of self-violence in the whole of the history of art (—even Alfieri, who in other respects is his next-of-kin, is outdone by him. The note of a Torinese).

12

This view, that our actors have become more worthy of respect than heretofore, does not imply that I believe them to have become less dangerous…. But who is in any doubt as to what I want,—as to what the three requisitions are concerning which my wrath and my care and love of art, have made me open my mouth on this occasion?

That the stage should not become master of the arts.
That the actor should not become the corrupter of the genuine.
That music should not become an art of lying.

Postscript

The gravity of these last words allows me at this point to introduce a few sentences out of an unprinted essay which will at least leave no doubt as to my earnestness in regard to this question. The title of this essay is: "What Wagner has cost us."

One pays dearly for having been a follower of Wagner. Even to-day a vague feeling that this is so, still prevails. Even Wagner's success, his triumph, did not uproot this feeling thoroughly. But formerly it was strong, it was terrible, it was a gloomy hate throughout almost three-quarters of Wagner's life. The resistance which he met with among us Germans cannot be too highly valued or too highly honoured. People guarded themselves against him as against an illness,—not with arguments—it is impossible to refute an illness,—but with obstruction, with mistrust, with repugnance, with loathing, with sombre earnestness, as though he were a great rampant danger. The æsthetes gave themselves away when out of three schools of German philosophy they waged an absurd war against Wagner's principles with "ifs" and "fors"—what did he care about principles, even his own!—The Germans themselves had enough instinctive good sense to dispense with every "if" and "for" in this matter. An instinct is weakened when it becomes conscious: for by becoming conscious it makes itself feeble. If there were any signs that in spite of the universal character of European decadence there was still a modicum of health, still an instinctive premonition of what is harmful and dangerous, residing in the German soul, then it would be precisely this blunt resistance to Wagner which I should least like to see underrated. It does us honour, it gives us some reason to hope: France no longer has such an amount of health at her disposal. The Germans, these loiterers par excellence, as history shows, are to-day the most backward among the civilised nations of Europe; this has its advantages,—for they are thus relatively the youngest.

One pays dearly for having been a follower of Wagner. It is only quite recently that the Germans have overcome a sort of dread of him,—the desire to be rid of him occurred to them again and again.[12] Does anybody remember a very curious occurrence in which, quite unexpectedly towards the end, this old feeling once more manifested itself? It happened at Wagner's funeral. The first Wagner Society, the one in Munich, laid a wreath on his grave with this inscription, which immediately became famous: "Salvation to the Saviour!" Everybody admired the lofty inspiration which had dictated this inscription, as also the taste which seemed to be the privilege of the followers of Wagner. Many also, however (it was singular enough), made this slight alteration in it: "Salvation from the Saviour"—People began to breathe again—

One pays dearly for having been a follower of Wagner. Let us try to estimate the influence of this worship upon culture. Whom did this movement press to the front? What did it make ever more and more pre-eminent?—In the first place the layman's arrogance, the arrogance of the art-maniac. Now these people are organising societies, they wish to make their taste prevail, they even wish to pose as judges in rebus musicis et musicantibus. Secondly: an ever increasing indifference towards severe, noble and conscientious schooling in the service of art, and in its place the belief in genius, or in plain English, cheeky dilettantism (—the formula for this is to be found in the Mastersingers). Thirdly, and this is the worst of all: Theatrocracy—, the craziness of a belief in the pre-eminence of the theatre, in the right of the theatre to rule supreme over the arts, over Art in general.... But this should be shouted into the face of Wagnerites a hundred times over: that the theatre is something lower than art, something secondary, something coarsened, above all something suitably distorted and falsified for the mob. In this respect Wagner altered nothing: Bayreuth is grand Opera—and not even good opera.... The stage is a form of Demolatry in the realm of taste, the stage is an insurrection of the mob, a plébiscite against good taste.... The case of Wagner proves this fact: he captivated the masses—he depraved taste, he even perverted our taste for opera!—

One pays dearly for having been a follower of Wagner. What has Wagner-worship made out of spirit? Does Wagner liberate the spirit? To him belong that ambiguity and equivocation and all other qualities which can convince the uncertain without making them conscious of why they have been convinced. In this sense Wagner is a seducer on a grand scale. There is nothing exhausted, nothing effete, nothing dangerous to life, nothing that slanders the world in the realm of spirit, which has not secretly found shelter in his art, he conceals the blackest obscurantism in the luminous orbs of the ideal. He flatters every nihilistic (Buddhistic) instinct and togs it out in music; he flatters every form of Christianity, every religious expression of decadence. He that hath ears to hear let him hear: everything that has ever grown out of the soil of impoverished life, the whole counterfeit coinage of the transcendental and of a Beyond found its most sublime advocate in Wagner's art, not in formulæ (Wagner is too clever to use formulæ), but in the persuasion of the senses which in their turn makes the spirit weary and morbid. Music in the form of Circe ... in this respect his last work is his greatest masterpiece. In the art of seduction "Parsifal" will for ever maintain its rank as a stroke of genius.... I admire this work. I would fain have composed it myself. Wagner was never better inspired than towards the end. The subtlety with which beauty and disease are united here, reaches such a height, that it casts so to speak a shadow upon all Wagner's earlier achievements: it seems too bright, too healthy. Do ye understand this? Health and brightness acting like a shadow? Almost like an objection?... To this extent are we already pure fools.... Never was there a greater Master in heavy hieratic perfumes—Never on earth has there been such a connoisseur of paltry infinities, of all that thrills, of extravagant excesses, of all the feminism from out the vocabulary of happiness! My friends, do but drink the philtres of this art! Nowhere will ye find a more pleasant method of enervating your spirit, of forgetting your manliness in the shade of a rosebush.... Ah, this old magician, mightiest of Klingsors; how he wages war against us with his art, against us free spirits! How he appeals to every form of cowardice of the modern soul with his charming girlish notes! There never was such a mortal hatred of knowledge! One must be a very cynic in order to resist seduction here. One must be able to bite in order to resist worshipping at this shrine. Very well, old seducer! The cynic cautions you—cave canem....

One pays dearly for having been a follower of Wagner. I contemplate the youthlets who have long been exposed to his infection. The first relatively innocuous effect of it is the corruption of their taste. Wagner acts like chronic recourse to the bottle. He stultifies, he befouls the stomach. His specific effect: degeneration of the feeling for rhythm. What the Wagnerite calls rhythmical is what I call, to use a Greek metaphor, "stirring a swamp." Much more dangerous than all this, however, is the corruption of ideas. The youthlet becomes a moon-calf, an "idealist". He stands above science, and in this respect he has reached the master's heights. On the other hand, he assumes the airs of a philosopher, he writes for the Bayreuth Journal; he solves all problems in the name of the Father, the Son, and the Holy Master. But the most ghastly thing of all is the deterioration of the nerves. Let any one wander through a large city at night, in all directions he will hear people doing violence to instruments with solemn rage and fury, a wild uproar breaks out at intervals. What is happening? It is the disciples of Wagner in the act of worshipping him.... Bayreuth is another word for a Hydro. A typical telegram from Bayreuth would read bereits bereut (I already repent). Wagner is bad for young men; he is fatal for women. What medically speaking is a female Wagnerite? It seems to me that a doctor could not be too serious in putting this alternative of conscience to young women; either one thing or the other. But they have already made their choice. You cannot serve two Masters when one of these is Wagner. Wagner redeemed woman; and in return woman built Bayreuth for him. Every sacrifice, every surrender: there was nothing that they were not prepared to give him. Woman impoverishes herself in favour of the Master, she becomes quite touching, she stands naked before him. The female Wagnerite, the most attractive equivocality that exists to-day: she is the incarnation of Wagner's cause: his cause triumphs with her as its symbol.... Ah, this old robber! He robs our young men: he even robs our women as well, and drags them to his cell.... Ah, this old Minotaur! What has he not already cost us? Every year processions of the finest young men and maidens are led into his labyrinth that he may swallow them up, every year the whole of Europe cries out "Away to Crete! Away to Crete!"....

Second Postscript

It seems to me that my letter is open to some misunderstanding. On certain faces I see the expression of gratitude; I even hear modest but merry laughter. I prefer to be understood here as in other things. But since a certain animal, the worm of Empire, the famous Rhinoxera, has become lodged in the vineyards of the German spirit, nobody any longer understands a word I say. The Kreus-Zeitung has brought this home to me, not to speak of the Litterarisches Centralblatt. I have given the Germans the deepest books that they have ever possessed—a sufficient reason for their not having understood a word of them.... If in this essay I declare war against Wagner—and incidentally against a certain form of German taste, if I seem to use strong language about the cretinism of Bayreuth, it must not be supposed that I am in the least anxious to glorify any other musician. Other musicians are not to be considered by the side of Wagner. Things are generally bad. Decay is universal. Disease lies at the very root of things. If Wagner's name represents the ruin of music, just as Bernini's stands for the ruin of sculpture, he is not on that account its cause. All he did was to accelerate the fall,—though we are quite prepared to admit that he did it in a way which makes one recoil with horror from this almost instantaneous decline and fall to the depths. He possessed the ingenuousness of decadence: this constituted his superiority. He believed in it. He did not halt before any of its logical consequences. The others hesitated—that is their distinction. They have no other. What is common to both Wagner and "the others" consists in this: the decline of all organising power, the abuse of traditional means, without the capacity or the aim that would justify this. The counterfeit imitation of grand forms, for which nobody nowadays is strong, proud, self-reliant and healthy enough, excessive vitality in small details; passion at all costs; refinement as an expression of impoverished life, ever more nerves in the place of muscle. I know only one musician who to-day would be able to compose an overture as an organic whole: and nobody else knows him.[13] He who is famous now, does not write better music than Wagner, but only less characteristic, less definite music:—less definite, because half measures, even in decadence, cannot stand by the side of completeness. But Wagner was complete, Wagner represented thorough corruption, Wagner has had the courage, the will, and the conviction for corruption. What does Johannes Brahms matter?… It was his good fortune to be misunderstood by Germany; he was taken to be an antagonist of Wagner—people required an antagonist!—But he did not write necessary music, above all he wrote too much music!—When one is not rich one should at least have enough pride to be poor!… The sympathy which here and there was meted out to Brahms, apart from party interests and party misunderstandings, was for a long time a riddle to me, until one day through an accident, almost, I discovered that he affected a particular type of man. He has the melancholy of impotence. His creations are not the result of plenitude, he thirsts after abundance. Apart from what he plagiarises, from what he borrows from ancient or exotically modern styles—he is a master in the art of copying,—there remains as his most individual quality a longing.… And this is what the dissatisfied of all kinds, and all those who yearn, divine in him. He is much too little of a personality, too little of a central figure.… The "impersonal," those who are not self-centred, love him for this. He is especially the musician of a species of dissatisfied women. Fifty steps further on, and we find the female Wagnerite—just as we find Wagner himself fifty paces ahead of Brahms.—The female Wagnerite is a more definite, a more interesting, and above all, a more attractive type. Brahms is touching so long as he dreams or mourns over himself in private—in this respect he is modern;—he becomes cold, we no longer feel at one with him when he poses as the child of the classics.… People like to call Brahms Beethoven's heir: I know of no more cautious euphemism—All that which to-day makes a claim to being the grand style in music is on precisely that account either false to us or false to itself. This alternative is suspicious enough: in itself it contains a casuistic question concerning the value of the two cases. The instinct of the majority protests against the alternative; "false to us"—they do not wish to be cheated;—and I myself would certainly always prefer this type to the other ("False to itself"). This is my taste.—Expressed more clearly for the sake of the "poor in spirit" it amounts to this: Brahms or Wagner.… Brahms is not an actor.—A very great part of other musicians may be summed up in the concept Brahms—I do not wish to say anything about the clever apes of Wagner, as for instance Goldmark: when one has "The Queen of Sheba" to one's name, one belongs to a menagerie,—one ought to put oneself on show.—Nowadays all things that can be done well and even with a master hand are small. In this department alone is honesty still possible. Nothing, however, can cure music as a whole of its chief fault, of its fate, which is to be the expression of general physiological contradiction,—which is, in fact, to be modern.

The best instruction, the most conscientious schooling, the most thorough familiarity, yea, and even isolation, with the Old Masters,—all this only acts as a palliative, or, more strictly speaking, has but an illusory effect, because the first condition of the right thing is no longer in our bodies; whether this first condition be the strong race of a Handel or the overflowing animal spirits of a Rossini. Not everyone has the right to every teacher: and this holds good of whole epochs.—In itself it is not impossible that there are still remains of stronger natures, typical unadapted men, somewhere in Europe: from this quarter the advent of a somewhat belated form of beauty and perfection, even in music, might still be hoped for. But the most that we can expect to see are exceptional cases. From the rule, that corruption is paramount, that corruption is a fatality,—not even a God can save music.

Epilogue

And now let us take breath and withdraw a moment from this narrow world which necessarily must be narrow, because we have to make enquiries relative to the value of persons. A philosopher feels that he wants to wash his hands after he has concerned himself so long with the "Case of Wagner". I shall now give my notion of what is modern. According to the measure of energy of every age, there is also a standard that determines which virtues shall be allowed and which forbidden. The age either has the virtues of ascending life, in which case it resists the virtues of degeneration with all its deepest instincts. Or it is in itself an age of degeneration, in which case it requires the virtues of declining life,—in which case it hates everything that justifies itself, solely as being the outcome of a plenitude, or a superabundance of strength. Æsthetic is inextricably bound up with these biological principles: there is decadent æsthetic, and classical æsthetic,—"beauty in itself" is just as much a chimera as any other kind of idealism.—Within the narrow sphere of the so-called moral values, no greater antithesis could be found than that of master-morality and the morality of Christian valuations: the latter having grown out of a thoroughly morbid soil. (—The gospels present us with the same physiological types, as do the novels of Dostoiewsky), the master-morality ("Roman," "pagan," "classical," "Renaissance"), on the other hand, being the symbolic speech of well-constitutedness, of ascending life, and of the Will to Power as a vital principle. Master-morality affirms just as instinctively as Christian morality denies ("God," "Beyond," "self-denial,"—all of them negations). The first reflects its plenitude upon things,—it transfigures, it embellishes, it rationalises the world,—the latter impoverishes, bleaches, mars the value of things; it suppresses the world. "World" is a Christian term of abuse. These antithetical forms in the optics of values, are both necessary: they are different points of view which cannot be circumvented either with arguments or counter-arguments. One cannot refute Christianity: it is impossible to refute a diseased eyesight. That people should have combated pessimism as if it had been a philosophy, was the very acme of learned stupidity. The concepts "true" and "untrue" do not seem to me to have any sense in optics.—That, alone, which has to be guarded against is the falsity, the instinctive duplicity which would fain regard this antithesis as no antithesis at all: just as Wagner did,—and his mastery in this kind of falseness was of no mean order. To cast side-long glances at master-morality, at noble morality (—Icelandic saga is perhaps the greatest documentary evidence of these values), and at the same time to have the opposite teaching, the "gospel of the lowly," the doctrine of the need of salvation, on one's lips!... Incidentally, I admire the modesty of Christians who go to Bayreuth. As for myself, I could not endure to hear the sound of certain words on Wagner's lips. There are some concepts which are too good for Bayreuth ... What? Christianity adjusted for female Wagnerites, perhaps by female Wagnerites—for, in his latter days Wagner was thoroughly feminini generis—? Again I say, the Christians of to-day are too modest for me.... If Wagner were a Christian, then Liszt was perhaps a Father of the Church!—The need of salvation, the quintessence of all Christian needs, has nothing in common with such clowns; it is the most straightforward expression of decadence, it is the most convincing and most painful affirmation of decadence, in sublime symbols and practices. The Christian wishes to be rid of himself. Le moi est toujours haissable. Noble morality, master-morality, on the other hand, is rooted in a triumphant saying of yea to one's self,—it is the self-affirmation and self-glorification of life; it also requires sublime symbols and practices; but only "because its heart is too full." The whole of beautiful art and of great art belongs here; their common essence is gratitude. But we must allow it a certain instinctive repugnance to décadents, and a scorn and horror of the latter's symbolism: such things almost prove it. The noble Romans considered Christianity as a fœda superstitio: let me call to your minds the feelings which the last German of noble taste—Goethe—had in regard to the cross. It is idle to look for more valuable, more necessary contrasts.[14]

But the kind of falsity which is characteristic of the Bayreuthians is not exceptional to-day. We all know the hybrid concept of the Christian gentleman. This innocence in contradiction, this "clean conscience" in falsehood, is rather modern par excellence, with it modernity is almost defined. Biologically, modern man represents a contradiction of values, he sits between two stools, he says yea and nay in one breath. No wonder that it is precisely in our age that falseness itself became flesh and blood, and even genius! No wonder Wagner dwelt amongst us! It was not without reason that I called Wagner the Cagliostro of modernity.... But all of us, though we do not know it, involuntarily have values, words, formulæ, and morals in our bodies, which are quite antagonistic in their origin—regarded from a physiological standpoint, we are false.... How would a diagnosis of the modern soul begin? With a determined incision into this agglomeration of contradictory instincts, with the total suppression of its antagonistic values, with vivisection applied to its most instructive case. To philosophers the "Case of Wagner" is a windfall—this essay, as you observe, was inspired by gratitude.

Nietzsche Contra Wagner
THE BRIEF OF A PSYCHOLOGIST

Preface

The following chapters have been selected from past works of mine, and not without care. Some of them date back as far as 1877. Here and there, of course, they will be found to have been made a little more intelligible, but above all, more brief. Read consecutively, they can leave no one in any doubt, either concerning myself, or concerning Wagner: we are antipodes. The reader will come to other conclusions, too, in his perusal of these pages: for instance, that this is an essay for psychologists and not for Germans.... I have my readers everywhere, in Vienna, St Petersburg, Copenhagen, Stockholm, Paris, and New York—but I have none in Europe's Flat-land—Germany.... And I might even have something to say to Italians whom I love just as much as I ... Quousque tandem, Crispi ... Triple alliance: a people can only conclude a mésalliance with the "Empire."...

Friedrich Nietzsche.

Turin, Christmas 1888.

Wherein I Admire Wagner

I believe that artists very often do not know what they are best able to do. They are much too vain. Their minds are directed to something prouder than merely to appear like little plants, which, with freshness, rareness, and beauty, know how to sprout from their soil with real perfection. The ultimate goodness of their own garden and vineyard is superciliously under-estimated by them, and their love and their insight are not of the same quality. Here is a musician who is a greater master than anyone else in the discovering of tones, peculiar to suffering, oppressed, and tormented souls, who can endow even dumb misery with speech. Nobody can approach him in the colours of late autumn, in the indescribably touching joy of a last, a very last, and all too short gladness; he knows of a chord which expresses those secret and weird midnight hours of the soul, when cause and effect seem to have fallen asunder, and at every moment something may spring out of nonentity. He is happiest of all when creating from out the nethermost depths of human happiness, and, so to speak, from out man's empty bumper, in which the bitterest and most repulsive drops have mingled with the sweetest for good or evil at last. He knows that weary shuffling along of the soul which is no longer able either to spring or to fly, nay, which is no longer able to walk, he has the modest glance of concealed suffering, of understanding without comfort, of leave-taking without word or sign; verily as the Orpheus of all secret misery he is greater than anyone, and many a thing was introduced into art for the first time by him, which hitherto had not been given expression, had not even been thought worthy of art—the cynical revolts, for instance, of which only the greatest sufferer is capable, also many a small and quite microscopical feature of the soul, as it were the scales of its amphibious nature—yes indeed, he is the master of everything very small. But this he refuses to be! His tastes are much more in love with vast walls and with daring frescoes!... He does not see that his spirit has another desire and bent—a totally different outlook—that it prefers to squat peacefully in the corners of broken-down houses: concealed in this way, and hidden even from himself, he paints his really great masterpieces, all of which are very short, often only one bar in length—there, only, does he become quite good, great and perfect, perhaps there alone.—Wagner is one who has suffered much—and this elevates him above other musicians.—I admire Wagner wherever he sets himself to music—

Wherein I Raise Objections

With all this I do not wish to imply that I regard this music as healthy, and least of all in those places where it speaks of Wagner himself. My objections to Wagner's music are physiological objections. Why should I therefore begin by clothing them in æsthetic formulæ? Æsthetic is indeed nothing more than applied physiology—The fact I bring forward, my "petit fait vrai," is that I can no longer breathe with ease when this music begins to have its effect upon me; that my foot immediately begins to feel indignant at it and rebels: for what it needs is time, dance, march; even the young German Kaiser could not march to Wagner's Imperial March,—what my foot demands in the first place from music is that ecstasy which lies in good walking, stepping and dancing. But do not my stomach, my heart, my circulation also protest? Are not my intestines also troubled? And do I not become hoarse unawares? … in order to listen to Wagner I require Géraudel's Pastilles.… And then I ask myself, what is it that my whole body must have from music in general? for there is no such thing as a soul.… I believe it must have relief: as if all animal functions were accelerated by means of light, bold, unfettered, self-reliant rhythms, as if brazen and leaden life could lose its weight by means of delicate and smooth melodies. My melancholy would fain rest its head in the haunts and abysses of perfection; for this reason I need music. But Wagner makes one ill—What do I care about the theatre? What do I care about the spasms of its moral ecstasies in which the mob—and who is not the mob to-day?—rejoices? What do I care about the whole pantomimic hocus-pocus of the actor? You are beginning to see that I am essentially anti-theatrical at heart. For the stage, this mob art par excellence, my soul has that deepest scorn felt by every artist to-day. With a stage success a man sinks to such an extent in my esteem as to drop out of sight; failure in this quarter makes me prick my ears, makes me begin to pay attention. But this was not so with Wagner, next to the Wagner who created the most unique music that has ever existed there was the Wagner who was essentially a man of the stage, an actor, the most enthusiastic mimomaniac that has perhaps existed on earth, even as a musician. And let it be said en passant that if Wagner's theory was "drama is the object, music is only a means"—his practice was from beginning to end "the attitude is the end, drama and even music can never be anything else than means." Music as the manner of accentuating, of strengthening, and deepening dramatic poses and all things which please the senses of the actor; and Wagnerian drama only an opportunity for a host of interesting attitudes!—Alongside of all other instincts he had the dictatorial instinct of a great actor in everything and, as I have already said, as a musician also.—On one occasion, and not without trouble, I made this clear to a Wagnerite pur sang,—clearness and a Wagnerite! I won't say another word. There were reasons for adding; "For heaven's sake, be a little more true unto yourself! We are not in Bayreuth now. In Bayreuth people are only upright in the mass; the individual lies, he even lies to himself. One leaves oneself at home when one goes to Bayreuth, one gives up all right to one's own tongue and choice, to one's own taste and even to one's own courage, one knows these things no longer as one is wont to have them and practise them before God and the world and between one's own four walls. In the theatre no one brings the finest senses of his art with him, and least of all the artist who works for the theatre,—for here loneliness is lacking; everything perfect does not suffer a witness.… In the theatre one becomes mob, herd, woman, Pharisee, electing cattle, patron, idiot—Wagnerite: there, the most personal conscience is bound to submit to the levelling charm of the great multitude, there the neighbour rules, there one becomes a neighbour."

Wagner As À Danger

1

The aim after which more modern music is striving, which is now given the strong but obscure name of "unending melody," can be clearly understood by comparing it to one's feelings on entering the sea. Gradually one loses one's footing and one ultimately abandons oneself to the mercy or fury of the elements: one has to swim. In the solemn, or fiery, swinging movement, first slow and then quick, of old music—one had to do something quite different; one had to dance. The measure which was required for this and the control of certain balanced degrees of time and energy, forced the soul of the listener to continual sobriety of thought.—Upon the counterplay of the cooler currents of air which came from this sobriety, and from the warmer breath of enthusiasm, the charm of all good music rested—Richard Wagner wanted another kind of movement,—he overthrew the physiological first principle of all music before his time. It was no longer a matter of walking or dancing,—we must swim, we must hover.… This perhaps decides the whole matter. "Unending melody" really wants to break all the symmetry of time and strength; it actually scorns these things—Its wealth of invention resides precisely in what to an older ear sounds like rhythmic paradox and abuse. From the imitation or the prevalence of such a taste there would arise a danger for music—so great that we can imagine none greater—the complete degeneration of the feeling for rhythm, chaos in the place of rhythm.... The danger reaches its climax when such music cleaves ever more closely to naturalistic play-acting and pantomime, which governed by no laws of form, aim at effect and nothing more.... Expressiveness at all costs and music a servant, a slave to attitudes—this is the end....

2

What? would it really be the first virtue of a performance (as performing musical artists now seem to believe), under all circumstances to attain to a haut-relief which cannot be surpassed? If this were applied to Mozart, for instance, would it not be a real sin against Mozart's spirit,—Mozart's cheerful, enthusiastic, delightful and loving spirit? He who fortunately was no German, and whose seriousness is a charming and golden seriousness and not by any means that of a German clodhopper.... Not to speak of the earnestness of the "marble statue".... But you seem to think that all music is the music of the "marble statue"?—that all music should, so to speak, spring out of the wall and shake the listener to his very bowels?... Only thus could music have any effect! But on whom would the effect be made? Upon something on which a noble artist ought never to deign to act,—upon the mob, upon the immature! upon the blasés! upon the diseased! upon idiots! upon Wagnerites!...

A Music Without A Future

Of all the arts which succeed in growing on the soil of a particular culture, music is the last plant to appear; maybe because it is the one most dependent upon our innermost feelings, and therefore the last to come to the surface—at a time when the culture to which it belongs is in its autumn season and beginning to fade. It was only in the art of the Dutch masters that the spirit of mediæval Christianity found its expression—, its architecture of sound is the youngest, but genuine and legitimate, sister of the Gothic. It was only in Handel's music that the best in Luther and in those like him found its voice, the Judeo-heroic trait which gave the Reformation a touch of greatness-the Old Testament, not the New, become music. It was left to Mozart, to pour out the epoch of Louis XIV., and of the art of Racine and Claude Lorrain, in ringing gold; only in Beethoven's and Rossini's music did the Eighteenth Century sing itself out—the century of enthusiasm, broken ideals, and fleeting joy. All real and original music is a swan song—Even our last form of music, despite its prevalence and its will to prevail, has perhaps only a short time to live, for it sprouted from a soil which was in the throes of a rapid subsidence,—of a culture which will soon be submerged. A certain catholicism of feeling, and a predilection for some ancient indigenous (so-called national) ideals and eccentricities, was its first condition. Wagner's appropriation of old sagas and songs, in which scholarly prejudice taught us to see something German par excellence—now we laugh at it all, the resurrection of these Scandinavian monsters with a thirst for ecstatic sensuality and spiritualisation—the whole of this taking and giving on Wagner's part, in the matter of subjects, characters, passions, and nerves, would also give unmistakable expression to the spirit of his music provided that this music, like any other, did not know how to speak about itself save ambiguously: for musica is a woman.... We must not let ourselves be misled concerning this state of things, by the fact that at this very moment we are living in a reaction, in the heart itself of a reaction. The age of international wars, of ultramontane martyrdom, in fact, the whole interlude-character which typifies the present condition of Europe, may indeed help an art like Wagner's to sudden glory, without, however, in the least ensuring its future prosperity. The Germans themselves have no future....

We Antipodes

Perhaps a few people, or at least my friends, will remember that I made my first plunge into life armed with some errors and some exaggerations, but that, in any case, I began with hope in my heart. In the philosophical pessimism of the nineteenth century, I recognised—who knows by what by-paths of personal experience—the symptom of a higher power of thought, a more triumphant plenitude of life, than had manifested itself hitherto in the philosophies of Hume, Kant and Hegel!—I regarded tragic knowledge as the most beautiful luxury of our culture, as its most precious, most noble, most dangerous kind of prodigality; but, nevertheless, in view of its overflowing wealth, as a justifiable luxury. In the same way, I began by interpreting Wagner's music as the expression of a Dionysian powerfulness of soul. In it I thought I heard the earthquake by means of which a primeval life-force, which had been constrained for ages, was seeking at last to burst its bonds, quite indifferent to how much of that which nowadays calls itself culture, would thereby be shaken to ruins. You see how I misinterpreted, you see also, what I bestowed upon Wagner and Schopenhauer—myself.... Every art and every philosophy may be regarded either as a cure or as a stimulant to ascending or declining life: they always presuppose suffering and sufferers. But there are two kinds of sufferers:—those that suffer from overflowing vitality, who need Dionysian art and require a tragic insight into, and a tragic outlook upon, the phenomenon life,—and there are those who suffer from reduced vitality, and who crave for repose, quietness, calm seas, or else the intoxication, the spasm, the bewilderment which art and philosophy provide. Revenge upon life itself—this is the most voluptuous form of intoxication for such indigent souls!... Now Wagner responds quite as well as Schopenhauer to the twofold cravings of these people,—they both deny life, they both slander it but precisely on this account they are my antipodes.—The richest creature, brimming over with vitality,—the Dionysian God and man, may not only allow himself to gaze upon the horrible and the questionable; but he can also lend his hand to the terrible deed, and can indulge in all the luxury of destruction, disaggregation, and negation,—in him evil, purposelessness and ugliness, seem just as allowable as they are in nature—because of his bursting plenitude of creative and rejuvenating powers, which are able to convert every desert into a luxurious land of plenty. Conversely, it is the greatest sufferer and pauper in vitality, who is most in need of mildness, peace and goodness—that which to-day is called humaneness—in thought as well as in action, and possibly of a God whose speciality is to be a God of the sick, a Saviour, and also of logic or the abstract intelligibility of existence even for idiots (—the typical "free-spirits," like the idealists, and "beautiful souls," are décadents—); in short, of a warm, danger-tight, and narrow confinement, between optimistic horizons which would allow of stultification.... And thus very gradually, I began to understand Epicurus, the opposite of a Dionysian Greek, and also the Christian who in fact is only a kind of Epicurean, and who, with his belief that "faith saves," carries the principle of Hedonism as far as possible—far beyond all intellectual honesty.... If I am ahead of all other psychologists in anything, it is in this fact that my eyes are more keen for tracing those most difficult and most captious of all deductions, in which the largest number of mistakes have been made,—the deduction which makes one infer something concerning the author from his work, something concerning the doer from his deed, something concerning the idealist from the need which produced this ideal, and something concerning the imperious craving which stands at the back of all thinking and valuing—In regard to all artists of what kind soever, I shall now avail myself of this radical distinction: does the creative power in this case arise from a loathing of life, or from an excessive plenitude of life? In Goethe, for instance, an overflow of vitality was creative, in Flaubert—hate: Flaubert, a new edition of Pascal, but as an artist with this instinctive belief at heart: "Flaubert est toujours haissable, l'homme n'est rien, l'œuvre est tout".... He tortured himself when he wrote, just as Pascal tortured himself when he thought—the feelings of both were inclined to be "non-egoistic." ... "Disinterestedness"—principle of decadence, the will to nonentity in art as well as in morality.

Where Wagner Is At Home

Even at the present day, France is still the refuge of the most intellectual and refined culture in Europe, it remains the high school of taste: but one must know where to find this France of taste. The North-German Gazette, for instance, or whoever expresses his sentiments in that paper, thinks that the French are "barbarians,"—as for me, if I had to find the blackest spot on earth, where slaves still required to be liberated, I should turn in the direction of Northern Germany.... But those who form part of that select France take very good care to conceal themselves; they are a small body of men, and there may be some among them who do not stand on very firm legs—a few may be fatalists, hypochondriacs, invalids; others may be enervated, and artificial,—such are those who would fain be artistic,—but all the loftiness and delicacy which still remains to this world, is in their possession. In this France of intellect, which is also the France of pessimism, Schopenhauer is already much more at home than he ever was in Germany, his principal work has already been translated twice, and the second time so excellently that now I prefer to read Schopenhauer in French (—he was an accident among Germans, just as I am—the Germans have no fingers wherewith to grasp us; they haven't any fingers at all,—but only claws). And I do not mention Heine—l'adorable Heine, as they say in Paris—who long since has passed into the flesh and blood of the more profound and more soulful of French lyricists. How could the horned cattle of Germany know how to deal with the délicatesses of such a nature!—And as to Richard Wagner, it is obvious, it is even glaringly obvious, that Paris is the very soil for him, the more French music adapts itself to the needs of l'âme moderne, the more Wagnerian it will become,—it is far enough advanced in this direction already.—In this respect one should not allow one's self to be misled by Wagner himself—it was simply disgraceful on Wagner's part to scoff at Paris, as he did, in its agony in 1871.... In spite of it all, in Germany Wagner is only a misapprehension.—who could be more incapable of understanding anything about Wagner than the Kaiser, for instance?—To everybody familiar with the movement of European culture, this fact, however, is certain, that French romanticism and Richard Wagner are most intimately related. All dominated by literature, up to their very eyes and ears—the first European artists with a universal literary culture,—most of them writers, poets, mediators and minglers of the senses and the arts, all fanatics in expression, great discoverers in the realm of the sublime as also of the ugly and the gruesome, and still greater discoverers in passion, in working for effect, in the art of dressing their windows,—all possessing talent far above their genius,—virtuosos to their backbone, knowing of secret passages to all that seduces, lures, constrains or overthrows; born enemies of logic and of straight lines, thirsting after the exotic, the strange and the monstrous, and all opiates for the senses and the understanding. On the whole, a daring dare-devil, magnificently violent, soaring and high-springing crew of artists, who first had to teach their own century—it is the century of the mob—what the concept "artist" meant. But they were ill....

Wagner As The Apostle Of Chastity

1

Is this the German way? Comes this low bleating forth from German hearts? Should Teutons, sin repenting, lash themselves, Or spread their palms with priestly unctuousness, Exalt their feelings with the censer's fumes, And cower and quake and bend the trembling knee, And with a sickly sweetness plead a prayer? Then ogle nuns, and ring the Ave-bell, And thus with morbid fervour out-do heaven? Is this the German way? Beware, yet are you free, yet your own Lords. What yonder lures is Rome, Rome's faith sung without words.

2

There is no necessary contrast between sensuality and chastity, every good marriage, every genuine love affair is above this contrast; but in those cases where the contrast exists, it is very far from being necessarily a tragic one. This, at least, ought to hold good of all well-constituted and good-spirited mortals, who are not in the least inclined to reckon their unstable equilibrium between angel and petite bête, without further ado, among the objections to existence, the more refined and more intelligent like Hafis and Goethe, even regarded it as an additional attraction. It is precisely contradictions of this kind which lure us to life.... On the other hand, it must be obvious, that when Circe's unfortunate animals are induced to worship chastity, all they see and worship therein, is their opposite—oh! and with what tragic groaning and fervour, may well be imagined—that same painful and thoroughly superfluous opposition which, towards the end of his life, Richard Wagner undoubtedly wished to set to music and to put on the stage, And to what purpose? we may reasonably ask.

3

And yet this other question can certainly not be circumvented: what business had he actually with that manly (alas! so unmanly) "bucolic simplicity," that poor devil and son of nature—Parsifal, whom he ultimately makes a catholic by such insidious means—what?—was Wagner in earnest with Parsifal? For, that he was laughed at, I cannot deny, any more than Gottfried Keller can.... We should like to believe that "Parsifal" was meant as a piece of idle gaiety, as the closing act and satyric drama, with which Wagner the tragedian wished to take leave of us, of himself, and above all of tragedy, in a way which befitted him and his dignity, that is to say, with an extravagant, lofty and most malicious parody of tragedy itself, of all the past and terrible earnestness and sorrow of this world, of the most ridiculous form of the unnaturalness of the ascetic ideal, at last overcome. For Parsifal is the subject par excellence for a comic opera.... Is Wagner's "Parsifal" his secret laugh of superiority at himself, the triumph of his last and most exalted state of artistic freedom, of artistic transcendence—is it Wagner able to laugh at himself? Once again we only wish it were so; for what could Parsifal be if he were meant seriously? Is it necessary in his case to say (as I have heard people say) that "Parsifal" is "the product of the mad hatred of knowledge, intellect, and sensuality?" a curse upon the senses and the mind in one breath and in one fit of hatred? an act of apostasy and a return to Christianly sick and obscurantist ideals? And finally even a denial of self, a deletion of self, on the part of an artist who theretofore had worked with all the power of his will in favour of the opposite cause, the spiritualisation and sensualisation of his art? And not only of his art, but also of his life? Let us remember how enthusiastically Wagner at one time walked in the footsteps of the philosopher Feuerbach. Feuerbach's words "healthy sensuality" struck

Wagner in the thirties and forties very much as they struck many other Germans—they called themselves the young Germans—that is to say, as words of salvation. Did he ultimately change his mind on this point? It would seem that he had at least had the desire of changing his doctrine towards the end.... Had the hatred of life become dominant in him as in Flaubert? For "Parsifal" is a work of rancour, of revenge, of the most secret concoction of poisons with which to make an end of the first conditions of life, it is a bad work. The preaching of chastity remains an incitement to unnaturalness: I despise anybody who does not regard "Parsifal" as an outrage upon morality.—

How I Got Rid Of Wagner

1

Already in the summer of 1876, when the first festival at Bayreuth was at its height, I took leave of Wagner in my soul. I cannot endure anything double-faced. Since Wagner had returned to Germany, he had condescended step by step to everything that I despise—even to anti-Semitism.... As a matter of fact, it was then high time to bid him farewell: but the proof of this came only too soon. Richard Wagner, ostensibly the most triumphant creature alive; as a matter of fact, though, a cranky and desperate décadent, suddenly fell helpless and broken on his knees before the Christian cross.... Was there no German at that time who had the eyes to see, and the sympathy in his soul to feel, the ghastly nature of this spectacle? Was I the only one who suffered from it?—Enough, the unexpected event, like a flash of lightning, made me see only too clearly what kind of a place it was that I had just left,—and it also made me shudder as a man shudders who unawares has just escaped a great danger. As I continued my journey alone, I trembled. Not long after this I was ill, more than ill—I was tired;—tired of the continual disappointments over everything which remained for us modern men to be enthusiastic about, of the energy, industry, hope, youth, and love that are squandered everywhere; tired out of loathing for the whole world of idealistic lying and conscience-softening, which, once again, in the case of Wagner, had scored a victory over a man who was of the bravest; and last but not least, tired by the sadness of a ruthless suspicion—that I was now condemned to be ever more and more suspicious, ever more and more contemptuous, ever more and more deeply alone than I had been theretofore. For I had no one save Richard Wagner.... I was always condemned to the society of Germans....

2

Henceforward alone and cruelly distrustful of myself, I then took up sides—not without anger—against myself and for all that which hurt me and fell hard upon me; and thus I found the road to that courageous pessimism which is the opposite of all idealistic falsehood, and which, as it seems to me, is also the road to me—to my mission.... That hidden and dominating thing, for which for long ages we have had no name, until ultimately it comes forth as our mission,—this tyrant in us wreaks a terrible revenge upon us for every attempt we make either to evade him or to escape him, for every one of our experiments in the way of befriending people to whom we do not belong, for every active occupation, however estimable, which may make us diverge from our principal object:—aye, and even for every virtue which would fain protect us from the rigour of our most intimate sense of responsibility. Illness is always the answer, whenever we venture to doubt our right to our mission, whenever we begin to make things too easy for ourselves. Curious and terrible at the same time! It is for our relaxation that we have to pay most dearly! And should we wish after all to return to health, we then have no choice: we are compelled to burden ourselves more heavily than we had been burdened before....

The Psychologist Speaks

1

The oftener a psychologist—a born, an unavoidable psychologist and soul-diviner—turns his attention to the more select cases and individuals, the greater becomes his danger of being suffocated by sympathy: he needs greater hardness and cheerfulness than any other man. For the corruption, the ruination of higher men, is in fact the rule: it is terrible to have such a rule always before our eyes. The manifold torments of the psychologist who has discovered this ruination, who discovers once, and then discovers almost repeatedly throughout all history, this universal inner "hopelessness" of higher men, this eternal "too late!" in every sense—may perhaps one day be the cause of his "going to the dogs" himself. In almost every psychologist we may see a tell-tale predilection in favour of intercourse with commonplace and well-ordered men: and this betrays how constantly he requires healing, that he needs a sort of flight and forgetfulness, away from what his insight and incisiveness—from what his "business"—has laid upon his conscience. A horror of his memory is typical of him. He is easily silenced by the judgment of others, he hears with unmoved countenance how people honour, admire, love, and glorify, where he has opened his eyes and seen—or he even conceals his silence by expressly agreeing with some obvious opinion. Perhaps the paradox of his situation becomes so dreadful that, precisely where he has learnt great sympathy, together with great contempt, the educated have on their part learnt great reverence. And who knows but in all great instances, just this alone happened: that the multitude worshipped a God, and that the "God" was only a poor sacrificial animal! Success has always been the greatest liar—and the "work" itself, the deed, is a success too; the great statesman, the conqueror, the discoverer, are disguised in their creations until they can no longer be recognised, the "work" of the artist, of the philosopher, only invents him who has created it, who is reputed to have created it, the "great men," as they are reverenced, are poor little fictions composed afterwards; in the world of historical values counterfeit coinage prevails.

2

Those great poets, for example, such as Byron, Musset, Poe, Leopardi, Kleist, Gogol (I do not dare to mention much greater names, but I imply them), as they now appear, and were perhaps obliged to be: men of the moment, sensuous, absurd, versatile, light-minded and quick to trust and to distrust, with souls in which usually some flaw has to be concealed, often taking revenge with their works for an internal blemish, often seeking forgetfulness in their soaring from a too accurate memory, idealists out of proximity to the mud:—what a torment these great artists are and the so-called higher men in general, to him who has once found them out! We are all special pleaders in the cause of mediocrity. It is conceivable that it is just from woman—who is clairvoyant in the world of suffering, and, alas! also unfortunately eager to help and save to an extent far beyond her powers—that they have learnt so readily those outbreaks of boundless sympathy which the multitude, above all the reverent multitude, overwhelms with prying and self-gratifying interpretations. This sympathising invariably deceives itself as to its power; woman would like to believe that love can do everything—it is the superstition peculiar to her. Alas, he who knows the heart finds out how poor, helpless, pretentious, and blundering even the best and deepest love is—how much more readily it destroys than saves....

3

The intellectual loathing and haughtiness of every man who has suffered deeply—the extent to which a man can suffer, almost determines the order of rank—the chilling uncertainty with which he is thoroughly imbued and coloured, that by virtue of his suffering he knows more than the shrewdest and wisest can ever know, that he has been familiar with, and "at home" in many distant terrible worlds of which "you know nothing!"—this silent intellectual haughtiness, this pride of the elect of knowledge, of the "initiated," of the almost sacrificed, finds all forms of disguise necessary to protect itself from contact with gushing and sympathising hands, and in general from all that is not its equal in suffering. Profound suffering makes noble; it separates.—One of the most refined forms of disguise is Epicurism, along with a certain ostentatious boldness of taste which takes suffering lightly, and puts itself on the defensive against all that is sorrowful and profound. There are "cheerful men" who make use of good spirits, because they are misunderstood on account of them—they wish to be misunderstood. There are "scientific minds" who make use of science, because it gives a cheerful appearance, and because love of science leads people to conclude that a person is shallow—they wish to mislead to a false conclusion. There are free insolent spirits which would fain conceal and deny that they are at bottom broken, incurable hearts—this is Hamlet's case: and then folly itself can be the mask of an unfortunate and alas! all too dead-certain knowledge.

Epilogue

1

I have often asked myself whether I am not much more deeply indebted to the hardest years of my life than to any others. According to the voice of my innermost nature, everything necessary, seen from above and in the light of a superior economy, is also useful in itself—not only should one bear it, one should love it.... Amor fati: this is the very core of my being—And as to my prolonged illness, do I not owe much more to it than I owe to my health? To it I owe a higher kind of health, a sort of health which grows stronger under everything that does not actually kill it!—To it, I owe even my philosophy.... Only great suffering is the ultimate emancipator of spirit, for it teaches one that vast suspiciousness which makes an X out of every U, a genuine and proper X, i.e., the antepenultimate letter. Only great suffering; that great suffering, under which we seem to be over a fire of greenwood, the suffering that takes its time—forces us philosophers to descend into our nethermost depths, and to let go of all trustfulness, all good-nature, all whittling-down, all mildness, all mediocrity,—on which things we had formerly staked our humanity. I doubt whether such suffering improves a man; but I know that it makes him deeper.... Supposing we learn to set our pride, our scorn, our strength of will against it, and thus resemble the Indian who, however cruelly he may be tortured, considers himself revenged on his tormentor by the bitterness of his own tongue. Supposing we withdraw from pain into nonentity, into the deaf, dumb, and rigid sphere of self-surrender, self-forgetfulness, self-effacement: one is another person when one leaves these protracted and dangerous exercises in the art of self-mastery, one has one note of interrogation the more, and above all one has the will henceforward to ask more, deeper, sterner, harder, more wicked, and more silent questions, than anyone has ever asked on earth before.... Trust in life has vanished; life itself has become a problem.—But let no one think that one has therefore become a spirit of gloom or a blind owl! Even love of life is still possible,—but it is a different kind of love.... It is the love for a woman whom we doubt....

2

The rarest of all things is this: to have after all another taste—a second taste. Out of such abysses, out of the abyss of great suspicion as well, a man returns as though born again, he has a new skin, he is more susceptible, more full of wickedness; he has a finer taste for joyfulness; he has a more sensitive tongue for all good things; his senses are more cheerful; he has acquired a second, more dangerous, innocence in gladness; he is more childish too, and a hundred times more cunning than ever he had been before.

Oh, how much more repulsive pleasure now is to him, that coarse, heavy, buff-coloured pleasure, which is understood by our pleasure-seekers, our "cultured people," our wealthy folk and our rulers! With how much more irony we now listen to the hubbub as of a country fair, with which the "cultured" man and the man about town allow themselves to be forced through art, literature, music, and with the help of intoxicating liquor, to "intellectual enjoyments." How the stage-cry of passion now stings our ears; how strange to our taste the whole romantic riot and sensuous bustle, which the cultured mob are so fond of, together with its aspirations to the sublime, to the exalted and the distorted, have become. No: if we convalescents require an art at all, it is another art—-a mocking, nimble, volatile, divinely undisturbed, divinely artificial art, which blazes up like pure flame into a cloudless sky! But above all, an art for artists, only for artists! We are, after all, more conversant with that which is in the highest degree necessary—cheerfulness, every kind of cheerfulness, my friends!... We men of knowledge, now know something only too well: oh how well we have learnt by this time, to forget, not to know, as artists!... As to our future: we shall scarcely be found on the track of those Egyptian youths who break into temples at night, who embrace statues, and would fain unveil, strip, and set in broad daylight, everything which there are excellent reasons to keep concealed.[15] No, we are disgusted with this bad taste, this will to truth, this search after truth "at all costs;" this madness of adolescence, "the love of truth;" we are now too experienced, too serious, too joyful, too scorched, too profound for that.... We no longer believe that truth remains truth when it is unveiled,—we have lived enough to understand this.... To-day it seems to us good form not to strip everything naked, not to be present at all things, not to desire to "know" all. "Tout comprendre c'est tout mépriser."... "Is it true," a little girl once asked her mother, "that the beloved Father is everywhere?—I think it quite improper,"—a hint to philosophers.... The shame with which Nature has concealed herself behind riddles and enigmas should be held in higher esteem. Perhaps truth is a woman who has reasons for not revealing her reasons?... Perhaps her name, to use a Greek word is Baubo?—Oh these Greeks, they understood the art of living! For this it is needful to halt bravely at the surface, at the fold, at the skin, to worship appearance, and to believe in forms, tones, words, and the whole Olympus of appearance! These Greeks were superficial—from profundity.... And are we not returning to precisely the same thing, we dare-devils of intellect who have scaled the highest and most dangerous pinnacles of present thought, in order to look around us from that height, in order to look down from that height? Are we not precisely in this respect—Greeks? Worshippers of form, of tones, of words? Precisely on that account—artists?

SELECTED APHORISMS FROM NIETZSCHE'S RETROSPECT OF HIS YEARS OF FRIENDSHIP WITH WAGNER.

(Summer 1878.)

1. My blunder was this, I travelled to Bayreuth with an ideal in my breast, and was thus doomed to experience the bitterest disappointment. The preponderance of ugliness, grotesqueness and strong pepper thoroughly repelled me.

2. I utterly disagree with those who were dissatisfied with the decorations, the scenery and the mechanical contrivances at Bayreuth. Far too much industry and ingenuity was applied to the task of chaining the imagination to matters which did not belie their epic origin. But as to the naturalism of the attitudes, of the singing, compared with the orchestra!! What affected, artificial and depraved tones, what a distortion of nature, were we made to hear!

3. We are witnessing the death agony of the last Art: Bayreuth has convinced me of this.

4. My picture of Wagner, completely surpassed him; I had depicted an ideal monster—one, however, which is perhaps quite capable of kindling the enthusiasm of artists. The real Wagner, Bayreuth as it actually is, was only like a bad, final proof, pulled on inferior paper from the engraving which was my creation. My longing to see real men and their motives, received an extraordinary impetus from this humiliating experience.

5. This, to my sorrow, is what I realised; a good deal even struck me with sudden fear. At last I felt, however, that if only I could be strong enough to take sides against myself and what I most loved I would find the road to truth and get solace and encouragement from it—and in this way I became filled with a sensation of joy far greater than that upon which I was now voluntarily turning my back.

6. I was in love with art, passionately in love, and in the whole of existence saw nothing else than art—and this at an age when, reasonably enough, quite different passions usually possess the soul.

7. Goethe said: "The yearning spirit within me, which in earlier years I may perhaps have fostered too earnestly, and which as I grew older I tried my utmost to combat, did not seem becoming in the man, and I therefore had to strive to attain to more complete freedom." Conclusion?—I have had to do the same.

8. He who wakes us always wounds us.

9. I do not possess the talent of being loyal, and what is still worse, I have not even the vanity to try to appear as if I did.

10. He who accomplishes anything that lies beyond the vision and the experience of his acquaintances,—provokes envy and hatred masked as pity,—prejudice regards the work as decadence, disease, seduction. Long faces.

11. I frankly confess that I had hoped that by means of art the Germans would become thoroughly disgusted with decaying Christianity—I regarded German mythology as a solvent, as a means of accustoming people to polytheism.

What a fright I had over the Catholic revival!!

12. It is possible neither to suffer sufficiently acutely from life, nor to be so lifeless and emotionally weak, as to have need of Wagner's art, as to require it as a medium. This is the principal reason of one's opposition to it, and not baser motives; something to which we are not driven by any personal need, and which we do not require, we cannot esteem so highly.

13. It is a question either of no longer requiring Wagner's art, or of still requiring it.

Gigantic forces lie concealed in it: it drives one beyond its own domain.

14. Goethe said: "Are not Byron's audacity, sprightliness and grandeur all creative? We must beware of always looking for this quality in that which is perfectly pure and moral. All greatness is creative the moment we realise it." This should be applied to Wagner's art.

15. We shall always have to credit Wagner with the fact that in the second half of the nineteenth century he impressed art upon our memory as an important and magnificent thing. True, he did this in his own fashion, and this was not the fashion of upright and far-seeing men.

16. Wagner versus the cautious, the cold and the contented of the world—in this lies his

greatness—he is a stranger to his age—he combats the frivolous and the super-smart—But he also fights the just, the moderate, those who delight in the world (like Goethe), and the mild, the people of charm, the scientific among men—this is the reverse of the medal.

17. Our youth was up in arms against the soberness of the age. It plunged into the cult of excess, of passion, of ecstasy, and of the blackest and most austere conception of the world.

18. Wagner pursues one form of madness, the age another form. Both carry on their chase at the same speed, each is as blind and as unjust as the other.

19. It is very difficult to trace the course of Wagner's inner development—no trust must be placed in his own description of his soul's experiences. He writes party-pamphlets for his followers.

20. It is extremely doubtful whether Wagner is able to bear witness about himself.

21. There are men who try in vain to make a principle out of themselves. This was the case with Wagner.

22. Wagner's obscurity concerning final aims; his non-antique fogginess.

23. All Wagner's ideas straightway become manias; he is tyrannised over by them. How can such a man allow himself to be tyrannised over in this way! For instance by his hatred of Jews. He kills his themes like his "ideas," by means of his violent love of repeating them. The problem of excessive length and breadth; he bores us with his raptures.

24. "C'est la rage de voulour penser et sentir au delà de sa force" (Doudan). The Wagnerites.

25. Wagner whose ambition far exceeds his natural gifts, has tried an incalculable number of times to achieve what lay beyond his powers—but it almost makes one shudder to see some one assail with such persistence that which defies conquest—the fate of his constitution.

26. He is always thinking of the most extreme expression,—in every word. But in the end superlatives begin to pall.

27. There is something which is in the highest degree suspicious in Wagner, and that is Wagner's suspicion. It is such a strong trait in him, that on two occasions I doubted whether he were a musician at all.

28. The proposition: "in the face of perfection there is no salvation save love,"[16] is thoroughly Wagnerian. Profound jealousy of everything great from which he can draw fresh ideas. Hatred of all that which he cannot approach, the Renaissance, French and Greek art in style.

29. Wagner is jealous of all periods that have shown restraint: he despises beauty and grace, and finds only his own virtues in the "Germans," and even attributes all his failings to them.

30. Wagner has not the power to unlock and liberate the soul of those he frequents. Wagner is not sure of himself, but distrustful and arrogant. His art has this effect upon artists, it is envious of all rivals.

31. Plato's Envy. He would fain monopolise Socrates. He saturates the latter with himself, pretends to adorn him (καλὸς Σωκράτης), and tries to separate all Socratists from him in order himself to appear as the only true apostle. But his historical presentation of him is false, even to a parlous degree: just as Wagner's presentation of Beethoven and Shakespeare is false.

32. When a dramatist speaks about himself he plays a part: this is inevitable. When Wagner speaks about Bach and Beethoven he speaks like one for whom he would fain be taken. But he impresses only those who are already convinced, for his dissimulation and his genuine nature are far too violently at variance.

33. Wagner struggles against the "frivolity" in his nature, which to him the ignoble (as opposed to Goethe) constituted the joy of life.

34. Wagner has the mind of the ordinary man who prefers to trace things to one cause. The Jews do the same: one aim, therefore one Saviour. In this way he simplifies German and culture; wrongly but strongly.

35. Wagner admitted all this to himself often enough when in private communion with his soul. I only wish he had also admitted it publicly. For what constitutes the greatness of a character if it is not this, that he who possesses it is able to take sides even against himself in favour of truth.

Wagner's Teutonism

36. That which is un-German in Wagner. He lacks the German charm and grace of a Beethoven, a Mozart, a Weber; he also lacks the flowing, cheerful fire (Allegro con brio) of Beethoven and Weber. He cannot be free and easy without being grotesque. He lacks modesty, indulges in big drums, and always tends to surcharge his effect. He is not the good official that Bach was. Neither has he that Goethean calm in regard to his rivals.

37. Wagner always reaches the high-water mark of his vanity when he speaks of the German nature (incidentally it is also the height of his imprudence); for, if Frederick the Great's justice, Goethe's nobility and freedom from envy, Beethoven's sublime resignation, Bach's delicately transfigured spiritual life,—if steady work performed without any thought of glory and success, and

without envy, constitute the true German qualities, would it not seem as if Wagner almost wished to prove he is no German?

38. Terrible wildness, abject sorrow, emptiness, the shudder of joy, unexpectedness,—in short all the qualities peculiar to the Semitic race! I believe that the Jews approach Wagner's art with more understanding than the Aryans do.

39. A passage concerning the Jews, taken from Taine.—As it happens, I have misled the reader, the passage does not concern Wagner at all.—But can it be possible that Wagner is a Jew? In that case we could readily understand his dislike of Jews.[17]

40. Wagner's art is absolutely the art of the age: an æsthetic age would have rejected it. The more subtle people amongst us actually do reject it even now. The coarsifying of everything æsthetic.—Compared with Goethe's ideal it is very far behind. The moral contrast of these self-indulgent burningly loyal creatures of Wagner, acts like a spur, like an irritant and even this sensation is turned to account in obtaining an effect.

41. What is it in our age that Wagner's art expresses? That brutality and most delicate weakness which exist side by side, that running wild of natural instincts, and nervous hyper-sensitiveness, that thirst for emotion which arises from fatigue and the love of fatigue.—All this is understood by the Wagnerites.

42. Stupefaction or intoxication constitute all Wagnerian art. On the other hand I could mention instances in which Wagner stands higher, in which real joy flows from him.

43. The reason why the figures in Wagner's art behave so madly, is because he greatly feared lest people would doubt that they were alive.

44. Wagner's art is an appeal to inartistic people; all means are welcomed which help towards obtaining an effect. It is calculated not to produce an artistic effect but an effect upon the nerves in general.

45. Apparently in Wagner we have an art for everybody, because coarse and subtle means seem to be united in it. Albeit its pre-requisite may be musico-æsthetic education, and particularly with moral indifference.

46. In Wagner we find the most ambitious combination of all means with the view of obtaining the strongest effect whereas genuine musicians quietly develop individual genres.

47. Dramatists are borrowers—their principal source of wealth—artistic thoughts drawn from the epos. Wagner borrowed from classical music besides. Dramatists are constructive geniuses, they are not inventive and original as the epic poets are. Drama takes a lower rank than the epos: it presupposes a coarser and more democratic public.

48. Wagner does not altogether trust music. He weaves kindred sensations into it in order to lend it the character of greatness. He measures himself on others; he first of all gives his listeners intoxicating drinks in order to lead them into believing that it was the music that intoxicated them.

49. The same amount of talent and industry which makes the classic, when it appears some time too late, also makes the baroque artist like Wagner.

50. Wagner's art is calculated to appeal to short-sighted people—one has to get much too close up to it (Miniature): it also appeals to long-sighted people, but not to those with normal sight.

Contradictions in the Idea of Musical Drama

51. Just listen to the second act of the "Götterdämmerung," without the drama. It is chaotic music, as wild as a bad dream, and it is as frightfully distinct as if it desired to make itself clear even to deaf people. This volubility with nothing to say is alarming. Compared with it the drama is a genuine relief.—Is the fact that this music when heard alone, is, as a whole intolerable (apart from a few intentionally isolated parts) in its favour? Suffice it to say that this music without its accompanying drama, is a perpetual contradiction of all the highest laws of style belonging to older music: he who thoroughly accustoms himself to it, loses all feeling for these laws. But has the drama been improved thanks to this addition? A symbolic interpretation has been affixed to it, a sort of philological commentary, which sets fetters upon the inner and free understanding of the imagination—it is tyrannical. Music is the language of the commentator, who talks the whole of the time and gives us no breathing space. Moreover his is a difficult language which also requires to be explained. He who step by step has mastered, first the libretto (language!), then converted it into action in his mind's eye, then sought out and understood, and became familiar with the musical symbolism thereto: aye, and has fallen in love with all three things: such a man then experiences a great joy. But how exacting! It is quite impossible to do this save for a few short moments,—such tenfold attention on the part of one's eyes, ears, understanding, and feeling, such acute activity in apprehending without any productive reaction, is far too exhausting!—Only the very fewest behave in this way: how is it then that so many are affected? Because most people are only intermittingly attentive, and are inattentive for sometimes whole passages

at a stretch; because they bestow their undivided attention now upon the music, later upon the drama, and anon upon the scenery—that is to say they take the work to pieces.—But in this way the kind of work we are discussing is condemned: not the drama but a moment of it is the result, an arbitrary selection. The creator of a new genre should consider this! The arts should not always be dished up together,—but we should imitate the moderation of the ancients which is truer to human nature.

52. Wagner reminds one of lava which blocks its own course by congealing, and suddenly finds itself checked by dams which it has itself built. There is no Allegro con fuoco for him.

53. I compare Wagner's music, which would fain have the same effect as speech, with that kind of sculptural relief which would have the same effect as painting. The highest laws of style are violated, and that which is most sublime can no longer be achieved.

54. The general heaving, undulating and rolling of Wagner's art.

55. In regard to Wagner's rejection of form, we are reminded of Goethe's remark in conversation with Eckermann: "there is no great art in being brilliant if one respects nothing."

56. Once one theme is over, Wagner is always embarrassed as to how to continue. Hence the long preparation, the suspense. His peculiar craftiness consisted in transvaluing his weakness into virtues.—

57. The lack of melody and the poverty of melody in Wagner. Melody is a whole consisting of many beautiful proportions, it is the reflection of a well-ordered soul. He strives after melody; but if he finds one, he almost suffocates it in his embrace.

58. The natural nobility of a Bach and a Beethoven, the beautiful soul (even of a Mendelssohn) are wanting in Wagner. He is one degree lower.

59. Wagner imitates himself again and again—mannerisms. That is why he was the quickest among musicians to be imitated. It is so easy.

60. Mendelssohn who lacked the power of radically staggering one (incidentally this was the talent of the Jews in the Old Testament), makes up for this by the things which were his own, that is to say: freedom within the law, and noble emotions kept within the limits of beauty.

61. Liszt, the first representative of all musicians, but no musician. He was the prince, not the statesman. The conglomerate of a hundred musicians' souls, but not enough of a personality to cast his own shadow upon them.

62. The most wholesome phenomenon is Brahms, in whose music there is more German blood than in that of Wagner's. With these words I would say something complimentary, but by no means wholly so.

63. In Wagner's writings there is no greatness or peace, but presumption. Why?

64. Wagner's Style.—The habit he acquired, from his earliest days, of having his say in the most important matters without a sufficient knowledge of them, has rendered him the obscure and incomprehensible writer that he is. In addition to this he aspired to imitating the witty newspaper article, and finally acquired that presumption which readily joins hands with carelessness "and, behold, it was very good."

65. I am alarmed at the thought of how much pleasure I could find in Wagner's style, which is so careless as to be unworthy of such an artist.

66. In Wagner, as in Brahms, there is a blind denial of the healthy, in his followers this denial is deliberate and conscious.

67. Wagner's art is for those who are conscious of an essential blunder in the conduct of their lives. They feel either that they have checked a great nature by a base occupation, or squandered it through idle pursuits, a conventional marriage, &c. &c.

In this quarter the condemnation of the world is the outcome of the condemnation of the ego.

68. Wagnerites do not wish to alter themselves in any way, they live discontentedly in insipid, conventional and brutal circumstances—only at intervals does art have to raise them as by magic above these things. Weakness of will.

69. Wagner's art is for scholars who do not dare to become philosophers: they feel discontented with themselves and are generally in a state of obtuse stupefaction—from time to time they take a bath in the opposite conditions.

70. I feel as if I had recovered from an illness: with a feeling of unutterable joy I think of Mozart's Requiem. I can once more enjoy simple fare.

71. I understand Sophocles' development through and through—it was the repugnance to pomp and pageantry.

72. I gained an insight into the injustice of idealism, by noticing that I avenged myself on Wagner for the disappointed hopes I had cherished of him.

73. I leave my loftiest duty to the end, and that is to thank Wagner and Schopenhauer publicly, and to make them as it were take sides against themselves.

74. I counsel everybody not to fight shy of such paths (Wagner and Schopenhauer). The wholly unphilosophic feeling of remorse, has become quite strange to me.

Wagner's Effects.

75. We must strive to oppose the false after-effects of Wagner's art. If he, in order to create Parsifal, is forced to pump fresh strength from religious sources, this is not an example but a danger.

76. I entertain the fear that the effects of Wagner's art will ultimately pour into that torrent which takes its rise on the other side of the mountains, and which knows how to flow even over mountains.[18]

Footnotes:

1. It should be noted that the first and second editions of these essays on Wagner appeared in pamphlet form, for which the above first preface was written.
2. Fisher Unwin, 1911.
3. T. N. Foulis, 1910.
4. See Richard Wagner, by Houston Stuart Chamberlain (translated by G. A. Hight), pp. 15, 16.
5. Constable & Co., 1911.
6. See Author's Preface to "The Case of Wagner" in this volume.
7. Senta is the heroine in the "Flying Dutchman"—Tr.
8. A character in "Tannhauser."—Tr.
9. See "The Will to Power," vol. ii., authorised English edition.—Tr.

10 Note.—It was a real disaster for æsthetics when the word drama got to be translated by "action." Wagner is not the only culprit here, the whole world does the same,—even the philologists who ought to know better. What ancient drama had in view was grand pathetic scenes,—it even excluded action (or placed it before the piece or behind the scenes). The word drama is of Doric origin, and according to the usage of the Dorian language it meant "event," "history,"—both words in a hieratic sense. The oldest drama represented local legends, "sacred history," upon which the foundation of the cult rested (—thus it was not "action," but fatality. δρᾶν in Doric has nothing to do with action).

11. Hegel and his school wrote notoriously obscure German.—Tr.
12. Was Wagner a German at all? There are reasons enough for putting this question. It is difficult to find a single German trait in his character. Great learner that he was, he naturally imitated a great deal that was German—but that is all. His very soul contradicts everything which hitherto has been regarded as German, not to mention German musicians!—His father was an actor of the name of Geyer.... That which has been popularised hitherto as "Wagner's life" is fable convenue if not something worse. I confess my doubts on any point which is vouched for by Wagner alone. He was not proud enough to be able to suffer the truth about himself. Nobody had less pride than he. Like Victor Hugo he remained true to himself even in his biography,—he remained an actor.
13. This undoubtedly refers to Nietzsche's only disciple and friend, Peter Gast—Tr.
14. My "Genealogy of Morals" contains the best exposition of the antithesis "noble morality" and "Christian morality"; a more decisive turning point in the history of religious and moral science does not perhaps exist. This book, which is a touchstone by which I can discover who are my peers, rejoices in being accessible only to the most elevated and most severe minds: the others have not the ears to hear me. One must have one's passion in things, wherein no one has passion nowadays.
15. An allusion to Schiller's poem: "Das verschleierte Bild zu Sais."—Tr.
16. What Schiller said of Goethe.—Tr.
17. See note above.
18. It should be noted that the German Catholic party is called the Ultramontane Party. The river which can thus flow over mountains is Catholicism, towards which Nietzsche thought Wagner's art to be tending.—Tr.

The Dawn of Day

Translated by John McFarland Kennedy

There are many dawns which have yet to shed their light.—RIG-VEDA.

Originally Published by:
New York, The MacMillan Company, 1911

INTRODUCTION

When Nietzsche called his book The Dawn of Day, he was far from giving it a merely fanciful title to attract the attention of that large section of the public which judges books by their titles rather than by their contents. The Dawn of Day represents, figuratively, the dawn of Nietzsche's own philosophy. Hitherto he had been considerably influenced in his outlook, if not in his actual thoughts, by Schopenhauer, Wagner, and perhaps also Comte. Human, all-too-Human, belongs to a period of transition. After his rupture with Bayreuth, Nietzsche is, in both parts of that work, trying to stand on his own legs, and to regain his spiritual freedom; he is feeling his way to his own philosophy. The Dawn of Day, written in 1881 under the invigorating influence of a Genoese spring, is the dawn of this new Nietzsche. "With this book I open my campaign against morality," he himself said later in his autobiography, the Ecce Homo.

Just as in the case of the books written in his prime—The Joyful Wisdom, Zarathustra, Beyond Good and Evil, and The Genealogy of Morals—we cannot fail to be impressed in this work by Nietzsche's deep psychological insight, the insight that showed him to be a powerful judge of men and things unequalled in the nineteenth or, perhaps, any other century. One example of this is seen in his searching analysis of the Apostle Paul (Aphorism 68), in which the soul of the "First Christian" is ruthlessly and realistically laid bare to us. Nietzsche's summing-up of the Founder of Christianity—for of course, as is now generally recognised, it was Paul, and not Christ, who founded the Christian Church—has not yet called forth those bitter attacks from theologians that might have been expected, though one reason for this apparent neglect is no doubt that the portrait is so true, and in these circumstances silence is certainly golden on the part of defenders of the faith, who are otherwise, as a rule, loquacious enough. Nor has the taunt in Aphorism 84 elicited an answer from the quarter whither it was directed; and the "free" (not to say dishonest) interpretation of the Bible by Christian scholars and theologians, which is still proceeding merrily, is now being turned to Nietzsche's own writings. For the philosopher's works are now being "explained away" by German theologians in a most naïve and daring fashion, and with an ability which has no doubt been acquired as the result of centuries of skilful interpretation of the Holy Writ.

Nor are professional theologians the only ones who have failed to answer Nietzsche; for in other than religious matters the majority of savants have not succeeded in plumbing his depths. There is, for example, the question of race. Ten years ago, twenty years after the publication of The Dawn of Day, Nietzsche's countrymen enthusiastically hailed a book which has recently been translated into English, Chamberlain's Foundations of

the Nineteenth Century. In this book the Teutons are said to be superior to all the other peoples in the world, the reason given being that they have kept their race pure. It is due to this purity of race that they have produced so many great men; for every "good" man in history is a Teuton, and every bad man something else. Considerable skill is exhibited by the author in filching from his opponents the Latins their best trump cards, and likewise the trump card, Jesus Christ, from the Jews; for Jesus Christ, according to Chamberlain's very plausible argument, was not a Jew but an Aryan, i.e. a member of that great family of which the Teutons are a branch.

What would Nietzsche have said to this legerdemain? He has constantly pointed out that the Teutons are so far from being a pure race that they have, on the contrary, done everything in their power to ruin even the idea of a pure race for ever. For the Teutons, through their Reformation and their Puritan revolt in England, and the philosophies developed by the democracies that necessarily followed, were the spiritual forbears of the French Revolution and of the Socialistic régime under which we are beginning to suffer nowadays. Thus this noble race has left nothing undone to blot out the last remnant of race in Europe, and it even stands in the way of the creation of a new race. And with such a record in history the Germans write books, eulogising themselves as the salt of the earth, the people of peoples, the race of races, while in truth they are nothing else than nouveaux-riches endeavouring to draw up a decent pedigree for themselves. We know that honesty is not a prerequisite of such pedigrees, and that patriotism may be considered as a good excuse even for a wrong pedigree; but the race-pandemonium that followed the publication of Mr. Chamberlain's book in Germany was really a very unwise proceeding in view of the false and misleading document produced. What, it may be asked again, would Nietzsche have said if he had heard his countrymen screaming odes to their own glory as the "flower of

Europe"? He would assuredly have dismissed their exalted pretensions with a good-natured smile; for his study of history had shown him that even slaves must have their saturnalia now and then. But as to his philosophical answer there can be no doubt; for in Aphorism 272 of The Dawn of Day there is a single sentence which completely refutes the view of modern racemongers like Chamberlain and his followers: "It is probable," we read, "that there are no pure races, but only races which have become purified, and even these are extremely rare." There are even stronger expressions to be met with in "Peoples and Countries" (Aphorism 20; see the Genealogy of Morals, p. 226): "What quagmires and mendacity must there be about if it is possible, in the modern European hotch-potch, to raise the question of 'race'!" and again, in Aphorism 21: "Maxim—to associate with no man who takes any part in the mendacious race-swindle."

A man like Nietzsche, who makes so little impression upon mankind in general, is certainly not, as some people have thought and openly said, a public danger, so the guardians of the State need not be uneasy. There is little danger of Nietzsche's revolutionising either the masses or the classes; for, as Goethe used to say, "Seulement celui qui ressemble le peuple, l'émeut." Nietzsche's voice has as yet hardly been lifted in this country; and, until it is fully heard, both masses and classes will calmly proceed on their way to the extremes of democracy and anarchy, as they now appear to be doing. Anarchy, though, may be too strong a word; for there is some doubt whether, throughout Europe and America at all events, the people are not now too weak even for anarchy. A revolt is a sign of strength in a slave; but our modern slaves have no strength left.

In the meantime, however, it will have become clear that Nietzsche tried to stop this threatening degradation of the human race, that he endeavoured to supplant the morality of altruism—the cause of this degradation—by another, a super-Christian morality, and that he has succeeded in this aim, if not where the masses and the classes are concerned, at any rate in the case of that small minority of thinkers to which he really wished to appeal. And this minority is naturally grateful to the philosopher for having supplied them with a morality which enables them to be "good" without being fools—an unpleasant combination which, unfortunately, the Nazarene morality is seldom able to avoid. This Nazarene morality has doubtless its own merits, and its "good" and "evil" in many cases coincide with ours; but common sense and certain intellectual qualities are not too highly appreciated in the table of Christian values (see, for instance, 1 Cor. iii. 19), whence it will be observed that the enlightenment of a Christian is not always quite equal to his otherwise excellent intentions. We Nietzschians, however, must show that patience to them which they always pretend to show to their opponents. Nietzsche himself, indeed, recommends this in Aphorism 103 of this book, an aphorism which is almost too well known to need repetition; for it likewise disproves the grotesque though widely circulated supposition that all kinds of immorality would be indulged in under the sway of the "Immoralistic" philosopher:

"I should not, of course, deny—unless I were a fool—that many actions which are called immoral should be avoided and resisted; and in the same way that many which are called moral should be performed and encouraged; but I hold that in both cases these actions should be performed from motives other than those which have prevailed up to the present time. We must learn anew in order that at last, perhaps very late in the day, we may be able to do something more: feel anew."

In regard to the translation itself—which owes a good deal to many excellent suggestions made by Mr. Thomas Common—it adheres, as a rule, closely to the German text; and in only two or three instances has a slightly freer rendering been adopted in order to make the sense quite clear. There are one or two cases in which a punning or double meaning could not be adequately rendered in English: e.g. Aphorism 50, where the German word "Rausch" means both "intoxication" and also "elation" (i.e. the exalted feelings of the religious fanatic). Again, we have "Einleid," "Einleidigkeit," in Aphorism 63—words which do not quite correspond to pity, compassion, or fellow-feeling, and which, indeed, are not yet known to German lexicographers. A literal translation, "one-feeling," would be almost meaningless. What is actually signified is that both sufferer and sympathiser have nerves and feelings in common: an experience which Schopenhauer, as Nietzsche rightly points out, mistook for compassion or pity ("Mitleid"), and which lacked a word, even in German, until the later psychologist coined "Einleid." Again, in Aphorism 554 we have a play upon the words "Vorschritt" (leading, guidance) and "Fortschritt" (progress).

All these, however, are trifling matters in comparison with the substance of the book, and they are of more interest to philologists than to psychologists. It is for psychologists that this book was written; and such minds, somewhat rare in our time, may read in it with much profit.

J. M. Kennedy.

LONDON, September 1911.

AUTHORS PREFACE

In this book we find a "subterrestrial" at work, digging, mining, undermining. You can see him, always provided that you have eyes for such deep work,—how he makes his way slowly, cautiously, gently but surely, without showing signs of the weariness that usually accompanies a long privation of light and air. He might even be called happy, despite his labours in the dark. Does it not seem as if some faith were leading him on, some solace recompensing him for his toil? Or that he himself desires a long period of darkness, an unintelligible, hidden, enigmatic something, knowing as he does that he will in time have his own morning, his own redemption, his own rosy dawn?—Yea, verily he will return: ask him not what he seeketh in the depths; for he himself will tell you, this apparent Trophonius and subterrestrial, whensoever he once again becomes man. One easily unlearns how to hold one's tongue when one has for so long been a mole, and all alone, like him.—

2

Indeed, my indulgent friends, I will tell you—here, in this late preface,[1] which might easily have become an obituary or a funeral oration—what I sought in the depths below: for I have come back, and—I have escaped. Think not that I will urge you to run the same perilous risk! or that I will urge you on even to the same solitude! For whoever proceeds on his own path meets nobody: this is the feature of one's "own path." No one comes to help him in his task: he must face everything quite alone—danger, bad luck, wickedness, foul weather. He goes his own way; and, as is only right, meets with bitterness and occasional irritation because he pursues this "own way" of his: for instance, the knowledge that not even his friends can guess who he is and whither he is going, and that they ask themselves now and then: "Well? Is he really moving at all? Has he still ... a path before him?"—At that time I had undertaken something which could not have been done by everybody: I went down into the deepest depths; I tunnelled to the very bottom; I started to investigate and unearth an old faith which for thousands of years we philosophers used to build on as the safest of all foundations—which we built on again and again although every previous structure fell in: I began to undermine our faith in morals. But ye do not understand me?—

3

So far it is on Good and Evil that we have meditated least profoundly: this was always too dangerous a subject. Conscience, a good reputation, hell, and at times even the police, have not allowed and do not allow of impartiality; in the presence of morality, as before all authority, we must not even think, much less speak: here we must obey! Ever since the beginning of the world, no authority has permitted itself to be made the subject of criticism; and to criticise morals—to look upon morality as a problem, as problematic—what! was that not—is that not—immoral?—But morality has at its disposal not only every means of intimidation wherewith to keep itself free from critical hands and instruments of torture: its security lies rather in a certain art of enchantment, in which it is a past master—it knows how to "enrapture." It can often paralyse the critical will with a single look, or even seduce it to itself: yea, there are even cases where morality can turn the critical will against itself; so that then, like the scorpion, it thrusts the sting into its own body. Morality has for ages been an expert in all kinds of devilry in the art of convincing: even at the present day there is no orator who would not turn to it for assistance (only hearken to our anarchists, for instance: how morally they speak when they would fain convince! In the end they even call themselves "the good and the just"). Morality has shown herself to be the greatest mistress of seduction ever since men began to discourse and persuade on earth—and, what concerns us philosophers even more, she is the veritable Circe of philosophers. For, to what is it due that, from Plato onwards, all the philosophic architects in Europe have built in vain? that everything which they themselves honestly believed to be aere perennius threatens to subside or is already laid in ruins? Oh, how wrong is the answer which, even in our own day, rolls glibly off the tongue when this question is asked: "Because they have all neglected the prerequisite, the examination of the foundation, a critique of all reason"—that fatal answer made by Kant, who has certainly not thereby attracted us modern philosophers to firmer and less treacherous ground! (and, one may ask apropos of this, was it not rather strange to demand that an instrument should criticise its own value and effectiveness? that the intellect itself should "recognise" its own worth, power, and limits? was it not even just a little ridiculous?) The right answer would rather have been, that all philosophers, including Kant himself were building under the seductive influence of morality—that they aimed at certainty and "truth" only in appearance; but that in reality their attention was directed towards "majestic moral edifices," to use once more Kant's innocent mode of expression, who deems it his "less brilliant, but not undeserving" task and work "to level the ground and prepare a solid foundation for the erection of those majestic moral edifices" (Critique of Pure Reason, ii. 257). Alas! He did not succeed in his aim, quite the contrary—as we must acknowledge to-day. With this exalted aim, Kant was merely a true son of his century, which more than any other may justly be called the century of exaltation: and this he fortunately continued to be in respect to the more valuable side of this century (with that solid piece of sensuality, for example, which he introduced into his theory of knowledge). He, too, had been bitten by the moral tarantula, Rousseau; he, too, felt weighing on his soul that moral fanaticism of which another disciple of Rousseau's, Robespierre, felt and proclaimed himself to be the executor: de fonder sur la terre l'empire de la sagesse, de la justice, et de la vertu. (Speech of June 4th, 1794.) On the other hand, with such a French fanaticism in his heart, no one could have cultivated it in a less French, more deep, more thorough and more German manner—if the word German is still permissible in this sense—than Kant did: in order to make room for his "moral kingdom," he found himself compelled to add to it an indemonstrable world, a logical "beyond"—that was why he required his critique of pure reason! In other words, he would not have wanted it, if he had not deemed one thing to be more important than all the others: to render his moral kingdom unassailable by—or, better still, invisible to, reason,—for he felt too strongly the vulnerability of a moral order of things in the face of reason. For, when confronted with nature and history, when confronted with the ingrained immorality of nature and history, Kant was, like all good Germans from the earliest times, a pessimist: he believed in morality, not because it is demonstrated through nature and history, but despite its being steadily contradicted by them. To understand this "despite," we should perhaps recall a somewhat similar trait in Luther, that other great pessimist, who once urged it upon his friends with true Lutheran audacity: "If we could conceive by reason alone how that God who shows so much wrath and malignity could be merciful and just, what use should we have for faith?" For, from the earliest times, nothing has ever made a deeper impression upon the German soul, nothing has ever "tempted" it more, than that deduction, the most dangerous of all, which for every true Latin is a sin against the intellect: credo quia absurdum est.—With it German logic enters for the first time into the history of Christian dogma; but even to-day, a thousand years later, we Germans of the present, late Germans in every way, catch the scent of truth, a possibility of truth, at the back of the famous fundamental principle of dialectics with which Hegel secured the victory of the German spirit over Europe—"contradiction moves the world; all things contradict themselves." We are pessimists—even in logic.

4

But logical judgments are not the deepest and most fundamental to which the daring of our suspicion descends: the confidence in reason which is inseparable from the validity of these judgments, is, as confidence, a moral phenomenon ... perhaps German pessimism has yet to take its last step? Perhaps it has once more to draw up its "credo" opposite its "absurdum" in a terrible manner? And if this book is pessimistic even in regard to morals, even above the confidence in morals—should it not be a German book for that very reason? For, in fact, it represents a contradiction, and one which it does not fear: in it confidence in morals is retracted—but why? Out of morality! Or how shall we call that which takes place in it—in us? for our taste inclines to the employment of more modest phrases. But there is no doubt that to us likewise there speaketh a "thou shalt"; we likewise obey a strict law which is set above us—and this is the last cry of morals which is still audible to us, which we too must live: here, if anywhere, are we still men of conscience, because, to put the matter in plain words, we will not return to that which we look upon as decayed, outlived, and superseded, we will not return to something "unworthy of belief," whether it be called God, virtue, truth, justice, love of one's neighbour, or what not; we will not permit ourselves to open up a lying path to old ideals; we are thoroughly and unalterably opposed to anything that would intercede and mingle with us; opposed to all forms of present-day faith and Christianity; opposed to the lukewarmness of all romanticism and fatherlandism; opposed also to the artistic sense of enjoyment and lack of principle which would fain make us worship where we no longer believe—for we are artists—opposed, in short, to all this European feminism (or idealism, if this term be thought preferable) which everlastingly "draws upward," and which in consequence everlastingly "lowers" and "degrades." Yet, being men of this conscience, we feel that we are related to that German uprightness and piety which dates back thousands of years, although we immoralists and atheists may be the late and uncertain offspring of these virtues—yea, we even consider ourselves, in a certain respect, as their heirs, the executors of their inmost will: a pessimistic will, as I have already pointed out, which is not afraid to deny itself, because it denies itself with joy! In us is consummated, if you desire a formula—the autosuppression of morals.

5

But, after all, why must we proclaim so loudly and with such intensity what we are, what we want, and what we do not want? Let us look at this more calmly and wisely; from a higher and more distant point of view. Let us proclaim it, as if among ourselves, in so low a tone that all the world fails to hear it and us! Above all, however, let us say it slowly.... This preface comes late, but not too late: what, after all, do five or six years matter? Such a book, and such a problem, are in no hurry; besides, we are friends of the lento, I and my book. I have not been a philologist in vain—perhaps I am one yet: a teacher of slow reading. I even come to write slowly. At present it is not only my habit, but even my taste—a perverted taste, maybe—to write nothing but what will drive to despair every one who is "in a hurry." For philology is that venerable art which exacts from its followers one thing above all—to step to one side, to leave themselves spare moments, to grow silent, to become slow—the leisurely art of the goldsmith applied to language: an art which must carry out slow, fine work, and attains nothing if not lento. For this very reason philology is now more desirable than ever before; for this very reason it is the highest attraction and incitement in an age of "work": that is to say, of haste, of unseemly and immoderate hurry-skurry, which is intent upon "getting things done" at once, even every book, whether old or new. Philology itself, perhaps, will not "get things done" so hurriedly: it teaches how to read well: i.e. slowly, profoundly, attentively, prudently, with inner thoughts, with the mental doors ajar, with delicate fingers and eyes ... my patient friends, this book appeals only to perfect readers and philologists: learn to read me well!

RUTA, NEAR GENOA,
Autumn, 1886.

BOOK I

1. SUBSEQUENT JUDGMENT.—All things that endure for a long time are little by little so greatly permeated by reason that their origin in unreason becomes improbable. Does not almost every exact statement of an origin strike us as paradoxical and sacrilegious? Indeed, does not the true historian constantly contradict?

2. PREJUDICE OF THE LEARNED.—Savants are quite correct in maintaining the proposition that men in all ages believed that they knew what was good and evil, praiseworthy and blamable. But it is a prejudice of the learned to say that we now know it better than any other age.

3. A TIME FOR EVERYTHING.—When man assigned a sex to all things, he did not believe that he was merely playing; but he thought, on the contrary, that he had acquired a profound insight:—it was only at a much later period, and then only partly, that he acknowledged the enormity of his error. In the same way, man has attributed a moral relationship to everything that exists, throwing the cloak of ethical significance over the world's shoulders. One day all that will be of just as much value, and no more, as the amount of belief existing to-day in the masculinity or femininity of the sun.[2]

4. AGAINST THE FANCIFUL DISHARMONY OF THE SPHERES.—We must once more sweep out of the world all this false grandeur, for it is contrary to the justice that all things about us may claim. And for this reason we must not see or wish the world to be more disharmonic than it is!

5. BE THANKFUL!—The most important result of the past efforts of humanity is that we need no longer go about in continual fear of wild beasts, barbarians, gods, and our own dreams.

6. THE JUGGLER AND HIS COUNTERPART.—That which is wonderful in science is contrary to that which is wonderful in the art of the juggler. For the latter would wish to make us believe that we see a very simple causality, where, in reality, an exceedingly complex causality is in operation. Science, on the other hand, forces us to give up our belief in the simple causality exactly where everything looks so easily comprehensible and we are merely the victims of appearances. The simplest things are very "complicated"—we can never be sufficiently astonished at them!

7. RECONCEIVING OUR FEELING OF SPACE.—Is it real or imaginary things which have built up the greater proportion of man's happiness? It is certain, at all events, that the extent of the distance between the highest point of happiness and the lowest point of unhappiness has been established only with the help of imaginary things. As a consequence, this kind of a conception of space is always, under the influence of science, becoming smaller and smaller: in the same way as science has taught us, and is still teaching us, to look upon the earth as small—yea, to look upon the entire solar system as a mere point.

8. TRANSFIGURATION.—Perplexed sufferers, confused dreamers, the hysterically ecstatic—here we have the three classes into which Raphael divided mankind. We no longer consider the world in this light—and Raphael himself dare not do so: his own eyes would show him a new transfiguration.

9. CONCEPTION OF THE MORALITY OF CUSTOM.—In comparison with the mode of life which prevailed among men for thousands of years, we men of the present day are living in a very immoral age: the power of custom has been weakened to a remarkable degree, and the sense of morality is so refined and elevated that we might almost describe it as volatilised. That is why we late comers experience such difficulty in obtaining a fundamental conception of the origin of morality: and even if we do obtain it, our words of explanation stick in our throats, so coarse would they sound if we uttered them! or to so great an extent would they seem to be a slander upon morality! Thus, for example, the fundamental clause: morality is nothing else (and, above all, nothing more) than obedience to customs, of whatsoever nature they may be. But customs are simply the traditional way of acting and valuing. Where there is no tradition there is no morality; and the less life is governed by tradition, the narrower the circle of morality. The free man is immoral, because it is his will to depend upon himself and not upon tradition: in all the primitive states of humanity "evil" is equivalent to "individual," "free," "arbitrary," "unaccustomed," "unforeseen," "incalculable." In such primitive conditions, always measured by this standard, any action performed—not because tradition commands it, but for other reasons (e.g. on account of its individual utility), even for the same reasons as had been formerly established by custom—is termed immoral, and is felt to be so even by the very man who performs it, for it has not been done out of obedience to the tradition.

What is tradition? A higher authority, which is obeyed, not because it commands what is useful to us, but merely because it commands. And in what way can this feeling for tradition be distinguished from a general feeling of fear? It is the fear of a higher intelligence which commands, the fear of an incomprehensible power, of something that is more than personal—there is superstition in this fear. In primitive times the domain of morality included education and hygienics, marriage, medicine, agriculture, war, speech and silence, the relationship between man and man, and between man and the gods—morality required that a man should observe her prescriptions without thinking of himself as individual. Everything, therefore, was originally custom, and whoever wished to raise himself above it, had first of all to make himself a kind of lawgiver and medicine-man, a sort of demi-god—in other words, he had to create customs, a dangerous and fearful thing to do!—Who is the most moral man? On the one hand, he who most frequently obeys the law: e.g. he who, like the Brahmins, carries a consciousness of the law about with him wherever he may go, and introduces it into the smallest divisions of time, continually exercising his mind in finding opportunities for obeying the law. On the other hand, he who obeys the law in the most difficult cases. The most moral man is he who makes the greatest sacrifices to morality; but what are the greatest sacrifices? In answering this question several different kinds of morality will be developed: but the distinction between the morality of the most frequent obedience and the morality of the most difficult obedience is of the greatest importance. Let us not be deceived as to the motives of that moral law which requires, as an indication of morality, obedience to custom in the most difficult cases! Self-conquest is required, not by reason of its useful consequences for the individual; but that custom and tradition may appear to be dominant, in spite of all individual counter desires and advantages. The individual shall sacrifice himself—so demands the morality of custom.

On the other hand, those moralists who, like the followers of Socrates, recommend self-control and sobriety to the individual as his greatest possible advantage and the key to his greatest personal happiness, are exceptions—and if we ourselves do not think so, this is simply due to our having been brought up under their influence. They all take a new path, and thereby bring down upon themselves the utmost disapproval of all the representatives of the morality of custom. They sever their connection with the community, as immoralists, and are, in the fullest sense of the word, evil ones. In the same way, every Christian who "sought, above all things, his own salvation," must have seemed evil to a virtuous Roman of the old school. Wherever a community exists, and consequently also a morality of custom, the feeling prevails that any punishment for the violation of a custom is inflicted, above all, on the community: this punishment is a supernatural punishment, the manifestations and limits of which are so difficult to understand, and are investigated with such superstitious fear. The community can compel any one member of it to make good, either to an individual or to the community itself, any ill consequences which may have followed upon such a member's action. It can also call down a sort of vengeance upon the head of the individual by endeavouring to show that, as the result of his action, a storm of divine anger has burst over the community,—but, above all, it regards the guilt of the individual more particularly as its own guilt, and bears the punishment of the isolated individual as its own punishment—"Morals," they bewail in their innermost heart, "morals have grown lax, if such deeds as these are possible." And every individual action, every individual mode of thinking, causes dread. It is impossible to determine how much the more select, rare, and original minds must have suffered in the course of time by being considered as evil and dangerous, yea, because they even looked upon themselves as such. Under the dominating influence of the morality of custom, originality of every kind came to acquire a bad conscience; and even now the sky of the best minds seems to be more overcast by this thought than it need be.

10. COUNTER-MOTION BETWEEN THE SENSE OF MORALITY AND THE SENSE OF CAUSALITY.—As the sense of causality increases, so does the extent of the domain of morality decrease: for every time one has been able to grasp the necessary effects, and to conceive them as distinct from all incidentals and chance possibilities (post hoc), one has, at the same time, destroyed an enormous number of imaginary causalities, which had hitherto been believed in as the basis of morals—the real world is much smaller than the world of our imagination—and each time also one casts away a certain amount of one's anxiousness and coercion, and some of our reverence for the authority of custom is lost: morality in general undergoes a diminution. He who, on the other hand, wishes to increase it must know how to prevent results from becoming controllable.

11. MORALS AND MEDICINES OF THE PEOPLE.—Every one is continuously occupied in bringing more or less influence to bear upon the morals which prevail in a community: most of the people bring forward example after example to show the alleged relationship between cause and effect, guilt and punishment, thus upholding it as well founded and adding to the belief in it. A few make new observations upon the actions and their consequences, drawing conclusions therefrom and laying down laws; a smaller number raise objections and allow belief in these things to become weakened.—But they are all alike in the crude and unscientific manner in which they set about their work: if it is a question of objections to a law, or examples or observations of it, or of its proof, confirmation, expression or refutation, we always find the material and method entirely valueless, as valueless as the material and

form of all popular medicine. Popular medicines and popular morals are closely related, and should not be considered and valued, as is still customary, in so different a way: both are most dangerous and make-believe sciences.

12. CONSEQUENCE AS ADJUVANT CAUSE.—Formerly the consequences of an action were considered, not as the result of that action, but a voluntary adjuvant—i.e. on the part of God. Can a greater confusion be imagined? Entirely different practices and means have to be brought into use for actions and effects!

13. TOWARDS THE NEW EDUCATION OF MANKIND.—Help us, all ye who are well-disposed and willing to assist, lend your aid in the endeavour to do away with that conception of punishment which has swept over the whole world! No weed more harmful than this! It is not only to the consequences of our actions that this conception has been applied—and how horrible and senseless it is to confuse cause and effect with cause and punishment!—but worse has followed: the pure accidentality of events has been robbed of its innocence by this execrable manner of interpreting conception of punishment. Yea, they have even pushed their folly to such extremes that they would have us look upon existence itself as a punishment—from which it would appear that the education of mankind had hitherto been confided to cranky gaolers and hangmen.

14. THE SIGNIFICATION OF MADNESS IN THE HISTORY OF MORALITY.—If, despite that formidable pressure of the "morality of custom," under which all human communities lived—thousands of years before our own era, and during our own era up to the present day (we ourselves are dwelling in the small world of exceptions, and, as it were, in an evil zone):—if, I say, in spite of all this, new and divergent ideas, valuations, and impulses have made their appearance time after time, this state of things has been brought about only with the assistance of a dreadful associate: it was insanity almost everywhere that paved the way for the new thought and cast off the spell of an old custom and superstition. Do ye understand why this had to be done through insanity? by something which is in both voice and appearance as horrifying and incalculable as the demoniac whims of wind and sea, and consequently calling for like dread and respect? by something bearing upon it the signs of entire lack of consciousness as clearly as the convulsions and foam of the epileptic, which appeared to typify the insane person as the mask and speaking-trumpet of some divine being? by something that inspired even the bearer of the new thought with awe and fear of himself, and that, suppressing all remorse, drove him on to become its prophet and martyr?—Well, in our own time, we continually hear the statement reiterated that genius is tinctured with madness instead of good sense. Men of earlier ages were far more inclined to believe that, wherever traces of insanity showed themselves, a certain proportion of genius and wisdom was likewise present—something "divine," as they whispered to one another. More than this, they expressed their opinions on the point with sufficient emphasis. "All the greatest benefits of Greece have sprung from madness," said Plato, setting on record the opinion of the entire ancient world. Let us take a step further: all those superior men, who felt themselves irresistibly urged on to throw off the yoke of some morality or other, had no other resource—if they were not really mad—than to feign madness, or actually to become insane. And this holds good for innovators in every department of life, and not only in religion and politics. Even the reformer of the poetic metre was forced to justify himself by means of madness. (Thus even down to gentler ages madness remained a kind of convention in poets, of which Solon, for instance, took advantage when urging the Athenians to reconquer Salamis.)—"How can one make one's self mad when one is not mad and dare not feign to be so?" Almost all the eminent men of antiquity have given themselves up to this dreadful mode of reasoning: a secret doctrine of artifices and dietetic jugglery grew up around this subject and was handed down from generation to generation, together with the feeling of the innocence, even sanctity, of such plans and meditations. The means of becoming a medicine-man among the Indians, a saint among Christians of the Middle Ages, an angecok among Greenlanders, a Pagee among Brazilians, are the same in essence: senseless fasting, continual abstention from sexual intercourse, isolation in a wilderness, ascending a mountain or a pillar, "sitting on an aged willow that looks out upon a lake," and thinking of absolutely nothing but what may give rise to ecstasy or mental derangements.

Who would dare to glance at the desert of the bitterest and most superfluous agonies of spirit, in which probably the most productive men of all ages have pined away? Who could listen to the sighs of those lonely and troubled minds: "O ye heavenly powers, grant me madness! Madness, that I at length may believe in myself! Vouchsafe delirium and convulsions, sudden flashes of light and periods of darkness; frighten me with such shivering and feverishness as no mortal ever experienced before, with clanging noises and haunting spectres; let me growl and whine and creep about like a beast, if only I can come to believe in myself! I am devoured by doubt. I have slain the law, and I now dread the law as a living person dreads a corpse. If I am not above the law, I am the most abandoned of wretches. Whence cometh this new spirit that dwelleth within me but from you? Prove to me, then, that I am one of you—nothing but madness will prove it to me." And only too often does such a fervour attain its object: at the very time when Christianity was giving the greatest proof of its fertility in the production of saints and martyrs, believing that it was thus proving itself, Jerusalem contained large lunatic asylums for shipwrecked saints, for those whose last spark of good sense had been quenched by the floods of insanity.

15. THE MOST ANCIENT MEANS OF SOLACE.—First stage: In every misfortune or discomfort man sees something for which he must make somebody else suffer, no matter who—in this way he finds out the amount of power still remaining to him; and this consoles him. Second stage: In every misfortune or discomfort, man sees a punishment, i.e. an expiation of guilt and the means by which he may get rid of the malicious enchantment of a real or apparent wrong. When he perceives the advantage which misfortune bring with it, he believes he need no longer make another person suffer for it—he gives up this kind of satisfaction, because he now has another.

16. FIRST PRINCIPLE OF CIVILISATION.—Among savage tribes there is a certain category of customs which appear to aim at nothing but custom. They therefore lay down strict, and, on the whole, superfluous regulations (e.g. the rules of the Kamchadales, which forbid snow to be scraped off the boots with a knife, coal to be stuck on the point of a knife, or a piece of iron to be put into the fire—and death to be the portion of every one who shall act contrariwise!) Yet these laws serve to keep people continually reminded of the custom, and the imperative necessity on their parts to conform to it: and all this in support of the great principle which stands at the beginning of all civilisation: any custom is better than none.

17. GOODNESS AND MALIGNITY.—At first men imposed their own personalities on Nature: everywhere they saw themselves and their like, i.e. their own evil and capricious temperaments, hidden, as it were, behind clouds, thunder-storms, wild beasts, trees, and plants: it was then that they declared Nature was evil. Afterwards there came a time, that of Rousseau, when they sought to distinguish themselves from Nature: they were so tired of each other that they wished to have separate little hiding-places where man and his misery could not penetrate: then they invented "nature is good."

18. THE MORALITY OF VOLUNTARY SUFFERING.—What is the highest enjoyment for men living in a state of war in a small community, the existence of which is continually threatened, and the morality of which is the strictest possible? i.e. for souls which are vigorous, vindictive, malicious, full of suspicion, ready to face the direst events, hardened by privation and morality? The enjoyment of cruelty: just as, in such souls and in such circumstances, it would be regarded as a virtue to be ingenious and insatiable in cruelty. Such a community would find its delight in performing cruel deeds, casting aside, for once, the gloom of constant anxiety and precaution. Cruelty is one of the most ancient enjoyments at their festivities. As a consequence it is believed that the gods likewise are pleased by the sight of cruelty and rejoice at it—and in this way the belief is spread that voluntary suffering, self-chosen martyrdom, has a high signification and value of its own. In the community custom gradually brings about a practice in conformity with this belief: henceforward people become more suspicious of all exuberant well-being, and more confident as they find themselves in a state of great pain; they think that the gods may be unfavourable to them on account of happiness, and favourable on account of pain—not compassionate! For compassion is looked upon with contempt, and unworthy of a strong and awe-inspiring soul—but agreeable to them, because the sight of human suffering put these gods into good humour and makes them feel powerful, and a cruel mind revels in the sensation of power. It was thus that the "most moral man" of the community was considered as such by virtue of his frequent suffering, privation, laborious existence, and cruel mortification—not, to repeat it again and again, as a means of discipline or self-control or a desire for individual happiness—but a a virtue which renders the evil gods well-disposed towards the community, a virtue which continually wafts up to them the odour of an expiatory sacrifice. All those intellectual leaders of the nations who reached the point of being able to stir up the sluggish though prolific mire of their customs had to possess this factor of voluntary martyrdom as well as insanity in order to obtain belief—especially, and above all, as is always the case, belief in themselves! The more their minds followed new paths, and were consequently tormented by pricks of conscience, the more cruelly they battled against their own flesh, their own desires, and their own health—as if they were offering the gods a compensation in pleasure, lest these gods should wax wroth at the neglect of ancient customs and the setting up of new aims.

Let no one be too hasty in thinking that we have now entirely freed ourselves from such a logic of feeling! Let the most heroic souls among us question themselves on this very point. The least step forward in the domain of free thought and individual life has been achieved in all ages to the accompaniment of physical and intellectual tortures: and not only the mere step forward, no! but every form of movement and change has rendered necessary innumerable martyrs, throughout the entire course of thousands of years which sought their paths and laid down their foundation-stones, years, however, which we do not think of when we speak about "world-history," that ridiculously small division of mankind's existence. And even in this so-called world-history, which in the main is merely a great deal of noise about the latest novelties, there is no more important theme than the old, old tragedy of the martyrs who tried to move the mire. Nothing has been more dearly bought than the minute portion of human reason and feeling of liberty upon which we now pride ourselves. But it is this very pride which makes it almost impossible for us to-day to be conscious of that enormous lapse of time, preceding the period of "world-history" when "morality of custom" held the field, and to consider this lapse of time as the real and decisive epoch that established the character of mankind: an epoch when suffering was considered as a virtue, cruelty as a virtue, hypocrisy as a virtue, revenge as a virtue, and the denial of the reason as a virtue, whereas, on the other hand, well-being was regarded as a danger, longing for knowledge as a danger, peace as a danger, compassion as a danger: an epoch when being pitied was looked upon as an insult, work as an insult, madness as a divine attribute, and every kind of change as immoral and pregnant with ruin! You imagine that all this has changed, and that humanity must likewise have changed its character? Oh, ye poor psychologists, learn to know yourselves better!

19. MORALITY AND STUPEFACTION.—Custom represents the experiences of men of earlier times in regard to what they considered as useful and harmful; but the feeling of custom (morality) does not relate to these feelings as such, but to the age, the sanctity, and the unquestioned authority of the custom. Hence this feeling hinders our acquiring new experiences and amending morals: i.e. morality is opposed to the formation of new and better morals: it stupefies.

20. FREE-DOERS AND FREE-THINKERS.—Compared with free-thinkers, free-doers are at a disadvantage, because it is evident that men suffer more from the consequences of actions than of thoughts. If we remember, however, that both seek their own satisfaction, and that free-thinkers have already found their satisfaction in reflection upon and utterance of forbidden things, there is no difference in the motives; but in respect of the consequences the issue will be decided against the free-thinker, provided that it be not judged from the most superficial and vulgar external appearance, i.e. not as every one would judge it. We must make up for a good deal of the calumny with which men have covered all those who have, by their actions, broken away from the authority of some custom—they are generally called criminals. Every one who has hitherto overthrown a law of established morality has always at first been considered as a wicked man: but when it was afterwards found impossible to re-establish the law, and people gradually became accustomed to the change, the epithet was changed by slow degrees. History deals almost exclusively with these wicked men, who later on came to be recognised as good men.

21. "FULFILMENT OF THE LAW."—In cases where the observance of a moral precept has led to different consequence from that expected and promised, and does not bestow upon the moral man the happiness he had hoped for, but leads rather to misfortune and misery, the conscientious and timid man has always his excuse ready: "Something was lacking in the proper carrying out of the law." If the worst comes to the worst, a deeply-suffering and down-trodden humanity will even decree: "It is impossible to carry out the precept faithfully: we are too weak and sinful, and, in the depths of our soul, incapable of morality: consequently we have no claim to happiness and success. Moral precepts and promises have been given for better beings than ourselves."

22. WORKS AND FAITH.—Protestant teachers are still spreading the fundamental error that faith only is of consequence, and that works must follow naturally upon faith. This doctrine is certainly not true, but it is so seductive in appearance that it has succeeded in fascinating quite other intellects than that of Luther (e.g. the minds of Socrates and Plato): though the plain evidence and experience of our daily life prove the contrary. The most assured knowledge and faith cannot give us either the strength or the dexterity required for action, or the practice in that subtle and complicated mechanism which is a prerequisite for anything to be changed from an idea into action. Then, I say, let us first and foremost have works! and this means practice! practice! practice! The necessary faith will come later—be certain of that!

23. IN WHAT RESPECT WE ARE MOST SUBTLE.—By the fact that, for thousands of years, things (nature, tools, property of all kinds) were thought to be alive and to possess souls, and able to hinder and interfere with the designs of man, the feeling of impotence among men has become greater and more frequent than it need have been: for one had to secure one's things like men and beasts, by means of force, compulsion, flattery, treaties, sacrifices—and it is here that we may find the origin of the greater number of superstitious customs, i.e. of an important, perhaps paramount, and nevertheless wasted and useless division of mankind's activity!—But since the feeling of impotence and fear was so strong, and for such a length of time in a state of constant stimulation, the feeling of power in man has been developed in so subtle a manner that, in this respect, he can compare favourably with the most delicately-adjusted balance. This feeling has become his strongest propensity: and the means he discovered for creating it form almost the entire history of culture.

24. THE PROOF OF A PRECEPT.—The worth or worthlessness of a recipe—that for baking bread, for example—is proved, generally speaking, by the result expected coming to pass or not, provided, of course, that the directions given have been carefully followed. The case is different, however, when we come to deal with moral precepts, for here the results cannot be ascertained, interpreted, and divined. These precepts, indeed, are based upon hypotheses of but little scientific value, the proof or refutation of which by means of results is impossible:—but in former ages, when all science was crude and primitive, and when a matter was taken for granted on the smallest evidence, then the worth or worthlessness of a moral recipe was determined as we now determine any other precept: by

reference to the results. If the natives of Alaska believe in a command which says: "Thou shalt not throw a bone into the fire or give it to a dog," this will be proved by the warning: "If thou dost thou wilt have no luck when hunting." Yet, in one sense or another, it almost invariably happens that one has "no luck when hunting." It is no easy matter to refute the worth of the precept in this way, the more so as it is the community, and not the individual, which is regarded as the bearer of the punishment; and, again, some occurrence is almost certain to happen which seems to prove the rule.

25. CUSTOMS AND BEAUTY.—In justice to custom it must not be overlooked that, in the case of all those who conform to it whole-heartedly from the very start, the organs of attack and defence, both physical and intellectual, begin to waste away; i.e. these individuals gradually become more beautiful! For it is the exercise of these organs and their corresponding feelings that brings about ugliness and helps to preserve it. It is for this reason that the old baboon is uglier than the young one, and that the young female baboon most closely resembles man, and is hence the most handsome.—Let us draw from this our own conclusions as to the origin of female beauty!

26. ANIMALS AND MORALS.—The rules insisted upon in polite society, such, for example, as the avoidance of everything ridiculous, fantastic, presumptuous; the suppression of one's virtues just as much as of one's most violent desires, the instant bringing of one's self down to the general level, submitting one's self to etiquette and self-depreciation: all this, generally speaking, is to be found, as a social morality, even in the lowest scale of the animal world—and it is only in this low scale that we see the innermost plan of all these amiable precautionary regulations: one wishes to escape from one's pursuers and to be aided in the search for plunder. Hence animals learn to control and to disguise themselves to such an extent that some of them can even adapt the colour of their bodies to that of their surroundings (by means of what is known as the "chromatic function"). Others can simulate death, or adopt the forms and colours of other animals, or of sand, leaves, moss, or fungi (known to English naturalists as "mimicry").

It is in this way that an individual conceals himself behind the universality of the generic term "man" or "society," or adapts and attaches himself to princes, castes, political parties, current opinions of the time, or his surroundings: and we may easily find the animal equivalent of all those subtle means of making ourselves happy, thankful, powerful, and fascinating. Even that sense of truth, which is at bottom merely the sense of security, is possessed by man in common with the animals: we do not wish to be deceived by others or by ourselves; we hear with some suspicion the promptings of our own passions, we control ourselves and remain on the watch against ourselves. Now, the animal does all this as well as man; and in the animal likewise self-control originates in the sense of reality (prudence). In the same way, the animal observes the effects it exercises on the imagination of other beasts: it thus learns to view itself from their position, to consider itself "objectively"; it has its own degree of self-knowledge. The animal judges the movements of its friends and foes, it learns their peculiarities by heart and acts accordingly: it gives up, once and for all, the struggle against individual animals of certain species, and it likewise recognises, in the approach of certain varieties, whether their intentions are agreeable and peaceful. The beginnings of justice, like those of wisdom—in short, everything which we know as the Socratic virtues—are of an animal nature: a consequence of those instincts which teach us to search for food and to avoid our enemies. If we remember that the higher man has merely raised and refined himself in the quality of his food and in the conception of what is contrary to his nature, it may not be going too far to describe the entire moral phenomenon as of an animal origin.

27. THE VALUE OF THE BELIEF IN SUPERHUMAN PASSIONS.—The institution of marriage stubbornly upholds the belief that love, although a passion, is nevertheless capable of duration as such, yea, that lasting, lifelong love may be taken as a general rule. By means of the tenacity of a noble belief, in spite of such frequent and almost customary refutations—thereby becoming a pia fraus—marriage has elevated love to a higher rank. Every institution which has conceded to a passion the belief in the duration of the latter, and responsibility for this duration, in spite of the nature of the passion itself, has raised the passion to a higher level: and he who is thenceforth seized with such a passion does not, as formerly, think himself lowered in the estimation of others or brought into danger on that account, but on the contrary believes himself to be raised, both in the opinion of himself and of his equals. Let us recall institutions and customs which, out of the fiery devotion of a moment, have created eternal fidelity; out of the pleasure of anger, eternal vengeance; out of despair, eternal mourning; out of a single hasty word, eternal obligation. A great deal of hypocrisy and falsehood came into the world as the result of such transformations; but each time, too, at the cost of such disadvantages, a new and superhuman conception which elevates mankind.

28. STATE OF MIND AS ARGUMENT.—Whence arises within us a cheerful readiness for action?—such is the question which has greatly occupied the attention of men. The most ancient answer, and one which we still hear, is: God is the cause; in this way He gives us to understand that He approves of our actions. When, in former ages, people consulted the oracles, they did so that they might return home strengthened by this cheerful readiness; and every one answered the doubts which came to him, if alternative actions suggested themselves, by saying: "I shall do whatever brings about that

feeling." They did not decide, in other words, for what was most reasonable, but upon some plan the conception of which imbued the soul with courage and hope. A cheerful outlook was placed in the scales as an argument and proved to be heavier than reasonableness; for the state of mind was interpreted in a superstitious manner as the action of a god who promises success; and who, by this argument, lets his reason speak as the highest reasonableness. Now, let the consequences of such a prejudice be considered when shrewd men, thirsting for power, availed themselves of it—and still do so! "Bring about the right state of mind!"—in this way you can do without all arguments and overcome every objection!

29. ACTORS OF VIRTUE AND SIN.—Among the ancients who became celebrated for their virtue there were many, it would seem, who acted to themselves, especially the Greeks, who, being actors by nature, must have acted quite unconsciously, seeing no reason why they should not do so. In addition, every one was striving to outdo some one else's virtue with his own, so why should they not have made use of every artifice to show off their virtues, especially among themselves, if only for the sake of practice! Of what use was a virtue which one could not display, and which did not know how to display itself!—Christianity put an end to the career of these actors of virtue; instead it devised the disgusting ostentation and parading of sins: it brought into the world a state of mendacious sinfulness (even at the present day this is considered as bon ton among orthodox Christians).

30. REFINED CRUELTY AS VIRTUE.—Here we have a morality which is based entirely upon our thirst for distinction—do not therefore entertain too high an opinion of it! Indeed, we may well ask what kind of an impulse it is, and what is its fundamental signification? It is sought, by our appearance, to grieve our neighbour, to arouse his envy, and to awaken his feelings of impotence and degradation; we endeavour to make him taste the bitterness of his fate by dropping a little of our honey on his tongue, and, while conferring this supposed benefit on him, looking sharply and triumphantly into his eyes.

Behold such a man, now become humble, and perfect in his humility—and seek those for whom, through his humility, he has for a long time been preparing a torture; for you are sure to find them! Here is another man who shows mercy towards animals, and is admired for doing so—but there are certain people on whom he wishes to vent his cruelty by this very means. Look at that great artist: the pleasure he enjoyed beforehand in conceiving the envy of the rivals he had outstripped, refused to let his powers lie dormant until he became a great man—how many bitter moments in the souls of other men has he asked for as payment for his own greatness! The nun's chastity: with what threatening eyes she looks into the faces of other women who live differently from her! what a vindictive joy shines in those eyes! The theme is short, and its variations, though they might well be innumerable, could not easily become tiresome—for it is still too paradoxical a novelty, and almost a painful one, to affirm that the morality of distinction is nothing, at bottom, but joy in refined cruelty. When I say "at bottom," I mean here, every time in the first generation. For, when the habit of some distinguished action becomes hereditary, its root, so to speak, is not transmitted, but only its fruits (for only feelings, and not thoughts, can become hereditary): and, if we presuppose that this root is not reintroduced by education, in the second generation the joy in the cruelty is no longer felt: but only pleasure in the habit as such. This joy, however, is the first degree of the "good."

31. PRIDE IN SPIRIT.—The pride of man, which strives to oppose the theory of our own descent from animals and establishes a wide gulf between nature and man himself—this pride is founded upon a prejudice as to what the mind is; and this prejudice is relatively recent. In the long prehistorical period of humanity it was supposed that the mind was everywhere, and men did not look upon it as a particular characteristic of their own. Since, on the contrary, everything spiritual (including all impulses, maliciousness, and inclinations) was regarded as common property, and consequently accessible to everybody, primitive mankind was not ashamed of being descended from animals or trees (the noble races thought themselves honoured by such legends), and saw in the spiritual that which unites us with nature, and not that which severs us from her. Thus man was brought up in modesty—and this likewise was the result of a prejudice.

32. THE BRAKE.—To suffer morally, and then to learn afterwards that this kind of suffering was founded upon an error, shocks us. For there is a unique consolation in acknowledging, by our suffering, a "deeper world of truth" than any other world, and we would much rather suffer and feel ourselves above reality by doing so (through the feeling that, in this way, we approach nearer to that "deeper world of truth"), than live without suffering and hence without this feeling of the sublime. Thus it is pride, and the habitual fashion of satisfying it, which opposes this new interpretation of morality. What power, then, must we bring into operation to get rid of this brake? Greater pride? A new pride?

33. THE CONTEMPT OF CAUSES, CONSEQUENCES, AND REALITY.—Those unfortunate occurrences which take place at times in the community, such as sudden storms, bad harvests, or plagues, lead members of the community to suspect that offences against custom have been committed, or that new customs must be invented to appease a new demoniac power and caprice. Suspicion and reasoning of this kind, however, evade an inquiry into the real and natural causes, and take the

demoniac cause for granted. This is one source of the hereditary perversion of the human intellect; and the other one follows in its train, for, proceeding on the same principle, people paid much less attention to the real and natural consequences of an action than to the supernatural consequences (the so-called punishments and mercies of the Divinity). It is commanded, for instance, that certain baths are to be taken at certain times: and the baths are taken, not for the sake of cleanliness, but because the command has been made. We are not taught to avoid the real consequences of dirt, but merely the supposed displeasure of the gods because a bath has been omitted. Under the pressure of superstitious fear, people began to suspect that these ablutions were of much greater importance than they seemed; they ascribed inner and supplementary meanings to them, gradually lost their sense of and pleasure in reality, and finally reality is considered as valuable only to the extent that it is a symbol. Hence a man who is under the influence of the morality of custom comes to despise causes first of all, secondly consequences, and thirdly reality, and weaves all his higher feelings (reverence, sublimity, pride, gratitude, love) into an imaginary world: the so-called higher world. And even to-day we can see the consequences of this: wherever, and in whatever fashion, man's feelings are raised, that imaginary world is in evidence. It is sad to have to say it; but for the time being all higher sentiments must be looked upon with suspicion by the man of science, to so great an extent are they intermingled with illusion and extravagance. Not that they need necessarily be suspected per se and for ever; but there is no doubt that, of all the gradual purifications which await humanity, the purification of the higher feelings will be one of the slowest.

34. MORAL FEELINGS AND CONCEPTIONS.—It is clear that moral feelings are transmitted in such a way that children perceive in adults violent predilections and aversions for certain actions, and then, like born apes, imitate such likes and dislikes. Later on in life, when they are thoroughly permeated by these acquired and well-practised feelings, they think it a matter of propriety and decorum to provide a kind of justification for these predilections and aversions. These "justifications," however, are in no way connected with the origin or the degree of the feeling: people simply accommodate themselves to the rule that, as rational beings, they must give reasons for their pros and cons, reasons which must be assignable and acceptable into the bargain. Up to this extent the history of the moral feelings is entirely different from the history of moral conceptions. The first-mentioned are powerful before the action, and the latter especially after it, in view of the necessity for making one's self clear in regard to them.

35. FEELINGS AND THEIR DESCENT FROM JUDGMENTS.—"Trust in your feelings!" But feelings comprise nothing final, original; feelings are based upon the judgments and valuations which are transmitted to us in the shape of feelings (inclinations, dislikes). The inspiration which springs from a feeling is the grandchild of a judgment—often an erroneous judgment!—and certainly not one's own judgment! Trusting in our feelings simply means obeying our grandfather and grandmother more than the gods within ourselves: our reason and experience.

36. A FOOLISH PIETY, WITH ARRIÈRE-PENSÉES.—What! the inventors of ancient civilisations, the first makers of tools and tape lines, the first builders of vehicles, ships, and houses, the first observers of the laws of the heavens and the multiplication tables—is it contended that they were entirely different from the inventors and observers of our own time, and superior to them? And that the first slow steps forward were of a value which has not been equalled by the discoveries we have made with all our travels and circumnavigations of the earth? It is the voice of prejudice that speaks thus, and argues in this way to depreciate the importance of the modern mind. And yet it is plain to be seen that, in former times, hazard was the greatest of all discoverers and observers and the benevolent prompter of these ingenious ancients, and that, in the case of the most insignificant invention now made, a greater intellect, discipline, and scientific imagination are required than formerly existed throughout long ages.

37. WRONG CONCLUSIONS FROM USEFULNESS.—When we have demonstrated the highest utility of a thing, we have nevertheless made no progress towards an explanation of its origin; in other words, we can never explain, by mere utility, the necessity of existence. But precisely the contrary opinion has been maintained up to the present time, even in the domain of the most exact science. In astronomy, for example, have we not heard it stated that the (supposed) usefulness of the system of satellites—(replacing the light which is diminished in intensity by the greater distance of the sun, in order that the inhabitants of the various celestial bodies should not want for light)—was the final object of this system and explained its origin? Which may remind us of the conclusions of Christopher Columbus The earth has been created for man, ergo, if there are countries, they must be inhabited. "Is it probable that the sun would throw his rays on nothing, and that the nocturnal vigils of the stars should be wasted upon untravelled seas and unpeopled countries?"

38. IMPULSES TRANSFORMED BY MORAL JUDGMENTS.—The same impulse, under the impression of the blame cast upon it by custom, develops into the painful feeling of cowardice, or else the pleasurable feeling of humility, in case a morality, like that of Christianity, has taken it to its heart and called it good. In other words, this instinct will fall under the influence of either a good conscience or a bad one! In itself, like every instinct, it does not possess either this or indeed any other moral character and name, or even a definite accompanying feeling of pleasure or displeasure; it does not

acquire all these qualities as its second nature until it comes into contact with impulses which have already been baptized as good and evil, or has been recognised as the attribute of beings already weighed and valued by the people from a moral point of view. Thus the ancient conception of envy differed entirely from ours. Hesiod reckons it among the qualities of the good, benevolent Eris, and it was not considered as offensive to attribute some kind of envy even to the gods. This is easy to understand in a state of things inspired mainly by emulation, but emulation was looked upon as good, and valued accordingly.

The Greeks were likewise different from us in the value they set upon hope: they conceived it as blind and deceitful. Hesiod in one of his poems has made a strong reference to it—a reference so strong, indeed, that no modern commentator has quite understood it; for it runs contrary to the modern mind, which has learnt from Christianity to look upon hope as a virtue. Among the Greeks, on the other hand, the portal leading to a knowledge of the future seemed only partly closed, and, in innumerable instances, it was impressed upon them as a religious obligation to inquire into the future, in those cases where we remain satisfied with hope. It thus came about that the Greeks, thanks to their oracles and seers, held hope in small esteem, and even lowered it to the level of an evil and a danger.

The Jews, again, took a different view of anger from that held by us, and sanctified it: hence they have placed the sombre majesty of the wrathful man at an elevation so high that a European cannot conceive it. They moulded their wrathful and holy Jehovah after the images of their wrathful and holy prophets. Compared with them, all the Europeans who have exhibited the greatest wrath are, so to speak, only second-hand creatures.

39. THE PREJUDICE CONCERNING “PURE SPIRIT.”—Wherever the doctrine of pure spirituality has prevailed, its excesses have resulted in the destruction of the tone of the nerves: it taught that the body should be despised, neglected, or tormented, and that, on account of his impulses, man himself should be tortured and regarded with contempt. It gave rise to gloomy, strained, and downcast souls—who, besides, thought they knew the reason of their misery and how it might possibly be relieved! “It must be in the body! For it still thrives too well!”—such was their conclusion, whilst the fact was that the body, through its agonies, protested time after time against this never-ending mockery. Finally, a universal and chronic hyper-nervousness seized upon those virtuous representatives of the pure spirit: they learned to recognise joy only in the shape of ecstasies and other preliminary symptoms of insanity—and their system reached its climax when it came to look upon ecstasy as the highest aim of life, and as the standard by which all earthly things must be condemned.

40. MEDITATIONS UPON OBSERVANCES.—Numerous moral precepts, carelessly drawn from a single event, quickly became incomprehensible; it was as difficult a matter to deduce their intentions with any degree of certainty as it was to recognise the punishment which was to follow the breaking of the rule. Doubts were even held regarding the order of the ceremonies; but, while people guessed at random about such matters, the object of their investigations increased in importance, it was precisely the greatest absurdity of an observance that developed into a holy of holies. Let us not think too little of the energy wasted by man in this regard throughout thousands of years, and least of all of the effects of such meditations upon observances! Here we find ourselves on the wide training-ground of the intellect—not only do religions develop and continue to increase within its boundaries: but here also is the venerable, though dreadful, primeval world of science; here grow up the poet, the thinker, the physician, the lawgiver. The dread of the unintelligible, which, in an ambiguous fashion, demanded ceremonies from us, gradually assumed the charm of the intricate, and where man could not unravel he learnt to create.

41. TO DETERMINE THE VALUE OF THE VITA CONTEMPLATIVA.—Let us not forget, as men leading a contemplative life, what kind of evil and misfortunes have overtaken the men of the vita activa as the result of contemplation—in short, what sort of contra-account the vita activa has to offer us, if we exhibit too much boastfulness before it with respect to our good deeds. It would show us, in the first place, those so-called religious natures, who predominate among the lovers of contemplation and consequently represent their commonest type. They have at all times acted in such a manner as to render life difficult to practical men, and tried to make them disgusted with it, if possible: to darken the sky, to obliterate the sun, to cast suspicion upon joy, to depreciate hope, to paralyse the active hand—all this they knew how to do, just as, for miserable times and feelings, they had their consolations, alms, blessings, and benedictions. In the second place, it can show us the artists, a species of men leading the vita contemplativa, rarer than the religious element, but still often to be met with. As beings, these people are usually intolerable, capricious, jealous, violent, quarrelsome: this, however, must be deduced from the joyous and exalting effects of their works.

Thirdly, we have the philosophers, men who unite religious and artistic qualities, combined, however, with a third element, namely, dialectics and the love of controversy. They are the authors of evil in the same sense as the religious men and artists, in addition to which they have wearied many of their fellow-men with their passion for dialectics, though their number has always been very small. Fourthly, the thinkers and scientific workers. They but rarely strove after effects, and contented themselves with silently sticking to their own groove. Thus they brought about little envy and discomfort, and often, as objects of mockery and derision, they served, without wishing to do so, to make life easier for the men of the vita activa. Lastly, science ended by becoming of much advantage to all; and if, on account of this utility, many of the men who were destined for the vita activa are now slowly making their way along the road to science in the sweat of their brow, and not without brain-racking and maledictions, this is not the fault of the crowd of thinkers and scientific workers: it is "self-wrought pain."[3]

42. ORIGIN OF THE VITA CONTEMPLATIVA.—During barbarous ages, when pessimistic judgments held sway over men and the world, the individual, in the consciousness of his full power, always endeavoured to act in conformity with such judgments, that is to say, he put his ideas into action by means of hunting, robbery, surprise attacks, brutality, and murder: including the weaker forms of such acts, as far as they are tolerated within the community. When his strength declines, however, and he feels tired, ill, melancholy, or satiated—consequently becoming temporarily void of wishes or desires—he is a relatively better man, that is to say, less dangerous; and his pessimistic ideas will now discharge themselves only in words and reflections—upon his companions, for example, or his wife, his life, his gods,—his judgments will be evil ones. In this frame of mind he develops into a thinker and prophet, or he adds to his superstitions and invents new observances, or mocks his enemies. Whatever he may devise, however, all the productions of his brain will necessarily reflect his frame of mind, such as the increase of fear and weariness, and the lower value he attributes to action and enjoyment. The substance of these productions must correspond to the substance of these poetic, thoughtful, and priestly moods; the evil judgment must be supreme.

In later years, all those who acted continuously as this man did in those special circumstances—i.e. those who gave out pessimistic judgments, and lived a melancholy life, poor in action—were called poets, thinkers, priests, or "medicine-men." The general body of men would have liked to disregard such people, because they were not active enough, and to turn them out of the community; but there was a certain risk in doing so: these inactive men had found out and were following the tracks of superstition and divine power, and no one doubted that they had unknown means of power at their disposal. This was the value which was set upon the ancient race of contemplative natures—despised as they were in just the same degree as they were not dreaded! In such a masked form, in such an ambiguous aspect, with an evil heart and often with a troubled head, did Contemplation make its first appearance on earth: both weak and terrible at the same time, despised in secret, and covered in public with every mark of superstitious veneration. Here, as always, we must say: pudenda origo!

43. HOW MANY FORCES MUST NOW BE UNITED IN A THINKER.—To rise superior to considerations of the senses, to raise one's self to abstract contemplations: this is what was formerly regarded as elevation; but now it is not practicable for us to share the same feelings. Luxuriating in the most shadowy images of words and things; playing with those invisible, inaudible, imperceptible beings, was considered as existence in another and higher world, a world that sprang from the deep contempt felt for the world which was perceptible to the senses, this seductive and wicked world of ours. "These abstracta no longer mislead us, but they may lead us"—with such words men soared aloft. It was not the substance of these intellectual sports, but the sports themselves, which was looked upon as "the higher thing" in the primeval ages of science. Hence we have Plato's admiration for dialectics, and his enthusiastic belief in the necessary relationship of dialectics to the good man who has risen superior to the considerations of his senses. It was not only knowledge that was discovered little by little, but also the different means of acquiring it, the conditions and operations which precede knowledge in man. And it always seemed as if the newly-discovered operation or the newly-experienced condition were not a means of acquiring knowledge, but was even the substance, goal, and sum-total of everything that was worth knowing. What does the thinker require?—imagination, inspiration, abstraction, spirituality, invention, presentiment, induction, dialectics, deduction, criticism, ability to collect materials, an impersonal mode of thinking, contemplation, comprehensiveness, and lastly, but not least, justice, and love for everything that exists—but each one of these means was at one time considered, in the history of the vita contemplativa, as a goal and final purpose, and they all secured for their inventors that perfect happiness which fills the human soul when its final purpose dawns upon it.

44. ORIGIN AND MEANING.—Why does this thought come into my mind again and again, always in more and more vivid colours?—that, in former times, investigators, in the course of their search for the origin of things, always thought that they found something which would be of the highest importance for all kinds of action and judgment: yea, that they even invariably postulated that the salvation of mankind depended upon insight into the origin of things—whereas now, on the other hand, the more we examine into origins, the less do they concern our interests: on the contrary, all the valuations and interestedness which we have placed upon things begin to lose their meaning, the more we retrogress where knowledge is concerned and approach the things themselves. The origin becomes of less significance in proportion as we acquire insight into it; whilst things nearest to ourselves, around

and within us, gradually begin to manifest their wealth of colours, beauties, enigmas, and diversity of meaning, of which earlier humanity never dreamed. In former ages thinkers used to move furiously about, like wild animals in cages, steadily glaring at the bars which hemmed them in, and at times springing up against them in a vain endeavour to break through them: and happy indeed was he who could look through a gap to the outer world and could fancy that he saw something of what lay beyond and afar off.

45. A TRAGIC TERMINATION TO KNOWLEDGE.—Of all the means of exaltation, human sacrifices have at times done most to elevate man. And perhaps the one powerful thought—the idea of self-sacrificing humanity—might be made to prevail over every other aspiration, and thus to prove the victor over even the most victorious. But to whom should the sacrifice be made? We may already swear that, if ever the constellation of such an idea appeared on the horizon, the knowledge of truth would remain the single but enormous object with which a sacrifice of such a nature would be commensurate—because no sacrifice is too great for it. In the meantime the problem has never been expounded as to how far humanity, considered as a whole, could take steps to encourage the advancement of knowledge; and even less as to what thirst for knowledge could impel humanity to the point of sacrificing itself with the light of an anticipated wisdom in its eyes. When, perhaps, with a view to the advancement of knowledge, we are able to enter into communication with the inhabitants of other stars, and when, during thousands of years, wisdom will have been carried from star to star, the enthusiasm of knowledge may rise to such a dizzy height!

46. DOUBT IN DOUBT.—"What a good pillow doubt is for a well-balanced head!" This saying of Montaigne always made Pascal angry, for nobody ever wanted a good pillow so much as he did. Whatever was the matter with him?

47. WORDS BLOCK UP OUR PATH.—Wherever primitive men put down a word, they thought they had made a discovery. How different the case really was!—they had come upon a problem, and, while they thought they had solved it, they had in reality placed an obstacle in the way of its solution. Now, with every new piece of knowledge, we stumble over petrified words and mummified conceptions, and would rather break a leg than a word in doing so.

48. "KNOW THYSELF" IS THE WHOLE OF SCIENCE.—Only when man shall have acquired a knowledge of all things will he be able to know himself. For things are but the boundaries of man.

49. THE NEW FUNDAMENTAL FEELING: OUR FINAL CORRUPTIBILITY.—In former times people sought to show the feeling of man's greatness by pointing to his divine descent. This, however, has now become a forbidden path, for the ape stands at its entrance, and likewise other fearsome animals, showing their teeth in a knowing fashion, as if to say, No further this way! Hence people now try the opposite direction: the road along which humanity is proceeding shall stand as an indication of their greatness and their relationship to God. But alas! this, too, is useless! At the far end of this path stands the funeral urn of the last man and grave-digger (with the inscription, Nihil humani a me alienum puto). To whatever height mankind may have developed—and perhaps in the end it will not be so high as when they began!—there is as little prospect of their attaining to a higher order as there is for the ant and the earwig to enter into kinship with God and eternity at the end of their career on earth. What is to come will drag behind it that which has passed: why should any little star, or even any little species on that star, form an exception to that eternal drama? Away with such sentimentalities!

50. BELIEF IN INEBRIATION.—Those men who have moments of sublime ecstasy, and who, on ordinary occasions, on account of the contrast and the excessive wearing away of their nervous forces, usually feel miserable and desolate, come to consider such moments as the true manifestation of their real selves, of their "ego," and their misery and dejection, on the other hand, as the effect of the "non-ego". This is why they think of their environment, the age in which they live, and the whole world in which they have their being, with feelings of vindictiveness. This intoxication appears to them as their true life, their actual ego; and everywhere else they see only those who strive to oppose and prevent this intoxication, whether of an intellectual, moral, religious, or artistic nature.

Humanity owes no small part of its evils to these fantastic enthusiasts; for they are the insatiable sowers of the weed of discontent with one's self and one's neighbour, of contempt for the world and the age, and, above all, of world-lassitude. An entire hell of criminals could not, perhaps, bring about such unfortunate and far-reaching consequences, such heavy and disquieting effects that corrupt earth and sky, as are brought about by that "noble" little community of unbridled, fantastic, half-mad people—of geniuses, too—who cannot control themselves, or experience any inward joy, until they have lost themselves completely: while, on the other hand, the criminal often gives a proof of his admirable self-control, sacrifice, and wisdom, and thus maintains these qualities in those who fear him. Through him life's sky may at times seem overcast and threatening, but the atmosphere ever remains brisk and vigorous.—Furthermore, these enthusiasts bring their entire strength to bear on the task of imbuing mankind with belief in inebriation as in life itself: a dreadful belief! As savages are now quickly corrupted and ruined by "fire-water," so likewise has mankind in general been slowly though thoroughly corrupted by these spiritual "fire-waters" of intoxicating feelings and by those who keep alive the craving for them. It may yet be ruined thereby.

51. SUCH AS WE STILL ARE.—"Let us be indulgent to the great one-eyed!" said Stuart Mill, as if it were necessary to ask for indulgence when we are willing to believe and almost to worship them. I say: Let us be indulgent towards the two-eyed, both great and small; for, such as we are now, we shall never rise beyond indulgence!

52. WHERE ARE THE NEW PHYSICIANS OF THE SOUL?—It is the means of consolation which have stamped life with that fundamental melancholy character in which we now believe: the worst disease of mankind has arisen from the struggle against diseases, and apparent remedies have in the long run brought about worse conditions than those which it was intended to remove by their use. Men, in their ignorance, used to believe that the stupefying and intoxicating means, which appeared to act immediately, the so-called "consolations," were the true healing powers: they even failed to observe that they had often to pay for their immediate relief by a general and profound deterioration in health, that the sick ones had to suffer from the after-effects of the intoxication, then from the absence of the intoxication, and, later on, from a feeling of disquietude, depression, nervous starts, and ill-health. Again, men whose illness had advanced to a certain extent never recovered from it—those physicians of the soul, universally believed in and worshipped as they were, took care of that.

It has been justly said of Schopenhauer that he was one who again took the sufferings of humanity seriously: where is the man who will at length take the antidotes against these sufferings seriously, and who will pillory the unheard-of quackery with which men, even up to our own age, and in the most sublime nomenclature, have been wont to treat the illnesses of their souls?

53. ABUSE OF THE CONSCIENTIOUS ONES.—It is the conscientious, and not the unscrupulous, who have suffered so greatly from exhortations to penitence and the fear of hell, especially if they happened to be men of imagination. In other words, a gloom has been cast over the lives of those who had the greatest need of cheerfulness and agreeable images—not only for the sake of their own consolation and recovery from themselves, but that humanity itself might take delight in them and absorb a ray of their beauty. Alas, how much superfluous cruelty and torment have been brought about by those religions which invented sin! and by those men who, by means of such religions, desired to reach the highest enjoyment of their power!

54. THOUGHTS ON DISEASE.—To soothe the imagination of the patient, in order that he may at least no longer keep on thinking about his illness, and thus suffer more from such thoughts than from the complaint itself, which has been the case hitherto—that, it seems to me, is something! and it is by no means a trifle! And now do ye understand our task?

55. THE "WAYS."—So-called "short cuts" have always led humanity to run great risks: on hearing the "glad tidings" that a "short cut" had been found, they always left the straight path—and lost their way.

56. THE APOSTATE OF THE FREE SPIRIT.—Is there any one, then, who seriously dislikes pious people who hold formally to their belief? Do we not, on the contrary, regard them with silent esteem and pleasure, deeply regretting at the same time that these excellent people do not share our own feelings? But whence arises that sudden, profound, and unreasonable dislike for the man who, having at one time possessed freedom of spirit, finally becomes a "believer"? In thinking of him we involuntarily experience the sensation of having beheld some loathsome spectacle, which we must quickly efface from our recollection. Should we not turn our backs upon even the most venerated man if we entertained the least suspicion of him in this regard? Not, indeed, from a moral point of view, but because of sudden disgust and horror! Whence comes this sharpness of feeling? Perhaps we shall be given to understand that, at bottom, we are not quite certain of our own selves? Or that, early in life, we build round ourselves hedges of the most pointed contempt, in order that, when old age makes us weak and forgetful, we may not feel inclined to brush our own contempt away from us?

Now, speaking frankly, this suspicion is quite erroneous, and whoever forms it knows nothing of what agitates and determines the free spirit: how little, to him, does the changing of an opinion seem contemptible per se! On the contrary, how highly he prizes the ability to change an opinion as a rare and valuable distinction, especially if he can retain it far into old age! And his pride (not his pusillanimity) even reaches so high as to be able to pluck the fruits of the spernere se sperni and the spernere se ipsum: without his being troubled by the sensation of fear of vain and easy-going men. Furthermore, the doctrine of the innocence of all opinions appears to him to be as certain as the doctrine of the innocence of all actions: how could he act as judge and hangman before the apostate of intellectual liberty! On the contrary, the sight of such a person would disgust him as much as the sight of a nauseous illness disgusts the physician: the physical repulsion caused by everything spongy, soft, and suppurating momentarily overcomes reason and the desire to help. Hence our goodwill is overcome by the conception of the monstrous dishonesty which must have gained the upper hand in the apostate from the free spirit: by the conception of a general gnawing which is eating its way down even to the framework of the character.

57. OTHER FEARS, OTHER SAFETIES.—Christianity overspread life with a new and unlimited

insecurity, thereby creating new safeties, enjoyments and recreations, and new valuations of all things. Our own century denies the existence of this insecurity, and does so with a good conscience, yet it clings to the old habit of Christian certainties, enjoyments, recreations, and valuations!—even in its noblest arts and philosophies. How feeble and worn out must all this now seem, how imperfect and clumsy, how arbitrarily fanatical, and, above all, how uncertain: now that its horrible contrast has been taken away—the ever-present fear of the Christian for his eternal salvation!

58. CHRISTIANITY AND THE EMOTIONS.—In Christianity we may see a great popular protest against philosophy: the reasoning of the sages of antiquity had withdrawn men from the influence of the emotions, but Christianity would fain give men their emotions back again. With this aim in view, it denies any moral value to virtue such as philosophers understood it—as a victory of the reason over the passions—generally condemns every kind of goodness, and calls upon the passions to manifest themselves in their full power and glory: as love of God, fear of God, fanatic belief in God, blind hope in God.

59. ERROR AS A CORDIAL.—Let people say what they will, it is nevertheless certain that it was the aim of Christianity to deliver mankind from the yoke of moral engagements by indicating what it believed to be the shortest way to perfection: exactly in the same manner as a few philosophers thought they could dispense with tedious and laborious dialectics, and the collection of strictly-proved facts, and point out a royal road to truth. It was an error in both cases, but nevertheless a great cordial for those who were worn out and despairing in the wilderness.

60. ALL SPIRIT FINALLY BECOMES VISIBLE.—Christianity has assimilated the entire spirituality of an incalculable number of men who were by nature submissive, all those enthusiasts of humiliation and reverence, both refined and coarse. It has in this way freed itself from its own original rustic coarseness—of which we are vividly reminded when we look at the oldest image of St. Peter the Apostle—and has become a very intellectual religion, with thousands of wrinkles, arrière-pensées, and masks on its face. It has made European humanity more clever, and not only cunning from a theological standpoint. By the spirit which it has thus given to European humanity—in conjunction with the power of abnegation, and very often in conjunction with the profound conviction and loyalty of that abnegation—it has perhaps chiselled and shaped the most subtle individualities which have ever existed in human society: the individualities of the higher ranks of the Catholic clergy, especially when these priests have sprung from a noble family, and have brought to their work, from the very beginning, the innate grace of gesture, the dominating glance of the eye, and beautiful hands and feet. Here the human face acquires that spiritualisation brought about by the continual ebb and flow of two kinds of happiness (the feeling of power and the feeling of submission) after a carefully-planned manner of living has conquered the beast in man. Here an activity, which consists in blessing, forgiving sins, and representing the Almighty, ever keeps alive in the soul, and even in the body, the consciousness of a supreme mission; here we find that noble contempt concerning the perishable nature of the body, of well-being, and of happiness, peculiar to born soldiers: their pride lies in obedience, a distinctly aristocratic trait; their excuse and their idealism arise from the enormous impossibility of their task. The surpassing beauty and subtleties of these princes of the Church have always proved to the people the truth of the Church; a momentary brutalisation of the clergy (such as came about in Luther's time) always tended to encourage the contrary belief. And would it be maintained that this result of beauty and human subtlety, shown in harmony of figure, intellect, and task, would come to an end with religions? and that nothing higher could be obtained, or even conceived?

61. THE NEEDFUL SACRIFICE.—Those earnest, able, and just men of profound feelings, who are still Christians at heart, owe it to themselves to make one attempt to live for a certain space of time without Christianity! they owe it to their faith that they should thus for once take up their abode "in the wilderness"—if for no other reason than that of being able to pronounce on the question as to whether Christianity is needful. So far, however, they have confined themselves to their own narrow domain and insulted every one who happened to be outside of it: yea, they even become highly irritated when it is suggested to them that beyond this little domain of theirs lies the great world, and that Christianity is, after all, only a corner of it! No; your evidence on the question will be valueless until you have lived year after year without Christianity, and with the inmost desire to continue to exist without it: until, indeed, you have withdrawn far, far away from it. It is not when your nostalgia urges you back again, but when your judgment, based on a strict comparison, drives you back, that your homecoming has any significance!—Men of coming generations will deal in this manner with all the valuations of the past; they must be voluntarily lived over again, together with their contraries, in order that such men may finally acquire the right of shifting them.

62. ON THE ORIGIN OF RELIGIONS.—How can any one regard his own opinion of things as a revelation? This is the problem of the formation of religions: there has always been some man in whom this phenomenon was possible. A postulate is that such a man already believed in revelations. Suddenly, however, a new idea occurs to him one day, his idea; and the entire blessedness of a great personal hypothesis, which embraces all existence and the whole world, penetrates with such force into his

conscience that he dare not think himself the creator of such blessedness, and he therefore attributes to his God the cause of this new idea and likewise the cause of the cause, believing it to be the revelation of his God. How could a man be the author of so great a happiness? ask his pessimistic doubts. But other levers are secretly at work: an opinion may be strengthened by one's self if it be considered as a revelation; and in this way all its hypothetic nature is removed; the matter is set beyond criticism and even beyond doubt: it is sanctified. It is true that, in this way, a man lowers himself to playing the rôle of "mouthpiece," but his thought will end by being victorious as a divine thought—the feeling of finally gaining the victory conquers the feeling of degradation. There is also another feeling in the background: if a man raises his products above himself, and thus apparently detracts from his own worth, there nevertheless remains a kind of joyfulness, paternal love, and paternal pride, which compensates man—more than compensates man—for everything.

63. HATRED OF ONE'S NEIGHBOUR.—Supposing that we felt towards our neighbour as he does himself—Schopenhauer calls this compassion, though it would be more correct to call it auto-passion, fellow-feeling—we should be compelled to hate him, if, like Pascal, he thought himself hateful. And this was probably the general feeling of Pascal regarding mankind, and also that of ancient Christianity, which, under Nero, was "convicted" of odium generis humani, as Tacitus has recorded.

64. THE BROKEN-HEARTED ONES.—Christianity has the instinct of a hunter for finding out all those who may by hook or by crook be driven to despair—only a very small number of men can be brought to this despair. Christianity lies in wait for such as those, and pursues them. Pascal made an attempt to find out whether it was not possible, with the help of the very subtlest knowledge, to drive everybody into despair. He failed: to his second despair.

65. BRAHMINISM AND CHRISTIANITY.—There are certain precepts for obtaining a consciousness of power: on the one hand, for those who already know how to control themselves, and who are therefore already quite used to the feeling of power; and, on the other hand, for those who cannot control themselves. Brahminism has given its care to the former type of man; Christianity to the latter.

66. THE FACULTY OF VISION.—During the whole of the Middle Ages it was believed that the real distinguishing trait of higher men was the faculty of having visions—that is to say, of having a grave mental trouble. And, in fact, the rules of life of all the higher natures of the Middle Ages (the religiosi) were drawn up with the object of making man capable of vision! Little wonder, then, that the exaggerated esteem for these half-mad fanatics, so-called men of genius, has continued even to our own days. "They have seen things that others do not see"—no doubt! and this fact should inspire us with caution where they are concerned, and not with belief!

67. THE PRICE OF BELIEVERS.—He who sets such a value on being believed in has to promise heaven in recompense for this belief: and every one, even a thief on the Cross, must have suffered from a terrible doubt and experienced crucifixion in every form: otherwise he would not buy his followers so dearly.

68. THE FIRST CHRISTIAN.—The whole world still believes in the literary career of the "Holy Ghost," or is still influenced by the effects of this belief: when we look into our Bibles we do so for the purpose of "edifying ourselves," to find a few words of comfort for our misery, be it great or small—in short, we read ourselves into it and out of it. But who—apart from a few learned men—know that it likewise records the history of one of the most ambitious and importunate souls that ever existed, of a mind full of superstition and cunning: the history of the Apostle Paul? Nevertheless, without this singular history, without the tribulations and passions of such a mind, and of such a soul, there would have been no Christian kingdom; we should have scarcely have even heard of a little Jewish sect, the founder of which died on the Cross. It is true that, if this history had been understood in time, if we had read, really read, the writings of St. Paul, not as the revelations of the "Holy Ghost," but with honest and independent minds, oblivious of all our personal troubles—there were no such readers for fifteen centuries—it would have been all up with Christianity long ago: so searchingly do these writings of the Jewish Pascal lay bare the origins of Christianity, just as the French Pascal let us see its destiny and how it will ultimately perish. That the ship of Christianity threw overboard no inconsiderable part of its Jewish ballast, that it was able to sail into the waters of the heathen and actually did do so: this is due to the history of one single man, this apostle who was so greatly troubled in mind and so worthy of pity, but who was also very disagreeable to himself and to others.

This man suffered from a fixed idea, or rather a fixed question, an ever-present and ever-burning question: what was the meaning of the Jewish Law? and, more especially, the fulfilment of this Law? In his youth he had done his best to satisfy it, thirsting as he did for that highest distinction which the Jews could imagine—this people, which raised the imagination of moral loftiness to a greater elevation than any other people, and which alone succeeded in uniting the conception of a holy God with the idea of sin considered as an offence against this holiness. St. Paul became at once the fanatic defender and guard-of-honour of this God and His Law. Ceaselessly battling against and lying in wait for all transgressors of this Law and those who presumed to doubt it, he was pitiless and cruel towards all evil-doers, whom he would fain have punished in the most rigorous fashion possible.

Now, however, he was aware in his own person of the fact that such a man as himself—violent, sensual, melancholy, and malicious in his hatred—could not fulfil the Law; and furthermore, what seemed strangest of all to him, he saw that his boundless craving for power was continually provoked to break it, and that he could not help yielding to this impulse. Was it really "the flesh" which made him a trespasser time and again? Was it not rather, as it afterwards occurred to him, the Law itself, which continually showed itself to be impossible to fulfil, and seduced men into transgression with an irresistible charm? But at that time he had not thought of this means of escape. As he suggests here and there, he had many things on his conscience—hatred, murder, sorcery, idolatry, debauchery, drunkenness, and orgiastic revelry,—and to however great an extent he tried to soothe his conscience, and, even more, his desire for power, by the extreme fanaticism of his worship for and defence of the Law, there were times when the thought struck him: "It is all in vain! The anguish of the unfulfilled Law cannot be overcome." Luther must have experienced similar feelings, when, in his cloister, he endeavoured to become the ideal man of his imagination; and, as Luther one day began to hate the ecclesiastical ideal, and the Pope, and the saints, and the whole clergy, with a hatred which was all the more deadly as he could not avow it even to himself, an analogous feeling took possession of St. Paul. The Law was the Cross on which he felt himself crucified. How he hated it! What a grudge he owed it! How he began to look round on all sides to find a means for its total annihilation, that he might no longer be obliged to fulfil it himself! And at last a liberating thought, together with a vision—which was only to be expected in the case of an epileptic like himself—flashed into his mind: to him, the stern upholder of the Law—who, in his innermost heart, was tired to death of it—there appeared on the lonely path that Christ, with the divine effulgence on His countenance, and Paul heard the words: "Why persecutest thou Me?"

What actually took place, then, was this: his mind was suddenly enlightened, and he said to himself: "It is unreasonable to persecute this Jesus Christ! Here is my means of escape, here is my complete vengeance, here and nowhere else have I the destroyer of the Law in my hands!" The sufferer from anguished pride felt himself restored to health all at once, his moral despair disappeared in the air; for morality itself was blown away, annihilated—that is to say, fulfilled, there on the Cross! Up to that time that ignominious death had seemed to him to be the principal argument against the "Messiahship" proclaimed by the followers of the new doctrine: but what if it were necessary for doing away with the Law? The enormous consequences of this thought, of this solution of the enigma, danced before his eyes, and he at once became the happiest of men. The destiny of the Jews, yea, of all mankind, seemed to him to be intertwined with this instantaneous flash of enlightenment: he held the thought of thoughts, the key of keys, the light of lights; history would henceforth revolve round him! For from that time forward he would be the apostle of the annihilation of the Law! To be dead to sin—that meant to be dead to the Law also; to be in the flesh—that meant to be under the Law! To be one with Christ—that meant to have become, like Him, the destroyer of the Law; to be dead with Him—that meant likewise to be dead to the Law. Even if it were still possible to sin, it would not at any rate be possible to sin against the Law: "I am above the Law," thinks Paul; adding, "If I were now to acknowledge the Law again and to submit to it, I should make Christ an accomplice in the sin"; for the Law was there for the purpose of producing sin and setting it in the foreground, as an emetic produces sickness. God could not have decided upon the death of Christ had it been possible to fulfil the Law without it; henceforth, not only are all sins expiated, but sin itself is abolished; henceforth the Law is dead; henceforth "the flesh" in which it dwelt is dead—or at all events dying, gradually wasting away. To live for a short time longer amid this decay!—this is the Christian's fate, until the time when, having become one with Christ, he arises with Him, sharing with Christ the divine glory, and becoming, like Christ, a "Son of God." Then Paul's exaltation was at its height, and with it the importunity of his soul—the thought of union with Christ made him lose all shame, all submission, all constraint, and his ungovernable ambition was shown to be revelling in the expectation of divine glories.

Such was the first Christian, the inventor of Christianity! before him there were only a few Jewish sectaries.

69. INIMITABLE.—There is an enormous strain and distance between envy and friendship, between self-contempt and pride: the Greek lived in the former, the Christian in the latter.

70. THE USE OF A COARSE INTELLECT.—The Christian Church is an encyclopædia of primitive cults and views of the most varied origin; and is, in consequence, well adapted to missionary work: in former times she could—and still does—go wherever she would, and in doing so always found something resembling herself, to which she could assimilate herself and gradually substitute her own spirit for it. It is not to what is Christian in her usages, but to what is universally pagan in them, that we have to attribute the development of this universal religion. Her thoughts, which have their origin at once in the Judaic and in the Hellenic spirit, were able from the very beginning to raise themselves above the exclusiveness and subtleties of races and nations, as above prejudices. Although we may admire the power which makes even the most difficult things coalesce, we must nevertheless not

overlook the contemptible qualities of this power—the astonishing coarseness and narrowness of the Church's intellect when it was in process of formation, a coarseness which permitted it to accommodate itself to any diet, and to digest contradictions like pebbles.

71. THE CHRISTIAN VENGEANCE AGAINST ROME.—Perhaps nothing is more fatiguing than the sight of a continual conqueror: for more than two hundred years the world had seen Rome overcoming one nation after another, the circle was closed, all future seemed to be at an end, everything was done with a view to its lasting for all time—yea, when the Empire built anything it was erected with a view to being aere perennius. We, who know only the "melancholy of ruins," can scarcely understand that totally different melancholy of eternal buildings, from which men endeavoured to save themselves as best they could—with the light-hearted fancy of a Horace, for example. Others sought different consolations for the weariness which was closely akin to despair, against the deadening knowledge that from henceforth all progress of thought and heart would be hopeless, that the huge spider sat everywhere and mercilessly continued to drink all the blood within its reach, no matter where it might spring forth. This mute, century-old hatred of the wearied spectators against Rome, wherever Rome's domination extended, was at length vented in Christianity, which united Rome, "the world," and "sin" into a single conception. The Christians took their revenge on Rome by proclaiming the immediate and sudden destruction of the world; by once more introducing a future—for Rome had been able to transform everything into the history of its own past and present—a future in which Rome was no longer the most important factor; and by dreaming of the last judgment—while the crucified Jew, as the symbol of salvation, was the greatest derision on the superb Roman prætors in the provinces; for now they seemed to be only the symbols of ruin and a "world" ready to perish.

72. THE "LIFE AFTER DEATH."—Christianity found the idea of punishment in hell in the entire Roman Empire: for the numerous mystic cults have hatched this idea with particular satisfaction as being the most fecund egg of their power. Epicurus thought he could do nothing better for his followers than to tear this belief up by the roots: his triumph found its finest echo in the mouth of one of his disciples, the Roman Lucretius, a poet of a gloomy, though afterwards enlightened, temperament. Alas! his triumph had come too soon: Christianity took under its special protection this belief in subterranean horrors, which was already beginning to die away in the minds of men; and that was clever of it. For, without this audacious leap into the most complete paganism, how could it have proved itself victorious over the popularity of Mithras and Isis? In this way it managed to bring timorous folk over to its side—the most enthusiastic adherents of a new faith! The Jews, being a people which, like the Greeks, and even in a greater degree than the Greeks, loved and still love life, had not cultivated that idea to any great extent: the thought of final death as the punishment of the sinner, death without resurrection as an extreme menace: this was sufficient to impress these peculiar men, who did not wish to get rid of their bodies, but hoped, with their refined Egypticism, to preserve them for ever. (A Jewish martyr, about whom we may read in the Second Book of the Maccabees, would not think of giving up his intestines, which had been torn out: he wanted to have them at the resurrection: quite a Jewish characteristic!)

Thoughts of eternal damnation were far from the minds of the early Christians: they thought they were delivered from death, and awaited a transformation from day to day, but not death. (What a curious effect the first death must have produced on these expectant people! How many different feelings must have been mingled together—astonishment, exultation, doubt, shame, and passion! Verily, a subject worthy of a great artist!) St. Paul could say nothing better in praise of his Saviour than that he had opened the gates of immortality to everybody—he did not believe in the resurrection of those who had not been saved: more than this, by reason of his doctrine of the impossibility of carrying out the Law, and of death considered as a consequence of sin, he even suspected that, up to that time, no one had become immortal (or at all events only a very few, solely owing to special grace and not to any merits of their own): it was only in his time that immortality had begun to open its gates—and only a few of the elect would finally gain admittance, as the pride of the elect cannot help saying.

In other places, where the impulse towards life was not so strong as among the Jews and the Christian Jews, and where the prospect of immortality did not appear to be more valuable than the prospect of a final death, that pagan, yet not altogether un-Jewish addition of Hell became a very useful tool in the hands of the missionaries: then arose the new doctrine that even the sinners and the unsaved are immortal, the doctrine of eternal damnation, which was more powerful than the idea of a final death, which thereafter began to fade away. It was science alone which could overcome this idea, at the same time brushing aside all other ideas about death and an after-life. We are poorer in one particular: the "life after death" has no further interest for us! an indescribable blessing, which is as yet too recent to be considered as such throughout the world. And Epicurus is once more triumphant.

73. FOR THE "TRUTH"!—"The truth of Christianity was attested by the virtuous lives of the Christians, their firmness in suffering, their unshakable belief and above all by the spread and increase of the faith in spite of all calamities."—That's how you talk even now. The more's the pity. Learn, then, that all this proves nothing either in favour of truth or against it; that truth must be demonstrated differently from conscientiousness, and that the latter is in no respect whatever an argument in favour of

the former.

74. A CHRISTIAN ARRIÈRE-PENSÉE.—Would not this have been a general reservation among Christians of the first century: "It is better to persuade ourselves into the belief that we are guilty rather than that we are innocent; for it is impossible to ascertain the disposition of so powerful a judge—but it is to be feared that he is looking out only for those who are conscious of guilt. Bearing in mind his great power, it is more likely that he will pardon a guilty person than admit that any one is innocent, in his presence." This was the feeling of poor provincial folk in the presence of the Roman prætor: "He is too proud for us to dare to be innocent." And may not this very sentiment have made its influence felt when the Christians endeavoured to picture to themselves the aspect of the Supreme Judge?

75. NEITHER EUROPEAN NOR NOBLE.—There is something Oriental and feminine in Christianity, and this is shown in the thought, "Whom the Lord loveth, He chasteneth"; for women in the Orient consider castigations and the strict seclusion of their persons from the world as a sign of their husband's love, and complain if these signs of love cease.

76. IF YOU THINK IT EVIL, YOU MAKE IT EVIL.—The passions become evil and malignant when regarded with evil and malignant eyes. It is in this way that Christianity has succeeded in transforming Eros and Aphrodite—sublime powers, capable of idealisation—into hellish genii and phantom goblins, by means of the pangs which every sexual impulse was made to raise in the conscience of the believers. Is it not a dreadful thing to transform necessary and regular sensations into a source of inward misery, and thus arbitrarily to render interior misery necessary and regular in the case of every man! Furthermore, this misery remains secret with the result that it is all the more deeply rooted, for it is not all men who have the courage, which Shakespeare shows in his sonnets, of making public their Christian gloom on this point.

Must a feeling, then, always be called evil against which we are forced to struggle, which we must restrain even within certain limits, or, in given cases, banish entirely from our minds? Is it not the habit of vulgar souls always to call an enemy evil! and must we call Eros an enemy? The sexual feelings, like the feelings of pity and adoration, possess the particular characteristic that, in their case, one being gratifies another by the pleasure he enjoys—it is but rarely that we meet with such a benevolent arrangement in nature. And yet we calumniate and corrupt it all by our bad conscience! We connect the procreation of man with a bad conscience!

But the outcome of this diabolisation of Eros is a mere farce: the "demon" Eros becomes an object of greater interest to mankind than all the angels and saints put together, thanks to the mysterious Mumbo-Jumboism of the Church in all things erotic: it is due to the Church that love stories, even in our own time, have become the one common interest which appeals to all classes of people—with an exaggeration which would be incomprehensible to antiquity, and which will not fail to provoke roars of laughter in coming generations. All our poetising and thinking, from the highest to the lowest, is marked, and more than marked, by the exaggerated importance bestowed upon the love story as the principal item of our existence. Posterity may perhaps, on this account, come to the conclusion that its entire legacy of Christian culture is tainted with narrowness and insanity.

77. THE TORTURES OF THE SOUL.—The whole world raises a shout of horror at the present day if one man presumes to torture the body of another: the indignation against such a being bursts forth almost spontaneously. Nay; we tremble even at the very thought of torture being inflicted on a man or an animal, and we undergo unspeakable misery when we hear of such an act having been accomplished. But the same feeling is experienced in a very much lesser degree and extent when it is a question of the tortures of the soul and the dreadfulness of their infliction. Christianity has introduced such tortures on an unprecedented scale, and still continues to preach this kind of martyrdom—yea, it even complains innocently of backsliding and indifference when it meets with a state of soul which is free from such agonies. From all this it now results that humanity, in the face of spiritual racks, tortures of the mind, and instruments of punishment, behaves even to-day with the same awesome patience and indecision which it exhibited in former times in the presence of the cruelties practised on the bodies of men or animals. Hell has certainly not remained merely an empty sound; and a new kind of pity has been devised to correspond to the newly-created fears of hell—a horrible and ponderous compassion, hitherto unknown; with people "irrevocably condemned to hell," as, for example, the Stony Guest gave Don Juan to understand, and which, during the Christian era, should often have made the very stones weep.

Plutarch presents us with a gloomy picture of the state of mind of a superstitious man in pagan times: but this picture pales when compared with that of a Christian of the Middle Ages, who supposes that nothing can save him from "torments everlasting." Dreadful omens appear to him: perhaps he sees a stork holding a snake in his beak and hesitating to swallow it. Or all nature suddenly becomes pale; or bright, fiery colours appear across the surface of the earth. Or the ghosts of his dead relations approach him, with features showing traces of dreadful sufferings. Or the dark walls of the room in which the man is sleeping are suddenly lighted up, and there, amidst a yellow flame, he perceives instruments of torture and a motley horde of snakes and devils. Christianity has surely turned this world of ours into a fearful habitation by raising the crucifix in all parts and thereby proclaiming the earth to be a place "where the just man is tortured to death!" And when the ardour of some great preacher for once disclosed to the public the secret sufferings of the individual, the agonies of the lonely souls, when, for example, Whitefield preached "like a dying man to the dying," now bitterly weeping, now violently stamping his feet, speaking passionately, in abrupt and incisive tones, without fearing to turn the whole force of his attack upon any one individual present, excluding him from the assembly with excessive harshness—then indeed did it seem as if the earth were being transformed into a "field of evil." The huge crowds were then seen to act as if seized with a sudden attack of madness: many were in fits of anguish; others lay unconscious and motionless; others, again, trembled or rent the air with their piercing shrieks. Everywhere there was a loud breathing, as of half-choked people who were gasping for the breath of life. "Indeed," said an eye-witness once, "almost all the noises appeared to come from people who were dying in the bitterest agony."

Let us never forget that it was Christianity which first turned the death-bed into a bed of agony, and that, by the scenes which took place there, and the terrifying sounds which were made possible there for the first time, it has poisoned the senses and the blood of innumerable witnesses and their children. Imagine the ordinary man who can never efface the recollection of words like these: "Oh, eternity! Would that I had no soul! Would that I had never been born! My soul is damned, damned; lost for ever! Six days ago you might have helped me. But now all is over. I belong to the devil, and with him I will go down to hell. Break, break, ye poor hearts of stone! Ye will not break? What more can be done for hearts of stone? I am damned that ye may be saved! There he is! Yea; there he is! Come, good devil! Come!"

78. AVENGING JUSTICE.—Misfortune and guilt: these two things have been put on one scale by Christianity; so that, when the misfortune which follows a fault is a serious one, this fault is always judged accordingly to be a very heinous one. But this was not the valuation of antiquity, and that is why Greek tragedy—in which misfortune and punishment are discussed at length, and yet in another sense—forms part of the great liberators of the mind to an extent which even the ancients themselves could not realise. They remained ingenuous enough not to set up an "adequate relation" between guilt and misfortune. The guilt of their tragic heroes is, indeed, the little pebble that makes them stumble, and on which account they sometimes happen to break an arm or knock out an eye. Upon this the feeling of antiquity made the comment, "Well, he should have gone his way with more caution and less pride." It was reserved for Christianity, however, to say: "Here we have a great misfortune, and behind this great misfortune there must lie a great fault, an equally serious fault, though we cannot clearly see it! If, wretched man, you do not feel it, it is because your heart is hardened—and worse than this will happen to you!"

Besides this, antiquity could point to examples of real misfortunes, misfortunes that were pure and innocent; it was only with the advent of Christianity that all punishment became well-merited punishment: in addition to this it renders the imagination of the sufferer still more suffering, so that the victim, in the midst of his distress, is seized with the feeling that he has been morally reproved and cast away. Poor humanity! The Greeks had a special word to stand for the feeling of indignation which was experienced at the misfortune of another: among Christian peoples this feeling was prohibited and was not permitted to develop; hence the reason why they have no name for this more virile brother of pity.

79. A PROPOSAL.—If, according to the arguments of Pascal and Christianity, our ego is always hateful, how can we permit and suppose other people, whether God or men, to love it? It would be contrary to all good principles to let ourselves be loved when we know very well that we deserve nothing but hatred—not to speak of other repugnant feelings. "But this is the very Kingdom of Grace." Then you look upon your love for your neighbour as a grace? Your pity as a grace? Well, then, if you can do all this, there is no reason why you should not go a step further: love yourselves through grace, and then you will no longer find your God necessary, and the entire drama of the Fall and Redemption of mankind will reach its last act in yourselves!

80. THE COMPASSIONATE CHRISTIAN.—A Christian's compassion in the presence of his neighbour's suffering has another side to it: viz. his profound suspicion of all the joy of his neighbour, of his neighbour's joy in everything that he wills and is able to do.

81. THE SAINT'S HUMANITY.—A saint had fallen into the company of believers, and could no longer stand their continually expressed hatred for sin. At last he said to them: "God created all things, except sin: therefore it is no wonder that He does not like it. But man has created sin, and why, then, should he disown this only child of his merely because it is not regarded with a friendly eye by God, its grandfather? Is that human? Honour to whom honour is due—but one's heart and duty must speak, above all, in favour of the child—and only in the second place for the honour of the grandfather!"

82. THE THEOLOGICAL ATTACK.—"You must arrange that with yourself; for your life is at stake!"—Luther it is who suddenly springs upon us with these words and imagines that we feel the knife at our throats. But we throw him off with the words of one higher and more considerate than he: "We need form no opinion in regard to this or that matter, and thus save our souls from trouble. For, by their very nature, the things themselves cannot compel us to express an opinion."

83. POOR HUMANITY!—A single drop of blood too much or too little in the brain may render our life unspeakably miserable and difficult, and we may suffer more from this single drop of blood than Prometheus from his vulture. But the worst is when we do not know that this drop is causing our sufferings—and we think it is "the devil!" Or "sin!"

84. THE PHILOLOGY OF CHRISTIANITY.—How little Christianity cultivates the sense of honesty can be inferred from the character of the writings of its learned men. They set out their conjectures as audaciously as if they were dogmas, and are but seldom at a disadvantage in regard to the interpretation of Scripture. Their continual cry is: "I am right, for it is written"—and then follows an explanation so shameless and capricious that a philologist, when he hears it, must stand stock-still between anger and laughter, asking himself again and again: Is it possible? Is it honest? Is it even decent?

It is only those who never—or always—attend church that underestimate the dishonesty with which this subject is still dealt in Protestant pulpits; in what a clumsy fashion the preacher takes advantage of his security from interruption; how the Bible is pinched and squeezed; and how the people are made acquainted with every form of the art of false reading.

When all is said and done, however, what can be expected from the effects of a religion which, during the centuries when it was being firmly established, enacted that huge philological farce concerning the Old Testament? I refer to that attempt to tear the Old Testament from the hands of the Jews under the pretext that it contained only Christian doctrines and belonged to the Christians as the true people of Israel, while the Jews had merely arrogated it to themselves without authority. This was followed by a mania of would-be interpretation and falsification, which could not under any circumstances have been allied with a good conscience. However strongly Jewish savants protested, it was everywhere sedulously asserted that the Old Testament alluded everywhere to Christ, and nothing but Christ, more especially His Cross, and thus, wherever reference was made to wood, a rod, a ladder, a twig, a tree, a willow, or a staff, such a reference could not but be a prophecy relating to the wood of the Cross: even the setting-up of the Unicorn and the Brazen Serpent, even Moses stretching forth his hands in prayer—yea, the very spits on which the Easter lambs were roasted: all these were allusions to the Cross, and, as it were, preludes to it! Did any one who kept on asserting these things ever believe in them? Let it not be forgotten that the Church did not shrink from putting interpolations in the text of the Septuagint (e.g. Ps. xcvi. 10), in order that she might later on make use of these interpolated passages as Christian prophecies. They were engaged in a struggle, and thought of their foes rather than of honesty.

85. SUBTLETY IN PENURY.—Take care not to laugh at the mythology of the Greeks merely because it so little resembles your own profound metaphysics! You should admire a people who checked their quick intellect at this point, and for a long time afterwards had tact enough to avoid the danger of scholasticism and hair-splitting superstition.

86. THE CHRISTIAN INTERPRETERS OF THE BODY.—Whatever originates in the stomach, the intestines, the beating of the heart, the nerves, the bile, the seed—all those indispositions, debilities, irritations, and the whole contingency of that machine about which we know so little—a Christian like Pascal considers it all as a moral and religious phenomenon, asking himself whether God or the devil, good or evil, salvation or damnation, is the cause. Alas for the unfortunate interpreter! How he must distort and worry his system! How he must distort and worry himself in order to gain his point!

87. THE MORAL MIRACLE.—In the domain of morality, Christianity knows of nothing but the miracle; the sudden change in all valuations, the sudden renouncement of all habits, the sudden and irresistible predilection for new things and persons. Christianity looks upon this phenomenon as the work of God, and calls it the act of regeneration, thus giving it a unique and incomparable value. Everything else which is called morality, and which bears no relation to this miracle, becomes in consequence a matter of indifference to the Christian, and indeed, so far as it is a feeling of well-being and pride, an object of fear. The canon of virtue, of the fulfilled law, is established in the New Testament, but in such a way as to be the canon of impossible virtue: men who still aspire to moral perfections must come to understand, in the face of this canon, that they are further and further removed from their aim; they must despair of virtue, and end by throwing themselves at the feet of the Merciful One.

It is only in reaching a conclusion like this that moral efforts on the part of the Christian can still be regarded as possessing any value: the condition that these efforts shall always remain sterile, painful, and melancholy is therefore indispensable; and it is in this way that those efforts could still avail to bring about that moment of ecstasy when man experiences the "overflow of grace" and the moral miracle. This struggle for morality is, however, not necessary; for it is by no means uncommon for this miracle to happen to the sinner at the very moment when he is, so to speak, wallowing in the mire of sin: yea, the leap from the deepest and most abandoned sinfulness into its contrary seems easier, and, as a clear proof of the miracle, even more desirable.

What, for the rest, may be the signification of such a sudden, unreasonable, and irresistible revolution, such a change from the depths of misery into the heights of happiness? (might it be a disguised epilepsy?) This should at all events be considered by alienists, who have frequent opportunities of observing similar "miracles"—for example, the mania of murder or suicide. The relatively "more pleasant consequences" in the case of the Christian make no important difference.

88. LUTHER, THE GREAT BENEFACTOR.—Luther's most important result is the suspicion which he awakened against the saints and the entire Christian vita contemplativa; only since his day has an un-Christian vita contemplativa again become possible in Europe, only since then has contempt for laymen and worldly activity ceased. Luther continued to be an honest miner's son even after he had been shut up in a monastery, and there, for lack of other depths and "borings," he descended into himself, and bored terrifying and dark passages through his own depths—finally coming to recognise that an introspective and saintly life was impossible to him, and that his innate "activity" in body and soul would end by being his ruin. For a long time, too long, indeed, he endeavoured to find the way to holiness through castigations; but at length he made up his mind, and said to himself: "There is no real vita contemplativa! We have been deceived. The saints were no better than the rest of us." This was truly a rustic way of gaining one's case; but for the Germans of that period it was the only proper way. How edified they felt when they could read in their Lutheran catechism: "Apart from the Ten Commandments there is no work which could find favour in the eyes of God—these much-boasted spiritual works of the saints are purely imaginary!"

89. DOUBT AS SIN.—Christianity has done all it possibly could to draw a circle round itself, and has even gone so far as to declare doubt itself to be a sin. We are to be precipitated into faith by a miracle, without the help of reason, after which we are to float in it as the clearest and least equivocal of elements—a mere glance at some solid ground, the thought that we exist for some purpose other than floating, the least movement of our amphibious nature: all this is a sin! Let it be noted that, following this decision, the proofs and demonstration of the faith, and all meditations upon its origin, are prohibited as sinful. Christianity wants blindness and frenzy and an eternal swan-song above the waves under which reason has been drowned!

90. EGOISM VERSUS EGOISM.—How many are there who still come to the conclusion: "Life would be intolerable were there no God!" Or, as is said in idealistic circles: "Life would be intolerable if its ethical signification were lacking." Hence there must be a God—or an ethical signification of existence! In reality the case stands thus: He who is accustomed to conceptions of this sort does not desire a life without them, hence these conceptions are necessary for him and his preservation—but what a presumption it is to assert that everything necessary for my preservation must exist in reality! As if my preservation were really necessary! What if others held the contrary opinion? if they did not care to live under the conditions of these two articles of faith, and did not regard life as worth living if they were realised!—And that is the present position of affairs.

91. THE HONESTY OF GOD.—An omniscient and omnipotent God who does not even take care that His intentions shall be understood by His creatures—could He be a God of goodness? A God, who, for thousands of years, has permitted innumerable doubts and scruples to continue unchecked as if they were of no importance in the salvation of mankind, and who, nevertheless, announces the most dreadful consequences for any one who mistakes his truth? Would he not be a cruel god if, being himself in possession of the truth, he could calmly contemplate mankind, in a state of miserable torment, worrying its mind as to what was truth?

Perhaps, however, he really is a God of goodness, and was unable to express Himself more clearly? Perhaps he lacked intelligence enough for this? Or eloquence? All the worse! For in such a case he may have been deceived himself in regard to what he calls his "truth," and may not be far from being another "poor, deceived devil!" Must he not therefore experience all the torments of hell at seeing His creatures suffering so much here below—and even more, suffering through all eternity—when he himself can neither advise nor help them, except as a deaf and dumb person, who makes all kinds of equivocal signs when his child or his dog is threatened with the most fearful danger? A distressed believer who argues thus might be pardoned if his pity for the suffering God were greater than his pity for his "neighbours"; for they are his neighbours no longer if that most solitary and primeval being is also the greatest sufferer and stands most in need of consolation.

Every religion shows some traits of the fact that it owes its origin to a state of human intellectuality which was as yet too young and immature: they all make light of the necessity for speaking the truth: as yet they know nothing of the duty of God, the duty of being clear and truthful in His communications with men. No one was more eloquent than Pascal in speaking of the "hidden God" and the reasons why He had to keep Himself hidden, all of which indicates clearly enough that Pascal himself could never make his mind easy on this point: but he speaks with such confidence that one is led to imagine that he must have been let into the secret at some time or other. He seemed to have some idea that the deus absconditus bore a few slight traces of immorality; and he felt too much ashamed and afraid of acknowledging this to himself: consequently, like a man who is afraid, he spoke as loudly as he could.

92. AT THE DEATH-BED OF CHRISTIANITY.—All truly active men now do without inward

Christianity, and the most moderate and thoughtful men of the intellectual middle classes possess only a kind of modified Christianity; that is, a peculiarly simplified Christianity. A God who, in his love, ordains everything so that it may be best for us, a God who gives us our virtue and our happiness and then takes them away from us, so that everything at length goes on smoothly and there is no reason left why we should take life ill or grumble about it: in short, resignation and modesty raised to the rank of divinities—that is the best and most lifelike remnant of Christianity now left to us. It must be remembered, however, that in this way Christianity has developed into a soft moralism: instead of "God, freedom, and immortality," we have now a kind of benevolence and honest sentiments, and the belief that, in the entire universe, benevolence and honest sentiments will finally prevail: this is the euthanasia of Christianity.

93. WHAT IS TRUTH?—Who will not be pleased with the conclusions which the faithful take such delight in coming to?—"Science cannot be true; for it denies God. Hence it does not come from God; and consequently it cannot be true—for God is truth." It is not the deduction but the premise which is fallacious. What if God were not exactly truth, and if this were proved? And if he were instead the vanity, the desire for power, the ambitions, the fear, and the enraptured and terrified folly of mankind?

94. REMEDY FOR THE DISPLEASED.—Even Paul already believed that some sacrifice was necessary to take away the deep displeasure which God experienced concerning sin: and ever since then Christians have never ceased to vent the ill-humour which they felt with themselves upon some victim or another—whether it was "the world," or "history," or "reason," or joy, or the tranquillity of other men—something good, no matter what, had to die for their sins (even if only in effigie)!

95. THE HISTORICAL REFUTATION AS THE DECISIVE ONE.—Formerly it was sought to prove that there was no God—now it is shown how the belief that a God existed could have originated, and by what means this belief gained authority and importance: in this way the counterproof that there is no God becomes unnecessary and superfluous.—In former times, when the "evidences of the existence of God" which had been brought forward were refuted, a doubt still remained, viz. whether better proofs could not be found than those which had just been refuted: at that time the atheists did not understand the art of making a tabula rasa.

96. "IN HOC SIGNO VINCES."—To whatever degree of progress Europe may have attained in other respects, where religious affairs are concerned it has not yet reached the liberal naïveté of the ancient Brahmins, which proves that, in India, four thousand years ago, people meditated more profoundly and transmitted to their descendants more pleasure in meditating than is the case in our own days. For those Brahmins believed in the first place that the priests were more powerful than the gods, and in the second place that it was observances which constituted the power of the priests: as a result of which their poets were never tired of glorifying those observances (prayers, ceremonies, sacrifices, chants, improvised melodies) as the real dispensers of all benefits. Although a certain amount of superstition and poetry was mingled with all this, the principles were true! A step further, and the gods were cast aside—which Europe likewise will have to do before very long! One more step further, and priests and intermediaries could also be dispensed with—and then Buddha, the teacher of the religion of self-redemption, appeared. How far Europe is still removed from this degree of culture! When at length all the customs and observances, upon which rests the power of gods, priests, and saviours, shall have been destroyed, when as a consequence morality, in the old sense, will be dead, then there will come ... yea, what will come then? But let us refrain from speculating; let us rather make certain that Europe will retrieve that which, in India, amidst this people of thinkers, was carried out thousands of years ago as a commandment of thought!

Scattered among the different nations of Europe there are now from ten to twenty millions of men who no longer "believe in God"—is it too much to ask that they should give each other some indication or password? As soon as they recognise each other in this way, they will also make themselves known to each other; and they will immediately become a power in Europe, and, happily, a power among the nations! among the classes! between rich and poor! between those who command, and those who obey! between the most restless and the most tranquil, tranquillising people!

BOOK II

97. ONE BECOMES MORAL—but not because one is moral! Submission to morals may be due to slavishness or vanity, egoism or resignation, dismal fanaticism or thoughtlessness. It may, again, be an act of despair, such as submission to the authority of a ruler; but there is nothing moral about it per se.

98. ALTERATIONS IN MORALS.—Morals are constantly undergoing changes and transformations, occasioned by successful crimes. (To these, for example, belong all innovations in moral judgments.)

99. WHEREIN WE ARE ALL IRRATIONAL.—We still continue to draw conclusions from judgments which we consider as false, or doctrines in which we no longer believe,—through our feelings.

100. AWAKING FROM A DREAM.—Noble and wise men once upon a time believed in the music of the spheres; there are still noble and wise men who believe in "the moral significance of existence," but there will come a day when this music of the spheres also will no longer be audible to them. They will awake and perceive that their ears have been dreaming.

101. OPEN TO DOUBT.—To accept a belief simply because it is customary implies that one is dishonest, cowardly, and lazy.—Must dishonesty, cowardice, and laziness, therefore, be the primary conditions of morality?

102. THE MOST ANCIENT MORAL JUDGMENTS.—What attitude do we assume towards the acts of our neighbour?—In the first place, we consider how they may benefit ourselves—we see them only in this light. It is this effect which we regard as the intention of the acts,—and in the end we come to look upon these intentions of our neighbour as permanent qualities in him, and we call him, for example, "a dangerous man." Triple error! Triple and most ancient mistake! Perhaps this inheritance comes to us from the animals and their faculty of judgment! Must not the origin of all morality be sought in these detestable narrow-minded conclusions: "Whatever injures me is evil (something injurious in itself), whatever benefits me is good (beneficial and profitable in itself), whatever injures me once or several times is hostile per se; whatever benefits me once or several times is friendly per se." O pudenda origo! Is not this equivalent to interpreting the contemptible, occasional, and often merely accidental relations of another person to us as his primary and most essential qualities, and affirming that towards himself and every one else he is only capable of such actions as we ourselves have experienced at his hands once or several times! And is not this thorough folly based upon the most immodest of all mental reservations: namely, that we ourselves must be the standard of what is good, since we determine good and evil?

103. THERE ARE TWO CLASSES OF PEOPLE WHO DENY MORALITY.—To deny morality may mean, in the first place, to deny the moral inducements which, men pretend, have urged them on to their actions,—which is equivalent to saying that morality merely consists of words and forms, part of that coarse and subtle deceit (especially self-deceit) which is characteristic of mankind, and perhaps more especially of those men who are celebrated for their virtues. In the second place, it may mean our denying that moral judgments are founded on truths. It is admitted in such a case that these judgments are, in fact, the motives of the actions, but that in this way it is really errors as the basis of all moral judgments which urge men on to their moral actions. This is my point of view; but I should be far from denying that in very many cases a subtle suspicion in accordance with the former point of view—i.e. in the spirit of La Rochefoucauld—is also justifiable, and in any case of a high general utility.—Therefore I deny morality in the same way as I deny alchemy, i.e. I deny its hypotheses; but I do not deny that there have been alchemists who believed in these hypotheses and based their actions upon them. I also deny immorality—not that innumerable people feel immoral, but that there is any true reason why they should feel so. I should not, of course, deny—unless I were a fool—that many actions which are called immoral should be avoided and resisted; and in the same way that many which are called moral should be performed and encouraged; but I hold that in both cases these actions should be performed from motives other than those which have prevailed up to the present time. We must learn anew in order that at last, perhaps very late in the day, we may be able to do something more: feel anew.

104. OUR VALUATIONS.—All actions may be referred back to valuations, and all valuations are either one's own or adopted, the latter being by far the more numerous. Why do we adopt them?

Through fear, i.e. we think it more advisable to pretend that they are our own, and so well do we accustom ourselves to do so that it at last becomes second nature to us. A valuation of our own, which is the appreciation of a thing in accordance with the pleasure or displeasure it causes us and no one else, is something very rare indeed!—But must not our valuation of our neighbour—which is prompted by the motive that we adopt his valuation in most cases—proceed from ourselves and by our own decision? Of course, but then we come to these decisions during our childhood, and seldom change them. We often remain during our whole lifetime the dupes of our childish and accustomed judgments in our manner of judging our fellow-men (their minds, rank, morality, character, and reprehensibility), and we find it necessary to subscribe to their valuations.

105. PSEUDO-EGOISM.—The great majority of people, whatever they may think and say about their "egoism," do nothing for their ego all their life long, but only for a phantom of this ego which has been formed in regard to them by their friends and communicated to them. As a consequence, they all live in a haze of impersonal and half-personal opinions and of arbitrary and, as it were, poetic valuations: the one always in the head of another, and this head, again, in the head of somebody else—a queer world of phantoms which manages to give itself a rational appearance! This haze of opinions and habits grows in extent and lives almost independently of the people it surrounds; it is it which gives rise to the immense effect of general judgments on "man"—all those men, who do not know themselves, believe in a bloodless abstraction which they call "man," i.e. in a fiction; and every change caused in this abstraction by the judgments of powerful individualities (such as princes and philosophers) produces an extraordinary and irrational effect on the great majority,—for the simple reason that not a single individual in this haze can oppose a real ego, an ego which is accessible to and fathomed by himself, to the universal pale fiction, which he could thereby destroy.

106. AGAINST DEFINITIONS OF MORAL AIMS.—On all sides we now hear the aim of morals defined as the preservation and advancement of humanity; but this is merely the expression of a wish to have a formula and nothing more. Preservation wherein? advancement whither? These are questions which must at once be asked. Is not the most essential point, the answer to this wherein? and whither? left out of the formula? What results therefrom, so far as our own actions and duties are concerned, which is not already tacitly and instinctively understood? Can we sufficiently understand from this formula whether we must prolong as far as possible the existence of the human race, or bring about the greatest possible disanimalisation of man? How different the means, i.e. the practical morals, would have to be in the two cases! Supposing that the greatest possible rationality were given to mankind, this certainly would not guarantee the longest possible existence for them! Or supposing that their "greatest happiness" was thought to be the answer to the questions put, do we thereby mean the highest degree of happiness which a few individuals might attain, or an incalculable, though finally attainable, average state of happiness for all? And why should morality be the way to it? Has not morality, considered as a whole, opened up so many sources of displeasure as to lead us to think that man up to the present, with every new refinement of morality, has become more and more discontented with himself, with his neighbour, and with his own lot? Has not the most moral of men hitherto believed that the only justifiable state of mankind in the face of morals is that of the deepest misery?

107. OUR RIGHT TO OUR FOLLY.—How must we act? Why must we act? So far as the coarse and immediate needs of the individual are concerned, it is easy to answer these questions, but the more we enter upon the more important and more subtle domains of action, the more does the problem become uncertain and the more arbitrary its solution. An arbitrary decision, however, is the very thing that must be excluded here,—thus commands the authority of morals: an obscure uneasiness and awe must relentlessly guide man in those very actions the objects and means of which he cannot at once perceive. This authority of morals undermines our thinking faculty in regard to those things concerning which it might be dangerous to think wrongly,—it is in this way, at all events, that morality usually justifies itself to its accusers. Wrong in this place means dangerous; but dangerous to whom? It is not, as a rule, the danger of the doer of the action which the supporters of authoritative morals have in view, but their own danger; the loss which their power and influence might undergo if the right to act according to their own greater or lesser reason, however wilfully and foolishly, were accorded to all men. They on their part make unhesitating use of their right to arbitrariness and folly,—they even command in cases where it is hardly possible, or at all events very difficult, to answer the questions, "How must they act, why must they act?" And if the reason of mankind grows with such extraordinary slowness that it was often possible to deny its growth during the whole course of humanity, what is more to blame for this than this solemn presence, even omnipresence, of moral commands, which do not even permit the individual question of how and why to be asked at all? Have we not been educated precisely in such a way as to make us feel pathetic, and thus to obscure our vision at the very time when our reason should be able to see as clearly and calmly as possible—i.e. in all higher and more important circumstances?

108. SOME THESES.—We should not give the individual, in so far as he desires his own happiness, any precepts or recommendations as to the road leading to happiness; for individual happiness arises from particular laws that are unknown to anybody, and such a man will only be

hindered or obstructed by recommendations which come to him from outside sources. Those precepts which are called moral are in reality directed against individuals, and do not by any means make for the happiness of such individuals. The relationship of these precepts to the "happiness and well-being of mankind" is equally slight, for it is quite impossible to assign a definite conception to these words, and still less can they be employed as guiding stars on the dark sea of moral aspirations. It is a prejudice to think that morality is more favourable to the development of the reason than immorality. It is erroneous to suppose that the unconscious aim in the development of every conscious being (namely, animal, man, humanity, etc.) is its "greatest happiness": on the contrary, there is a particular and incomparable happiness to be attained at every stage of our development, one that is neither high nor low, but quite an individual happiness. Evolution does not make happiness its goal; it aims merely at evolution, and nothing else. It is only if humanity had a universally recognised goal that we could propose to do this or that: for the time being there is no such goal. It follows that the pretensions of morality should not be brought into any relationship with mankind: this would be merely childish and irrational. It is quite another thing to recommend a goal to mankind: this goal would then be something that would depend upon our own will and pleasure. Provided that mankind in general agreed to adopt such a goal, it could then impose a moral law upon itself, a law which would, at all events, be imposed by their own free will. Up to now, however, the moral law has had to be placed above our own free will: strictly speaking, men did not wish to impose this law upon themselves; they wished to take it from somewhere, to discover it, or to let themselves be commanded by it from somewhere.

109. SELF-CONTROL AND MODERATION, AND THEIR FINAL MOTIVE.—I find not more than six essentially different methods for combating the vehemence of an impulse. First of all, we may avoid the occasion for satisfying the impulse, weakening and mortifying it by refraining from satisfying it for long and ever-lengthening periods. Secondly, we may impose a severe and regular order upon ourselves in regard to the satisfying of our appetites. By thus regulating the impulse and limiting its ebb and flow to fixed periods, we may obtain intervals in which it ceases to disturb us; and by beginning in this way we may perhaps be able to pass on to the first method. In the third place, we may deliberately give ourselves over to an unrestrained and unbounded gratification of the impulse in order that we may become disgusted with it, and to obtain by means of this very disgust a command over the impulse: provided, of course, that we do not imitate the rider who rides his horse to death and breaks his own neck in doing so. For this, unhappily, is generally the outcome of the application of this third method.

In the fourth place, there is an intellectual trick, which consists in associating the idea of the gratification so firmly with some painful thought, that after a little practice the thought of gratification is itself immediately felt as a very painful one. (For example, when the Christian accustoms himself to think of the presence and scorn of the devil in the course of sensual enjoyment, or everlasting punishment in hell for revenge by murder; or even merely of the contempt which he will meet with from those of his fellow-men whom he most respects, if he steals a sum of money, or if a man has often checked an intense desire for suicide by thinking of the grief and self-reproaches of his relations and friends, and has thus succeeded in balancing himself upon the edge of life: for, after some practice, these ideas follow one another in his mind like cause and effect.) Among instances of this kind may be mentioned the cases of Lord Byron and Napoleon, in whom the pride of man revolted and took offence at the preponderance of one particular passion over the collective attitude and order of reason. From this arises the habit and joy of tyrannising over the craving and making it, as it were, gnash its teeth. "I will not be a slave of any appetite," wrote Byron in his diary. In the fifth place, we may bring about a dislocation of our powers by imposing upon ourselves a particularly difficult and fatiguing task, or by deliberately submitting to some new charm and pleasure in order thus to turn our thoughts and physical powers into other channels. It comes to the same thing if we temporarily favour another impulse by affording it numerous opportunities of gratification, and thus rendering it the squanderer of the power which would otherwise be commandeered, so to speak, by the tyrannical impulse. A few, perhaps, will be able to restrain the particular passion which aspires to domination by granting their other known passions a temporary encouragement and license in order that they may devour the food which the tyrant wishes for himself alone.

In the sixth and last place, the man who can stand it, and thinks it reasonable to weaken and subdue his entire physical and psychical organisation, likewise, of course, attains the goal of weakening a single violent instinct; as, for example, those who starve their sensuality and at the same time their vigour, and often destroy their reason into the bargain, such as the ascetics.—Hence, shunning the opportunities, regulating the impulse, bringing about satiety and disgust in the impulse, associating a painful idea (such as that of discredit, disgust, or offended pride), then the dislocation of one's forces, and finally general debility and exhaustion: these are the six methods. But the will to combat the violence of a craving is beyond our power, equally with the method we adopt and the success we may have in applying it. In all this process our intellect is rather merely the blind instrument of another rival craving, whether it be the impulse to repose, or the fear of disgrace and other evil consequences, or love. While "we" thus imagine that we are complaining of the violence of an impulse, it is at bottom merely one impulse which is complaining of another, i.e. the perception of the violent suffering which is being caused us presupposes that there is another equally or more violent impulse, and that a struggle is impending in which our intellect must take part.

110. THAT WHICH OPPOSES.—We may observe the following process in ourselves, and I should like it to be often observed and confirmed. There arises in us the scent of a kind of pleasure hitherto unknown to us, and consequently a new craving. Now, the question is, What opposes itself to this craving? If it be things and considerations of a common kind, or people whom we hold in no very high esteem, the aim of the new craving assumes the appearance of a "noble, good, praiseworthy feeling, and one worthy of sacrifice": all the moral dispositions which have been inherited will adopt it and will add it to the number of those aims which we consider as moral—and now we imagine that we are no longer striving after a pleasure, but after a morality, which greatly increases our confidence in our aspirations.

111. TO THE ADMIRERS OF OBJECTIVENESS.—He who, as a child, has observed in his parents and acquaintances in the midst of whom he has grown up, certain varied and strong feelings, with but little subtle discernment and inclination for intellectual justice, and has therefore employed his best powers and his most precious time in imitating these feelings, will observe in himself when he arrives at years of discretion that every new thing or man he meets with excites in him either sympathy or aversion, envy or contempt. Under the domination of this experience, which he is powerless to shake off, he admires neutrality of feeling or "objectivity" as an extraordinary thing, as something connected with genius or a very rare morality, and he cannot believe that even this neutrality is merely the product of education and habit.

112. ON THE NATURAL HISTORY OF DUTY AND RIGHT.—Our duties are the claims which others have upon us. How did they acquire these claims? By the fact that they considered us as capable of making and holding agreements and contracts, by assuming that we were their like and equals, and by consequently entrusting something to us, bringing us up, educating us, and supporting us. We do our duty, i.e. we justify that conception of our power for the sake of which all these things were done for us. We return them in proportion as they were meted out to us. It is thus our pride that orders us to do our duty—we desire to re-establish our own independence by opposing to that which others have done for us something that we do for them, for in that way the others invade our sphere of power, and would for ever have a hand in it if we did not make reprisals by means of "duty," and thus encroach upon their power. The rights of others can only have regard to that which lies within our power; it would be unreasonable on their part to require something from us which does not belong to us. To put the matter more accurately, their rights can only relate to what they imagine to be in our power, provided that it is something that we ourselves consider as being in our power. The same error may easily occur on either side. The feeling of duty depends upon our having the same belief in regard to the extent of our power as other people have, i.e. that we can promise certain things and undertake to do them freely ("free will").

My rights consist of that part of my power which others have not only conceded to me, but which they wish to maintain for me. Why do they do it? On the one hand they are actuated by wisdom, fear and prudence: whether they expect something similar from us (the protection of their rights), whether they consider a struggle with us as dangerous or inopportune, or whether they see a disadvantage to themselves in every diminution of our power, since in that case we should be ill adapted for an alliance with them against a hostile third power. On the other hand rights are granted by donations and cessions. In this latter case, the other people have not only enough power, but more than enough, so that they can give up a portion and guarantee it to the person to whom they give it: whereby they presuppose a certain restricted sense of power in the person upon whom they have bestowed the gift. In this way rights arise: recognised and guaranteed degrees of power. When the relations of powers to one another are materially changed, rights disappear and new ones are formed, as is demonstrated by the constant flux and reflux of the rights of nations. When our power diminishes to any great extent, the feelings of those who hitherto guaranteed it undergo some change: they consider whether they shall once again restore us to our former possession, and if they do not see their way to do this they deny our "rights" from that time forward. In the same way, if our power increases to a considerable extent the feelings of those who previously recognised it, and whose recognition we no longer require, likewise change: they will then try to reduce our power to its former dimensions, and they will endeavour to interfere in our affairs, justifying their interference by an appeal to their "duty." But this is merely useless word-quibbling. Where right prevails, a certain state and degree of power is maintained, and all attempts at its augmentation and diminution are resisted. The right of others is the concession of our feeling of power to the feeling of power in these others. Whenever our power shows itself to be thoroughly shattered and broken, our rights cease: on the other hand, when we have become very much stronger, the rights of others cease in our minds to be what we have hitherto admitted them to be. The man who aims at being just, therefore, must keep a constant lookout for the changes in the indicator of the scales in order that he may properly estimate the degrees of power and right which, with the customary transitoriness of human things, retain their equilibrium for only a short time and in most cases continue to rise and fall. As a consequence it is thus very difficult to be "just," and requires much experience, good intentions, and an unusually large amount of good sense.

113. STRIVING FOR DISTINCTION.—When we strive after distinction we must ceaselessly keep our eyes fixed on our neighbour and endeavour to ascertain what his feelings are; but the sympathy and knowledge which are necessary to satisfy this desire are far from being inspired by harmlessness, compassion, or kindness. On the contrary, we wish to perceive or find out in what way our neighbour suffers from us, either internally or externally, how he loses control over himself and yields to the impression which our hand or even our mere appearance makes on him. Even when he who aspires to distinction makes or wishes to make a joyful, elevating, or cheerful impression, he does not enjoy this success in that he rejoices, exalts, or cheers his neighbour, but in that he leaves his impress on the latter's soul, changing its form and dominating it according to his will. The desire for distinction is the desire to subject one's neighbour, even if it be merely in an indirect fashion, one only felt or even only dreamt of. There is a long series of stages in this secretly-desired will to subdue, and a very complete record of them would perhaps almost be like an excellent history of culture from the early distortions of barbarism down to the caricatures of modern over-refinement and sickly idealism.

This desire for distinction entails upon our neighbour—to indicate only a few rungs of the long ladder—torture first of all, followed by blows, then terror, anxious surprise, wonder, envy, admiration, elevation, pleasure, joy, laughter, derision, mockery, sneers, scourging and self-inflicted torture. There at the very top of the ladder stands the ascetic and martyr, who himself experiences the utmost satisfaction, because he inflicts on himself, as a result of his desire for distinction, that pain which his opposite, the barbarian on the first rung of the ladder, inflicts upon those others, upon whom and before whom he wishes to distinguish himself. The triumph of the ascetic over himself, his introspective glance, which beholds a man split up into a sufferer and a spectator, and which henceforth never looks at the outside world but to gather from it, as it were, wood for his own funeral pyre: this final tragedy of the desire for distinction which shows us only one person who, so to speak, is consumed internally—that is an end worthy of the beginning: in both cases there is an inexpressible happiness at the sight of torture; indeed, happiness considered as a feeling of power developed to the utmost, has perhaps never reached a higher pitch of perfection on earth than in the souls of superstitious ascetics. This is expressed by the Brahmins in the story of King Visvamitra, who obtained so much strength by thousands of years of penance that he undertook to construct a new heaven. I believe that in the entire category of inward experiences the people of our time are mere novices and clumsy guessers who "try to have a shot at it": four thousand years ago much more was known about these execrable refinements of self-enjoyment. Perhaps at that time the creation of the world was imagined by some Hindu dreamer to have been an ascetic operation which a god took upon himself! Perhaps this god may have wished to join himself to a mobile nature as an instrument of torture in order thus to feel his happiness and power doubled! And even supposing him to have been a god of love: what a delight it would have been for him to create a suffering mankind in order that he himself might suffer divinely and super-humanly from the sight of the continual torture of his creatures, and thus to tyrannise over himself! And, again, supposing him to have been not only a god of love, but also a god of holiness, we can scarcely conceive the ecstasies of this divine ascetic while creating sins and sinners and eternal punishment, and an immense place of eternal torture below his throne where there is a continual weeping and wailing and gnashing of teeth!

It is not by any means impossible that the soul of a St. Paul, a Dante, or a Calvin, and people like them, may once have penetrated into the terrifying secrets of such voluptuousness of power, and in view of such souls we may well ask whether the circle of this desire for distinction has come to a close with the ascetic. Might it not be possible for the course of this circle to be traversed a second time, by uniting the fundamental idea of the ascetic, and at the same time that of a compassionate Deity? In other words, pain would be given to others in order that pain might be given to one's self, so that in this way one could triumph over one's self and one's pity to enjoy the extreme voluptuousness of power.—Forgive me these digressions, which come to my mind when I think of all the possibilities in the vast domain of psychical debaucheries to which one may be led by the desire for power!

114. ON THE KNOWLEDGE OF THE SUFFERER.—The state of sick men who have suffered long and terribly from the torture inflicted upon them by their illness, and whose reason has nevertheless not been in any way affected, is not without a certain amount of value in our search for knowledge—quite apart from the intellectual benefits which follow upon every profound solitude and every sudden and justified liberation from duties and habits. The man who suffers severely looks forth with terrible calmness from his state of suffering upon outside things: all those little lying enchantments, by which things are usually surrounded when seen through the eye of a healthy person, have vanished from the sufferer; his own life even lies there before him, stripped of all bloom and colour. If by chance it has happened that up to then he has lived in some kind of dangerous fantasy, this extreme disenchantment through pain is the means, and possibly the only means, of extricating him from it. (It is possible that this is what happened to the Founder of Christianity when suspended from the Cross; for

the bitterest words ever pronounced, "My God, My God, why hast Thou forsaken Me?" if understood in their deepest sense, as they ought to be understood, contain the evidence of a complete disillusionment and enlightenment in regard to the deceptions of life: in that moment of supreme suffering Christ obtained a clear insight into Himself, just as in the poet's narrative did the poor dying Don Quixote.)

The formidable tension of the intellect that wishes to hold its own against pain shows everything that one now looks upon in a new light, and the inexpressible charm of this new light is often powerful enough to withstand all the seductiveness of suicide and to make the continuation of life seem very desirable to the sufferer. His mind scornfully turns to the warm and comfortable dream-world in which the healthy man moves about thoughtlessly, and he thinks with contempt of the noblest and most cherished illusions in which he formerly indulged. He experiences delight in conjuring up this contempt as if from the depths of hell, and thus inflicting the bitterest sufferings upon his soul: it is by this counterpoise that he bears up against physical suffering—he feels that such a counterpoise is now essential! In one terrible moment of clear-sightedness he says to himself, "Be for once thine own accuser and hangman; for once regard thy suffering as a punishment which thou hast inflicted on thyself! Enjoy thy superiority as a judge: better still, enjoy thine own will and pleasure, thy tyrannical arbitrariness! Raise thyself above thy life as above thy suffering, and look down into the depth of reason and unreason!"

Our pride revolts as it never did before, it experiences an incomparable charm in defending life against such a tyrant as suffering and against all the insinuations of this tyrant, who would fain urge us to give evidence against life,—we are taking the part of life in the face of this tyrant. In this state of mind we take up a bitter stand against all pessimism in order that it may not appear to be a consequence of our condition, and thus humiliate us as conquered ones. The charm of being just in our judgments was also never greater than now; for now this justice is a triumph over ourselves and over so irritated a state of mind that unfairness of judgment might be excused,—but we will not be excused, it is now, if ever, that we wish to show that we need no excuse. We pass through downright orgies of pride.

And now appears the first ray of relief, of recovery, and one of its first effects is that we turn against the preponderance of our pride: we call ourselves foolish and vain, as if we had undergone some unique experience. We humiliate ungratefully this all-powerful pride, the aid of which enabled us to endure the pain we suffered, and we call vehemently for some antidote for this pride: we wish to become strangers to ourselves and to be freed from our own person after pain has forcibly made us personal too long. "Away with this pride," we cry, "it was only another illness and convulsion!" Once more we look longingly at men and nature and recollect with a sorrowful smile that now since the veil has fallen we regard many things concerning them in a new and different light,—but we are refreshed by once more seeing the softened lights of life, and emerge from that fearfully dispassionate daylight in which we as sufferers saw things and through things. We do not get angry when we see the charms of health resume their play, and we contemplate the sight as if transformed, gently and still fatigued. In this state we cannot listen to music without weeping.

115. THE SO-CALLED "EGO."—Language and the prejudices upon which language is based very often act as obstacles in our paths when we proceed to explore internal phenomena and impulses: as one example, we may instance the fact that there are only words to express the superlative degrees of these phenomena and impulses. Now, it is our habit no longer to observe accurately when words fail us, since it is difficult in such cases to think with precision: in former times, even, people involuntarily came to the conclusion that where the domain of words ceased, the domain of existence ceased also. Wrath, hatred, love, pity, desire, recognition, joy, pain: all these are names indicating extreme conditions; the milder and middle stages, and even more particularly the ever active lower stages, escape our attention, and yet it is they which weave the warp and woof of our character and destiny. It often happens that these extreme outbursts—and even the most moderate pleasure or displeasure of which we are actually conscious, whether in partaking of food or listening to a sound, is possibly, if properly estimated, merely an extreme outburst,—destroy the texture and are then violent exceptions, in most cases the consequences of some congestions,—and how easily as such can they mislead the observer! as indeed they mislead the person acting! We are all of us not what we appear to be according to the conditions for which alone we have consciousness and words, and consequently praise and blame. We fail to recognise ourselves after these coarse outbursts which are known to ourselves alone, we draw conclusions from data where the exceptions prove stronger than the rules; we misinterpret ourselves in reading our own ego's pronouncements, which appeared to be so clear. But our opinion of ourselves, this so-called ego which we have arrived at by this wrong method, contributes henceforth to form our character and destiny.

116. THE UNKNOWN WORLD OF THE "SUBJECT."—What men have found it so difficult to understand from the most ancient times down to the present day is their ignorance in regard to themselves, not merely with respect to good and evil, but something even more essential. The oldest of illusions lives on, namely, that we know, and know precisely in each case, how human action is originated. Not only "God who looks into the heart," not only the man who acts and reflects upon his

action, but everybody does not doubt that he understands the phenomena of action in every one else. "I know what I want and what I have done, I am free and responsible for my act, and I make others responsible for their acts; I can mention by its name every moral possibility and every internal movement which precedes an act,—ye may act as ye will, I understand myself and I understand you all!" Such was what every one thought once upon a time, and almost every one thinks so even now. Socrates and Plato, who in this matter were great sceptics and admirable innovators, were nevertheless intensely credulous in regard to that fatal prejudice, that profound error, which holds that "The right knowledge must necessarily be followed by the right action." In holding this principle they were still the heirs of the universal folly and presumption that knowledge exists concerning the essence of an action.

"It would indeed be dreadful if the comprehension of the essence of a right action were not followed by that right action itself"—this was the only manner in which these great men thought it necessary to demonstrate this idea, the contrary seemed to them to be inconceivable and mad; and nevertheless this contrary corresponds to the naked reality which has been demonstrated daily and hourly from time immemorial. Is it not a "dreadful" truth that all that we know about an act is never sufficient to accomplish it, that the bridge connecting the knowledge of the act with the act itself has never yet been built? Acts are never what they appear to us to be. We have taken great pains to learn that external things are not as they appear to us.—Well! It is the same with internal phenomena. All moral acts are in reality "something different,"—we cannot say anything more about them, and all acts are essentially unknown to us. The general belief, however, has been and still is quite the contrary: the most ancient realism is against us: up to the present humanity has thought, "An action is what it appears to be." (In re-reading these words a very expressive passage from Schopenhauer occurs to me, and I will quote it as a proof that he, too, without the slightest scruple, continued to adhere to this moral realism: "Each one of us is in reality a competent and perfect moral judge, knowing exactly good and evil, made holy by loving good and despising evil,—such is every one of us in so far as the acts of others and not his own are under consideration, and when he has merely to approve or disapprove, whilst the burden of the performance of the acts is borne by other shoulders. Every one is therefore justified in occupying as confessor the place of God.")

117. IN PRISON.—My eye, whether it be keen or weak, can only see a certain distance, and it is within this space that I live and move: this horizon is my immediate fate, greater or lesser, from which I cannot escape. Thus, a concentric circle is drawn round every being, which has a centre and is peculiar to himself. In the same way our ear encloses us in a small space, and so likewise does our touch. We measure the world by these horizons within which our senses confine each of us within prison walls. We say that this is near and that is far distant, that this is large and that is small, that one thing is hard and another soft; and this appreciation of things we call sensation—but it is all an error per se! According to the number of events and emotions which it is on an average possible for us to experience in a given space of time, we measure our lives; we call them short or long, rich or poor, full or empty; and according to the average of human life we estimate that of other beings,—and all this is an error per se!

If we had eyes a hundred times more piercing to examine the things that surround us, men would seem to us to be enormously tall; we can even imagine organs by means of which men would appear to us to be of immeasurable stature. On the other hand, certain organs could be so formed as to permit us to view entire solar systems as if they were contracted and brought close together like a single cell: and to beings of an inverse order a single cell of the human body could be made to appear in its construction, movement, and harmony as if it were a solar system in itself. The habits of our senses have wrapped us up in a tissue of lying sensations which in their turn lie at the base of all our judgments and our "knowledge,"—there are no means of exit or escape to the real world! We are like spiders in our own webs, and, whatever we may catch in them, it will only be something that our web is capable of catching.

118. WHAT IS OUR NEIGHBOUR?—What do we conceive of our neighbour except his limits: I mean that whereby he, as it were, engraves and stamps himself in and upon us? We can understand nothing of him except the changes which take place upon our own person and of which he is the cause, what we know of him is like a hollow, modelled space. We impute to him the feelings which his acts arouse in us, and thus give him a wrong and inverted positivity. We form him after our knowledge of ourselves into a satellite of our own system, and if he shines upon us, or grows dark, and we in any case are the ultimate cause of his doing so, we nevertheless still believe the contrary! O world of phantoms in which we live! O world so perverted, topsy-turvy and empty, and yet dreamt of as full and upright!

119. EXPERIENCE AND INVENTION.—To however high a degree a man can attain to knowledge of himself, nothing can be more incomplete than the conception which he forms of the instincts constituting his individuality. He can scarcely name the more common instincts: their number and force, their flux and reflux, their action and counteraction, and, above all, the laws of their nutrition, remain absolutely unknown to him. This nutrition, therefore, becomes a work of chance: the daily experiences of our lives throw their prey now to this instinct and now to that, and the instincts gradually

seize upon it; but the ebb and flow of these experiences does not stand in any rational relationship to the nutritive needs of the total number of the instincts. Two things, then, must always happen: some cravings will be neglected and starved to death, while others will be overfed. Every moment in the life of man causes some polypous arms of his being to grow and others to wither away, in accordance with the nutriment which that moment may or may not bring with it. Our experiences, as I have already said, are all in this sense means of nutriment, but scattered about with a careless hand and without discrimination between the hungry and the overfed. As a consequence of this accidental nutrition of each particular part, the polypus in its complete development will be something just as fortuitous as its growth.

To put this more clearly: let us suppose that an instinct or craving has reached that point when it demands gratification,—either the exercise of its power or the discharge of it, or the filling up of a vacuum (all this is metaphorical language),—then it will examine every event that occurs in the course of the day to ascertain how it can be utilised with the object of fulfilling its aim: whether the man runs or rests, or is angry, or reads or speaks or fights or rejoices, the unsatiated instinct watches, as it were, every condition into which the man enters, and, as a rule, if it finds nothing for itself it must wait, still unsatisfied. After a little while it becomes feeble, and at the end of a few days or a few months, if it has not been satisfied, it will wither away like a plant which has not been watered. This cruelty of chance would perhaps be more conspicuous if all the cravings were as vehement in their demands as hunger, which refuses to be satisfied with imaginary dishes; but the great majority of our instincts, especially those which are called moral, are thus easily satisfied,—if it be permitted to suppose that our dreams serve as compensation to a certain extent for the accidental absence of "nutriment" during the day. Why was last night's dream full of tenderness and tears, that of the night before amusing and gay, and the previous one adventurous and engaged in some continual obscure search? How does it come about that in this dream I enjoy indescribable beauties of music, and in that one I soar and fly upwards with the delight of an eagle to the most distant heights?

These inventions in which our instincts of tenderness, merriment, or adventurousness, or our desire for music and mountains, can have free play and scope—and every one can recall striking instances—are interpretations of our nervous irritations during sleep, very free and arbitrary interpretations of the movements of our blood and intestines, and the pressure of our arm and the bed coverings, or the sound of a church bell, the weathercocks, the moths, and so on. That this text, which on the whole is very much the same for one night as another, is so differently commented upon, that our creative reason imagines such different causes for the nervous irritations of one day as compared with another, may be explained by the fact that the prompter of this reason was different to-day from yesterday—another instinct or craving wished to be satisfied, to show itself, to exercise itself and be refreshed and discharged: this particular one being at its height to-day and another one being at its height last night. Real life has not the freedom of interpretation possessed by dream life; it is less poetic and less unrestrained—but is it necessary for me to show that our instincts, when we are awake, likewise merely interpret our nervous irritations and determine their "causes" in accordance with their requirements? that there is no really essential difference between waking and dreaming! that even in comparing different degrees of culture, the freedom of the conscious interpretation of the one is not in any way inferior to the freedom in dreams of the other! that our moral judgments and valuations are only images and fantasies concerning physiological processes unknown to us, a kind of habitual language to describe certain nervous irritations? that all our so-called consciousness is a more or less fantastic commentary of an unknown text, one which is perhaps unknowable but yet felt?

Consider some insignificant occurrence. Let us suppose that some day as we pass along a public street we see some one laughing at us. In accordance with whatever craving has reached its culminating point within us at that moment, this incident will have this or that signification for us; and it will be a very different occurrence in accordance with the class of men to which we belong. One man will take it like a drop of rain, another will shake it off like a fly, a third person will try to pick a quarrel on account of it, a fourth will examine his garments to see if there is anything about them likely to cause laughter, and a fifth will in consequence think about what is ridiculous per se, a sixth will be pleased at having involuntarily contributed to add a ray of sunshine and mirth to the world,—in all these cases some craving is gratified, whether anger, combativeness, meditation, or benevolence. This instinct, whatever it may be, has seized upon that incident as its prey: why that particular one? Because, hungry and thirsty, it was lying in ambush.

Not long ago at 11 o'clock in the morning a man suddenly collapsed and fell down in front of me as if struck by lightning. All the women who were near at once gave utterance to cries of horror, while I set the man on his feet again and waited until he recovered his speech. During this time no muscle of my face moved and I experienced no sensation of fear or pity; I simply did what was most urgent and reasonable and calmly proceeded on my way. Supposing some one had told me on the previous evening that at 11 o'clock on the following day a man would fall down in front of me like this, I should have suffered all kinds of agonies in the interval, lying awake all night, and at the decisive moment should also perhaps have fallen down like the man instead of helping him; for in the meantime all the imaginable cravings within me would have had leisure to conceive and to comment upon this incident. What are our experiences, then? Much more what we attribute to them than what they really are. Or should we perhaps say that nothing is contained in them? that experiences in themselves are merely works of fancy?

120. TO TRANQUILLISE THE SCEPTIC.—"I don't know at all what I am doing. I don't know in the least what I ought to do!"—You are right, but be sure of this: you are being done at every moment! Mankind has at all times mistaken the active for the passive: it is its eternal grammatical blunder.

121. CAUSE AND EFFECT.—On this mirror—and our intellect is a mirror—something is going on that indicates regularity: a certain thing is each time followed by another certain thing. When we perceive this and wish to give it a name, we call it cause and effect,—fools that we are! as if in this we had understood or could understand anything! For, of course, we have seen nothing but the images of causes and effects, and it is just this figurativeness which renders it impossible for us to see a more substantial relation than that of sequence!

122. THE PURPOSES IN NATURE.—Any impartial investigator who examines the history of the eye and its form in the lower creatures, and sees how the visual organ was slowly developed, cannot help recognising that sight was not the first purpose of the eye, but probably only asserted itself when pure hazard had contributed to bring together the apparatus. One single example of this kind, and the "final purposes" fall from our eyes like scales.

123. REASON.—How did reason come into the world? As is only proper, in an irrational manner; by accident. We shall have to guess at this accident as a riddle.

124. WHAT IS VOLITION?—We laugh at a man who, stepping out of his room at the very minute when the sun is rising, says, "It is my will that the sun shall rise"; or at him who, unable to stop a wheel, says, "I wish it to roll"; or, again, at him who, thrown in a wrestling match, says, "Here I lie, but here I wish to lie." But, joking apart, do we not act like one of these three persons whenever we use the expression "I wish"?

125. ON THE DOMAIN OF FREEDOM.—We can think many more things than we can do and experience—i.e. our faculty of thinking is superficial and is satisfied with what lies on the surface, it does not even perceive this surface. If our intellect were strictly developed in proportion to our power, and our exercise of this power, the primary principle of our thinking would be that we can understand only that which we are able to do—if, indeed, there is any understanding at all. The thirsty man is without water, but the creations of his imagination continually bring the image of water to his sight, as if nothing could be more easily procured. The superficial and easily satisfied character of the intellect cannot understand real need, and thus feels itself superior. It is proud of being able to do more, to run faster, and to reach the goal almost within the twinkling of an eye: and in this way the domain of thought, when contrasted with the domain of action, volition, and experience, appears to be the domain of liberty, while, as I have already stated, it is nothing but the domain of superficiality and self-sufficiency.

126. FORGETFULNESS.—It has never yet been proved that there is such a thing as forgetfulness: all that we know is that we have no power over recollection. In the meantime we have filled up this gap in our power with the word "forgetfulness," exactly as if it were another faculty added to our list. But, after all, what is within our power? If that word fills up a gap in our power, might not the other words be found capable of filling up a gap in the knowledge which we possess of our power?

127. FOR A DEFINITE PURPOSE.—Of all human actions probably the least understood are those which are carried out for a definite purpose, because they have always been regarded as the most intelligible and commonplace to our intellect. The great problems can be picked up in the highways and byways.

128. DREAMING AND RESPONSIBILITY.—You would wish to be responsible for everything except your dreams! What miserable weakness, what lack of logical courage! Nothing contains more of your own work than your dreams! Nothing belongs to you so much! Substance, form, duration, actor, spectator—in these comedies you act as your complete selves! And yet it is just here that you are afraid and ashamed of yourselves, and even Oedipus, the wise Oedipus, derived consolation from the thought that we cannot be blamed for what we dream. From this I must conclude that the great majority of men must have some dreadful dreams to reproach themselves with. If it were otherwise, to how great an extent would these nocturnal fictions have been exploited in the interests of man's pride! Need I add that the wise Oedipus was right, that we are really not responsible for our dreams any more than for our waking hours, and that the doctrine of free will has as its parents man's pride and sense of power! Perhaps I say this too often; but that does not prove that it is not true.

129. THE ALLEGED COMBAT OF MOTIVES.—People speak of the "combat of motives," but they designate by this expression that which is not a combat of motives at all. What I mean is that, in our meditative consciousness, the consequences of different actions which we think we are able to carry

out present themselves successively, one after the other, and we compare these consequences in our mind. We think we have come to a decision concerning an action after we have established to our own satisfaction that the consequences of this action will be favourable. Before we arrive at this conclusion, however, we often seriously worry because of the great difficulties we experience in guessing what the consequences are likely to be, and in seeing them in their full importance, without exception—and, after all this, we must reckon up any fortuitous elements that are likely to arise. Then comes the chief difficulty: all the consequences which we have with such difficulty determined one by one must be weighed on some scales against each other; and it only too often comes about that, owing to the difference in the quality of all the conceivable consequences, both scales and weights are lacking for this casuistry of advantage.

Even supposing, however, that in this case we are able to overcome the difficulty, and that mere hazard has placed in our scales results which permit of a mutual balance, we have now, in the idea of the consequences of a particular action, a motive for performing this very action, but only one motive! When we have finally decided to act, however, we are fairly often influenced by another order of motives than those of the "image of the consequences." What brings this about may be the habitual working of our inner machinery, or some little encouragement on the part of a person whom we fear or honour or love, or the love of comfort which prefers to do that which lies nearest; or some stirring of the imagination provoked at the decisive moment by some event of trifling importance; or some physical influence which manifests itself quite unexpectedly; a mere whim brings it about; or the outburst of a passion which, as it accidentally happens, is ready to burst forth—in a word, motives operate which we do not understand very well, or which we do not understand at all, and which we can never balance against one another in advance.

It is probable that a contest is going on among these motives too, a driving backwards and forwards, a rising and lowering of the parts, and it is this which would be the real "contest of motives," something quite invisible and unknown to us. I have calculated the consequences and the successes, and in doing so have set a very necessary motive in the line of combat with the other motives,—but I am as little able to draw up this battle line as to see it: the battle itself is hidden from my sight, as likewise is the victory, as victory; for I certainly come to know what I shall finally do, but I cannot know what motive has in the end proved to be the victor. Nevertheless, we are decidedly not in the habit of taking all these unconscious phenomena into account, and we generally conceive of the preliminary stages of an action only so far as they are conscious: thus we mistake the combat of the motives for a comparison of the possible consequences of different actions,—a mistake that brings with it most important consequences, and consequences that are most fatal to the development of morals.

130. AIMS? WILL?—We have accustomed ourselves to believe in two kingdoms, the domain of purposes and volition, and the domain of chance. In this latter domain everything is done senselessly, there is a continual going to and fro without any one being able to say why or wherefore. We stand in awe of this powerful realm of the great cosmic stupidity, for in most instances we learn to know it when it falls down upon the other world, that of aims and intentions, like a slate from a roof, always overwhelming some beautiful purpose of ours.

This belief in these two kingdoms arises from ancient romanticism and legend: we clever dwarfs, with all our will and aims, are interfered with, knocked down, and very often crushed to death by those ultra-stupid giants, the accidents,—but in spite of this we should not like to be deprived of the fearful poetry of their proximity, for these monsters very often make their appearance when life in the spider's web of definite aims has become too tiresome or too anxious for us, and they sometimes bring about a divine diversion when their hands for once tear the whole web in pieces,—not that these irrational beings ever intend to do what they do, or even observe it. But their coarse and bony hands rend our web as if it were thin air.

Moira was the name given by the Greeks to this realm of the incalculable and of sublime and eternal limitedness; and they set it round their gods like a horizon beyond which they could neither see nor act,—with that secret defiance of the gods which one meets with in different nations; the gods are worshipped, but a final trump card is held in readiness to play against them. As instances of this we may recollect that the Indians and the Persians, who conceived all their gods as having to depend upon the sacrifices of mortals, so that if it came to the worst the mortals could, at least, let the gods die of starvation; or the gods of the stubborn and melancholy Scandinavians, who enjoyed a quiet revenge in the thought that a twilight of the gods was to come as some compensation for the perpetual fear which their evil gods caused them. The case of Christianity was very different, for its essential feelings were not those of the Indians, Persians, Greeks, or Scandinavians. Christianity commanded its disciples to worship in the dust the spirit of power, and to kiss the very dust. It gave the world to understand that this omnipotent "realm of stupidity" was not so stupid as it seemed, and that we, on the contrary, were stupid when we could not perceive that behind this realm stood God Himself: He who, although fond of dark, crooked and wonderful ways, at last brought everything to a "glorious end." This new myth of God, who had hitherto been mistaken for a race of giants or Moira, and who was now Himself the spinner and weaver of webs and purposes even more subtle than those of our own intellect—so subtle, indeed, that they appear to be incomprehensible and even unreasonable—this myth was so bold a transformation and so daring a paradox that the over-refined ancient world could not resist it, however extravagant and contradictory the thing seemed: for, let it be said in confidence, there was a contradiction in it,—if our intellect cannot divine the intellect and aims of God, how did it divine this quality of its intellect and this quality of God's intellect?

In more modern times, indeed, the doubt has increased as to whether the slate that falls from the roof is really thrown by "Divine love," and mankind again harks back to the old romance of giants and dwarfs. Let us learn then, for it is time we did so, that even in our supposed separate domain of aims and reason the giants likewise rule. And our aims and reason are not dwarfs, but giants. And our own webs are just as often and as clumsily rent by ourselves as by the slate. And not everything is purpose that is called purpose, and still less is everything will that is called will. And if you come to the conclusion, "Then there is only one domain, that of stupidity and hazard?" it must be added that possibly there is only one domain, possibly there is neither will nor aim, and we may only have imagined these things. Those iron hands of necessity that shake the dice-box of chance continue their game indefinitely: hence, it must happen that certain throws perfectly resemble every degree of appropriateness and good sense. It may be that our own voluntary acts and purposes are merely such throws, and that we are too circumscribed and vain to conceive our extremely circumscribed state! that we ourselves shake the dice-box with iron hands, and do nothing in our most deliberate actions but play the game of necessity. Possibly! To rise beyond this "possibly" we should indeed have been guests in the Underworld, playing at dice and betting with Proserpine at the table of the goddess herself.

131. MORAL FASHIONS.—How moral judgments as a whole have changed! The greatest marvels of the morality of antiquity, such as Epictetus, knew nothing of the glorification, now so common, of the spirit of sacrifice, of living for others: after the fashion of morality now prevailing we should really call them immoral; for they fought with all their strength for their own ego and against all sympathy for others, especially for the sufferings and moral imperfections of others. Perhaps they would reply to us by saying, "If you feel yourselves to be such dull and ugly people, by all means think of others more than yourselves. You will be quite right in doing so!"

132. THE LAST ECHOES OF CHRISTIANITY IN MORALS.—"On n'est bon que par la pitié: il faut donc qu'il y ait quelque pitié dans tous nos sentiments"—so says morality nowadays. And how does this come about? The fact that the man who performs social, sympathetic, disinterested, and benevolent actions is now considered as the moral man: this is perhaps the most general effect, the most complete transformation, that Christianity has produced in Europe; perhaps in spite of itself, and not by any means because this was part of its essential doctrine. But this was the residuum of those Christian feelings that prevailed at the time when the contrary and thoroughly selfish faith in the "one thing needful," the absolute importance of eternal and personal salvation, together with the dogmas upon which this belief had rested, were gradually receding, and when the auxiliary beliefs in "love" and "love of one's neighbour," harmonising with the extraordinary practice of charity by the Church, were thereby coming to the front. The more people gradually became separated from the dogmas, the more did they seek some sort of justification for this separation in a cult of the love of humanity: not to fall short in this respect of the Christian ideal, but to excel it if possible, was the secret stimulus of all the French free-thinkers from Voltaire to Auguste Comte; and this latter with his famous moral formula "vivre pour autrui" has indeed out-christianised even Christianity!

It was Schopenhauer in Germany and John Stuart Mill in England who were the means of bringing into the greatest prominence this doctrine of sympathetic affections and of pity or utility to others as a principle of action; but these men themselves were only echoes. From about the time of the French Revolution these doctrines have manifested themselves in various places with enormous force. Since then they have shown themselves in their coarsest as well has their most subtle form, and all Socialistic principles have almost involuntarily taken their stand on the common ground of this doctrine. At the present time there is perhaps no more widely spread prejudice than that of thinking that we know what really and truly constitutes morality. Every one now seems to learn with satisfaction that society is beginning to adapt the individual to the general needs, and that it is at the same time the happiness and sacrifice of each one to consider himself as a useful member and instrument of the whole. They have still, however, doubts as to the form in which this whole is to be looked for, whether in a state already existing, or in one which has yet to be established, or in a nation, or in an international brotherhood, or in new and small economic communities. On this point there is still much reflection, doubt, struggling, excitement, and passion; but it is pleasant and wonderful to observe the unanimity with which the "ego" is called upon to practice self-denial, until, in the form of adaptation to the whole, it once again secures its own fixed sphere of rights and duties,—until, indeed, it has become something quite new and different. Nothing else is being attempted, whether admitted or not, than the complete transformation, even the weakening and suppression of the individual: the supporters of the majority never tire of enumerating and anathematising all that is bad, hostile, lavish, expensive, and luxurious in the form of individual existence that has hitherto prevailed; they hope that society may be administered in a cheaper, less dangerous, more uniform, and more harmonious way when nothing is left but large corporations and their members. All that is considered as good which in any way corresponds to this desire for grouping men into one particular society, and to the minor cravings which necessarily accompany this desire,—this is the chief moral current of our time; sympathy and social feelings are working hand in glove. (Kant is still outside of this movement: he expressly teaches that we should be insensible to the sufferings of others if our benevolence is to have any moral value,—a doctrine which Schopenhauer, very angrily, as may easily be imagined, described as the Kantian absurdity.)

133. "NO LONGER THINKING OF ONE'S SELF."—Let us seriously consider why we should jump into the water to rescue some one who has just fallen in before our eyes, although we may have no particular sympathy for him. We do it for pity's sake; no one thinks now but of his neighbour,—so says thoughtlessness. Why do we experience grief and uneasiness when we see some one spit blood, although we may be really ill-disposed towards him and wish him no good? Out of pity; we have ceased to think of ourselves,—so says thoughtlessness again. The truth is that in our pity—I mean by this what we erroneously call "pity"—we no longer think consciously of ourselves, but quite unconsciously, exactly as when slipping we unconsciously make the best counter-motions possible in order to recover our balance, and in doing so clearly use all our intelligence. A mishap to another offends us; it would bring our impotence, or perhaps our cowardice, into strong relief if we could do nothing to help him; or in itself it would give rise to a diminution of our honour in the eyes of others and of ourselves. Or again, accidents that happen to others act as finger-posts to point out our own danger, and even as indications of human peril and frailty they can produce a painful effect upon us. We shake off this kind of pain and offence, and balance it by an act of pity behind which may be hidden a subtle form of self-defence or even revenge. That at bottom we strongly think of ourselves may easily be divined from the decision that we arrive at in all cases where we can avoid the sight of those who are suffering or starving or wailing. We make up our minds not to avoid such people when we can approach them as powerful and helpful ones, when we can safely reckon upon their applause, or wish to feel the contrast of our own happiness, or, again, when we hope to get rid of our own boredom. It is misleading to call the suffering that we experience at such a sight, and which may be of a very different kind, commiseration. For in all cases it is a suffering from which the suffering person before us is free: it is our own suffering, just as his suffering is his own. It is thus only this personal feeling of misery that we get rid of by acts of compassion. Nevertheless, we never act thus from one single motive: as it is certain that we wish to free ourselves from suffering thereby, it is also certain that by the same action we yield to an impulse of pleasure. Pleasure arises at the sight of a contrast to our own condition, at the knowledge that we should be able to help if only we wished to do so, at the thought of the praise and gratitude which we should gain if we did help, at the very act of helping, in so far as this might prove successful (and because something which is gradually seen to be successful gives pleasure to the doer); but even more particularly at the feeling that our intervention brings to an end some deplorable injustice,—even the outburst of one's indignation is invigorating.

All this, including even things still more subtle, comprises "pity." How clumsily with this one word does language fall foul of such a complex and polyphonous organism! That pity, on the other hand, is identical with the suffering the sight of which brings it about, or that it has a particularly subtle and penetrating comprehension of it: this is in contradiction to experience, and he who has glorified pity under these two heads lacked sufficient experience in the domain of morals. That is why I am seized with some doubts when reading of the incredible things attributed by Schopenhauer to pity. It is obvious that he thereby wished to make us believe in the great novelty he brought forward, viz., that pity—the pity which he observed so superficially and described so badly—was the source of all and every past and future moral action,—and all this precisely because of those faculties which he had begun by attributing to it.

What is it in the end that distinguishes men without pity from men who are really compassionate? In particular, to give merely an approximate indication, they have not the sensitive feeling for fear, the subtle faculty for perceiving danger: nor yet is their vanity so easily wounded if something happens which they might have been able to prevent,—the caution of their pride commands them not to interfere uselessly with the affairs of others; they even act on the belief that every one should help himself and play his own cards. Again, in most cases they are more habituated to bearing pain than compassionate men, and it does not seem at all unjust to them that others should suffer, since they themselves have suffered. Lastly, the state of soft-heartedness is as painful to them as is the state of stoical impassability to compassionate men: they have only disdainful words for sensitive hearts, as they think that such a state of feeling is dangerous to their own manliness and calm bravery,—they conceal their tears from others and wipe them off, angry with themselves. They belong to a different type of egoists from the compassionate men,—but to call them, in a distinct sense, evil and the compassionate ones good, is merely a moral fashion which has had its innings, just as the reverse fashion had also its innings, and a long innings, too.

134. TO WHAT EXTENT WE MUST BEWARE OF PITY.—Pity, in so far as it actually gives rise to suffering—and this must be our only point of view here—is a weakness, like every other indulgence in an injurious emotion. It increases suffering throughout the world, and although here and there a certain amount of suffering may be indirectly diminished or removed altogether as a consequence of pity, we must not bring forward these occasional consequences, which are on the whole insignificant, to justify the nature of pity which, as has already been stated, is prejudicial. Supposing that it prevailed, even if only for one day, it would bring humanity to utter ruin. In itself the nature of pity is no better than that of any other craving; it is only where it is called for and praised—and this happens when people do not understand what is injurious in it, but find in it a sort of joy—that a good conscience becomes attached to it; it is only then that we willingly yield to it, and do not shrink from acknowledging it. In other circumstances where it is understood to be dangerous, it is looked upon as a weakness; or, as in the case of the Greeks, as an unhealthy periodical emotion the danger of which might be removed by temporary and voluntary discharges. If a man were to undertake the experiment of deliberately devoting his attention to the opportunities afforded by practical life for the exercise of pity, and were over and over again to picture in his own mind the misery he might meet with in his immediate surroundings, he would inevitably become melancholy and ill. If, however, he wished in any sense of the word to serve humanity as a physician, he would have to take many precautions with respect to this feeling, as otherwise it would paralyse him at all critical moments, undermine the foundations of his knowledge, and unnerve his helpful and delicate hand.

135. AROUSING PITY.—Among savages men think with a moral shudder of the possibility of becoming an object of pity, for such a state they regard as deprived of all virtue. Pitying is equivalent to despising: they do not want to see a contemptible being suffer, for this would afford them no enjoyment. On the other hand, to behold one of their enemies suffering, some one whom they look upon as their equal in pride, but whom torture cannot induce to give up his pride, and in general to see some one suffer who refuses to lower himself by appealing for pity—which would in their eyes be the most profound and shameful humiliation—this is the very joy of joys. Such a spectacle excites the deepest admiration in the soul of the savage, and he ends by killing such a brave man when it is in his power, afterwards according funeral honours to the unbending one. If he had groaned, however; if his countenance had lost its expression of calm disdain; if he had shown himself to be contemptible,—well, in such a case he might have been allowed to live like a dog: he would no longer have aroused the pride of the spectator, and pity would have taken the place of admiration.

136. HAPPINESS IN PITY.—If, as is the case among the Hindus, we decree the end and aim of all intellectual activity to be the knowledge of human misery, and if for generation after generation this dreadful resolution be steadily adhered to, pity in the eyes of such men of hereditary pessimism comes to have a new value as a preserver of life, something that helps to make existence endurable, although it may seem worthy of being rejected with horror and disgust. Pity becomes an antidote to suicide, a sentiment which brings pleasure with it and enables us to taste superiority in small doses. It gives some diversion to our minds, makes our hearts full, banishes fear and lethargy, and incites us to speak, to complain, or to act: it is a relative happiness when compared with the misery of the knowledge that hampers the individual on every side, bewilders him, and takes away his breath. Happiness, however, no matter of what nature it may be, gives us air and light and freedom of movement.

137. WHY DOUBLE THE "EGO"?—To view our own experiences in the same light as we are in the habit of looking at those of others is very comforting and an advisable medicine. On the other hand, to look upon the experiences of others and adopt them as if they were our own—which is called for by the philosophy of pity—would ruin us in a very short time: let us only make the experiment without trying to imagine it any longer! The first maxim is, in addition, undoubtedly more in accordance with reason and goodwill towards reason; for we estimate more objectively the value and significance of an event when it happens to others,—the value, for instance, of a death, loss of money or slander. But pity, taking as its principle of action the injunction, "Suffer the misfortune of another as much as he himself," would lead the point of view of the ego with all its exaggerations and deviations to become the point of view of the other person, the sympathiser: so that we should have to suffer at the same time from our own ego and the other's ego. In this way we would voluntarily overload ourselves with a double irrationality, instead of making the burden of our own as light as possible.

138. BECOMING MORE TENDER.—Whenever we love some one and venerate and admire him, and afterwards come to perceive that he is suffering—which always causes us the utmost astonishment, since we cannot but feel that the happiness we derive from him must flow from a superabundant source of personal happiness—our feelings of love, veneration, and admiration are essentially changed: they become more tender; that is, the gap that separates us seems to be bridged over and there appears to be an approach to equality. It now seems possible to give him something in return, whilst we had previously imagined him as being altogether above our gratitude. Our ability to requite him for what we have received from him arouses in us feelings of much joy and pleasure. We endeavour to ascertain what can best calm the grief of our friend, and we give it to him; if he wishes for kind words, looks,

attentions, services, or presents, we give them; but, above all, if he would like to see us suffering from the sight of his suffering, we pretend to suffer, for all this secures for us the enjoyment of active gratitude, which is equivalent in a way to good-natured revenge. If he wants none of these things, and refuses to accept them from us, we depart from him chilled and sad, almost mortified; it appears to us as if our gratitude had been declined, and on this point of honour even the best of men is still somewhat touchy. It results from all this that even in the best case there is something humiliating in suffering, and something elevating and superior in sympathy,—a fact which will keep the two feelings apart for ever and ever.

139. HIGHER IN NAME ONLY.—You say that the morality of pity is a higher morality than that of stoicism? Prove it! But take care not to measure the "higher" and "lower" degrees of morality once more by moral yardsticks; for there are no absolute morals. So take your yardstick from somewhere else, and be on your guard!

140. PRAISE AND BLAME.—When a war has come to an unsuccessful conclusion we try to find the man who is to blame for the war; when it comes to a successful conclusion we praise the man who is responsible for it. In all unsuccessful cases attempts are made to blame somebody, for non-success gives rise to dejection, against which the single possible remedy is involuntarily applied; a new incitement of the sense of power; and this incitement is found in the condemnation of the "guilty" one. This guilty one is not perhaps the scapegoat of the faults of others; he is merely the victim of the feeble, humiliated, and depressed people who wish to prove upon some one that they have not yet lost all their power. Even self-condemnation after a defeat may be the means of restoring the feeling of power.

On the other hand, glorification of the originator is often but an equally blind result of another instinct that demands its victim,—and in this case the sacrifice appears to be sweet and attractive even for the victim. This happens when the feeling of power is satiated in a nation or a society by so great and fascinating a success that a weariness of victory supervenes and pride wishes to be discharged: a feeling of self-sacrifice is aroused and looks for its object. Thus, whether we are blamed or praised we merely, as a rule, provide opportunities for the gratification of others, and are only too often caught up and whirled away for our neighbours to discharge upon us their accumulated feelings of praise or blame. In both cases we confer a benefit upon them for which we deserve no credit and they no thanks.

141. MORE BEAUTIFUL BUT LESS VALUABLE.—Picturesque morality: such is the morality of those passions characterised by sudden outbursts, abrupt transitions; pathetic, impressive, dreadful, and solemn attitudes and gestures. It is the semi-savage stage of morality: never let us be tempted to set it on a higher plane merely on account of its æsthetic charms.

142. SYMPATHY.—In order to understand our neighbour, that is, in order to reproduce his sentiments in ourselves, we often, no doubt, plumb the cause of his feelings, as, for example, by asking ourselves, Why is he sad? in order that we may become sad ourselves for the same reason. But we much more frequently neglect to act thus, and we produce these feelings in ourselves in accordance with the effects which they exhibit in the person we are studying,—by imitating in our own body the expression of his eyes, his voice, his gait, his attitude (or, at any rate, the likeness of these things in words, pictures, and music), or we may at least endeavour to mimic the action of his muscles and nervous system. A like feeling will then spring up in us as the result of an old association of movements and sentiments which has been trained to run backwards and forwards. We have developed to a very high pitch this knack of sounding the feelings of others, and when we are in the presence of any one else we bring this faculty of ours into play almost involuntarily,—let the inquirer observe the animation of a woman's countenance and notice how it vibrates and quivers with animation as the result of the continual imitation and reflection of what is going on around her.

It is music, however, more than anything else that shows us what past-masters we are in the rapid and subtle divination of feelings and sympathy; for even if music is only the imitation of an imitation of feelings, nevertheless, despite its distance and vagueness, it often enables us to participate in those feelings, so that we become sad without any reason for feeling so, like the fools that we are, merely because we hear certain sounds and rhythms that somehow or other remind us of the intonation and the movements, or perhaps even only of the behaviour, of sorrowful people. It is related of a certain Danish king that he was wrought up to such a pitch of warlike enthusiasm by the song of a minstrel that he sprang to his feet and killed five persons of his assembled court: there was neither war nor enemy; there was rather the exact opposite; yet the power of the retrospective inference from a feeling to the cause of it was sufficiently strong in this king to overpower both his observation and his reason. Such, however, is almost invariably the effect of music (provided that it thrills us), and we have no need of such paradoxical instances to recognise this,—the state of feeling into which music transports us is almost always in contradiction to the appearance of our actual state, and of our reasoning power which recognises this actual state and its causes.

If we inquire how it happened that this imitation of the feelings of others has become so common, there will be no doubt as to the answer: man being the most timid of all beings because of his subtle and delicate nature has been made familiar through his timidity with this sympathy for, and rapid comprehension of, the feelings of others, even of animals. For century after century he saw danger in everything that was unfamiliar to him, in anything that happened to be alive, and whenever the spectacle of such things and creatures came before his eyes he imitated their features and attitude, drawing at the same time his own conclusion as to the nature of the evil intentions they concealed. This interpretation of all movements and all facial characteristics in the sense of intentions, man has even brought to bear on things inanimate,—urged on as he was by the illusion that there was nothing inanimate. I believe that this is the origin of everything that we now call a feeling for nature, that sensation of joy which men experience at the sight of the sky, the fields, the rocks, the forests, the storms, the stars, the landscapes, and spring: without our old habits of fear which forced us to suspect behind everything a kind of second and more recondite sense, we should now experience no delight in nature, in the same way as men and animals do not cause us to rejoice if we have not first been deterred by that source of all understanding, namely, fear. For joy and agreeable surprise, and finally the feeling of ridicule, are the younger children of sympathy, and the much younger brothers and sisters of fear. The faculty of rapid perception, which is based on the faculty of rapid dissimulation, decreases in proud and autocratic men and nations, as they are less timid; but, on the other hand, every category of understanding and dissimulation is well known to timid peoples, and among them is to be found the real home of imitative arts and superior intelligence.

When, proceeding from the theory of sympathy such as I have just outlined, I turn my attention to the theory, now so popular and almost sacrosanct, of a mystical process by means of which pity blends two beings into one, and thus permits them immediately to understand one another, when I recollect that even so clear a brain as Schopenhauer's delighted in such fantastic nonsense, and that he in his turn transplanted this delight into other lucid and semi-lucid brains, I feel unlimited astonishment and compassion. How great must be the pleasure we experience in this senseless tomfoolery! How near must even a sane man be to insanity as soon as he listens to his own secret intellectual desires!—Why did Schopenhauer really feel so grateful, so profoundly indebted to Kant? He revealed on one occasion the undoubted answer to this question. Some one had spoken of the way in which the qualitias occulta of Kant's Categorical Imperative might be got rid of, so that the theory itself might be rendered intelligible. Whereupon Schopenhauer gave utterance to the following outburst: "An intelligible Categorical Imperative! Preposterous idea! Stygian darkness! God forbid that it should ever become intelligible! The fact that there is actually something unintelligible, that this misery of the understanding and its conceptions is limited, conditional, final, and deceptive,—this is beyond question Kant's great gift." Let any one consider whether a man can be in possession of a desire to gain an insight into moral things when he feels himself comforted from the start by a belief in the inconceivableness of these things! one who still honestly believes in illuminations from above, in magic, in ghostly appearances, and in the metaphysical ugliness of the toad!

143. WOE TO US IF THIS IMPULSE SHOULD RAGE!—Supposing that the impulse towards devotion and care for others ("sympathetic affection") were doubly as strong as it now is, life on earth could not be endured. Let it only be considered how many foolish things every one of us does day by day and hour by hour, merely out of solicitude and devotion for himself, and how unbearable he seems in doing so: and what then would it be like if we were to become for other people the object of the stupidities and importunities with which up to the present they have only tormented themselves! Should we not then take precipitately to our heels as soon as one of our neighbours came towards us? And would it not be necessary to overwhelm this sympathetic affection with the abuse that we now reserve for egoism?

144. CLOSING OUR EARS TO THE COMPLAINTS OF OTHERS.—When we let our sky be clouded by the complaints and suffering of other mortals, who must bear the consequences of such gloom? No doubt those other mortals, in addition to all their other burdens! If we are merely to be the echoes of their complaints, we cannot accord them either help or comfort; nor can we do so if we were continually keeping our ears open to listen to them,—unless we have learnt the art of the Olympians, who, instead of trying to make themselves unhappy, endeavoured to feel edified by the misfortunes of mankind. But this is something too Olympian for us, although, in our enjoyment of tragedy, we have already taken a step towards this ideal divine cannibalism.

145. "UNEGOISTIC."—This man is empty and wishes to be filled, that one is over-full and wishes to be emptied: both of them feel themselves urged on to look for an individual who can help them. And this phenomenon, interpreted in a higher sense, is in both cases known by the same name, "love." Well? and could this love be something unegoistic?

146. LOOKING BEYOND OUR NEIGHBOUR.—What? Ought the nature of true morality to consist for us in fixing our eyes upon the most direct and immediate consequences of our action for other people, and in our coming to a decision accordingly? This is only a narrow and bourgeois morality, even though it may be a morality: but it seems to me that it would be more superior and liberal to look beyond these immediate consequences for our neighbour in order to encourage more distant purposes, even at the risk of making others suffer,—as, for example, by encouraging the spirit of

knowledge in spite of the certainty that our free-thought will have the instant effect of plunging others into doubt, grief, and even worse afflictions. Have we not at least the right to treat our neighbour as we treat ourselves? And if, where we are concerned, we do not think in such a narrow and bourgeois fashion of immediate consequences and sufferings, why should we be compelled to act thus in regard to our neighbour? Supposing that we felt ready to sacrifice ourselves, what is there to prevent us from sacrificing our neighbour together with ourselves,—just as States and Sovereigns have hitherto sacrificed one citizen to the others, "for the sake of the general interest," as they say?

We too, however, have general interests, perhaps even more general than theirs: so why may we not sacrifice a few individuals of this generation for the benefit of generations to come? so that their affliction, anxiety, despair, blunders, and misery may be deemed essential because a new plough is to break up the ground and render it fertile for all. Finally, we communicate the disposition to our neighbour by which he is enabled to feel himself a victim: we persuade him to carry out the task for which we employ him. Are we then devoid of all pity? If, however, we wish to achieve a victory over ourselves beyond our pity, is not this a higher and more liberal attitude and disposition than that in which we only feel safe after having ascertained whether an action benefits or harms our neighbour? On the contrary, it is by means of such sacrifice—including the sacrifice of ourselves, as well as of our neighbours—that we should strengthen and elevate the general sense of human power, even supposing that we attain nothing more than this. But even this itself would be a positive increase of happiness. Then, if even this ... but not a word more! You have understood me at a glance.

147. THE CAUSE OF "ALTRUISM."—Men have on the whole spoken of love with so much emphasis and adoration because they have hitherto always had so little of it, and have never yet been satiated with this food: in this way it became their ambrosia. If a poet wished to show universal benevolence in the image of a Utopia, he would certainly have to describe an agonising and ridiculous state of things, the like of which was never seen on earth,—every one would be surrounded, importuned, and sighed for, not as at present, by one lover, but by thousands, by everybody indeed, as the result of an irresistible craving which would then be as vehemently insulted and cursed as selfishness has been by men of past ages. The poets of this new condition of things, if they had sufficient leisure to write, would be dreaming of nothing but the blissful and loveless past, the divine selfishness of yore, and the wonderful possibilities in former times of remaining alone, not being run after by one's friends, and of even being hated and despised—or any other odious expressions which the beautiful animal world in which we live chooses to coin.

148. LOOKING FAR AHEAD.—If, in accordance with the present definition, only those actions are moral which are done for the sake of others, and for their sake only, then there are no moral actions at all! If, in accordance with another definition, only those actions are moral which spring from our own free will, then there are no moral actions in this case either! What is it, then, that we designate thus, which certainly exists and wishes as a consequence to be explained? It is the result of a few intellectual blunders; and supposing that we were able to free ourselves from these errors, what would then become of "moral actions"? It is due to these errors that we have up to the present attributed to certain actions a value superior to what was theirs in reality: we separated them from "egoistic" and "non-free" actions. When we now set them once more in the latter categories, as we must do, we certainly reduce their value (their own estimate of value) even below its reasonable level, because "egoistic" and "non-free" actions have up to the present been under-valued owing to that alleged profound and essential difference.

In future, then, will these very actions be less frequently performed, since they will be less highly esteemed? Inevitably! Or at all events for a fairly long time, as long as the scale of valuations remains under the reacting influence of former mistakes! But we make some return for this by giving back to men their good courage for the carrying out of actions that are now reputed to be selfish, and thus restore their value,—we relieve men's bad consciences! and as up to the present egoistic actions have been by far the most frequent, and will be so to all eternity, we free the whole conception of these actions and of life from its evil appearance! This is a very high and important result. When men no longer believe themselves to be evil, they cease to be so.

BOOK III

149. LITTLE UNCONVENTIONAL ACTIONS ARE NECESSARY!—To act occasionally in matters of custom against our own better judgments; to yield in practice while reserving our own intellectual liberty; to behave like everybody else and thus to show ourselves amiable and considerate to all, to compensate them, as it were, even if only to some extent, for our unconventional opinions—all this among many tolerably liberal-minded men is looked upon not only as permissible but even as "honourable," "humane," "tolerant," and "unpedantic," or whatever fine words may be used to lull to sleep the intellectual conscience. So, for example, one man, although he may be an atheist, has his infant baptized in the usual Christian fashion; another goes through his period of military service, though he may severely condemn all hatred between nations; and a third runs into the Church with a girl because she comes from a religious family, and makes his vows to a priest without feeling ashamed of it. "It is of no importance if one of us does what every one else does and has done"—so says ignorant prejudice! What a profound mistake! For nothing is of greater importance than that a powerful, long-established, and irrational custom should be once again confirmed by the act of some one who is recognised as rational. In this way the proceeding is thought to be sanctioned by reason itself! All honour to your opinions! but little unconventional actions are of still greater value.

150. THE HAZARD OF MARRIAGES.—If I were a god, and a benevolent god, the marriages of men would cause me more displeasure than anything else. An individual can make very great progress within the seventy years of his life—yea, even within thirty years: such progress, indeed, as to surprise even the gods! But when we then see him exposing the inheritance and legacy of his struggles and victories, the laurel crown of his humanity, on the first convenient peg where any female may pick it to pieces for him; when we observe how well he can acquire and how little he is capable of preserving his acquisitions, and how he does not even dream that by procreation he might prepare a still more victorious life,—we then, indeed, become impatient and say, "Nothing can in the end result from humanity, individuals are wasted, for all rationality of a great advance of humanity is rendered impossible by the hazard of marriages: let us cease from being the assiduous spectators and fools of this aimless drama!" It was in this mood that the gods of Epicurus withdrew long ago to their divine seclusion and felicity: they were tired of men and their love affairs.

151. HERE ARE NEW IDEALS TO INVENT.—At a time when a man is in love he should not be allowed to come to a decision about his life and to determine once and for all the character of his society on account of a whim. We ought publicly to declare invalid the vows of lovers, and to refuse them permission to marry: and this because we should treat marriage itself much more seriously, so that in cases where it is now contracted it would not usually be allowed in future! Are not the majority of marriages such that we should not care to have them witnessed by a third party? And yet this third party is scarcely ever lacking—the child—and he is more than a witness; he is the whipping-boy and scapegoat.

152. FORMULA OF OATH.—"If I am now telling a lie I am no longer an honourable man, and every one may say so to my face." I recommend this formula in place of the present judicial oath and its customary invocation to the Deity: it is stronger. There is no reason why even religious men should oppose it; for as soon as the customary oath no longer serves, all the religious people will have to turn to their catechism, which says, "Thou shalt not take the name of the Lord thy God in vain."

153. THE MALCONTENT.—He is one of the brave old warriors: angry with civilisation because he believes that its object is to make all good things—honour, rewards, and fair women—accessible even to cowards.

154. CONSOLATION AMID PERILS.—The Greeks, in the course of a life that was always surrounded by great dangers and cataclysms, endeavoured to find in meditation and knowledge a kind of security of feeling, a last refugium. We, who live in a much more secure state, have introduced danger into meditation and knowledge, and it is in life itself that we endeavour to find repose, a refuge from danger.

155. EXTINCT SCEPTICISM.—Hazardous enterprises are rarer in modern times than in antiquity and in the Middle Ages, probably because modern times have no more belief in omens, oracles, stars, and soothsayers. In other words, we have become incapable of believing in a future which is reserved for us, as the ancients did, who—in contradistinction to ourselves—were much less sceptical regarding

that which is to be than that which is.

156. EVIL THROUGH EXUBERANCE.—"Oh, that we should not feel too happy!"—such was the secret fear of the Greeks in their best age. That is why they preached moderation to themselves. And we?

157. THE WORSHIP OF NATURAL SOUNDS.—What signification can we find in the fact that our culture is not only indulgent to the manifestations of grief, such as tears, complaints, reproaches, and attitudes of rage and humility, but even approves them and reckons them among the most noble and essential things?—while, on the other hand, the spirit of ancient philosophy looked down upon them with contempt, without admitting their necessity in any way. Let us remember how Plato—who was by no means one of the most inhuman of the philosophers—speaks of the Philoctetus of the tragic stage. Is it possible that our modern culture is wanting in "philosophy"? or, in accordance with the valuations of those old philosophers, do we perhaps all form part of the "mob"?

158. THE CLIMATE FOR FLATTERY.—In our day flatterers should no longer be sought at the courts of kings, since these have all acquired a taste for militarism, which cannot tolerate flattery. But this flower even now often grows in abundance in the neighbourhood of bankers and artists.

159. THE REVIVERS.—Vain men value a fragment of the past more highly from the moment when they are able to revive it in their imagination (especially if it is difficult to do so), they would even like if possible to raise it from the dead. Since, however, the number of vain people is always very large, the danger presented by historical studies, if an entire epoch devotes its attention to them, is by no means small: too great an amount of strength is then wasted on all sorts of imaginable resurrections. The entire movement of romanticism is perhaps best understood from this point of view.

160. VAIN, GREEDY, AND NOT VERY WISE.—Your desires are greater than your understanding, and your vanity is even greater than your desires,—to people of your type a great deal of Christian practice and a little Schopenhauerian theory may be strongly recommended.

161. BEAUTY CORRESPONDING TO THE AGE.—If our sculptors, painters, and musicians wish to catch the significance of the age, they should represent beauty as bloated, gigantic, and nervous: just as the Greeks, under the influence of their morality of moderation, saw and represented beauty in the Apollo di Belvedere. We should, indeed, call him ugly! But the pedantic "classicists" have deprived us of all our honesty!

162. THE IRONY OF THE PRESENT TIME.—At the present day it is the habit of Europeans to treat all matters of great importance with irony, because, as the result of our activity in their service, we have no time to take them seriously.

163. AGAINST ROUSSEAU.—If it is true that there is something contemptible about our civilisation, we have two alternatives: of concluding with Rousseau that, "This despicable civilisation is to blame for our bad morality," or to infer, contrary to Rousseau's view, that "Our good morality is to blame for this contemptible civilisation. Our social conceptions of good and evil, weak and effeminate as they are, and their enormous influence over both body and soul, have had the effect of weakening all bodies and souls and of crushing all unprejudiced, independent, and self-reliant men, the real pillars of a strong civilisation: wherever we still find the evil morality to-day, we see the last crumbling ruins of these pillars." Thus let paradox be opposed by paradox! It is quite impossible for the truth to lie with both sides: and can we say, indeed, that it lies with either? Decide for yourself.

164. PERHAPS PREMATURE.—It would seem at the present time that, under many different and misleading names, and often with a great want of clearness, those who do not feel themselves attached to morals and to established laws are taking the first initial steps to organise themselves, and thus to create a right for themselves; whilst hitherto, as criminals, free-thinkers, immoral men and miscreants, they have lived beyond the pale of the law, under the bane of outlawry and bad conscience, corrupted and corrupting. On the whole, we should consider this as right and proper, although it may result in insecurity for the coming century and compel every one to bear arms.—There is thereby a counterforce which continually reminds us that there is no exclusively moral-making morality, and that a morality which asserts itself to the exclusion of all other morality destroys too much sound strength and is too dearly bought by mankind. The non-conventional and deviating people, who are so often productive and inventive, must no longer be sacrificed: it must never again be considered as a disgrace to depart from morality either in actions or thought; many new experiments must be made upon life and society, and the world must be relieved from a huge weight of bad conscience. These general aims must be recognised and encouraged by all those upright people who are seeking truth.

165. A MORALITY WHICH DOES NOT BORE ONE.—The principal moral commandments which a nation permits its teachers to emphasise again and again stand in relation to its chief defects, and that is why it does not find them tiresome. The Greeks, who so often failed to employ moderation, coolness, fair-mindedness, and rationality in general, turned a willing ear to the four Socratic virtues,—they stood in such need of them, and yet had so little talent for them!

166. AT THE PARTING OF THE WAYS.—Shame! You wish to form part of a system in which you must be a wheel, fully and completely, or risk being crushed by wheels! where it is understood that

each one will be that which his superiors make of him! where the seeking for "connections" will form part of one's natural duties! where no one feels himself offended when he has his attention drawn to some one with the remark, "He may be useful to you some time"; where people do not feel ashamed of paying a visit to ask for somebody's intercession, and where they do not even suspect that by such a voluntary submission to these morals, they are once and for all stamped as the common pottery of nature, which others can employ or break up of their free will without feeling in any way responsible for doing so,—just as if one were to say, "People of my type will never be lacking, therefore, do what you will with me! Do not stand on ceremony!"

167. UNCONDITIONAL HOMAGE.—When I think of the most read German philosopher, the most popular German musician, and the most distinguished German statesman, I cannot but acknowledge that life is now rendered unusually arduous for these Germans, this nation of unconditional sentiments, and that, too, by their own great men. We see three magnificent spectacles spread out before us: on each occasion there is a river rushing along in the bed which it has made for itself, and even so agitated that one thinks at times it intends to flow uphill. And yet, however we might admire Schopenhauer, who would not, all things considered, like to have other opinions than his? Who in all greater and smaller things would now share the opinions of Richard Wagner, although there may be truth in the view expressed by some one: viz. that wherever Wagner gave or took offence some problem lay hidden,—which, however, he did not unearth for us. And, finally, how many are there who would be willing and eager to agree with Bismarck, if only he could always agree with himself, or were even to show some signs of doing so for the future! It is true that it is by no means astonishing to find statesmen without principles, but with dominant instincts; a versatile mind, actuated by these dominant and violent instincts, and hence without principles—these qualities are looked upon as reasonable and natural in a statesman. But, alas, this has up to the present been so un-German; as un-German as the fuss made about music and the discord and bad temper excited around the person of the musician; or as un-German as the new and extraordinary position taken up by Schopenhauer: he did not feel himself to be either above things or on his knees before them—one or other of these alternatives might still have been German—but he assumed an attitude against things! How incredible and disagreeable! to range one's self with things and nevertheless be their adversary, and finally the adversary of one's self,—what can the unconditional admirer do with such an example? And what, again, can he do with three such examples who cannot keep the peace towards one another! Here we see Schopenhauer as the antagonist of Wagner's music, Wagner attacking Bismarck's politics, and Bismarck attacking Wagnerism and Schopenhauerism. What remains for us to do? Where shall we flee with our thirst for wholesale hero-worship! Would it not be possible to choose from the music of the musician a few hundred bars of good music which appealed to the heart, and which we should like to take to heart because they are inspired by the heart,—could we not stand aside with this small piece of plunder, and forget the rest? And could we not make a similar compromise as regards the philosopher and the statesman,—select, take to heart, and in particular forget the rest?

Yes, if only forgetfulness were not so difficult! There was once a very proud man who would never on any account accept anything, good or evil, from others,—from any one, indeed, but himself. When he wanted to forget, however, he could not bestow this gift upon himself, and was three times compelled to conjure up the spirits. They came, listened to his desire, and said at last, "This is the only thing it is not in our power to give!" Could not the Germans take warning by this experience of Manfred? Why, then, should the spirits be conjured up? It is useless. We never forget what we endeavour to forget. And how great would be the "balance" which we should have to forget if we wished henceforth to continue wholesale admirers of these three great men! It would therefore be far more advisable to profit by the excellent opportunity offered us to try something new, i.e. to advance in the spirit of honesty towards ourselves and become, instead of a nation of credulous repetition and of bitter and blind animosity, a people of conditional assent and benevolent opposition. We must come to learn in the first place, however, that unconditional homage to people is something rather ridiculous, that a change of view on this point would not discredit even Germans, and that there is a profound and memorable saying: "Ce qui importe, ce ne sont point les personnes: mais les choses." This saying is like the man who uttered it—great, honest, simple, and silent,—just like Carnot, the soldier and Republican. But may I at the present time speak thus to Germans of a Frenchman, and a Republican into the bargain? Perhaps not: perhaps I must not even recall what Niebuhr in his time dared to say to the Germans: that no one had made such an impression of true greatness upon him as Carnot.

168. A MODEL.—What do I like about Thucydides, and how does it come that I esteem him more highly than Plato? He exhibits the most wide-spread and artless pleasure in everything typical in men and events, and finds that each type is possessed of a certain quantity of good sense: it is this good sense which he seeks to discover. He likewise exhibits a larger amount of practical justice than Plato; he never reviles or belittles those men whom he dislikes or who have in any way injured him in the course of his life. On the contrary: while seeing only types, he introduces something noble and additional into all things and persons; for what could posterity, to which he dedicates his work, do with things not

typical! Thus this culture of the disinterested knowledge of the world attains in him, the poet-thinker, a final marvellous bloom,—this culture which has its poet in Sophocles, its statesman in Pericles, its doctor in Hippocrates, and its natural philosopher in Democritus: this culture which deserves to be called by the name of its teachers, the Sophists, and which, unhappily, from the moment of its baptism at once begins to grow pale and incomprehensible to us,—for henceforward we suspect that this culture, which was combated by Plato and all the Socratic schools, must have been very immoral! The truth of this matter is so complicated and entangled that we feel unwilling to unravel it: so let the old error (error veritate simplicior) run its old course.

169. THE GREEK GENIUS FOREIGN TO US.—Oriental or modern, Asiatic or European: compared with the ancient Greeks, everything is characterised by enormity of size and by the revelling in great masses as the expression of the sublime, whilst in Paestum, Pompeii, and Athens we are astonished, when contemplating Greek architecture, to see with what small masses the Greeks were able to express the sublime, and how they loved to express it thus. In the same way, how simple were the Greeks in the idea which they formed of themselves! How far we surpass them in the knowledge of man! Again, how full of labyrinths would our souls and our conceptions of our souls appear in comparison with theirs! If we had to venture upon an architecture after the style of our own souls—(we are too cowardly for that!)—a labyrinth would have to be our model. That music which is peculiar to us, and which really expresses us, lets this be clearly seen! (for in music men let themselves go, because they think there is no one who can see them hiding behind their music).

170. ANOTHER POINT OF VIEW.—How we babble about the Greeks! What do we understand of their art, the soul of which was the passion for naked masculine beauty! It was only by starting therefrom that they appreciated feminine beauty. For the latter they had thus a perspective quite different from ours. It was the same in regard to their love for women: their worship was of a different kind, and so also was their contempt.

171. THE FOOD OF THE MODERN MAN.—He has learned to digest many things; nay, almost everything; it is his ambition to do so. He would, however, be really of a higher order if he did not understand this so well: homo pamphagus is not the finest type of the human race. We live between a past which had a more wayward and deranged taste than we, and a future which will possibly have a more select taste,—we live too much midway.

172. TRAGEDY AND MUSIC.—Men of essentially warlike disposition, such, for example, as the ancient Greeks in the time of Æschylus, are difficult to rouse, and when pity once triumphs over their hardness they are seized as by a kind of giddiness or a "demoniacal power,"—they feel themselves overpowered and thrilled by a religious horror. After this they become sceptical about their condition; but as long as they are in it they enjoy the charm of being, as it were, outside themselves, and the delight of the marvellous mixed with the bitterest gall of suffering: this is the proper kind of drink for fighting men,—something rare, dangerous, and bitter-sweet, which does not often fall to one's lot.

Tragedy appeals to souls who feel pity in this way, to those fierce and warlike souls which are difficult to overcome, whether by fear or pity, but which lose nothing by being softened from time to time. Of what use, however, is tragedy to those who are as open to the "sympathetic affections" as the sails of a ship to the wind! When at the time of Plato the Athenians had become more softened and sensitive, oh, how far they were still removed from the gushing emotions of the inhabitants of our modern towns and villages! And yet even then the philosophers were beginning to complain of the injurious nature of tragedy. An epoch full of danger such as that now beginning, in which bravery and manliness are rising in value, will perhaps again harden souls to such an extent that they will once more stand in need of tragic poèts: but in the meantime these are somewhat superfluous, to put it mildly. For music, too, a better age may be approaching (it will certainly be a more evil age!) when artists will have to make their music appeal to strongly individual beings, beings which will have become hard and which will be dominated by the gloomy earnestness of their own passion; but of what use is music to the little souls of the present age which is fast passing away, souls that are too unsteady, ill-developed, half-personal, inquisitive, and covetous of everything?

173. THE FLATTERERS OF WORK.—In the glorification of "work" and the never-ceasing talk about the "blessing of labour," I see the same secret arrière-pensée as I do in the praise bestowed on impersonal acts of a general interest, viz. a fear of everything individual. For at the sight of work—that is to say, severe toil from morning till night—we have the feeling that it is the best police, viz. that it holds every one in check and effectively hinders the development of reason, of greed, and of desire for independence. For work uses up an extraordinary proportion of nervous force, withdrawing it from reflection, meditation, dreams, cares, love, and hatred; it dangles unimportant aims before the eyes of the worker and affords easy and regular gratification. Thus it happens that a society where work is continually being performed will enjoy greater security, and it is security which is now venerated as the supreme deity.—And now, horror of horrors! it is the "workman" himself who has become dangerous; the whole world is swarming with "dangerous individuals," and behind them follows the danger of dangers—the individuum!

174. THE MORAL FASHION OF A COMMERCIAL COMMUNITY.—Behind the principle of the present moral fashion: "Moral actions are actions performed out of sympathy for others," I see the social instinct of fear, which thus assumes an intellectual disguise: this instinct sets forth as its supreme, most important, and most immediate principle that life shall be relieved of all the dangerous characteristics which it possessed in former times, and that every one must help with all his strength towards the attainment of this end. It is for that reason that only those actions which keep in view the general security and the feeling of security of society are called "good." How little joy must men now have in themselves when such a tyranny of fear prescribes their supreme moral law, if they make no objection when commanded to turn their eyes from themselves and to look aside from themselves! And yet at the same time they have lynx eyes for all distress and suffering elsewhere! Are we not, then, with this gigantic intention of ours of smoothing down every sharp edge and corner in life, utilising the best means of turning mankind into sand! Small, soft, round, infinite sand! Is that your ideal, ye harbingers of the "sympathetic affections"? In the meantime even the question remains unanswered whether we are of more use to our neighbour in running immediately and continually to his help,—which for the most part can only be done in a very superficial way, as otherwise it would become a tyrannical meddling and changing,—or by transforming ourselves into something which our neighbour can look upon with pleasure,—something, for example, which may be compared to a beautiful, quiet, and secluded garden, protected by high walls against storms and the dust of the roads, but likewise with a hospitable gate.

175. FUNDAMENTAL BASIS OF A CULTURE OF TRADERS.—We have now an opportunity of watching the manifold growth of the culture of a society of which commerce is the soul, just as personal rivalry was the soul of culture among the ancient Greeks, and war, conquest, and law among the ancient Romans. The tradesman is able to value everything without producing it, and to value it according to the requirements of the consumer rather than his own personal needs. "How many and what class of people will consume this?" is his question of questions. Hence, he instinctively and incessantly employs this mode of valuation and applies it to everything, including the productions of art and science, and of thinkers, scholars, artists, statesmen, nations, political parties, and even entire ages: with respect to everything produced or created he inquires into the supply and demand in order to estimate for himself the value of a thing. This, when once it has been made the principle of an entire culture, worked out to its most minute and subtle details, and imposed upon every kind of will and knowledge, this is what you men of the coming century will be proud of,—if the prophets of the commercial classes are right in putting that century into your possession! But I have little belief in these prophets. Credat Judæus Apella—to speak with Horace.

176. THE CRITICISM OF OUR ANCESTORS.—Why should we now endure the truth, even about the most recent past? Because there is now always a new generation which feels itself in contradiction to the past and enjoys in this criticism the first-fruits of its sense of power. In former times the new generation, on the contrary, wished to base itself on the old and began to feel conscious of its power, not only in accepting the opinions of its ancestors but, if possible, taking them even more seriously. To criticise ancestral authority was in former times a vice; but at the present time our idealists begin by making it their starting-point.

177. TO LEARN SOLITUDE.—O ye poor fellows in the great centres of the world's politics, ye young and talented men, who, urged on by ambition, think it your duty to propound your opinion of every event of the day,—for something is always happening,—who, by thus making a noise and raising a cloud of dust, mistake yourselves for the rolling chariot of history; who, because ye always listen, always suit the moment when ye can put in your word or two, thereby lose all real productiveness. Whatever may be your desire to accomplish great deeds, the deep silence of pregnancy never comes to you! The event of the day sweeps you along like straws before the wind whilst ye lie under the illusion that ye are chasing the event,—poor fellows! If a man wishes to act the hero on the stage he must not think of forming part of the chorus; he should not even know how the chorus is made up.

178. DAILY WEAR AND TEAR.—These young men are lacking neither in character, nor talent, nor zeal, but they have never had sufficient time to choose their own path; they have, on the contrary, been habituated from the most tender age to have their path pointed out to them. At the time when they were ripe enough to be sent into the "desert," something else was done with them. They were turned to account, estranged from themselves, and brought up in such a way that they became accustomed to be worn out by their daily toil. This was imposed on them as a duty, and now they cannot do without it; they would not wish it to be otherwise. The only thing that cannot be refused to these poor beasts of burden is their "holidays"—such is the name they give to this ideal of leisure in an overworked century; "holidays," in which they may for once be idle, idiotic, and childish to their heart's content.

179. AS LITTLE STATE AS POSSIBLE!—All political and economic matters are not of such great value that they ought to be dealt with by the most talented minds: such a waste of intellect is at bottom worse than any state of distress. These matters are, and ever will be, the province of smaller minds, and others than the smaller minds should not be at the service of this workshop: it would be better to let the machinery work itself to pieces again! But as matters stand at the present time, when not

only do all people believe that they must know all about it day by day, but wish likewise to be always busy about it, and in so doing neglect their own work, it is a great and ridiculous mistake. The price that has to be paid for the "public safety" is far too high, and, what is maddest of all, we effect the very opposite of "public safety" a fact which our own dear century has undertaken to prove, as if this had never been proved before! To make society secure against thieves and fire, and to render it thoroughly fit for all kinds of trade and traffic, and to transform the State in a good and evil sense into a kind of Providence—these aims are low, mediocre, and not by any means indispensable; and we should not seek to attain them by the aid of the highest means and instruments which exist—means which we should reserve precisely for our highest and rarest aims! Our epoch, however much it may babble about economy, is a spendthrift: it wastes intellect, the most precious thing of all.

180. WARS.—The great wars of our own day are the outcome of historical study.

181. GOVERNING.—Some people govern because of their passion for governing; others in order that they may not be governed,—the latter choose it as the lesser of two evils.

182. ROUGH AND READY CONSISTENCY.—People say of a man with great respect, "He is a character"—that is, when he exhibits a rough and ready consistency, when it is evident even to the dullest eye. But, whenever a more subtle and profound intellect sets itself up and shows consistency in a higher manner, the spectators deny the existence of any character. That is why cunning statesmen usually act their comedy under the cloak of a kind of rough and ready consistency.

183. THE OLD AND THE YOUNG.—"There is something immoral about Parliaments,"—so many people still think,—"for in them views even against the Government may be expressed."—"We should always adopt that view of a subject which our gracious Lord commands,"—this is the eleventh commandment in many an honest old head, especially in Northern Germany. We laugh at it as an out-of-date fashion, but in former times it was the moral law itself. Perhaps we shall again some day laugh at that which is now considered as moral by a generation brought up under a parliamentary régime, namely, the policy of placing one's party before one's own wisdom, and of answering every question concerning the public welfare in such a way as to fill the sails of the party with a favourable gust of wind. "We must take that view of a subject which the position of our party calls for"—such would be the canon. In the service of such morals we may now behold every kind of sacrifice, even martyrdom and conquest over one's self.

184. THE STATE AS A PRODUCTION OF ANARCHISTS.—In countries inhabited by tractable men there are always a few backsliders and intractable people. For the present the latter have joined the Socialists more than any other party. If it should happen that these people once come to have the making of the laws, they may be relied upon to impose iron chains upon themselves, and to practise a dreadful discipline,—they know themselves! and they will endure these harsh laws with the knowledge that they themselves have imposed them—the feeling of power and of this particular power will be too recent among them and too attractive for them not to suffer anything for its sake.

185. BEGGARS.—Beggars ought to be suppressed; because we get angry both when we help them and when we do not.

186. BUSINESS MEN.—Your business is your greatest prejudice, it binds you to your locality, your society and your tastes. Diligent in business but lazy in thought, satisfied with your paltriness and with the cloak of duty concealing this contentment: thus you live, and thus you like your children to be.

187. A POSSIBLE FUTURE.—Is it impossible for us to imagine a social state in which the criminal will publicly denounce himself and dictate his own punishment, in the proud feeling that he is thus honouring the law which he himself has made, that he is exercising his power, the power of a lawmaker, in thus punishing himself? He may offend for once, but by his own voluntary punishment he raises himself above his offence, and not only expiates it by his frankness, greatness, and calmness, but adds to it a public benefit.—Such would be the criminal of a possible future, a criminal who would, it is true, presuppose a future legislation based upon this fundamental idea: "I yield in great things as well as in small only to the law which I myself have made." How many experiments must yet be made! How many futures have yet to dawn upon mankind!

188. STIMULANTS AND FOOD.—Nations are deceived so often because they are always looking for a deceiver, i.e. a stimulating wine for their senses. When they can only have this wine they are glad to put up even with inferior bread. Intoxication is to them more than nutriment—this is the bait with which they always let themselves be caught! What, to them, are men chosen from among themselves—although they may be the most expert specialists—as compared with the brilliant conquerors, or ancient and magnificent princely houses! In order that he may inspire them with faith, the demagogue must at least exhibit to them a prospect of conquest and splendour. People will always obey, and even do more than obey, provided that they can become intoxicated in doing so. We may not even offer them repose and pleasure without this laurel crown and its maddening influence.

This vulgar taste which ascribes greater importance to intoxication than nutrition did not by any means originate in the lower ranks of the population: it was, on the contrary, transplanted there, and on this backward soil it grows in great abundance, whilst its real origin must be sought amongst the highest intellects, where it flourished for thousands of years. The people is the last virgin soil upon which this brilliant weed can grow. Well, then, is it really to the people that we should entrust politics in order that they may thereby have their daily intoxication?

189. HIGH POLITICS.—Whatever may be the influence in high politics of utilitarianism and the vanity of individuals and nations, the sharpest spur which urges them onwards is their need for the feeling of power—a need which rises not only in the souls of princes and rulers, but also gushes forth from time to time from inexhaustible sources in the people. The time comes again and again when the masses are ready to stake their lives and their fortunes, their consciences and their virtue, in order that they may secure that highest of all enjoyments and rule as a victorious, tyrannical, and arbitrary nation over other nations (or at all events think that they do).

On occasions such as these, feelings of prodigality, sacrifice, hope, confidence, extraordinary audacity, and enthusiasm will burst forth so abundantly that a sovereign who is ambitious or far-sighted will be able to seize the opportunity for making war, counting upon the good conscience of his people to hide his injustice. Great conquerors have always given utterance to the pathetic language of virtue; they have always been surrounded by crowds of people who felt themselves, as it were, in a state of exaltation and would listen to none but the most elevated oratory. The strange madness of moral judgments! When man experiences the sensation of power he feels and calls himself good; and at exactly the same time the others who have to endure his power call him evil!—Hesiod, in his fable of the epochs of man, has twice in succession depicted the same epoch, that of the heroes of Homer, and has thus made two epochs out of one: to those who lived under the terrible iron heel of those adventurous despots, or had heard their ancestors speak of them, the epoch appeared to be evil; but the descendants of those chivalric races worshipped it as the "good old times," and as an almost ideally blissful age. The poet could thus not help doing what he did,—his audience probably included the descendants of both races.

190. FORMER GERMAN CULTURE.—When the Germans began to interest other European nations, which is not so very long ago, it was owing to a culture which they no longer possess to-day, and which they have indeed shaken off with a blind ardour, as if it had been some disease; and yet they have not been able to replace it by anything better than political and national lunacy. They have in this way succeeded in becoming even more interesting to other nations than they were formerly through their culture: and may that satisfy them! It is nevertheless undeniable that this German culture has fooled Europeans, and that it did not deserve the interest shown in it, and much less the imitation and emulation displayed by other nations in trying to rival it.

Let us look back for a moment upon Schiller, Wilhelm von Humboldt, Schleiermacher, Hegel, and Schelling; let us read their correspondence and mingle for a time with the large circle of their followers: what have they in common, what characteristics have they, that fill us, as we are now, partly with a feeling of nausea and partly with pitiful and touching emotions? First and foremost, the passion for appearing at all costs to be morally exalted, and then the desire for giving utterance to brilliant, feeble, and inconsequential remarks, together with their fixed purpose of looking upon everything (characters, passions, times, customs) as beautiful—"beautiful," alas, in accordance with a bad and vague taste, which nevertheless pretended to be of Hellenic origin. We behold in these people a weak, good-natured, and glistening idealism, which, above all, wished to exhibit noble attitudes and noble voices, something at once presumptuous and inoffensive, and animated by a cordial aversion to "cold" or "dry" reality—as also to anatomy, complete passions, and every kind of philosophical continence and scepticism, but especially towards the knowledge of nature in so far as it was impossible to use it as religious symbolism.

Goethe, in his own characteristic fashion, observed from afar these movements of German culture: placing himself beyond their influence, gently remonstrating, silent, more and more confirmed in his own better course. A little later, and Schopenhauer also was an observer of these movements—a great deal of the world and devilry of the world had again been revealed to him, and he spoke of it both roughly and enthusiastically, for there is a certain beauty in this devilry! And what was it, then, that really seduced the foreigners and prevented them from viewing this movement as did Goethe and Schopenhauer, or, better, from ignoring it altogether? It was that faint lustre, that inexplicable starlight which formed a mysterious halo around this culture. The foreigners said to themselves: "This is all very very remote from us; our sight, hearing, understanding, enjoyment, and powers of valuations are lost here, but in spite of that there may be some stars! There may be something in it! Is it possible that the Germans have quietly discovered some corner of heaven and settled there? We must try to come nearer to these Germans." So they did begin to come nearer to the Germans, while not so very long afterwards the Germans put themselves to some trouble to get rid of this starlight halo: they knew only too well that they had not been in heaven, but only in a cloud!

191. BETTER MEN.—They tell me that our art is meant for the men of the present day, these greedy, unsatisfied, undisciplined, disgusted, and harassed spirits, and that it exhibits to them a picture of happiness, exaltation, and unworldliness beside that of their own brutality, so that for once they may

forget and breathe freely; nay, perhaps find that they may derive some encouragement towards flight and conversion from that oblivion. Poor artists, with such a public as this; half of whose thoughts require the attention of a priest, and the other half the attention of an alienist! How much happier was Corneille—"Our great Corneille!" as Madame de Sévigné exclaimed, with the accent of a woman in the presence of a whole man,—how far superior was his audience, which he could please with pictures of chivalric virtues, strict duty, generous devotion, and heroic self-denial! How differently did he and they love existence, not as coming from blind and confused "will," which we curse because we cannot destroy it; but loving existence as a place, so to speak, where greatness joined with humanity is possible, and where even the greatest restraint of form, such as submission to the caprice of priests and princes, could not suppress either the pride, chivalric feeling, the grace or the intellect of individuals, but could, on the contrary, be felt as a charm and incentive, as a welcome contrast to innate self-glorification and distinction and the inherited power of volition and passion.

192. THE DESIRE FOR PERFECT OPPONENTS.—It cannot be denied that the French have been the most Christian nation in the world, not because the devotion of masses in France has been greater than elsewhere, but because those Christian ideals which are most difficult to realise have become incarnated here instead of merely remaining fancies, intentions, or imperfect beginnings. Take Pascal, for example, the greatest of all Christians in his combination of ardour, intellect, and honesty, and consider what elements had to be combined in his case! Take Fénelon, the most perfect and attractive embodiment of ecclesiastical culture in all its power: a sublime golden mean of whom a historian would be tempted to prove the impossibility, whilst in reality he was merely the perfection of something exceedingly difficult and improbable. Take Madame de Guyon among her companions, the French Quietists: and everything that the eloquence and ardour of the Apostle Paul has endeavoured to divine with regard to the Christian's state of semi-divinity, this most sublime, loving, silent, and ecstatic state is seen verified in her, without, however, that Jewish obtrusiveness that Paul showed towards God—due in the case of Madame de Guyon to the real old French artlessness in words and gestures, artlessness at once womanly, subtle, and distinguished. Consider, again, the founder of the Trappists—the last person who really took seriously the ascetic ideal of Christianity, not because he was an exception among Frenchmen, but because he was a true Frenchman: for up to our own day his gloomy organisation has not been able to acclimatise itself and to prosper, except among Frenchmen; and it has followed them into Alsace and Algeria.

Let us not forget the Huguenots, either: that combination of a martial and industrial spirit, refined manners and Christian severity, has never been more beautifully exhibited. And it was at Port Royal that the great Christian erudition beheld its last era of prosperity; and in France more than anywhere else great men know how to prosper. Though not at all superficial, a great Frenchman has always his apparent superficiality;—he has, so to speak, a natural skin for his real contents and depth,—while, on the other hand, the depth of a great German is generally, as it were, closed up in an ugly-shaped box, like an elixir, which, by means of a hard and curious covering, endeavours to preserve itself from the light of day and the touch of thoughtless hands. And now let us endeavour to find out why a people like the French, so prolific in perfect types of Christians, likewise necessarily brought forth the perfect contrary types, those of unchristian free-thought! The French free-thinker, in his own inward being, had to fight against truly great men, and not, like the free-thinkers of other nations, merely against dogmas and sublime abortions.

193. ESPRIT AND MORALS.—The German, who possesses the secret of knowing how to be tedious in spite of wit, knowledge, and feeling, and who has habituated himself to consider tediousness as moral, is in dread in thè presence of French esprit lest it should tear out the eyes of morality—but a dread mingled with "fascination," like that experienced by the little bird in the presence of the rattlesnake. Amongst all the celebrated Germans none possessed more esprit than Hegel, but he also had that great German dread of it which brought about his peculiar and defective style. For the nature of this style resembles a kernel, which is wrapped up so many times in an outer covering that it can scarcely peep through, now and then glancing forth bashfully and inquisitively, like "young women peeping through their veils," to use the words of that old woman-hater, Æschylus. This kernel, however, is a witty though often impertinent joke on intellectual subjects, a subtle and daring combination of words, such as is necessary in a society of thinkers as gilding for a scientific pill—but, enveloped as it is in an almost impenetrable cover, it exhibits itself as the most abstruse science, and likewise as the worst possible moral tediousness. Here the Germans had a permissible form of esprit and they revelled in it with such boundless delight that even Schopenhauer's unusually fine understanding could not grasp it—during the whole of his life he thundered against the spectacle that the Germans offered to him, but he could never explain it.

194. VANITY OF THE TEACHERS OF MORALS.—The relatively small success which teachers of morals have met with may be explained by the fact that they wanted too much at once, i.e. they were too ambitious and too fond of laying down precepts for everybody. In other words, they were beating the air and making speeches to animals in order to turn them into men; what wonder, then, that

the animals thought this tedious! We should rather choose limited circles and endeavour to find and promote morals for them: for instance, we should make speeches to wolves with the object of turning them into dogs; but, above all, the greatest success will remain for the man who does not seek to educate either everybody or certain limited circles, but only one single individual, and who cannot be turned to the right or left from his straight purpose. The last century was superior to ours precisely because it possessed so many individually educated men, as well as educators in the same proportion, who had made this their life's task, and who with this task were dignified not only in their own eyes but in those of all the remaining "good society."

195. THE SO-CALLED CLASSICAL EDUCATION.—Alas! we discover that our life is consecrated to knowledge and that we should throw it away, nay, that we should even have to throw it away if this consecration did not protect us from ourselves: we repeat this couplet, and not without deep emotion:

Thee, Fate, I follow, though I fain would not,
And yet I must, with many a sigh and groan!

And then, in looking backwards over the course of our lives, we discover that there is one thing that cannot be restored to us: the wasted period of our youth, when our teachers did not utilise these ardent and eager years to lead us to the knowledge of things, but merely to this so-called "classical education"! Only think of this wasted youth, when we were inoculated clumsily and painfully with an imperfect knowledge of the Greeks and Romans as well as of their languages, contrary to the highest principle of all culture, which holds that we should not give food except to those who hunger for it! Think of that period of our lives when we had mathematics and physics forced down our throats, instead of being first of all made acquainted with the despair of ignorance, instead of having our little daily life, our activities, and everything occurring in our houses, our workshops, in the sky, and in nature, split up into thousands of problems, painful, humiliating and irritating problems—and thus having our curiosity made acquainted with the fact that we first of all require a mathematical and mechanical knowledge before we can be allowed to rejoice in the absolute logic of this knowledge! If we had only been imbued with reverence for those branches of science, if we had only been made to tremble with emotion—were it only for once—at the struggles, the defeats, and the renewed combats of those great men, of the martyrdom which is the history of pure science! But, on the contrary, we were allowed to develop a certain contempt for those sciences in favour of historical training, formal education[4] and "classicism."

And we allowed ourselves to be so easily deceived! Formal education! Might we not have pointed to the best teachers at our high schools and asked laughingly, "Where then do they keep their formal education? and, if it is wanting in them, how can they teach it?" And classicism! Did we get any of that instruction which the ancients used to impart to their youth? Did we learn to speak or to write like them? Did we ceaselessly exercise ourselves in that duel of speech, dialectic? Did we learn to move as beautifully and proudly as they did, and to excel as they did in wrestling, throwing, and boxing? Did we learn anything of that practical asceticism of all the Greek philosophers? Did we receive any training in a single ancient virtue, and in the way in which the ancients were trained in it? Was not all meditation upon morals wanting in our education?—And how much more the only possible criticism on the subject of morality, those courageous and earnest attempts to live according to this or that morality! Did our teachers ever stir up a feeling in us which the ancients valued more highly than moderns? Did they in the spirit of the ancients indicate to us the divisions of the day and of life, and those aims by which the lives of the ancients were guided? Did we learn the ancient languages as we now learn the modern ones, viz. that we might speak them fluently and well? Nowhere can we find a real proficiency or any new faculty as the result of those toilsome years! only the knowledge of what men had learnt and were able to do in past ages!

And what knowledge! Nothing becomes clearer to me year by year than the fact that the entire Greek and ancient mode of life, however simple and evident it must seem to our eyes, is in truth very difficult to understand, and even scarcely accessible, and that the customary ease with which we babble about the ancients is either giddy levity or the old hereditary conceit of our thoughtlessness. We are deceived by words and ideas which appear to resemble our own, but behind them there is always concealed a feeling which must be strange, incomprehensible, or painful to our modern conceptions. And these are realms in which boys are allowed to roam about! Enough: we roamed about them in our childhood, and there we became seized with an almost ineradicable antipathy for all antiquity, the antipathy arising from an intimacy which was apparently too great! For so great is the conceit of our classical teachers, who would almost make it appear that they had gained full control over the ancients, that they pass on this conceit to their pupils, together with the suspicion that such a possession is of little use for making people happy, but is good enough for honest, foolish old book-worms. "Let them brood over their treasure: it is well worthy of them!"—It is with this unexpressed thought that we completed our classical education. It can't be changed now—for us, at all events! But let us not think of ourselves alone!

196. THE MOST PERSONAL QUESTIONS OF TRUTH.—What am I really doing, and what do I mean by doing it? That is the question of truth which is not taught under our present system of education, and consequently not asked, because there is no time for it. On the other hand, we have always time and inclination for talking nonsense with children, rather than telling them the truth; for flattering women who will later on be mothers, rather than telling them the truth; and for speaking with young men about their future and their pleasures, rather than about the truth!

But what, after all, are seventy years!—Time passes, and they soon come to an end; it matters as little to us as it does to the wave to know how and whither it is rolling! No, it might even be wisdom not to know it.

"Agreed; but it shows a want of pride not even to inquire into the matter; our culture does not tend to make people proud."

"So much the better!"

"Is it really?"

197. ENMITY OF THE GERMANS TOWARDS ENLIGHTENMENT.—Let us consider the contributions which in the first half of this century the Germans made to general culture by their intellectual work. In the first place, let us take the German philosophers: they went back to the first and oldest stage of speculation, for they were content with conceptions instead of explanations, like the thinkers of dreamy epochs—a pre-scientific type of philosophy was thus revived by them. Secondly, we have the German historians and romanticists: their efforts on the whole aimed at restoring to the place of honour certain old and primitive sentiments, especially Christianity, the "soul of the people," folk-lore, folk-speech, mediævalism, Oriental asceticism, and Hinduism. In the third place, there are the natural philosophers who fought against the spirit of Newton and Voltaire, and, like Goethe and Schopenhauer, endeavoured to re-establish the idea of a deified or diabolised nature, and of its absolute ethical and symbolical meaning. The main general tendency of the Germans was directed against enlightenment and against those social revolutions which were stupidly mistaken for the consequences of enlightenment: the piety towards everything that existed tried to become piety towards everything that had ever existed, only in order that heart and mind might be permitted to fill themselves and gush forth again, thus leaving no space for future and novel aims. The cult of feeling took the place of the cult of reason, and the German musicians, as the best exponents of all that is invisible, enthusiastic, legendary, and passionate, showed themselves more successful in building up the new temple than all the other artists in words and thoughts.

If, in considering these details, we have taken into account the fact that many good things were said and investigated, and that many things have since then been more fairly judged than on any previous occasion, there yet remains to be said of the whole that it was a general danger, and one by no means small, to set knowledge altogether below feeling under the appearance of an entire and definitive acquaintance with the past—and, to use that expression of Kant, who thus defined his own particular task—"To make way again for belief by fixing the limits of knowledge." Let us once more breathe freely, the hour of this danger is past! And yet, strange to say, the very spirits which these Germans conjured up with such eloquence have at length become the most dangerous for the intentions of those who did conjure them up: history, the comprehension of origin and development, sympathy with the past, the new passion for feeling and knowledge, after they had been for a long time at the service of this obscure exalted and retrograde spirit, have once more assumed another nature, and are now soaring with outstretched wings above the heads of those who once upon a time conjured them forth, as new and stronger genii of that very enlightenment to combat which they had been resuscitated. It is this enlightenment which we have now to carry forward,—caring nothing for the fact that there has been and still is "a great revolution," and again a great "reaction" against it: these are but playful crests of foam when compared with the truly great current on which we float, and want to float.

198. ASSIGNING PRESTIGE TO ONE'S COUNTRY.—It is the men of culture who determine the rank of their country, and they are characterised by an innumerable number of great inward experiences, which they have digested and can now value justly. In France and Italy this fell to the lot of the nobility; in Germany, where up to now the nobility has been, as a rule, composed of men who had not much intellect to boast about (perhaps this will soon cease to be the case), it was the task of the priests, the school teachers and their descendants.

199. WE ARE NOBLER.—Fidelity, generosity, concern for one's good reputation: these three qualities, combined in one sentiment, we call noble, distinguished, aristocratic; and in this respect we excel the Greeks. We do not wish to give this up at any cost under the pretext that the ancient objects of these virtues have rightly fallen in esteem, but we wish cautiously to substitute new objects for these most precious and hereditary impulses. To understand why the sentiments of the noblest Greeks must be considered as inferior and scarcely respectable in the present age, where we are still under the influence of the chivalric and feudal nobility, we must recall the words of consolation to which Ulysses gave utterance in the midst of the most humiliating situations, "Bear with it, my dear heart, bear with it! Thou

hast borne with many more swinish things[5] than these!" As an instance of this mythical example, consider also the tale of that Athenian officer, who, when threatened with a stick by another officer in the presence of the entire general staff, shook off his disgrace with the words, "Strike, but listen to me." (This was Themistocles, that ingenious Ulysses of the classical epoch, who was just the man at the moment of disgrace to address to his "dear heart" that verse of comfort and affliction.)

The Greeks were far from making light of life and death because of an insult, as we, influenced by a hereditary spirit of chivalric adventurousness and self-devotion, are in the habit of doing; or from looking for opportunities of honourably risking life and death, as in duels; or from valuing the preservation of an unstained name (honour) more than the acquirement of an evil reputation, when the latter was compatible with glory and the feeling of power; or from remaining faithful to the prejudices and the articles of faith of a caste, when these could prevent them from becoming tyrants. For this is the ignoble secret of the good Greek aristocrat: out of sheer jealousy he treats every one of the members of his caste as being on an equal footing with himself, but he is ready at every moment to spring like a tiger on his prey—despotism. What matter lies, murders, treason, or the betrayal of his native city to him! Justice was an extremely difficult matter for people of this kind to understand—nay, justice was almost something incredible. "The just man" was to the Greeks what "the saint" was to the Christians. When Socrates, however, laid down the axiom, "The most virtuous man is the happiest," they could not trust their ears; they thought they had heard a madman speaking. For, as a picture of the happiest man, every nobleman had in his mind the cheeky audacity and devilry of the tyrant who sacrifices everything and every one to his own exuberance and pleasure. Among people whose imagination secretly raved about such happiness, the worship of the State could not, of course, have been too deeply implanted—but I think that men whose desire for power does not rage so blindly as that of the Greek noblemen no longer stand in need of such idolatry of the State, by means of which, in past ages, such a passion was kept within due bounds.

200. ENDURANCE OF POVERTY.—There is one great advantage in noble extraction: it makes us endure poverty better.

201. THE FUTURE OF THE NOBILITY.—The bearing of the aristocratic classes shows that, in all the members of their body the consciousness of power is continually playing its fascinating game. Thus people of aristocratic habits, men or women, never sink worn out into a chair; when every one else makes himself comfortable, as in a train, for example, they avoid reclining at their ease; they do not appear to get tired after standing at Court for hours at a stretch; they do not furnish their houses in a comfortable manner, but in such a way as to produce the impression of something grand and imposing, as if they had to serve as a residence for greater and taller beings; they reply to a provoking speech with dignity and clearness of mind, and not as if scandalised, crushed, shamed, or out of breath in the plebeian fashion. As the aristocrat is able to preserve the appearance of being possessed of a superior physical force which never leaves him, he likewise wishes by his aspect of constant serenity and civility of disposition, even in the most trying circumstances, to convey the impression that his mind and soul are equal to all dangers and surprises. A noble culture may resemble, so far as passions are concerned, either a horseman who takes pleasure in making his proud and fiery animal trot in the Spanish fashion,—we have only to recollect the age of Louis XIV.,—or like the rider who feels his horse dart away with him like the elemental forces, to such a degree that both horse and rider come near losing their heads, but, owing to the enjoyment of the delight, do keep very clear heads: in both these cases this aristocratic culture breathes power, and if very often in its customs only the appearance of the feeling of power is required, nevertheless the real sense of superiority continues constantly to increase as the result of the impression which this display makes upon those who are not aristocrats.

This indisputable happiness of aristocratic culture, based as it is on the feeling of superiority, is now beginning to rise to ever higher levels; for now, thanks to the free spirits, it is henceforth permissible and not dishonourable for people who have been born and reared in aristocratic circles to enter the domain of knowledge, where they may secure more intellectual consecrations and learn chivalric services even higher than those of former times, and where they may look up to that ideal of victorious wisdom which as yet no age has been able to set before itself with so good a conscience as the period which is about to dawn. Lastly, what is to be the occupation of the nobility in the future if it becomes more evident from day to day that it is less and less indecorus to take any part in politics?

202. THE CARE OF THE HEALTH.—We have scarcely begun to devote any attention to the physiology of criminals, and yet we have already reached the inevitable conclusion that between criminals and madmen there is no really essential difference: if we suppose that the current moral fashion of thinking is a healthy way of thinking. No belief, however, is nowadays more firmly believed in than this one, so we should not therefore shrink from drawing the inevitable conclusion and treating the criminal like a lunatic—above all, not with haughty pitifulness, but with medical skill and good will. He may perhaps be in need of a change of air, a change of society, or temporary absence: perhaps of solitude and new occupations—very well! He may perhaps feel that it would be to his advantage to live under surveillance for a short time in order thus to obtain protection from himself and from a

troublesome tyrannical impulse—very well! We should make clear to him the possibility and the means of curing him (the extermination, transformation, and sublimation of these impulses), and also, in the worst cases, the improbability of a cure; and we should offer to the incurable criminal, who has become a useless burden to himself, the opportunity of committing suicide. While holding this in reserve as an extreme measure of relief, we should neglect nothing which would tend above all to restore to the criminal his good courage and freedom of spirit; we should free his soul from all remorse, as if it were something unclean, and show him how he may atone for a wrong which he may have done some one by benefiting some one else, perhaps the community at large, in such way that he might even do more than balance his previous offence.

All this must be done with the greatest tact! The criminal must, above all, remain anonymous or adopt an assumed name, changing his place of residence frequently, so that his reputation and future life may suffer as little as possible. At the present time it is true that the man who has been injured, apart altogether from the manner in which this injury might be redressed, wishes for revenge in addition, and applies to the courts that he may obtain it—and this is why our dreadful penal laws are still in force: Justice, as it were, holding up a pair of shopkeeper's scales and endeavouring to balance the guilt by punishment; but can we not take a step beyond this? Would it not be a great relief to the general sentiment of life if, while getting rid of our belief in guilt, we could also get rid of our old craving for vengeance, and gradually come to believe that it is a refined wisdom for happy men to bless their enemies and to do good to those who have offended them, exactly in accordance with the spirit of Christian teaching! Let us free the world from this idea of sin, and take care to cast out with it the idea of punishment. May these monstrous ideas henceforth live banished far from the abodes of men—if, indeed, they must live at all, and do not perish from disgust with themselves.

Let us not forget also, however, that the injury caused to society and to the individual by the criminal is of the same species as that caused by the sick: for the sick spread cares and ill-humour; they are non-productive, consume the earnings of others, and at the same time require attendance, doctors, and support, and they really live on the time and strength of the healthy. In spite of this, however, we should designate as inhuman any one who, for this reason, would wish to wreak vengeance on the sick. In past ages, indeed, this was actually done: in primitive conditions of society, and even now among certain savage peoples, the sick man is treated as a criminal and as a danger to the community, and it is believed that he is the resting-place of certain demoniacal beings who have entered into his body as the result of some offence he has committed—those ages and peoples hold that the sick are the guilty!

And what of ourselves? Are we not yet ripe for the contrary conception? Shall we not be allowed to say, "The guilty are the sick"? No; the hour for that has not yet come. We still lack, above all, those physicians who have learnt something from what we have hitherto called practical morals and have transformed it into the art and science of healing. We still lack that intense interest in those things which some day perhaps may seem not unlike the "storm and stress" of those old religious ecstasies. The Churches have not yet come into the possession of those who look after our health; the study of the body and of dietary are not yet amongst the obligatory subjects taught in our primary and secondary schools; there are as yet no quiet associations of those people who are pledged to one another to do without the help of law courts, and who renounce the punishment and vengeance now meted out to those who have offended against society. No thinker has as yet been daring enough to determine the health of society, and of the individuals who compose it, by the number of parasites which it can support; and no statesman has yet been found to use the ploughshare in the spirit of that generous and tender saying, "If thou wilt till the land, till it with the plough; then the bird and the wolf, walking behind thy plough, will rejoice in thee—all creatures will rejoice in thee."

203. AGAINST BAD DIET.—Fie upon the meals which people nowadays eat in hotels and everywhere else where the well-off classes of society live! Even when eminent men of science meet together their tables groan under the weight of the dishes, in accordance with the principle of the bankers: the principle of too many dishes and too much to eat. The result of this is that dinners are prepared with a view to their mere appearance rather than the consequences that may follow from eating them, and that stimulating drinks are required to help in driving away the heaviness in the stomach and in the brain. Fie on the dissoluteness and extreme nervousness which must follow upon all this! Fie upon the dreams that such repasts bring! Fie upon the arts and books which must be the desert of such meals! Despite all the efforts of such people their acts will taste of pepper and ill-temper, or general weariness! (The wealthy classes in England stand in great need of their Christianity in order to be able to endure their bad digestions and their headaches.) Finally, to mention not only the disgusting but also the more pleasant side of the matter, these people are by no means mere gluttons: our century and its spirit of activity has more power over the limbs than the belly. What then is the meaning of these banquets? They represent! What in Heaven's name do they represent? Rank?—no, money! There is no rank now! We are all "individuals"! but money now stands for power, glory, pre-eminence, dignity, and influence; money at the present time acts as a greater or lesser moral prejudice for a man in proportion to the amount he may possess. Nobody wishes to hide it under a bushel or display it in heaps on a table:

hence money must have some representative which can be put on the table—so behold our banquets!

204. DANÆ AND THE GOD OF GOLD.—Whence arises this excessive impatience in our day which turns men into criminals even in circumstances which would be more likely to bring about the contrary tendency? What induces one man to use false weights, another to set his house on fire after having insured it for more than its value, a third to take part in counterfeiting, while three-fourths of our upper classes indulge in legalised fraud, and suffer from the pangs of conscience that follow speculation and dealings on the Stock Exchange: what gives rise to all this? It is not real want,—for their existence is by no means precarious; perhaps they have even enough to eat and drink without worrying,—but they are urged on day and night by a terrible impatience at seeing their wealth pile up so slowly, and by an equally terrible longing and love for these heaps of gold. In this impatience and love, however, we see re-appear once more that fanaticism of the desire for power which was stimulated in former times by the belief that we were in the possession of truth, a fanaticism which bore such beautiful names that we could dare to be inhuman with a good conscience (burning Jews, heretics, and good books, and exterminating entire cultures superior to ours, such as those of Peru and Mexico). The means of this desire for power are changed in our day, but the same volcano is still smouldering, impatience and intemperate love call for their victims, and what was once done "for the love of God" is now done for the love of money, i.e. for the love of that which at present affords us the highest feeling of power and a good conscience.

205. THE PEOPLE OF ISRAEL.—One of the spectacles which the next century will invite us to witness is the decision regarding the fate of the European Jews. It is quite obvious now that they have cast their die and crossed their Rubicon: the only thing that remains for them is either to become masters of Europe or to lose Europe, as they once centuries ago lost Egypt, where they were confronted with similar alternatives. In Europe, however, they have gone through a schooling of eighteen centuries such as no other nation has ever undergone, and the experiences of this dreadful time of probation have benefited not only the Jewish community but, even to a greater extent, the individual. As a consequence of this, the resourcefulness of the modern Jews, both in mind and soul, is extraordinary. Amongst all the inhabitants of Europe it is the Jews least of all who try to escape from any deep distress by recourse to drink or to suicide, as other less gifted people are so prone to do. Every Jew can find in the history of his own family and of his ancestors a long record of instances of the greatest coolness and perseverance amid difficulties and dreadful situations, an artful cunning in fighting with misfortune and hazard. And above all it is their bravery under the cloak of wretched submission, their heroic spernere se sperni that surpasses the virtues of all the saints.

People wished to make them contemptible by treating them contemptibly for nearly twenty centuries, and refusing them access to all honourable positions and dignities, and by pushing them further down into the meaner trades—and under this process indeed they have not become any cleaner. But contemptible? They have never ceased for a moment from believing themselves qualified for the very highest functions, nor have the virtues of the suffering ever ceased to adorn them. Their manner of honouring their parents and children, the rationality of their marriages and marriage customs, distinguishes them amongst all Europeans. Besides this, they have been able to create for themselves a sense of power and eternal vengeance from the very trades that were left to them (or to which they were abandoned). Even in palliation of their usury we cannot help saying that, without this occasional pleasant and useful torture inflicted on their scorners, they would have experienced difficulty in preserving their self-respect for so long. For our self-respect depends upon our ability to make reprisals in both good and evil things. Nevertheless, their revenge never urges them on too far, for they all have that liberty of mind, and even of soul, produced in men by frequent changes of place, climate, and customs of neighbours and oppressors, they possess by far the greatest experience in all human intercourse, and even in their passions they exercise the caution which this experience has developed in them. They are so certain of their intellectual versatility and shrewdness that they never, even when reduced to the direst straits, have to earn their bread by manual labour as common workmen, porters, or farm hands. In their manners we can still see that they have never been inspired by chivalric and noble feelings, or that their bodies have ever been girt with fine weapons: a certain obtrusiveness alternates with a submissiveness which is often tender and almost always painful.

Now, however, that they unavoidably inter-marry more and more year after year with the noblest blood of Europe, they will soon have a considerable heritage of good intellectual and physical manners, so that in another hundred years they will have a sufficiently noble aspect not to render themselves, as masters, ridiculous to those whom they will have subdued. And this is important! and therefore a settlement of the question is still premature. They themselves know very well that the conquest of Europe or any act of violence is not to be thought of; but they also know that some day or other Europe may, like a ripe fruit, fall into their hands, if they do not clutch at it too eagerly. In the meantime, it is necessary for them to distinguish themselves in all departments of European distinction and to stand in the front rank: until they shall have advanced so far as to determine themselves what distinction shall mean. Then they will be called the pioneers and guides of the Europeans whose modesty they will no longer offend.

And then where shall an outlet be found for this abundant wealth of great impressions accumulated during such an extended period and representing Jewish history for every Jewish family, this wealth of passions, virtues, resolutions, resignations, struggles, and conquests of all kinds—where can it find an outlet but in great intellectual men and works! On the day when the Jews will be able to exhibit to us as their own work such jewels and golden vessels as no European nation, with its shorter and less profound experience, can or could produce, when Israel shall have changed its eternal vengeance into an eternal benediction for Europe: then that seventh day will once more appear when old Jehovah may rejoice in Himself, in His creation, in His chosen people—and all, all of us, will rejoice with Him!

206. THE IMPOSSIBLE CLASS.—Poverty, cheerfulness, and independence—it is possible to find these three qualities combined in one individual; poverty, cheerfulness, and slavery—this is likewise a possible combination: and I can say nothing better to the workmen who serve as factory slaves; presuming that it does not appear to them altogether to be a shameful thing to be utilised as they are, as the screws of a machine and the stopgaps, as it were, of the human spirit of invention. Fie on the thought that merely by means of higher wages the essential part of their misery, i.e. their impersonal enslavement, might be removed! Fie, that we should allow ourselves to be convinced that, by an increase of this impersonality within the mechanical working of a new society, the disgrace of slavery could be changed into a virtue! Fie, that there should be a regular price at which a man should cease to be a personality and become a screw instead! Are you accomplices in the present madness of nations which desire above all to produce as much as possible, and to be as rich as possible? Would it not be your duty to present a counter-claim to them, and to show them what large sums of internal value are wasted in the pursuit of such an external object?

But where is your internal value when you no longer know what it is to breathe freely; when you have scarcely any command over your own selves, and often feel disgusted with yourselves as with some stale food; when you zealously study the newspapers and look enviously at your wealthy neighbour, made covetous by the rapid rise and fall of power, money, and opinions; when you no longer believe in a philosophy in rags, or in the freedom of spirit of a man who has few needs; when a voluntary and idyllic poverty without profession or marriage, such as should suit the more intellectual ones among you, has become for you an object of derision? On the other hand, the piping of the Socialistic rat-catchers who wish to inspire you with foolish hopes is continually sounding in your ears: they tell you to be ready and nothing further, ready from this day to the next, so that you wait and wait for something to come from outside, though living in all other respects as you lived before—until this waiting is at length changed into hunger and thirst and fever and madness, and the clay of the bestia triumphans at last dawns in all its glory. Every one of you should on the contrary say to himself: "It would be better to emigrate and endeavour to become a master in new and savage countries, and especially to become master over myself, changing my place of abode whenever the least sign of slavery threatens me, endeavouring to avoid neither adventure nor war, and, if things come to the worst, holding myself ready to die: anything rather than continuing in this state of disgraceful thraldom, this bitterness, malice and rebelliousness!" This would be the proper spirit: the workmen in Europe ought to make it clear that their position as a class has become a human impossibility, and not merely, as they at present maintain, the result of some hard and aimless arrangement of society. They should bring about an age of great swarming forth from the European beehive such as has never yet been seen, protesting by this voluntary and huge migration against machines and capital and the alternatives that now threaten them either of becoming slaves of the State or slaves of some revolutionary party.

May Europe be freed from one-fourth of her inhabitants! Both she and they will experience a sensation of relief. It is only far in the distance, in the undertaking of vast colonisations, that we shall be able to observe how much rationality, fairness, and healthy suspicion mother Europe has incorporated in her sons—these sons who could no longer endure life in the home of the dull old woman, always running the danger of becoming as bad-tempered, irritable, and pleasure-seeking as she herself. The European virtues will travel along with these workmen far beyond the boundaries of Europe; and those very qualities which on their native soil had begun to degenerate into a dangerous discontent and criminal inclinations will, when abroad, be transformed into a beautiful, savage naturalness and will be called heroism; so that at last a purer air would again be wafted over this old, over-populated, and brooding Europe of ours. What would it matter if there was a scarcity of "hands"? Perhaps people would then recollect that they had accustomed themselves to many wants merely because it was easy to gratify them—it would be sufficient to unlearn some of these wants! Perhaps also Chinamen would be called in, and these would bring with them their modes of living and thinking, which would be found very suitable for industrious ants. They would also perhaps help to imbue this fretful and restless Europe with some of their Asiatic calmness and contemplation, and—what is perhaps most needful of all—their Asiatic stability.

207. THE ATTITUDE OF THE GERMANS TO MORALITY.—A German is capable of great

things, but he is unlikely to accomplish them, for he obeys whenever he can, as suits a naturally lazy intellect. If he is ever in the dangerous situation of having to stand alone and cast aside his sloth, when he finds it no longer possible to disappear like a cipher in a number (in which respect he is far inferior to a Frenchman or an Englishman), he shows his true strength: then he becomes dangerous, evil, deep, and audacious, and exhibits to the light of day that wealth of latent energy which he had previously carried hidden in himself, and in which no one, not even himself, had ever believed. When in such a case a German obeys himself—it is very exceptional for him to do so—he does so with the same heaviness, inflexibility, and endurance with which he obeys his prince and performs his official duties: so that, as I have said, he is then capable of great things which bear no relation to the "weak disposition" he attributes to himself.

As a rule, however, he is afraid of depending upon himself alone, he is afraid of taking the initiative: that is why Germany uses up so many officials and so much ink. Light-heartedness is a stranger to the German; he is too timid for it: but in entirely new situations which rouse him from his torpor he exhibits an almost frivolous spirit—he then delights in the novelty of his new position as if it were some intoxicating drink, and he is, as we know, quite a connoisseur in intoxication. It thus happens that the German of the present day is almost always frivolous in politics, though even here he has the advantage and prejudice of thoroughness and seriousness; and, although he may take full advantage of these qualities in negotiations with other political powers, he nevertheless rejoices inwardly at being able for once in his life to feel enthusiastic and capricious, to show his fondness for innovations, and to change persons, parties, and hopes as if they were masks. Those learned German scholars, who hitherto have been considered as the most German of Germans, were and perhaps still are as good as the German soldiers on account of their profound and almost childish inclination to obey in all external things, and on account of being often compelled to stand alone in science and to answer for many things: if they can only preserve their proud, simple, and patient disposition, and their freedom from political madness at those times when the wind changes, we may yet expect great things from them—such as they are or such as they were, they are the embryonic stage of something higher.

So far the advantages and disadvantages of the Germans, including even their learned men, have been that they were more given to superstition and showed greater eagerness to believe than any of the other nations; their vices are, and always have been, their drunkenness and suicidal inclinations (the latter a proof of the clumsiness of their intellect, which is easily tempted to throw away the reins). Their danger is to be sought in everything that binds down the faculties of reason and unchains the passions (as, for example, the excessive use of music and spirits), for the German passion acts contrarily to its own advantage, and is as self-destructive as the passions of the drunkard. Indeed, German enthusiasm is worth less than that of other nations, for it is barren. When a German ever did anything great it was done at a time of danger, or when his courage was high, with his teeth firmly set and his prudence on the alert, and often enough in a fit of generosity.—Intercourse with these Germans is indeed advisable, for almost every one of them has something to give, if we can only understand how to make him find it, or rather recover it (for he is very untidy in storing away his knowledge).

Well: when people of this type occupy themselves with morals, what precisely will be the morality that will satisfy them? In the first place, they will wish to see idealised in their morals their sincere instinct for obedience. "Man must have something which he can implicitly obey"—this is a German sentiment, a German deduction; it is the basis of all German moral teaching. How different is the impression, however, when we compare this with the entire morality of the ancient world! All those Greek thinkers, however varied they may appear to us, seem to resemble, as moralists, the gymnastic teacher who encourages his pupils by saying, "Come, follow me! Submit to my discipline! Then perhaps you may carry off the prize from all the other Greeks." Personal distinction: such was the virtue of antiquity. Submission, obedience, whether public or private: such is German virtue. Long before Kant set forth his doctrine of the Categorical Imperative, Luther, actuated by the same impulse, said that there surely must be a being in whom man could trust implicitly—it was his proof of the existence of God; it was his wish, coarser and more popular than that of Kant, that people should implicitly obey a person and not an idea, and Kant also finally took his roundabout route through morals merely that he might secure obedience for the person. This is indeed the worship of the German, the more so as there is now less worship left in his religion.

The Greeks and Romans had other opinions on these matters, and would have laughed at such "there must be a being": it is part of the boldness of their Southern nature to take up a stand against "implicit belief," and to retain in their inmost heart a trace of scepticism against all and every one, whether God, man, or idea. The thinker of antiquity went even further, and said nil admirari: in this phrase he saw reflected all philosophy. A German, Schopenhauer, goes so far in the contrary direction as to say: admirari id est philosophari. But what if, as happens now and then, the German should attain to that state of mind which would enable him to perform great things? if the hour of exception comes, the hour of disobedience? I do not think Schopenhauer is right in saying that the single advantage the Germans have over other nations is that there are more atheists among them than elsewhere; but I do know this: whenever the German reaches the state in which he is capable of great things, he invariably raises himself above morals! And why should he not? Now he has something new to do, viz. to command—either himself or others! But this German morality of his has not taught him how to command! Commanding has been forgotten in it.

BOOK IV

208. A QUESTION OF CONSCIENCE.—"Now, in summa, tell me what this new thing is that you want."—"We no longer wish causes to be sinners and effects to be executioners."

209. THE UTILITY OF THE STRICTEST THEORIES.—People are indulgent towards a man's moral weaknesses, and in this connection they use a coarse sieve, provided that he always professes to hold the most strict moral theories. On the other hand, the lives of free-thinking moralists have always been examined closely through a microscope, in the tacit belief that an error in their lives would be the best argument against their disagreeable knowledge.[6]

210. THE "THING IN ITSELF."—We used to ask formerly: What is the ridiculous?—as if there were something above and beyond ourselves that possessed the quality of provoking laughter, and we exhausted ourselves in trying to guess what it was (a theologian even held that it might be "the naïveté of sin"). At the present time we ask: What is laughter? how does it arise? We have considered the point, and finally reached the conclusion that there is nothing which is good, beautiful, sublime, or evil in itself; but rather that there are conditions of soul which lead us to attribute such qualities to things outside ourselves and in us. We have taken back their predicates from things; or we have at all events recollected that we have merely lent the things these predicates. Let us be careful that this insight does not cause us to lose the faculty of lending, and that we do not become at the same time wealthier and more avaricious.

211. TO THOSE WHO DREAM OF IMMORTALITY.—So you desire the everlasting perpetuity of this beautiful consciousness of yourselves? Is it not shameful? Do you forget all those other things which would in their turn have to support you for all eternity, just as they have borne with you up to the present with more than Christian patience? Or do you think that you can inspire them with an eternally pleasant feeling towards yourself? A single immortal man on earth would imbue everyone around him with such a disgust for him that a general epidemic of murder and suicide would be brought about. And yet, ye petty dwellers on earth, with your narrow conceptions of a few thousand little minutes of time, ye would wish to be an everlasting burden on this everlasting universal existence! Could anything be more impertinent? After all, however, let us be indulgent towards a being of seventy years: he has not been able to exercise his imagination in conceiving his own "eternal tediousness"—he had not time enough for that!

212. WHEREIN WE KNOW OURSELVES.—As soon as one animal sees another it mentally compares itself with it; and men of uncivilised ages did the same. The consequence is that almost all men come to know themselves only as regards their defensive and offensive faculties.

213. MEN WHOSE LIVES HAVE BEEN FAILURES.—Some men are built of such stuff that society is at liberty to do what it likes with them—they will do well in any case, and will not have to complain of having failed in life. Other men are formed of such peculiar material—it need not be a particularly noble one, but simply rarer—that they are sure to fare ill except in one single instance: when they can live according to their own designs,—in all other cases the injury has to be borne by society. For everything that seems to the individual to be a wasted or blighted life, his entire burden of discouragement, powerlessness, sickness, irritation, covetousness, is attributed by him to society—and thus a heavy, vitiated atmosphere is gradually formed round society, or, in the most favourable cases, a thundercloud.

214. WHAT INDULGENCE!—You suffer, and call upon us to be indulgent towards you, even when in your suffering you are unjust towards things and men! But what does our indulgence matter! You, however, should take greater precautions for your own sake! That's a nice way of compensating yourself for your sufferings, by imposing still further suffering on your own judgment! Your own revenge recoils upon yourselves when you start reviling something: you dim your own eyes in this way, and not the eyes of others; you accustom yourself to looking at things in the wrong way, and with a squint.

215. THE MORALITY OF VICTIMS.—"Enthusiastic sacrifice," "self-immolation"—these are the catch-words of your morality, and I willingly believe that you, as you say, "mean it honestly": but I know you better than you know yourselves, if your "honesty" is capable of going arm in arm with such a morality. You look down from the heights of this morality upon that other sober morality which calls for self-control, severity, and obedience; you even go so far as to call it egoistic—and you are indeed

frank towards yourselves in saying that it displeases you—it must displease you! For, in sacrificing and immolating yourselves with such enthusiasm, you delight in the intoxication of the thought that you are now one with the powerful being, God or man, to whom you are consecrating yourselves: you revel in the feeling of his power, which is again attested by this sacrifice.

In reality, however, you only appear to sacrifice yourselves; for your imagination turns you into gods and you enjoy yourselves as such. Judged from the point of view of this enjoyment, how poor and feeble must that other "egoistic" morality of obedience, duty, and reason seem to you: it is displeasing to you because in this instance true self-sacrifice and self-surrender are called for, without the victim thinking himself to be transformed into a god, as you do. In a word, you want intoxication and excess, and this morality which you despise takes up a stand against intoxication and excess—no wonder it causes you some displeasure!

216. EVIL PEOPLE AND MUSIC.—Should the full bliss of love, which consists in unlimited confidence, ever have fallen to the lot of persons other than those who are profoundly suspicious, evil, and bitter? For such people enjoy in this bliss the gigantic, unlooked-for, and incredible exception of their souls! One day they are seized with that infinite, dreamy sensation which is entirely opposed to the remainder of their private and public life, like a delicious enigma, full of golden splendour, and impossible to be described by mere words or similes. Implicit confidence makes them speechless—there is even a species of suffering and heaviness in this blissful silence; and this is why souls that are overcome with happiness generally feel more grateful to music than others and better ones do: for they see and hear through music, as through a coloured mist, their love becoming, as it were, more distant, more touching, and less heavy. Music is the only means that such people have of observing their extraordinary condition and of becoming aware of its presence with a feeling of estrangement and relief. When the sound of music reaches the ears of every lover he thinks: "It speaks of me, it speaks in my stead; it knows everything!"

217. THE ARTIST.—The Germans wish to be transported by the artist into a state of dreamy passion; by his aid the Italians wish to rest from their real passions; the French wish him to give them an opportunity of showing their judgment and of making speeches. So let us be just!

218. TO DEAL LIKE AN ARTIST WITH ONE'S WEAKNESSES.—If we must positively have weaknesses and come in the end to look upon them as laws beyond ourselves, I wish that everybody may be possessed of as much artistic capacity as will enable him to set off his virtues by means of his weaknesses, and to make us, through his weaknesses, desirous of acquiring his virtues: a power which great musicians have possessed in quite an exceptional degree. How frequently do we notice in Beethoven's music a coarse, dogmatic, and impatient tone; in Mozart, the joviality of an honest man, whose heart and mind have not overmuch to give us; in Richard Wagner, an abrupt and aggressive restlessness, in the midst of which, just as the most patient listener is on the point of losing his temper, the composer regains his powers, and likewise the others. Through their very weaknesses, these musicians have created in us an ardent desire for their virtues, and have given us a palate which is ten times more sensitive to every note of this tuneful intellect, tuneful beauty, and tuneful goodness.

219. DECEIT IN HUMILIATION.—By your foolishness you have done a great wrong to your neighbour and destroyed his happiness irretrievably—and then, having overcome your vanity, you humble yourself before him, surrender your foolishness to his contempt, and fancy that, after this difficult scene, which is an exceedingly painful one for you, everything has been set right, that your own voluntary loss of honour compensates your neighbour for the injury you have done to his happiness. With this feeling you take your leave comforted, believing that your virtue has been re-established.

Your neighbour, however, suffers as intensely as before. He finds nothing to comfort him in the fact that you have been irrational and have told him so: on the contrary, he remembers the painful appearance you presented to him when you were disparaging yourself in his presence—it is as if another wound had been inflicted on him. He does not think of revenging himself, however; and cannot conceive how a proper balance can be struck between you and him. In point of fact, you have been acting that scene for yourself and before yourself: you invited a witness to be present, not on his account, but on your own—don't deceive yourself!

220. DIGNITY AND TIMIDITY.—Ceremonies, official robes and court dresses, grave countenances, solemn aspects, the slow pace, involved speech—everything, in short, known as dignity—are all pretences adopted by those who are timid at heart: they wish to make themselves feared (themselves or the things they represent). The fearless (i.e. originally those who naturally inspire others with awe) have no need of dignity and ceremonies: they bring into repute—or, still more, into ill-repute—honesty and straightforward words and bearing, as characteristics of their self-confident awefulness.

221. THE MORALITY OF SACRIFICE.—The morality which is measured by the spirit of sacrifice is that of a semi-civilised state of society. Reason in this instance gains a hard-fought and bloody victory within the soul; for there are powerful contrary instincts to be overcome. This cannot be brought about without the cruelty which the sacrifices to cannibal gods demand.

222. WHERE FANATICISM IS TO BE DESIRED.—Phlegmatic natures can be rendered enthusiastic only by being fanaticised.

223. THE DREADED EYE.—Nothing is dreaded more by artists, poets, and writers than the eye which sees through their little deceptions and subsequently notices how often they have stopped at the boundary where the paths branch off either to innocent delight in themselves or to the straining after effect; the eye which checks them when they try to sell little things dear, or when they try to exalt and adorn without being exalted themselves; the eye which, despite all the artifices of their art, sees the thought as it first presented itself to them, perhaps as a charming vision of light, perhaps also, however, as a theft from the whole world, or as an everyday conception which they had to expand, contract, colour, wrap up, and spice, in order to make something out of it, instead of the thought making something out of them.—Oh, this eye, which sees in your work all your restlessness, inquisitiveness, and covetousness, your imitation and exaggeration (which is only envious imitation) which knows both your blush of shame and your skill in concealing it from others and interpreting it to yourselves!

224. THE "EDIFYING" ELEMENT IN OUR NEIGHBOUR'S MISFORTUNE.—He is in distress, and straightway the "compassionate" ones come to him and depict his misfortune to him. At last they go away again, satisfied and elevated, after having gloated over the unhappy man's misfortune and their own, and spent a pleasant Sunday afternoon.

225. TO BE QUICKLY DESPISED.—A man who speaks a great deal, and speaks quickly, soon sinks exceedingly low in our estimation, even when he speaks rationally—not only to the extent that he annoys us personally, but far lower. For we conjecture how great a burden he has already proved to many other people, and we thus add to the discomfort which he causes us all the contempt which we presume he has caused to others.

226. RELATIONS WITH CELEBRITIES.—A. But why do you shun this great man?—B. I should not like to misunderstand him. Our defects are incompatible with one another: I am short-sighted and suspicious, and he wears his false diamonds as willingly as his real ones.

227. THE CHAIN-WEARERS.—Beware of all those intellects which are bound in chains! clever women, for example, who have been banished by fate to narrow and dull surroundings, amid which they grow old. True, there they lie in the sun, apparently lazy and half-blind; but at every unknown step, at everything unexpected, they start up to bite: they revenge themselves on everything that has escaped their kennel.

228. REVENGE IN PRAISE.—Here we have a written page which is covered with praise, and you call it flat; but when you find out that revenge is concealed in this praise you will find it almost too subtle, and you will experience a great deal of pleasure in its numerous delicate and bold strokes and similes. It is not the man himself, but his revenge, which is so subtle, rich, and ingenious: he himself is scarcely aware of it.

229. PRIDE.—Ah, not one of you knows the feeling of the tortured man after he has been put to the torture, when he is being carried back to his cell, and his secret with him!—he still holds it in a stubborn and tenacious grip. What know ye of the exultation of human pride?

230. "UTILITARIAN."—At the present time men's sentiments on moral things run in such labyrinthic paths that, while we demonstrate morality to one man by virtue of its utility, we refute it to another on account of this utility.

231. ON GERMAN VIRTUE.—How degenerate in its taste, how servile to dignities, ranks, uniforms, pomp, and splendour must a nation have been, when it began to consider the simple as the bad, the simple man (schlicht) as the bad man (schlecht)! We should always oppose the moral bumptiousness of the Germans with this one little word "bad," and nothing else.

232. FROM A DISPUTE.—A. Friend, you have talked yourself hoarse.—B. Then I am refuted, so let's drop the subject.

233. THE "CONSCIENTIOUS" ONES.—Have you noticed the kind of men who attach the greatest value to the most scrupulous conscientiousness? Those who are conscious of many mean and petty sentiments, who are anxiously thinking of and about themselves, are afraid of others, and are desirous of concealing their inmost feelings as far as possible. They endeavour to impose upon themselves by means of this strict conscientiousness and rigorousness of duty, and by the stern and harsh impression which others, especially their inferiors, cannot fail to receive of them.

234. DREAD OF FAME.—A. The endeavour to avoid one's renown, the intentional offending of one's panegyrists, the dislike of hearing opinions about one's self, and all through fear of renown: instances like these are to be met with; they actually exist—believe it or not!—B. They are found, no doubt! They exist! A little patience, Sir Arrogance!

235. REFUSING THANKS.—We are perfectly justified in refusing a request, but it is never right to refuse thanks—or, what comes to the same thing, to accept them coldly and conventionally. This gives deep offence—and why?

236. PUNISHMENT.—A strange thing, this punishment of ours! It does not purify the criminal; it is not a form of expiation; but, on the contrary, it is even more defiling than the crime itself.

237. PARTY GRIEVANCES.—In almost every party there is a ridiculous, but nevertheless somewhat dangerous grievance. The sufferers from it are those who have long been the faithful and honourable upholders of the doctrine propagated by the party, and who suddenly remark that one day a much stronger figure than themselves has got the ear of the public. How can they bear being reduced to silence? So they raise their voices, sometimes changing their notes.

238. TRIVING FOR GENTLENESS.—When a vigorous nature has not an inclination towards cruelty, and is not always preoccupied with itself; it involuntarily strives after gentleness—this is its distinctive characteristic. Weak natures, on the other hand, have a tendency towards harsh judgments—they associate themselves with the heroes of the contempt of mankind, the religious or philosophical traducers of existence,.or they take up their position behind strict habits and punctilious "callings": in this way they seek to give themselves a character and a kind of strength. This is likewise done quite involuntarily.

239. A HINT TO MORALISTS.—Our musicians have made a great discovery. They have found out that interesting ugliness is possible even in their art; this is why they throw themselves with such enthusiastic intoxication into this ocean of ugliness, and never before has it been so easy to make music. It is only now that we have got the general, dark-coloured background, upon which every luminous ray of fine music, however faint, seems tinged with golden emerald lustre; it is only now that we dare to inspire our audience with feelings of impetuosity and indignation, taking away their breath, so to speak, in order that we may afterwards, in an interval of restful harmony, inspire them with a feeling of bliss which will be to the general advantage of a proper appreciation of music.

We have discovered the contrast: it is only now that the strongest effects are possible—and cheap. No one bothers any more about good music. But you must hurry up! When any art has once made this discovery, it has but a short space of time to live.—Oh, if only our thinkers could probe into the depths of the souls of our musicians when listening to their music! How long we must wait until we again have an opportunity of surprising the inward man in the very act of his evil doing, and his innocence of this act! For our musicians have not the slightest suspicion that it is their own history, the history of the disfigurement of the soul, which they are transposing into music. In former times a good musician was almost forced by the exigencies of his art to become a good man—and now!

240. THE MORALITY OF THE STAGE.—The man who imagines that the effect of Shakespeare's plays is a moral one, and that the sight of Macbeth irresistibly induces us to shun the evil of ambition, is mistaken, and he is mistaken once more if he believes that Shakespeare himself thought so. He who is truly obsessed by an ardent ambition takes delight in beholding this picture of himself; and when the hero is driven to destruction by his passion, this is the most pungent spice in the hot drink of this delight. Did the poet feel this in another way? How royally and with how little of the knave in him does his ambitious hero run his course from the moment of his great crime! It is only from this moment that he becomes "demoniacally" attractive, and that he encourages similar natures to imitate him.—There is something demoniacal here: something which is in revolt against advantage and life, in favour of a thought and an impulse. Do you think that Tristan and Isolde are warnings against adultery, merely because adultery has resulted in the death of both of them? This would be turning poets upside down, these poets who, especially Shakespeare, are in love with the passions in themselves, and not less so with the readiness for death which they give rise to: this mood in which the heart no more clings to life than a drop of water does to the glass. It is not the guilt and its pernicious consequences which interests these poets—Shakespeare as little as Sophocles (in the Ajax, Philoctetes, Œdipus)—however easy it might have been in the cases just mentioned to make the guilt the lever of the play, it was carefully avoided by the poets.

In the same way the tragic poet by his images of life does not wish to set us against life. On the contrary, he exclaims; "It is the charm of charms, this exciting, changing, and dangerous existence of ours, so often gloomy and so often bathed in sun! Life is an adventure—whichever side you may take in life it will always retain this character!"—Thus speaks the poet of a restless and vigorous age, an age which is almost intoxicated and stupefied by its superabundance of blood and energy, in an age more evil than our own: and this is why it is necessary for us to adapt and accommodate ourselves first to the purpose of a Shakespearian play, that is, by misunderstanding it.

241. FEAR AND INTELLIGENCE.—If that which is now expressly maintained is true, viz. that the cause of the black pigment of the skin must not be sought in light, might this phenomenon perhaps be the ultimate effect of frequent fits of passion accumulated for century after century (and an afflux of blood under the skin)? while in other and more intelligent races the equally frequent spasms of fear and blanching may have resulted in the white colour of the skin?—For the degree of timidity is the standard by which the intelligence may be measured; and the fact that men give themselves up to blind anger is an indication that their animal nature is still near the surface, and is longing for an opportunity to make its presence felt once more. Thus a brownish-grey would probably be the primitive colour of man—something of the ape and the bear, as is only proper.

242. INDEPENDENCE.—Independence (which in its weakest form is called "freedom of

thought") is the type of resignation which the tyrannical man ends by accepting—he who for a long time had been looking for something to govern, but without finding anything except himself.

243. THE TWO COURSES.—When we endeavour to examine the mirror in itself we discover in the end that we can detect nothing there but the things which it reflects. If we wish to grasp the things reflected we touch nothing in the end but the mirror.—This is the general history of knowledge.

244. DELIGHT IN REALITY.—Our present inclination to take delight in reality—for almost every one of us possesses it—can only be explained by the fact that we have taken delight in the unreal for such a long time that we have got tired of it. This inclination in its present form, without choice and without refinement, is not without danger—its least danger is its want of taste.

245. THE SUBTLETY OF THE FEELING OF POWER.—Napoleon was greatly mortified at the fact that he could not speak well, and he did not deceive himself in this respect: but his thirst for power, which never despised the slightest opportunity of showing itself, and which was still more subtle than his subtle intellect, led him to speak even worse than he might have done. It was in this way that he revenged himself upon his own mortification (he was jealous of all his emotions because they possessed power) in order to enjoy his autocratic pleasure.

He enjoyed this pleasure a second time in respect to the ears and judgment of his audience, as if it were good enough for them to be addressed in this way. He even secretly enjoyed the thought of bewildering their judgment and good taste by the thunder and lightning of his highest authority—that authority which lies in the union of power and genius—while both his judgment and his good taste held fast proudly and indifferently to the truth that he did not speak well.—Napoleon, as the complete and fully developed type of a single instinct, belongs to ancient humanity, whose characteristic—the simple construction and ingenious development and realisation of a single motive or a small number of motives—may be easily enough recognised.

246. ARISTOTLE AND MARRIAGE.—Insanity makes its appearance in the children of great geniuses, and stupidity in those of the most virtuous—so says Aristotle. Did he mean by this to invite exceptional men to marry?

247. THE ORIGIN OF A BAD TEMPERAMENT.—Injustice and instability in the minds of certain men, their disordered and immoderate manner, are the ultimate consequences of the innumerable logical inexactitudes, superficialities, and hasty conclusions of which their ancestors have been guilty. Men of a good temperament, on the other hand, are descended from solid and meditative races which have set a high value upon reason—whether for praiseworthy or evil purposes is of no great importance.

248. DISSIMULATION AS A DUTY.—Kindness has been best developed by the long dissimulation which endeavoured to appear as kindness: wherever great power existed the necessity for dissimulation of this nature was recognised—it inspires security and confidence, and multiplies the actual sum of our physical power. Falsehood, if not actually the mother, is at all events the nurse of kindness. In the same way, honesty has been brought to maturity by the need for a semblance of honesty and integrity: in hereditary aristocracies. The persistent exercise of such a dissimulation ends by bringing about the actual nature of the thing itself: the dissimulation in the long run suppresses itself, and organs and instincts are the unexpected fruits in this garden of hypocrisy.

249. WHO, THEN, IS EVER ALONE.—The faint-hearted wretch does not know what it means to be lonely. An enemy is always prowling in his tracks. Oh, for the man who could give us the history of that subtle feeling called loneliness!

250. NIGHT AND MUSIC.—It was only at night time, and in the semi-obscurity of dark forests and caverns, that the ear, the organ of fear, was able to develop itself so well, in accordance with the mode of living of the timid—that is, the longest human epoch which has ever yet existed: when it is clear daylight the ear is less necessary. Hence the character of music, which is an art of night and twilight.

251. STOICAL.—The Stoic experiences a certain sense of cheerfulness when he feels oppressed by the ceremonial which he has prescribed for himself: he enjoys himself then as a ruler.

252. CONSIDER.—The man who is being punished is no longer he who has done the deed. He is always the scapegoat.

253. APPEARANCE.—Alas! what must be best and most resolutely proved is appearance itself; for only too many people lack eyes to observe it. But it is so tiresome!

254. THOSE WHO ANTICIPATE.—What distinguishes poetic natures, but is also a danger for them, is their imagination, which exhausts itself in advance: which anticipates what will happen or what may happen, which enjoys and suffers in advance, and which at the final moment of the event or the action is already fatigued. Lord Byron, who was only too familiar with this, wrote in his diary: "If ever I have a son he shall choose a very prosaic profession—that of a lawyer or a pirate."

255. CONVERSATION ON MUSIC.—

A. What do you say to that music?

B. It has overpowered me, I can say nothing about it. Listen! there it is beginning again.

A. All the better! This time let us do our best to overpower it. Will you allow me to add a few words to this music? and also to show you a drama which perhaps at your first hearing you did not wish to observe?

B. Very well, I have two ears and even more if necessary; move up closer to me.

A. We have not yet heard what he wishes to say to us, up to the present he has only promised to say something—something as yet unheard, so he gives us to understand by his gestures, for they are gestures. How he beckons! How he raises himself up! How he gesticulates! and now the moment of supreme tension seems to have come to him: two more fanfares, and he will present us with his superb and splendidly-adorned theme, rattling, as it were, with precious stones.

Is it a handsome woman? or a beautiful horse? Enough, he looks about him as if enraptured, for he must assemble looks of rapture. It is only now that his theme quite pleases him: it is only now that he becomes inventive and risks new and audacious features. How he forces out his theme! Ah, take care!—he not only understands how to adorn, but also how to gloss it over! Yes, he knows what the colour of health is, and he knows how to make it up,—he is more subtle in his self-consciousness than I thought. And now he is convinced that he has convinced his hearers; he sets off his impromptus as if they were the most important things under the sun: he points to his theme with an insolent finger as if it were too good for this world.—Ah, how distrustful he is! He is afraid we may get tired!—that is why he buries his melody in sweet notes.—Now he even appeals to our coarser senses that he may excite us and thus get us once again into his power. Listen to him as he conjures up the elementary force of tempestuous and thundering rhythms!

And now that he sees that these things have captivated our attention, strangle us, and almost overwhelm us, he once again ventures to introduce his theme amidst this play of the elements in order to convince us, confused and agitated as we are, that our confusion and agitation are the effects of his miraculous theme. And from now onwards his hearers believe in him: as soon as the theme is heard once more they are reminded of its thrilling elementary effects. The theme profits by this recollection—now it has become demoniacal! What a connoisseur of the soul he is! He gains command over us by all the artifices of the popular orator. But the music has stopped again.

B. And I am glad of it; for I could no longer bear listening to your observations! I should prefer ten times over to let myself be deceived to knowing the truth once after your version.

A. That is just what I wished to hear from you. The best people now are just like you: you are quite content to let yourselves be deceived. You come here with coarse, lustful ears, and you do not bring with you your conscience of the art of listening. On the way here you have cast away your intellectual honesty, and thus you corrupt both art and artists. Whenever you applaud and cheer you have in your hands the conscience of the artists—and woe to art if they get to know that you cannot distinguish between innocent and guilty music! I do not indeed refer to "good" and "bad" music—we meet with both in the two kinds of music mentioned! but I call innocent music that which thinks only of itself and believes only in itself, and which on account of itself has forgotten the world at large—this spontaneous expression of the most profound solitude which speaks of itself and with itself, and has entirely forgotten that there are listeners, effects, misunderstandings and failures in the world outside. In short, the music which we have just heard is precisely of this rare and noble type; and everything I said about it was a fable—pardon my little trick if you will!

B. Oh, then you like this music, too? In that case many sins shall be forgiven you!

256. THE HAPPINESS OF THE EVIL ONES.—These silent, gloomy, and evil men possess a peculiar something which you cannot dispute with them—an uncommon and strange enjoyment in the dolce far niente; a sunset and evening rest, such as none can enjoy but a heart which has been too often devoured, lacerated, and poisoned by the passions.

257. WORDS PRESENT IN OUR MINDS.—We always express our thoughts with those words which lie nearest to hand. Or rather, if I may reveal my full suspicion; at every moment we have only the particular thought for the words that are present in our minds.

258. FLATTERING THE DOG.—You have only to stroke this dog's coat once, and he immediately splutters and gives off sparks like any other flatterer—and he is witty in his own way. Why should we not endure him thus?

259. THE QUONDAM PANEGYRIST.—"He has now become silent now in regard to me, although he knows the truth and could tell it; but it would sound like vengeance—and he values truth so highly, this honourable man!"

260. THE AMULET OF DEPENDENT MEN.—He who is unavoidably dependent upon some master ought to possess something by which he can inspire his master with fear, and keep him in check: integrity, for example, or probity, or an evil tongue.

261. WHY SO SUBLIME!—Oh, I know them well this breed of animals! Certainly it pleases them better to walk on two legs "like a god"—but it pleases me better when they fall back on their four feet. This is incomparably more natural for them!

262. THE DEMON OF POWER.—Neither necessity nor desire, but the love of power, is the demon of mankind. You may give men everything possible—health, food, shelter, enjoyment—but they

are and remain unhappy and capricious, for the demon waits and waits; and must be satisfied. Let everything else be taken away from men, and let this demon be satisfied, and then they will nearly be happy—as happy as men and demons can be; but why do I repeat this? Luther has already said it, and better than I have done, in the verses:

"And though they take our life,
Goods, honour, children, wife,
Yet is their profit small,
These things shall vanish all,
The Kingdom it remaineth."
The Kingdom! there it is again![7]

263. CONTRADICTION INCARNATE AND ANIMATED.—There is a physiological contradiction in what is called genius: genius possesses on the one hand a great deal of savage disorder and involuntary movement, and on the other hand a great deal of superior activity in this movement. Joined to this a genius possesses a mirror which reflects the two movements beside one another, and within one another, but often opposed to one another. Genius in consequence of this sight is often unhappy, and if it feels its greatest happiness in creating, it is because it forgets that precisely then, with the highest determinate activity, it does something fantastic and irrational (such is all art) and cannot help doing it.

264. DECEIVING ONE'S SELF.—Envious men with a discriminating intuition endeavour not to become too closely acquainted with their rivals in order that they may feel themselves superior to them.

265. THERE IS A TIME FOR THE THEATRE.—When the imagination of a people begins to diminish, there arises the desire to have its legends represented on the stage: it then tolerates the coarse substitutes for imagination. In the age of the epic rhapsodist, however, the theatre itself, and the actor dressed up as a hero, form an obstacle in the path of the imagination instead of acting as wings for it—too near, too definite, too heavy, and with too little of dreamland and the flights of birds about them.

266. WITHOUT CHARM.—He lacks charm and knows it. Ah, how skilful he is in masking this defect! He does it by a strict virtue, gloomy looks, and acquired distrust of all men, and of existence itself; by coarse jests, by contempt for a more refined manner of living, by pathos and pretensions, and by a cynical philosophy—yea, he has even developed into a character through the continual knowledge of his deficiency.

267. WHY SO PROUD?—A noble character is distinguished from a vulgar one by the fact that the latter has not at ready command a certain number of habits and points of view like the former: fate willed that they should not be his either by inheritance or by education.

268. THE ORATOR'S SCYLLA AND CHARYBDIS.—How difficult it was in Athens to speak in such a way as to win over the hearers to one's cause without repelling them at the same time by the form in which one's speech was cast, or withdrawing their attention from the cause itself by this form! How difficult it still is to write thus in France!

269. SICK PEOPLE AND ART.—For all kinds of sadness and misery of soul we should first of all try a change of diet and severe manual labour; but in such cases men are in the habit of having recourse to mental intoxicants, to art for example—which is both to their own detriment and that of art! Can you not see that when you call for art as sick people you make the artists themselves sick?

270. APPARENT TOLERATION.—Those are good, benevolent, and rational words on and in favour of science, but, alas! I see behind these words your toleration of science. In a corner of your inmost mind you think, in spite of all you say, that it is not necessary for you, that it shows magnanimity on your part to admit and even to advocate it, more especially as science on its part does not exhibit this magnanimity in regard to your opinion! Do you know that you have no right whatever to exercise this toleration? that this condescension of yours is an even coarser disparagement of science than any of that open scorn which a presumptuous priest or artist might allow himself to indulge in towards science? What is lacking in you is a strong sense for everything that is true and actual, you do not feel grieved and worried to find that science is in contradiction to your own sentiments, you are unacquainted with that intense desire for knowledge ruling over you like a law, you do not feel a duty in the need of being present with your own eyes wherever knowledge exists, and to let nothing that is "known" escape you. You do not know that which you are treating with such toleration! and it is only because you do not know it that you can succeed in adopting such a gracious attitude towards it. You, forsooth, would look upon science with hatred and fanaticism if it for once cast its shining and illuminating glance upon you! What does it matter to us, then, if you do exhibit toleration—and towards a phantom! and not even towards us!—and what do we matter!

271. FESTIVE MOODS.—It is exactly those men who aspire most ardently towards power who feel it indescribably agreeable to be overpowered! to sink suddenly and deeply into a feeling as into a whirlpool! To suffer the reins to be snatched out of their hand, and to watch a movement which takes

them they know not where! Whatever or whoever may be the person or thing that renders us this service, it is nevertheless a great service: we are so happy and breathless, and feel around us an exceptional silence, as if we were in the most central bowels of the earth. To be for once entirely powerless! the plaything of the elementary forces of nature! There is a restfulness in this happiness, a casting away of the great burden, a descent without fatigue, as if one had been given up to the blind force of gravity.

This is the dream of the mountain climber, who, although he sees his goal far above him, nevertheless falls asleep on the way from utter exhaustion, and dreams of the happiness of the contrast—this effortless rolling down hill. I describe happiness as I imagine it to be in our present-day society, the badgered, ambitious society of Europe and America. Now and then they wish to fall back into impotence—this enjoyment is offered them by wars, arts, religions, and geniuses. When a man has temporarily abandoned himself to a momentary impression which devours and crushes everything—and this is the modern festive mood—he afterwards becomes freer, colder, more refreshed, and more strict, and again strives tirelessly after the contrary of all this: power.

272. THE PURIFICATION OF RACES.—It is probable that there are no pure races, but only races which have become purified, and even these are extremely rare.[8] We more often meet with crossed races, among whom, together with the defects in the harmony of the bodily forms (for example when the eyes do not accord with the mouth) we necessarily always find defects of harmony in habits and appreciations. (Livingstone heard some one say, "God created white and black men, but the devil created the half-castes.")

Crossed races are always at the same time crossed cultures and crossed moralities: they are, as a rule, more evil, cruel, and restless. Purity is the final result of innumerable adjustments, absorptions, and eliminations; and progress towards purity in a race is shown by the fact that the latent strength in the race is more and more restricted to a few special functions, whilst it formerly had to carry out too many and often contradictory things. Such a restriction will always have the appearance of an impoverishment, and must be judged with prudence and moderation. In the long run, however, when the process of purification has come to a successful termination, all those forces which were formerly wasted in the struggle between the disharmonious qualities are at the disposal of the organism as a whole, and this is why purified races have always become stronger and more beautiful.—The Greeks may serve us as a model of a purified race and culture!—and it is to be hoped that some day a pure European race and culture may arise.

273. PRAISE.—Here is some one who, you perceive, wishes to praise you: you bite your lips and brace up your heart: Oh, that that cup might go hence! But it does not, it comes! let us therefore drink the sweet impudence of the panegyrist, let us overcome the disgust and profound contempt that we feel for the innermost substance of his praise, let us assume a look of thankful joy—for he wished to make himself agreeable to us! And now that it is all over we know that he feels greatly exalted; he has been victorious over us. Yes, and also over himself, the villain!—for it was no easy matter for him to wring this praise from himself.

274. THE RIGHTS AND PRIVILEGES OF MAN.—We human beings are the only creatures who, when things do not go well with us, can blot ourselves out like a clumsy sentence,—whether we do so out of honour for humanity or pity for it, or on account of the aversion we feel towards ourselves.

275. THE TRANSFORMED BEING.—Now he becomes virtuous; but only for the sake of hurting others by being so. Don't pay so much attention to him.

276. HOW OFTEN! HOW UNEXPECTED!—How may married men have some morning awakened to the fact that their young wife is dull, although she thinks quite the contrary! not to speak of those wives whose flesh is willing but whose intellect is weak!

277. WARM AND COLD VIRTUES.—Courage is sometimes the consequence of cold and unshaken resolution, and at other times of a fiery and reckless élan. For these two kinds of courage there is only the one name!—but how different, nevertheless, are cold virtues and warm virtues! and the man would be a fool who could suppose that "goodness" could only be brought about by warmth, and no less a fool he who would only attribute it to cold. The truth is that mankind has found both warm and cold courage very useful, yet not often enough to prevent it from setting them both in the category of precious stones.

278. THE GRACIOUS MEMORY.—A man of high rank will do well to develop a gracious memory, that is, to note all the good qualities of people and remember them particularly; for in this way he holds them in an agreeable dependence. A man may also act in this way towards himself: whether or not he has a gracious memory determines in the end the superiority, gentleness, or distrust with which he observes his own inclinations and intentions, and finally even the nature of these inclinations and intentions.

279. WHEREIN WE BECOME ARTISTS.—He who makes an idol of some one endeavours to justify himself in his own eyes by idealising this person: in other words, he becomes an artist that he may have a clear conscience. When he suffers he does not suffer from his ignorance, but from the lie he

has told himself to make himself ignorant. The inmost misery and desire of such a man—and all passionate lovers are included in this category—cannot be exhausted by normal means.

280. CHILDLIKE.—Those who live like children—those who have not to struggle for their daily bread, and do not think that their actions have any ultimate signification—remain childlike.

281. OUR EGO DESIRES EVERYTHING.—It would seem as if men in general were only inspired by the desire to possess: languages at least would permit of this supposition, for they view past actions from the standpoint that we have been put in possession of something—"I have spoken, struggled, conquered"—as if to say, I am now in possession of my word, my struggle, my victory. How greedy man appears in this light! he cannot even let the past escape him: he even wishes to have it still!

282. DANGER IN BEAUTY.—This woman is beautiful and intelligent: alas, how much more intelligent she would have become if she had not been beautiful!

283. DOMESTIC AND MENTAL PEACE.—Our habitual mood depends upon the mood in which we maintain our habitual entourage.

284. NEW THINGS AS OLD ONES.—Many people seem irritated when something new is told them: they feel the ascendancy which the news has given to the person who has learnt it first.

285. WHAT ARE THE LIMITS OF THE EGO.—The majority of people take under their protection, as it were, something that they know, as if the fact of knowing it was sufficient in itself to make it their property. The acquisitiveness of the egoistic feeling has no limits: Great men speak as if they had behind them the whole of time, and had placed themselves at the head of this enormous host; and good women boast of the beauty of their children, their clothes, their dog, their physician, or their native town, but the only thing they dare not say is, "I am all that." Chi non ha non è—as they say in Italy.

286. DOMESTIC ANIMALS, PETS AND THE LIKE.—Could there be anything more repugnant than the sentimentality which is shown to plants and animals—and this on the part of a creature who from the very beginning has made such ravages among them as their most ferocious enemy,—and who ends by even claiming affectionate feelings from his weakened and mutilated victims! Before this kind of "nature" man must above all be serious, if he is any sort of a thinking being.

287. TWO FRIENDS.—They were friends once, but now they have ceased to be so, and both of them broke off the friendship at the same time, the one because he believed himself to be too greatly misunderstood, and the other because he thought he was known too intimately—and both were wrong! For neither of them knew himself well enough.

288. THE COMEDY OF THE NOBLE SOULS.—Those who cannot succeed in exhibiting a noble and cordial familiarity endeavour to let the nobleness of their nature be seen by their exercise of reserve and strictness, and a certain contempt for familiarity, as if their strong sense of confidence were ashamed to show itself.

289. WHERE WE MAY SAY NOTHING AGAINST VIRTUE.—Among cowards it is thought bad form to say anything against bravery, for any expression of this kind would give rise to some contempt; and unfeeling people are irritated when anything is said against pity.[9]

290. A WASTE.—We find that with irritable and abrupt people their first words and actions generally afford no indication of their actual character—they are prompted by circumstances, and are to some extent simply reproductions of the spirit of these circumstances. Because, however, as the words have been uttered and the deeds done, the subsequent words and deeds, indicating the real nature of such people, have often to be used to reconcile, amend, or extinguish the former.

291. ARROGANCE.—Arrogance is an artificial and simulated pride; but it is precisely the essential nature of pride tò be incapable of artifice, simulation, or hypocrisy—and thus arrogance is the hypocrisy of the incapacity for hypocrisy, a very difficult thing, and one which is a failure in most cases. But if we suppose that, as most frequently happens, the presumptuous person betrays himself, then a treble annoyance falls to his lot: people are angry with him because he has endeavoured to deceive them, and because he wished to show himself superior to them, and finally they laugh at him because he failed in both these endeavours. How earnestly, therefore, should we dissuade our fellow-men from arrogance!

292. A SPECIES OF MISCONCEPTION.—When we hear somebody speak it is often sufficient for his pronunciation of a single consonant (the letter r, for example) to fill us with doubts as to the honesty of his feelings: we are not accustomed to this particular pronunciation, and should have to make it ourselves as it were arbitrarily—it sounds "forced" to us. This is the domain of the greatest possible misconception: and it is the same with the style of a writer who has certain habits which are not the habits of everybody. His "artlessness" is felt as such only by himself, and precisely in regard to that which he himself feels to be "forced" (because he has yielded in this matter to the prevailing fashion and to so called "good taste"), he may perhaps give pleasure and inspire confidence.

293. THANKFUL.—One superfluous grain of gratitude and piety makes one suffer as from a vice—in spite of all one's independence and honesty one begins to have a bad conscience.

294. SAINTS.—It is the most sensual men who find it necessary to avoid women and to torture

their bodies.

295. THE SUBTLETY OF SERVING.—One of the most subtle tasks in the great art of serving is that of serving a more than usually ambitious man, who, indeed, is excessively egoistic in all things, but is entirely adverse to being thought so (this is part of his ambition). He requires that everything shall be according to his own will and humour, yet in such a way as to give him the appearance of always having sacrificed himself, and of rarely desiring anything for himself alone.

296. DUELLING.—I think it a great advantage, said some one, to be able to fight a duel—if, of course, it is absolutely necessary; for I have at all times brave companions about me. The duel is the last means of thoroughly honourable suicide left to us; but it is unfortunately a circuitous means, and not even a certain one.

297. PERNICIOUS.—A young man can be most surely corrupted when he is taught to value the like-minded more highly than the differently minded.

298. HERO-WORSHIP AND ITS FANATICS.—The fanatic of an ideal that possesses flesh and blood is right as a rule so long as he assumes a negative attitude, and he is terrible in his negation: he knows what he denies as well as he knows himself, for the simple reason that he comes thence, that he feels at home there, and that he has always the secret fear of being forced to return there some day. He therefore wishes to make his return impossible by the manner of his negation. As soon as he begins to affirm, however, he partly shuts his eyes and begins to idealise (frequently merely for the sake of annoying those who have stayed at home). We might say that there was something artistic about this—agreed, but there is also something dishonest about it.

The idealist of a person imagines this person to be so far from him that he can no longer see him distinctly, and then he travesties that which he can just perceive into something "beautiful"—that is to say, symmetrical, vaguely outlined, uncertain. Since he wishes to worship from afar that ideal which floats on high in the distance, he finds it essential to build a temple for the object of his worship as a protection from the profanum vulgus. He brings into this temple for the object of his worship all the venerable and sanctified objects which he still possesses, so that his ideal may benefit by their charm, and that, nourished in this way, it may grow more and more divine. In the end he really succeeds in forming his God, but, alas for him! there is some one who knows how all this has been done, viz. his intellectual conscience; and there is also some one who, quite unconsciously, begins to protest against these things, viz. the deified one himself, who, in consequence of all this worship, praise, and incense, now becomes completely unbearable and shows himself in the most obvious and dreadful manner to be non-divine, and only too human.

In a case like this there is only one means of escape left for such a fanatic; he patiently suffers himself and his fellows to be maltreated, and interprets all this misery in maiorem dei gloriam by a new kind of self-deceit and noble falsehood. He takes up a stand against himself, and in doing so experiences, as an interpreter and ill-treated person, something like martyrdom—and in this way he climbs to the height of his conceit. Men of this kind to be found, for example, in the entourage of Napoleon: indeed, perhaps it may have been he who inspired the soul of his century with that romantic prostration in the presence of the "genius" and the "hero," which was so foreign to the spirit of rationalism of the nineteenth century—a man about whom even Byron was not ashamed to say that he was a "worm compared with such a being." (The formulæ of this prostration have been discovered by Thomas Carlyle, that arrogant old muddle-head and grumbler, who spent his long life in trying to romanticise the common sense of his Englishmen: but in vain!)

299. THE APPEARANCE OF HEROISM.—Throwing ourselves in the midst of our enemies may be a sign of cowardice.

300. CONDESCENDING TOWARDS THE FLATTERER.—It is the ultimate prudence of insatiably ambitious men not only to conceal their contempt for man which the sight of flatterers causes them: but also to appear even condescending to them, like a God who can be nothing if not condescending.

301. "STRENGTH OF CHARACTER."—"What I have said once I will do"—This manner of thinking is believed to indicate great strength of character. How many actions are accomplished, not because they have been selected as being the most rational, but because at the moment when we thought of them they influenced our ambition and vanity by some means or another, so that we do not stop until we have blindly carried them out. Thus they strengthen in us our belief in our character and our good conscience, in short our strength; whilst the choice of the most rational acts possible brings about a certain amount of scepticism towards ourselves, and thus encourages a sense of weakness in us.

302. ONCE, TWICE, AND THRICE TRUE.—Men lie unspeakably and often, but they do not think about it afterwards, and generally do not believe in it.

303. THE PASTIME OF THE PSYCHOLOGIST.—He thinks he knows me, and fancies himself to be subtle and important when he has any kind of relations with me; and I take care not to undeceive him. For in such a case I should suffer for it, while now he wishes me well because I arouse in him a feeling of conscious superiority.—There is another, who fears that I think I know him, and feels a sense

of inferiority at this. As a result he behaves in a timid and vacillating manner, in my presence, and endeavours to mislead me in regard to himself so that he may regain an ascendancy over me.

304. THE DESTROYERS OF THE WORLD.—When some men fail to accomplish what they desire to do they exclaim angrily, "May the whole world perish!" This odious feeling is the height of envy which reasons thus: because I cannot have one thing the whole world in general must have nothing! the whole world shall not exist!

305. GREED.—When we set out to buy something our greed increases with the cheapness of the object—Why? Is it because the small differences in price make up the little eye of greed?

306. THE GREEK IDEAL.—What did the Greeks admire in Ulysses? Above all his capacity for lying and for taking a shrewd and dreadful revenge, his being equal to circumstances, his appearing to be nobler than the noblest when necessary, his ability to be everything he desired, his heroic pertinacity, having all means within his command, possessing genius—the genius of Ulysses is an object of the admiration of the gods, they smile when they think of it—all this is the Greek ideal! What is most remarkable about it is that the contradiction between seeming and being was not felt in any way, and that as a consequence it could not be morally estimated. Were there ever such accomplished actors?

307. FACTA! YES, FACTA FICTA!—The historian need not concern himself with events which have actually happened, but only those which are supposed to have happened; for none but the latter have produced an effect. The same remark applies to the imaginary heroes. His theme—this so-called world-history—what is it but opinions on imaginary actions and their imaginary motives, which in their turn give rise to opinions and actions the reality of which, however, is at once evaporated, and is only effective as vapour,—a continual generating and impregnating of phantoms above the dense mists of unfathomable reality. All historians record things which have never existed, except in imagination.

308. NOT TO UNDERSTAND TRADE IS NOBLE.—To sell one's virtue only at the highest price, or even to carry on usury with it as a teacher, a civil servant, or an artist, for instance, brings genius and talent down to the level of the common tradesman. We must be careful not to be clever with our wisdom!

309. FEAR AND LOVE.—The general knowledge of mankind has been furthered to a greater extent by fear than by love; for fear endeavours to find out who the other is, what he can do, and what he wants: it would be dangerous and prejudicial to be deceived on this point. On the other hand, love is induced by its secret craving to discover as many beautiful qualities as possible in the loved object, or to raise this loved object as high as possible: it is a joy and an advantage to love to be deceived in this way—and this is why it does it.

310. GOOD-NATURED PEOPLE.—Good-natured people have acquired their character from the continual fear of foreign attacks in which their ancestors lived,—these ancestors, who were in the habit of mitigating and tranquillising, humbling themselves, preventing, distracting, flattering, and apologising, concealing their grief and anger, and preserving an unruffled countenance,—and they ultimately bequeathed all this delicate and well-formed mechanism to their children and grandchildren. These latter, thanks to their more favourable lot, did not experience this feeling of dread, but they nevertheless continue in the same groove.

311. THE SO-CALLED SOUL.—The sum-total of those internal movements which come naturally to men, and which they can consequently set in motion readily and gracefully, is called the soul—men are looked upon as void of soul when they let it be seen that their inward emotions are difficult and painful to them.

312. THE FORGETFUL ONES.—In outbursts of passion and the delusions of dreams and madness, man rediscovers his own primitive history, and that of humanity: animality and its savage grimaces. For once his memory stretches back into the past, while his civilised condition is developed from the forgetfulness of these primitive experiences, that is to say, from the failing of this memory. He who, as a forgetful man of a higher nature, has always remained aloof from these things, does not understand men—but it is an advantage if from time to time there are individuals who do not understand men, individuals who are, so to speak, created from the divine seed and born of reason.

313. THE FRIEND WHOM WE WANT NO LONGER.—That friend whose hopes we cannot satisfy we should prefer to have as an enemy.

314. IN THE SOCIETY OF THINKERS.—In the midst of the ocean of becoming we adventurers and birds of passage wake up on an island no larger than a small boat, and here we look round us for a moment with as much haste and curiosity as possible; for how quickly may some gale blow us away or some wave sweep over the little island and leave nothing of us remaining! Here, however, upon this little piece of ground we meet with other birds of passage and hear of still earlier ones,—and thus we live together for one precious minute of recognition and divining, amid the cheerful fluttering of wings and joyful chirping, and then adventure in spirit far out on the ocean, feeling no less proud than the ocean itself.

315. PARTING WITH SOMETHING.—To give up some of our property, or to waive a right, gives pleasure when it denotes great wealth. Generosity may be placed in this category.

316. WEAK SECTS.—Those sects which feel that they will always remain weak hunt up a few intelligent individual adherents, wishing to make up in quality what they lack in quantity. This gives rise to no little danger for intelligent minds.

317. THE JUDGMENT OF THE EVENING.—The man who meditates upon his day's and life's work when he has reached the end of his journey and feels weary, generally arrives at a melancholy conclusion; but this is not the fault of the day or his life, but of weariness.—In the midst of creative work we do not take time, as a rule, to meditate upon life and existence, nor yet in the midst of our pleasures: but if by a chance this did happen once we should no longer believe him to be right who waited for the seventh day and for repose to find everything that exists very beautiful.—He had missed the right moment.

318. BEWARE OF SYSTEMISERS!—There is a certain amount of comedy about systemisers: in trying to complete a system and to round off its horizon they have to try to let their weaker qualities appear in the same style as their stronger ones.—They wish to represent complete and uniformly strong natures.

319. HOSPITALITY.—The object of hospitality is to paralyse all hostile feeling in a stranger. When we cease to look upon strangers as enemies, hospitality diminishes; it flourishes so long as its evil presupposition does.

320. THE WEATHER.—An exceptional and uncertain state of the weather makes men suspicious even of one another: at the same time they come to like innovations, for they must diverge from their accustomed habits. This is why despots like those countries where the weather is moral.

321. DANGER IN INNOCENCE.—Innocent people become easy victims in all circumstances because their lack of knowledge prevents them from distinguishing between moderation and excess, and from being betimes on their guard against themselves. It is as a result of this that innocent, that is, ignorant young women become accustomed to the frequent enjoyment of sexual intercourse, and feel the want of it very much in later years when their husbands fall ill or grow prematurely old. It is on account of this harmless and orthodox conception, as if frequent sexual intercourse were right and proper, that they come to experience a need which afterwards exposes them to the severest tribulations, and even worse.

Considering the matter, however, from a higher and more general point of view, whoever loves a man or a thing without knowing him or it, falls a prey to something which he would not love if he could see it. In all cases where experience, precautions, and prudent steps are required, it is the innocent man who will be most thoroughly corrupted, for he has to drink with closed eyes the dregs and most secret poison of everything put before him. Let us consider the procedure of all princes, churches, sects, parties, and corporations: Is not the innocent man always used as the sweetest bait for the most dangerous and wicked traps?—just as Ulysses availed himself of the services of the innocent Neoptolemos to cheat the old and infirm anchorite and ogre of Lemnos out of his bow and arrows. Christianity, with its contempt for the world, has made ignorance a virtue—innocence, perhaps because the most frequent result of this innocence is precisely, as I have indicated above, guilt, the sense of guilt, and despair: In other words, a virtue which leads to Heaven by the circuitous route of Hell; for only then can the gloomy propylæa of Christian salvation be thrown open, and only then is the promise of a posthumous second innocence effective. This is one of the finest inventions of Christianity!

322. LIVING WITHOUT A DOCTOR WHEN POSSIBLE.—It seems to me that a sick man lives more carelessly when he is under medical observation than when he attends to his own health. In the first case it suffices for him to obey strictly all his Doctor's prescriptions; but in the second case he gives more attention to the ultimate object of these prescriptions, namely, his health; he observes much more, and submits himself to a more severe discipline than the directions of his physician would compel him to do.

All rules have this effect: they distract our attention from the fundamental aim of the rule, and make us more thoughtless. But to what heights of immoderation and destruction would men have risen if ever they had completely and honestly left everything to the Godhead as to their physician, and acted in accordance with the words "as God will"!

323. THE DARKENING OF THE HEAVENS.—Do you know the vengeance of those timid people who behave in society just as if they had stolen their limbs? The vengeance of the humble, Christian-like souls who just manage to slink quietly through the world? The vengeance of those who always judge hastily, and are as hastily said to be in the wrong? The vengeance of all classes of drunkards, for whom the morning is always the most miserable part of the day? and also of all kinds of invalids and sick and depressed people who have no longer the courage to become healthy?

The number of these petty vengeful people, and, even more, the number of their petty acts of revenge, is incalculable. The air around us is continually whizzing with the discharged arrows of their malignity, so that the sun and the sky of their lives become darkened thereby,—and, alas! not only theirs, but more often ours and other men's: and this is worse than the frequent wounds which they make on our skins and hearts. Do we not occasionally deny the existence of the sun and sky merely because we have not seen them for so long?—Well then, solitude! because of this, solitude!

324. THE PSYCHOLOGY OF THE ACTOR.—It is the blissful illusion of all great actors to imagine that the historical personages whom they are representing were really in the same state of mind as they themselves are when interpreting them—but in this they are very much mistaken. Their powers of imitation and divination, which they would fain exhibit as a clairvoyant faculty, penetrate only far enough to explain gestures, accent, and looks, and in general anything exterior: that is, they can grasp the shadow of the soul of a great hero, statesman, or warrior, or of an ambitious, jealous, or desperate person—they penetrate fairly near to the soul, but they never reach the inmost spirit of the man they are imitating.

It would, indeed, be a fine thing to discover that instead of thinkers, psychologists, or experts we required nothing but clairvoyant actors to throw light upon the essence of any condition. Let us never forget, whenever such pretensions are heard, that the actor is nothing but an ideal ape—so much of an ape is he, indeed, that he is not capable of believing in the "essence" or in the "essential": everything becomes for him merely performance, intonation, attitude, stage, scenery, and public.

325. LIVING AND BELIEVING APART.—The means of becoming the prophet and wonder-worker of one's age are the same to-day as in former times: one must live apart, with little knowledge, some ideas, and a great deal of presumption—we then finish by believing that mankind cannot do without us, because it is clear that we can do without it. When we are inspired with this belief we find faith. Finally, a piece of advice to him who needs it (it was given to Wesley by Boehler, his spiritual teacher): "Preach faith until you have it; then you will preach it because you have it!"

326. KNOWING OUR CIRCUMSTANCES.—We may estimate our powers, but not our power. Not only do circumstances conceal it from us and show it to us time about, but they even exaggerate or diminish it. We must consider ourselves as variable quantities whose productive capacity may in favourable circumstances reach the greatest possible heights: we must therefore reflect upon these circumstances, and spare no pains in studying them.

327. A FABLE.—The Don Juan of knowledge—no philosopher or poet has yet succeeded in discovering him. He is wanting in love for the things he recognises, but he possesses wit, a lust for the hunting after knowledge, and the intrigues in connection with it, and he finds enjoyment in all these, even up to the highest and most distant stars of knowledge—until at last there is nothing left for him to pursue but the absolutely injurious side of knowledge, just as the drunkard who ends by drinking absinthe and aquafortis. That is why last of all he feels a longing for hell, for this is the final knowledge which seduces him. Perhaps even this would disappoint him, as all things do which one knows! and then he would have to stand still for all eternity, a victim to eternal deception, and transformed into his enemy, the Stony Guest, who longs for an evening meal of knowledge which will never more fall to his share! for the whole world of things will not have another mouthful left to offer to these hungry men.

328. WHAT IDEALISTIC THEORIES DISCLOSE.—We are most certain to find idealistic theories among unscrupulously practical men; for such men stand in need of the lustre of these theories for the sake of their reputation. They adopt them instinctively without by any means feeling hypocritical in doing so—no more hypocritical than Englishmen with their Christianity and their Sabbath-keeping. On the other hand, contemplative natures who have to keep themselves on the guard against all kinds of fantasies and who dread to be reputed as enthusiasts, are only to be satisfied with hard realistic theories: they take possession of them under the same instinctive compulsion without thereby losing their honesty.

329. THE CALUMNIATORS OF CHEERFULNESS.—People who have been deeply wounded by the disappointments of life look with suspicion upon all cheerfulness as if it were something childish and puerile, and revealed a lack of common sense that moves them to pity and tenderness, such as one would experience when seeing a dying child caressing his toys on his death-bed. Such men appear to see hidden graves under every rose; rejoicings, tumult, and cheerful music appear to them to be the voluntary illusions of a man who is dangerously ill and yet wishes to take a momentary draught from the intoxicating cup of life. But this judgment about cheerfulness is merely the reflection of the latter on the dark background of weariness and ill-health: in itself it is something touching, irrational, and pitiable, even childlike and puerile, but connected with that second childhood which follows in the train of old age, and is the harbinger of death.

330. NOT YET ENOUGH!—It is not sufficient to prove a case, we must also tempt or raise men to it: hence the wise man must learn to convey his wisdom; and often in such a manner that it may sound like foolishness!

331. RIGHT AND LIMITS.—Asceticism is the proper mode of thinking for those who must extirpate their carnal instincts, because these are ferocious beasts,—but only for such people!

332. THE BOMBASTIC STYLE.—An artist who does not wish to put his elevated feelings into a work and thus unburden himself, but who rather wishes to impart these feelings of elevation to others, becomes pompous, and his style becomes the bombastic style.

333. "HUMANITY."—We do not consider animals as moral beings. But do you think that

animals consider us as moral beings? An animal which had the power of speech once said: "Humanity is a prejudice from which we animals at least do not suffer."

334. THE CHARITABLE MAN.—The charitable man gratifies a need of his own inward feelings when doing good. The stronger this need is the less does such a man try to put himself in the place of those who serve the purpose of gratifying his desire: he becomes indelicate and sometimes even offensive. (This remark applies to the benevolence and charity of the Jews, which, as is well known, is somewhat more effusive than that of other peoples.)[10]

335. THAT LOVE MAY BE FELT AS LOVE.—We must be honest towards ourselves, and must know ourselves very well indeed, to be able to practise upon others that humane dissimulation known as love and kindness.

336. WHAT ARE WE CAPABLE OF?—A man who had been tormented all day by his wicked and malicious son slew him in the evening, and then with a sigh of relief said to the other members of his family: "Well now we can sleep in peace." Who knows what circumstances might drive us to!

337. "NATURAL."—To be natural, at least in his deficiencies, is perhaps the last praise that can be bestowed upon an artificial artist, who is in other respects theatrical and half genuine. Such a man will for this very reason boldly parade his deficiencies.

338. CONSCIENCE-SUBSTITUTE.—One man is another's conscience: and this is especially important when the other has none else.

339. THE TRANSFORMATION OF DUTIES.—When our duties cease to be difficult of accomplishment, and after long practice become changed into agreeable delights and needs, then the rights of others to whom our duties (though now our inclinations) refer change into something else: that is, they become the occasion of pleasant feelings for us. Henceforth the "other," by virtue of his rights, becomes an object of love to us instead of an object of reverence and awe as formerly. It is our own pleasure we seek when we recognise and maintain the extent of his power. When the Quietists no longer felt their Christian faith as a burden, and experienced their delight only in God, they took the motto: "Do all to the glory of God." Whatever they performed henceforth in this sense was no longer a sacrifice, it was as much as to say, "Everything for the sake of our pleasure." To demand that duty should be always rather burdensome, as Kant does, is to demand that it shall never develop into a habit or custom. There is a small residue of ascetic cruelty in this demand.

340. APPEARANCES ARE AGAINST THE HISTORIAN.—It is a sufficiently demonstrated fact that human beings come from the womb; nevertheless when children grow up and stand by the side of their mother this hypothesis appears very absurd—all appearances are against it.

341. THE ADVANTAGE OF IGNORANCE.—Some one has said that in his childhood he experienced such a contempt for the caprices and whims of a melancholy temperament that, until he had grown up and had become a middle-aged man, he did not know what his own temperament was like: it was precisely a melancholy temperament. He declared that this was the best of all possible kinds of ignorance.

342. DO NOT BE DECEIVED!—Yes, he examined the matter from every side and you think him to be a man of profound knowledge. But he only wishes to lower the price—he wants to buy it!

343. A MORAL PRETENCE.—You refuse to be dissatisfied with yourselves or to suffer from yourselves, and this you call your moral tendency! Very well; another may perhaps call it your cowardice! One thing, however, is certain, and that is that you will never take a trip round the world (and you yourselves are this world), and you will always remain in yourselves an accident and a clod on the face of the earth! Do you fancy that we who hold different views from you are merely exposing ourselves out of pure folly to the journey through our own deserts, swamps, and glaciers, and that we are voluntarily choosing grief and disgust with ourselves, like the Stylites?

344. SUBTLETY IN MISTAKES.—If Homer, as they say, sometimes nodded, he was wiser than all the artists of sleepless ambition. We must allow admirers to stop for a time and take breath by letting them find fault now and then; for nobody can bear an uninterruptedly brilliant and untiring excellence—and instead of doing good such a master would merely become a taskmaster, whom we hate while he precedes us.

345. OUR HAPPINESS IS NOT AN ARGUMENT EITHER PRO OR CON.—Many men are only capable of a small share of happiness: and it is not an argument against their wisdom if this wisdom is unable to afford them a greater degree of happiness, any more than it is an argument against medical skill that many people are incurable, and others always ailing. May every one have the good fortune to discover the conception of existence which will enable him to realise his greatest share of happiness! though this will not necessarily prevent his life from being miserable and not worth envying.

346. THE ENEMIES OF WOMEN.—"Woman is our enemy"—The man who speaks to men in this way exhibits an unbridled lust which not only hates itself but also its means.

347. THE SCHOOL OF THE ORATOR.—When a man has kept silence for a whole year he learns to stop chattering, and to discourse instead. The Pythagoreans were the best statesmen of their age.

348. THE FEELING OF POWER.—Note the distinction: the man who wishes to acquire the feeling of power seizes upon any means, and looks upon nothing as too petty which can foster this feeling. He who already possesses power, however, has grown fastidious and refined in his tastes; few things can be found to satisfy him.

349. NOT SO VERY IMPORTANT.—When we are present at a death-bed there regularly arises in us a thought that we immediately suppress from a false sense of propriety: the thought that the act of dying is less important than the customary veneration of it would wish us to believe, and that the dying man has probably lost in his life things which were more important than he is now about to lose by his death. In this case the end is certainly not the goal.

350. THE BEST WAY TO PROMISE.—When a man makes a promise it is not merely the word that promises, but what lies unexpressed behind the word. Words indeed weaken a promise by discharging and using up a power which forms part of that power which promises. Therefore shake hands when making a promise, but put your finger on your lips—in this way you will make the safest promises.

351. GENERALLY MISUNDERSTOOD.—In conversation we sometimes observe people endeavouring to set a trap in which to catch others—not out of evil-mindedness, as one might suppose, but from delight in their own shrewdness. Others again prepare a joke so that some one else may utter it, they tie the knot so that others may undo it: not out of goodwill, as might be supposed, but from wickedness, and their contempt for coarse intellects.

352. CENTRE.—The feeling, "I am the centre of the world," forcibly comes to us when we are unexpectedly overtaken by disgrace: we then feel as if we were standing dazed in the midst of a surge, and dazzled by the glance of one enormous eye which gazes down upon us from all sides and looks us through and through.

353. FREEDOM OF SPEECH.—"The truth must be told, even if the world should be shivered in fragments"—so cries the eminent and grandiloquent Fichte.—Yes, certainly; but we must have it first.—What he really means, however, is that each man should speak his mind, even if everything were to be turned upside down. This point, however, is open to dispute.

354. THE COURAGE FOR SUFFERING.—Such as we now are, we are capable of bearing a tolerable amount of displeasure, and our stomach is suited to such indigestible food. If we were deprived of it, indeed, we should perhaps think the banquet of life insipid; and if it were not for our willingness to suffer pain we should have to let too many pleasures escape us!

355. ADMIRERS.—The man who admires up to the point that he would be ready to crucify any one who did not admire, must be reckoned among the executioners of his party—beware of shaking hands with him, even when he belongs to your own side.

356. THE EFFECT OF HAPPINESS.—The first effect of happiness is the feeling of power, and this feeling longs to manifest itself, whether towards ourselves or other men, or towards ideas and imaginary beings. Its most common modes of manifestation are making presents, derision, and destruction—all three being due to a common fundamental instinct.

357. MORAL MOSQUITOES.—Those moralists who are lacking in the love of knowledge, and who are only acquainted with the pleasure of giving pain, have the spirit and tediousness of provincials. Their pastime, as cruel as it is lamentable, is to observe their neighbour with the greatest possible closeness, and, unperceived, to place a pin in such position that he cannot help pricking himself with it. Such men have preserved something of the wickedness of schoolboys, who cannot amuse themselves without hunting and torturing either the living or the dead.

358. REASONS AND THEIR UNREASON.—You feel a dislike for him, and adduce innumerable reasons for this dislike, but I only believe in your dislike and not in your reasons! You flatter yourself by adducing as a rational conclusion, both to yourself and to me, that which happens to be merely a matter of instinct.

359. APPROVING OF SOMETHING.—We approve of marriage in the first place because we are not yet acquainted with it, in the second place because we have accustomed ourselves to it, and in the third place because we have contracted it—that is to say, in most cases. And yet nothing has been proved thereby in favour of the value of marriage in general.

360. NO UTILITARIANS.—"Power which has greatly suffered both in deed and in thought is better than powerlessness which only meets with kind treatment"—such was the Greek way of thinking. In other words, the feeling of power was prized more highly by them than any mere utility or fair renown.

361. UGLY IN APPEARANCE.—Moderation appears to itself to be quite beautiful: it is unaware of the fact that in the eyes of the immoderate it seems coarse and insipid, and consequently ugly.

362. DIFFERENT IN THEIR HATRED.—There are men who do not begin to hate until they feel weak and tired: in other respects they are fair-minded and superior. Others only begin to hate when they see an opportunity for revenge: in other respects they carefully avoid both secret and open wrath, and overlook it whenever there is any occasion for it.

363. MEN OF CHANCE.—It is pure hazard which plays the essential part in every invention, but most men do not meet with this hazard.

364. CHOICE OF ENVIRONMENT.—We should beware of living in an environment where we are neither able to maintain a dignified silence nor to express our loftier thoughts, so that only our complaints and needs and the whole story of our misery are left to be told. We thus become dissatisfied with ourselves and with our surroundings, and to the discomfort which brings about our complaints we add the vexation which we feel at always being in the position of grumblers. But we should, on the contrary, live in a place where we should be ashamed to speak of ourselves and where it would not be necessary to do so.—Who, however, thinks of such things, or of the choice in such things? We talk about our "fate," brace up our shoulders, and sigh, "Unfortunate Atlas that I am!"

365. VANITY.—Vanity is the dread of appearing to be original. Hence it is a lack of pride, but not necessarily a lack of originality.

366. THE CRIMINAL'S GRIEF.—The criminal who has been found out does not suffer because of the crime he has committed, but because of the shame and annoyance caused him either by some blunder which he has made or by being deprived of his habitual element; and keen discernment is necessary to distinguish such cases. Every one who has had much experience of prisons and reformatories is astonished at the rare instances of really genuine "remorse," and still more so at the longing shown to return to the old wicked and beloved crime.

367. ALWAYS APPEARING HAPPY.—When, in the Greece of the third century, philosophy had become a matter of public emulation, there were not a few philosophers who became happy through the thought that others who lived according to different principles, and suffered from them, could not but feel envious of their happiness. They thought they could refute these other people with their happiness better than anything else, and to achieve this object they were content to appear to be always happy; but, following this practice, they were obliged to become happy in the long run! This, for example, was the case of the cynics.

368. THE CAUSE OF MUCH MISUNDERSTANDING.—The morality of increasing nervous force is joyful and restless; the morality of diminishing nervous force, towards evening, or in invalids and old people, is passive, calm, patient, and melancholy, and not rarely even gloomy. In accordance with what we may possess of one or other of these moralities, we do not understand that which we lack, and we often interpret it in others as immorality and weakness.

369. RAISING ONE'S SELF ABOVE ONE'S OWN LOWNESS.—"Proud" fellows they are indeed, those who, in order to establish a sense of their own dignity and importance, stand in need of other people whom they may tyrannise and oppress—those whose powerlessness and cowardice permits some one to make sublime and furious gestures in their presence with impunity, so that they require the baseness of their surroundings to raise themselves for one short moment above their own baseness!—For this purpose one man requires a dog, another a friend, a third a wife, a fourth a party, a fifth, again, one very rarely to be met with, a whole age.

370. TO WHAT EXTENT THE THINKER LOVES HIS ENEMY.—Make it a rule never to withhold or conceal from yourself anything that may be thought against your own thoughts. Vow it! This is the essential requirement of honest thinking. You must undertake such a campaign against yourself every day. A victory and a conquered position are no longer your concern, but that of truth—and your defeat also is no longer your concern!

371. THE EVIL OF STRENGTH.—Violence as the outcome of passion, for example, of rage, must be understood from the physiological point of view as an attempt to avoid an imminent fit of suffocation. Innumerable acts arising from animal spirits and vented upon others are simply outlets for getting rid of sudden congestion by a violent muscular exertion: and perhaps the entire "evil of strength" must be considered from this point of view. (This evil of strength wounds others unintentionally—it must find an outlet somewhere; while the evil of weakness wishes to wound and to see signs of suffering.)

372. TO THE CREDIT OF THE CONNOISSEUR.—As soon as some one who is no connoisseur begins to pose as a judge we should remonstrate, whether it is a male or female whipper-snapper. Enthusiasm or delight in a thing or a human being is not an argument; neither is repugnance or hatred.

373. TREACHEROUS BLAME.—"He has no knowledge of men" means in the mouth of some "He does not know what baseness is"; and in the mouths of others, "He does not know the exception and knows only too well what baseness means."

374. THE VALUE OF SACRIFICE.—The more the rights of states and princes are questioned as to their right to sacrifice the individual (for example, in the administration of justice, conscription, etc.), the more will the value of self-sacrifice rise.

375. SPEAKING TOO DISTINCTLY.—There are several reasons why we articulate our words too distinctly: in the first place, from distrust of ourselves when using a new and unpractised language; secondly, when we distrust others on account of their stupidity or their slowness of comprehension. The same remark applies to intellectual matters: our communications are sometimes too distinct, too painful,

because if it were otherwise those to whom we communicate our ideas would not understand us. Consequently the perfect and easy style is only permissible when addressing a perfect audience.

376. PLENTY OF SLEEP.—What can we do to arouse ourselves when we are weary and tired of our ego? Some recommend the gambling table, others Christianity, and others again electricity. But the best remedy, my dear hypochondriac, is, and always will be, plenty of sleep in both the literal and figurative sense of the word. Thus another morning will at length dawn upon us. The knack of worldly wisdom is to find the proper time for applying this remedy in both its forms.

377. WHAT WE MAY CONCLUDE FROM FANTASTIC IDEALS.—Where our deficiencies are, there also is our enthusiasm. The enthusiastic principle "love your enemies" had to be invented by the Jews, the best haters that ever existed; and the finest glorifications of chastity have been written by those who in their youth led dissolute and licentious lives.

378. CLEAN HANDS AND CLEAN WALLS.—Do not paint the picture either of God or the devil on your walls: for in so doing you will spoil your walls as well as your surroundings.[11]

379. PROBABLE AND IMPROBABLE.—A woman secretly loved a man, raised him far above her, and said to herself hundreds of times in her inmost heart, "If a man like that were to love me, I should look upon it as a condescension before which I should have to humble myself in the dust."—And the man entertained the same feelings towards the woman, and in his inmost heart he felt the very same thought. When at last both their tongues were loosened, and they had communicated their most secret thoughts to one another, a deep and meditative silence ensued. Then the woman said in a cold voice: "The thing is quite clear! We are neither of us that which we loved! If you are what you say you are, and nothing more, then I have humbled myself in vain and loved you; the demon misled me as well as you." This very probable story never happens—and why doesn't it?

380. TESTED ADVICE.—Of all the means of consolation there is none so efficacious for him who has need of it as the declaration that in his case no consolation can be given. This implies such a distinction that the afflicted person will at once raise his head again.

381. KNOWING ONE'S "INDIVIDUALITY".—We too often forget that in the eyes of strangers who see us for the first time we are quite different beings from what we consider ourselves to be—in most cases we exhibit nothing more than one particular characteristic which catches the eye of the stranger, and determines the impression we make on him. Thus the most peaceful and fair-minded man, if only he has a big moustache, may, as it were, repose in the shade of this moustache; for ordinary eyes will merely see in him the accessory of a big moustache, that is to say, a military, irascible, and occasionally violent character, and will act accordingly.

382. GARDENERS AND GARDENS.—Wet dreary days, loneliness, and unkind words give rise within us to conclusions like fungi; some morning we find that they have grown up in front of us we know not whence, and there they scowl at us, sullen and morose. Woe to the thinker who instead of being the gardener of his plants, is merely the soil from which they spring.

383. THE COMEDY OF PITY.—However much we may feel for an unhappy friend of ours, we always act with a certain amount of insincerity in his presence: we refrain from telling him everything we think, and how we think it, with all the circumspection of a doctor standing by the bedside of a patient who is seriously ill.

384. CURIOUS SAINTS.—There are pusillanimous people who have a bad opinion of everything that is best in their works, and who at the same time interpret and comment upon them badly: but also, by a kind of revenge, they entertain a bad opinion of the sympathy of others, and do not believe in sympathy at all; they are ashamed to appear to be carried away from themselves, and feel a defiant comfort in appearing or becoming ridiculous.—States of soul like these are to be found in melancholy artists.

385. VAIN PEOPLE.—We are like shop-windows, where we ourselves are constantly arranging, concealing, or setting in the foreground those supposed qualities which others attribute to us—in order to deceive ourselves.

386. PATHETIC AND NAÏVE.—It may be a very vulgar habit to let no opportunity slip of assuming a pathetic air for the sake of the enjoyment to be experienced in imagining the spectator striking his breast and feeling himself to be small and miserable. Consequently it may also be the indication of a noble mind to make fun of pathetic situations, and to behave in an undignified manner in them. The old, warlike nobility of France possessed that kind of distinction and delicacy.

387. A REFLECTION BEFORE MARRIAGE.—Supposing she loved me, what a burden she would be to me in the long run! and supposing that she did not love me, what a much greater burden she would be to me in the long run! We have to choose between two different kinds of burdens; therefore let us marry.

388. RASCALITY WITH A GOOD CONSCIENCE.—It is exceedingly annoying to be cheated in small bargains in certain countries,—in the Tyrol, for example,—because, in addition to the bad bargain, we are compelled to accept the evil countenance and coarse greediness of the man who has cheated us, together with his bad conscience and his hostile feeling against us. At Venice, on the other

hand, the cheater is highly delighted at his successful fraud, and is not in the least angry with the man he has cheated—nay, he is even inclined to show him some kindness, and above all to have a hearty laugh with him if he likes.—In short, one must possess wit and a good conscience in order to be a knave, and this will almost reconcile the cheated one with the cheat.[12]

389. RATHER TOO AWKWARD.—Good people who are too awkward to be polite and amiable promptly endeavour to return an act of politeness by an important service, or by a contribution beyond their power. It is touching to see them timidly producing their gold coins when others have offered them their gilded coppers!

390. HIDING ONE'S INTELLIGENCE.—When we surprise some one in the act of hiding his intelligence from us we call him evil: the more so if we suspect that it is his civility and benevolence which have induced him to do so.

391. THE EVIL MOMENT.—Lively dispositions only lie for a moment: after this they have deceived themselves, and are convinced and honest.

392. THE CONDITION OF POLITENESS.—Politeness is a very good thing, and really one of the four chief virtues (although the last), but in order that it may not result in our becoming tiresome to one another the person with whom I have to deal must be either one degree more or less polite than I—otherwise we should never get on, and the ointment would not only anoint us, but would cement us together.

393. DANGEROUS VIRTUES.—"He forgets nothing, but forgives everything"—wherefore he shall be doubly detested, for he causes us double shame by his memory and his magnanimity.

394. WITHOUT VANITY.—Passionate people think little of what others may think; their state of mind raises them above vanity.

395. CONTEMPLATION.—In some thinkers the contemplative state peculiar to a thinker is always the consequence of a state of fear, in others always of desire. In the former, contemplation thus seems allied to the feeling of security, in the latter to the feeling of surfeit—in other words, the former are spirited in their mood, the latter over-satiated and neutral.

396. HUNTING.—The one is hunting for agreeable truths, the other for disagreeable ones. But even the former takes greater pleasure in the hunt than in the booty.

397. EDUCATION.—Education is a continuation of procreation, and very often a kind of supplementary varnishing of it.

398. HOW TO RECOGNISE THE CHOLERIC.—Of two persons who are struggling together, or who love and admire one another, the more choleric will always be at a disadvantage. The same remark applies to two nations.

399. SELF-EXCUSE.—Many men have the best possible right to act in this or that way; but as soon as they begin to excuse their actions we no longer believe that they are right—and we are mistaken.

400. MORAL PAMPERING.—There are tender, moral natures who are ashamed of all their successes and feel remorse after every failure.

401. DANGEROUS UNLEARNING.—We begin by unlearning to love others, and end by finding nothing lovable in ourselves.

402. ANOTHER FORM OF TOLERATION.—"To remain a minute too long on red-hot coals and to be burnt a little does no harm either to men or to chestnuts. The slight bitterness and hardness makes the kernel all the sweeter."—Yes, this is your opinion, you who enjoy the taste! You sublime cannibals!

403. DIFFERENT PRIDE.—Women turn pale at the thought that their lover may not be worthy of them; Men turn pale at thè thought that they may not be worthy of the women they love. I speak of perfect women, perfect men. Such men, who are self-reliant and conscious of power at ordinary times, grow diffident and doubtful of themselves when under the influence of a strong passion. Such women, on the other hand, though always looking upon themselves as the weak and devoted sex, become proud and conscious of their power in the great exception of passion,—they ask: "Who then is worthy of me?"

404. WHEN WE SELDOM DO JUSTICE.—Certain men are unable to feel enthusiasm for a great and good cause without committing a great injustice in some other quarter: this is their kind of morality.

405. LUXURY.—The love of luxury is rooted in the depths of a man's heart: it shows that the superfluous and immoderate is the sea wherein his soul prefers to float.

406. TO IMMORTALISE.—Let him who wishes to kill his opponent first consider whether by doing so he will not immortalise him in himself.

407. AGAINST OUR CHARACTER.—If the truth which we have to utter goes against our character—as very often happens—we behave as if we had uttered a clumsy falsehood, and thus rouse suspicion.

408. WHERE A GREAT DEAL OF GENTLENESS IS NEEDED.—Many natures have only the choice of being either public evil-doers or secret sorrow-bearers.

409. ILLNESS.—Among illness are to be reckoned the premature approach of old age, ugliness, and pessimistic opinions—three things that always go together.

410. TIMID PEOPLE.—It is the awkward and timid people who easily become murderers: they do not understand slight but sufficient means of defence or revenge, and their hatred, owing to their lack of intelligence and presence of mind, can conceive of no other expedient than destruction.

411. WITHOUT HATRED.—You wish to bid farewell to your passion? Very well, but do so without hatred against it! Otherwise you have a second passion.—The soul of the Christian who has freed himself from sin is generally ruined afterwards by the hatred for sin. Just look at the faces of the great Christians! they are the faces of great haters.

412. INGENIOUS AND NARROW-MINDED.—He can appreciate nothing beyond himself, and when he wishes to appreciate other people he must always begin by transforming them into himself. In this, however, he is ingenious.

413. PRIVATE AND PUBLIC ACCUSERS.—Watch closely the accuser and inquirer,—for he reveals his true character; and it is not rare for this to be a worse character than that of the victim whose crime he is investigating. The accuser believes in all innocence that the opponent of a crime and criminal must be by nature of good character, or at least must appear as such—and this is why he lets himself go, that is to say, he drops his mask.

414. VOLUNTARY BLINDNESS.—There is a kind of enthusiastic and extreme devotion to a person or a party which reveals that in our inmost hearts we feel ourselves superior to this person or party, and for this reason we feel indignant with ourselves. We blind ourselves, as it were, of our own free will to punish our eyes for having seen too much.

415. REMEDIUM AMORIS.—That old radical remedy for love is now in most cases as effective as it always was: love in return.

416. WHERE IS OUR WORST ENEMY?—He who can look after his own affairs well, and knows that he can do so, is as a rule conciliatory towards his adversary. But to believe that we have right on our side, and to know that we are incapable of defending it—this gives rise to a fierce and implacable hatred against the opponent of our cause. Let every one judge accordingly where his worst enemies are to be sought.

417. THE LIMITS OF ALL HUMILITY.—Many men may certainly have attained that humility which says credo quia absurdum est, and sacrifices its reason; but, so far as I know, not one has attained to that humility which after all is only one step further, and which says creda quia absurdus sum.

418. ACTING THE TRUTH.—Many a man is truthful, not because he would be ashamed to exhibit hypocritical feelings, but because he would not succeed very well in inducing others to believe in his hypocrisy. In a word, he has no confidence in his talent as an actor, and therefore prefers honestly to act the truth.

419. COURAGE IN A PARTY.—The poor sheep say to their bell-wether: “Only lead us, and we shall never lack courage to follow you.” But the poor bell-wether thinks in his heart: “Only follow me, and I shall never lack courage to lead you.”

420. CUNNING OF THE VICTIM.—What a sad cunning there is in the wish to deceive ourselves with respect to the person for whom we have sacrificed ourselves, when we give him an opportunity in which he must appear to us as we should wish him to be!

421. THROUGH OTHERS.—There are men who do not wish to be seen except through the eyes of others: a wish which implies a great deal of wisdom.

422. MAKING OTHERS HAPPY.—Why is the fact of our making others happy more gratifying to us than all other pleasures?—Because in so doing we gratify fifty cravings at one time. Taken separately they would, perhaps, be very small pleasures; but when put into one hand, that hand will be fuller than ever before—and the heart also.

BOOK V

423. IN THE GREAT SILENCE.—Here is the sea, here may we forget the town. It is true that its bells are still ringing the Angelus—that solemn and foolish yet sweet sound at the junction between day and night,—but one moment more! now all is silent. Yonder lies the ocean, pale and brilliant; it cannot speak. The sky is glistening with its eternal mute evening hues, red, yellow, and green: it cannot speak. The small cliffs and rocks which stretch out into the sea as if each one of them were endeavouring to find the loneliest spot—they too are dumb. Beautiful and awful indeed is this vast silence, which so suddenly overcomes us and makes our heart swell.

Alas! what deceit lies in this dumb beauty! How well could it speak, and how evilly, too, if it wished! Its tongue, tied up and fastened, and its face of suffering happiness—all this is but malice, mocking at your sympathy: be it so! I do not feel ashamed to be the plaything of such powers! but I pity thee, oh nature, because thou must be silent, even though it be only malice that binds thy tongue: nay, I pity thee for the sake of thy malice!

Alas! the silence deepens, and once again my heart swells within me: it is startled by a fresh truth—it, too, is dumb; it likewise sneers when the mouth calls out something to this beauty; it also enjoys the sweet malice of its silence. I come to hate speaking; yea, even thinking. Behind every word I utter do I not hear the laughter of error, imagination, and insanity? Must I not laugh at my pity and mock my own mockery? Oh sea, oh evening, ye are bad teachers! Ye teach man how to cease to be a man. Is he to give himself up to you? Shall he become as you now are, pale, brilliant, dumb, immense, reposing calmly upon himself?—exalted above himself?

424. FOR WHOM THE TRUTH EXISTS.—Up to the present time errors have been the power most fruitful in consolations: we now expect the same effects from accepted truths, and we have been waiting rather too long for them. What if these truths could not give us this consolation we are looking for? Would that be an argument against them? What have these truths in common with the sick condition of suffering and degenerate men that they should be useful to them? It is, of course, no proof against the truth of a plant when it is clearly established that it does not contribute in any way to the recovery of sick people. Formerly, however, people were so convinced that man was the ultimate end of nature that they believed that knowledge could reveal nothing that was not beneficial and useful to man—nay, there could not, should not be, any other things in existence.

Perhaps all this leads to the conclusion that truth as an entity and a coherent whole exists only for those natures who, like Aristotle, are at once powerful and harmless, joyous and peaceful: just as none but these would be in a position to seek such truths; for the others seek remedies for themselves—however proud they may be of their intellect and its freedom, they do not seek truth. Hence it comes about that these others take no real joy in science, but reproach it for its coldness, dryness, and inhumanity. This is the judgment of sick people about the games of the healthy.—Even the Greek gods were unable to administer consolation; and when at length the entire Greek world fell ill, this was a reason for the destruction of such gods.

425. WE GODS IN EXILE.—Owing to errors regarding their descent, their uniqueness, their mission, and by claims based upon these errors, men have again and again "surpassed themselves"; but through these same errors the world has been filled with unspeakable suffering, mutual persecution, suspicion, misunderstanding, and an even greater amount of individual misery. Men have become suffering creatures in consequence of their morals, and the sum-total of what they have obtained by those morals is simply the feeling that they are far too good and great for this world, and that they are enjoying merely a transitory existence on it. As yet the "proud sufferer" is the highest type of mankind.

426. THE COLOUR-BLINDNESS OF THINKERS.—How differently from us the Greeks must have viewed nature, since, as we cannot help admitting, they were quite colour-blind in regard to blue and green, believing the former to be a deeper brown, and the latter to be yellow. Thus, for instance, they used the same word to describe the colour of dark hair, of the corn-flower, and the southern sea; and again they employed exactly the same expression for the colour of the greenest herbs, the human skin, honey, and yellow raisins: whence it follows that their greatest painters reproduced the world they lived in only in black, white, red, and yellow. How different and how much nearer to mankind, therefore, must nature have seemed to them, since in their eyes the tints of mankind predominated also in nature, and nature was, as it were, floating in the coloured ether of humanity! (blue and green more

than anything else dehumanise nature). It is this defect which developed the playful facility that characterised the Greeks of seeing the phenomena of nature as gods and demi-gods—that is to say, as human forms.

Let this, however, merely serve as a simile for another supposition. Every thinker paints his world and the things that surround him in fewer colours than really exist, and he is blind to individual colours. This is something more than a mere deficiency. Thanks to this nearer approach and simplification, he imagines he sees in things those harmonies of colours which possess a great charm, and may greatly enrich nature. Perhaps, indeed, it was in this way that men first learnt to take delight in viewing existence, owing to its being first of all presented to them in one or two shades, and consequently harmonised. They practised these few shades, so to speak, before they could pass on to any more. And even now certain individuals endeavour to get rid of a partial colour-blindness that they may obtain a richer faculty of sight and discernment, in the course of which they find that they not only discover new pleasures, but are also obliged to lose and give up some of their former ones.

427. THE EMBELLISHMENT OF SCIENCE.—In the same way that the feeling that "nature is ugly, wild, tedious—we must embellish it (embellir la nature)"—brought about rococo horticulture, so does the view that "science is ugly, difficult, dry, dreary and weary, we must embellish it," invariably gives rise to something called philosophy. This philosophy sets out to do what all art and poetry endeavour to do, viz., giving amusement above all else; but it wishes to do this, in conformity with its hereditary pride, in a higher and more sublime fashion before an audience of superior intellects. It is no small ambition to create for these intellects a kind of horticulture, the principal charm of which—like that of the usual gardening—is to bring about an optical illusion (by means of temples, perspective, grottos, winding walks, and waterfalls, to speak in similes), exhibiting science in a condensed form and in all kinds of strange and unexpected illuminations, infusing into it as much indecision, irrationality, and dreaminess as will enable us to walk about in it "as in savage nature," but without trouble and boredom.

Those who are possessed of this ambition even dream of making religion superfluous—religion, which among men of former times served as the highest kind of entertainment. All this is now running its course, and will one day attain its highest tide. Even now hostile voices are being raised against philosophy, exclaiming: "Return to science, to nature, and the naturalness of science!" and thus an age may begin which may discover the most powerful beauty precisely in the "savage and ugly" domains of science, just as it is only since the time of Rousseau that we have discovered the sense for the beauty of high mountains and deserts.

428. TWO KINDS OF MORALISTS.—To see a law of nature for the first time, and to see it whole (for example, the law of gravity or the reflection of light and sound), and afterwards to explain such a law, are two different things and concern different classes of minds. In the same way, those moralists who observe and exhibit human laws and habits—moralists with discriminating ears, noses, and eyes—differ entirely from those who interpret their observations. These latter must above all be inventive, and must possess an imagination untrammelled by sagacity and knowledge.

429. THE NEW PASSION.—Why do we fear and dread a possible return to barbarism? Is it because it would make people less happy than they are now? Certainly not! the barbarians of all ages possessed more happiness than we do: let us not deceive ourselves on this point!—but our impulse towards knowledge is too widely developed to allow us to value happiness without knowledge, or the happiness of a strong and fixed delusion: it is painful to us even to imagine such a state of things! Our restless pursuit of discoveries and divinations has become for us as attractive and indispensable as hapless love to the lover, which on no account would he exchange for indifference,—nay, perhaps we, too, are hapless lovers! Knowledge within us has developed into a passion, which does not shrink from any sacrifice, and at bottom fears nothing but its own extinction. We sincerely believe that all humanity, weighed down as it is by the burden of this passion, are bound to feel more exalted and comforted than formerly, when they had not yet overcome the longing for the coarser satisfaction which accompanies barbarism.

It may be that mankind may perish eventually from this passion for knowledge!—but even that does not daunt us. Did Christianity ever shrink from a similar thought? Are not love and death brother and sister? Yes, we detest barbarism,—we all prefer that humanity should perish rather than that knowledge should enter into a stage of retrogression. And, finally, if mankind does not perish through some passion it will perish through some weakness: which would we prefer? This is the main question. Do we wish its end to be in fire and light, or in the sands?

430. LIKEWISE HEROIC.—To do things of the worst possible odour, things of which we scarcely dare to speak, but which are nevertheless useful and necessary, is also heroic. The Greeks were not ashamed of numbering even the cleansing of a stable among the great tasks of Hercules.

431. THE OPINIONS OF OPPONENTS.—In order to measure the natural subtlety or weakness of even the cleverest heads, we must consider the manner in which they take up and reproduce the opinions of their adversaries, for the natural measure of any intellect is thereby revealed. The perfect

sage involuntarily idealises his opponent and frees his inconsistencies from all defects and accidentalities: he only takes up arms against him when he has thus turned his opponent into a god with shining weapons.

432. INVESTIGATOR AND ATTEMPTER.—There is no exclusive method of knowing in science. We must deal with things tentatively, treating them by turns harshly or justly, passionately or coldly. One investigator deals with things like a policeman, another like a confessor, and yet a third like an inquisitive traveller. We force something from them now by sympathy and now by violence: the one is urged onward and led to see clearly by the veneration which the secrets of the things inspire in him, and the other again by the indiscretion and malice met with in the explanation of these secrets. We investigators, like all conquerors, explorers, navigators, and adventurers, are men of a daring morality, and we must put up with our liability to be in the main looked upon as evil.

433. SEEING WITH NEW EYES.—Presuming that by the term "beauty in art" is always implied the imitation of something that is happy—and this I consider to be true—according as an age or a people or a great autocratic individuality represents happiness: what then is disclosed by the so-called realism of our modern artists in regard to the happiness of our epoch? It is undoubtedly its type of beauty which we now understand most easily and enjoy best of any. As a consequence, we are induced to believe that this happiness which is now peculiar to us is based on realism, on the sharpest possible senses, and on the true conception of the actual—that is to say, not upon reality, but upon what we know of reality. The results of science have already gained so much in depth and extent that the artists of our century have involuntarily become the glorifiers of scientific "blessings" per se.

434. INTERCESSION.—Unpretentious regions are subjects for great landscape painters; remarkable and rare regions for inferior painters: for the great things of nature and humanity must intercede in favour of their little, mediocre, and vain admirers—whereas the great man intercedes in favour of unassuming things.

435. NOT TO PERISH UNNOTICED.—It is not only once but continuously that our excellence and greatness are constantly crumbling away; the weeds that grow among everything and cling to everything ruin all that is great in us—the wretchedness of our surroundings, which we always try to overlook and which is before our eyes at every hour of the day, the innumerable little roots of mean and petty feelings which we allow to grow up all about us, in our office, among our companions, or our daily labours. If we permit these small weeds to escape our notice we shall perish through them unnoticed!—And, if you must perish, then do so immediately and suddenly; for in that case you will perhaps leave proud ruins behind you! and not, as is now to be feared, merely molehills, covered with grass and weeds—these petty and miserable conquerors, as humble as ever, and too wretched even to triumph.

436. CASUISTIC.—We are confronted with a very bitter and painful dilemma, for the solution of which not every one's bravery and character are equal: when, as passengers on board a steamer, we discover that the captain and the helmsman are making dangerous mistakes, and that we are their superiors in nautical science—and then we ask ourselves: "What would happen if we organised a mutiny against them, and made them both prisoners? Is it not our duty to do so in view of our superiority? and would not they in their turn be justified in putting us in irons for encouraging disobedience?"

This is a simile for higher and worse situations; and the final question to be decided is, What guarantees our superiority and our faith in ourselves in such a case? Success? but in order to do that we must do the very thing in which all the danger lies—not only dangerous for ourselves, but also for the ship.

437. PRIVILEGES.—The man who really owns himself, that is to say, he who has finally conquered himself, regards it as his own right to punish, to pardon, or to pity himself: he need not concede this privilege to any one, though he may freely bestow it upon some one else—a friend, for example—but he knows that in doing this he is conferring a right, and that rights can only be conferred by one who is in full possession of power.

438. MAN AND THINGS.—Why does the man not see the things? He himself is in the way: he conceals the things.

439. CHARACTERISTICS OF HAPPINESS.—There are two things common to all sensations of happiness: a profusion of feelings, accompanied by animal spirits, so that, like the fishes, we feel ourselves to be in our element and play about in it. Good Christians will understand what Christian exuberance means.

440. NEVER RENOUNCE.—Renouncing the world without knowing it, like a nun, results in a fruitless and perhaps melancholy solitude. This has nothing in common with the solitude of the vita contemplativa of the thinker: when he chooses this form of solitude he wishes to renounce nothing; but he would on the contrary regard it as a renunciation, a melancholy destruction of his own self, if he were obliged to continue in the vita practica. He forgoes this latter because he knows it, because he knows himself. So he jumps into his water, and thus gains his cheerfulness.

441. WHY THE NEAREST THINGS BECOME EVER MORE DISTANT FOR US.—The more we give up our minds to all that has been and will be, the paler will become that which actually is. When we live with the dead and participate in their death, what are our "neighbours" to us? We grow lonelier simply because the entire flood of humanity is surging round about us. The fire that burns within us, and glows for all that is human, is continually increasing—and hence we look upon everything that surrounds us as if it had become more indifferent, more shadowy,—but our cold glance is offensive.

442. THE RULE.—"The rule always appears to me to be more interesting than the exception"—whoever thinks thus has made considerable progress in knowledge, and is one of the initiated.

443. ON EDUCATION.—I have gradually come to see daylight in regard to the most general defect in our methods of education and training: nobody learns, nobody teaches, nobody wishes, to endure solitude.

444. SURPRISE AT RESISTANCE.—Because we have reached the point of being able to see through a thing we believe that henceforth it can offer us no further resistance—and then we are surprised to find that we can see through it and yet cannot penetrate through it. This is the same kind of foolishness and surprise as that of the fly on a pane of glass.

445. WHERE THE NOBLEST ARE MISTAKEN.—We give some one at length our dearest and most valued possession, and then love has nothing more to give: but the recipient of the gift will certainly not consider it as his dearest possession, and will consequently be wanting in that full and complete gratitude which we expect from him.

446. HIERARCHY.—First and foremost, there are the superficial thinkers, and secondly the profound thinkers—such as dive into the depths of a thing,—thirdly, the thorough thinkers, who get to the bottom of a thing—which is of much greater importance than merely diving into its depths,—and, finally, those who leap head foremost into the marsh: though this must not be looked upon as indicating either depth or thoroughness! these are the lovers of obscurity.[13]

447. MASTER AND PUPIL.—By cautioning his pupils against himself the teacher shows his humanity.

448. HONOURING REALITY.—How can we look at this exulting multitude without tears and acquiescence? at one time we thought little of the object of their exultation, and we should still think so if we ourselves had not come through a similar experience. And what may these experiences lead us to! what are our opinions! In order that we may not lose ourselves and our reason we must fly from experiences. It was thus that Plato fled from actuality, and wished to contemplate things only in their pale mental concepts: he was full of sensitiveness, and knew how easily the waves of this sensitiveness would drown his reason.—Must the sage therefore say, "I will honour reality, but I will at the same time turn my back to it because I know and dread it?" Ought he to behave as certain African tribes do in the presence of their sovereign, whom they approach backwards, thus showing their reverence at the same time as their dread?

449. WHERE ARE THE POOR IN SPIRIT?—Oh, how greatly it goes against my grain to impose my own thoughts upon others! How I rejoice over every mood and secret change within me as the result of which the thoughts of others are victorious over my own! but from time to time I enjoy an even greater satisfaction, when I am allowed to give away my intellectual possessions, like the confessor sitting in his box and anxiously awaiting the arrival of some distressed person who stands in need of consolation, and will be only too glad to relate the full misery of his thoughts so that the listener's hand and heart will once again be filled, and the troubled soul eased! Not only has the confessor no desire for renown: he would fain shùn gratitude as well, for it is obtrusive, and does not stand in awe of solitude or silence.

But to live without a name, and even to be slightly sneered at; too obscure to arouse envy or enmity; with a head free from fever, a handful of knowledge, and a pocketful of experience; a physician, as it were, of the poor in spirit, helping this one or that one whose head is troubled with opinions, without the latter perceiving who has actually helped him! without any desire to appear to be in the right in the presence of his patient, or to carry off a victory. To speak to him in such a way that, after a short and almost imperceptible hint or objection, the listener may find out for himself what is right and proudly walk away! To be like an obscure and unknown inn which turns no one away who is in need, but which is afterwards forgotten and laughed at! To be without any advantages over others—neither possessing better food nor purer air, nor a more cheerful mind—but always to be giving away, returning, communicating, and becoming poorer! To know how to be humble in order to be accessible to many people and humiliating to none! To take a great deal of injustice on his shoulders and creep through the cracks and crannies of all kinds of errors, in order that we may reach many obscure souls on their secret paths! ever in possession of some kind of love, and some kind of egoism and self-enjoyment! in possession of power, and yet at the same time hidden and resigned! constantly basking in the sunshine and sweetness of grace, and yet knowing that quite near to us stands the ladder leading to the sublime!—that would be life! that would indeed be a reason for a long life!

450. THE TEMPTATIONS OF KNOWLEDGE.—A glance through the gate of science acts upon passionate spirits as the charm of charms: they will probably become dreamers, or in the most favourable cases poets, so great is their desire for the happiness of the man who can discern. Does it not enter into all your senses, this note of sweet temptation by which science has announced its joyful message in a thousand ways, and in the thousand and first way, the noblest of all, "Begone, illusion! for then 'Woe is me' also vanished, and with it woe itself is gone" (Marcus Aurelius).

451. FOR WHOM A COURT JESTER IS NEEDFUL.—Those who are very beautiful, very good, and very powerful scarcely ever learn the full and naked truth about anything,—for in their presence we involuntarily lie a little, because we feel their influence, and in view of this influence convey a truth in the form of an adaptation (by falsifying the shades and degrees of facts, by omitting or adding details, and withholding that which is insusceptible of adaptation). If, however, in spite of all this, people of this description insist upon hearing the truth, they must keep a court jester—a being with the madman's privilege of being unable to adapt himself.

452. IMPATIENCE.—There is a certain degree of impatience in men of thought and action, which in cases of failure at once drives them to the opposite camp, induces them to take a great interest in it, and to give themselves up to new undertakings—until here again the slowness of their success drives them away. Thus they rove about, like so many reckless adventurers, through the practices of many kingdoms and natures; and in the end, as the result of their wide knowledge of men and things, acquired by their unheard of travel and practice, and with a certain moderation of their craving, they become powerful practical men. Hence a defect in character may become the school of genius.

453. A MORAL INTERREGNUM.—Who is now in a position to describe that which will one day supplant moral feelings and judgments!—however certain we may be that these are founded on error, and that the building erected upon such foundations cannot be repaired: their obligation must gradually diminish from day to day, in so far as the obligation of reason does not diminish! To carry out the task of re-establishing the laws of life and action is still beyond the power of our sciences of physiology and medicine, society and solitude: though it is only from them that we can borrow the foundation-stones of new ideals (but not the ideals themselves). Thus we live a preliminary or after existence, according to our tastes and talents, and the best we can do in this interregnum is to be as much as possible our own "reges," and to establish small experimental states. We are experiments: if we want to be so!

454. A DIGRESSION.—A book like this is not intended to be read through at once, or to be read aloud. It is intended more particularly for reference, especially on our walks and travels: we must take it up and put it down again after a short reading, and, more especially, we ought not to be amongst our usual surroundings.

455. THE PRIMARY NATURE.—As we are now brought up, we begin by acquiring a secondary nature, and we possess it when the world calls us mature, of age, efficient. A few have sufficient of the serpent about them to cast this skin some day, when their primary nature has come to maturity under it. But in the majority of people the germ of it withers away.

456. A VIRTUE IN PROCESS OF BECOMING.—Such assertions and promises as those of the ancient philosophers on the unity of virtue and felicity, or that of Christianity, "Seek ye first the Kingdom of God and His righteousness, and all these things shall be added unto you," have never been made with absolute sincerity, but always without a bad conscience nevertheless. People were in the habit of boldly laying down principles—which they wished to be true—exactly as if they were truth itself, in spite of all appearances to the contrary, and in doing this they felt neither religious nor moral compunction; for it was in honorem maiorem of virtue or of God that one had gone beyond truth, without, however, any selfish intention!

Many good people still act up to this degree of truthfulness: when they feel unselfish they think it permissible to treat truth more lightly. Let it be remembered that the word honesty is neither to be found among the Socratic nor the Christian virtues: it is one of our most recent virtues, not yet quite mature, frequently misconstrued and misunderstood, scarcely conscious of itself—something in embryo, which we may either promote or check according to our inclination.

457. FINAL TACITURNITY.—There are some men who fare like the digger after hidden treasures: they quite accidentally discover the carefully-preserved secrets of another's soul, and as a result come into the possession of knowledge which it is often a heavy burden to bear. In certain circumstances we may know the living and the dead, and sound their inmost thoughts to such an extent that it becomes painful to us to speak to others about them: at every word we utter we are afraid of being indiscreet.—I can easily imagine a sudden silence on the part of the wisest historian.

458. THE GREAT PRIZE.—There is a very rare thing, but a very delightful one, viz. the man with a nobly-formed intellect who possesses at the same time the character and inclinations, and even meets with the experiences, suited to such an intellect.

459. THE MAGNANIMITY OF THE THINKER.—Both Rousseau and Schopenhauer were proud enough to inscribe upon their lives the motto, Vitam impendere vero. And how they both must

have suffered in their pride because they could not succeed in verum impendere vitæ!—verum, such as each of them understood it,—when their lives ran side by side with their knowledge like an uncouth bass which is not in tune with the melody.

Knowledge, however, would be in a bad way if it were measured out to every thinker only in proportion as it can be adapted to his own person. And thinkers would be in a bad way if their vanity were so great that they could only endure such an adaptation, for the noblest virtue of a great thinker is his magnanimity, which urges him on in his search for knowledge to sacrifice himself and his life unshrinkingly, often shamefacedly, and often with sublime scorn, and smiling.

460. UTILISING OUR HOURS OF DANGER.—Those men and conditions whose every movement may mean danger to our possessions, honour, and life or death, and to those most dear to us, we shall naturally learn to know thoroughly. Tiberius, for instance, must have meditated much more deeply on the character and methods of government of the Emperor Augustus, and must have known far more about them than even the wisest historian.

At the present day we all live, relatively speaking, in a security which is much too great to make us true psychologists: some survey their fellow-men as a hobby, others out of ennui, and others again merely from habit; but never to the extent they would do if they were told "Discern or perish!" As long as truths do not cut us to the quick we assume an attitude of contempt towards them: they still appear to us too much like the "winged dreams," as if we could or could not have them at our discretion, as if we could likewise be aroused from these truths as from a dream!

461. HIC RHODUS, HIC SALTA.—Our music, which can and must change into everything, because like the demon of the sea, it has no character of its own: this music in former times devoted its attention to the Christian savant, and transposed his ideals into sounds: why cannot it likewise find those brighter, more cheerful, and universal sounds which correspond to the ideal thinker?—a music which could rock itself at ease in the vast floating vaults of the soul? So far our music has been so great and so good; nothing seemed impossible to its powers. May it therefore prove possible to create these three sensations at one time: sublimity, deep and warm light, and rapture of the greatest possible consistency!

462. SLOW CURES.—Chronic illnesses of the soul, like those of the body, are very rarely due to one gross offence against physical and mental reason, but as a general rule they arise from innumerable and petty negligences of a minor order.—A man, for example, whose breathing becomes a trifle weaker every day, and whose lungs, by inhaling too little air, are deprived of their proper amount of exercise, will end by being struck down by some chronic disease of the lungs. The only remedy for cases like these is a countless number of minor exercises of a contrary tendency—making it a rule, for example, to take a long and deep breath every quarter of an hour, lying flat on the ground if possible. For this purpose a clock which strikes the quarters should be chosen as a lifelong companion.

All these remedies are slow and trifling; but yet the man who wishes to cure his soul will carefully consider a change, even in his least important habits. Many a man will utter a cold and angry word to his surroundings ten times a day without thinking about it, and he will forget that after a few years it will have become a regular habit with him to put his surroundings out of temper ten times a day. But he can also acquire the habit of doing good to them ten times.

463. ON THE SEVENTH DAY.—"You praise this as my creation? but I have only put aside what was a burden to me! my soul is above the vanity of creators.—You praise this as my resignation? but I have only stripped myself of what had become burdensome! My soul is above the vanity of the resigned ones!"

464. THE DONOR'S MODESTY.—There is such a want of generosity in always posing as the donor and benefactor, and showing one's face when doing so! But to give and bestow, and at the same time to conceal one's name and favour! or not to have a name at all, like nature, in whom this fact is more refreshing to us than anything else—here at last we no more meet with the giver and bestower, no more with a "gracious countenance."—It is true that you have now forfeited even this comfort, for you have placed a God in this nature—and now everything is once again fettered and oppressed! Well? are we never to have the right of remaining alone with ourselves? are we always to be watched, guarded, surrounded by leading strings and gifts? If there is always some one round about us, the best part of courage and kindness will ever remain impossible of attainment in this world. Are we not tempted to fly to hell before this continual obtrusiveness of heaven, this inevitable supernatural neighbour? Never mind, it was only a dream; let us wake up!

465. AT A MEETING.—

A. What are you looking at? you have been standing here for a very long time.

B. Always the new and the old over again! the helplessness of a thing urges me on to plunge into it so deeply that I end by penetrating to its deepest depths, and perceive that in reality it is not worth so very much. At the end of all experiences of this kind we meet with a kind of sorrow and stupor. I experience this on a small scale several times a day.

466. A LOSS OF RENOWN.—What an advantage it is to be able to speak as a stranger to mankind! When they take away our anonymity, and make us famous, the gods deprive us of "half our

virtue."

467. DOUBLY PATIENT.—"By doing this you will hurt many people."—I know that, and I also know that I shall have to suffer for it doubly: in the first place out of pity for their suffering, and secondly from the revenge they will take on me. But in spite of this I cannot help doing what I do.

468. THE KINGDOM OF BEAUTY IS GREATER.—We move about in nature, cunning and cheerful, in order that we may surprise everything in the beauty peculiar to it; we make an effort, whether in sunshine or under a stormy sky, to see a distant part of the coast with its rocks, bays, and olive and pine trees under an aspect in which it achieves its perfection and consummation. Thus also we should walk about among men as their discoverers and explorers, meting out to them good and evil in order that we may unveil the peculiar beauty which is seen with some in the sunshine, in others under thunder-clouds, or with others again only in twilight and under a rainy sky.

Are we then forbidden to enjoy the evil man like some savage landscape which possesses its own bold and daring lines and luminous effects, while this same man, so long as he behaves well, and in conformity with the law, appears to us to be an error of drawing, and a mere caricature which offends us like a defect in nature?—Yes, this is forbidden: for as yet we have only been permitted to seek beauty in anything that is morally good,—and this is sufficient to explain why we have found so little and have been compelled to look for beauty without either flesh or bones!—in the same way as evil men are familiar with innumerable kinds of happiness which the virtuous never dream of, we may also find among them innumerable types of beauty, many of them as yet undiscovered.

469. THE INHUMANITY OF THE SAGE.—The heavy and grinding progress of the sage, who in the words of the Buddhist song, "Wanders lonely like the rhinoceros," now and again stands in need of proofs of a conciliatory and softened humanity, and not only proofs of those accelerated steps, those polite and sociable witticisms; not only of humour and a certain self-mockery, but likewise of contradictions and occasional returns to the predominating inconsistencies. In order that he may not resemble the heavy roller that rolls along like fate, the sage who wishes to teach must take advantage of his defects, and utilise them for his own adornment; and when saying "despise me" he will implore permission to be the advocate of a presumptuous truth.

This sage wishes to lead you to the mountains, and he will perhaps endanger your life: therefore as the price of his enjoyment he willingly authorises you to take your revenge either before or afterwards on such a guide. Do you remember what thoughts came into your head when he once led you to a gloomy cavern over a slippery path? Your distrustful heart beat rapidly, and said inwardly, "This guide might surely do something better than crawl about here! he is one of those idle people who are full of curiosity—is it not doing him too much honour to appear to attach any value at all to him by following him?"

470. MANY AT THE BANQUET.—How happy we are when we are fed like the birds by the hand of some one who throws them their crumbs without examining them too closely, or inquiring into their worthiness! To live like a bird which comes and flies away, and does not carry its name on its beak! I take great pleasure in satisfying my appetite at the banquet of the many.

471. ANOTHER TYPE OF LOVE FOR ONE'S NEIGHBOUR.—Everything that is agitated, noisy, fitful, and nervous forms a contrast to the great passion which, glowing in the heart of man like a quiet and gloomy flame, and gathering about it all that is flaming and ardent, gives to man the appearance of coldness and indifference, and stamps a certain impassiveness on his features. Such men are occasionally capable of showing their love for their neighbour, but this love is different from that of sociable people who are anxious to please. It is a mild, contemplative, and calm amiability: these people, as it were, look out of the windows of the castle which serves them as a stronghold, and consequently as a prison; for the outlook into the far distance, the open air, and a different world is so pleasant for them!

472. NOT JUSTIFYING ONESELF.—

A. But why are you not willing to justify yourself?

B. I could do it in this instance, as in dozens of others; but I despise the pleasure which lies in justification, for all that matters little to me, and I would rather bear a stained reputation than give those petty folks the spiteful pleasure of saying, "He takes these things very seriously." This is not true. Perhaps I ought to have more consideration for myself, and look upon it as a duty to rectify erroneous opinions about myself—I am too indifferent and too indolent regarding myself, and consequently also regarding everything that is brought about through my agency.

473. WHERE TO BUILD ONE'S HOUSE.—If you feel great and productive in solitude, society will belittle and isolate you, and vice versa. A powerful mildness such as that of a father:—wherever this feeling takes possession of you, there build your house, whether in the midst of the multitude, or on some silent spot. Ubi pater sum, ibi patria.[14]

474. THE ONLY MEANS.—"Dialectic is the only means of reaching the divine essence, and penetrating behind the veil of appearance." This declaration of Plato in regard to dialectic is as solemn and passionate as that of Schopenhauer in regard to the contrary of dialectic—and both are wrong. For

that to which they wish to point out the way to us does not exist.—And so far have not all the great passions of mankind been passions for something non-existent?—and all their ceremonies—ceremonies for something non-existent also?

475. BECOMING HEAVY.—You know him not; whatever weights he may attach to himself he will nevertheless be able to raise them all with him. But you, judging from the weak flapping of your own wings, come to the conclusion that he wishes to remain below, merely because he does burden himself with those weights.

476. AT THE HARVEST THANKSGIVING OF THE INTELLECT.—There is a daily increase and accumulation of experiences, events, opinions upon these experiences and events, and dreams upon these opinions—a boundless and delightful display of wealth! its aspect dazzles the eyes: I can no longer understand how the poor in spirit can be called blessed! Occasionally, however, I envy them when I am tired: for the superintendence of such vast wealth is no easy task, and its weight frequently crushes all happiness.—Alas, if only the mere sight of it were sufficient! If only we could be misers of our knowledge!

477. FREED FROM SCEPTICISM.—

A. Some men emerge from a general moral scepticism bad-tempered and feeble, corroded, worm-eaten, and even partly consumed—but I on the other hand, more courageous and healthier than ever, and with my instincts conquered once more. Where a strong wind blows, where the waves are rolling angrily, and where more than usual danger is to be faced, there I feel happy. I did not become a worm, although I often had to work and dig like a worm.

B. You have just ceased to be a sceptic; for you deny!

A. And in doing so I have learnt to say yea again.

478. LET US PASS BY.—Spare him! Leave him in his solitude! Do you wish to crush him down entirely? He became cracked like a glass into which some hot liquid was poured suddenly—and he was such a precious glass!

479. LOVE AND TRUTHFULNESS.—Through our love we have become dire offenders against truth, and even habitual dissimulators and thieves, who give out more things as true than seem to us to be true. On this account the thinker must from time to time drive away those whom he loves (not necessarily those who love him), so that they may show their sting and wickedness, and cease to tempt him. Consequently the kindness of the thinker will have its waning and waxing moon.

480. INEVITABLE.—No matter what your experience may be, any one who does not feel well disposed towards you will find in this experience some pretext for disparaging you! You may undergo the greatest possible revolutions of mind and knowledge, and at length, with the melancholy smile of the convalescent, you may be able to step out into freedom and bright stillness, and yet some one will say: "This fellow looks upon his illness as an argument, and takes his impotence to be a proof of the impotence of all others—he is vain enough to fall ill that he may feel the superiority of the sufferer." And again, if somebody were to break the chains that bound him down, and wounded himself severely in doing so, some one else would point at him mockingly and cry: "How awkward he is! there is a man who had got accustomed to his chains, and yet he is fool enough to burst them asunder!"

481. TWO GERMANS.—If we compare Kant and Schopenhauer with Plato, Spinoza, Pascal, Rousseau, and Goethe, with reference to their souls and not their intellects, we shall see that the two first-named thinkers are at a disadvantage: their thoughts do not constitute a passionate history of their souls—we are not led to expect in them romance, crises, catastrophies, or death struggles. Their thinking is not at the same time the involuntary biography of a soul, but in the case of Kant merely of a head; and in the case of Schopenhauer again merely the description and reflection of a character ("the invariable") and the pleasure which this reflection causes, that is to say, the pleasure of meeting with an intellect of the first order.

Kant, when he shimmers through his thoughts, appears to us as an honest and honourable man in the best sense of the words, but likewise as an insignificant one: he is wanting in breadth and power; he had not come through many experiences, and his method of working did not allow him sufficient time to undergo experiences. Of course, in speaking of experiences, I do not refer to the ordinary external events of life, but to those fatalities and convulsions which occur in the course of the most solitary and quiet life which has some leisure and glows with the passion for thinking. Schopenhauer has at all events one advantage over him; for he at least was distinguished by a certain fierce ugliness of disposition, which showed itself in hatred, desire, vanity, and suspicion: he was of a rather more ferocious disposition, and had both time and leisure to indulge this ferocity. But he lacked "development," which was also wanting in his range of thought: he had no "history."

482. SEEKING ONE'S COMPANY.—Are we then looking for too much when we seek the company of men who have grown mild, agreeable to the taste, and nutritive, like chestnuts which have been put into the fire and taken out just at the right moment? Of men who expect little from life, and prefer to accept this little as a present rather than as a merit of their own, as if it were carried to them by birds and bees? Of men who are too proud ever to feel themselves rewarded, and too serious in their

passion for knowledge and honesty to have time for or pleasure in fame? Such men we should call philosophers; but they themselves will always find some more modest designation.

483. SATIATED WITH MANKIND.—

A. Seek for knowledge! Yes! but always as a man! What? must I always be a spectator of the same comedy, and always play a part in the same comedy, without ever being able to observe things with other eyes than those? and yet there may be countless types of beings whose organs are better adapted for knowledge than ours! At the end of all their searching for knowledge what will men at length come to know? Their organs! which perhaps is as much as to say: the impossibility of knowledge! misery and disgust!

B. This is a bad attack you have—reason is attacking you! to-morrow, however, you will again be in the midst of knowledge, and hence of irrationality—that is to say, delighted about all that is human. Let us go to the sea!

484. GOING OUR OWN WAY.—When we take the decisive step, and make up our minds to follow our own path, a secret is suddenly revealed to us: it is clear that all those who had hitherto been friendly to us and on intimate terms with us judged themselves to be superior to us, and are offended now. The best among them are indulgent, and are content to wait patiently until we once more find the "right path"—they know it, apparently. Others make fun of us, and pretend that we have been seized with a temporary attack of mild insanity, or spitefully point out some seducer. The more malicious say we are vain fools, and do their best to blacken our motives; while the worst of all see in us their greatest enemy, some one who is thirsting for revenge after many years of dependence,—and are afraid of us. What, then, are we to do? My own opinion is that we should begin our sovereignty by promising to all our acquaintances in advance a whole year's amnesty for sins of every kind.

485. FAR-OFF PERSPECTIVES.—

A. But why this solitude?

B. I am not angry with anybody. But when I am alone it seems to me that I can see my friends in a clearer and rosier light than when I am with them; and when I loved and felt music best I lived far from it. It would seem that I must have distant perspectives in order that I may think well of things.

486. GOLD AND HUNGER.—Here and there we meet with a man who changes into gold everything that he touches. But some fine evil day he will discover that he himself must starve through this gift of his. Everything around him is brilliant, superb, and unapproachable in its ideal beauty, and now he eagerly longs for things which it is impossible for him to turn into gold—and how intense is this longing! like that of a starving man for a meal! Query: What will he seize?

487. SHAME.—Look at that noble steed pawing the ground, snorting, longing for a ride, and loving its accustomed rider—but, shameful to relate, the rider cannot mount to-day, he is tired.—Such is the shame felt by the weary thinker in the presence of his own philosophy!

488. AGAINST THE WASTE OF LOVE.—Do we not blush when we surprise ourselves in a state of violent aversion? Well, then, we should also blush when we find ourselves possessed of strong affections on account of the injustice contained in them. More: there are people who feel their hearts weighed down and oppressed when some one gives them the benefit of his love and sympathy to the extent that he deprives others of a share. The tone of his voice reveals to us the fact that we have been specially selected and preferred! but, alas! I am not thankful for being thus selected: I experience within myself a certain feeling of resentment against him who wishes to distinguish me in this way—he shall not love me at the expense of others! I shall always try to look after myself and to endure myself, and my heart is often filled to overflowing, and with some reason. To such a man nothing ought to be given of which others stand so greatly in need.

489. FRIENDS IN NEED.—We may occasionally remark that one of our friends sympathises with another more than with us. His delicacy is troubled thereby, and his selfishness is not equal to the task of breaking down his feelings of affection: in such a case we should facilitate the separation for him, and estrange him in some way in order to widen the distance between us.—This is also necessary when we fall into a habit of thinking which might be detrimental to him: our affection for him should induce us to ease his conscience in separating himself from us by means of some injustice which we voluntarily take upon ourselves.

490. THOSE PETTY TRUTHS.—"You know all that, but you have never lived through it—so I will not accept your evidence. Those 'petty truths'—you deem them petty because you have not paid for them with your blood!"—But are they really great, simply because they have been bought at so high a price? and blood is always too high a price!—"Do you really think so? How stingy you are with your blood!"

491. SOLITUDE, THEREFORE!—

A. So you wish to go back to your desert?

B. I am not a quick thinker; I must wait for myself a long time—it is always later and later before the water from the fountain of my own ego spurts forth, and I have often to go thirsty longer than suits my patience. That is why I retire into solitude in order that I may not have to drink from the common cisterns. When I live in the midst of the multitude my life is like theirs, and I do not think like myself; but after some time it always seems to me as if the multitude wished to banish me from myself and to rob me of my soul. Then I get angry with all these people, and afraid of them; and I must have the desert to become well disposed again.

492. UNDER THE SOUTH WIND.—

A. I can no longer understand myself! It was only yesterday that I felt myself so tempestuous and ardent, and at the same time so warm and sunny and exceptionally bright! but to-day! Now everything is calm, wide, oppressive, and dark like the lagoon at Venice. I wish for nothing, and draw a deep breath, and yet I feel inwardly indignant at this "wish for nothing"—so the waves rise and fall in the ocean of my melancholy.

B. You describe a petty, agreeable illness. The next wind from the north-east will blow it away.

A. Why so?

493. ON ONE'S OWN TREE.—

A. No thinker's thoughts give me so much pleasure as my own: this, of course, proves nothing in favour of their value; but I should be foolish to neglect fruits which are tasteful to me only because they happen to grow on my own tree!—and I was once such a fool.

B. Others have the contrary feeling: which likewise proves nothing in favour of their thoughts, nor yet is it any argument against their value.

494. THE LAST ARGUMENT OF THE BRAVE MAN.—There are snakes in this little clump of trees.—Very well, I will rush into the thicket and kill them.—But by doing that you will run the risk of falling a victim to them, and not they to you.—But what do I matter?

495. OUR TEACHERS.—During our period of youth we select our teachers and guides from our own times, and from those circles which we happen to meet with: we have the thoughtless conviction that the present age must have teachers who will suit us better than any others, and that we are sure to find them without having to look very far. Later on we find that we have to pay a heavy penalty for this childishness: we have to expiate our teachers in ourselves, and then perhaps we begin to look for the proper guides. We look for them throughout the whole world, including even present and past ages—but perhaps it may be too late, and at the worst we discover that they lived when we were young—and that at that time we lost our opportunity.

496. THE EVIL PRINCIPLE.—Plato has marvellously described how the philosophic thinker must necessarily be regarded as the essence of depravity in the midst of every existing society: for as the critic of all its morals he is naturally the antagonist of the moral man, and, unless he succeeds in becoming the legislator of new morals, he lives long in the memory of men as an instance of the "evil principle." From this we may judge to how great an extent the city of Athens, although fairly liberal and fond of innovations, abused the reputation of Plato during his lifetime. What wonder then that he—who, as he has himself recorded, had the "political instinct" in his body—made three different attempts in Sicily, where at that time a united Mediterranean Greek State appeared to be in process of formation?

It was in this State, and with its assistance, that Plato thought he could do for the Greeks what Mohammed did for the Arabs several centuries later: viz. establishing both minor and more important customs, and especially regulating the daily life of every man. His ideas were quite practicable just as certainly as those of Mohammed were practicable; for even much more incredible ideas, those of Christianity, proved themselves to be practicable! a few hazards less and a few hazards more—and then the world would have witnessed the Platonisation of Southern Europe; and, if we suppose that this state of things had continued to our own days, we should probably be worshipping Plato now as the "good principle." But he was unsuccessful, and so his traditional character remains that of a dreamer and a Utopian—stronger epithets than these passed away with ancient Athens.

497. THE PURIFYING EYE.—We have the best reason for speaking of "genius" in men—for example, Plato, Spinoza, and Goethe—whose minds appear to be but loosely linked to their character and temperament, like winged beings which easily separate themselves from them, and then rise far above them. On the other hand, those who never succeeded in cutting themselves loose from their temperament, and who knew how to give to it the most intellectual, lofty, and at times even cosmic expression (Schopenhauer, for instance) have always been very fond of speaking about their genius.

These geniuses could not rise above themselves, but they believed that, fly where they would, they would always find and recover themselves—this is their "greatness," and this can be greatness!—The others who are entitled to this name possess the pure and purifying eye which does not seem to have sprung out of their temperament and character, but separately from them, and generally in contradiction to them, and looks out upon the world as on a God whom it loves. But even people like these do not come into possession of such an eye all at once: they require practice and a preliminary school of sight, and he who is really fortunate will at the right moment also fall in with a teacher of pure sight.

498. NEVER DEMAND!—You do not know him! it is true that he easily and readily submits both to men and things, and that he is kind to both—his only wish is to be left in peace—but only in so far as men and things do not demand his submission. Any demand makes him proud, bashful, and warlike.

499. THE EVIL ONE.—"Only the solitary are evil!"—thus spake Diderot, and Rousseau at once felt deeply offended. Thus he proved that Diderot was right. Indeed, in society, or amid social life, every evil instinct is compelled to restrain itself, to assume so many masks, and to press itself so often into the Procrustean bed of virtue, that we are quite justified in speaking of the martyrdom of the evil man. In solitude, however, all this disappears. The evil man is still more evil in solitude—and consequently for him whose eye sees only a drama everywhere he is also more beautiful.

500. AGAINST THE GRAIN.—A thinker may for years at a time force himself to think against the grain: that is, not to pursue the thoughts that spring up within him, but, instead, those which he is compelled to follow by the exigencies of his office, an established division of time, or any arbitrary duty which he may find it necessary to fulfil. In the long run, however, he will fall ill; for this apparently moral self-command will destroy his nervous system as thoroughly and completely as regular debauchery.

501. MORTAL SOULS.—Where knowledge is concerned perhaps the most useful conquest that has ever been made is the abandonment of the belief in the immortality of the soul. Humanity is henceforth at liberty to wait: men need no longer be in a hurry to swallow badly-tested ideas as they had to do in former times. For in those times the salvation of this poor "immortal soul" depended upon the extent of the knowledge which could be acquired in the course of a short existence: decisions had to be reached from one day to another, and "knowledge" was a matter of dreadful importance!

Now we have acquired good courage for errors, experiments, and the provisional acceptance of ideas—all this is not so very important!—and for this very reason individuals and whole races may now face tasks so vast in extent that in former years they would have looked like madness, and defiance of heaven and hell. Now we have the right to experiment upon ourselves! Yes, men have the right to do so! the greatest sacrifices have not yet been offered up to knowledge—nay, in earlier periods it would have been sacrilege, and a sacrifice of our eternal salvation, even to surmise such ideas as now precede our actions.

502. ONE WORD FOR THREE DIFFERENT CONDITIONS.—When in a state of passion one man will be forced to let loose the savage, dreadful, unbearable animal. Another when under the influence of passion will raise himself to a high, noble, and lofty demeanour, in comparison with which his usual self appears petty. A third, whose whole person is permeated with nobility of feeling, has also the most noble storm and stress: and in this state he represents Nature in her state of savageness and beauty, and stands only one degree lower than Nature in her periods of greatness and serenity, which he usually represents. It is while in this state of passion, however, that men understand him better, and venerate him more highly at these moments—for then he is one step nearer and more akin to them. They feel at once delighted and horrified at such a sight and call it—divine.

503. FRIENDSHIP.—The objection to a philosophic life that it renders us useless to our friends would never have arisen in a modern mind: it belongs rather to classical antiquity. Antiquity knew the stronger bonds of friendship, meditated upon it, and almost took it to the grave with it. This is the advantage it has over us: we, on the other hand, can point to our idealisation of sexual love. All the great excellencies of ancient humanity owed their stability to the fact that man was standing side by side with man, and that no woman was allowed to put forward the claim of being the nearest and highest, nay even sole object of his love, as the feeling of passion would teach. Perhaps our trees do not grow so high now owing to the ivy and the vines that cling round them.

504. RECONCILIATION.—Should it then be the task of philosophy to reconcile what the child has learnt with what the man has come to recognise? Should philosophy be the task of young men because they stand midway between child and man and possess intermediate necessities? It would almost appear to be so if you consider at what ages of their life philosophers are now in the habit of setting forth their conceptions: at a time when it is too late for faith and too early for knowledge.

505. PRACTICAL PEOPLE.—We thinkers have the right of deciding good taste in all things, and if necessary of decreeing it. The practical people finally receive it from us: their dependence upon us is incredibly great, and is one of the most ridiculous spectacles in the world, little though they themselves know it and however proudly they like to carp at us unpractical people. Nay, they would even go so far as to belittle their practical life if we should show a tendency to despise it—whereto at times we might be urged on by a slightly vindictive feeling.

506. THE NECESSARY DESICCATION OF EVERYTHING GOOD.—What! must we conceive of a work exactly in the spirit of the age that has produced it? but we experience greater delight and surprise, and get more information out of it when we do not conceive it in this spirit! Have you not remarked that every new and good work, so long as it is exposed to the damp air of its own age is least valuable—just because it still has about it all the odour of the market, of opposition, of modern ideas, and of all that is transient from day to day? Later on, however, it dries up, its "actuality" dies away: and then only does it obtain its deep lustre and its perfume—and also, if it is destined for it, the calm eye of eternity.

507. AGAINST THE TYRANNY OF TRUTH.—Even if we were mad enough to consider all our

opinions as truth, we should nevertheless not wish them alone to exist. I cannot see why we should ask for an autocracy and omnipotence of truth: it is sufficient for me to know that it is a great power. Truth, however, must meet with opposition and be able to fight, and we must be able to rest from it at times in falsehood—otherwise truth will grow tiresome, powerless, and insipid, and will render us equally so.

508. NOT TO TAKE A THING PATHETICALLY.—What we do to benefit ourselves should not bring us in any moral praise, either from others or from ourselves, and the same remark applies to those things which we do to please ourselves. It is looked upon as bon ton among superior men to refrain from taking things pathetically in such cases, and to refrain from all pathetic feelings: the man who has accustomed himself to this has retrieved his naïveté.

509. THE THIRD EYE.—What! You are still in need of the theatre! are you still so young? Be wise, and seek tragedy and comedy where they are better acted, and where the incidents are more interesting, and the actors more eager. It is indeed by no means easy to be merely a spectator in these cases—but learn! and then, amid all difficult or painful situations, you will have a little gate leading to joy and refuge, even when your passions attack you. Open your stage eye, that big third eye of yours, which looks out into the world through the other two.

510. ESCAPING FROM ONE'S VIRTUES.—Of what account is a thinker who does not know how to escape from his own virtues occasionally! Surely a thinker should be more than "a moral being"!

511. THE TEMPTRESS.—Honesty is the great temptress of all fanatics.[15] What seemed to tempt Luther in the guise of the devil or a beautiful woman, and from which he defended himself in that uncouth way of his, was probably nothing but honesty, and perhaps in a few rarer cases even truth.

512. BOLD TOWARDS THINGS.—The man who, in accordance with his character, is considerate and timid towards persons, but is courageous and bold towards things, is afraid of new and closer acquaintances, and limits his old ones in order that he may thus make his incognito and his inconsiderateness coincide with truth.

513. LIMITS AND BEAUTY.—Are you looking for men with a fine culture? Then you will have to be satisfied with restricted views and sights, exactly as when you are looking for fine countries.—There are, of course, such panoramic men: they are like panoramic regions, instructive and marvellous: but not beautiful.

514. TO THE STRONGER.—Ye stronger and arrogant intellects, we ask you for only one thing: throw no further burdens upon our shoulders, but take some of our burdens upon your own, since ye are stronger! but ye delight in doing the exact contrary: for ye wish to soar, so that we must carry your burden in addition to our own—we must crawl!

515. THE INCREASE OF BEAUTY.—Why has beauty increased by the progress of civilisation? because the three occasions for ugliness appear ever more rarely among civilised men: first, the wildest outbursts of ecstasy; secondly, extreme bodily exertion, and, thirdly, the necessity of inducing fear by one's very sight and presence—a matter which is so frequent and of so great importance in the lower and more dangerous stages of culture that it even lays down the proper gestures and ceremonials and makes ugliness a duty.

516. NOT TO IMBUE OUR NEIGHBOURS WITH OUR OWN DEMON.—Let us in our age continue to hold the belief that benevolence and beneficence are the characteristics of a good man; but let us not fail to add "provided that in the first place he exhibits his benevolence and beneficence towards himself." For if he acts otherwise—that is to say, if he shuns, hates, or injures himself—he is certainly not a good man. He then merely saves himself through others: and let these others take care that they do not come to grief through him, however well disposed he may appear to be to them!—but to shun and hate one's own ego, and to live in and for others, this has up to the present, with as much thoughtlessness as conviction, been looked upon as "unselfish," and consequently as "good."

517. TEMPTING INTO LOVE.—We ought to fear a man who hates himself; for we are liable to become the victims of his anger and revenge. Let us therefore try to tempt him into self-love.

518. RESIGNATION.—What is resignation? It is the most comfortable position of a patient, who, after having suffered a long time from tormenting pains in order to find it, at last became tired—and then found it.

519. DECEPTION.—When you wish to act you must close the door upon doubt, said a man of action.—And are you not afraid of being deceived in doing so? replied the man of a contemplative mind.

520. ETERNAL OBSEQUIES.—Both within and beyond the confines of history we might imagine that we were listening to a continual funeral oration: we have buried, and are still burying, all that we have loved best, our thoughts, and our hopes, receiving in exchange pride, gloria mundi—that is, the pomp of the graveside speech. It is thus that everything is made good! Even at the present time the funeral orator remains the greatest public benefactor.

521. EXCEPTIONAL VANITY.—Yonder man possesses one great quality which serves as a consolation for him: his look passes with contempt over the remainder of his being, and almost his entire character is included in this. But he recovers from himself when, as it were, he approaches his

sanctuary; already the road leading to it appears to him to be an ascent on broad soft steps—and yet, ye cruel ones, ye call him vain on this account!

522. WISDOM WITHOUT EARS.—To hear every day what is said about us, or even to endeavour to discover what people think of us, will in the end kill even the strongest man. Our neighbours permit us to live only that they may exercise a daily claim upon us! They certainly would not tolerate us if we wished to claim rights over them, and still less if we wished to be right! In short, let us offer up a sacrifice to the general peace, let us not listen when they speak of us, when they praise us, blame us, wish for us, or hope for us—nay, let us not even think of it.

523. A QUESTION OF PENETRATION.—When we are confronted with any manifestation which some one has permitted us to see, we may ask: what is it meant to conceal? What is it meant to draw our attention from? What prejudices does it seek to raise? and again, how far does the subtlety of the dissimulation go? and in what respect is the man mistaken?

524. THE JEALOUSY OF THE LONELY ONES.—This is the difference between sociable and solitary natures, provided that both possess an intellect: the former are satisfied, or nearly satisfied, with almost anything whatever; from the moment that their minds have discovered a communicable and happy version of it they will be reconciled even with the devil himself! But the lonely souls have their silent rapture, and their speechless agony about a thing: they hate the ingenious and brilliant display of their inmost problems as much as they dislike to see the women they love too loudly dressed—they watch her mournfully in such a case, as if they were just beginning to suspect that she was desirous of pleasing others. This is the jealousy which all lonely thinkers and passionate dreamers exhibit with regard to the esprit.

525. THE EFFECT OF PRAISE.—Some people become modest when highly praised, others insolent.

526. UNWILLING TO BE A SYMBOL.—I sympathise with princes: they are not at liberty to discard their high rank even for a short time, and thus they come to know people only from the very uncomfortable position of constant dissimulation—their continual compulsion to represent something actually ends by making solemn ciphers of them.—Such is the fate of all those who deem it their duty to be symbols.

527. THE HIDDEN MEN.—Have you never come across those people who check and restrain even their enraptured hearts, and who would rather become mute than lose the modesty of moderation? and have you never met those embarrassing, and yet so often good-natured people who do not wish to be recognised, and who time and again efface the tracks they have made in the sand? and who even deceive others as well as themselves in order to remain obscure and hidden?

528. UNUSUAL FORBEARANCE.—It is often no small indication of kindness to be unwilling to criticise some one, and even to refuse to think of him.

529. HOW MEN AND NATIONS GAIN LUSTRE.—How many really individual actions are left undone merely because before performing them we perceive or suspect that they will be misunderstood!—those actions, for example, which have some intrinsic value, both in good and evil. The more highly an age or a nation values its individuals, therefore, and the more right and ascendancy we accord them, the more will actions of this kind venture to make themselves known,—and thus in the long run a lustre of honesty, of genuineness in good and evil, will spread over entire ages and nations, so that they—the Greeks, for example—like certain stars, will continue to shed light for thousands of years after their sinking.

530. DIGRESSIONS OF THE THINKER.—The course of thought in certain men is strict and inflexibly bold. At times it is even cruel towards such men, although considered individually they may be gentle and pliable. With well-meaning hesitation they will turn the matter ten times over in their heads, but will at length continue their strict course. They are like streams that wind their way past solitary hermitages: there are places in their course where the stream plays hide and seek with itself, and indulges in short idylls with islets, trees, grottos, and cascades—and then it rushes ahead once more, passes by the rocks, and forces its way through the hardest stones.

531. DIFFERENT FEELINGS TOWARDS ART.—From the time when we begin to live as a hermit, consuming and consumed, our only company being deep and prolific thoughts, we expect from art either nothing more, or else something quite different from what we formerly expected—in a word, we change our taste. For in former times we wished to penetrate for a moment by means of art into the element in which we are now living permanently: at that time we dreamt ourselves into the rapture of a possession which we now actually possess. Indeed, flinging away from us for the time being what we now have, and imagining ourselves to be poor, or to be a child, a beggar, or a fool, may now at times fill us with delight.

532. "LOVE EQUALISES."—Love wishes to spare the other to whom it devotes itself any feeling of strangeness: as a consequence it is permeated with disguise and simulation; it keeps on deceiving continuously, and feigns an equality which in reality does not exist. And all this is done so instinctively that women who love deny this simulation and constant tender trickery, and have even the audacity to

assert that love equalises (in other words that it performs a miracle)!

This phenomenon is a simple matter if one of the two permits himself or herself to be loved, and does not deem it necessary to feign, but leaves this to the other. No drama, however, could offer a more intricate and confused instance than when both persons are passionately in love with one another; for in this case both are anxious to surrender and to endeavour to conform to the other, and finally they are both at a loss to know what to imitate and what to feign. The beautiful madness of this spectacle is too good for this world, and too subtle for human eyes.

533. WE BEGINNERS.—How many things does an actor see and divine when he watches another on the stage! He notices at once when a muscle fails in some gesture; he can distinguish those little artificial tricks which are so calmly practised separately before the mirror, and are not in conformity with the whole; he feels when the actor is surprised on the stage by his own invention, and when he spoils it amid this surprise.—How differently, again, does a painter look at some one who happens to be moving before him! He will see a great deal that does not actually exist in order to complete the actual appearance of the person, and to give it its full effect. In his mind he attempts several different illuminations of the same object, and divides the whole by an additional contrast.—Oh, that we now possessed the eyes of such an actor and such a painter for the province of the human soul!

534. SMALL DOSES.—If we wish a change to be as deep and radical as possible, we must apply the remedy in minute doses, but unremittingly for long periods. What great action can be performed all at once? Let us therefore be careful not to exchange violently and precipitately the moral conditions with which we are familiar for a new valuation of things,—nay, we may even wish to continue living in the old way for a long time to come, until probably at some very remote period we become aware of the fact that the new valuation has made itself the predominating power within us, and that its minute doses to which we must henceforth become accustomed have set up a new nature within us.—We now also begin to understand that the last attempt at a great change of valuations—that which concerned itself with political affairs (the "great revolution")—was nothing more than a pathetic and sanguinary piece of quackery which, by means of sudden crises, was able to inspire a credulous Europe with the hope of a sudden recovery, and has therefore made all political invalids impatient and dangerous up to this very moment.

535. TRUTH REQUIRES POWER.—Truth in itself is no power at all, in spite of all that flattering rationalists are in the habit of saying to the contrary. Truth must either attract power to its side, or else side with power, for otherwise it will perish again and again. This has already been sufficiently demonstrated, and more than sufficiently!

536. THE THUMBSCREW.—It is disgusting to observe with what cruelty every one charges his two or three private virtues to the account of others who may perhaps not possess them, and whom he torments and worries with them. Let us therefore deal humanely with the "sense of honesty," although we may possess in it a thumbscrew with which we can worry to death all these presumptuous egoists who even yet wish to impose their own beliefs upon the whole world—we have tried this thumbscrew on ourselves!

537. MASTERY.—We have reached mastery when we neither mistake nor hesitate in the achievement.

538. THE MORAL INSANITY OF GENIUS.—In a certain category of great intellects we may observe a painful and partly horrible spectacle: in their most productive moments their flights aloft and into the far distance appear to be out of harmony with their general constitution and to exceed their power in one way or another, so that each time there remains a deficiency, and also in the long run a defectiveness in the entire machinery, which latter is manifested among those highly intellectual natures by various kinds of moral and intellectual symptoms more regularly than by conditions of bodily distress.

Thus those incomprehensible characteristics of their nature—all their timidity, vanity, hatefulness, envy, their narrow and narrowing disposition—and that too personal and awkward element in natures like those of Rousseau and Schopenhauer, may very well be the consequences of a periodical attack of heart disease; and this in its turn may be the result of a nervous complaint, and this latter the consequence of ——[16]

So long as genius dwells within us we are full of audacity, yea, almost mad, and heedless of health, life, and honour; we fly through the day as free and swift as an eagle, and in the darkness we feel as confident as an owl.—But let genius once leave us and we are instantly overcome by a feeling of the most profound despondency: we can no longer understand ourselves; we suffer from everything that we experience and do not experience; we feel as if we were in the midst of shelterless rocks with the tempest raging round us, and we are at the same time like pitiful childish souls, afraid of a rustle or a shadow.—Three-fourths of all the evil committed in the world is due to timidity; and this is above all a physiological process.

539. DO YOU KNOW WHAT YOU WANT?—Have you never been troubled by the fear that you might not be at all fitted for recognising what is true? by the fear that your senses might be too dull,

and even your delicacy of sight far too blunt? If you could only perceive, even once, to what extent your volition dominates your sight! How, for example, you wished yesterday to see more than some one else, while to-day you wish to see it differently! and how from the start you were anxious to see something which would be in conformity with or in opposition to anything that people thought they had observed up to the present. Oh, those shameful cravings! How often you keep your eyes open for what is efficacious, for what is soothing, just because you happen to be tired at the moment! Always full of secret predeterminations of what truth should be like, so that you—you, forsooth!—might accept it! or do you think that to-day, because you are as frozen and dry as a bright winter morning, and because nothing is weighing on your mind, you have better eyesight! Are not ardour and enthusiasm necessary to do justice to the creations of thought?—and this indeed is what is called sight! as if you could treat matters of thought any differently from the manner in which you treat men. In all relations with thought there is the same morality, the same honesty of purpose, the same arrière-pensée, the same slackness, the same faint-heartedness—your whole lovable and hateful self! Your physical exhaustion will lend the things pale colours whilst your feverishness will turn them into monsters! Does not your morning show the things in a different light from the evening? Are you not afraid of finding in the cave of all knowledge your own phantom, the veil in which truth is wrapped up and hidden from your sight? Is it not a dreadful comedy in which you so thoughtlessly wish to take part?

540. LEARNING.—Michelangelo considered Raphael's genius as having been acquired by study, and upon his own as a natural gift: learning as opposed to talent; though this is mere pedantry, with all due respect to the great pedant himself. For what is talent but a name for an older piece of learning, experience, exercise, appropriation, and incorporation, perhaps as far back as the times of our ancestors, or even earlier! And again: he who learns forms his own talents, only learning is not such an easy matter and depends not only upon our willingness, but also upon our being able to learn at all.

Jealousy often prevents this in an artist, or that pride which, when it experiences any strange feeling, at once assumes an attitude of defence instead of an attitude of scholarly receptiveness. Raphael, like Goethe, lacked this pride, on which account they were great learners, and not merely the exploiters of those quarries which had been formed by the manifold genealogy of their forefathers. Raphael vanishes before our eyes as a learner in the midst of that assimilation of what his great rival called his "nature": this noblest of all thieves daily carried off a portion of it; but before he had appropriated all the genius of Michelangelo he died—and the final series of his works, because it is the beginning of a new plan of study, is less perfect and good, for the simple reason that the great student was interrupted by death in the midst of his most difficult task, and took away with him that justifying and final goal which he had in view.

541. HOW WE SHOULD TURN TO STONE.—By slowly, very, very slowly, becoming hard like a precious stone, and at last lie still, a joy to all eternity.

542. THE PHILOSOPHER AND OLD AGE.—It is not wise to permit evening to act as a judge of the day; for only too often in this case weariness becomes the judge of success and good will. We should also take the greatest precautions in regard to everything connected with old age and its judgment upon life, more especially since old age, like the evening, is fond of assuming a new and charming morality, and knows well enough how to humiliate the day by the glow of the evening skies, twilight and a peaceful and wistful silence. The reverence which we feel for an old man, especially if he is an old thinker and sage, easily blinds us to the deterioration of his intellect, and it is always necessary to bring to light the hidden symptoms of such a deterioration and lassitude, that is to say, to uncover the physiological phenomenon which is still concealed behind the old man's moral judgments and prejudices, in case we should be deceived by our veneration for him, and do something to the disadvantage of knowledge. For it is not seldom that the illusion of a great moral renovation and regeneration takes possession of the old man. Basing his views upon this, he then proceeds to express his opinions on the work and development of his life as if he had only then for the first time become clearsighted—and nevertheless it is not wisdom, but fatigue, which prompts his present state of well-being and his positive judgments.

The most dangerous indication of this weariness is above all the belief in genius, which as a rule only arises in great and semi-great men of intellect at this period of their lives: the belief in an exceptional position, and exceptional rights. The thinker who thus believes himself to be inspired by genius henceforth deems it permissible for him to take things more easily, and takes advantage of his position as a genius to decree rather than to prove. It is probable, however, that the need felt by the weary intellect for alleviation is the main source of this belief—it precedes it in time, though appearances may indicate the contrary.

At this time too, as the result of the love which all weary and old people feel for enjoyment, such men as those I am speaking of wish to enjoy the results of their thinking instead of again testing them and scattering the seeds abroad once more. This leads them to make their thoughts palatable and enjoyable, and to take away their dryness, coldness, and want of flavour; and thus it comes about that the old thinker apparently raises himself above his life's work, while in reality he spoils it by infusing into it a certain amount of fantasy, sweetness, flavour, poetic mists, and mystic lights. This is how Plato ended, as did also that great and honest Frenchman, Auguste Comte, who, as a conqueror of the exact sciences, cannot be matched either among the Germans or the Englishmen of this century.

There is a third symptom of fatigue: that ambition which actuated the great thinker when he was young, and which could not then find anything to satisfy it, has also grown old, and, like one that has no more time to lose, it begins to snatch at the coarser and more immediate means of its gratification, means which are peculiar to active, dominating, violent, and conquering dispositions. From this time onwards the thinker wishes to found institutions which shall bear his name, instead of erecting mere brain-structures. What are now to him the ethereal victories and honours to be met with in the realm of proofs and refutations, or the perpetuation of his fame in books, or the thrill of exultation in the soul of the reader? But the institution, on the other hand, is a temple, as he well knows—a temple of stone, a durable edifice, which will keep its god alive with more certainty than the sacrifices of rare and tender souls.[17]

Perhaps, too, at this period of his life the old thinker will for the first time meet with that love which is fitted for a god rather than for a human being, and his whole nature becomes softened and sweetened in the rays of such a sun, like fruit in autumn. Yes, he grows more divine and beautiful, this great old man,—and nevertheless it is old age and weariness which permit him to ripen in this way, to grow more silent, and to repose in the luminous adulation of a woman. Now it is all up with his former desire—a desire which was superior even to his own ego—for real disciples, followers who would carry on his thought, that is, true opponents. This desire arose from his hitherto undiminished energy, the conscious pride he felt in being able at any time to become an opponent himself,—nay, even the deadly enemy of his own doctrine,—but now his desire is for resolute partisans, unwavering comrades, auxiliary forces, heralds, a pompous train of followers. He is now no longer able to bear that dreadful isolation in which every intellect that advances beyond the others is compelled to live. From this time forward he surrounds himself with objects of veneration, companionship, tenderness, and love; but he also wishes to enjoy the privileges of all religious people, and to worship what he venerates most highly in his little community—he will even go as far as to invent a religion for the purpose of having a community.

Thus lives the wise old man, and in living thus he falls almost imperceptibly into such a deplorable proximity to priestly and poetic extravagances that it is difficult to recollect all his wise and severe period of youth, the former rigid morality of his mind, and his truly virile dread of fancies and misplaced enthusiasm. When he was formerly in the habit of comparing himself with the older thinkers, he did so merely that he might measure his weakness against their strength, and that he might become colder and more audacious towards himself; but now he only makes this comparison to intoxicate himself with his own delusions. Formerly he looked forward with confidence to future thinkers, and he even took a delight in imagining himself to be cast into the shade by their brighter light. Now, however, he is mortified to think that he cannot be the last: he endeavours to discover some way of imposing upon mankind, together with the inheritance which he is leaving to them, a restriction of sovereign thinking. He fears and reviles the pride and the love of freedom of individual minds: after him no one must allow his intellect to govern with absolute unrestriction: he himself wishes to remain for ever the bulwark on which the waves of ideas may break—these are his secret wishes, and perhaps, indeed, they are not always secret.

The hard fact upon which such wishes are based, however, is that he himself has come to a halt before his teaching, and has set up his boundary stone, his "thus far and no farther." In canonising himself he has drawn up his own death warrant: from now on his mind cannot develop further. His race is run; the hour-hand stops. Whenever a great thinker tries to make himself a lasting institution for posterity, we may readily suppose that he has passed the climax of his powers, and is very tired, very near the setting of his sun.

543. WE MUST NOT MAKE PASSION AN ARGUMENT FOR TRUTH.—Oh, you kind-hearted and even noble enthusiasts, I know you! You wish to seem right in our eyes as well as in your own, but especially in your own!—and an irritable and subtle evil conscience so often spurs you on against your very enthusiasm! How ingenious you then become in deceiving your conscience, and lulling it to sleep! How you hate honest, simple, and clean souls; how you avoid their innocent glances! That better knowledge whose representatives they are, and whose voice you hear only too distinctly within yourselves when it questions your belief,—how you try to cast suspicion upon it as a bad habit, as a disease of the age, as the neglect and infection of your own intellectual health! It drives you on to hate even criticism, science, reason! You must falsify history to make it testify in your favour; you must deny virtues in case they should obscure those of your own idols and ideals.

Coloured images where arguments are needed! Ardour and power of expression! Silver mists! Ambrosian nights! well do you know how to enlighten and to darken—to darken by means of light! and indeed when your passion can no longer be kept within bounds the moment comes when you say to yourselves, "Now I have won for myself a good conscience, now I am exalted, courageous, self-denying, magnanimous; now I am honest!" How you long for these moments when your passion will confer upon you full and absolute rights, and also, as it were, innocence. How happy you are when engaged in battle and inspired with ecstasy or courage, when you are elated beyond yourself, when gnawing doubt has left you, and when you can even decree: "Any man who is not in ecstasy as we are cannot by any chance know what or where truth is." How you long to meet with those who share your belief in this state—which is a state of intellectual depravity—and to set your own fire alight with their flames! Oh, for your martyrdom, your victory of the sanctified lie! Must you really inflict so much pain upon yourselves?—Must you?

544. HOW PHILOSOPHY IS NOW PRACTISED.—I can see quite well that our philosophising youths, women, and artists require from philosophy exactly the opposite of what the Greeks derived from it. What does he who does not hear the continual exultation that resounds through every speech and counter-argument in a Platonic dialogue, this exultation over the new invention of rational thinking, know about Plato or about ancient philosophy? At that time souls were filled with enthusiasm when they gave themselves up to the severe and sober sport of ideas, generalisations, refutations,—that enthusiasm which perhaps those old, great, severe, and prudent contrapuntists in music have also known. At that time the Greek palate still possessed that older and formerly omnipotent taste: and by the side of this taste their new taste appeared to be enveloped in so much charm that the divine art of dialectic was sung by hesitating voices as if its followers were intoxicated with the frenzy of love. That old form of thinking, however, was thought within the bounds of morality, and for it nothing existed but fixed judgments and established facts, and it had no reasons but those of authority. Thinking, therefore, was simply a matter of repetition, and all the enjoyment of speech and dialogue could only lie in their form.

Wherever the substance of a thing is looked upon as eternal and universally approved, there is only one great charm, the charm of variable forms, that is, of fashion. Even in the poets ever since the time of Homer, and later on in the case of the sculptors, the Greeks did not enjoy originality, but its contrary. It was Socrates who discovered another charm, that of cause and effect, of reason and sequence, and we moderns have become so used to it, and have been brought up to the necessity of logic that we look upon it as the normal taste, and as such it cannot but be repugnant to ardent and presumptuous people. Such people are pleased by whatever stands out boldly from the normal: their more subtle ambition leads them to believe only too readily that they are exceptional souls, not dialectic and rational beings, but, let us say, "intuitive" beings gifted with an "inner sense," or with a certain "intellectual perception." Above all, however, they wish to be "artistic natures" with a genius in their heads, and a demon in their bodies, and consequently with special rights in this world and in the world to come—especially the divine privilege of being incomprehensible.

And people like these are "going in for" philosophy nowadays! I fear they will discover one day that they have made a mistake—what they are looking for is religion!

545. BUT WE DO NOT BELIEVE YOU.—You would fain pass for psychologists, but we shall not allow it! Are we not to notice that you pretend to be more experienced, profound, passionate, and perfect than you actually are?—just as we notice in yonder painter that there is a trifling presumptuousness in his manner of wielding the brush, and in yonder musician that he brings forward his theme with the desire to make it appear superior to what it really is. Have you experienced history within yourselves, commotions, earthquakes, long and profound sadness, and sudden flashes of happiness? Have you acted foolishly with great and little fools? Have you really undergone the delusions and woe of the good people? and also the woe and the peculiar happiness of the most evil? Then you may speak to me of morality, but not otherwise!

546. SLAVE AND IDEALIST.—The followers of Epictetus would doubtless not be to the taste of those who are now striving after the ideal. The constant tension of his being, the indefatigable inward glance, the prudent and reserved incommunicativeness of his eye whenever it happens to gaze upon the outer world, and above all, his silence or laconic speech: all these are characteristics of the strictest fortitude,—and what would our idealists, who above all else are desirous of expansion, care for this? But in spite of all this the Stoic is not fanatical. He detests the display and boasting of our idealists: his pride, however great it may be, is not eager to disturb others. It permits of a certain gentle approach, and has no desire to spoil anybody's good humour—nay, it can even smile. A great deal of ancient humanity is to be seen exemplified in this ideal. The most excellent feature about it, however, is that the thinker is completely free from the fear of God, strictly believes in reason, and is no preacher of penitence.

Epictetus was a slave: his ideal man is without any particular rank, and may exist in any grade of society, but above all he is to be sought in the deepest and lowest social classes, as the silent and self-sufficient man in the midst of a general state of servitude, a man who defends himself alone against the outer world, and is constantly living in a state of the highest fortitude. He is distinguished from the Christian especially, because the latter lives in hope in the promise of "unspeakable glory," permits presents to be made to him, and expects and accepts the best things from divine love and grace, and not from himself. Epictetus, on the other hand, neither hopes nor allows his best treasure to be given him—

he possesses it already, holds it bravely in his hand, and defies the world to take it away from him. Christianity was devised for another class of ancient slaves, for those who had a weak will and weak reason—that is to say, for the majority of slaves.

547. THE TYRANTS OF THE INTELLECT.—The progress of science is at the present time no longer hindered by the purely accidental fact that man attains to about seventy years, which was the case far too long. In former times people wished to master the entire extent of knowledge within this period, and all the methods of knowledge were valued according to this general desire. Minor questions and individual experiments were looked upon as unworthy of notice: people wanted to take the shortest path under the impression that, since everything in this world seemed to be arranged with a view to man's needs, even the acquirement of knowledge was regulated in view of the limits of human life.

To solve everything at a single stroke, with one word—this was the secret desire; and the task was represented in the symbol of the Gordian knot or the egg of Columbus. No one doubted that it was possible to reach the goal of knowledge after the manner of Alexander or Columbus, and to settle all questions with one answer. "There is a mystery to be solved," seemed to be the aim of life in the eyes of the philosopher: it was necessary in the first place to find out what this enigma was, and to condense the problem of the world into the simplest enigmatical formula possible. The boundless ambition and delight of being the "unraveller of the world" charmed the dreams of many a thinker: nothing seemed to him worth troubling about in this world but the means of bringing everything to a satisfactory conclusion. Philosophy thus became a kind of supreme struggle for the tyrannical sway over the intellect, and no one doubted that such a tyrannical domination was reserved for some very happy, subtle, ingenious, bold, and powerful person—a single individual!—and many (the last was Schopenhauer) fancied themselves to be this privileged person.

From this it follows that, on the whole, science has up to the present remained in a rather backward state owing to the moral narrow-mindedness of its disciples, and that henceforth it will have to be pursued from a higher and more generous motive. "What do I matter?" is written over the door of the thinker of the future.

548. VICTORY OVER POWER.—If we consider all that has been venerated up to the present as "superhuman intellect" or "genius," we must come to the sad conclusion that, considered as a whole, the intellectuality of mankind must have been extremely low and poor: so little mind has hitherto been necessary in order to feel at once considerably superior to all this! Alas for the cheap glory of "genius"! How quickly has it been raised to the throne, and its worship grown into a custom! We still fall on our knees before power—according to the old custom of slaves—and nevertheless, when the degree of venerability comes to be determined, only the degree of reason in the power will be the deciding factor. We must find out, indeed, to how great an extent power has been overcome by something higher, which it now obeys as a tool and instrument.

As yet, however, there have been too few eyes for such investigations: even in the majority of cases the mere valuation of genius has almost been looked upon as blasphemy. And thus perhaps everything that is most beautiful still takes place in the midst of darkness and vanishes in endless night almost as soon as it has made its appearance,—I refer to the spectacle of that power which a genius does not lay out upon works, but upon himself as a work, that is, his own self-control, the purifying of his own imagination, the order and selection in his inspirations and tasks. The great man ever remains invisible in the greatest thing that claims worship, like some distant star: his victory over power remains without witnesses, and hence also without songs and singers. The hierarchy of the great men in all the past history of the human race has not yet been determined.

549. FLIGHT FROM ONE'S SELF.—Those sufferers from intellectual spasms who are impatient towards themselves and look upon themselves with a gloomy eye—such as Byron or Alfred de Musset—and who, in everything that they do, resemble runaway horses, and from their own works derive only a transient joy and an ardent passion which almost bursts their veins, followed by sterility and disenchantment—how are they able to bear up! They would fain attain to something "beyond themselves." If we happen to be Christians, and are seized by such a desire as this, we strive to reach God and to become one with Him; if we are a Shakespeare we shall be glad to perish in images of a passionate life; if we are like Byron we long for actions, because these detach us from ourselves to an even greater extent than thoughts, feelings, and works.

And should the desire for performing great deeds really be at bottom nothing but a flight from our own selves?—as Pascal would ask us. And indeed this assertion might be proved by considering the most noble representations of this desire for action: in this respect let us remember, bringing the knowledge of an alienist to our aid, that four of the greatest men of all ages who were possessed of this lust for action were epileptics—Alexander the Great, Cæsar, Mohammed, and Napoleon; and Byron likewise was subject to the same complaint.

550. KNOWLEDGE AND BEAUTY.—If men, as they are still in the habit of doing, reserve their veneration and feelings of happiness for works of fancy and imagination, we should not be surprised if they feel chilled and displeased by the contrary of fancy and imagination. The rapture which arises from

even the smallest, sure, and definite step in advance into insight, and which our present state of science yields to so many in such abundance—this rapture is in the meantime not believed in by all those who are in the habit of feeling enraptured only when they leave reality altogether and plunge into the depths of vague appearance—romanticism. These people look upon reality as ugly, but they entirely overlook the fact that the knowledge of even the ugliest reality is beautiful, and that the man who can discern much and often is in the end very far from considering as ugly the main items of that reality, the discovery of which has always inspired him with the feeling of happiness.

Is there anything "beautiful in itself"? The happiness of those who can recognise augments the beauty of the world, bathing everything that exists in a sunnier light: discernment not only envelops all things in its own beauty, but in the long run permeates the things themselves with its beauty—may ages to come bear witness to the truth of this statement! In the meantime let us recall an old experience: two men so thoroughly different in every respect as Plato and Aristotle were agreed in regard to what constituted superior happiness—not merely their own and that of men in general, but happiness in itself, even the happiness of the gods. They found this happiness to lie in knowledge, in the activity of a well practised and inventive understanding (not in "intuition" like the German theologians and semi-theologians; not in visions, like the mystics; and not in work, like the merely practical men). Similar opinions were expressed by Descartes and Spinoza. What great delight must all these men have felt in knowledge! and how great was the danger that their honesty might give way, and that they themselves might become panegyrists of things!

551. FUTURE VIRTUES.—How has it come about that, the more intelligible the world has become, the more all kinds of ceremonies have diminished? Was fear so frequently the fundamental basis of that awe which overcame us at the sight of anything hitherto unknown and mysterious, and which taught us to fall upon our knees before the unintelligible, and to beg for mercy? And has the world, perhaps, through the very fact that we have grown less timid, lost some of the charms it formerly had for us? Is it not possible that our own dignity and stateliness, our formidable character, has decreased together with our spirit of dread? Perhaps we value the world and ourselves less highly since we have begun to think more boldly about it and ourselves? Perhaps there will come a moment in the future when this courageous spirit of thinking will have reached such a point that it will feel itself soaring in supreme pride, far above men and things—when the wise man, being also the boldest, will see himself and even more particularly existence, the lowest of all beneath himself?

This type of courage, which is not far removed from excessive generosity, has been lacking in humanity up to the present.—Oh, that our poets might once again become what they once were: seers, telling us something about what might possibly happen! now that what is real and what is past are being ever more and more taken from them, and must continue to be taken from them—for the time of innocent counterfeiting is at an end! Let them try to enable us to anticipate future virtues, or virtues that will never be found on earth, although they may exist somewhere in the world!—purple-glowing constellations and whole Milky Ways of the beautiful! Where are ye, ye astronomers of the ideal?

552. IDEAL SELFISHNESS.—Is there a more sacred state than that of pregnancy? To perform every one of our actions in the silent conviction that in one way or another it will be to the benefit of that which is being generated within us—that it must augment its mysterious value, the very thought of which fills us with rapture? At such a time we refrain from many things without having to force ourselves to do so: we suppress the angry word, we grasp the hand forgivingly; our child must be born from all that is best and gentlest. We shun our own harshness and brusqueness in case it should instil a drop of unhappiness into the cup of the beloved unknown. Everything is veiled, ominous; we know nothing about what is going on, but simply wait and try to be prepared. During this time, too, we experience a pure and purifying feeling of profound irresponsibility, similar to that felt by a spectator before a drawn curtain; it is growing, it is coming to light; we have nothing to do with determining its value, or the hour of its arrival. We are thrown back altogether upon indirect, beneficent and defensive influences. "Something greater than we are is growing here"—such is our most secret hope: we prepare everything with a view to his birth and prosperity—not merely everything that is useful, but also the noblest gifts of our souls.

We should, and can, live under the influence of such a blessed inspiration! Whether what we are looking forward to is a thought or a deed, our relationship to every essential achievement is none other than that of pregnancy, and all our vainglorious boasting about "willing" and "creating" should be cast to the winds! True and ideal selfishness consists in always watching over and restraining the soul, so that our productiveness may come to a beautiful termination. Thus in this indirect manner we must provide for and watch over the good of all; and the frame of mind, the mood in which we live, is a kind of soothing oil which spreads far around us on the restless souls.—Still, these pregnant ones are funny people! let us therefore dare to be funny also, and not reproach others if they must be the same. And even when this phenomenon becomes dangerous and evil we must not show less respect to that which is generating within us or others than ordinary worldly justice, which does not allow the judge or the hangman to interfere with a pregnant woman.

553. CIRCUITOUS ROUTES.—Where does all this philosophy mean to end with its circuitous routes? Does it do more than transpose into reason, so to speak, a continuous and strong impulse—a craving for a mild sun, a bright and bracing atmosphere, southern plants, sea breezes, short meals of meat, eggs, and fruit, hot water to drink, quiet walks for days at a time, little talking, rare and cautious reading, living alone, pure, simple, and almost soldier-like habits—a craving, in short, for all things which are suited to my own personal taste? a philosophy which is in the main the instinct for a personal regimen—an instinct that longs for my air, my height, my temperature, and my kind of health, and takes the circuitous route of my head to persuade me to it!

There are many other and certainly more lofty philosophies, and not only such as are more gloomy and pretentious than mine—and are they perhaps, taking them as a whole, nothing but intellectual circuitous routes of the same kind of personal impulses?—In the meantime I look with a new eye upon the mysterious and solitary flight of a butterfly high on the rocky banks of the lake where so many plants are growing: there it flies hither and thither, heedless of the fact that its life will last only one more day, and that the night will be too cold for its winged fragility. For it, too, a philosophy might be found, though it might not be my own.

554. LEADING.[18]—When we praise progress we only praise the movement and those who do not let us remain on the same spot, and in the circumstances this is certainly something, especially if we live among Egyptians. In changeable Europe, however, where movement is "understood," to use their own expression, "as a matter of course"—alas, if we only understood something about it too!—I praise leaders and forerunners: that is to say, those who always leave themselves behind, and do not care in the least whether any one is following them or not. "Wherever I halt I find myself alone: why should I halt! the desert is still so wide!"—such is the sentiment of the true leader.

555. THE LEAST IMPORTANT ARE SUFFICIENT.—We ought to avoid events when we know that even the least important of them frequently enough leave a strong impression upon us—and these we cannot avoid.—The thinker must possess an approximate canon of all the things he still wishes to experience.

556. THE FOUR VIRTUES.—Honest towards ourselves, and to all and everything friendly to us; brave in the face of our enemy; generous towards the vanquished; polite at all times: such do the four cardinal virtues wish us to be.

557. MARCHING AGAINST AN ENEMY.—How pleasant is the sound of even bad music and bad motives when we are setting out to march against an enemy!

558. NOT CONCEALING ONE'S VIRTUES.—I love those men who are as transparent as water, and who, to use Pope's expression, hide not from view the turbid bottom of their stream. Even they, however, possess a certain vanity, though of a rare and more sublimated kind: some of them would wish us to see nothing but the mud, and to take no notice of the clearness of the water which enables us to look right to the bottom. No less a man than Gautama Buddha has imagined the vanity of these few in the formula, "Let your sins appear before men, and conceal your virtues." But this would exhibit a disagreeable spectacle to the world—it would be a sin against good taste.

559. "NOTHING IN EXCESS!"—How often is the individual recommended to set up a goal which it is beyond his power to reach, in order that he may at least attain that which lies within the scope of his abilities and most strenuous efforts! Is it really so desirable, however, that he should do so? Do not the best men who try to act according to this doctrine, together with their best deeds, necessarily assume a somewhat exaggerated and distorted appearance on account of their excessive tension? and in the future will not a grey mist of failure envelop the world, owing to the fact that we may see everywhere struggling athletes and tremendous gestures, but nowhere a conqueror crowned with the laurel, and rejoicing in his victory?

560. WHAT WE ARE FREE TO DO.—We can act as the gardeners of our impulses, and—which few people know—we may cultivate the seeds of anger, pity, vanity, or excessive brooding, and make these things fecund and productive, just as we can train a beautiful plant to grow along trellis-work. We may do this with the good or bad taste of a gardener, and as it were, in the French, English, Dutch, or Chinese style. We may let nature take its own course, only trimming and embellishing a little here and there; and finally, without any knowledge or consideration, we may even allow the plants to spring up in accordance with their own natural growth and limitations, and fight out their battle among themselves,—nay, we can even take delight in such chaos, though we may possibly have a hard time with it! All this is at our option: but how many know that it is? Do not the majority of people believe in themselves as complete and perfect facts? and have not the great philosophers set their seal on this prejudice through their doctrine of the unchangeability of character?

561. LETTING OUR HAPPINESS ALSO SHINE.—In the same way as painters are unable to reproduce the deep brilliant hue of the natural sky, and are compelled to use all the colours they require for their landscapes a few shades deeper than nature has made them—just as they, by means of this trick, succeed in approaching the brilliancy and harmony of nature's own hues, so also must poets and philosophers, for whom the luminous rays of happiness are inaccessible, endeavour to find an

expedient. By picturing all things a shade or two darker than they really are, their light, in which they excel, will produce almost exactly the same effect as the sunlight, and will resemble the light of true happiness.—The pessimist, on the other hand, who paints all things in the blackest and most sombre hues, only makes use of bright flames, lightning, celestial glories, and everything that possesses a glaring, dazzling power, and bewilders our eyes: to him light only serves the purpose of increasing the horror, and of making us look upon things as being more dreadful than they really are.

562. THE SETTLED AND THE FREE.—It is only in the Underworld that we catch a glimpse of that gloomy background of all that bliss of adventure which forms an everlasting halo around Ulysses and his like, rivalling the eternal phosphorescence of the sea,—that background which we can never forget: the mother of Ulysses died of grief and yearning for her child. The one is driven on from place to place, and the heart of the other, the tender stay-at-home friend, breaks through it—so it always is. Affliction breaks the hearts of those who live to see that those whom they love best are deserting their former views and faith,—it is a tragedy brought about by the free spirits,—a tragedy which, indeed, occasionally comes to their own knowledge. Then, perhaps, they too, like Ulysses, will be forced to descend among the dead to get rid of their sorrow and to relieve their affliction.

563. THE ILLUSION OF THE MORAL ORDER OF THE UNIVERSE.—There is no "eternal justice" which requires that every fault shall be atoned and paid for,—the belief that such a justice existed was a terrible delusion, and useful only to a limited extent; just as it is also a delusion that everything is guilt which is felt as such. It is not the things themselves, but the opinions about things that do not exist, which have been such a source of trouble to mankind.

564. BY THE SIDE OF EXPERIENCE.—Even great intellects have only a hand-breadth experience—in the immediate proximity of this experience their reflection ceases, and its place is taken by unlimited vacuity and stupidity.

565. DIGNITY AND IGNORANCE.—Wherever we understand we become amiable, happy, and ingenious; and when we have learnt enough, and have trained our eyes and ears, our souls show greater plasticity and charm. We understand so little, however, and are so insufficiently informed, that it rarely happens that we seize upon a thing and make ourselves lovable at the same time,—on the contrary we pass through cities, nature, and history with stiffness and indifference, at the same time taking a pride in our stiff and indifferent attitude, as if it were simply due to superiority. Thus our ignorance and our mediocre desire for knowledge understand quite well how to assume a mask of dignity and character.

566. LIVING CHEAPLY.—The cheapest and most innocent mode of life is that of the thinker; for, to mention at once its most important feature, he has the greatest need of those very things which others neglect and look upon with contempt. In the second place he is easily pleased and has no desire for any expensive pleasures. His task is not difficult, but, so to speak, southern; his days and nights are not wasted by remorse; he moves, eats, drinks, and sleeps in a manner suited to his intellect, in order that it may grow calmer, stronger, and clearer. Again, he takes pleasure in his body and has no reason to fear it; he does not require society, except from time to time in order that he may afterwards go back to his solitude with even greater delight. He seeks and finds in the dead compensation for the living, and can even replace his friends in this way—viz., by seeking out among the dead the best who have ever lived.—Let us consider whether it is not the contrary desires and habits which have made the life of man expensive, and as a consequence difficult and often unbearable. In another sense, however, the thinker's life is certainly the most expensive, for nothing is too good for him; and it would be an intolerable privation for him to be deprived of the best.

567. IN THE FIELD.—"We should take things more cheerfully than they deserve; especially because for a very long time we have taken them more seriously than they deserved." So speak the brave soldiers of knowledge.

568. POET AND BIRD.—The bird Phœnix showed the poet a glowing scroll which was being gradually consumed in the flames. "Be not alarmed," said the bird, "it is your work! It does not contain the spirit of the age, and to a still less extent the spirit of those who are against the age: so it must be burnt. But that is a good sign. There is many a dawn of day."

569. TO THE LONELY ONES.—If we do not respect the honour of others in our soliloquies as well as in what we say publicly, we are not gentlemen.

570. LOSSES.—There are some losses which communicate to the soul a sublimity in which it ceases from wailing, and wanders about silently, as if in the shade of some high and dark cypresses.

571. THE BATTLE-FIELD DISPENSARY OF THE SOUL.—What is the most efficacious remedy?—Victory.

572. LIFE SHALL COMFORT US.—If, like the thinker, we live habitually amid the great current of ideas and feelings, and even our dreams follow this current, we expect comfort and peacefulness from life, while others wish to rest from life when they give themselves up to meditation.

573. CASTING ONE'S SKIN.—The snake that cannot cast its skin perishes. So too with those minds which are prevented from changing their views: they cease to be minds.

574. NEVER FORGET!—The higher we soar the smaller we appear to those who cannot fly.

575. WE AERONAUTS OF THE INTELLECT.—All those daring birds that soar far and ever farther into space, will somewhere or other be certain to find themselves unable to continue their flight, and they will perch on a mast or some narrow ledge—and will be grateful even for this miserable accommodation! But who could conclude from this that there was not an endless free space stretching far in front of them, and that they had flown as far as they possibly could? In the end, however, all our great teachers and predecessors have come to a standstill, and it is by no means in the noblest or most graceful attitude that their weariness has brought them to a pause: the same thing will happen to you and me! but what does this matter to either of us? Other birds will fly farther! Our minds and hopes vie with them far out and on high; they rise far above our heads and our failures, and from this height they look far into the distant horizon and see hundreds of birds much more powerful than we are, striving whither we ourselves have also striven, and where all is sea, sea, and nothing but sea!

And where, then, are we aiming at? Do we wish to cross the sea? whither does this over-powering passion urge us, this passion which we value more highly than any other delight? Why do we fly precisely in this direction, where all the suns of humanity have hitherto set? Is it possible that people may one day say of us that we also steered westward, hoping to reach India—but that it was our fate to be wrecked on the infinite? Or, my brethren? or—?

Footnotes:

1. The book was first published in 1881, the preface being added to the second edition, 1886.—TR.

2. This refers, of course, to the different genders of the nouns in other languages. In German, for example, the sun is feminine, and in French masculine.—TR.

3. M. Henri Albert points out that this refers to a line of Paul Gerhardt's well-known song: "Befiel du deine Wege." TR.

4. "Formal education" is the name given in Germany to those branches of learning which tend to develop the logical faculties, as opposed to "material" education which deals with the acquisition of facts and all kinds of "useful" knowledge.—TR.

5. The reference is to the Odyssey, XX. 18: "Τέτλαθι δή, κραδίη; καὶ κύντερον ἄλλο ποτ᾽ ἔτλης..." etc. Κύντερος, from κύων, "a dog," lit. more dog-like, i.e. shameless, horrible, audacious.—TR.

6. If this aphorism seems obscure, the reader may take Tolstoi as an example of the first class and Nietzsche as an example of the second. Tolstoi's inconsistencies are generally glossed over, because he professed the customary moral theories of the age, while Nietzsche has had to endure the most searching criticism because he did not. In Nietzsche's case, however, the scrutiny has been in vain; for, having no unworkable Christian theories to uphold, unlike Tolstoi, Nietzsche's life is not a series of compromises. The career of the great pagan philosopher was, in essence, much more saintly than that of the great Christian. How different from Tolstoi, too, was that noble Christian, Pascal, who, from the inevitable clash of his creed and his nature, died at thirty-eight, while his weaker epigone lived in the fulness of his fame until he was over eighty!—TR.

7. A hit at the German Empire, which Nietzsche always despised, since it led to the utter extinction of the old German spirit. "Kingdom" (in "Kingdom of God") and "Empire" are both represented by the one German word Reich.—TR.

8. This sentence is a complete refutation of a book which caused so much stir in Germany about a decade ago, and in England quite recently, Chamberlain's Nineteenth Century, in which a purely imaginary Teutonic race is held up as the Chosen People of the world. Nietzsche says elsewhere, "Peoples and Countries," aphorism 21, "Associate with no man who takes part in the mendacious race-swindle."—TR.

9. The fiercest protests against Nietzsche's teaching even now come from the "unfeeling people." Hence the difficulty—now happily past—of introducing him into Anglo-Saxon countries.—TR.

10. The German Jews are well known for their charity, by means of which they probably wish to prove that they are not so bad as the Anti-Semites paint them.—TR.

11. That is, do not speak either of God or the devil. The German proverb runs: "Man soll den Teufel nicht an die Wand malen, sonst kommt er."—TR.

12. The case of that other witty Venetian, Casanova.—TR.

13. The play upon the words gründlich (thorough) thinkers, and Untergründlichen (lit. those underground) cannot be rendered in English.—TR.

14. A variation of the well-known proverb, Ubi bene, ibi patria.—TR.

15. Hence the violence of all fanatics, who do not wish to shout down the outer world so much as to shout down their own inner enemy, viz. truth.—TR.

16. This omission is in the original.—TR.

17. This, of course, refers to Richard Wagner, as does also the following paragraph.—TR.

18. The play upon the words Vorschritt (leading) and Fortschritt (progress) cannot be rendered in English.—TR.

www.ingramcontent.com/pod-product-compliance
Lightning Source LLC
Chambersburg PA
CBHW060328100426
42812CB00003B/911

* 9 7 8 1 9 8 8 2 9 7 6 6 8 *